HOLLAND
2ND EDITION

Where to Stay and Eat
for All Budgets

Must-See Sights
and Local Secrets

Ratings You Can Trust

Fodor's Travel Publications   New York, Toronto, London, Sydney, Auckland
www.fodors.com

FODOR'S HOLLAND

Editor: Robert I. C. Fisher

Editorial Production: Tom Holton

Editorial Contributors: Shirley J. S. Agudo, Derek Brookman, Carol Conover, Anne Hodgkinson, Steve Korver, Anna Lambert, Jonette Stabbert, Charlotte A. R. Vaudrey

Maps: David Lindroth and Ed Jacobus, *cartographers;* Rebecca Baer and Robert Blake, *map editors*

Design: Fabrizio La Rocca, *creative director;* Guido Caroti, *art director;* Melanie Marin, *senior picture editor*

Production/Manufacturing: Colleen Ziemba

Cover Photo (cyclist riding past windmills, Noord-Holland): Suzanne and Nick Geary/Stone

Second Edition

ISBN 1–4000–1338–0

ISSN 1537-5617

SPECIAL SALES

This book is available for special discounts for bulk purchases for sales promotions or premiums. Special editions, including personalized covers, excerpts of existing books, and corporate imprints, can be created in large quantities for special needs. For more information, write to Special Markets/Premium Sales, 1745 Broadway, MD 6-2, New York, New York 10019 or e-mail specialmarkets@randomhouse.com. Inquiries from Canada should be directed to your local Canadian bookseller or sent to Random House of Canada, Ltd., Marketing Department, 2775 Matheson Boulevard East, Mississauga, Ontario L4W 4P7. Inquiries from the United Kingdom should be sent to Fodor's Travel Publications, 20 Vauxhall Bridge Road, London SW1V 2SA, England.

AN IMPORTANT TIP & AN INVITATION

Although all prices, opening times, and other details in this book are based on information supplied to us at press time, changes occur all the time in the travel world, and Fodor's cannot accept responsibility for facts that become outdated or for inadvertent errors or omissions. So **always confirm information when it matters,** especially if you're making a detour to visit a specific place. Your experiences—positive and negative—matter to us. If we have missed or misstated something, **please write to us.** We follow up on all suggestions. Contact the Holland editor at editors@fodors.com or c/o Fodor's at 1745 Broadway, New York, New York 10019.

PRINTED IN THE UNITED STATES OF AMERICA

10 9 8 7 6 5 4 3 2 1

DESTINATION: HOLLAND

Coming into view as the mist rises on time-burnished canals, like a curtain being raised on a play, are the iconic images of Holland. First, the water-locked, seemingly unassuming land. Then the farmers, their clog-shod feet still as entrenched in the fields as Van Gogh's potato eaters. In the north, the sky takes center stage, its vastness interrupted only by the spires of church towers, standing sentrylike over this land of low horizons. But head to the cities and you'll see that The Netherlands is so much more than windmills and wooden shoes. A museum in itself, Amsterdam is packed with monuments, statues, Rembrandts, and diamonds. Rotterdam sparkles with some of the 21st century's most distinctive architecture. Then, within the span of a single day, you can roll back the centuries by visiting a 14th-century castle at Muiden or the dreamy lassitude of historic Hoorn. You can feast your eyes on field after field of tulips, pursue the ghost of Frans Hals through the streets of Haarlem, and marvel at the wonder of a dike that stretches across open water for nearly twenty miles. Best of all may be those villages that remind you of Vermeer-stock lasses adorned with pearl earrings, bowing to the audience, clear pigments of your imagination.

Karen Cure, Editorial Director

CONTENTS

ABOUT THIS BOOK

There's no doubt that the best source for travel advice is a like-minded friend who's just been where you're headed. But with or without that friend, you'll have a better trip with a Fodor's guide in hand. Once you've learned to find your way around its pages, you'll be in great shape to find your way around your destination.

SELECTION

Our goal is to cover the best properties, sights, and activities in their category, as well as the most interesting communities to visit. We make a point of including local food lovers' hot spots as well as neighborhood options, and we avoid all that's touristy unless it's really worth your time. You can go on the assumption that everything you read about in this book is recommended wholeheartedly by our writers and editors. It goes without saying that no property mentioned in the book has paid to be included.

RATINGS

Orange stars ★ denote sights and properties that our editors and writers consider the very best in the area covered by the entire book. Many of these, the best of the best, are listed in the Fodor's Choice section in the front of the book. Black stars ★ highlight the sights and properties we deem Highly Recommended, the don't-miss sights within any region. Fodor's Choice and Highly Recommended options in each region are usually listed on the title page of the chapter covering that region. Use the index to find complete descriptions. In cities, sights pinpointed with numbered map bullets ❶ in the margins tend to be more important than those without bullets.

SPECIAL SPOTS

Pleasures & Pastimes focuses on types of experiences that reveal the spirit of the destination. Watch for Off the Beaten Path sights. Some are out of the way, some are quirky, and all are worth your while. If the munchies hit while you're exploring, look for Need a Break? suggestions.

TIME IT RIGHT

Wondering when to go? Check On the Calendar up front and chapters' Timing sections for weather and crowd overviews and best days and times to visit.

SEE IT ALL

Use Fodor's exclusive Great Itineraries as a model for your trip. (For a good overview of the entire destination, follow those that begin the book, or mix regional itineraries from several chapters.) In cities, Good Walks guide you to important sights in each neighborhood; ☞ indicates the starting points of walks and itineraries in the text and on the map.

BUDGET WELL

Hotel and restaurant price categories from ¢ to $$$$ are defined in the opening pages of each chapter—expect to find a balanced selection for every budget, from amazing bargains to luxurious blowouts. For attractions, we always give standard adult admission fees; reductions are usually available for children, students, and senior citizens.

BASIC INFO

Smart Travel Tips lists travel essentials for the entire area covered by the book; city- and region-specific basics end each chapter in the A to Z sections. To find the best way to get around, see the transportation section; see individual modes of travel ("By Car," "By Train") for details. We assume you'll check Web sites or call for particulars.

ON THE MAPS	**Maps** throughout the book show you what's where and help you find your way around. Black and orange numbered bullets ❶ ❶ in the text correlate to bullets on maps.
BACKGROUND	In general, we give background information within the chapters in the course of explaining sights as well as in **CloseUp** boxes and in **Understanding Holland** at the end of the book. To get in the mood, review the suggestions in **Further Reading**. The **Dutch Vocabulary** can be invaluable to get you started.
FIND IT FAST	Within the book, chapters are arranged in a roughly corkscrew direction spiraling out from Amsterdam and encompassing all areas of Holland, beginning with the Randstad area (famed for the cities of Haarlem, Leiden, Delft, and Rotterdam) and The Hague, continuing south to the Border Provinces, then heading back north to the Green Heart, Friesland, Groningen, Drenthe, and the Wadden Sea islands. Chapters are divided into small regions, within which towns are covered in logical geographical order; attractive routes and interesting places between towns are flagged as **En Route**. Heads at the top of each page help you find what you need within a chapter.
DON'T FORGET	**Restaurants** are open for lunch and dinner daily unless we state otherwise; we mention dress only when there's a specific requirement and reservations only when they're essential or not accepted— it's always best to book ahead. Unless we note otherwise, most **hotels** have private baths, phone, TVs, and air-conditioning and operate on the European Plan (a.k.a. EP, meaning without meals). We always list facilities but not whether you'll be charged extra to use them, so when pricing accommodations, find out what's included.
SYMBOLS	

Many Listings

- ★ Fodor's Choice
- ★ Highly recommended
- ⊠ Physical address
- ✛ Directions
- 🕮 Mailing address
- ☎ Telephone
- 🖷 Fax
- ⊕ On the Web
- ✉ E-mail
- 🎫 Admission fee
- ☉ Open/closed times
- ▶ Start of walk/itinerary
- Ⓜ Metro stations
- ▱ Credit cards

Outdoors

- ⛳ Golf
- ⛺ Camping

Hotels & Restaurants

- 🏨 Hotel
- 🛏 Number of rooms
- ⬧ Facilities
- 🍽 Meal plans
- ✕ Restaurant
- ⬨ Reservations
- 🏛 Dress code
- ↘ Smoking
- 🍷 BYOB
- ✕🏨 Hotel with restaurant that warrants a visit

Other

- ☺ Family-friendly
- ℹ Contact information
- ⇨ See also
- ⊠ Branch address
- ☞ Take note

ON THE ROAD WITH FODOR'S

A trip takes you out of yourself. Concerns of life at home completely disappear, driven away by more immediate thoughts—about, say, what marvels will beguile the next day, or where you'll have dinner. That's where Fodor's comes in. We make sure that you know all your options, so that you don't miss something that's around the next bend just because you didn't know it was there. Because the best memories of your trip might well have nothing to do with what you came to Holland to see, we guide you to sights large and small all over the country. You might set out to enjoy the famous 17th-century "Golden Age" landscape paintings in Amsterdam's Rijksmuseum, but back at home you find yourself unable to forget exploring the nearby Vondelpark, luminous as a Ruysdael canvas after a wintry storm. With Fodor's at your side, serendipitous discoveries are never far away. Our success in showing you every corner of Holland is a credit to our extraordinary writers.

After years of travel subsidized by carpentry, set design, and B-movie acting, **Steve Korver** came to Amsterdam to reverse the journey his Dutch parents had made as immigrants to Canada. A decade later, he is established as a lover of raw herring and an obsessive expert on all things Amsterdam, as readers will see once they open his chapter on that amazing city. In between his bouts of Fodorifying Holland, he has written articles on film, books, art, food, and media for such publications as *Time Out, Globe & Mail* and *Condé Nast Traveler*. And when the Dutch metropolis starts feeling too cute and claustrophobic, he goes to Russia in search of Yuri Gagarin, the first man in space (a book on which should appear by the author in 2004) or to the former Yugoslavia to find the perfect plum brandy. He is also working on a book, based on years' worth of columns and essays, that will be a relentless attempt to spicily reinterpret Amsterdam's past, present, and mythical realities. He divides his writing time between the streets of Amsterdam and the trees of his brother's farm in Ontario. For this edition, Steve wrote the complete Exploring, Where to Eat, Nightlife and the Arts, and Sports & the Outdoors sections of our Amsterdam chapter, along with the "Going Dutch" essay in our Understanding Holland chapter.

From the moment she first smelled Dutch cocoa wafting on the breeze, confirmed chocoholic **Jonette Stabbert** knew she was here to stay in Holland. After all, breathing chocolate is only second best to eating it, but since becoming acclimated, she regularly makes the rounds of *chocolateries*. A native New Yorker—Brooklyn! (to use Breukelen's American spelling)—Jonette traded New for Old Amsterdam in 1970 and is still in love with the Dutch city. Researching this guide was like a vacation encompassing her favorite activities—she got to visit cutting-edge boutiques, frozen-in-amber museums, and enjoyed heavenly day trips, such as the Bollenstreek Bulb Route. Theories abound that living close to water is conducive to creativity. Opting for total immersion, Jonette is a writer, artist, and designer, and also teaches corporate creativity seminars and art and writing workshops. As a writer whose short stories are regularly published, she sometimes acts as a "media escort," guiding visiting novelists and journalists around town. A "people person," networking through numerous professional organizations has brought her in contact with "everybody," which has gained her access to the newest information. The Fodor's reader is the clear winner. For this edition, she researched and updated the Smart Travel Tips chapter, the Metropolitan Holland chapter, and the Where to Stay, Shopping, and Side Trips sections of the Amsterdam chapter.

For this book, **Charlotte Vaudrey** careered around much of her turf on Rollerblades, Dictaphone in one hand as she talked her way across the cities in the Randstad. The summer was hot, but the breeze was cool, and the Dutch (themselves so graceful on blades, be they roller or ice, with an intrinsic, quintessentially Dutch sense of balance) have an enormous respect for those non-naturals who give it a go. Charlotte lived in North America before stints in London, Paris, and now Delft, the robust yet dreamy city that gave us Vermeer. She has worked as a regular contributor for *Roundabout, Rush on Amsterdam,* and various *WHERE* publications. For this book she wrote most of the Metropolitan Holland: Rotterdam & the Randstad chapter and crafted the Smart Travel Tips chapter.

After taking a music degree in sunny California, **Anne Hodgkinson** left for windswept Holland and its thriving early music ("oude muziek") scene in 1989. While touring much of Europe with Dutch, Belgian, and German choirs, her interest in other aspects of its culture was whetted. Now settled in Utrecht, she sings the occasional solo in a Bach cantata or other oratorio and has diversified into translating and writing. The early years in Holland were hard and, feeling oppressed by the meat-and-potatoes culture prevailing at the time, she often sought solace by finding obscure ingredients ("like garlic!—how do these people *survive?*") in far-away neighborhoods. Despite being an enthusiastic cook and bon vivant, she keeps (relatively) trim by cycling all over town for ingredients and taking long walking trips. Updater of our chapter on The Hague, and a fan of the network of long-distance footpaths crisscrossing Europe, she especially enjoys places of natural beauty that intersect with culture, such as the "Dutch Alps" around Maastricht. She and her husband are working on a gastronomical hiking guide.

Two years ago, **Anna Lambert** happened to sample a Dutch *stroopwafel* in a London deli and realized that a move to The Netherlands was vital (she's since gained 8 pounds in her bid to track down the definitive example of this syrup-filled cookie). Anna now lives just outside Arnhem in a picture-perfect—if damp—thatched cottage, where she combines writing with traveling throughout Holland and exercising her Dutch-language skills on long-suffering native friends. Writing her chapters on The Hague and on the Border Provinces, she's discovered that the best things about her adopted homeland are the frankness of its people, the beauty of its architecture—both ancient and modern—and the glorious bouquets of flowers that are displayed everywhere. Anna has written for a variety of publications, including the *Financial Times*, *Elle Decor*, and *Vogue Living and Entertaining*.

In 1985 **Derek Brookman** left his native Scotland to see whether the grass was greener on the Dutch side of the North Sea: the rest, as they say, is history. Enamored by the diversity of life—there's a Vietnamese restaurant, West African cultural center, Turkish café, and a grow-your-own marijuana shop all within fifty yards of his front door—he spread his roots ever deeper in the loamy Eindhoven soil, especially now that there are two Brookmanettes on the scene. More than two years traveling in Asia taught Derek the value of a reliable and informative guidebook, and for the Border Provinces chapter he explored the region extensively, combining work with the opportunity to charge down forest paths at night on his mountain bike or delighting in the unpretentious grandeur of Limburg's many châteaux. These days he works as a freelance writer, covering subjects ranging from football to architecture and environmental issues, and is nearly finished writing his first novel.

A true Netherlandphile who lived in the northeast of Holland for five years before moving to Paris, **Shirley Agudo** openly admits that she prefers the backroads of the rural province of Drenthe to the brazen City of Lights. An American expatriate with a witty sarcasm born out of survival in foreign cultures, Shirley worked for many years in corporate public relations in the States and subsequently as editor of *Pittsburgh's Parent* magazine before trading in her steel-toed shoes for wooden ones. She now writes for Dutch magazines, including *Roundabout*, and book publishers, specializing in travel and expatriate issues. Her latest books include *The Holland Handbook*, *Holland Events Diary*, and a forthcoming opus on the subject of networking. After traversing five Dutch provinces and five islands to research the chapters on The Green Heart and The North & the Wadden Sea Islands of this book, Shirley reports that she's even more passionately in love with this lyrical country below sea level and, as of 2003, has now returned to live in Holland. Only a megahole in a dike, she says, could ever drive her away.

Assisting Shirley with the updating of this current edition is **Carol Conover**, an American who settled in Amersfoort. After studying at the Netherlands Carillon School, she began a new venture, Byways Holland, a private tour business catering to those who prefer Holland on a platter, complete with an English-speaking guide (www.bywaysholland.com).

Holland: The Provinces

GRONINGEN

FRIESLAND

DRENTHE

OVERIJSSEL

FLEVOLAND

NOORD-HOLLAND

Winschoten

Emmen

Delfzijl

Groningen

Assen

Hoogeveen

Enschede

Hengelo

Almelo

Zwolle

Deventer

Apeldoorn

Meppel

Drachten

Dokkum

Sneek

Leeuwarden

Bolsward

Harlingen

Lelystad

Enkhuizen

Hoorn

Purmerend

Amsterdam

Zaanstad

Alkmaar

Den Helder

Borkum

Rottumeroog

Rottumerplatt

Simonszand

Schiermonnikoog

Ameland

Terschelling

Vlieling

Texel

IJsselmeer

Waddenzee

Noordzee

N34

N36

N35

N41

A28/E232

A32

A6

N371

N34

N48

A1/E30

A28/E232

A7/E22

A7/E22

A6

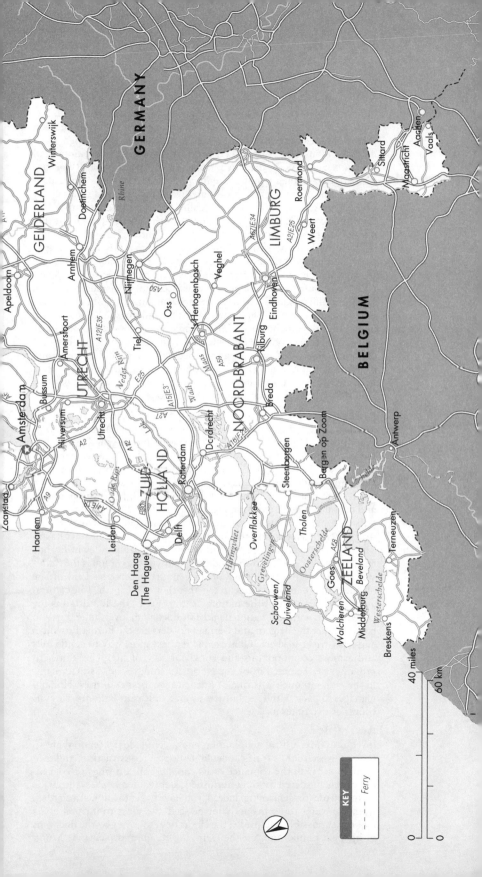

Nearly a doll's house of a country, custom-made for the traveler in a hurry, The Netherlands is just about half the size of the state of Maine. The country is too small for there to be vast natural areas, and it's too precariously close to sea level, even at its highest points, for there to be dramatic landscapes. Instead, Holland is what the Dutch jokingly call a big green city. As the delta of Europe, it is where the great Rhine and Maas rivers and their tributaries empty into the North Sea. Amsterdam serves as the country's focal point and is the inspired and chaotic hub of a 50-km (31-mi) circle of cities called the Randstad—the true cultural and economic heart of the nation—which includes The Hague (the nation's seat of government and the world's center of international justice), Rotterdam (the nation's industrial center and the world's largest port), and the historic university cities of Haarlem, Leiden, Delft, and Utrecht. In contrast, the northern and eastern provinces are rural and quiet, with only the unique province of Friesland occasionally making some grumbling sounds, in its own separate language, about its 500-year history as part of The Netherlands. Grumblings, and only grumblings, they remain, however: inner conflicts have long taken on kinder and gentler dimensions in Holland. Indeed, the historical chasm between the north, populated with tough-minded and practical Calvinists, and the Catholic southern provinces that hug the Belgian border has long been crossed with a tradition of tolerance that grew from a sea-battling land's awareness that one cannot survive alone.

Nearly half of this democratic monarchy has been reclaimed from the sea, and the doughty inhabitants have been working for generations to keep it from slipping back. Hence the special look of the Dutch landscape, the subject of some of the most beautiful old-master paintings ever created. In scenery and structure, the country's north and south regions differ little, for both have the same North Sea beach line on the northwestern side, the same sand dunes and bulb fields in the center, and the same type of rivers on their land borders. Yet each of the country's five main regions—Amsterdam, the Randstad, the Green Heart, the Border Provinces, and the North—possesses its own distinct flavor. The capital, Amsterdam, is one of the most amazing cities in Europe and The Netherlands' "shop window." South of the capital is the Randstad (Ridge City), comprising four adjacent urban centers—Leiden, The Hague, Rotterdam, and Utrecht; together they make up the true cultural and economic heart of the nation. To the east of the Randstad is the Green Heart, with vast national parks studded with lovely museums and palaces. Near the Belgian and German borders are the Border Provinces and Maastricht—where billiard-table flatness gives way to gentle hills and a more cosmopolitan and convivial way of life. The Northern provinces are hemmed in by the North Sea and, to the east, Germany. In the end, although it is one of Europe's smallest countries, Holland manages to pack within its borders as many pleasures and treasures as countries five times its size.

① Amsterdam

It requires only a little imagination and a gentle dose of moonlight to replace Amsterdam's traffic, telephone booths, construction, and souvenir shops with the romance of its canals. Built on rings of concentric canals bordered by time-burnished, step-gabled houses, the city is custom made for sightseeing. Indeed, you have to get to know Amsterdam from the water to be properly introduced and glass-roof canal boats make that possible. Helpfully, the city is held together by the linchpins of its great public squares: the Dam, the Rembrandtplein, the Munt, and the Leidseplein. The Dam, an open square overlooked by the Royal Dam Palace, is a godsend to visitors as a landmark, for even the worst student of foreign languages can easily obtain help if lost by asking for the "Dam."

The sector you first see upon leaving the storybook gates of Amsterdam's Centraal Station, the eastern half of the Centrum (or Old Center) literally drips with history—a history where sex and religion come equally represented. But the **Red Light District**, or Rosse Buurt, remains reined in—and surprisingly safe—and goes almost as far to seemingly gel seamlessly with the city's oldest church, the Oude Kerk, itself now a venue for modern art exhibitions. The Red Light District is part and parcel of the city region known as the **Oude Zijde**, or Old Side. Top sights hereabouts include the medieval square of **Nieuwmarkt** (now festooned with Chinese restaurants), which is landmarked by the great Waag weigh house; the 17th-century **Trippenhuis** mansion; the grand museum of Golden Age Amsterdam known as **Amstelkring** (with its hidden Our Dear Lord in the Attic church), replete with sumptuous period rooms; and the last-but-not-least Red Light District, often called *de Walletjes* ("the little walls"), itself studded with historic jewels such as the "In the Monkeys" half-timbered house. Here, too, by the waterfront area, is the **Schreierstoren**—the "Weeping Tower"—where Henry Hudson set off to fail in discovering a passage to the East (but then stumbled over Manhattan as a slight recompense). In short: everything that makes Amsterdam familiar to the global imagination. To the west of the Old Side is the city district known as the New Side, or the **Nieuwe Zijde**. This is really just as ancient—relatively speaking—as the Old Side, from which it is eparated by the Oudezijds Voorburgwal street. The center spotlight of the Nieuwe Zijde is always shining upon the city's focal square, the bustling **Dam**, with its opulent **Koninklijk palace** and **Nieuwe Kerk**. Near the Spui square is the **Amsterdam Historical Museum**, where a visit will ensure that any further wanderings of the city will be amplified by what you witnessed and absorbed there. Here, too, is the classic modernist architecture of the **Beurs van Berlage** and the *gezellig* (cozy and congenial) and centuries-old **Begijnhof**, one of the city's most famous inner courtyards.

Set to the west and south of the city center is the famous Grachtengordel. Call it a "belt" or a "girdle," but the Golden Age product that consists of the three main encircling canals—Prinsengracht (Princes' Canal), Keizersgracht (Emperors' Canal), and Herengracht (Gentlemen's Canal)—form a ring of unparalleled historical beauty. The point where these canals intersected with Nieuwe Spiegelstraat became known as the Golden Bend—the *Gouden Bocht*—since houses here were occupied by the richest families of Amsterdam. Heading a few blocks over to what is called the Eastern Canal Ring you'll find assorted treasures, including Baroque-era interiors on view at the magnificent 17th-century **Willet-Holthuysen Museum**; the scenic **Munt Toren** tower; the period-room-rich **Museum van Loon**; the noted Magere Brug bridge; and even a stretch or two of canal benches (fairly rare, in fact) to help drink in the canal views. To the north of the Golden Bend is the western half of the Grachtengordel, the first canal sector to be built and one that harbors not only miles of gabled residences that reflect most sweetly and surreally in the canal waters below but also intersecting streets that harbor a plethora of high-quality/quirky shopping and eating (especially on the "Nine Streets"). The northern sectors of the Grachtengordel center around Amsterdam's beloved Jordaan (probably derived from the French for "garden," *jardin*). Although this cozy, scenic, and singular neighborhood's working class roots have long sprouted branches of gentrification, it remains a wanderers' paradise where you can take in leafy canals, funky galleries, yet funkier shops, hidden courtyards *(hofjes)*, and cafés/bars/restaurants of both the posh and charmingly local persuasion—the latter often involving a terrace with a view and an interior with massive nicotine staining, which color-codes nicely with a congenial sense of warmth and humor. This area—bound by those famously scenic canals, the Brouwersgracht, Elandsgracht, Lijnbaansgracht, and Prinsengracht—is also the setting of some of Amsterdam's most memorable sights. The most famous is the **Anne Frank House.** Nearby is the fabulous **Bartolotti Huis,** a spectacular 17th-century Dutch Renaissance residence, now the Netherlands Theater Museum.

Near the southern end of the city, the Museum District–centered around the Museumplein square—gives you, in short, the history of art at your fingertips (not to mention, your potentially blistered toe tips) as Rembrandts, Van Goghs, and Bill Violas are all on evocative display in the city's three main art museums: the **Rijksmuseum** (sadly going through a massive rebuilding over the next many years, so call/surf ahead for their varying hours and exhibition locations), the **Van Gogh Museum** (more than 200 of the artist's paintings are on view), and the **Stedelijk Museum of Modern Art.** Set to the south of the Museum District is Amsterdam Zuid, or South Amsterdam, a neighborhood which harbors many posh residences, not to mention the most elitist shopping options along the country's most famous fashion strip, **PC Hooftstraat.** To the east of the center-city Oude Zijde and the city's aorta, the wide Amstel River, lies the extension of the Old Jewish Neighborhood known as the stately and serene **Plantage** (plantation). It was on the eastern bank of the Amstel in the 17th century that Jewish refugees from Portugal quickly colonized the area as their own. And it was here, not far from today's glitteringly modern "Stopera," or Stadhuis-Muzietktheater opera and concert house, that Rembrandt set up shop in one of Amsterdam's grandest houses. The former home of Rembrandt, the **Museum het Rembrandthuis,** tops the bill of fare here, but there are many other destinations, including such 17th-century treasures as the grand **Zuiderkerk** church; the renowned **Joods Historisch Museum,** and the old-world knickknack marketeering of the Waterlooplein flea market. Everywhere you walk you'll find one of Amsterdam's thousands of those stained-by-time *bruine kroegjes* (brown cafés), where *koffie* is the drink of choice. Offering The Netherlands' hottest nightlife, impressive concerts, and fine restaurants, Amsterdam reinvents itself with every sunset.

And when it comes to day-tripping, Amsterdammers are undeniably lucky. Droves of stressed-out city residents tie their bicycles to the roof racks of their Mercedes on Saturday and Sunday; vacationers in Amsterdam can share in the natives' pleasure in these destinations any day of the week. For just north of the city, in the province of Noord-Holland, are many of the famed "folkoric towns." **Monnickendam** has a harbor brimming with history, an 18th-century town hall, and many dainty gabled houses. Human Dutch dolls walk the streets of nearby **Volendam.** For more history, Hoorn and Enkhuizen are musts. **Hoorn** was once a leading seaport of The Netherlands and gave its name to Cape Horn. After the 17th century it fell asleep. So did **Enkhuizen,** whose restored village of the Zuiderzeemuseum will fascinate those interested in boats, fishing, peasant furniture, or regional costumes. Here you'll find a gallery of costumed dummies, each in a room furnished appropriately to the locality, that don't ask you if you want to take their pictures. **Alkmaar** also has a historic cheese market, but don't miss the rest of the town, packed with medieval courtyards, windmills, and gabled houses. Near **Zaandam**—where Peter the Great once learned the craft of shipbuilding—the windmill-filled Zaanse Schans region demonstrates the many uses of windmill-produced power throughout The Netherlands.

② Metropolitan Holland: Rotterdam & the Randstad

Like filings around the end of a magnet, four major urban centers cluster in a heart-of-Holland arc, commonly known as the Randstad, just to the south of Amsterdam. Although the capital, Amsterdam, remains a world-class city, these four offer a truer look at Dutch culture and society. West of the city the **Bloemen Route** (Flower Road) leads from Aalsmeer—one of the greatest floral villages in Europe—to the famed Keukenhof gardens and the town of **Lisse**. This is the Holland of tulips, hyacinths, and narcissi, aglow with the colors of Easter in spring and generally a rainbow of color year-round. It is a short step from this ocean of seasonal color to a haven of perennial color—the city of **Haarlem**, the earliest center of Dutch art, which gave rise to one of the most important schools of landscape painting in the 17th century. Here are the excellent Frans Hals and Teylers museums and the church of St. Bavo. **Leiden,** the birthplace of Rembrandt and site of a great university, remains a charming town where windmills rise over the cityscape. Here also is the Pieterskerk, church of the Pilgrim Fathers who worshipped in it for 10 years before setting sail for America in 1620. The tree-lined canals, humpbacked bridges, and step-gabled houses of **Delft** preserve the atmosphere of the 16th and 17th centuries better than any other city in the country, captured unforgettably in the canvases of Vermeer and Pieter de Hoogh. Delft, of course, colored the world with its unique blue, best found in its famous blue-and-white Delftware china. The city is, in a sense, the national shrine of The Netherlands with its venerable Prinsenhof, where William the Silent lived and was assassinated. Grotius, the founder of international law, was born here and now reposes in the Nieuwe Kerk not far from the mighty William and other members of the House of Orange.

Rotterdam, a true phoenix of a city, rose from the ashes of World War II to become one of the busiest ports in Europe. Today, 21st-century architectural innovations, in quirky colors and shapes, are at nearly every turn. But here, too, is the historic Delfshaven harbor and the magnificent Museum Boijmans van Beuningen, home to the fabled painting of Pieter Brueghel the Elder's *Tower of Babel,* Hieronymus Bosch's *Prodigal Son,* and Jan van Eyck's *Three Maries.* In **Utrecht'**s history-soaked town center, not far from the Oude Gracht (Old Canal), stands the 338-foot tower of "the Cathedral That Is Missing." This city is the centerpiece of a region that is considered by many Dutch to be the most beautiful in the country: the landscape fairly bursts with lovely old trees (a rarity in the polders, or countryside reclaimed from the sea) and storybook castle-châteaux. Other destinations include **Brielle**—the redoubt of the legendary Sea Beggars; the famous 19 windmills of **Kinderdijk; Dordrecht,** whose historic town center is replete with delightful and typical Dutch canal vistas; **Gouda,** whose name brings to mind a weekly cheese market, the manufacture of clay pipes, and the priceless stained glass in the Sint Janskerk; and the **Kasteel de Haar,** Holland's most opulent, fairy-tale castle.

3 The Hague

Called 's-Gravenhage or Den Haag by the Dutch (and "the Largest Village in Europe" by residents), **The Hague** is a royal and regal city—filled with patrician mansions and gracious parks and home to Queen Beatrix and the International Court of Justice. Its downtown is stuffed with fine restaurants and posh antiques shops. Although Amsterdam is the nation's constitutional capital, The Hague is the seat of the Dutch government and the International Court of Justice. If the city center near Centraal Station is dominated by postmodern high-rise towers, the ritzy dwellings of the rich and famous of centuries gone by are still here to enchant. At the heart of the Centrum—the historic city center—is the **Ridderzaal**, or Knights' Hall, which stands alone in the middle of the Binnenhof, or Inner Court, its 13th-century towers recalling an era when architects were as much concerned with defense as shelter, its shape suggesting more a church than a castle. On the far side of the Binnenhof is the fabled **Mauritshuis** (much more intimate than the Rijksmuseum), where the canvases on display are world famous—Vermeer's *View of Delft* and *Girl with a Pearl Earring* are just two. As in other museums, you can spend hours here, but unlike other collections, you waste no time on second-rate work. Here, too, you'll find other museums that still are perfumed with the age of long-ago Holland, notably that connoisseur's delight, the **Museum Mesdag,** whose period rooms are lined with 19th-century daubs and paintings of The Hague School; the **Haags Gemeentemuseum,** which contains the world's largest collection of Piet Mondriaan paintings; the **Museum Bredius**; and the regal **Prince William V Painting Gallery.** Beyond the town borders lies the miniature-size Holland on view at **Madurodam** and the windswept beach resort of **Scheveningen,** which still offers some of the best herring in the world.

4 The Border Provinces & Maastricht

In most Dutch provinces the sea presses in to the land, constantly striving to win a foothold; Zeeland, to the contrary, pushes out into the water, invading the invader's territory and looking for trouble. On strips of land, like thumbs of a right hand, pointing westward toward the North Sea, Zeeland remains an ancient and romantic place. **Zierikzee** is a yachting port, and **Veere** is relentlessly picturesque; **Middelburg, Breda,** and **'s-Hertogenbosch** all have historic significance, the latter as the hometown of that 16th-century surrealist Hieronymus Bosch. The southernmost province of The Netherlands, Limburg, differs from the rest of the country in many ways, most especially in its rolling hills and dense forests. Here lies **Maastricht,** the oldest city in The Netherlands. Wedged somewhat hesitatingly between Belgium and Germany, the town remains an intoxicating mixture of three languages, times, currencies, and customs. There are imposing Romanesque and Gothic churches, hundreds of historic gable-stone houses, and fabulous French food (where else can you enjoy breakfast with champagne in The Netherlands?). The milder southern climate in this region contributes its share to the city's exuberant and sophisticated street life. Each March, the European Fine Art Fair—some say this is the best art fair in Europe—draws Prince Bernhard, high rollers, and the richest collectors of old-master paintings in the world.

(5) The Green Heart

Although as steeped in history as any other Dutch region, Gelderland seems to put the emphasis on the beauties of outdoor life, for it is a province studded with national parks and Edenic forests. Glorying in the title "The Largest Garden City in The Netherlands," **Apeldoorn** is so lavishly endowed with trees, natives challenge visitors to find the place. Thousands do every year, mostly to visit the incomparably charming yet superbly elegant 17th-century **Palace Het Loo**—the Dutch Baroque castle and hunting lodge that was home to William and Mary (who went on to become king and queen of England). Set within **De Hoge Veluwe,** the nation's largest natural preserve, is the celebrated **Kröller-Müller Museum,** which has extraordinary paintings of the postimpressionists as well as a multitude of works by Van Gogh, including his *Sunflowers* and *Potato Eaters.* This region is, above all, a walking and bicycling paradise, and hikes through lush woods and moors can often end delightfully at grand country mansions, such as Het Wezenveld, Bruggenbosch, and Hunderen, outside Apeldoorn. The major towns of the region—**Zwolle, Deventer, Zutphen**—all have historic churches or town squares. The capital of the region is **Arnhem,** best known for "the bridge too far" of World War II. Its chief attractions are the battlefields, memorials, and war cemeteries that have become sacred places of pilgrimages, set in a region rich in scenic beauty.

(6) The North & the Wadden Sea Islands

Leeuwarden is the capital of Friesland and birthplace of Saskia, Rembrandt's wife, and of the mysterious Mata Hari. Crafts are a highlight here: the fine Netherlands Ceramic Museum and the Fries Museum are a great introduction to the cultural heritage of the province. Along the IJsselmeer coastline, now protected from the ravages of the sea and tides, there are plenty of quaint, though defunct, fishing villages. Out on a promontory, the former port of **Hindeloopen** seems to have been lost in time. In nearby **Makkum** is Tichelaar's Royal Makkum Pottery and Tile Factory. Flotillas of yachts tack across the myriad interconnected lakes around **Sloten** and **Sneek,** where the province's connection with the sea and water is most evident. The **Wadden Sea Islands,** just a short ferry ride from the Mainland, are also home to seafarers. The largest of these five islands, **Texel,** is easy to reach from Amsterdam to the port of Den Helder. The other islands are more remote, though the roadway across the **Afsluitdijk** (Enclosing Dike) at the northern end of the IJsselmeer reduces journey times considerably. **Terschelling** is the most popular island, with bustling terraces during the high season and the extraordinary theatrical events of the Oerol Festival in June. The more exclusive, secluded, car-free island of **Schiermonnikoog,** an oasis of unspoiled nature on bird migration routes, is a favorite weekend getaway for the Dutch. Farther east is **Groningen,** a sophisticated university town, filled with architectural delights, pretty canals, and the magnificent gardens of the Prinsenhoftuin, where 250 years of topiary, lawn making, and hedge growing have produced a masterpiece on nature's canvas. Here and there, distinctive storks' nests mounted atop wheels perch high upon poles—a fitting icon for this lovely, verdant agricultural region.

As packed as a Lionel model village and practically crawling with history, Holland continues to offer far more mileage per tourist euro than many a larger country. Many travelers use Holland's small size (a couple of hours' traveling will take them halfway across the country) as a rationale to "do" its destinations on day trips. Availing themselves of its terrific trains, they find it entirely possible to base themselves in Amsterdam and head out by day to Leiden, Delft, Utrecht, Haarlem, The Hague, and Rotterdam. Of course, this leaves them too little time to appreciate the unexpectedly rich rewards that await beyond Amsterdam. Some may joke that Holland is now just a virtual extension of the town limits of Amsterdam, but the serious traveler who heads out to explore the entire country will enjoy the last laugh. You could happily spend a week just getting to know Amsterdam. Two to three weeks would be ideal for exploring the rest of the country.

The crowded, shining cities will beckon you first but before long the far horizons will call. You certainly won't be conscious of any overpopulation problem as you travel through Holland's green countryside, spacious and flat, laced with blue canals and beech-bordered roads. The biggest slopes are those leading up to the canal bridges; the tallest objects are the windmills with their white cloth sails stretched to pick up the slightest breeze. Look for them and you will undoubtedly find nearby cozy villages, the kind that were painted by Hobbema. Here, if you are lucky, you'll find interiors that conjure up the glowing chambers of Vermeer, natives who beam with the inner radiance found in Rembrandt's portraits, and cafés where people live out the rich-hued scenes of the Old Masters.

If You Have 3 Days

After arriving in **Amsterdam** and viewing the famous gables from the comfort of a canal boat (tours take one to two hours), feast your eyes on Rembrandts and Van Goghs in the city's museums. Your first night is spent in Amsterdam, so there's plenty of time to explore the backstreets of the Jordaan (Amsterdam's version of Greenwich Village) and to find a cozy restaurant. Next morning, check out some of Amsterdam's quirkier shops—or visit a diamond-cutting factory if that's more your style. Then set off along the A4 for **The Hague** to visit a palace or two and the Madurodam miniature village in **Scheveningen**. End the day with a rijsttafel in one of The Hague's excellent Indonesian restaurants. In the morning, take a tram (20 minutes) to nearby **Delft** and visit its renowned porcelain factory; then set off back along the A4 to **Leiden**. If it's springtime, take the N206 out of town and through the bulb fields to the spectacular Keukenhof gardens. Otherwise, spend the afternoon exploring this attractive old university town, for many years home to the Pilgrim Fathers. Leiden is just half an hour from Schiphol Airport, along the A4.

If You Have 5 Days

Your first night is in **Amsterdam**. This gives you a day on either side for exploring canals, museums, bustling markets, and the Jordaan district. In the afternoon of your second day, head off along the A4 to **Leiden**. If it's springtime, follow instead the A9 and the N208 through the bulb fields, allowing an hour for visiting the Keukenhof gardens on the way. After a morning spent seeing Leiden's 15th-century church and beautifully restored windmill, continue along the A4 to **The Hague**, seat of the government and home to some excellent art collections. Next day, take a tram to **Delft**, one of the most beautifully preserved historic towns in the country, conveniently situated on the outskirts of The Hague. Then take the A12 to **Utrecht**, where you can climb the Gothic Domtoren, the highest church tower in The Netherlands, for a panoramic view of the countryside. Back on ground level, you can visit a delightful museum of music boxes, player pianos, and barrel organs. On the fifth day take the A28, then the A1, out to the Hoge Veluwe national park, near **Apeldoorn**, where you can spend time walking in the forest or visiting the Kröller-Müller Museum with its extraordinary collection of Van Goghs and modern art. From Apeldoorn, you can continue your journey into Germany or take the A1 back to Amsterdam.

If You Have 9 Days

Two days and two nights in **Amsterdam** give you time for a leisurely exploration of the city. On the third day, follow the A4 to **Leiden** (or take the N208 bulb route if it's springtime), and then travel on to **The Hague**. Visit the historic center and porcelain factory of **Delft** on the morning of the fourth day; then head across to **Utrecht** on the A12. On the way, stop off in **Gouda**, famed not only for its cheeses but also for its medieval city hall and the magnificent stained glass in the Sint Janskerk. From Utrecht take the A2 south, stopping for the night in an ancient Limburg manor house or castle, such as the medieval Kasteel Wittem near **Heerlen**. Spend Day 6 in **Maastricht** (just a short drive from Wittem on the N278), which has an abundance of sidewalk cafés and a carefree French air. Maastricht also boasts the Bonnefantenmuseum, which is well stocked with superb religious carvings and intriguing contemporary art. Then travel along the German border to the Hoge Veluwe national park near **Apeldoorn** (take the A2 out of Maastricht, turn off onto the N271, and follow it up to Nijmegen, from which the A325 and the A50 take you into the park). The pretty little town of **Zutphen**, which has a library of rare and beautiful early manuscripts, makes a good overnight stop (follow the N345 out of Apeldoorn). There are now two possibilities in the northern provinces. Option one: On Day 8 travel north to **Leeuwarden** (follow the A50 to Zwolle, then the A28 to Meppel, and turn finally onto the A32). After visiting the National Ceramics Museum and viewing some of Leeuwarden's elegant 18th-century facades, you can take the A31 to the IJsselmeer coastline. Take the dike road (N31), exploring coastal towns such as the pottery town of **Makkum**, the former fishing village of **Hindeloopen** with its painted traditional furniture, and the port of Harlingen along the way. If you have additional time, you can take the ferry from here to the island of **Terschelling**. Option two: On Day 8 travel north to **Groningen** (follow A50 to Zwolle, then A28 to Meppel, and turn finally onto A32). If time allows, spend a night on the restful island of **Schiermonnikoog** (take N361 northbound to the Lauwersoog ferry terminal).

In both cases, return to Amsterdam on the A7, which takes you over the Afsluitdijk, the long dike that closes off the IJsselmeer from the North Sea. If you are heading straight back to Amsterdam, stay on the A7. The island of **Texel** is only a small detour (take N99 and N250 to the ferry terminal at Den Helder). Return to the A7. The picturesque towns of **Enkhuizen** and **Hoorn** (take the N302 turnoff from the A7) are typical of the former fishing ports of West Friesland and merit an overnight stay or a short visit to their museums.

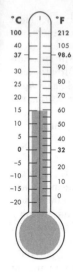

°C / °F
100 / 212
40 / 105
37 / 98.6
30 / 90
25 / 80
20 / 70
15 / 60
10 / 50
5 / 40
0 / 32
-5 / 20
-10 / 10
-15 / 10
-20 / 0

The Netherlands is at its best when the temperatures climb and cafés and restaurants spill across sidewalks to lure happy groups to dine on canal boats moored alongside. Unfortunately, because such weather is so transient, you could find yourself sharing your sun-dappled experience with too many others for comfort. Because the famous tulip fields bloom during April and May, this is perhaps the best time to visit Holland. Spring is also the driest time of the year. Rain, however, can arrive year-round to dampen your sightseeing, so, like the locals, always have an umbrella at the ready, as sunny afternoons are often preceded by stormy mornings.

From tulip time (mid-April to mid-May) onward, it becomes increasingly difficult to obtain accommodations reservations. In addition, with the approach of summer, museums, galleries, and tourist sights heave with visitors. Some say that if you are making an extended tour of Europe, you should consider scheduling Holland for the beginning or end of your itinerary, saving July and August for exploring less crowded countries.

But if you have to visit in high summer, be sure to take a vacation from your Amsterdam vacation and discover the cities that have that quaint Dutch beauty (not to mention cultural and social happenings plus historical interest), all without the crush. Optimum times to visit are May through June and September through October. Swimming is possible from May or June onward but is reserved for the hardy. The main cultural calendar runs from September through June, but happily there are so many festivals and open-air events scheduled in summer that no one really notices.

Climate

Weather-wise, the best months for sightseeing are April, May, June, September, and October, when the days are long and the summer crowds have not yet filled the beaches and the museums to capacity. The maritime climate of The Netherlands is very changeable, though, and during these months expect weather ranging from cool to pleasant to wet and windy to hot and surprisingly humid. Eastern and southeastern provinces edge toward a more Continental climate, with warmer summers and colder winters than along the North Sea coast, which can itself be very cold from December through February and March.

🗐 Forecasts **Weather Channel Connection** ☎ 900/932–8437, 95¢ per min from a Touch-Tone phone ⊕ www.weather.com.

AMSTERDAM

Jan.	40F	4C	May	61F	16C	Sept.	65F	18C
	34	1		50	10		56	13
Feb.	41F	5C	June	65F	18C	Oct.	56	13C
	34	1		56	13		49	9
Mar.	47F	8C	July	70F	21C	Nov.	47F	8C
	38	3		59	15		41	5
Apr.	52F	11C	Aug.	68F	20C	Dec.	41F	5C
	43	6		59	15		36	2

ON THE CALENDAR

Jan.–Feb.

The widely acclaimed **International Film Festival Rotterdam** (☎ 0900/403–4065) celebrates international avant-garde cinema. More than 300 noncommercial films are screened in the Pathé on the Stadschouwburgplein, the IMAX Waterstad Theater, Lantaren/Venster, and the Luxor (and others), and run over 10 days from the last week of January to the first week of February.

If it is cold enough—sometimes 20 years go by before the weather is deemed frigid enough—Friesland hosts its famous **Elfstedentocht**, a one-day, 11-city ice-skating race through some of Holland's prettiest medieval towns. There is no set day, but it usually happens sometime in January or February. Thousands of participants don garb to honor the glowing hues of the House of Orange and set out to Hans Brinker their way from Leeuwarden, capital of Friesland, through the circuit towns of Sneek, IJlst, Sloten, Stavoren, Hindeloopen, Workum, Bolsward, Harlingen, Franeker, and Dokkum. All of Holland watches the race on TV.

Feb.

Toward the end of February, just before Lent, the festivities of **Carnival** are kicked off in Limburg province, the most Catholic part of the country. The city of Maastricht is particularly famed for its merrymaking parades and events, although even Amsterdam up in Noord-Holland sports a Carnival parade.

Mar.

The **Stille Omgang (Silent Procession)** (☎ 023/524–6229) has local Amsterdam Catholics processing through the streets on the Saturday night after March 10 to commemorate the 1345 Miracle of the Host, which has traditionally been regarded as a founding date for the city proper.

Held at Maastricht's MECC Congress and Exhibition Hall, the **European Fine Art Fair** (☎ European Fine Art Foundation, Box 1035, 5200 BA 's-Hertogenbosch ☎ 073/614 5165 ⊕ www.tefaf.com) presents a panoply of old-master paintings that attracts one of the fanciest crowds of collectors from around the world for 10 glamorous days beginning every mid-March. A fabled team of experts examines items to weed out any pieces of dubious authenticity—of those items that pass the test, the best known and most sought after are probably the paintings of the Renaissance to Baroque eras.

Apr.

During the last Saturday in April, the *Bloemen Corso,* or **Bulb District Flower Parade** (☎ 0252/434710) passes through Lisse to open the **National Floral Exhibition** (☎ 0252/465555) at Keukenhof Gardens, heralding the peak days for visiting the famous tulip fields. The 32-km (20-mi) route runs from Noordwijk to Haarlem. **National Museum Weekend** opens 450 museums across the country to visitors free or at a discount. April 30 is the unforgettable **Queen's Day,** the Dutch monarch's official birthday, when Amsterdam erupts with a citywide, all-day street party and the queen makes a more sedate official visit to a selected town in the provinces. This is actually the birth date of Queen Juliana, but her daughter Queen Beatrix now celebrates her B-day all the same. Because of a one-day, "free-license" law, thousands of Amsterdammers mount a gigantic "yard sale" by lining the streets with stalls filled with their attic bric-a-brac. April 29 sees an all-night party in some cities, with Utrecht being a center for the party-hearty crowd.

May

May 4 and 5 are **Remembrance and Liberation Day** respectively and are marked by solemnity on the former and huge frolicsome music festivals throughout the country on the latter. Every imaginable art form is represented at the annual arts fair in Amsterdam's southern suburb RAI convention center, **KunstRAI** (☎ 020/549–1212), usually beginning near the end of the month. **National Bicycle Day** (May 8) has both professionals and novices racing through The Netherlands. An international modern dance festival, **Spring Dance** (☎ 030/232–4125), bounds into Utrecht. Usually the second Saturday in May, **Nationale Molendag** is Holland's National Windmill Day, when more than half of the nation's 1,000 windmills are in action and open for visits by the public. Also in May, the **Asparagus Season** is upon kitchens across the land as chefs make hay to create concoctions with Holland's fabled bumper crop of "white gold."

SUMMER

June

Usually around June 3, the famed herring fleets of Scheveningen unfurl festive banners, decorate ships, and hold crafts markets to ceremoniously celebrate **Vlaggetjesdag** (or Flag Day), the traditional start of the herring season, by racing out to haul in the first barrel of *groene* (fresh) herring to grace the table of Queen Beatrix. Green thumbers and lovers of luxury will love the **Open Garden Days** (☎ 020/320–3660), sponsored by Stichting de Amsterdamse Grachtentuin, when private houses along the posh Herengracht, Keizersgracht, and Prinsengracht open their private gardens and salons for several days in mid-June. Over a period of 10 days, the **Amsterdam Roots Festival** (☎ 0900/0191) brings together the best global acts in the city's best venues. **Holland Festival of the Performing Arts** (☎ 020/530–7110) captures Amsterdam, spilling over to The Hague, Rotterdam, and Utrecht, making this the biggest national fête for the performing arts. Most opera, dance, theater, and concert presentations are held in Amsterdam, and tickets usually go on sale May 1. **Parkpop** (☎ 070/361–8888), a pop music festival, livens up The Hague. To enjoy open-air concerts and theater, check out the **Vondelpark Theater** (☎ 020/673–1499) and its summer calendar, running from June through August.

July

Rotterdam's **Metropolis Pop Festival** hosts national and international performances on three stages in the Zuiderpark on the first Sunday of July. The Hague hosts the **North Sea Jazz Festival** (☎ 015/214–8900) with live performances by top international artists. The **International Organ Competition** (☎ 023/511–5733) brings musicians to Haarlem in even-number years.

Aug.

The Amsterdam **Canal Festival** brings flotillas of boats for classical music performances on a floating stage on the canal. For two weeks **Parade** (☎ 033/465–4577) re-creates and updates a Breughel painting by bringing together absurd theatrics in Martin Luther Park. The

Gay Pride Boat Parade (☎ 020/620–8807) fills Amsterdam's canals with over-the-top spectacle and the canal sides with as many as a quarter million spectators on the first Saturday in August. Rotterdam mounts a **Heineken Jazz and Blues Festival** in various locations during August. Around August 20, Scheveningen Pier and Boulevard, not far from The Hague, hosts a three-day **Fireworks Festival.**

FALL

Sept.

The **Bloemen Corso Floral Parade** (☎ 0297/325100) makes a daylong procession of floats from Aalsmeer to Amsterdam in early September; **Gaudeamus International Music Week** (☎ 020/694–7349) honors contemporary classical music and its young composers in Amsterdam; and the **Opening of Parliament** (☎ 070/356–4000) takes place in The Hague on the third Tuesday—the queen arrives in her golden coach in a ceremonial promenade that heads out from the "office palace" of Noordeinde to the famed medieval complex at the Binnenhof. During the first Saturday in September, **Open Monumentendag** means that you can enter many historic buildings normally closed to the public. The famous collection of historic windmills in Zaandam takes center stage every September 30 during **Zaanse Windmill Day** in the Zaanse Schans area, just to the north of Amsterdam.

Oct.

The **Holland Dance Festival** (☎ 0900/340–3505) brings ballet and other dance companies to The Hague. After a few years in Amsterdam, **Crossing Border** (☎ www.crossingborder.nl) has returned to The Hague to continue its good work as a "literary festival that rocks."

Nov.–Dec.

With the **St. Nicolaas Parade** (☎ 0900/400–4040) in Amsterdam on November 18 and in cities throughout the country, the arrival of Sinter Klaas launches the Christmas season. Indeed, the American Santa Claus is a holiday descendant of the Dutch saint, who, with little padding (wouldn't you know, the jolly fat Santa is an American invention) arrives then to dispense ginger cookies. The biggest day is Sinterklaasvond, December 5. People offer poems heralding their friends, and many towns host St. Nicholas, who gallops from house to house, leaving gag presents behind. In Amsterdam, Santa arrives by barge near Sint Nicholasskerk, along with his "Moorish" helper, Zwarte Piet (Black Peter). Real presents are often saved for the more commercial festivities on December 25. Amsterdam's Christmas Market in the Museumplein square is held December 7–24. Unfortunately, because of global warming, the canals of Amsterdam freeze up more and more infrequently, but when a frigid cold wave moves in from the North Sea, the locals hope the city will permit skating on the canals, often under the stars. Of a much more adult nature, **High Times Cannabis Cup** (☎ 020/624–1777) employs the Melkweg avenue to celebrate harvest season with five days of wastedness punctuated with bands, banquets, and much-coveted awards for farming abilities. Around December 19, Gouda hosts a beautiful **Gouda by Candlelight** festival. The globally prestigious **International Documentary Film Festival** (☎ 020/626–1939) is centered around Leidseplein and attracts tens of thousands to its hundreds of screenings.

Diamonds & Delft

As old as Amsterdam is, some things never seem to change. The bustle and noise of crowds of shoppers in the area surrounding its Dam Square is reminiscent of the cattle drives that only a few centuries ago thundered to market through the Kalverstraat (Calf's Street), now one of the major shopping streets. The city's mercantile roots go as far back as Rembrandt's day, when the maritime Dutch West India and East India companies were busy colonizing a trading empire so far-flung the sun never set on it entirely. The resulting plunder—spices from Java, porcelains from China, furs from Russia, rugs from Turkey—made Amsterdammers into the very first shop-till-you-droppers. Today, Holland shines with equal radiance for shoppers, be they the millionaire trade or economy-minded nabobs. Whether you go for Baroque or for postmillennium, the variety of goods available in Amsterdam, The Hague, Rotterdam, and other cities energizes a continuous parade of boutiques, street markets, and department stores. Hunting in Holland for that special purchase is akin to grand entertainment. Thanks to the six-centuries-old Dutch history of savvy trading, you can save the money that a world cruise would cost and instead stay here to shop. Clothing, cosmetics, food, household items, furniture, gifts, and toys are on offer from every corner of the globe; there are even shops that deal with special-category goods from specific countries, such as Indonesian bric-a-brac. Of course you'll particularly want to shop for Dutch specialties.

Diamonds have always been an Amsterdammer's best friend. Starting with the Spanish conquest of 1576, many diamond experts fled north, from Antwerp to the Netherlandish capital. Shiploads of raw diamonds from India or Brazil led to a spate of feverish activity, lasting until the cargo was cut and the finished stone sent off, usually to Paris. This stream became a flood when the children of a Dutch farmer living near Hopetown, South Africa, discovered that pebbles in a nearby stream made marvelous toys. Soon, the diamond rush was on and Amsterdam became famed as the home of diamond cutters. A visit to one of the city's modern diamond centers (there are several around the Rokin) offers the visitor a brief education in this fascinating business.

What other gifts "say" Holland? Holland is a chocoholic's mecca, and everyone knows the mmmm-boy flavors crafted by Droste and Van Houten. Those good Dutch chocolates are available in prepackaged bars, but head to a shop such as Amsterdam's Puccini Bomboni, centrally located on the Singel canal, to stock up on large slabs or handmade bonbons with exotic fillings. Many travelers wind up delving into Delft. If you want to serve your choice Gouda in the proper manner back home, you may want to purchase a piece of authentic Delftware. The key word is "authentic." A variety of blue and white "delft" is available in a range of brands and prices, and you can pick up attractive souvenir-quality "delft" pieces at any giftware shop. But the real McCoy is known as Royal Delft, and it can be found in the better giftware shops, such as those on Amsterdam's Rokin and the PC Hooftstraat. No visit to Delft is complete without stopping off at the Royal Porcelain Factory to see plates and tulip vases being painted by hand and perhaps picking up a souvenir or two. These wares bear the worthy name of De Porceleyne Fles. On the bottom of each object is a triple signature: a plump vase topped by a straight line, the stylized letter "F" below it, and the word "Delft." Blue is no longer the only official color. In 1948, a rich red cracked glaze was premiered depicting profuse flowers, graceful birds, and leaping gazelles. There is New Delft, a range of green, gold, and black hues, whose exquisite minuscule figures are drawn to resemble an old Persian tapestry; the Pynacker Delft, borrowing Japanese motifs in rich oranges and golds; and the brighter Polychrome Delft, which can strike a brilliant sunflower-yellow effect. When shopping, keep in mind that there are many companies creating "delft," but only one crafting the porcelain that has colored the world since the 17th century with its unique blue. Holland's other famous ceramic is Makkum pottery, whose only genuine objects come from the firm of Koninklijke Tichelaar Makkum (Royal Tichelaar).

Dining in Any Language Her sons and daughters having ranged the
four corners of the earth for several centuries, Holland can offer you a large variety of cooking, and the frequent trips that Dutch businesspeople make to Paris have served to ensure that the French cuisine in Holland, when it is good, is very, very good. If your soul yearns for them, and your wallet can stand the strain, caviar sorbet, blue trout with white truffles, and passion-fruit soufflé are yours for the ordering. But real Dutch cooking is made of sterner stuff— or, at least they used to say so, in days of yore. Simple, solid nourishment, without any fancy trimmings that might hide the basic high quality of the food, is what warmed the cockles of the average Hollander's culinary heart. Happily, over the past two decades, the usual array of *erwtensoep,* a thick pea soup, and *hutspot,* a hotchpotch of a stew, watered-down beers, and plain boiled fish, have given way to an amazing array of dining delights, thanks to the nouvelle incursion that has taken the starch—literally—out of many Dutch menus. New chefs have now enlarged their purview to encompass most of the world. In the space of two weeks, diners in Amsterdam can cover as much tongue-tingling ground as in a two-week package tour of exotic, far-flung places, especially the Indonesian culinary classics (so delicious it was rumored that the Dutch invaded Java just for a good rijsttafel, or rice served with several small, spicy meat, poultry, and vegetable dishes).

One way the Dutch have always had a dining advantage over other Europeans is the quantity and quality of the fresh ingredients available to them. Their national green thumb produces the continent's best and greatest variety of vegetables and fruits, and their dairy farms supply a rich store of creams, cheeses, and butter for sauces. In recent years the traditional grassroots values of organic farming have been making inroads, in sharp contrast to the intensive greenhouse agriculture in which the Dutch excel. The forests yield game, and the sea dikes are covered with rare herbs and other vegetation that nourishes their lambs and calves, resulting in exceptionally tasty, tender meats year-round. The waters of The Netherlands, both salt and fresh, are well known for the quality and variety of the fish and shellfish they yield. Today, even in rural areas, imaginative dishes are prepared with the high-quality fresh ingredients so readily available. Many Dutch chefs have also spent time in the kitchens of France and Belgium to learn the techniques of both traditional and nouvelle haute cuisine. The rest of the population also travels far and wide, and this has influenced dining habits in The Netherlands. You find Chinese, Italian, Mexican, and Indian restaurants even in small cities. Traditional cooking and regional recipes with seasonal ingredients can still be savored in Old Dutch restaurants, which usually display the NEERLANDS DIS (Dutch dish) soup tureen sign.

Before fine restaurants started making an inroad, the main Amsterdam dining mainstay was the "brown café," or *bruine kroeg,* so called because they are rarely decorated with anything but the residue of three decades of pipe and cigarette smoke. A cross between a British pub and a French café, they still serve, for the most part, good inexpensive food and top it all off with a normally exuberant atmosphere. Whether it be in a cozy café, a reinvented industrial monument, a chic purveyor of international elegance, or a trendy eatery for hipsters, in Amsterdam and other major cities, dinner is served until 10 in most restaurants, though most diners eat between 7 and 9; elsewhere, dining hours vary by local custom. In the northern and eastern provinces, people dine from as early as 6, and in the southern provinces, dinner is later: from 8 to 9. However, even in Amsterdam and other large cities, it is difficult to find a place that will serve you after 10.

Rembrandt & Company An actual trip to Holland is not necessary
to savor this unique country; a short visit to any major museum will probably just as effectively transport the viewer—by way of the paintings of Rembrandt, Hals, Vermeer, De Hootch, Terborch, Van Ruysdael, Hobbema, and Van Gogh—to its legendary landscapes, city scenes, and domestic interiors. Few other countries can boast of having fathered so many great artists, but then again, Holland seems almost expressly composed for the artist by nature; its peaceful dells, rolling dunes, and verdant mantles of foliage seem so alluring they practically demand the artist pick up brush and palette. Holland is obviously much more than what can fit on an easel—but as the grand and glorious history of Dutch art proves, not that much more.

To begin, it is important to make the distinction between Flemish and Dutch painting. In the late 16th century, The Netherlands were divided into a Flemish, predominantly Roman Catholic south, still under Spanish rule, and an independent alliance of seven Dutch Protestant northern provinces. Until then, most of the painters hailed from the southern cities of Ghent, Antwerp, and Bruges, and their subject matter was mostly biblical and allegorical. A few of the most influential include Jan van Eyck (1385–1441), who founded the Flemish School and perfected the technique of oil painting, and Rogier van der Weyden (1399–1464), who swept the canvas clean and focused on the personalities of his subjects, injecting an emotional intensity into his work and straying from the typical devotional pictures that were crammed with detail and symbolism and showed static groups of bodies. Two other notables were Hieronymus Bosch (1450–1516), whose meticulously detailed, macabre allegorical paintings can take hours to decipher, and Pieter Bruegel the Elder (1525–69), whose scenes depicting peasant life in Flemish landscapes are an amalgam of color and texture.

In the northern provinces, around Haarlem, a different style of painting began to surface. Jan Mostaert (1475–1555) and Lucas van der Leyden (1489–1553) were on the cusp of this new movement, which brought a kind of realism into previously static and religious paintings. In Utrecht, meanwhile, followers of the Italian master Caravaggio made a complete break with mannerist painting. The chiaroscuro technique used light and shadow to play out dramatic contrasts and created realism as had never been seen on canvas before.

Gerrit van Honthorst (1590–1656) is probably the most well-known Dutch representative of this particular style.

Out of these two disparate schools flowed the 17th-century Golden Age of Dutch painting. Hals, Rembrandt, and Vermeer were all influenced by such diversity of technique. During the height of the Golden Age, paintings were mass produced and artists specialized in different genre paintings to keep up with the demands of the market. Religious paintings and portraits remained highly popular, but maritime, city, landscapes, and other genre paintings found an outlet as well.

Frans Hals (1581–1666) has been called the first modern painter. A fantastically adept and naturally gifted man, he could turn out a portrait in an hour. He delighted in capturing the emotions of a moment—a smile or a grimace—in an early manifestation of the same impressionist preferences that were to capture art in the 19th century. In his works he breaks with the static tradition, and his naturalistic portraits capture the emotional expression of his subjects while also giving the impression of an informal, relaxed scene. His psychological portraits, however, are not generally considered as perceptive as those of his most famous contemporary. Rembrandt van Rijn (1606–69) is regarded as the most versatile artist of the 17th century, and his fame is uncontested. Born in Leiden, the fifth child of a miller, he grew rich from painting and tuition paid by his pupils (two of whom, Govert Flinck and Ferdinand Bol, are now considered to be the authors of many a masterwork previously thought to have been painted by Rembrandt); for a while his wealth was such that he became a noted collector of art. Into his first works he painted a heap of over-ornamentation, but then, as the years went by, he dug deeper and deeper into the essence of his subjects and portrayed the incessant metaphysical struggle for inner beauty and reason. When his whole material world crashed about him, though he was blackmailed and ruined, he unaccountably continued to turn out art that grew greater and greater. His marvelously skilled use of light and shadow is a text and source of wonder. He began his career painting commissioned portraits for wealthy merchants but soon grew bored of pleasing the increasingly political and fickle rich. His quick temper and his interest in darker subjects made him unpopular in those more elite circles. The *Night Watch* (1642), his major group portrait, was considered artistically innovative but failed to please his audience, and he soon found himself at the margins of "good" society; still, he continued to work. Some of his most impressive work dates from that later period in his life.

Jan Vermeer (1632–72) is the third in this triumvirate of artists and is a different case altogether. He produced only 35 known paintings during his career, but these exquisite portraits of simple domestic life make him the most precious genre painter of his time. He brought genre art to its peak; in small canvases of a sometimes overwhelming realism, he painted the soft calm and everyday sameness of scenes from middle-class life, with the subjects caught and held fast in the net of their normal surroundings. A rather reticent man, he lived his whole life in Delft and died poor.

Around the middle of the century, Baroque influences began to permeate Dutch painting, bringing with it a trend for both the picturesque and the utterly natural. As for the latter, artists such as Jacob van Ruysdael, Salomon van Ruysdael, Albert Cuyp, and Meindert Hobbema started producing landscape painting, making landscape—once relegated to the background of most canvases—the primary subject. Their tranquil scenes of polder lanes, rustic hillocks, grazing cows, and windswept canals were coveted by 17th- and 18th-century collectors stuck in noisy cities and obviously offered a sort of "visual Valium" to them. Other masters were more playful in tone. Probably the most famous recorder of riotous scenes was the tavern keeper Jan Steen (1625–79). His lively, bitingly satiric, sometimes lewd domestic scenes are imbued with humor; a "Jan Steen household" suggests a scene of disorder. He was the painter par excellence of the Dutch shopkeeper and his family—the lower middle class. He had trouble finding a market for his art; when he died, he supposedly had 500 unsold canvases. Steen's works are still a joy to see today, even if some of the nuances are lost on us.

Gerard Terborch (1617–81) developed a mastery of painting textile texture and served up a series of thoughtful "conversation pieces" posing his subject talking. Pieter de Hooch (1629–after 1688) excelled in painting the haute bourgeois interior, often populated by elegant matrons and burgher masters—he remains a connoisseur's favorite. Leiden's Gerard Dou (1613–75) also is famous for his interior domestic scenes, often with stunning light by candlelight. His paintings became highly fashionable in the 19th century and were collected by the dozen by the Rothschilds.

With the deaths of Hals, Rembrandt, and Vermeer and the French invasion, the Golden Age was gone for good. Following French models, painting became overrefined and stylized, falling away from its earlier innovations. Even in landscape painting, formulaic daubs in the Classical style were created by such masters as Jan Both (1618–52) and Nicolaes Berchem (1620–83). Fortunately, the greatest Golden Age canvases are still adored by all visitors who discover, even in the largest Dutch cities, corners where the real world appears to dissolve and, just for a moment, they have the sensation of stepping into a 17th-century painting. Browse through a book of Dutch art before you come to Holland, and have a look at paintings of church interiors by Saenredam and De Witte, and views of Delft, of Utrecht, or of Haarlem's St. Bavokerk. Store them away in your mind's eye and, sure enough, as you look across a market square from a certain angle, turn a corner of a canal, or wander through a church, you'll feel as if you've stepped into a Hobbema or Vermeer.

Wheel Estate
Whether you fancy having a go while you're in the country, or just watching the locals ambling by on theirs, the *fiet* or bicycle, is one thing you can't ignore in The Netherlands. Cycling's not merely a pastime here, it's a way of life, providing a convenient means of transport for kids going to school, shoppers to market, and workers to the office. In this country of 15 million people there are 12 million bikes, making bike theft a major problem in the bigger towns. A lighthearted Dutch legend predicts that if you holler "That's my bike!" when a crowd of cyclists is whizzing past, at least

three of them will pull over, abandon their saddles, and head off to the nearest side street.

The flatness of The Netherlands makes it ideal cycling terrain, and throughout the country some 17,000 km (10,000 mi) of special lanes and pathways ensure that it's also very safe, which explains why only speed cyclists tend to wear any form of protective gear, such as helmets. That said, amateur cyclists engage in enough precarious riding styles to leave visitors wondering if helmets wouldn't be a good idea for everyone. There's the delicately balanced "side-saddle" passenger technique (a friend hops on to the bar at the back), for example, not to mention the pull-along wooden boxes that are attached to the bicycle and are sometimes seen holding as many as three small children, plus a dog and the week's groceries. In the bigger cities, watch out for all the special bike lanes. Even though the traffic may be flowing in one direction, bikers are allowed to head in both, and just because the light is red doesn't mean you might not be overtaken by a slew of bikers heading your way.

If you want to try it, bike rentals are nearly always available at train stations, and many of the larger hotels will have them, too. You'll probably need to have your passport at hand. Give your bike a short test ride before you going off with it, to be sure you haven't rented a *rammelkast,* or "bone shaker." Another thing to be aware of is the unusual factory-installed protective chain beneath the saddle that's then passed through the wheels. If you get one of these, make sure the bike shop shows you how it operates before you cycle off; the same applies to the lights, which sometimes have the switches in the most unexpected places. If you're planning on doing a lot of cycling, you may want to invest in a set of *panniers,* special canvas saddlebags that will easily hold the necessary essentials: picnic, map, water bottle, and sweater. You can pick these up cheaply from Hema stores (found in almost every larger town), and they simply strap onto your bicycle.

Once on the road, the signs to look for consist of direction pointers featuring red letters on a white background. A special lane or *fietspad* is indicated by a round blue sign with a white bike in the middle. Elsewhere, ultraclear signage allows you to cycle from one spot to another using numbers as your guide; maps of such cycle routes are available from any VVV and most railway stations. When it comes to an environmentally friendly and healthful mode of travel that will allow you to see everything at your own pace, the Dutch will assure you: a bike can't be beat. A car means you have to stop and get out to look around; on foot you don't cover ground. But on a bike you can interact with the people and the countryside, and blissfully hear the wind blowing through the fields.

FODOR'S CHOICE

The sights, restaurants, hotels, and other travel experiences listed below are our editors' top picks—the crème de la crème chosen from the lists of Fodor's Choices found on the opening pages of the chapters in this book. They're the best of their type in the area covered by the book. In addition, the list incorporates many of the highly recommended restaurants and hotels our reviewers have come to treasure. In the chapters that follow, you will find all the details.

LODGING

$$$$ **Amstel Inter-Continental, Amsterdam.** Elegant enough to please a queen, extroverted enough to welcome Madonna, the Rolling Stones, and Michael Jackson, this grand dowager has wowed all onlookers since it opened its doors in 1867. With its palatial five stories, sash windows, and historic roof dormers, you'll feel like a visiting dignitary when entering the magnificent lobby, a soaring salon covered with wedding-cake stucco trim and replete with a grand double staircase that demands you glide, not walk, down it.

$$$$ **Des Indes Inter-Continental, The Hague.** Stay here and you'll be following in the footsteps of Empress Josephine of France, Theodore Roosevelt, and the legendary ballerina Anna Pavlova, who all loved this stately grande dame of the Belle Epoque era.

$$$$ **Hotel Château St. Gerlach, Valkenburg.** This gorgeous hotel, in an old tenant farm on the château estate, offers visitors plush, Provençal-style rooms and Les Trois Corbeaux, which attracts gourmands from all over The Netherlands.

$$$$ **Seven One Seven, Amsterdam.** This classical 19th-century canal-side guest house contains salons that fuse grandeur with tasteful glamour; guest rooms are minimuseums filled with classical antiquities, framed art, and flowers, while the plush library enjoys a setting designed after Sherlock Holmes's own heart.

$$$$ **Spaarne 8, Haarlem.** This exclusive 1765 restored hotel, redesigned by Dick Beijer (renowned for his work for Elton John and Sir Terence Conran), is about super-luxury—the fact that it makes a design statement as well is just the topping.

$$$$ **Vuurtoren (Lighthouse), Harlingen.** For once in a lifetime, experience the unparalleled rush that accompanies sleeping at the top of a luxurious lighthouse—two people only, please.

$$$$ **Pulitzer Sheraton, Amsterdam.** A clutch of 17th- and 18th-century houses—25 in all—were combined to create this rambling hotel sprinkled with landscaped garden courtyards. Facing the Prinsengracht canal, it now has a certain irreverent postmodern quirkiness, a prizewinning wine cellar, and its own wooden boat for touring.

$$–$$$$ **Golden Tulip Efteling Hotel, Tilburg.** If you plan to stay late at the storybook realms of De Efteling amusement park, this on-site hotel is replet with fairy-tale-castle design and themed rooms—opt to sleep in canopy beds under a briar roof in the Sleeping Beauty suite (but don't prick your hand on the spinning wheel).

$–$$$$	**Bridges House, Delft.** The history of this exquisite hotel goes back to Jan Steen—one of the greatest painters of The Hague School—who lived and painted here. Helping to embody the age-old spirit of the city, antiques grace each spacious room.
$–$$$	**Hotel-Paleis Het Stadhouderlijk Hof, Leeuwarden.** History precedes you at this former royal palace, where the standard rates aren't princely but the room styles and quality of accommodations are fit for any king and his queen. Built in 1550, the palace was originally inhabited by William I, Prince of Orange, Duke of Nassau 1580–84. The red carpet now awaits *you*. Ideally located in the old part of town, it's the only place in The Netherlands where you can sleep in a royal palace.
$$$	**Ambassade, Amsterdam.** Ten 17th- and 18th-century houses have been folded into this hotel on the Herengracht, now home-away-from-home for such literati as Lessing, Le Carré, Eco, and Rushdie.
$$$	**De Keizerskroon Bilderberg, Apeldoorn.** Within walking distance of Paleis Het Loo, this grand country inn was once patronized by Czar Peter the Great and is still an obvious haunt of visiting royalty and those living vicariously.
$$–$$$	**Château de Havixhorst, Staphorst.** Both storks and gentry have landed at this 18th-century haven of manorial tranquility, ideal for some regal R&R with just the right infusion of fuss. The idea here is to be one with nature while perched, like the nesting and highly discriminating storks on the roof, in this moated castle (now a National Monument).
$$–$$$	**Kasteel Geulzicht, Heerlen.** Set amid gentle hills near the village of Houthem-St. Gerlach, this 19th-century fantasia of a Renaissance castle is a Disney-like vision, truly bristling with machicolations, stepped gables, and a looming tower. Inside, the guest rooms (some occupying the castle turrets and tower) are made for mortals, not legendary knights.
$–$$$	**Mercure De Draak, Bergen op Zoom.** Bursting with history, magnificent halls, and stylish guest rooms, the De Draak began life as an inn way back in 1397, so can claim to be Holland's oldest hotel. Headlined by its Great Hall and Markiezen Hall—spectacular set-pieces that still look ready to welcome the 17th-century burgomasters of Rembrandt—it also offers ravishingly updated guest quarters.
$–$$$	**Schimmelpenninck Huys, Groningen.** Reeking with history all the way back to the 11th century, this grand old patrician mansion with a Dutch *klok* gable from the 1600s has been cleverly melded into 50 pristine, modern boudoirs, and apartments.

BUDGET LODGING

$	**Het Rentmeesterhuis, Fraeylemaborg.** This bed-and-breakfast is set in a beautifully renovated house dating from 1720, which served as the steward's residence for the noted Fraeylemaborg manor-house museum. Awaken for the magnum of all breakfasts, served in the antiques-filled country kitchen.
$	**Hotel d'Orangerie, Maastricht.** Situated in a building that dates from 1752, this is a delightful, intimate little hotel with country-house

coziness and a breakfast room warmed by a marble fireplace, chandeliers, and pretty frescoed walls.

$ **Quentin England, Amsterdam.** A connoisseur's delight—adorned with a Tudor gable and five-step gable—the Quentin occupies two buildings created in 1884 as homages to England and Holland. The tiny breakfast room is particularly enchanting, with flower boxes on the windowsills, dark-wood tables, and fin-de-siècle decorations.

¢ **B&B Oosteinde, Delft.** Located behind the Beestenmarkt, near the fairytale twin towers of the city gate at Oostpoort, this welcoming house will make you feel like a Delft resident, not a visitor.

RESTAURANTS

$$$$ **Château Neercanne, Maastricht.** Built in 1698 as a pleasure dome for one of Maastricht's military governors, this spot was chosen by Queen Beatrix as the venue for state banquets. Walk off any excess calories in the magnificent Baroque-style garden.

$$$$ **De Librije, Zwolle.** Housed in the stunning, beamed, former library of a 15th-century monastery, owner-chef Jonnie Boer's restaurant walls are lined with accolades, searing his reputation as Holland's *crème de la crème*. His "Cuisine Pure" is a dazzler, based on local ingredients such as nettles, water mint, berries, rose hips, wild mushrooms, mustard, and even cat's tails (the plant version, of course).

$$$$ **Excelsior, Amsterdam.** For when only the classically elegant will do, take your primped-up selves here. Solicitous waiters, knowledgeable sommeliers, and towering dessert trolleys all waltz together in a setting of towering palms, tall candelabras, and shimmering chandeliers. Even more more delicious is the mouthwatering view of the Amstel River.

$$$$ **Kasteel Doorwerth, Arnhem.** If 200 candles lit in the chandeliers of a moated castle overlooking the Rhine don't "get you in the mood," then your significant other had better drop you off and drive on. The ultimate romantic dinner is what we're after here, only 8 km (5 mi) from Arnhem, and featuring a timbered dining room, once the castle's coach house, furnished with antiques, not that you'll notice.

$$$$ **La Rive, Amsterdam.** The Amstel Inter-Continental' restaurant is having no problem maintaining its reputation for celestial cuisine under chef Edwin Kats, whose creations will delight chubby-walleted epicureans.

$$$$ **Nolet's, Yerseke.** With an interior that doubles as a museum on Reymerswaele, with many excavated exhibits from the village that gave the world the famous Flemish painter Marinus van Reymerswaele, this place is legendary for its seafood (although the large aquarium on view might give some heartburn).

$$$$ **Vermeer, Amsterdam.** With its milk-white walls, dramatic black-and-white patterned floors, Delft plates, fireplace hearths, and Stern Old Dutch chandeliers, this stately place does conjure up the amber canvases of the great Johannes (if he ever did the decor for a fancy hotel chain, that is). Young chef Pascal Jalaij's creations are cosmic

in the way they balance texture and contrast (what this man does with fois gras!).

$$$-$$$$ **Breitner, Amsterdam.** With a formal interior of rich red carpeting and muted pastel colors, a grand vista over the City Hall complex, and fabulous food, it's no wonder the patrons do their share to show respect for Breitner by dressing smartly.

$$$-$$$$ **L'Orage, Delft.** As soon as you walk through the door you anticipate the sensational dining options on offer, thanks to Jannie Munk— Delft's very own Lady Chef (one of the many awards she has won)— who is now reaching out to a wider public thanks to the professional classes she offers in her kitchen.

$$$-$$$$ **Le Garage, Amsterdam.** A decade ago, this building's industrial roots were erased to make room for a brasserie of red plush seating and kaleidoscopically mirrored walls—handy for its clientele of Hollandwood glitterati who like to see and be seen. This is the home of the celebrity "Crazy Chef" Joop Braakhekke, whose Flemish *hennepotje*, a starter pâté of chicken, snails, and rabbit, is particularly sublime.

$$$-$$$$ **Marc Smeets, The Hague.** The Hague's top culinary temple is replete with shimmering chandeliers, gigantic red-orange banquettes, and more-than-nouvelle combinations that dazzle the tongue, such as his oven-cooked pheasant with sauerkraut and pancetta bacon. Deescrumptious.

$$$-$$$$ **Paul Fagel at Het Arsenaal, Naarden.** Past and future come together here in a high-concept renovation of a 17th-century arsenal masterminded by Jan des Bouvrie, who is to Holland what Philippe Starck is to France. Fagel, himself, is a whiz kid—as you'll see with his succulent oven-roasted lamb.

$$$-$$$$ **Toine Hermsen, Maastricht.** Unashamedly elegant—think crystal, crisp white napery, and gleaming silverware—but with food that is plain delicious, including the Bresse duck with tomato confit, bell peppers, and potatoes in Provençale sauce.

$$-$$$$ **De Poort, Amsterdam.** A showpiece in Old Dutch style (complete with polished woods and ceiling paintings), De Poort—part of the Die Poert van Cleve hotel complex—is, in fact, officially Old Dutch with its roots as a "steak brasserie" stretching back to 1870. By the time you read this, De Poort will have served 6 million of its acclaimed juicy slabs but don't forget the pea soup thick enough to eat with a fork.

$$$ **Manoir Inter Scaldes, Yerseke.** Maartje Boudeling's imaginative use of the products of the region—seafood, fish, lamb, wild game, and fresh herbs—is unrivaled. Not surprisingly, as the daughter of an oyster farmer, her selection of oysters is among the sweetest and most succulent you can sample.

$$-$$$ **It Rains Fishes, The Hague.** Near-neighbor Prince Willem Alexander, heir to the Dutch throne, has been known to pop in here to feast on predominantly aquatic specialties that combine Thai, Malaysian, Indonesian, and French flavors. Finish the night off with the Thai basil and chocolate sorbet.

$$–$$$	**Polman's Huis, Utrecht.** Tall windows and an impossibly distant stucco ceiling dwarf the coffee drinkers in this grandest of grand cafés.
$–$$	**Dudok Brasserie, The Hague.** These days, Dudok is *the* in place in The Hague, because it's ideal for people-of-every-stripe-watching, from politicians debating over a beer, to the *jeunesse d'orée* toying with their salads, to pensioners tucking into an afternoon tea of cream cakes and salmon sandwiches.
$–$$	**'T Goude Hooft, The Hague.** Magnificently dating from 1423 but rebuilt in 1660, the oldest restaurant in The Hague has a well-preserved interior, with plenty of wooden beams, brass chandeliers, and "antique" furniture all richly redolent of the Dutch Golden Age. Try the platter of *bitterballen*. (What are these croquettes made of? No one will tell you.)
¢–$$	**Winkel van Sinkel, Utrecht.** This Neoclassical *paleis* (palace) is fronted with columns and cast-iron statues of women, conjuring up images of Grecian luxe and abundance. If the terrace is packed, head inside to have a tasty lunch or dinner in the fantastic, high-ceilinged Grote Zaal.

BUDGET RESTAURANTS

¢–$	**Café Bern, Amsterdam.** This dark and woody café, as evocative as a Jan Steen 17th-century interior, has been serving the same cheese fondue for decades and for good reason: it's about perfect.
¢–$	**De Gevulde Koe, Amsterdam.** "The Stuffed Cow" has an ever-changing menu that tends to favor less—strange, considering its name—beef and more fish and ostrich (in truffle sauce!). In short: this is the ultimate in earthy Dutch eating cafés where a yuppie has yet to be sighted.
¢	**Keuken van 1870, Amsterdam.** The best and most economic foray into the satiating world of traditional Dutch cooking, as reassuring as a Dutch grandmother, the kitchen serves such warming singularities as *erwtensoep*, a sausage-fortified pea soup so thick you could eat it with a toothpick.
¢	**'t Pannekoekschip, Groningen.** Kids adore the more than 100 kinds of pancakes at this popular pancake ship—yes, it's literally a ship. Adults love these sizzling delights, too—but be aware that pancakes are not breakfast fare in Holland.

QUINTESSENTIAL HOLLAND

	Amsterdam canals at night. Walking along the canals of Amsterdam after dark is one of the simplest, cheapest, and most memorable experiences that Holland has to offer. Pedestrians (and cyclists) rule over traffic, the most beautiful gables are subtly lighted up, and the pretty humpbacked bridges are festooned with lights. Alternatively, get up early and stroll out before the city is awake as the mist gently rises off the water.

Begijnhof, Amsterdam. Feel the gentle breeze of history in the solitude of a serene courtyard that has hardly changed since the Pilgrim Fathers worshipped here centuries ago.

Bikes on dikes (most anywhere). Trundling along the top of a dike on a sit-up-and-beg Dutch bicycle, with the sea to one side of you, wetlands (alive with bird life) on the other, and the wind in your hair, is transporting in more ways than one. Enhance the delight by stopping over at one of myriad waterside cafés or charming villages along the way.

Carnival, Maastricht. Medieval Christian pageantry combines with pagan revelry in the last days before Lent. Join the merriment of parades and parties as the ebullient southern Dutch go all out for a jolly good time.

Grotten Sint Pieter, Maastricht. At the Caves of Mount St. Peter, you can wander along some of the 20,000 passages and into the dim, echoing halls of a vast subterranean complex of caves that provided a refuge for the people of Limburg from AD 50 up to the Second World War.

Prinsenhof, Delft. Sit quietly in the courtyard garden, and then explore the atmospheric 15th-century convent before strolling off along what is probably the oldest canal in The Netherlands. At times it seems that you are stepping right into Vermeer's *View of Delft.*

WHERE ART COMES FIRST

Groningen Museum, Groningen. One of The Netherlands' most adventurous contributions to modern architecture stands like a gateway to the city as you leave the train station. Three distinctive pavilions, designed by different architects, are connected by waterways. Exhibitions include local history and an innovative series dedicated to modern fashion designers.

Kröller-Müller Museum, Otterlo. Art collections based on the quirks of one person's taste are often the choicest ones, as is here proved by Hélène Müller's stash of Van Goghs and modern art. Not only is the art world-class, but the museum is in the heart of The Netherlands' most beautiful nature reserve.

Nieuwe Kerk, Delft. Here, typically Dutch building materials of brick and wood give even soaring Gothic buildings a down-to-earth feel. Inside, however, you'll find the magnificent marble mausoleum of the royal House of Orange.

Paleis Het Loo, Apeldoorn. Stroll through the elegant formal gardens, view the sumptuous Dutch Baroque palace that was home to the Dutch royal family until the 1960s, then pop inside to feast your eyes on the rich furnishings.

Rietveld-Schroeder House, Utrecht. A pinnacle of Dutch modernism awaits you in a suburb of Utrecht. With its white walls, plate-glass windows, and clean straight lines, this villa—designed by Gerrit Rietveld—set the mark for much 20th-century European design.

Rijksmuseum, Amsterdam. As if the best collection of Dutch Golden Age art in the world were not enough, "the Rijks" also offers a cornucopia of other aesthetic delights. The collection of applied arts is especially comprehensive, from early Oriental Buddhas to 17th-century four-poster beds swathed in tapestry. Rembrandt's enormous *Night Watch* is a hot contender for the title of "the world's most famous painting."

Vincent Van Gogh Museum, Amsterdam. It is difficult to pick a favorite from the more than 200 paintings by this great artist on view here, but *Sunflowers* is among the top choices. None of the versions you may have seen in reproduction can match the luster of the original, where brilliant blues appear unexpectedly between the bright yellows and greens.

TOWNS & VILLAGES

Alkmaar, Noord-Holland. As one of the "cheese towns," Alkmaar may be most noted for its traditional cheese market, but it is also worth visiting for its several hundred historical monuments, many windmills, and beautiful medieval courtyards—a concentration of all things Holland.

Amersfoort, Utrecht Province. Poised for battle with its fortress gates and double-ringed canal—the only such vein in all of Europe—this is a highly walkable town with winding, cobblestone streets, parts of which are closed to traffic, where you can almost hear the clack of hooves of jousting horses.

Bronkhorst, Gelderland Province. It's as though Dickens's Tiny Tim has left his thumbprint on Bronkhorst, the tiniest official town in The Netherlands. Wander along its cobblestone streets paved with nostalgia and punctuated with a Charles Dickens Museum and a lot of curiosity shops.

Giethoorn, Overijssel Province. Vying for first-place prize in photogenicity (some cynics might say photo infamy), Giethoorn is a verdant, miniature version of Venice—an irresistible punter's paradise flanked by a profusion of thatched-roof cottages. Are you in Hansel and Gretel's garden or Alice in Wonderland's fantasy?

Sloten, Friesland. As the elf of the 11-city Elfstedentocht ice-race towns, Sloten seems to have been frozen in time. Once a fortress at the southwestern gate to Friesland and settled around 1063, it can probably all be seen in about three hours, but there's not a drop in its bucket to be missed. The epitome of charming towns, Sloten has a sleepiness that is to be savored.

Veere, Zeeland. This famously pretty 16th-century town is crowned with a Gothic Town Hall, whose fairy-tale facade is decorated with statues commemorating Veere's former lords and ladies.

SMART TRAVEL TIPS

Half the fun of traveling is looking forward to your trip—but when you look forward, don't just daydream. There are plans to be made and things to learn about, and there is serious work to be done. The following chapter will give you helpful pointers on many of the questions that arise when planning your trip and also when you are on the road. Finding out about your destination before you leave home means you won't squander time organizing everyday minutiae once you've arrived. You'll be more streetwise when you hit the ground as well, better prepared to explore the aspects of The Netherlands that drew you here in the first place. The organizations in this section can provide information to supplement this guide; contact them for up-to-the-minute details. Many trips begin by contacting The Netherlands tourist bureau: consult their listings under Visitor Information, below. Happy landings!

ADDRESSES

Fittingly, for a country with a history as venerable as Holland's, the country's *straats,* or streets (and other places) are often named after its famous sons and daughters. In Delft, for one example, Hugo de Grootstraat is named in honor of the city's lawyer-philosopher. In a bigger city, you get all the variations: Jacob Catsstraat, Jacob Catskade, Jacob Catsplein, ad infinitum. Of course, kings and queens feature: Wilhelminastraat is named after Queen Wilhelmina, the grandmother of the current queen, Beatrix. In Amsterdam, Vondelpark is named after Holland's most celebrated poet, Joost van den Vondel, and Rembrandtplein is a touristy square, named after the artist who had a studio just across the canals. A *plein* is a square; a *grote markt* is a market square, usually an old town's historic center, such as the one you find in Haarlem.

Other geographical terms to keep in mind are a *dwarsstraat,* or street that runs perpendicular to a street or canal, such as the Leidsestraat and the Leidsedwarsstraat. A *straatje* is a small street; a *weg* is a road; a *gracht* is a canal; a *steeg* is a very small street; a *laan* is a lane. *Baan* is another name for a road, not quite a highway, but busier than an average street. Note that in The Netherlands, the house number always comes after the street name on addresses.

The Dutch have an infinite range of names for bodies of water, from *gracht* to *singel* to *kanaal* (all roughly equating to "canal"). A singel is is a major canal within a city. The difference between a singel and a gracht is hard to define, even for a Dutch person. In fact, the names can be confusing because sometimes there is *no* water at all—many grachten have been filled in by developers to make room for houses, roads, and so on. Near harbor areas you'll notice *havens* (harbors), named after the goods that ships used to bring in, like in Rotterdam, *Wijnhaven* (Wine Harbor) and *Vishaven* (Fish Harbor).

Don't let common address abbreviations confuse you. BG stands for *Begane Grond* (ground floor); SOUT for *Souterrain* (sublevel/basement apartment); HS for *Huis* (a ground-floor apartment or main entry). Some common geographical abbreviations are *str.* for *straat* (street); *gr.* for *gracht* (canal); and *pl.* for *plein* (square). For example: Leidsestr., Herengr., or Koningspl.

Finally, first things last. Every guidebook on The Netherlands is titled . . . Holland. In fact, Holland is a term that, legally, refers to only 2 out of the country's 12 provinces (i.e., Noord-Holland). But, as the term "Holland" has been generally favored for millennia, so this book, as common usage has it, uses it interchangeably with The Netherlands.

AIR TRAVEL

BOOKING

When you book **look for nonstop flights** and **remember that "direct" flights stop at least once.** Try to avoid connecting flights, which require a change of plane. Two airlines may operate a connecting flight jointly, so ask if your airline operates every segment of the trip; you may find that the carrier you prefer flies you only part of the way. For more booking tips and to check prices and make online flight reservations, log on to ⊕ www.fodors.com.

CARRIERS

When flying internationally to The Netherlands, you usually choose between a domestic carrier, the national flag carrier of the country, and a foreign carrier from a third country. You may, for example, choose to fly KLM Royal Dutch Airlines to The Netherlands for the basic reason

that, as the national flag carrier, it has the greatest number of nonstop flights. Domestic carriers offer connections to smaller destinations. Third-party carriers may have a price advantage.

KLM and its global alliance partner Northwest—together with their regional partner airlines—fly from Amsterdam's Schiphol Airport to more than 400 destinations in more than 80 countries worldwide. Nearly 100 of those are European destinations, with three to four daily flights to most airports and up to 17 flights a day to London alone. Northwest Airlines now handles all reservations and ticket office activities on behalf of KLM in the United States and Canada, with KLM's biggest North American hubs in Detroit and Minneapolis, as well as Memphis, New York, and Washington among its gateways. KLM's direct flights connect Amsterdam to Atlanta, Los Angeles, and Miami, and numerous others. Including connections via KLM's hubs, the airline flies to more than 100 destinations in the United States from Amsterdam. In Canada, KLM/Northwest serves Montreal, Toronto, and Vancouver. For more information, contact the airline at one of the reservation numbers below. For further information about schedules and special fare promotions, go to KLM/Northwest's Web site.

Other international carriers include American Airlines, Continental Airlines, Delta Air Lines, United Airlines, and US Airways, but none of these carriers makes a transatlantic flight to any of The Netherlands' regional airports. MartinAir Holland, however, along with Dutch Bird and other charters, does make transatlantic flights from some of the regional terminals. If your carrier offers Rotterdam as a final destination, you fly into Amsterdam then transfer. KLM Cityhopper and KLM Excel offer a varied schedule of flights connecting Amsterdam with the smaller regional airports, and British Airways provides a number of domestic flights; between them, the whole country is covered. Transavia Airlines flies from Amsterdam and Rotterdam to a number of European destinations, and many other carriers link European capitals with Amsterdam; for instance, Air France offers a direct route between Amsterdam and Paris. Check with your travel agent for details.

Ask your airline if it offers e-ticketing (electronic ticketing), which eliminates all paperwork: there's no ticket to pick up or misplace. You go directly to the gate and give the agent your ticket number instead of waiting in line at the counter while minutes tick by.

🔁 To & From The Netherlands KLM Royal Dutch Airlines ☎ 300/303747 in Australia, 020/474-7747 in The Netherlands, 09/309-1782 in New Zealand, 0870/243-0541 in U.K. ☎ 800/447-4747 for Northwest/KLM sales office in the U.S. and Canada ⊕ www.klm.com. American Airlines ☎ 800/433-7300 ⊕ www.aa.com. British Airways ☎ 0870/850-9850 in U.K., 020/346-9559 in The Netherlands ⊕ www.britishairways.com. British Midland ☎ 0870/607-0555 ⊕ www.flybml.com. Continental Airlines ☎ 800/231-0856 ⊕ www.continental.com. Delta Air Lines ☎ 800/241-4141 ⊕ www.delta.com. Dutch Bird ☎ 020/605-5800 ⊕ www.Dutchbird.com. MartinAir Holland ☎ 020/601-1767 ⊕ www.martinair.com. Transavia Airlines ☎ 020/406-0406 in The Netherlands ⊕ www.transavia.nl/home. United Airlines ☎ 800/538-2929 ⊕ www.ual.com. US Airways ☎ 800/428-4322 ⊕ www.usairways.com.

🔁 Around The Netherlands KLM (⇨ To & From the Netherlands, above). British Airways (⇨ To & From the Netherlands, above).

CHECK-IN & BOARDING

Always ask your carrier about its check-in policy. Plan to arrive at the airport about 2 hours before your scheduled departure time for domestic flights and 2½ to 3 hours before international flights.

Assuming that not everyone with a ticket will show up, airlines routinely overbook planes. When everyone does, airlines ask for volunteers to give up their seats. In return, these volunteers usually get a certificate for a free flight and are rebooked on the next flight out. If there are not enough volunteers, the airline must choose who will be denied boarding. The first to get bumped are passengers who checked in late and those flying on discounted tickets, so **get to the gate and check in as early as possible,** especially during peak periods.

Always **bring a government-issued photo ID to the airport;** even when it's not required, a passport is best.

CUTTING COSTS

The least expensive airfares to The Netherlands are priced for round-trip travel and must usually be purchased in advance. Airlines generally allow you to change your return date for a fee; most-low fare tickets, however, are nonrefundable. It's smart to **call a number of airlines,** and when you are quoted a good price, **book it on the spot**—the same fare may not be available the next day. Always **check different routings** and look into using alternate airports. Also, price off-peak flights, which may be significantly less expensive than others. Lower-priced charter flights to a range of Dutch destinations are available throughout the year. Travel agents, especially low-fare specialists(⇨ Discounts & Deals, *below*), are helpful.

Consolidators are another good source. They buy tickets for scheduled international flights at reduced rates from the airlines, then sell them at prices that beat the best fare available directly from the airlines. Sometimes you can even get your money back if you need to return the ticket. Carefully read the fine print detailing penalties for changes and cancellations, purchase the ticket with a credit card, and **confirm your consolidator reservation with the airline.**

When you **fly as a courier,** you trade your checked-luggage space for a ticket deeply subsidized by a courier service. There are restrictions on when you can book and how long you can stay. Some courier companies list with membership organizations, such as the Air Courier Association and the International Association of Air Travel Couriers; these require you to become a member before you can book a flight.

Many airlines, singly or in collaboration, offer discount air passes that allow foreigners to travel economically in a particular country or region. These visitor passes usually must be reserved and purchased before you leave home. Information about passes can be difficult to track down on airline Web sites, which tend to be geared to travelers departing from a given carrier's country rather than to those intending to visit that country. Try typing the name of the pass into a search engine, or search for "pass" within the carrier's Web site.

EasyJet has low fares to Amsterdam flying in from Barcelona, Belfast, Edinburgh, Geneva, Glasgow, Liverpool, London (Gatwick and Luton), and Nice. BasiqAir flies to Amsterdam and Rotterdam from Barcelona and Nice.

⁊ Consolidators & Low-Cost Airlines BasiqAir ☎ 0900/0737 in The Netherlands. Cheap Tickets ☎ 888/922-8849 ⊕ www.cheaptickets.com. Easy-Jet ☎ 023/568-4880 in The Netherlands ⊕ www. easyjet.com. Global Travel ☎ 416/516-1113 in Canada. Up & Away Travel ☎ 212/889-2345. World Courier of Canada ☎ 905/678-6007.
⁊ Discount Passes FlightPass EuropebyAir ☎ 888/387-2479 ⊕ www.europebyair.com. SAS Air Passes Scandinavian Airlines ☎ 800/221-2350 ⊕ www.scandinavian.net.

ENJOYING THE FLIGHT

All flights within The Netherlands are no-smoking. Smoking is allowed on an increasingly limited number of international flights; **contact your carrier about its smoking policy. State your seat preference** when purchasing your ticket, and then repeat it when you confirm and when you check in. For more legroom, you can request one of the few emergency-aisle seats at check-in, if you are capable of lifting at least 50 pounds—a Federal Aviation Administration requirement of passengers in these seats. Seats behind a bulkhead also offer more legroom, but they don't have under-seat storage. Don't sit in the row in front of the emergency aisle or in front of a bulkhead, where seats may not recline.

If you have dietary concerns, **ask for special meals when booking.** These can be vegetarian, low-cholesterol, or kosher, for example. It's a good idea to pack some healthful snacks and a small bottle (plastic) of water in your carry-on bag. On long flights, try to maintain a normal routine to help fight jet lag. At night, **get some sleep.** By day, **eat light meals, drink water** (not alcohol), and **move around the cabin** to stretch your legs. For additional jet-lag tips consult *Fodor's FYI: Travel Fit & Healthy* (available at bookstores everywhere).

FLYING TIMES

Flying time to Amsterdam is 21½ hours from Auckland; 1 hour from London; 10½ hours from Los Angeles; 7 hours from New York; 29 minutes from Amsterdam to Rotterdam; 20 hours from Sydney; and 8 hours from Toronto.

HOW TO COMPLAIN

If your baggage goes astray or your flight goes awry, complain right away. Most carriers require that you **file a claim immediately.** The Aviation Consumer Protection Division of the Department of Transportation publishes *Fly-Rights,* which discusses airlines and consumer issues and is available online.
⁊ Airline Complaints Aviation Consumer Protection Division ⊠ U.S. Department of Transportation, C-75, 400 7th St. SW, Washington, DC 20590 ☎ 202/366-2220 ⊕ www.dot.gov/airconsumer. Federal Aviation Administration Consumer Hotline ☎ 800/322-7873. A helpful Web site is ⊕ http://airconsumer.ost.dot.gov/problems.htm.

RECONFIRMING

Check the status of your flight before you leave for the airport. You can do this on your carrier's Web site, by linking to a flight-status checker (many Web booking services offer these), or by calling your carrier or travel agent. Always confirm international flights at least 72 hours ahead of the scheduled departure time.

AIRPORTS

Located just outside Amsterdam, **Luchthaven Schiphol** is the main passenger airport for Holland. With the annual number of passengers using Schiphol approaching 40 million, it is ranked among the world's top five best-connected airports. At Schiphol, transfers to and from inter-country flights are quick and easy, as both international and country services have been integrated into one terminal. If you plan to fly via Schiphol from a regional airport, transfer times are minimal, and the connection fares tend to be very reasonable.

Rotterdam is the biggest of the regional airport options and provides daily service to many European cities; other regional airports include Eindhoven, Groningen, and Maastricht. An increasing number of international charter flights choose these airports, as benefits include shorter check-in times and ample parking. However, there are no rail links that connect such regional airports with nearby cities, so passengers must resort to taking buses or taxis.
⁊ Airport Information Aachen Luchthaven (Airport) ✈ 15 km (8 mi) north of Maastricht ☎ 043/358-9898. Amsterdam Luchthaven (Airport) Schiphol ✈ 17 km (11 mi) southwest of Amsterdam ☎ 0900/0141. Eindhoven Luchthaven (Airport) ✈ 12 km (8 mi) northwest of Eindhoven ☎ 040/291-9818. Groningen Luchthaven (Airport) Eelde ✈ 5 km (3 mi) west of Groningen ☎ 050/308-1300

or 050/309-7070. **Rotterdam Luchthaven (Airport)** ⊹ 17 km (11 mi) northwest of Rotterdam ☎ 010/446-3444.

AIRPORT TRANSFERS

Once you disembark from your plane at Amsterdam Luchthaven (Airport) at Schiphol, you can travel to and from the city center in several ways. The Schiphol Rail Link operates between the airport and the city 24 hours a day, with service to Centraal Station—Amsterdam's central railway station—or to stations in the south of the city. From 6:30 AM to 12:30 AM, a train departs from or arrives at Schiphol every 15 minutes; other hours, there is one train every hour. The trip takes about 15 minutes and costs €3. Trains leave from the platforms of Schiphol Station, found beneath Schiphol Plaza. They head into the city using one of three routes. The most popular is the NS Schiphollijn, which runs to Centraal Station (with two stops in west Amsterdam). Another route heads to the Amsterdam Zuid/WTC (South/World Trade Center) station in south Amsterdam, and another line heads to the RAI section, near the big convention center. From these south Amsterdam stations, Tram 5 goes to Leidseplein and the Museum Quarter; from RAI, Tram 4 goes to Rembrandtplein. Keep in mind that Schiphol Station is one of Holland's busiest—make sure you catch the shuttle to Amsterdam and not a train heading to The Hague! As always, when arriving at Amsterdam's Centraal Station, keep an eye out for any stray pickpockets. Other than taxis, you may wish to hop aboard a tram or bus to get to your hotel, so go to one of the **Gemeentevervoerbedrijf (GVB) Amsterdam Municipal Transport** booths found in front of the Centraal Station. Here you can find directions, fare information, and schedules.

KLM Shuttle operates a shuttle bus service between Amsterdam Schiphol Airport and 16 of the city's major hotels (among them, the Krasnapolsky and the Toren), along with stops that are convenient to many other hotels in the city. The trip takes about half an hour and costs €10.50 one-way. Hours for this bus shuttle are 7 AM to 6 PM, every half hour; between 6 PM and 9 PM, departures are every hour.

Finally, there is a taxi stand directly in front of the arrival hall at Amsterdam Schiphol Airport. A service charge is in-cluded, but small additional tips are not unwelcome. New laws determine that taxi fares are now fixed from Schiphol to Amsterdam; depending on the neighborhood, a trip will cost between €25 and €30. When you're returning home, a ride to Schiphol from Amsterdam center city area, the Centrum, will cost €22. A new service that might be convenient for budget travelers who count every euro is the Schiphol Travel Taxi. The taxi needs to be booked at least 48 hours in advance and rides are shared, so the trip will take a bit longer, as the taxi stops to pick up passengers. **⑦ Taxis & Shuttles KLM Shuttle** ☎ 020/653-4975. **Schiphol Rail Link** ☎ 0900/9292. **Schiphol Travel Taxi** ☎ 020/0900-8876.

DUTY-FREE SHOPPING

Although the European Union eliminated duty-free shopping in airports in The Netherlands and in Europe, Schiphol's tax-free shopping center, See-Buy-Fly, maintains its ability to sell cheaper goods thanks to a subsidy from the airport; you can also make in-flight duty-free purchases.

BIKE TRAVEL

GETTING AROUND BY BICYCLE

To rent a bicycle, you'll pay from €6.50 per day, plus a deposit of about €50 per bike, and need a passport or other identification. The more days you rent, the cheaper the price, and rates by the week are even more competitive. Bikes can be rented at outlets near larger railway stations or by contacting local rental centers. In this flat country, with its 19,000 km (10,000 mi) of *fietspaden* (cycle paths) in and between cities, a bicycle is an ideal means of getting around. A fietspad might easily be mistaken for a pedestrian path. If you see a circular sign, with a bicycle ringed in blue, then only bikes can use the fietspad. If, however, there is also a *bromfiets* (moped) on the sign, then mopeds can use the path. The youngsters riding them tend to drive exceptionally fast, so beware of the potential hazards of meandering across a seemingly quiet fietspad.

Never leave your bike unlocked: there is a rapid turnover of stolen bikes no matter what quality or condition. Use a "D" lock, which can't be cut with the average thieves' tools, and lock your bike's frame to something that can't be shifted, such as a railing.

As a cyclist, you'll notice that most fellow cyclers don't really observe the traffic signs and rules, nor do they stay in the bicycle lanes marked out for them, unless the road has particularly heavy traffic. However, as a result of accidents caused by aggressive cyclists, fines and other penalties are being rigorously imposed (you can also be fined for riding at night with no lights, and for drunken cycling). Cars that are turning across your path are supposed to stop for you, but it is wise to watch out. Maps and route guides are available from the VVV (tourist information offices) representing the area you plan to explore, although bicycle tracks between towns are so well signposted that you do not have to rely on a map.*See* the A to Z section at the end of each regional chapter for information on where to rent bikes.

BIKES IN FLIGHT

Most airlines accommodate bikes as luggage, provided they are dismantled and boxed; check with individual airlines about packing requirements. Airlines sell bike boxes, which are often free at bike shops, for about $15 (bike bags start at $100). International travelers often can substitute a bike for a piece of checked luggage at no charge; otherwise, the cost is about $100. Domestic and Canadian airlines charge $40–$80 each way.

🔁 Bike Transport Information ⊕ www.bikeaccess. net

BOAT & FERRY TRAVEL

ARRIVING & DEPARTING BY BOAT & FERRY FROM ENGLAND

Traveling from the United Kingdom, there are two daily Stena line crossings between the **Hoek van Holland** (Corner of Holland, an industrial shipping area west of Rotterdam) to Harwich, on the fast car ferry, taking approximately 3 hours. The overnight crossing takes about 7 hours. These are the only ferry crossings that can be booked at the international travel window in large railway stations. There is one PO North Sea overnight crossing between the Europoort in Rotterdam and Hull, which takes about 14 hours, and one DFDS Seaways overnight crossing from Newcastle to IJmuiden, in Amsterdam, taking 15 hours.

Ferries and superfast hydrofoils are run between Harwich and Hook of Holland twice

daily by Stena Line. In England, ferries to The Netherlands are run daily from Harwich International Port in Harwich and also overnight between Hull and Rotterdam by PO North Sea Ferries. The trip takes 3 to 11 hours, depending on the route.

🔁 From the U.K. **DFDS Seaways** ⊠ Sluisplein 33, 1975 AG IJmuiden ☎ 0255/546666 🖶 0255/546655 ⊕ www.scansea.com.**Harwich International Port** ⊠ Harwich International Port, Parkeston Quay, Harwich, Essex CO12 4SR England ☎ 01255/242000. **PO North Sea Ferries** in The Netherlands ⊠ Beneluxhaven, Havennummer 5805, Rotterdam/Europoort ☎ 020/201-3333 ⊕ www.ponsf.com/index/ ⊠ King George Dock, Hedon Rd., Hull HU9 5QA England ☎ 08705/202020. **Stena Line** in The Netherlands ⊠ Hoek van Holland Terminal, Stationsweg 10, 3151 HS Hoek van Holland ☎ 0174/315800, 0900/8123 booking (10¢ per min) 🖶 0174/389389 ⊕ www.stenaline.nl.

BOAT & FERRY TRAVEL WITHIN HOLLAND

An extensive ferry system serves The Netherlands. DFDS Seaways is a leading carrier. Ferries run from several locations in Friesland, including Lauwersoog, Harlingen, Holwerd, to the Frisian Islands. Ferries cross the IJsselmeer from Enkhuizen to Stavoren (no cars) and to Urk. Ferries connect Den Helder to the island of Texel in Noord-Holland. Ferries in Zeeland have ports in Breskens and Vlissingen.

🔁 Boat & Ferry Information **Den Helder Ferries to Texel** ☎ 0222/369600. **DFDS Seaways** ⊠ Sluisplein 33, 1975 AG IJmuiden ☎ 0255/546666 🖶 0255/546655 ⊕ www.scansea.com. **Enkhuizen Ferries** ⊠ to Stavoren, no cars ☎ 0228/326-6667 ⊠ to Urk ☎ 0527/683407. **Friesland Ferries** ⊠ Lauwersoog ☎ 0519/349050 ⊠ Harlingen ☎ 0900/363-5736 ⊠ Holwerd ☎ 0900/363-5736. **Zeeland Ferries** ⊠ Breskens ☎ 0117/381663 ⊠ Vlissingen ☎ 0118/465905.

GETTING AROUND BY BOAT

Hire your own boat or take a guided city canal tour of Amsterdam, Leiden or Delft; alternatively, take a harbor tour to **check out Rotterdam's extensive Europoort,** the world's biggest harbor, and the flood barrier. There are pedestrian ferries behind Amsterdam's Centraal station across the IJ. For more specific information about guided tours, small-boat rental, and details about passenger and car ferries to the islands in the north of the country, including Texel, Terschelling, and Schiermonikoog, *see* individual regional chapters.

BUSINESS HOURS

BANKS & OFFICES

Banks are open weekdays 9:30 to 4 or 5, with some extending their business hours to coordinate with late-night shopping. Some banks are closed Monday mornings.

The main post office in each town is open weekdays, 9 to 5 or 6, Saturday 10 to 1:30. In every post office you'll also find the Postbank, a money-changing facility, which has the same opening hours.

BARS & RESTAURANTS

As a general guide, bars in the larger cities open at various times during the day and close at 1 AM throughout the week, at 2 or 3 AM on Friday and Saturday. Restaurants are open evenings 5–11, although some kitchens close as early as 9, and many are closed on Sunday and Monday.

MUSEUMS & SIGHTS

Major sights, such as Amsterdam's Koninklijk Paleis, have summer opening hours; churches and cathedrals are open 9–3; parks are open dawn to dusk; *hofjes* (almshouses) open at the discretion of their inhabitants. Museum hours vary; to give some Amsterdam instances, the city's famous Rijksmuseum is open 10–5, the Van Gogh museum is open 10–6, and the Anne Frank House is open 9–7 and until 9 in summer.

Note that when this book refers to summer hours, it means approximately Easter to October; winter hours run from November to Easter. The Keukenhof floral displays are open only in spring and late summer; VVV (tourist information centers) also have extended summer hours. Always check locally.

SHOPS

Most shops are open from noon to 6 on Monday, 9 to 6 Tuesday through Saturday. In smaller towns and villages, shops often close for lunch. Hairdressers are generally closed Sunday and Monday. In recreation and resort areas most shops are open from early morning until late at night and during weekends. In the centers of Amsterdam, Rotterdam, and Scheveningen, the coastal resort of The Hague, shops are open on Saturday and sometimes on Sunday from noon to 6. Thursday or Friday is a designated late-night shopping night in the larger towns. *Markts* (markets) selling fruit, flowers, and other wares run from 10 to 4 or sometimes 5. Larger settlements have bakeries open seven days a week in addition to small *avondwinkels* (late-night opening shops) selling food, wine, and toiletries, which are open from afternoon till midnight or later. Supermarkets are open weekdays until 8 or 10 PM and Saturday until 5 or 7 PM.

BUS TRAVEL

ARRIVING & DEPARTING BY COACH

Eurolines runs a coach service, which is essentially a well-equipped bus, to transfer passengers between countries but not between cities in the same country. You can travel from London, crossing via the Channel Tunnel or by ferry, or from Brussels to Rotterdam or Amsterdam, but the journeys are exhaustively long. With the advent of EasyJet, it is worth looking into noncommuter-time flights that beat the price of even a Euroline ticket.

🚌 Bus Information/Europe-Wide Travel Eurolines In The Netherlands ✉ Rokin 10, Amsterdam ☏ 020/421-7951 ⊕ www.eurolines.nl/ ✉ In England ✉ 4 Cardiff Rd., Luton, Bedfordshire. LU1 1PP England ☏ 0870/514-3219 in U.K., 845/228-0145 in U.S.

GETTING AROUND BY BUS, TRAM & METRO

The bus and tram systems within Holland provide excellent transport links within cities. Frequent bus services are available in all cities in the Randstad (the provinces of North and South Holland, and Utrecht) and most larger settlements throughout the rest of The Netherlands; trams run in Amsterdam, The Hague, between Delft and The Hague, and in Rotterdam. Amsterdam and Rotterdam also have subways, referred to as the metro. Amsterdam's metro system has lines running southeast and southwest; Rotterdam's metro system also has only two lines (east to west and north to south), which extend into the suburbs and cross in the city center for easy transfers. The newer metro trains are cleaner and more agreeable to use, but old and new operate on all lines, so you can't predict what you'll get.

Connexxion is one of the larger companies providing bus and tram services, and it operates across the country. Other companies include BBA and Arriva, in addition to the extra services provided in each larger urban settlement, where, for example, GVB provides additional services in Amsterdam; HTM in The Hague; GVU in Utrecht; and RET in Rotterdam. There are usually maps of each city's network in individual shelters, and diagrams of routes are found on board. Between stops, trams brake only when absolutely necessary, so listen for warning bells if you are walking or cycling near tram lines. Taxis use tram lines, but other cars are allowed to venture onto them only when turning right.

The newer fleets of buses are cleaner, therefore nicer to use, and bus lanes (shared only with taxis) remain uncongested, ensuring that you travel more swiftly than the rest of the traffic in rush hour. If the bus is very crowded, you may have to stand, so hold on to a handrail, as the buses can travel quite fast; to **avoid rush hour,** don't travel between 8 and 9 in the morning or between 4:30 and 5:30 in the afternoon.

TICKETS

The same ticket can be used in buses, trams, and metros throughout Holland. Called a *strippenkaart* (strip ticket), a 2- or 3-strip ticket can be bought directly from the bus driver. If you buy a ticket in advance, this works out much cheaper per journey: a 15-strip ticket is €6.20 and a 45-strip ticket costs €18.30. You can buy these at railway stations, post offices, and many bookshops and cigarette kiosks, and they remain valid until there are no further strips left, or for one year from the first stamp.

Each city is divided into zones, and the fare you pay depends on the number of zones you travel through. A small city is one zone (two strips), but to travel across The Hague takes you through four (five strips) zones. These zones are displayed on transport maps. Each journey you make costs one strip plus the number of zones you travel through. When you get on a bus, you show the driver your strippenkaart and simply say where your final destination is, or the number of zones you plan to travel through, and let him or her stamp the strips.

In a metro you have to stamp your ticket yourself in the small yellow machines found near the doors, and you can often do this in a tram. Count the number of strips you need (note that most tourists will be traveling within a one-zone area and therefore the tickets they buy directly from the driver only contain two or three strips), fold your ticket at the bottom of the last strip required, and stamp the final strip in the machine. A stamp on a strip uses that, and the strips above it. Two or more people can travel on the same strippenkaart, but the appropriate number of units must be stamped for each person. The newest trams in Amsterdam (recognizable by their large windows) have ticket control booths in the center of the tram. You may only board the tram there, unless you already have a valid stamp on your ticket, in which case you may board at the front and show your ticket to the driver. On older trams, you can usually board only at the rear, where you will encounter either a ticket controller (*conducteur*) or a stamping machine. This makes for a lot of confusion, as you need to be in the right place when the tram arrives. Follow the lead of other passengers to be sure you don't miss getting on.

The maps at the tram and bus stops show the zonal regions, and there are also map diagrams inside the trams. The stamp indicates the zone where the journey started, and the time, and remains valid for one hour, so you can travel within the zones you have stamped until the hour is up. If you make a mistake and stamp too many strips, tell the driver and he or she will put a sticker over the incorrect stamp.

Teams of ticket inspectors occasionally make spot checks. This doesn't happen often, but if you are checked and you don't have a stamped strippenkaart, you face a €27 fine.

⌘ Bus Information Information on public transportation, including schedules, fares for **trains, buses, trams, and ferries** ☎ 0900/9292. **Lost and found** ☎ 020/460–5858.

CUTTING COSTS

Paying the full travel fare, without using a pass or reduction card, means that toddlers under 3 travel for free; children from 4 to 11 have an automatic 40% reduction, and those over 12 are charged the full fare. If you plan to use buses, trams, and metros more often than four days a week, it is more economical for you to buy a weekly pass. Each different company offers slightly different reductions, so it depends on which cities you want to travel in, the extent of your travel, and the length of time you want the pass to remain valid. Ask a transport information officer which pass suits your plans best.

Ask about all reduction cards and passes by calling the public transport information line, asking at the local transport window in large railway stations, or dropping in to the nearest VVV (tourist office).

CAMERAS & PHOTOGRAPHY

For an invaluable guide to shooting great travel pictures, go to Fodor's Web site, where nearly 100 easy-to-follow photography tips have been integrated into the online Smart Travel Tips section. Take a look at the sections; then click on the topics that interest you. Our tips for taking travel pictures like a pro will open up in a separate browser window.

The *Kodak Guide to Shooting Great Travel Pictures* (available at bookstores everywhere) is loaded with tips.
🖪 Photo Help Fodor's Travel Publications ⊕ www.fodors.com. Kodak Information Center ☎ 800/242-2424 ⊕ www.kodak.com.

EQUIPMENT PRECAUTIONS

Don't pack film and equipment in checked luggage, where it is much more susceptible to damage. X-ray machines used to view checked luggage are becoming much more powerful and therefore are much more likely to ruin your film. Try to **ask for hand inspection of film,** which becomes clouded after repeated exposure to airport X-ray machines, and **keep videotapes and computer disks away from metal detectors.** Always **keep film, tape, and computer disks out of the sun.** Carry an extra supply of batteries, and **be prepared to turn on your camera, camcorder, or laptop** to prove to airport security personnel that the device is real.

VIDEOS

The local standard for videotape is Pal.

CAR RENTAL

Auto-verhuur (car rental) in The Netherlands is best for exploring the center, north, or east of the country, but is to be avoided in the heavily urbanized northwest, known as the Randstad, where the public transport infrastructure is excellent.

Signage on country roads is usually pretty good, but be prepared to patiently trail behind cyclists blithely riding two abreast (which is illegal), even when the road is not wide enough for you to pass. Major car-rental companies have boxy Renault cars and Peugeots in various sizes that are always in good condition.
🖪 Major Agencies **Alamo** ☎ 800/462-5266, 0208/750-2800 in U.K. ⊕ www.alamo.com. **Avis** ☎ 800/230-4898, 800/272-5871 in Canada, 02/9353-9000 in Australia, 0800/655111 in New Zealand, 0870/606-0100 in U.K. ⊕ www.avis.com. **Budget** ⊠ Overtoom 121, 1054 HE Amsterdam ☎ 020/604-1349, 0144/227-6266 in U.K. ⊕ www.budget.com ⊠ Griend 2, Maastricht ☎ 0900/1576 ⊠ Kuylstraat 101, Rotterdam ☎ 010/437-8622. **Dollar** ☎ 800/800-3665, 800/800-6000 in U.K., where it's affiliated with Sixt, 649/255-0620 in New Zealand ⊕ www.dollar.com. **Hertz** ☎ 800/654-3001, 800/263-0600 in Canada, 0870/844-8844 in U.K., 03/9698-2555 in Australia, 0800/654-321 in New Zealand ⊕ www.hertz.com. **National Car Rental** ☎ 800/227-7368, 020/8745-2800 in U.K. ⊕ www.nationalcar.com. For specific information about car-rental agencies across The Netherlands, see the A to Z section in each regional chapter.

CUTTING COSTS

Most major American rental-car companies have offices or affiliates in The Netherlands, but the rates are generally better if you make a reservation from abroad rather than from within Holland.

For a good deal, **book through a travel agent, who will shop around.**

Do **look into wholesalers,** companies that do not own fleets but rent in bulk from those that do and often offer better rates than traditional car-rental operations. Prices are best during off-peak periods. Rentals booked through wholesalers often must be paid for before you leave home.
🖪 Wholesalers **Auto Europe** ☎ 207/842-2000 or 888/223-5555 🖷 207/842-2222 ⊕ www.autoeurope.com. **Destination Europe Resources** (DER) ⊠ 9501 W. Devon Ave., Rosemont, IL 60018 ☎ 800/782-2424 🖷 800/282-7474 ⊕ www.dertravel.com. **Europe by Car** ☎ 212/581-3040 or 800/223-1516 🖷 212/246-1458 ⊕ www.europebycar.com. **Kemwel** ☎ 800/678-0678 or 207/842-2285 🖷 207/842-2286 ⊕ www.kemwel.com.

INSURANCE

When driving a rented car you are generally responsible for any damage to or loss of the vehicle. Collision policies that car-rental companies sell for European rentals typically do not cover stolen vehicles. Before you rent—and purchase collision or theft coverage—see what coverage you already have under the terms of your personal auto-insurance policy and credit cards.

SURCHARGES

Before you pick up a car in one city and leave it in another, **ask about drop-off charges or one-way service fees,** which can be substantial. Note, too, that some rental agencies charge extra if you return the car before the time specified in your contract. To avoid a hefty refueling fee, **fill the tank just before you turn in the car,** but be aware that gas stations near the rental outlet may overcharge. It's almost never a deal to buy the tank of gas in the car when you rent it; the understanding is that you'll return it empty, but some fuel usually remains.

CAR TRAVEL

A network of well-maintained superhighways and secondary roads makes car travel convenient, but traffic is exceptionally heavy around the bigger cities, especially on the roads in the Randstad, and those approaching the North Sea beaches on summer weekends. There are no tolls on roads or highways, and only one tunnel has a toll: Kiltunnel, near Dordrecht, which costs €3.40 round-trip.

Your driver's license may not be recognized outside your home country. International Driver's Permits (IDPs) are available from the American and Canadian automobile associations and, in the United Kingdom, from the Automobile Association and Royal Automobile Club. These international permits, valid only in conjunction with your regular driver's license, are universally recognized; having one may save you a problem with local authorities.

FROM THE U.K.

From Calais (north coast of France), you can drive along the coast in the direction of Ghent, Antwerp (both in Belgium) to Breda, Rotterdam, and Amsterdam.

EMERGENCY SERVICES

If you haven't joined a motoring organization, the **ANWB** (Royal Dutch Touring Club) charges €100 for 24-hour road assistance. If you aren't a member, you can call the ANWB after breaking down, but you must pay a €78 on-the-spot membership charge. Emergency crews may not accept credit cards or checks when they pick you up. If your automobile association is affiliated with the **Alliance International du Tourisme** (AIT), and you have proof of membership, you are entitled to free help.

To call for assistance push the help button on any yellow ANWB phone located every kilometer (½ mi) on highways, and a dispatch operator immediately finds you. Alternatively, ring their 24-hour emergency line or their information number for details about their road rescue service.
∄ ANWB (Royal Dutch Touring Club) ☎ 0800/0888 emergency number, 070/314-7147 office number ⊕ www.anwb.nl/.

GASOLINE

Gas stations are generally open Monday–Saturday 6 or 7 AM–8 PM or later, with longer opening times on Sunday. But note that in some towns, gas stations can be closed on Sunday. All stations have self-service pumps. Gas stations on the motorways are open 24 hours. Unleaded four-star costs about €1.30 per liter.

PARKING

Parking space is at a premium in Amsterdam as in most towns, but especially in the *centrum* (historic town centers), which have narrow, one-way streets with large areas given over to pedestrians. Most towns are metered from 9 AM to 7 PM, so it is a good idea (if not the only option) to **leave your car only in designated parking areas.** *Parkeren* (parking lots) are indicated by a white "P" in a blue square. Illegally parked cars get clamped and, after 24 hours, if you haven't paid for the clamp to be removed, towed. If you get clamped, a sticker on the windshield indicates where you should go to pay the fine (from €63 to more than €100).

ROAD MAPS

Michelin maps are regularly updated and are the best countrywide maps; they offer the advantage of being consistent with Michelin maps of other countries you may visit. They are available at newsagents and bookshops across the country. Free city maps are generally available at VVV (tourist offices), and more detailed city maps can be bought at bookshops or large gas stations.

RULES OF THE ROAD

Driving is on the right, and regulations are largely as in Britain and the United States. Speed limits are 120 kph (75 mph) on superhighways, 100 kph (62 mph) on urban-area highways, and 50 kph (30 mph) on suburban roads.

For safe driving, go with the flow, stay in the slow lane unless you want to pass, and make way for faster cars wanting to pass you. In cities and towns, approach crossings with care; local drivers may exercise the principle of priority for traffic from the right with some abandon. Although the majority of cyclists observe the stoplights and general road signs, many do not expect you, even as a driver, to give way. The latest ruling states that unless otherwise marked, all traffic coming from the right has priority, even bicycles.

The driver and front-seat passenger are required to wear seat belts, and backseat passengers are also required to wear available seat belts. Fines for driving after drinking are heavy, including the suspension of license and the additional possibility of six months' imprisonment.

CHILDREN IN HOLLAND

Be sure to plan ahead and involve your youngsters as you outline your trip. When packing, include things to keep them busy en route. On sightseeing days, try to schedule activities of special interest to your children. If you are renting a car, don't forget to **arrange for a car seat** when you reserve.

Discounts are prevalent, so always ask about a child's discount before purchasing tickets. Children under a certain age ride free on buses and trams. Children under 18 are sometimes admitted free or have a lowered rate on entry to museums and galleries. For general advice about traveling with children, consult *Fodor's FYI: Travel with Your Baby* (available in bookstores everywhere).

FLYING

If your children are two or older, **ask about children's airfares.** As a general rule, infants under two not occupying a seat fly at greatly reduced fares or even for free. When booking, **confirm carry-on allowances** if you're traveling with infants. In general, for babies charged 10% of the adult fare you are allowed one carry-on bag and a collapsible stroller; if the flight is full, the stroller may have to be checked or you may be limited to less.

Experts agree that it's a good idea to use safety seats aloft for children weighing less than 40 pounds. Airlines set their own policies: U.S. carriers usually require that the child be ticketed, even if he or she is young enough to ride free, since the seats must be strapped into regular seats. Do **check your airline's policy about using safety seats during takeoff and landing.** Safety seats are not allowed everywhere in the plane, so get your seat assignments as early as possible.

When reserving, **request children's meals or a freestanding bassinet** (not available at all airlines) if you need them. But note that bulkhead seats, where you must sit to use the bassinet, may lack an overhead bin or storage space on the floor.

SIGHTS & ATTRACTIONS

Places that are especially appealing to children are indicated by a rubber-duckie icon (🦆) in the margin.

CUSTOMS & DUTIES

When shopping abroad, **keep receipts** for all purchases. Upon reentering the country, **be ready to show customs officials what you've bought.** If you feel a duty is incorrect, appeal the assessment. If you object to the way your clearance was handled, note the inspector's badge number. In either case, first ask to see a supervisor. If the problem isn't resolved, write to the appropriate authorities, beginning with the port director at your point of entry.

IN AUSTRALIA

Australian residents who are 18 or older may bring home A$400 worth of souvenirs and gifts (including jewelry), 250 cigarettes or 250 grams of tobacco, and 1,125 ml of alcohol (including wine, beer, and spirits). Residents under 18 may bring back A$200 worth of goods. Prohibited items include meat products. Seeds, plants, and fruits need to be declared upon arrival.

🔲 **Australian Customs Service** 🗺 Regional Director, GPO 8, Sydney, NSW 2000 📠 02/9213-2000 🖨 02/9213-4043 🌐 www.customs.gov.au.

IN CANADA

Canadian residents who have been out of Canada for at least seven days may bring in C$750 worth of goods duty-free. If you've been away fewer than seven days but more than 48 hours, the duty-free allowance drops to C$200; if your trip lasts 24 to 48 hours, the allowance is C$50. You may not pool allowances with family members. Goods claimed under the C$750 exemption may follow you by mail; those claimed under the lesser exemptions must accompany you. Alcohol and tobacco products may be included in the seven-day and 48-hour exemptions but not in the 24-hour exemption. If you meet the age requirements of the province or territory through which you reenter Canada, you may bring in, duty-free, 1.5 liters of wine *or* 1.14 liters (40 imperial ounces) of liquor *or* 24 12-ounce cans or bottles of beer or ale. If you are 19 or older you may bring in, duty-free, 200 cigarettes and 50 cigars. Check ahead of time with the Canada Customs and Revenue Agency or the Department of Agriculture for policies regarding meat products, seeds, plants, and fruits.

You may send an unlimited number of gifts (only one gift per recipient, however) worth up to C$60 each duty-free to Canada. Label the package UNSOLICITED GIFT—VALUE UNDER $60. Alcohol and tobacco are excluded.

7 Canada Customs and Revenue Agency ⊠ 2265 St. Laurent Blvd. S, Ottawa, Ontario K1G 4K3 ☎ 204/983-3500, 506/636-5064, 800/461-9999 toll-free in Canada ⊕ www.ccra-adrc.gc.ca.

IN NEW ZEALAND

All homeward-bound residents may bring back NZ$700 worth of souvenirs and gifts; passengers may not pool their allowances, and children can claim only the concession on goods intended for their own use. For those 17 or older, the duty-free allowance also includes 4.5 liters of wine or beer; one 1,125-ml bottle of spirits; and either 200 cigarettes, 250 grams of tobacco, 50 cigars, *or* a combination of the three up to 250 grams. Meat products, seeds, plants, and fruits must be declared upon arrival to the Agricultural Services Department.

7 New Zealand Customs ⊠ Head Office, The Customhouse, 17–21 Whitmore St., Box 2218, Wellington ☎ 04/473-6099 ⊕ www.customs.govt.nz

IN THE U.K.

If you are a U.K. resident and your journey was wholly within the European Union, you probably won't have to pass through customs when you return to the United Kingdom. If you plan to bring back large quantities of alcohol or tobacco, check EU limits beforehand. In most cases, if you plan to bring back more than 200 cigars, 800 cigarettes, 10 liters of spirits, and/or 90 liters of wine, you will have to declare the goods upon return.

7 HM Customs and Excise ⊠ New King's Beam House, 22 Upper Ground, London, SE1 9PJ ☎ 020/620-1313 ⊕ www.hmce.gov.uk.

IN THE U.S.

U.S. residents who have been out of the country for at least 48 hours (and who have not used the $400 allowance or any part of it in the past 30 days) may bring home $400 worth of foreign goods duty-free; the duty-free allowance drops to $200 for fewer than 48 hours.

U.S. residents 21 and older may bring back 1 liter of alcohol duty-free. In addition, regardless of your age, you are allowed 200 cigarettes and 100 non-Cuban cigars. Antiques, which the U.S. Customs Service defines as objects more than 100 years old, enter duty-free, as do original works of art done entirely by hand, including paintings, drawings, and sculptures. You may also send packages home duty-free, with a limit of one parcel per addressee per day (except alcohol or tobacco products or perfume worth more than $5). You can mail up to $200 worth of goods for personal use; label the package PERSONAL USE and attach a list of its contents and their retail value. If the package contains your used personal belongings, mark it PERSONAL GOODS RETURNED to avoid paying duties. You may send up to $100 worth of goods as a gift; mark the package UNSOLICITED GIFT. Mailed items do not affect your duty-free allowance on your return.

7 U.S. Customs Service inquiries ⊠ 1300 Pennsylvania Ave. NW, Washington, DC 20229 ☎ 202/354-1000 ⊕ www.customs.gov ⊠ complaints ⊠ Customer Satisfaction Unit, 1300 Pennsylvania Ave. NW, Room 5.5A, Washington, DC 20229 ⊠ registration of equipment ⊠ Office of Passenger Programs, 1300 Pennsylvania Ave. NW, Room 5.4D, Washington, DC 20229 ☎ 202/927-0530.

DISABILITIES & ACCESSIBILITY

Although it is said that The Netherlands is a world leader in providing facilities for people with disabilities, the most obvious difficulty that people with disabilities face in The Netherlands is negotiating the cobbled streets of the older town centers. Businesses in the tourism and leisure industry are, however, making their premises more easily accessible, and when they are found to be independently accessible for wheelchair users, the International Accessibility Symbol (IAS) is awarded. For information on accessibility nationwide, relevant to travelers with disabilities, contact Access Wise (whose official title is the Vakantie Informatie Punt, or Holiday Information Center) or the NIZW (Nederlands Instituut voor Zorg en Welzijn, or National Institute for Care and Welfare).

Some cinemas and theaters have a forward-looking approach and are accessible. Train and bus stations are equipped with special telephones, elevators, and toilets in larger stations, and the metro is accessible to users of specific wheelchairs. Most trams, however, have high steps, making them inaccessible to wheelchair users, although the newer trams have low-mount doors. Visitors can obtain special passes to **ensure free escort travel on Dutch trains—** for general assistance contact the Nederlandse Spoorwegen (or NS, the Dutch Rail Service) before 2 PM at least one day in advance, or by 2 PM Friday for travel on Saturday, Sunday, or Monday, or public holidays, using the number below. For information on tours and exchanges for travelers with disabilities, contact Access Wise (Vakantie Informatie Punt), whose bank of information is partly sourced from Mobility International.

⚐ Local Resources **Access Wise** ☎ 026/370-6161 🖷 026/377-6420. **Nederlandse Spoorwegen** (Netherlands Railways) ☎ 030/230-5566. **NIZW** (National Institute of Care and Welfare) ✑ Postbus 19152, 3501 DD Utrecht ☎ 030/230-6311. **Wheelchair Hire** ✉ Haarlemmermeerstraat 49-53, 1058 JP Amsterdam ☎ 020/615-7188, €20 per week, with a security deposit of €200.

TRAVEL AGENCIES

⚐ Travelers with Mobility Problems **Access Adventures** ✉ 206 Chestnut Ridge Rd., Scottsville, NY 14624 ☎ 716/889-9096 ✑ dltravel@prodigy.net. **CareVacations** ✉ 5110-50 Ave., No. 5, Leduc, Al-

berta T9E 6V4 Canada ☎ 780/986-6404 or 877/478-7827 🖷 780/986-8332 ⊕ www.carevacations.com. **Flying Wheels Travel** ✉ 143 W. Bridge St., Box 382, Owatonna, MN 55060 ☎ 507/451-5005 or 800/535-6790 🖷 507/451-1685 ⊕ www.flyingwheelstravel.com.

DISCOUNTS & DEALS

Be a smart shopper and **compare all your options** before making decisions. A plane ticket bought with a promotional coupon from travel clubs, coupon books, and direct-mail offers or on the Internet may not be cheaper than the least expensive fare from a discount ticket agency. And always keep in mind that what you get is just as important as what you save.

DISCOUNT RESERVATIONS

To save money, **look into discount reservations services** with Web sites and toll-free numbers, which use their buying power to get a better price on hotels, airline tickets, even car rentals. When booking a room, always **call the hotel's local toll-free number** (if one is available) rather than the central reservations number—you'll often get a better price. Always ask about special packages or corporate rates.

When shopping for the best deal on hotels and car rentals, **look for guaranteed exchange rates,** which protect you against a falling dollar. With your rate locked in, you won't pay more, even if the price goes up in the local currency.

⚐ Airline Tickets 800/AIR-4LESS.
⚐ Hotel Rooms **International Marketing & Travel Concepts** ☎ 800/790-4682 ⊕ www.imtc-travel.com. **Steigenberger Reservation Service** ☎ 800/223-5652 ⊕ www.srs-worldhotels.com. **Travel Interlink** ☎ 800/888-5898 ⊕ www.travelinterlink.com. **Turbotrip.com** ☎ 800/473-7829 ⊕ www.turbotrip.com.

PACKAGE DEALS

Don't confuse packages and guided tours. When you buy a package, you travel on your own, just as though you had planned the trip yourself. Fly-drive packages, which combine airfare and car rental, are often a good deal. If you **buy a rail-drive pass,** you may save on train tickets and car rentals. All Eurail- and EuroPass holders get a discount on Eurostar fares through the Channel Tunnel.

EATING & DRINKING

The restaurants we list are the cream of the crop in each price category. Properties indicated by a ✗⊞ are lodging establishments whose restaurant warrants a special trip. For price categories, *see* the price charts found under the Where to Eat and Where to Stay sections in Chapter 1 (Amsterdam) and under the About the Restaurants & Hotels sections in the regional Chapters 2, 3, 4, 5, and 6.

RESERVATIONS & DRESS

Reservations are always a good idea; we mention them only when they're essential or not accepted. Book as far ahead as you can, and reconfirm as soon as you arrive. (Large parties should always call ahead to check the reservations policy.) We mention dress only when men are required to wear a jacket or a jacket and tie.

ELECTRICITY

To use electric-powered equipment purchased in the United States or Canada, **bring a converter and adapter.**

The electrical current in The Netherlands is 220 volts, 50 cycles alternating current (AC); wall outlets take Continental-type plugs, with two round prongs.

If your appliances are dual-voltage, you'll need only an adapter. Don't use 110-volt outlets marked FOR SHAVERS ONLY for high-wattage appliances such as blow-dryers. Most laptops operate equally well on 110 and 220 volts and so require only an adapter.

EMBASSIES

🇦🇺 Australia **Australian Embassy** ✉ Carnegielaan 4, The Hague ☎ 070/310-8200.
🇨🇦 Canada **Canadian Embassy** ✉ Sophialaan 7, The Hague ☎ 070/311-1600.
🇳🇿 New Zealand **New Zealand Embassy** ✉ Carnegielaan 10, The Hague ☎ 070/346-9324.
🇬🇧 United Kingdom **British Embassy** ✉ Lange Voorhout 10, The Hague ☎ 070/427-0427.
🇺🇸 United States **U.S. Embassy** ✉ Lange Voorhout 102, The Hague ☎ 070/310-9209.

EMERGENCIES

Police, ambulance, and fire (☎ 112 toll-free 24-hr switchboard for emergencies). The 24-hour help-line service **Afdeling Inlichtingen Apotheken** (☎ 020/694-8709)

(*apotheken* means "pharmacy") can direct you to your nearest open pharmacy; there is a rotating schedule to cover evenings, nights, and weekends—details are also posted at your local *apotheken,* and in your area's regional newspaper. The **Centraal Doktorsdienst/Atacom** (Medical Center; ☎ 020/592-3434) offers a 24-hour English-speaking help line providing advice about medical symptoms. In the case of minor accidents, phone **directory inquiries** (☎ 0900/8008) to get the number for the outpatients' department at your nearest *ziekenhuis* (hospital). **TBB** (☎ 020/570-9595 or 0900/821-2230) is a 24-hour dental service that refers callers to a dentist (or *tandarts*). Operators can also give details of pharmacies open outside normal hours.

For less urgent police matters, call the **central number** (☎ 0900/8844), or call directory inquiries for your local station (⇨ Telephones, Directory & Operator Assistance, *below*). For car breakdowns and other car-related emergencies call the big automobile agency in The Netherlands, the ANWB (⇨ Car Travel, Emergency Services, *above*).

Note that all numbers quoted above with the code 020 are for Amsterdam and surrounding area only, indicating that instead of a national central number for that service, help lines are centered on large towns, so also *see* Emergencies *in* the A to Z section in this guide's regional chapters.

ENGLISH- & DUTCH-LANGUAGE MEDIA

ENGLISH-LANGUAGE MEDIA

Roundabout is an English-language monthly magazine guide to what's going on culturally in The Netherlands for visitors and residents, with the main emphasis on the Rotterdam area.

The *International Herald Tribune,* an English-language newspaper with general world news, is available daily in The Netherlands from many newsagents, and the *Financieele Dagblad* has a daily page devoted to English. Daily English-language newspapers are available at bigger newsagents, but they are quite expensive, running at €5. Two English-language newspapers, *Amsterdam Weekly* and *Amsterdam Times,* are planning to launch their first issues in early 2004. Sunday papers have never taken off, but larger railway stations and Sunday-opening bookshops have international Sunday papers.

BOOKS

For Holland's largest selection of books in English, head to **Waterstone's Booksellers** (✉ Kalverstraat 152, just off Spui ☎ 020/638–3821), in Amsterdam; **American Book Center** (✉ Lange Poten 23 ☎ 070/364–2742), in The Hague; or **Donner Bookstore** (✉ Lijnbaan 150 ☎ 010/413–2070), in Rotterdam.

DUTCH-LANGUAGE NEWSPAPERS & MAGAZINES

The leading newspapers *NRC Handelsblad* and *De Volkskrant* are both considered a serious read, with the politically more right-wing *NRC* priced a little above the left-wing *Volkskrant*. *Algemeen Dagblaad* is popular with sports fans, and *De Telegraaf* is the closest thing Holland has to a tabloid press.

Each regional area also has a local paper, such as The Hague's *Haagsche Courant*. Early commuters pick up a copy of *Metro* or *Spits*, the free dailies distributed on weekdays in all public transport stations. In addition to containing national and international news, *Metro* has a good guide to the day's events, across the country; *Spits*, which shares its publisher with the *Telegraaf*, has a high human-interest gossip content. The *Gay Krant* is a biweekly Dutch-language newspaper aimed at the gay community and covers cultural happenings, legal and health issues, and any news relevant to lesbians and gay men.

Each major city publishes its own *Uitkrant* (Going Out), a free monthly detailing events in that specific city, which can be picked up at theaters, bookstores, and tourist information centers within the city of focus. Published in Dutch, the listings are nonetheless a useful guide. *Shark*, a low-budget biweekly, is found in bars and clubs, with movie and music reviews, and its supplement, *Queer Fish*, lists gay and lesbian events.

Chic Dutch-style magazines are glossy and thick and feature the latest, greatest, and chicest things on the scene. *Residence* leads the pack and is mostly devoted to antiques, antiques dealers, and beautiful homes. *Elegance* embraces an upmarket lifestyle, with attention to fashion and home decor. The focus of *Avenue* is wide, including stylish homes, fashion, and interviews with celebrities. Sometimes compared to the English magazine *The Face*, *BLVD* is among the hippest magazines and has been called a cyberglossy. It deals with the "now" in art, culture, and fashion and is produced and aimed at twentysomethings. For fashion, most turn to a Dutch-language, Holland-centric version of *Elle*.

RADIO & TELEVISION

All daily papers contain TV and radio programming listings, and you can also buy weekly guides. Each area has access to between 20 and 30 channels, which the local council selects. This includes three Dutch channels (news, weather, soaps; fairly mundane); six commercial Dutch channels (including SBS6 and Yorin); and regional channels, such as AT5, which is for Amsterdam viewers only. You can also tune in to TMF (The Music Factory), a Dutch take on MTV, as well as Discovery, Geographic, CNN, and British state-funded channels BBC1 and BBC2; there's also TV5, the French channel, as well as German and Italian channels. As with foreign films screened in The Netherlands, all channels are subtitled, not dubbed, into Dutch.

GAY & LESBIAN TRAVEL

Whether or not Amsterdam is the "Gay Capital of Europe," its reputation as being more tolerant of gays and lesbians than most other major world cities makes it a very popular mecca for both the gay and lesbian traveler. The Netherlands originally decriminalized homosexuality in 1811, the age of consent was lowered to 16 back in 1971, and there are stringent antidiscrimination laws. Legislation passed in April 2001 granted same-sex couples the right to marry when, previously, gay and lesbian couples could just register as partners. It's illegal for hotels to refuse accommodation to gays and lesbians, but there are details available of those specifically gay-owned. The Gay & Lesbian Switchboard can provide information on hotels that are gay- and lesbian-friendly. ⓘ **Local Contact** Helpful gay and lesbian organizations include **COC National** ✉ Rozenstraat 8, Jordaan, Amsterdam ☎ 020/623–4596. COC's head office deals with all matters relating to gays and lesbians. The local branch ✉ Rozenstraat 14, Amsterdam ☎ 020/626–3087 is a busy meeting place, dealing with the social side, and has an info-coffee shop. Well-informed members of the **Gay & Lesbian Switchboard** ☏ 020/623-6565 dispense information and advice, and staff at **SAD Schorerstichting** ✉ PC Hooftstraat 5, 107117 BL Amsterdam ☏ 020/662-4206 provide STD tests as well as general information and HIV advice.

⚑ Gay- & Lesbian-Friendly Travel Agencies Kennedy Travel ✉ 130 W. 42nd St., Suite 401, New York, NY 10036 ☏ 212/840-8659 or 800/237-7433 🖷 212/730-2269 ⊕ www.kennedytravel.com. **Now Voyager** ✉ 4406 18th St., San Francisco, CA 94114 ☏ 415/626-1169 or 800/255-6951 🖷 415/626-8626 ⊕ www.nowvoyager.com. **Skylink Travel and Tour** ✉ 1455 N. Dutton Ave., Suite A, Santa Rosa, CA 95401 ☏ 707/546-9888 or 800/225-5759 🖷 707/636-0951, serving lesbian travelers.

HEALTH

Drogists (pharmacists) sell toiletries and nonprescription drugs (⇨ *also* Emergencies, *above*). For prescription drugs go to an *apotheek* (pharmacy). While you are traveling in The Netherlands, the Centers for Disease Control and Prevention (CDC) in Atlanta recommends that you observe health precautions similar to those that would apply while traveling in the United States.

⚑ Medical Care For inquiries about medical care, contact the national health service agency: **GGD Nederland** ⊕ www.gdd.nl/.

HOLIDAYS

Nationale feestdagen (national holidays) are New Year's Day (January 1); Good Friday (April 9 in 2004, March 25 in 2005); Easter Sunday and Monday (April 11 and 12 in 2004, March 27 and 28 in 2005); Koninginnedag (Queen's Day, April 30); Remembrance Day (May 4); Liberation Day (May 5); Ascension Day (May 20 in 2004, May 5 in 2005); Whitsunday (Pentecost) and Monday (May 30 and 31 in 2004, May 15 and 16 in 2005); and Christmas (December 25 and 26). During these holidays, banks and schools are closed, as are many shops, restaurants, and museums. Some businesses close for May 4, Remembrance Day. Throughout the Netherlands, there is a two-minute silent pause from 8 to 8:02 PM, and even traffic stops. Take note and please respect this custom. For information on these and other holidays, *see also* "On the Calendar" in the front section of this book.

INSURANCE

The most useful travel-insurance plan is a comprehensive policy that includes coverage for trip cancellation and interruption, default, trip delay, and medical expenses (with a waiver for preexisting conditions).

Without insurance you will lose all or most of your money if you cancel your trip, regardless of the reason. Default insurance covers you if your tour operator, airline, or cruise line goes out of business. Trip-delay covers expenses that arise because of bad weather or mechanical delays. Study the fine print when comparing policies.

If you're traveling internationally, a key component of travel insurance is coverage for medical bills incurred if you get sick on the road. Such expenses are not generally covered by Medicare or private policies. U.K. residents can buy a travel-insurance policy valid for most vacations taken during the year in which it's purchased (but check preexisting-condition coverage). British and Australian citizens need extra medical coverage when traveling overseas.

Always **buy travel policies directly from the insurance company**; if you buy them from a cruise line, airline, or tour operator that goes out of business you probably will not be covered for the agency or operator's default, a major risk. Before making any purchase, **review your existing health and homeowner's policies** to find what they cover away from home.

⚑ Travel Insurers In the United States: **Access America** ✉ 6600 W. Broad St., Richmond, VA 23230 ☏ 866/807-3982 toll-free 🖷 800/346-9265 ⊕ www.accessamerica.com. **Travel Guard International** ✉ 1145 Clark St., Stevens Point, WI 54481 ☏ 800/826-4919, 715/345-0505 for international callers 🖷 800/955-8785 ⊕ www.travelguard.com.
⚑ Insurance Information In Australia: **Insurance Council of Australia** ✉ Level 3, 56 Pitt St., Sydney, NSW 2000 ☏ 02/9253-5100 🖷 02/9253-5111 ⊕ www.ica.com.au. In Canada: **RBC Travel Insurance** ✉ 6880 Financial Dr., Mississauga, Ontario L5N 7Y5 ☏ 800/565-3129 🖷 905/813-4704 ⊕ www.rbcinsurance.com. In New Zealand: **Insurance Council of New Zealand** ✉ Level 7, 111-115 Customhouse Quay, Box 474, Wellington ☏ 04/472-5230 🖷 04/473-3011 ⊕ www.icnz.org.nz. In the United Kingdom: **Association of British Insurers** ✉ 51 Gresham St., London EC2V 7HQ ☏ 020/7600-3333 🖷 020/7696-8999 ⊕ www.abi.org.uk.

LANGUAGE

There are two official Dutch languages: Dutch, used across the country, and Fries (Frisian), used in the north. In Amsterdam, as in all the other major cities and towns, English is widely spoken. State schools teach English to pupils as young as eight, and with English TV, youngsters often have a smattering of authentic-sounding vocabulary before they even get into learning English at school. Not only is it the country's strong second language, but the general public is very happy to help English-speaking visitors, to the extent that even if you ask in Dutch, they answer cheerfully in English. Signs and notices often have duplicated information in English, if not more languages. Even in more remote villages you can usually find someone who speaks at least a little English.

LODGING

Accommodations in the incredibly popular Randstad region are at a premium, so **you should book well in advance.** The lodgings we review in this book are the cream of the crop in each price category. We always list the facilities that are available—but we don't specify whether they cost extra: when pricing accommodations, always ask what's included and what costs extra. Extra fees can be charged for everything from breakfast to use of parking facilities. For price categories, consult the price charts found under the Where to Eat and Where to Stay sections in Chapter 1 (Amsterdam) and under the About the Restaurants & Hotels sections *in* Chapters 2, 3, 4, 5, and 6.

Properties indicated by a ✗⌖ are lodging establishments whose restaurants warrant a special trip. If a hotel offers a room rate that includes breakfast, this Breakfast Plan is noted in the hotel review as BP. Hotels that operate on the European Plan, without including breakfast in the room rate, are noted as EP. Breakfast often isn't included at government-rated four-star-and-above hotels. In general, all other hotel meals, when breakfast is included in the room rate, are extra in cost, but some resort and spa hotels offer a room-and-board package that mandates taking meals at the facility—check when making your reservations. In general, properties are assigned price categories based on the range from their least-expensive standard double

room at high season (excluding holidays) to the most expensive.

APARTMENT & HOUSE RENTALS

If you want a home base that's roomy enough for a family and comes with cooking facilities, **consider a furnished rental.** These can save you money, especially if you're traveling with a group. Home-exchange directories sometimes list rentals as well as exchanges.

City Mundo has an excellent network, and whatever your requirements, this creative city specialist directory will try to hook you up to your ideal spot, whether that's in a windmill or a houseboat. The price drops the longer you stay, up to the maximum of 21 nights, with a minimum of two nights. Book online, at the group's Web site (⇨ Web Sites, *below*), where visuals and descriptions are constantly updated as new facilities come in.

It's also worth contacting **Holiday Link**, an agency that provides contacts and addresses for home-exchange holidays and house-sitting during holiday periods; bed-and-breakfasts; rentals of private houses in Holland; and budget accommodations. The company is part of **HomeLink International**, the worldwide vacation organization in more than 50 countries, so it knows what's what.

Get in touch with the VVV (tourist information offices) of the region you plan to travel to, as they all have extensive accommodations listings. They can book reservations for you, according to your specific accommodations requirements. Call the number below for the local office in the area you plan to visit.

🛈 **International Agents Hideaways International** ✉ 767 Islington St., Portsmouth, NH 03801 ☎ 603/430-4433 or 800/843-4433 🖷 603/430-4444 ⊕ www.hideaways.com. **Villas International** ✉ 4340 Redwood Hwy., Suite D309, San Rafael, CA 94903 ☎ 415/499-9490 or 800/221-2260 🖷 415/499-9491 ⊕ www.villasintl.com.
🛈 **Local Agents Center Parcs** ⌖ Admiraliteitskade 40, 3063 ED Rotterdam ☎ 010/498-9898 ⊕ www.centerparcs.nl. **City Mundo** ✉ Schinkelkade 47 II, 1075VK Amsterdam ☎ 020/676-5270 ⊕ www.citymundo.co. **Duinrell Holiday Cottages** ✉ Duinrell 1, 2242 JP Wassenaar ☎ 070/515-5258 🖷 070/515-5370 ⊕ www.duinrell.nl. **Holiday Link** ⌖ Postbus 70-155, 9704 AD Groningen ☎ 050/313-2424 ⊕ www.holidaylink.com. **Holland Tulip Parcs** ✉ Marijke Meustraat 112, 4818 LW Breda ☎ 076/

520-0099 🖶 076/531-7920 ⊕ www.
hollandtulipparcs.nl/. **Landal Green Parks** 🖅 Box
910, 2270 AX Voorburg ☎ 070/300-3500 🖶 070/
300-3515 ⊕ www.landalgreenparks.com. **VVV
tourist offices** ☎ 0900/400-4040 (calls cost 55¢
per min). **Zilverberk Parken** 🖅 Box 2067, 3800 CB
Amersfoort ☎ 033/465-6300 🖶 033/461-6003
⊕ www.zilverberk.nl.

CAMPING

Camping is a good way to find reasonably
priced accommodations in an otherwise
overcrowded resort, and camping gear can
be rented at most resorts across The
Netherlands; contact your travel agent or
the **ANWB** (Royal Dutch Touring Club ;
⇨ *below*) for details. Permits and mem-
berships are not required for camping, but
rates are cheaper if you book with one.
Make sure you **stay only on authorized
campsites**—if caught *vrij kamperen* (camping for free), or sleeping in your car, you
face a €90 fine.

**You need your passport or alternative ID
to register** on arrival at your campsite,
unless you plan to stay on a Green campsite, for which you need ANWB's
"Green" camping membership. Green
sites are on farms where children can get
involved feeding animals. Details on
tented-only *natuurcampingen* (sites in
protected environments) can also be ob-
tained from the ANWB.

The ANWB publishes *Camping Gids Nederland* (Guide to Camping in The Netherlands); although it is in Dutch, it lists the
contact details of every site in The Netherlands and has a lot of visuals. It's available
from ANWB stores and larger bookshops
across Holland for €9.95. Call the ANWB
office for any questions about camping, to
obtain "Green" campsite membership, or
to find your nearest ANWB shop. When
you dial, just hold the line for an information officer.

The local VVV (tourist information office)
can also provide you with addresses of
campsites around The Netherlands. Call
the VVV number *below* for sites in the
area you plan to visit. Camp rates are seasonal, but for two people with a car and a
tent expect to pay between €19 and €33,
depending on where the campsite is and
what facilities it offers.

7 Directory of Campgrounds ANWB (Royal Dutch
Touring Club) ☎ 070/314-1420. **VVV Central Tourist
Offices** ☎ 0900/400-4040 (calls cost 55¢ per min).

See also the A to Z section at the end of the appropriate regional chapter to find VVVs in the area you
plan to visit.

HOSTELS

No matter what your age, you can **save on
lodging costs by staying at hostels**
(*jeugdherbergen*). In some 4,500 locations
in more than 70 countries around the
world, Hostelling International (HI), the
umbrella group for a number of national
youth-hostel associations, offers single-sex,
dorm-style beds and, at many hostels,
rooms for couples and family accommodations. Amsterdam is world famous for two
beloved hostels: the Flying Pig Palace and
the Stayokay Hostel in Vondelpark. Membership in any HI national hostel association, like the Dutch affiliation NJHC, or
Nederlandse Jeugdherberg Centrale, is
open to travelers of all ages and allows
you to stay in HI-affiliated hostels at member rates; one-year membership is about
$28 for adults (C$35 for a two-year minimum membership in Canada, £12.50 in
the United Kingdom, A$52 in Australia,
and NZ$40 in New Zealand); hostels run
about $10–$25 (€11–€27.60) per night.
Members have priority if the hostel is full;
they're also eligible for discounts around
the world, even on rail and bus travel in
some countries. NJHC (Stayokay/
Nederlandse Jeugdherberg Centrale) has
an excellent web site with visuals and information about the many hostels on offer
in The Netherlands.
**7 Organizations Hostelling International–Amer-
ican Youth Hostels** ✉ 8401 Colesville Rd., Suite
600, Silver Spring, MD 20910 ☎ 301/495-1240
🖶 301/495-6697 ⊕ www.hiayh.org. **Hostelling International–Canada** ✉ 400-205 Catherine St., Ottawa, Ontario K2P 1C3 ☎ 613/237-7884, 800/663-
5777 in Canada 🖶 613/237-7868 ⊕ www.hihostels.
ca. **NJHC** (Dutch Youth Hostel Association,) 🖅 Box
9191, 1006 AD Amsterdam ☎ 020/639-2929 🖶 020/
639-0199. **Stayokay (Nederlandse Jeugdherberg
Centrale)** ☎ 010/264-6064 ⊕ www.stayokay.com.
Youth Hostel Association Australia ✉ 10 Mallett
St., Camperdown, NSW 2050 ☎ 02/9565-1699
🖶 02/9565-1325 ⊕ www.yha.com.au. **Youth Hostel
Association of England and Wales** ✉ Trevelyan
House, 8 St. Stephen's Hill, St. Albans, Hertfordshire
AL1 2DY England ☎ 0870/870-8808 🖶 01727/
844126 ⊕ www.yha.org.uk. **Youth Hostel Association of New Zealand** ✉ Level 3, 193 Cashel St., Box
436, Christchurch ☎ 03/379-9970 🖶 03/365-4476
⊕ www.yha.org.nz.

HOTELS

In line with the international system, Dutch hotels are awarded stars (one to five) by a governmental agency based on their facilities and services. Those with three or more stars feature en-suite bathrooms where a shower is standard, and a tub is a four-star standard. Rooms in lodgings listed in this guide have a shower unless otherwise indicated. One Dutch peculiarity to watch out for is having twin beds pushed together instead of having one double. If you want a double bed (or *tweepersoonsbed*), you may have to pay more. Keep in mind that the star ratings are general indications and that a charming three-star might make for a better stay than a more expensive four-star. During low season, usually November to March (excluding Christmas and the New Year) when a hotel is not full, it is sometimes possible to **negotiate a discounted rate,** if one is not already offered. Prices in larger cities, particularly in the Randstad area, are significantly higher than those in outlying towns in rural areas, especially over the peak summer period. Room rates for deluxe and four-star rooms are on a par with those in other European cities, so in these categories, **ask for one of the better rooms,** since less desirable rooms—and there occasionally are some—don't measure up to what you are paying for.

Most hotels quote room rates excluding breakfast. When you book a room, specifically **ask whether the rate includes breakfast.** You are under no obligation to take breakfast at your hotel, but most hotels expect you to do so. It is encouraging to note that many of the hotels we recommend offer a wide selection at their buffet breakfast instead of the simple, even skimpy Continental breakfasts.

Check out your hotel's location, and **ask your hotelier about availability of a room with a view,** if you're not worried about the extra expense: hotels in the historic center with a pretty canal view are highly sought after.

Always ask if there is an elevator (called a lift) or if guests need to climb any stairs. Even if you are fairly fit, you may find traditional Dutch staircases intimidating and difficult to negotiate. It's worth considering if you plan to stay in a listed monument. The alternative is to request a ground-floor room.

In older hotels, the quality of the rooms may vary; if you don't like the room you're given, request another. This applies to noise, too. Front rooms may be larger or have a view, but they may also have a lot of street noise—so if you're a light sleeper, **request a quiet room when making reservations.** Remember to **specify whether you care to have a bath or shower,** since many bathrooms do not have tubs. It is always a good idea to **have your reservation, dates, and rate confirmed by fax.**

Aside from going directly to the hotels or booking a travel and hotel package with your travel agent, there are several ways of making reservations. The **Nederlands Reserverings Centrum** (the Dutch hoteliers' reservation service) handles bookings for the whole of The Netherlands on its Web site for cancellations and reservations only; bookings are made online. The VVV (Netherlands Board of Tourism) offer the same services; branches of the VVV can be found in Schiphol Airport and Amsterdam Centraal Station, and regional VVV offices specialize in their own area. Contact the office based in the region you plan to travel to, or go to the area's VVV's web site (listed under Visitor Information in the A to Z section found in the regional chapters of this book). Most agencies charge a booking fee, which starts at €9 per person.

A pleasant alternative to getting accommodations in a hotel is to stay at a bed-and-breakfast (B&B). The best way to track down B&B accommodations is through either creative city accommodations specialist City Mundo or Holiday Link, both of which deal with private accommodations and longer stays (⇨ Web Sites, *below*).

All hotels listed have private bath unless otherwise noted.

🛂 **Local Contact City Mundo** ✉ Schinkelkade 47 II, 1075 VK Amsterdam ☎ 020/676-5271. **Holiday Link** 🖅 Postbus 70-155, 9704 AD Groningen ☎ 050/313-2424. **Nederlands Reserverings Centrum** (Dutch Hoteliers' Reservation Service) ☎ 0299/689144 ⊕ www.hotelres.nl. **VVV Central Tourist Offices** ☎ 0900/400-4040 (calls cost 55¢ per min).

🛂 **Toll-Free Numbers Best Western** ☎ 800/780-7234 ⊕ www.bestwestern.com. **Choice** ☎ 800/654-6200 ⊕ www.choicehotels.com. **Hilton** ☎ 800/445-8667 ⊕ www.hilton.com. **Holiday Inn** ☎ 800/465-4329 ⊕ www.ichotelsgroup.com.

MAIL & SHIPPING

For mail destined for outside the local area, use the *overige bestemmingen* slot in mailboxes. The national postal service's logo is PTT POST (white letters on a red oblong). The Dutch mail system can be slower than you'd expect, so allow about 10 days for mail to and from the United States and Canada and up to a week to and from the United Kingdom. For postal information within The Netherlands call ☎ 0800/0417.

POSTAL RATES

Airmail letters (lightweight stationery) to the United States and Canada cost €.75 for the first 20 grams and €1.50 up to 50 grams. Always **stick the blue "priority" sticker on your envelope**, or write "priority" in big, clear letters to the side of the address. Postcards cost a universal €.54, no matter where they are destined. Letters (for the first 20 grams) to the United Kingdom, as well as to any other EU country, cost €.59. Letters sent within the Netherlands cost €.39 for the first 20 grams. You can buy *postzegels* (stamps) and postcards from tobacconists, the post office, the VVV, and souvenir shops.

RECEIVING MAIL

Correspondence can be addressed to you care of the Dutch post office. Letters should be addressed to your name, followed by "Poste Restante" on the next line, then the address of the main post office in a specific city. You can collect it from the post office in question by showing your passport or photo-bearing ID. American Express also has a general delivery service. There is no charge for cardholders, holders of American Express traveler's checks, or those who booked the vacation with American Express.

MONEY MATTERS

The price tags in The Netherlands' main cities are considered reasonable in comparison with those in neighboring countries. As you would expect, prices vary from region to region and are lower in the countryside than in the urban Randstad. Good value for money can still be had in many places, and as a tourist in this Anglophile country, you are a lot less likely to get ripped off in The Netherlands than in countries where English is less-widely embraced.

Here are some sample prices: admission to the Rijksmuseum is €9; cheapest seats at the Stadsschouwbourg theater run €12 for plays, €20 for opera; a movie ticket is €6.50–€9.50 (depending on time of show). Going to a Dutch nightclub might set you back €5–€20. A daily English-language newspaper is €5. An Amsterdam taxi ride (1⅓ km, or 1½ mi) costs about €4.55. An inexpensive hotel room for two, including breakfast, in Amsterdam, is about €65–€125; an inexpensive Amsterdam dinner is €20–€35 for two, and a half-liter carafe of house wine is €11. A simple sandwich item on the menu runs to about €2.50, a cup of coffee €2. A Coke is €1.40, and a half liter of beer is €2.95.

Prices throughout this guide are given for adults. Substantially reduced fees are almost always available for children, students, and senior citizens. For information on taxes, *see* Taxes, *below*.

ATMS

The Dutch word for ATM is *Pinautomaat*; many locals call the machines simply "pin."

CREDIT CARDS

Throughout this guide, the following abbreviations are used: **AE**, American Express; **DC**, Diners Club; **MC**, MasterCard; and **V**, Visa.

🚹 **Reporting Lost Cards American Express** ☎ 800/554-2639, 020/504-8666 Global Assist in The Netherlands. **Diners Club** ☎ 800/234-6377. **MasterCard** ☎ 0800/022-5821 in The Netherlands. **Visa** ☎ 0800/022-3110 in The Netherlands.

CURRENCY

The single European Union (EU) currency, the euro, is now the official currency of the 11 countries participating in the European Monetary Union (with the notable exceptions of Great Britain, Denmark, Sweden, and Greece).

On the other hand, the U.S. dollar (and all other currencies that are not part of the EU community) and the euro are in direct competition. In fact, this is the reason why the euro was created in the first place, so it could box with the big boys. The gloves are off, and you do have to pay close attention to where you change your money (that is, dollars into euros), thus following the old guidelines for exchanging currencies—**shop around for the best exchange rates (and also check the rates before** leaving home) when it comes to non-EU currencies, such as the U.S dollar, the Japanese yen, and the British pound.

Although it might take Europeans a little getting used to, the euro will make your life much, much easier. Gone are the days when a day trip to Germany meant changing money into yet another currency and paying whatever supplementary commission thereon. Before, a trip to Europe meant carting home a small plastic bag of faded notes in all colors of the rainbow and hundreds of coins you had to examine carefully to find the origin. Now with the euro, crossing borders will just be that much easier: first, you won't have to take all that time and energy following your trusty guidebook's expert advice on the best exchange locations; second, there won't be that awkward moment when you find you don't have enough local currency to buy a piece of gum; and third, you won't have to do all that math (hooray!). The euro was created as a direct competitor with the U.S. dollar, which means that their rates are quite similar: at press time (January 2004), 1 euro = 1.27 US$.

The euro system is classic; there are eight coins: 1 and 2 euros, plus 1, 2, 5, 10, 20, and 50 centimes, or cents, of the euro. All coins have one side that has the value of the euro on it and the other side with each country's own, unique national symbol. There are seven colorful notes: 5, 10, 20, 50, 100, 200, and 500 euros. Notes have the principal architectural styles from antiquity onward on one side and the map and the flag of Europe on the other and are the same for all countries.

CURRENCY EXCHANGE

These days, the **easiest way to get euros is through ATMs.** An ATM is called a *Pinautomaat*; you can find them in airports, train stations, and throughout the city. ATM rates are excellent because they are based on wholesale rates offered only by major banks. It's a good idea, however, to bring some euros with you from home and always to have some cash and traveler's checks as backup. For the best deal when exchanging currencies not within the Monetary Union purview (the U.S. dollar, the yen, and the English pound are examples), compare rates at banks (which usually have the most favorable rates) and booths and look for exchange booths that

clearly state "no commission." At exchange booths always confirm the rate with the teller before exchanging money. You won't do as well at exchange booths in airports or rail and bus stations, in hotels, in restaurants, or in stores. To avoid lines at airport exchange booths, **get some euros before you leave home.**
⟐ Exchange Services **International Currency Express** ☎ 888/278-6628 for orders ⊕ www. foreignmoney.com. **GWK (***bureau de change***)** branches are located near railway stations throughout the country ☎ 0900/0566. There's an office at **Amsterdam Schiphol Airport** ☎ 020/653-5121.

TRAVELER'S CHECKS

Do you need traveler's checks? It depends on where you're headed. If you're going to rural areas and villages, go with cash; traveler's checks are best used in cities and towns in the Randstad region and more popular destinations throughout the rest of the country. Lost or stolen checks can usually be replaced within 24 hours; to ensure a speedy refund, buy your own traveler's checks—don't let someone else pay for them, as irregularities like this can cause delays. The person who bought the checks should make the call to request a refund.

PACKING

When coming to The Netherlands, be flexible: pack an umbrella (or two—the topography results in a blustery wind, which makes short work of a lightweight frame); bring a raincoat, with a thick liner in winter; and always have a sweater or jacket handy. For daytime wear and casual evenings, turtlenecks and thicker shirts under a sweater are ideal for winter. Unpredictable summer weather means that a long-sleeve cotton shirt and jacket could be perfect one day, whereas the next, a T-shirt or vest top is as much as you can wear, making it hard to pack lightly. Bring a little something for all eventualities and you shouldn't get stuck.

Essentially, laid-back is the norm. Older locals in more rural areas sport shorts and clogs, so style-wise, anything goes. Men aren't required to wear ties or jackets anywhere, except in some smarter hotels and exclusive restaurants; jeans are very popular and worn to the office. Cobblestone streets make walking in high heels perilous—you don't want a wrenched ankle—and white sneakers are a dead giveaway that you are an American tourist; a better choice is a pair of dark-color, comfortable walking shoes.

In your carry-on luggage, **pack an extra pair of eyeglasses or contact lenses and enough of any medication** you take to last the entire trip. You may also ask your doctor to write a spare prescription using the drug's generic name, since brand names may vary from country to country. In luggage to be checked, **never pack prescription drugs or valuables.** And don't forget to carry with you the addresses of offices that handle refunds of lost traveler's checks. Check *Fodor's How to Pack* (available in bookstores everywhere) for more tips.

To avoid customs and security delays, carry medications in their original packaging; don't pack any sharp objects, including knives of any size or material, scissors, manicure tools, corkscrews, or anything else that might arouse suspicion. If you need such objects on your trip, consider shipping them to your destination or buying them there.

CHECKING LUGGAGE

You are allowed one carry-on bag and one personal article, such as a purse or a laptop computer. Make sure that everything you carry aboard will fit under the seat or in the overhead bin. Get to the gate early, so you can board as soon as possible.

Airline liability for baggage is limited to $2,500 per person on flights within the United States. On international flights it amounts to $9.07 per pound or $20 per kilogram for checked baggage (roughly $635 per 70-pound bag) and $400 per passenger for unchecked baggage. You can buy additional coverage at check-in for about $10 per $1,000 of coverage, but it excludes a rather extensive list of items, shown on your airline ticket.

PASSPORTS & VISAS

When traveling internationally, **carry your passport** even if you don't need one (it's always the best form of ID) and **make two photocopies of the data page** (one for someone at home and another for you, carried separately from your passport). If you lose your passport, promptly call the nearest embassy or consulate and the local police.

U.S. passport applications for children under age 14 require consent from both parents or legal guardians; both parents must appear together to sign the application. If only one parent appears, he or she must submit a written statement from the other parent authorizing passport issuance for the child. A parent with sole authority must present evidence of it when applying; acceptable documentation includes the child's certified birth certificate listing only the applying parent, a court order specifically permitting this parent's travel with the child, or a death certificate for the non-applying parent. Application forms and instructions are available on the Web site of the **U.S. State Department's Bureau of Consular Affairs** (⊕ www.travel.state.gov).

ENTERING THE NETHERLANDS

All U.S., Canadian, and U.K. citizens, even infants, need only a valid passport to enter The Netherlands for stays of up to 90 days.

PASSPORT OFFICES

The best time to apply for a passport or to renew is in fall and winter. Before any trip, check your passport's expiration date, and, if necessary, renew it as soon as possible.
➐ Australian Citizens **Australian State Passport Office** ☎ 131232 ⊕ www.passports.gov.au.
➐ Canadian Citizens **Passport Office** ☎ 819/994–3500, 800/567–6868 in Canada ⊕ www.ppt.gc.ca.
➐ New Zealand Citizens **New Zealand Passport Office** ☎ 0800/225–050, 04/474–8100 from overseas ⊕ www.passports.govt.nz.
➐ U.K. Citizens **London Passport Office** ☎ 0870/521–0410 ⊕ www.ukpa.gov.uk for application procedures and to request an emergency passport.
➐ U.S. Citizens **National Passport Information Center** ☎ 202/647–4000, 202/647–5225 hot line for American Travelers ⊕ www.travel.state.gov.

SAFETY

Most of the destinations in this guide are among the safest spots in The Netherlands. Amsterdam is unlike any other modern metropolis: although it has had certain problems with crime, and with abuse of legalized prostitution and soft drugs, the serious crime rate is exceptionally low, so having your bike stolen is the worst thing most likely to happen to you. Still, in crowded intersections and dark alleys, it is always best to be streetwise and take double precautions for your safety; it may be best to keep your money in a money belt and not flaunt your expensive camera. As always, be wary of pickpockets in crowds and while riding crowded city trams and at automated cash machines.

SENIOR-CITIZEN TRAVEL

To qualify for age-related discounts, **mention your senior-citizen status up front** when booking hotel reservations (not when checking out) and before you're seated in restaurants (not when paying the bill). Be sure to have identification on hand. When renting a car, ask about promotional car-rental discounts, which can be cheaper than senior-citizen rates.

⊡ Educational Programs Elderhostel ✉ 11 Ave. de Lafayette, Boston, MA 02111-1746 🕾 877/426-8056 🖷 877/426-2166 ⊕ www.elderhostel.org.

STUDENTS IN HOLLAND

The Netherlands is a popular student destination, and in the university towns there are lots of facilities geared toward students' needs (housing, information, and so forth). Students with identification cards (such as an ISIC, or International Student Identity Card) are usually entitled to discounts in shops, clubs, museums, galleries, cinemas, and entertainment venues. The main division of the Universiteit van Amsterdam (UvA) can be found in historic buildings stretching from Spui to Kloveniersburgwal. The Vrije Universiteit (VU) is about half the size of UvA and is housed in one big building in the south of Amsterdam. The Rijksuniversiteit van Leiden is scattered across town, as is Rotterdam's Erasmus Universiteit. Delft's Technische Universiteit isn't a campus as such, but the majority of its buildings are in one area. Eindhoven also has a technical university, and Tilburg's university is well known for its economics department. In Enschede, the Universiteit Twente is named after the region; it is a technical university but also teaches social studies. Groningen has an enormous student population, as does Utrecht, whereas Maastricht's university is considerably smaller.

LOCAL RESOURCES

The **Foreign Student Service** (FSS; ⇨ IDs and Services, *below*) promotes the well-being of foreign students, providing personal assistance and general information on studying in The Netherlands. It also runs the International Student Insurance

Service (ISIS) and organizes social activities. Accommodations agencies can help with finding a room, and for a small fee you can take part in accommodations agency lotteries (for multiple-night stays), usually held daily. Each university has a service and information center; UvA's center (⇨ IDs and Services, *below*) offers personal advice on studying and student life; contact individual universities for information about their accommodations agencies and services, help lines, libraries, summer courses, student unions, and student welfare.

STUDENT ACCOMMODATIONS

In addition to the YHA hostels, young visitors to Holland can stay at a youth hotel, or "sleep-in," which provides basic, inexpensive accommodations for young people. A list of these is available from the **NBT** (🕾 212/370-7360 in New York). In summer (and in some cases year-round), the **Vereniging voor Natuur en Milieu Educatie** (IVN; ⊡ IVN, Postbus 20123, 1000 HC Amsterdam 🕾 020/622-8115 ⊕ www.ivn.nl) organizes work camps in scenic locations, popular among English-speaking visitors age 15–30. Another organization to consider for volunteer work in Holland is **Internationale Vrijwilligers Projecten** (✉ Willemstraat 7, 3511 RJ Utrecht 🕾 030/231-7721 ⊕ www.siw.nl/en).

TRAVEL AGENCIES

To save money, **look into deals available through student-oriented travel agencies.** To qualify you'll need a bona fide student ID card. Members of international student groups are also eligible.

⊡ IDs & Services British Council Education Centre ✉ Weteringschans 85a 1017 RZ Amsterdam 🕾 020/524-7676. **Erasmus Universiteit Rotterdam** ✉ Burgermeisteroudlaan 50 🕾 010/408-1111. **Foreign Student Service** ✉ Oranje Nassaulaan 5, Amsterdam 🕾 020/671-5915. **Rijksuniversiteit Leiden** ✉ Rapenburg 70 🕾 071/527-8011. **STA Travel** (CIEE), ✉ 205 E. 42nd St., 15th fl., New York, NY 10017 🕾 212/822-2700, 972/699-0200 outside North America, call collect: 🖷 212/822-2699 ⊕ www.statravel.com. **Technische Universiteit Delft** ✉ Julianalaan 134 🕾 015/278-9111. **Travel Cuts** ✉ 187 College St., Toronto, Ontario M5T 1P7 Canada 🕾 416/979-2406, 866/246-9762 in Canada 🖷 416/979-8167 ⊕ www.travelcuts.com. **Universiteit van Amsterdam** ✉ Spui 21 🕾 020/525-9111. **UvA Service and Information Center** ✉ Binnengasthuisstraat 9, Amsterdam 🕾 020/525-8080.

TAXES

HOTEL

The service charge and the 6% VAT (Value-Added Tax) are included in the rate. Tourist tax is never included and is 5% extra.

RESTAURANT

In a restaurant you pay 5% service charge, 6% VAT on food items, and 19% VAT on all beverages, all of which are included in the menu prices.

VALUE-ADDED TAX

Referred to as the BTW in Holland, the Value-Added Tax (VAT) runs 19% on clothes and luxury goods, 6% on basic goods. On most consumer goods, it is already included in the amount on the price tag, so you can't actually see what percentage you're paying.

To **get an VAT refund,** you need to reside outside the European Union (EU) and you need to have spent €136 or more in the same shop on the same day (this is including tax). Provided that you personally carry the goods out of the country within 30 days, you may claim a refund at your point of departure from the EU. The simplest system is to **look for stores displaying Tax Free Shopping,** or Global Refund signs, like those at the Bijenkorf. Although Global Refund is the largest VAT refund service, note that there are also other private companies, such as Cash-Back, which help facilitate these transactions for a fee. Once you have made your purchases, go to their customer service department and **ask for a VAT or Tax Free form.** Normally you receive 15% back, but these refund service agents charge 5% commission. You then have these tax-refund forms stamped at customs at the airport where you finally depart from the European Union. It's also a good idea to carry your purchases in your hand luggage, in case customs wants to physically check what you've bought. Once stamped, the forms can be cashed at any bank in the airport, or you can opt to have the refund credited to your bank account.

🛈 VAT Refunds Global Refund ✉ 99 Main St., Suite 307, Nyack, NY 10960 ☎ 800/566–9828 🖷 845/348–1549 ⊕ www.globalrefund.com.

TELEPHONES

AREA & COUNTRY CODES

The country code for The Netherlands is 31. Here are area codes for major cities: Amsterdam, 020; Delft, 015; Eindhoven, 040; Groningen, 050; Leiden, 071; Maastricht 043; Rotterdam, 010; Utrecht, 030. Essentially, the region around every town or city uses the same area code. To call Amsterdam from within Amsterdam, you don't need the code: just dial the seven-digit number. To call Amsterdam from elsewhere in The Netherlands, dial 020 at the start of the number. In addition to the standard city codes, there are three other prefixes used: public information numbers starting with 0800 are free phone numbers, but the information lines with the prefix 0900 are charged at premium rates (35¢ a minute or more), and 06 numbers indicate mobile (cell) phones.

When dialing a Dutch number from abroad, you drop the initial 0 from the local area code, so someone calling from New York, for example, to Amsterdam would dial 011 + 31 + 20 + the seven-digit phone number. From the United Kingdom, dial 00 + 31 + 20 + phone number. When you are dialing from The Netherlands to someplace overseas, the country code is 00–1 for the United States and Canada, 00–61 for Australia, 00–64 for New Zealand, and 00–44 for the United Kingdom. All mobile and land-line phones in Holland are 10 digits long (some help lines and information centers, such as the rail inquiry line, have only 8 digits), with most area codes 3 digits and phone numbers 7 digits. Note that some smaller towns and villages have a 4-digit area code and a 6-digit local number.

DIRECTORY & OPERATOR ASSISTANCE

To ask directory inquiries for a telephone number outside The Netherlands, dial 0900/8418 (calls are charged at €1.15 an inquiry). For numbers within The Netherlands, dial 0900/8008 (calls are charged at €1.15).

To reach an international operator, make a collect call, or dial toll free to a number outside The Netherlands, dial 0800/0410; to speak to a local operator, or make a collect call within The Netherlands, dial 0800/0101.

LONG-DISTANCE SERVICES

AT&T, MCI, and Sprint access codes make calling long-distance relatively convenient, but you may find the local access number blocked in many hotel rooms. First ask the hotel operator to connect you. If the hotel operator balks, ask for an international operator, or dial the international operator yourself. One way to improve your odds of getting connected to your long-distance carrier is to travel with more than one company's calling card (a hotel may block Sprint, for example, but not MCI). If all else fails, call from a pay phone.

F7 Access Codes **AT&T Direct** ☎ 0800/022-9111. **MCI WorldPhone** ☎ 0800/022-9122. **Sprint International Access** ☎ 0800/022-9119.

PUBLIC PHONES

To make a call, lift the receiver, wait till you hear a dial tone, a low-pitched constant hum, then insert a phone card, credit card, or the appropriate amount of coins. Dial the number, and as soon as your correspondent picks up the receiver, you are connected. To make an international call, dial 00 followed by the country code, then drop the first 0 of the area code (see Area and Country codes, above).

Phone cards work only in booths affiliated with the card's company, so Telfort cards work only in blue Telfort booths, found on station platforms, and within towns; KPN cards can be used only in KPN booths, screened by green-edged glass.

Since the increase in cellular phones, the number of phone booths is decreasing. At every railway station there are pay phones, either in the ticket hall or on the platforms. There are clusters of pay phones around pedestrian squares, but the railway station phones are all Telfort and you can use only a Telfort card or coins, whereas the pay phones out on the street are KPN Telecom, where you need to use another card. Awkward, yes—and the reason is that the stations are the property of the NS (Nederlandse Spoorweg, or Dutch Train System), and so they have their own contract with Telfort, whereas public ground is owned by the government, which has a contract with former state firm KPN. The newest KPN phone booths also accept credit cards.

Telfort phone booths and public phones found in bars and cafés accept coins from €.10 to €2.

Off-peak rates apply weekdays 8–8 and all weekend. Phone cards worth €5, €8, and €10 (approximately) can be bought from VVVs (branches of the Netherlands Board of Tourism), post offices, train stations, newsagents, and tobacconists. Since hotels tend to overcharge for international calls, it is best to use a prepaid telephone card in a public phone.

TIME

The Netherlands is one hour ahead of Greenwich Mean Time (GMT). Daylight-saving time begins on the last Sunday in March, when clocks are set forward one hour; on the last Sunday in October, clocks are set back one hour. All clocks on Central European Time (CET) go forward and back on the same spring and autumn dates as GMT. The Netherlands operate on a 24-hour clock, so AM hours are listed as in the United States and Britain but PM hours continue through the cycle (1 PM is 13:00, 2 PM is 14:00, etc.) When it's 3 PM in Amsterdam, it is 2 PM in London, 9 AM in New York City, and 6 AM in Los Angeles. A telephone call will get you the **speaking clock** (☎ 0900/8002) in Dutch.

TIPPING

The following guidelines apply in Amsterdam, but the Dutch tip smaller amounts in smaller cities and towns. In restaurants a service charge of about 6% is included in menu prices. Tip 10% extra if you've really enjoyed the meal and gotten good service, and **leave the tip as change rather than putting it on your credit card.** If you're not satisfied, don't leave anything. Though a service charge is also included in hotel, taxi, bar, and café bills, the Dutch mostly round up the change to the nearest two euros for large bills and to the nearest euro for smaller ones. In taxis, round up the fare to 10% extra. Rest-room attendants expect only change, 25¢, and a cloakroom attendant in an average bar expects half a euro per coat (more in expensive hotels and restaurants).

TOURS & PACKAGES

Because everything is prearranged on a prepackaged tour or independent vacation, you spend less time planning—and often get it all at a good price.

BOOKING WITH AN AGENT

Travel agents are excellent resources. But it's a good idea to collect brochures from several agencies, as some agents' suggestions may be influenced by relationships with tour and package firms that reward them for volume sales. If you have a special interest, **find an agent with expertise in that area**; the American Society of Travel Agents (ASTA; ⇨ Travel Agencies, *below*) has a database of specialists worldwide.

Make sure your travel agent knows the accommodations and other services of the place being recommended. Ask about the hotel's location, room size, beds, and whether it has a pool, room service, or programs for children, if you care about these. Has your agent been there in person or sent others whom you can contact?

Do some homework on your own, too: local tourism boards can provide information about lesser-known and small-niche operators, some of which may sell only direct.

BUYER BEWARE

Each year consumers are stranded or lose their money when tour operators—even large ones with excellent reputations—go out of business. So **check out the operator.** Ask several travel agents about its reputation, and try to **book with a company that has a consumer-protection program.** (Look for information in the company's brochure.) In the United States, members of the National Tour Association and the United States Tour Operators Association are required to set aside funds to cover your payments and travel arrangements in the event that the company defaults. It's also a good idea to choose a company that participates in the American Society of Travel Agents' Tour Operator Program (TOP); ASTA will act as mediator in any disputes between you and your tour operator.

Remember that the more your package or tour includes the better you can predict the ultimate cost of your vacation. Make sure you know exactly what is covered, and **beware of hidden costs.** Are taxes, tips, and transfers included? Entertainment and excursions? These can add up.

🔢 Tour-Operator Recommendations **American Society of Travel Agents (** ⇨ Travel Agencies, *below*). **National Tour Association (NTA)** ✉ 546 E. Main St., Lexington, KY 40508 ☎ 859/226-4444 or 800/682-8886 🖷 859/226-4404 ⊕ www.ntaonline. com. **United States Tour Operators Association (USTOA)** ✉ 275 Madison Ave., Suite 2014, New York, NY 10016 ☎ 212/599-6599 or 800/468-7862 🖷 212/599-6744 ⊕ www.ustoa.com.

TRAIN TRAVEL

The Netherlands has a very compact network; the trains are among the most modern in Europe and are the quickest way to travel between city centers. Services are relatively frequent, with a minimum of two departures per hour for large cities for each routing. The carriages are modern and clean, and although many Dutch people complain about delays, the trains usually run exactly on time. Extra services are offered, such as the night train, which runs hourly all night, stopping at major cities and most staff speak English. Reserving a particular seat is not possible on Dutch trains, though. Stations in most towns are centrally located, usually within walking distance of major sights.

On the train you have the choice of *roken* (smoking) or *niet roken* (no-smoking), and first or second class, indicated with a large 1 or 2 painted on the outside of the train, for your reference as you get on, and at the end of each aisle. First-class travel costs about 50% more, which on local trains gives you a slightly larger seat in a compartment that is less likely to be full, but on long-distance trains you get wider seats, more legroom, and better ventilation and lighting. At peak travel times, first-class train travel is worth the difference.

The fastest trains on the Nederlandse Spoorwegen (or NS, The Netherlands Railway) are the Thalys trains (⊕ www. thalys.com) operating on the main line from Amsterdam to The Hague and Rotterdam, through to Brussels and Paris, and the I.C.E. trains traveling from Amsterdam to Utrecht, Arnhem, and destinations across Germany. You pay a supplement for traveling on these trains, and reservations are made when you buy your ticket. There is little aisle and luggage space, though there is a space near the door where you can put large bags. To avoid having to squeeze though narrow aisles, **board only at your carriage** (look for the number on your ticket). Carriage numbers are displayed on their exterior. Next fastest are international trains, for which you do not have to pay a supplement. Intercity trains are novel in that they can come double-decker; they have a few more stops than the international trains and travel only within the country. *Sneltreins* (express trains) also have two decks but take in more stops, so they are a little slower. *Stoptreins* (local trains) are the slowest.

If you have a reduction pass (⇨ Cutting Costs, *below*), you are restricted from using it before 9 AM; further, because all trains serve commuters, you most likely won't get a seat if you travel during rush hour, which makes later travel doubly appealing.

To avoid long lines at station ticket windows when you're in a hurry, **buy tickets in advance**. With the exception of the Thalys and I.C.E. trains, all tickets can be purchased at the last minute—tickets for these trains can be bought up to one hour before departure and up to three months in advance (Thalys) or up to two months (I.C.E.).

Normal tickets are either *enkele reis* (one-way) or *retour* (round-trip). Round-trip tickets cost approximately 74% of two single tickets. They are valid only on the day you buy them, unless you ask specifically for a ticket with a different date, or not dated. If you buy a nondated ticket, **you must stamp the date on your ticket before you board the train** on your day of travel. Use one of the small yellow machines near the tracks. Just hold the ticket flat and slide it in the gap until you hear a short ring. Once stamped, your ticket is valid for the rest of the day. You can get on and off at will at stops in between your destinations until midnight.

Most main-line rail ticket windows are open Monday–Thursday 6 AM–11 PM, Friday 6 AM–11:45 PM, Saturday 7 AM–11:45 PM, and Sunday 7 AM–11 PM, and no credit cards, debit cards, or traveler's checks are valid for payment. If you don't have Dutch cash, the GWK money exchange has branches in or near most large stations.

If you forget to stamp your ticket in the machine, or you didn't make it in time to buy a ticket, you can seek out an inspector and pay the on-board fare, a stinging 70% more expensive than at the railway station counter. As in a tram or metro, you often travel in a train without anyone asking to check your ticket. If you wait for the inspector to find out that you don't have a

valid ticket, he or she will insist that you buy a ticket at the higher rate—but there is no lesser penalty for owning up before being found out.

Apart from using the ticket window in a station, you can **buy tickets at the yellow ticket machines** in the main hall of the railway station, or on the platforms. These machines accept cash and cards, if you have a four-digit PIN code. Each city is allocated a number (which is also the city's postal code), which you select from the list on the machine. For example, Amsterdam is 1000, Rotterdam is 3000, and Delft is 2600. Key this in, and then choose which of the following you want as flashing lights highlight each pair of options: first or second class; full fare or with a reduction; same-day travel or without a date stamp; and, finally, one-way or round-trip.

Note that in some Dutch cities (including Amsterdam, Rotterdam, The Hague, and Delft) there are two or more stations, although one is the principal station *Centraal*. **Be sure of the exact name of the station** from which your train will depart, and at which you wish to get out.

There is a refreshment service on faster trains, from intercities to the Thalys, with roller carts or a cafeteria or dining car. It is not advised to drink tap water on trains, because the toilet facilities are cleaned only between journeys.
🚆 In The Netherlands **NS–Nederlandse Spoorwegen/Dutch Railways** ☎ 0900/8008 ⊕ www.ns.nl/.
🚆 From the U.K. **British Rail** ☎ 0845/748–4950.

CUTTING COSTS

Train fares in Holland are lower than in most other European countries, but you can still **save money by looking into rail passes**—there are a host of special saver tickets that make train travel even cheaper. Be aware, however, that if you don't plan to cover many miles, then you may as well buy individual tickets; a *dagkaart* (unlimited travel pass for one day) costs €37.10 second class, €59.40 first, but it is almost impossible to rack up enough miles to make it worthwhile.

Between July and the end of August, **check out the Zomertoer,** which allows second-class-only unlimited travel for three days within a 10-day period (€45 for one person and €59 for two people).

Once in Holland, **inquire about the Vo-ordeel-urenkaart,** a reduction card available for all ages, which costs €49 and entitles the holder to a 40% discount on all first- and second-class tickets, when traveling after 9 AM. You need a residential address to apply for this card, as well as passport photos and ID. The card proper will take between four and six weeks to be processed and arrive on your doorstep, but you are issued a valid card for the interim time.

The Netherlands is one of 17 countries in which you can **use a Eurailpass,** providing unlimited first-class travel in all 17 countries. If you plan to travel extensively, get a standard pass. Train travel is available for 15 days ($588), 21 days ($762), one month ($946), two months ($1,338), or three months ($1,654). Children aged 4–11 are charged half the adult fare, and children under 4 travel for free. You can also receive free or discounted travel on some ferry lines, and a Eurailpass Youth for second-class traveling at a lower fare is available to those under 26 ($414 for 15 days). If you plan to travel with one or more others, the Eurailpass Saver offers considerable discounts: 15 days is $498 per person.

Use the Eurail Selectpass if you can narrow down your travel: it offers unlimited first-class travel to three, four, or five countries, cutting the cost to you even further—Benelux (Belgium, The Netherlands, and Luxembourg) counts as one. Fares are as follows: travel for 5 days ($438), 6 days ($476), 8 days ($552), 10 days ($624), or 15 days ($794) in a two-month period. There is a catch, though: the chosen countries must be connected by a direct rail or shipping line. As before, those under 26 can travel on a Eurail Selectpass Youth second class for less: $307 for five days. If two to five people travel on a Eurail Selectpass Saver together, the individual cost drops to $374 for five days.

Order a free copy of the latest brochure, "Europe on Track," by calling **Eurail** (☎ 888/382–7245) in the United States to compare prices and options, or obtain all the information on their web site. Whichever pass you choose, **remember to buy your Eurailpass or Eurail Selectpass before you leave** for Europe. You can buy the passes in The Netherlands but at a 15% *hike-up* compared with buying at

home. You can get further information and order your tickets at the Rail Europe Web site.

Many travelers assume that the rail passes guarantee them seats on the trains they wish to ride, but **you need to book ahead,** even if you are using a rail pass. Seat reservations are required on most European high-speed trains and are a good idea on trains that may be crowded—particularly on popular summer routes.

🎫 Information & Passes All tickets for travel within The Netherlands can be purchased at any Dutch rail station. International passes can be bought at the international window of larger stations. Eurailpasses and Eurail Selectpasses are available through **Eurail** ⊕ www.eurail.com and through the travel agencies of **Rail Europe** ✉ 44 S. Broadway, No. 11, White Plains, NY 10601 ☎ 914/682–2999 ⊕ www.raileurope.com/us/, and **CIT North America, Ltd.** ✉ 15 W. 44th St., 10th fl., New York, NY 10036 ☎ 800/248–8687 ⊕ www.cit-rail.com.

TRAIN TAXIS

When you buy your ticket from a station ticket office, you can buy a *trein-taxi* ticket from some stations for a standard €3.80 per person, per ride. It doesn't matter where you're going, so long as it's within the city limits. The fare is so cheap because it's shared—but with waiting time at a guaranteed maximum of 10 minutes after your call, you won't be hanging around long. Larger cities don't have trein-taxi service. Trein-taxis are ideal for getting to sights on the outskirts of smaller towns. **Ask at the ticket windows in smaller stations,** or ring the transport inquiry number (⇨ Train Information, *below*).

🎫 Train Information Holland-wide **Public Transport Information** ☎ 0900/9292 information officer including schedules and fares. For **lost and found** ☎ 030/235–3923 (hold the line for an operator) on train lines and in stations, ask for a form at the nearest station. **Nederlandse Spoorwegen** (Dutch Rail Customer Service) ☎ 0900/202–1163 (calls cost 10¢ per min).

TRANSPORTATION AROUND THE NETHERLANDS

Public transportation is the fastest mode of travel between The Netherlands' cities, most especially in the Randstad. It is also relatively inexpensive compared with renting a car and paying for gas. Holland's cities are served by Nederlands Spoorwegen (⇨ Train Travel, *above*), with fast services on main lines (Amsterdam–Schiphol–Leiden–The Hague–Rotterdam–Dordrecht–Breda, and on to Brussels and Paris, Amsterdam–Arnhem and on to Germany, and Amsterdam–Utrecht–Eindhoven–Maastricht) that in most cases beat plane travel in time and cost.

Buses (⇨ Bus Travel, *above*) are as comfortable as trains, except when crowded, but are more expensive to travel longer distances; buses do offer more frequent services to certain smaller towns served only by secondary rail connections and are excellent for transport within a city.

The Netherlands has an intricate network of motorways and secondary roads, making renting a car (⇨ Car Rental, *above*) for travel between smaller towns and outlying visitor attractions in the north or east of the country a feasible but expensive alternative to public transport. Using a car in the Randstad, however, with the complex of one-way streets in city centers makes driving a real headache, let alone difficult when contemplating parking options and expense. In addition, there is also the consideration of traffic, especially around rush hour, where driving between Amsterdam and The Hague can take up to three times longer than traveling by train.

The levelness of the country means that bicycling (⇨ Bike Travel, *above*) is a seriously taken solution for most Dutch people. With well-maintained cycle lanes in and around every city and most towns, cycling enables you to see the sights at your own pace, and you can really make like a local.

TRAVEL AGENCIES

A good travel agent puts your needs first. Look for an agency that has been in business at least five years, emphasizes customer service, and has someone on staff who specializes in your destination. In addition, **make sure the agency belongs to a professional trade organization.** The American Society of Travel Agents (ASTA)—the largest and most influential in the field with more than 20,000 members in some 140 countries—maintains and enforces a strict code of ethics and will step in to help mediate any agent-client disputes involving ASTA members if necessary. ASTA (whose motto is

"Without a travel agent, you're on your own") also maintains a Web site that includes a directory of agents. (If a travel agency is also acting as your tour operator, *see* Buyer Beware *in* Tours & Packages, *above*.)

🔢 Local Agent Referrals **American Society of Travel Agents (ASTA)** ✉ 1101 King St., Suite 200, Alexandria, VA 22314 ☎ 703/739-2782 🖷 703/684-8319 🌐 www.astanet.com. **Association of British Travel Agents** ✉ 68-71 Newman St., London W1T 3AH England ☎ 020/7637-2444 🖷 020/7637-0713 🌐 www.abtanet.com. **Association of Canadian Travel Agents** ✉ 5025 Orbitor Dr., Bldg. 6, Suite 103, Mississauga, Ontario L4W 4Y5 ☎ 905/282-9294 🖷 905/282-9826 🌐 www.acta.net. **Australian Federation of Travel Agents** ✉ Level 3, 309 Pitt St., Sydney, NSW 2000 Australia ☎ 02/9264-3299 or 1300/363-416 🖷 02/9264-1085 🌐 www.afta.com.au. **Travel Agents' Association of New Zealand** ✉ Tourism and Travel House, 79 Boulcott St., Box 1888, Wellington 10033 New Zealand ☎ 04/499-0104 🖷 04/499-0786 🌐 www.taanz.org.nz.

🔢 International Agents, Approved by The Netherlands Board of Tourism **American Express Travel** ✉ 200 Vesey St., Lobby Level, 3 World Financial Center, New York, NY 10285 ☎ 212/640-5130 🖷 212/640-9365. **Connoisseur Travel** ✉ 13315 W. Washington Blvd., Los Angeles, CA 90066 ☎ 310/306-6050 🖷 310/578-1860. **Priority Travel** ✉ 35 E. Wacker Dr., Chicago, IL 60601 ☎ 312/782-7340 🖷 312/550-9167. British Agents: **Supranational Hotel Reservations** ☎ 0500/303030. Canadian agents: **Canada 3000 Tickets** ✉ TD Centre, 1201 Pender St. W, Vancouver, BC V6E 2V2 ☎ 604/609-3000. **Exclusive Tours (Merit Travel Group Inc.)** ✉ 145 King St. W, Toronto, M5H 1J8 Ontario ☎ 416/368-8332.

VISITOR INFORMATION

Each VVV (Netherlands Board of Tourism) within The Netherlands has information principally on its own region; **contact the VVV of the area you plan to travel to,** and ask directly for information. Alternatively, **contact The Netherlands Board of Tourism** at home, or in The Netherlands, for countrywide information. For specific VVV tourist offices for most cities and towns in The Netherlands, consult Visitor Information in the A to Z section found in the regional chapters of this book.

🔢 Tourist Offices in the U.S. **VVV–Netherlands Board of Tourism** ✉ 355 Lexington Ave., 21st fl., New York, NY 10017 ☎ 212/557-3500 or 212/370-7360 🖷 212/370-9507 🌐 www.goholland.com ✉ c/o Northwest Airlines, 11101 Aviation Blvd., Suite

200, Los Angeles, CA 90045 ☎ 310/348-9339 🖶 310/348-9344. **𝟕 Tourist Office in the U.K.** ✆ Box 30783, London WC2B 6DH England ☎ 0207/539-7950 🖶 0207/539-7953. **𝟕 Tourist Office in Canada** ✉ 25 Adelaide St. E, Suite 710, Toronto, M5C 1Y2 Ontario ☎ 416/363-1577 🖶 416/363-1470. **𝟕 Tourist Office in Australia Dutch Consulate General** ✆ Box 261, Bondi Junction 2022, NSW 1355 Australia ☎ 029/387-6644 🖶 029/387-3962. **𝟕 Tourist Office in New Zealand** ✆ Box 3816, Auckland 1 New Zealand ☎ 09/379-5399 🖶 09/379-5807. **𝟕 Tourist Office in The Netherlands Netherlands Board of Tourism** ☎ 070/370-5705 nationwide information. **VVV** ✉ Stationsplein 10, 1012 AB Amsterdam ☎ 0900/400-4040 regional specialists (calls cost 55¢ per min) ✉ Koningen Julianaplein 30, 2595 AA The Hague ☎ 0900/340-3505 regional specialists (calls cost 45¢ per min) ✉ Coolsingel 67, 3012 AC Rotterdam ☎ 0900/403-4065 regional specialists (calls cost 35¢ per min). For regional tourist offices, see the A to Z sections at the end of each regional chapter in this book. **𝟕 U.S. Government Advisories U.S. Department of State** ✉ Overseas Citizens Services Office, Room 4811, 2201 C St. NW, Washington, DC 20520 ☎ 202/647-5225 for interactive hot line ⊕ www.travel.state.gov; enclose a self-addressed, stamped, business-size envelope.

WEB SITES

Do check out the World Wide Web when planning your trip. You'll find everything from weather forecasts to virtual tours of famous cities. Be sure to **visit Fodors.com** (⊕ www.fodors.com), a complete travel-planning site. You can research prices and book plane tickets, hotel rooms, rental cars, vacation packages, and more. In addition, you can post your pressing questions in the Travel Talk section. Other planning tools include a currency converter and weather reports, and there are loads of links to travel resources. **𝟕 Suggested Web Sites** The official site for The Netherlands' Tourist Board is ⊕ www.holland.com.

The official Amsterdam site is ⊕ www.amsterdam.nl. More information is found at ⊕ www.visitamsterdam.nl. A Holland-wide site is ⊕ www.visiteurope.com/holland/. Other general sites are ⊕ www.visitholland.com and ⊕ www.amsterdamhotspots.nl. ⊕ www.channels.nl is a Web site that guides you through the city with the help of many colorful photographs. For more information on The Netherlands, visit ⊕ www.goholland.com. Go on a virtual tour of Dutch museums at ⊕ www.tribute.nl/hollandmuseums. The American Society of Travel Agents is at ⊕ www.astanet.com. For rail information and schedules, go to ⊕ www.ns.nl. For airport information, go to ⊕ www.schiphol.nl. For information about the national carrier go to ⊕ www.klm.com for KLM/Northwest flight information and reservations; check out the low tariffs on ⊕ www.easyjet.com/en/ and, for budget travelers, ⊕ www.airfair.nl.

Go to ⊕ www.citymundo.com to view City Mundo's creative city-specialist directory of accommodations. Make bookings online with Nederlands Reserverings Centrum (the Dutch hoteliers' reservation service) at ⊕ www.hotelres.nl. For budget accommodations, try ⊕ www.stayokay.com, which provides comprehensive information for The Netherlands—just click on "English" to access all information. At ⊕ www.iyhf.org Hostelling International has a site for worldwide reservations. For information on car-breakdown rescue service, camping, biking, hiking, and water sports, go to ⊕ www.anwb.nl, the Dutch Touring Club. Go to ⊕ www.raileurope.com for pan-Europe ticket sales, for U.S. residents, which also has links to sites for Australian, Canadian, New Zealand, and British residents; you'll find these at the top of the screen. At ⊕ www.weer.nl you can find out the weather forecasts for The Netherlands (in Dutch but with figures and visuals so it's accessible). For a fun site where you can learn a bit of Dutch, go to ⊕ www.learndutch.org. The English-language Dutch magazine *Expats Magazine* has online articles about news and current cultural events at ⊕ www.expatsonline.nl. One of the most informative English-language Web sites about The Netherlands is at ⊕ www.expatica.com. *Shark* is a free newspaper with alternative listings, and their site is at ⊕ www.underwateramsterdam.com.

AMSTERDAM

FODOR'S CHOICE

Amsterdams Historisch Museum, *a grand introduction*

Anne Frankhuis, *birthplace of* The Diary of Anne Frank

The Begijnhof, *so picturesque it will click your camera for you*

The Jordaan, *Amsterdam's most distinctive "village"*

The Gouden Bocht, *home to the 17th-century rich and famous*

Het Koninklijk Paleis, *the grandest palace in Holland*

Museum Amstelkring, *with its "Our Lord in the Attic" church*

Museum het Rembrandthuis, *the immortal artist lived here*

Museum Willet-Holthuysen, *for its Golden Age elegance*

Rijksmuseum, *home to Rembrandt's* Night Watch

Rijksmuseum Vincent Van Gogh, *a crescendo of color*

HIGHLY RECOMMENDED

RESTAURANTS   De Poort, *Nieuwe Zijde*

Kantjil en de Tijger, *Nieuwe Zijde*

Excelsior, *Oude Zijde*

La Rive, *East & Amstel*

Le Garage, *Museum District*

Vermeer, *Oude Zijde*

HOTELS   Ambassade, *Western Canal Ring*

Amstel Inter-Continental, *Plantage*

Dikker and Thijs Fenice, *Leidseplein*

Grand Sofitel Demeure Amsterdam, *Oude Zijde*

Seven One Seven, *Western Canal Ring*

Toren, *Jordaan*

Many other great sights, restaurants, and hotels enliven this city.
For other favorites, look for the black stars as you read this chapter.

By Steve
Korver and
Jonette
Stabbert

AMSTERDAM HAS AS MANY FACETS AS A 40-CARAT DIAMOND polished by one of the city's gem cutters: the capital, and spiritual "downtown," of a nation ingrained with the principles of tolerance; a veritable Babylon of old-world charm; a font for homegrown geniuses such as Rembrandt and Van Gogh; a cornucopia bursting with parrot tulips and other greener—more potent—blooms; and a unified social zone that takes in cozy bars, archetypal "brown" cafés, and outdoor markets. While impressive gabled houses bear witness to the Golden Age of the 17th century, their upside-down images reflected in the waters of the city's canals symbolize and magnify the contradictions within the broader Dutch society. With a mere 730,000 friendly souls and with almost everything a scant 10-minute bike ride away, Amsterdam is actually like a village—albeit a largish global one—but one that happens to pack the cultural wallop of a megalopolis. A wry bit of self-criticism has the city of Rotterdam making the money, the bureaucratic Hague figuring out what to do with the money, and Amsterdam spending the money.

However, this kind of thinking is fast losing ground as Amsterdam reinvents itself as the business "Gateway to Europe." Hundreds of foreign companies have established headquarters here to take advantage of Amsterdam's central position within the European Union. One result of this windfall is that the city is hastening to upgrade its infrastructure and to create new cityscapes that will, it is hoped, lure photographers away from the diversions of the Red Light District. Within a few years, the Eastern Docklands—once a bastion for squatters attracted to its abandoned warehouses—will be transformed into a new hub of culture and nightlife, with a boardwalk planned to be as image enhancing as Sydney's in Australia. Could this be the birth of a new "Golden Age"?

Still, it will take time to fully erase more than eight centuries of erratic history, much of which was of a spicy nature: Anabaptists running naked in the name of religious fervor in 1535; a go-go bar claiming tax-exempt status as representing the Church of Satan; mass suicides after the 1730s crash of the tulip bulb market; riots galore, from the Eel Riot of the 1880s to the squatter riots a hundred years later; famed trumpeter-turned-junkie Chet Baker's swan-song leap from a hotel window; the 1960s proto-hippie Provos playing mind games with city officials; the festival of Queen's Day, whereby the city transforms itself into a remarkably credible depiction of the Fall of Rome; and the endless debates—about sin, students, gayness, sex and drugs, even, yes, about coffee shops.

Rembrandt to Rock 'n' Roll
We tend to take stereotypes with a grain of salt, but, in the case of Amsterdam, go ahead and believe them. At the same time, we need to remember that there's so much more. To find the "more," one must be deliberate in planning explorations; otherwise some visitors may find themselves looping back—as have sailors for centuries—to the city's gravitational center, the Red Light District. After all, it is hoped that as a visitor, you are here, at least partly, to unburden yourself of some misconceptions. Certainly this town is endearing because of its kinder, gentler nature—a reputation for championing Sex, Drugs, and Rock 'n' Roll cannot alone account for Amsterdam's being the fourth most popular travelers' destination in Europe (after London, Paris, and Rome). Carrying far greater weight—cultural, moral, social—is the fact that within a single square mile the city is home to some of the greatest achievements in Western art. Is there a conscious inmate of our planet who doesn't revere Rembrandt, who doesn't love Van Gogh? The French writer J-K Huysmans called Amsterdam "a dream, an orgy of houses and

Perhaps Amsterdam's greatest charm is also its greatest enigma: How can such a gracious cultural center with an incomparable romance also multitask as the most offbeat metropolis in the world? Built on a latticework of concentric canals like an aquatic rainbow, this remains the City of Canals—but Amsterdam is no Venice, content to live on moonlight serenades and former glory. Rather, on nearly every street you'll find old and new side by side: quiet corners where time seems to be holding its breath next to neon-lit Kalverstraat, Red Light ladies strutting under the city's oldest church. Above all, today's visitors can enjoy the same streets hallowed by the spirits of Rembrandt, Van Gogh, and Anne Frank.

1

As you explore the great sights, remember Amsterdam is a great walking city because so many of its real treasures are untouted details: tiny alleyways barely visible on the map, hidden garden courtyards, shop windows, sudden vistas of church spires and gabled roofs. Also remember that Amsterdam can be rather damp. With the obvious precautions of comfortable, weatherproof shoes and an umbrella, walking might well become your favorite pastime.

**If you have
1 day**

So, you want to taste Amsterdam, gaze at its beauty, and inhale its special flair, all in one breathtaking (literally) day? Although you will never get into the casual groove of the city in a whirlwind visit, it's actually a super way to make notes as you go along to compile a Sinter Klaas (or Santa Claus) list for a plan of action for your more leisurely return trip. Still, one day can give you a real taste of the city. Leaving the main rail terminus, Centraal Station, head toward the right and the sector known as the Nieuwe Zijde ("New Side")—the westerly portion of Amsterdam's inner city, the Centrum. If it is your wont, you could head left into the Oude Zijde ("Old Side"), but hereabouts is the Red Light District—even though traditional gables vie with equally traditional leisure industries here, this sector is best left for night. So, from Centraal Station head south along the (unfortunately, tacky) Damrak street, turning right on Oudebrugsteeg for several blocks until you get to the Museum Amstelkring (at Oudezijds Voorburgwal 40), where you'll get a full blast of Golden Age splendor, thanks to spectacular period rooms and the famous "Our Lord in the Attic" church. After this dip into Vermeer's day, backtrack to the Damrak, turn left, and continue south—noting the famous Beurs van Berlage stock exchange along the way—until you reach the seething hub of the Dam, the broadest square in the old section of town. Landmarked by the Nieuwe Kerk—site of all Dutch coronations—it is also home to the magical 17th-century Het Koninklijk Paleis, which fills the western side of the square. Its richly decorated marble interiors are open to the public when the queen is not in residence. From the Dam, follow the busy pedestrian shopping street, Kalverstraat, south to the entrance to the Amsterdams Historisch Museum. Here you can get an enjoyable, easily digestible lesson on the city's past, including its freely accessible Schutters Gallery with its massive Golden Age group portraits.

Passing through the painting gallery of the Historisch Museum brings you to the entrance of the Begijnhof, a blissfully peaceful courtyard oasis. Behind the Begijnhof you come to an open square, the Spui, lined with popular sidewalk cafés, and to the Singel, the innermost of Amsterdam's concentric canals. Cut through the canals by way of the romantic Heisteeg alley and its continuation, the Wijde Heisteeg, turning left down the Herengracht to the corner of Leidsegracht. This is part of the prestigious Gouden Bocht, the grandest stretch of canal in town.

Continue down the Herengracht to the Vijzelstraat and turn right to the next canal, the Keizersgracht. Cross the Keizersgracht and turn left to find the Museum van Loon, an atmospheric canal house, still occupied by the family that has owned it for centuries but open to the public. Turn back down Keizersgracht until you reach the very posh Nieuwe Spiegelstraat; take another right and walk toward Museumplein. Rising up in front of you is the redbrick, neo-Gothic splendor of the Rijksmuseum, housing the world's greatest collection of Dutch art, or, for now, at least its "Best of the Golden Age" selection (with its world-famed Rembrandts and Vermeers) found in the only wing not undergoing massive renovation in the coming years. When you leave the Rijksmuseum, walk through the covered gallery under the building. Directly ahead is Museumplein itself; to your right is Paulus Potterstraat (look for the diamond factory on the far corner), where you'll find the Van Gogh Museum, which contains a unique collection of that tortured artist's work.

Continuing along Paulus Potterstraat, at the corner of Van Baerlestraat, you reach the Stedelijk Museum, where you can see modern art from Picasso to the present. Just around the corner, facing the back of the Rijksmuseum across Museumplein, is the magnificent 19th-century concert hall, the Concertgebouw. A short walk back up along Van Baerlestraat will bring you to the Vondelpark—acre after acre of parkland alive with people in summer.

If you have **3 days** Everyone's dream of Amsterdam is the grand, crescent-shape waterways of the *Grachtengordel* (girdle or ring of canals), lined with splendid buildings and pretty, gabled houses. On your second day, take full advantage of these delights—wander off the main thoroughfares, saunter along the smaller canals that crisscross them, and sample the charms of such historic city neighborhoods as the Jordaan. Begin at busy Dam Square and circle around behind the royal palace to follow the tram tracks into the wide and busy Raadhuisstraat. Once you cross the Herengracht, turn right along the canal, and at the bend in the first block you will see the Nederlands Theatermuseum, which occupies two gorgeous 17th-century houses. Return to the Raadhuisstraat and turn right, following it to the Westermarkt. Stop for a fish snack at the stall under the shadow of the tower of the Westerkerk, on the right, facing the next canal. This landmark is Rembrandt's burial place. Make a right past the church and follow the Prinsengracht canal to the Anne Frank House, where you can visit the attic hideaway in which Anne Frank wrote her diary.

The neighborhood to your left, across the canal, is the Jordaan, full of curious alleys and pretty canals, intriguing shops and cafés. At the intersection of the Prinsengracht and Brouwersgracht, discover the Brouwersgracht, one of the most picturesque canals in Amsterdam. Oozing with ancient charm, the Jordaan's higgledy-piggledy streets and arterial canals will offer a good setting for a digestive wander, with its local brown cafés, stained brown from chain-smoking regulars and stocked with every imaginable other digestive aid. Then enhance the romance factor by finding your way back to your hotel via the wonderfully lighted canal rings.

On your third day, start by exploring "Rembrandt's neighborhood," Amsterdam's historic Jewish Quarter. Begin at its heart, Waterlooplein. Today the square is dominated by the imposing modern Muziektheater/Stadhuis (Music Theater/Town Hall), which is surrounded by a large and lively flea market. East of Waterlooplein, on Jonas Daniël Meijerplein, is the Joods Historisch Museum, skillfully converted from a number of old synagogues. Just to the east of that, on the corner of Mr. Visserplein and Jonas Daniël Meijerplein, is the stately Portugees Israelitische Synagoge. Its interior is simple but awe-inspiring because of its vast size and floods of natural light.

Venturing over to the sylvan Plantage neighborhood, you'll find that the varied flora cultivated in the greenhouses of the Hortus Botanicus is just across the canal. Then you might want to make a short diversion to the Verzetsmuseum, which explains the Dutch resistance to the occupying forces, passive and active, during the Second World War. But for something more lighthearted, especially if you have children in tow, proceed to the Artis Zoo (which was attractively laid out in parklike surroundings in the 19th century and has a well-stocked aquarium). Time permitting, take Tram 9 or 14 farther east along Plantage Middonlaan, to the Tropenmuseum, which has riveting displays on tropical cultures and a special children's section.

Alternatively, you can walk from the synagogue up Jodenbreestraat, where—in the second house from the corner by the Zwanenburgwal—you'll find the Museum het Rembrandthuis, the mansion where Rembrandt lived at the height of his prosperity, which now houses a large collection of his etchings. Cross the bridge to St. Antoniebreestraat and follow it to the Zuiderkerk, whose rather Asian spire is the neighborhood's chief landmark. Take St. Antoniebreestraat north to Nieuwmarkt. Take Koningsstraat to the Kromboomssloot and turn left, then right at Rechtboomssloot (both pretty, leafy canals), and follow it through this homey neighborhood, the oldest in Amsterdam, to Montelbaanstraat; turn left and cut through to the broad Oude Waal canal. Follow it right to the Montelbaanstoren, a tower that dates back to the 16th century and was often sketched by Rembrandt. Up Kalkmarkt from the tower is Prins Hendrikkade, which runs along the eastern docks.

Following Prins Hendrikkade east you enter the modern world with a bang at the NEMO Science & Technology Center. A little farther on is the Nederlands Scheepvaartmuseum, where there is a fascinating replica of an old Dutch East India ship. Across the bridge on Hoogte Kadijk is the Museumwerf 't Kromhout, where wooden sailing boats are still restored and repaired. If, on the other hand, you go west along Prins Hendrikkade to Geldersekade, you can see the Schreierstoren, the tower where legend has it that women used to stand weeping and waiting for their men to return from sea. Here, Henry Hudson set sail for America in the 16th century, making for a fitting farewell finale for your third day.

If you have
5 days
A more extended stay can mean three things: stretching the above recommendations into a five-day period, going efficiently local by renting a bicycle, and having the time to choose from the mass of international concerts (perhaps there are still tickets left for a jazz legend at the Bimhuis, your fa-

vorite conductor at the Concertgebouw, or any manner of musical acts at the former church Paradiso or the former milk factory Melkweg). More time also means more flexibility in dealing with Amsterdam's propensity toward sudden bursts of rain. Besides equipping yourself with an umbrella, you can decide when it looks like there is to be a stretch of sun, the better to explore the Old Center or the Western Canal Ring and the Jordaan. A cloudy day should inspire a more lingering exploration of the Museum District or the Jewish District, both of which are rich with cultural refuges from rain. Of course, sunny late afternoons and evenings should be spent on a sunny terrace or in Vondelpark, whose light at this time gives off a similar glow as you may have witnessed earlier in a Golden Age painting at the Rijksmuseum. At least one of your dinners should be spent indulging in either a cheese fondue or a full-blown Indonesian rice table. Dessert, of course, will be a walk along a canal, or even better, an evening canal cruise that will have you admiring the city from its most complementary of vantage points.

Also to be considered is taking perhaps a full day to wander the harbor front from the evocatively ancient and nautical Westelijke Eilanden to the boardwalk arising beside Oostelijke Handelskade to the stunning residential architecture of the Java and KNSM islands and the Borneo and Sporenburg peninsulas. A pretty day can even inspire you to point your bike farther afield—say, up the Amstel River toward Oude Kerk (a favored route of Rembrandt) or north along the IJsselmeer to the fishing village of Marken. More time also means that you may have by now stumbled across a friendly brown café where you feel comfortable in establishing yourself as a temporary "regular." After all, Amsterdam by day offers such a multitude of globally statured cultural offerings, you may want to spend your nights taking advantage of the city's more "villagey," socially cozy aspects.

---

water." So true: the city of Amsterdam, when compared with other major European cities, is uniquely defined by houses, not palaces, estates, and other aristocratic folderol. With 7,000 registered monuments, most of which began as residences and warehouses of humble merchants, set on 160 man-made canals (stretching 75 km [50 mi]), Amsterdam has the largest historical inner city in Europe.

The city's advancement to the Golden Age of the 17th century actually began some time before the 13th century. A local legend has Amsterdam discovered by two fishermen who, while lost at sea with their dog, vowed to found a town on any bit of land that offered them safety—foreshadowing Amsterdam's future as a place of refuge. When they finally landed on terra firma, their dog was quick to baptize the spot with some "regurgitation"—and before you knew it, a little fishing hamlet rose on the boggy estuary at the mouth of the Amstel River. To keep the sea at bay, the plucky but essentially leaderless inhabitants were forced to join together in the building of dikes, creating a proto-democracy of sorts in the process. But Amsterdam's official voyage toward global domination began only in 1275, when it attracted members of the aristocracy: Floris V, count of Holland, decreed that the little settlement would be exempt from paying tolls. Consequently, this settlement of Amstelledamme was soon taking in tons of beer from Hamburg, along with a lot of thirsty settlers. Following the dictum that it takes money to make money, beer profits opened up other fields of endeavor, and by the 17th century, Amsterdam had become the richest and most powerful city in the world.

But to truly understand Amsterdam is not merely to look at its vertical time line. Like the canals' waters, the city's historical evolution follows a cyclical pattern of both down spins and upswings. Today's influx of multinationals, to name but one example, makes sense in a town that produced the world's first-ever multinational: the East India Company (VOC). The merchant traders of the day realized they could lose everything with the sinking of a single ship, so they cleverly banded together to buy shares in what was now their collective of sailing ships, thereby each losing only a percentage if a ship was lost. In short order, the VOC made trade with Asia efficient, and its massive profits led directly to Amsterdam's Golden Age, when it was called, in Voltaire's words, "the storage depot of the world."

Naturally, there was a downfall: unprecedented wealth led to cockiness, which in turn led to corruption, which in turn led—so the Calvinists believed—to the arrival of Napoléon. Although many factors led to the decline of the Golden Age—chief among them increasing competition from other colonial powers—there is no doubt that its "embarrassment of riches" did affect local character. With no king or monarch, the people of Amsterdam have always behaved in a progressive manner, indulging in their freedom to do their own thing. While the rest of Europe still felt it necessary to uphold the medieval tags of "honor" and "heroism," Amsterdam had the luxury of focusing just on money—and the means to make it. And with money came confidence and liberty. French historian Henri Mechoulan said, "all the people of the 17th-century say Amsterdam is a . . . 'Temple of Trade' but primarily Amsterdam must be regarded as the cradle of freedom." Certainly it's no coincidence that Amsterdam was the place where the noted 16th-century political thinker John Locke wrote his *Epistula de Tolerantia,* that a 17th-century scientist like Jan Swammerdam could lay the basis for entomology, that philosophers like Spinoza and Descartes could propound controversial world views, or that architects like Hendrick de Keyser, Joseph van Campen, and Daniel Stalpaert could pursue their own visions of the ideal. The Enlightenment was in fact ushered in by books, including those by Voltaire, that were not allowed to be published anywhere else but here. Even the United States Declaration of Independence's statement of freedom and equality was based on a manifesto written here in 1581 by Dutch rebels engaged in setting up a republic after freeing themselves from the rule of Phillip II.

A New Golden Age?

Amsterdam's arms, indeed, were spread wide to all rebels with a cause. But pragmatic motives were often behind such a welcoming posture. Consummate masters at "clinching the deal," Amsterdammers were known for a no-nonsense approach to business, and this, in turn, led to a broad tolerance for people of diverse cultures and religions. Such an attitude drew not only oppressed Jews, perhaps from Portugal and Eastern Europe, but also every other stripe of political or economic refugee, and from the whole continent. So, not merely "modern," Amsterdam has historically been "multicultural" *avant la lettre.* The onset of a second goldenish age in the late 19th century, through an escalation of Indonesian profits, the discovery of diamonds in South Africa, and the opening of the North Sea Channel, resulted in a doubling of the population. Then, with the post–World War II boom, another wave of immigrants, now from the former colonies of Indonesia, Suriname, and the Antilles as well as "guest workers" from Morocco and Turkey, thronged in. Today, as the "Gateway to Europe," Amsterdam finds itself scrambling to provide housing to employees of multinational companies from across Europe, North America, and the world at large.

The pragmatic laws of supply and demand also account for Amsterdam's eminence as a city of the arts. The iconic heroes of the first Golden Age—from Rembrandt to Steen—were basically commercial artists supplying services to a population with money to burn. If Van Gogh had not been distracted by personal problems, he might have been free to better exploit—as did many of his contemporaries—the favorable economic climate, and both to revolutionize art and make a viable living while doing so. In contrast to the art of the past, which was driven by inspiration, today's Dutch artistic revolutions are taking place more under the guise of "design," with many of the city's visually inclined professionals achieving instant acclaim for their dazzling configurations on the graphical "canvas" of the Internet. Because there is no going back, it makes sense that a tiny town, where space must be obsessively organized, should be at the precipice of this new virtual world.

Similarly, Amsterdam is enjoying a renaissance as a showcase for the newly voguish concepts of Dutch architecture (best represented by ambitious building projects like those along the Eastern Docklands and Ijburg). These may yet prove to be as enduring, influential, and image defining as were the canal-side gabled houses and the Amsterdam School of past boom years. However, visual smartness is not much in evidence in such inner-city areas as the Wallen, Damrak, Nieuwendijk, and Rembrandtsplein, which at present reflect an area heading straight for Disneyification. But for now, let us leave the complaining to the locals. Your assignment, while visiting this endlessly fascinating city, is strictly to enjoy yourself. It's remarkably easy to do: just take on the characteristics of the local waterways and go with the flow.

– Steve Korver

EXPLORING AMSTERDAM

By Steve Korver

This chapter divides Amsterdam into seven fascinating explorations. Heading out from Amsterdam's Centraal Station, the main transport hub, you first discover the Nieuwe Zijde—the "New Side," comprising the western half of the Centrum (city center). You then head westward to the Grachtengordel West, or Western Canal Ring, and its fascinating and funky Jordaan neighborhood. This section deposits you at the next sector, which begins at the northwest end of Grachtengordel Oost, or the Eastern Canal Ring, famed for its 17th-century Gouden Bocht ("Golden Ring") area. Continuing south, you head past the square of Leidseplein to Amsterdam's famous Museum District and, just beyond, De Pijp, the colorful district that sits shoulder to shoulder with Amsterdam Zuid, today, the poshest residential sector of Amsterdam (sorry, it has no historic sites). The chapter then heads back up north to cover the eastern half of Amsterdam, beginning again at Centraal Station and taking in the historic Oude Zijde—the "Old Side," comprising the eastern half of the Centrum. You then move south to cover two memorable neighborhoods, the Jewish Quarter—immortalized by Rembrandt—and the Plantage. Finally, you conclude with a tour of the sights of the city's waterfront and shipping district.

When it comes to getting your own bearings, Amsterdam can prove a challenge. Indeed, the city's shape and distinctive canal rings often remind first-time visitors of the wrinkles on their furrowed brows as they come to grip with the city's somewhat challenging layout. If you take an overview of the entire city from the sky, first imagine a horizontal line with a dip in the middle. The dip in the middle of our hypothetical line marks the point at which an artificial island was built to receive the Centraal Station (1889). The medieval core of Amsterdam, marked by

Amsterdam on Wheels

As soon as you step out of the train and leave Centraal Station, you are confronted with a great chaos of parked and moving bikes. When in Rome, you do as the Romans, so in Amsterdam you should rent a bike. It can make all the difference to your stay here and offer you an insider's perspective on this compact city. Taking the necessary care to watch for other traffic and pedestrians, you can get around on two wheels at a pace that still allows you to take in your surroundings. Most rental bikes are fitted with pedal brakes, rather than hand brakes. To stop, you pedal backward, which can take awhile to grow accustomed to. Rental bikes are usually one-speed, but this is sufficient for the flat city. Because Amsterdammers got on their bikes as soon as they were weaned, cycling lessons are anathema. If you are out of practice, wheel your bike to the Vondelpark, the city's "green lung," and start out on the grass for a soft landing without scrapes. Make sure you lock the frame of your bike to something fixed, such as a bike rack or railing, even when leaving it unattended for the shortest time. One essential thing you should be aware of while exploring Amsterdam is that the usually friendly local folks (whose uncanny English can be exploited whenever you find yourself forever looping about) can suddenly turn ugly when confronted while bicycling along the easily identifiable bike paths with a tourist checking a map—or, heaven forbid, a guidebook. So be warned or be prepared to have the fear of the God-like stature of the Dutch bicyclist drummed into you. You can brood sensitivity by renting a bicycle by yourself and attempting to find a Zen peace within the psychotically pedaling throngs.

Nowadays the Vondelpark is also the place for a leisurely in-line skate, though there are also the hip-and-trendy practicing their pirouettes. In summer you can rent skates and protective knee, elbow, and wrist pads from a booth at the southern end of the park. For the inexperienced it is certainly worth having a lesson with a friendly instructor, which adds only a little to the overall rental costs. Weather permitting, you can join the **Friday Night Skate** (⊕ www.fridaynightskate.nl), an initiative copied from the massively popular event in Paris. Here in Amsterdam, hundreds of skaters tour the streets of the city with guides and qualified first-aid officers on hand for any unlucky bumps. Join them at 8 PM outside the Nederlands Filmmuseum (Netherlands Film Museum; ⊠ Vondelpark 3, Museum District and Vondelpark) at the northeastern end of the Vondelpark.

Amsterdam's Hofjes—the Historic Almshouses

Hidden behind innocent-looking gateways throughout the city center, most notably along the main ring of canals and in the Jordaan neighborhood, are some of its most charming houses. There are about 30 *hofjes* (almshouses), mainly dating back to the 18th century, when the city's flourishing merchants established hospices for the old and needy—pensions and social security were unheard of then. Their philanthropy was supposed to be rewarded by a place in heaven. But be warned (and be prepared for disappointment): residents of these hofjes like their peace and quiet, and are often prone to locking their entrances to visitors in the name of maintaining that peace and quiet. Most famous is the Begijnhof, and others such as the Hofje Van Brienen and De Zon are included in the Exploring Amsterdam walking tours. Yet others include the **Sint Andrieshofje** (✉ Egelantiersgracht 107–114, Jordaan); founded in 1615, it is the second-oldest almshouse in Amsterdam. Notice the fine gables, including a step gable in the style of Hendrick de Keyser. The **Claes Claeszhofje** (✉ junction of Egelantiersstraat, Eerste Egelantiersdwarsstraat, and Tuinstraat, Jordaan) was established in 1626 by a Mennonite textile trader. The **Zevenkeurvorstenhofje** (✉ Tuinstraat 197–223) was founded around 1645, though the houses standing today are 18th century. The **Karthuizerhof** (✉ Karthuizerstraat 21–131, Jordaan) was founded in 1650 and now accommodates young people around a courtyard with two 17th-century pumps.

Dutch Modern While much of this chapter is devoted to Amsterdam's gorgeous Golden Age past, structures throughout the city attest to its role in creating some of the most striking landmarks of early-20th-century architecture and design. Some critics carp that Dutch architecture is as straitlaced as the people themselves. In fact, the intolerance of architecture-for-art's-sake found first fruition in the works of the loosely grouped architects of the Amsterdam School, who during World War I began to straddle late-19th-century expressionism and the purism of De Stijl, the Dutch movement founded by Theo van Doesburg in 1917 that propounded ideas similar to the Bauhaus in Germany. The cubist tendencies proclaimed by De Stijl had their roots in the order and conciseness of the great Dutch architectural innovator Hendrik Petrus Berlage (1856–1934), noted for his design for the city's Beurs van Berlage stock exchange. This, in turn, affected domestic interior design. While warm and cozy houses with overstuffed chairs, lace curtains, and carpeted floors prevail in most of Holland, modernist architects and furniture designers were fervently taken up by Amsterdammers. The city has a concentration of international design firms and shops with great contemporary furniture and accessories for the home, where the leading designer names include W. H. Gispen, Martin Visser, Benno Premsela, Piet Hein Eek, Henk Stallinga, and, most recently, Droog Design (Dry Design)—more a "mentality" than a "style"—which achieved international fame with its whimsical wobble vases and soft sinks. All in all, fans of *Wallpaper* magazine should be very happy in Amsterdam.

The Way of All Flesh The great French writer and philosopher Albert Camus probably described Amsterdam best when he observed that the city's concentric rings of canals dauntingly resembled the circles of hell. If we follow this logic, it is indeed a strong coincidence that the Red Light District would then be the central cauldron of damnation. And the fact that the rookie visitor often finds himself forever looping back to this area as if under the rigid control of some strange gravity just adds to the eeriness. However, one can hypothesize that this was a geographical trick fine-tuned through the centuries to keep that ever-arriving influx of sailors compartmentalized, thereby leaving the rest of the city to the residents—and the more savvy traveler. This theory may also help account for the endless press depicting Amsterdam as a capital of sin and depravity. But no two ways about it, sex is a big business in Amsterdam—it is also a centuries-long saga in the making, for the history of prostitution in Amsterdam, with its successful harbor, is almost as long as the history of the city. Men who were seeking companionship and comfort have been regular visitors since the Middle Ages. In the 16th century, the city's sheriff and his enforcement officials actually ran the brothels. When prostitution was outlawed, these government officials required significant raises in their salaries because of the loss of income. In the 17th century, window prostitutes were working out of their own homes. Others solicited on the streets or in taverns along the Zeedijk, but prostitution was limited to certain sections of the city. "Honest" labor for women was poorly paid, and, therefore, many women—particularly seamen's wives—supplemented their earnings with prostitution.

The 19th century saw a dramatic rise in the urban poor and a razing of slum areas. Newly built dwellings were too expensive for craftsmen and artisans to maintain, so people started renting rooms to prostitutes and students to supplement their income. The often-privileged students, prostitutes, and artists coming together in the neighborhood stimulated a carefree and fun atmosphere that still dominates in today's Red Light District. Prostitution in Amsterdam has been appreciatively and informatively portrayed in John Irving's book *A Widow for One Year.*

Dutch pragmatism is evident in the city government's approach to the unsavory aspects of life: the goal is to control and maintain public order and safety through tolerance of existing activities. There are three official locations for window prostitution: the infamous and central Red Light District 9 (in Dutch referred to as the Rosse Buurt or De Walletjes); along part of the Spuistraat on the Nieuwe Zijde; and on the Ruysdaelkade on the periphery of De Pijp. As of 2000, the permit/license system introduced in the 1990s, primarily to prevent the spread of sexually transmitted diseases by targeting the prostitutes with information and help, was extended to brothels. The women now have legal recourse should the brothel not meet the standards the license demands. The Red Light District is active day and night. Most of the women (men's forays into the window trade have always met with failure) are scantily dressed and dance or bounce their breasts in windows and doors surrounded with red and blue fluorescent light to highlight their costumes. Prostitutes come in all sizes, shapes, and nationalities and a rainbow of color. The narrowness of the streets, with windows on both sides, has an "in your face" boldness, and the new visitor will certainly feel confronted. When visiting the Red Light District, make your first stop the Prostitute Information Center, or PIC, which is also Dutch slang for "penis" (Enge Kerksteeg 3, ☎ 020/420–7328). Founded and staffed by former prostitutes, the center provides information to prostitutes, customers, and tourists on the new laws, codes of behavior, and the neighborhood in general. For those who feel more comfortable in groups, PIC recommends tours organized by **Lindbergh Excursions** (✉ 26 Damrak, Nieuwe Zijde ☎ 020/622–2766).

---

a confusion of waterways that have since been partially filled in (Damrak and Rokin were once canals), is directly below this dip and thus within a few minutes' walk of the station itself. Around this core you'll notice four semicircular rings of canals, with two more at a somewhat greater distance. Everything within the Lijnbaansgracht, or outermost canal, is called the Centrum; everything beyond belongs to the modern development of Amsterdam and is subdivided into West, *Zuid* (south), and *Oost* (east). With this noted, we seriously advise you to do your exploring with map in hand. The concentrically circular nature of the city's layout makes it terribly easy to start walking in exactly the opposite direction from the one you thought you were going.

Amsterdam:
Nieuwe Zijde
to the Museum District

JORDAAN

WESTERN
CANAL
RING

GOUDE
BOCH

MUSEUM
DISTRICT

Vondelpark

Museum
Plein

KEY

Canal bus
Ferry
Metro lines
Rail lines
Start of walk
Tram lines

The Centrum—or inner Old Center—is handily sliced in half into a westerly "New Side" and an easterly "Old Side" (with its enjoining former Jewish Quarter). It is here, within the encircling Golden Age–built canals (Herengracht, Keizersgracht, and Prinsengracht) with their equally image-defining grandly gabled canal houses, and the Museum District (located on this horseshoe's southerly hump)—that you'll find most of the famous attractions of Amsterdam. To most short-term visitors, the Museum District and Vondelpark are the city's furthest frontier, but on either side of these are two of the city's more vibrant neighborhoods: the still staunchly individualistic Jordaan to the west and the ultimately multicultural De Pijp to the east. Originally built to house the ever arriving migrants and workers, these neighborhoods are probably the best places to go to get a sense of the real Amsterdam today.

Finally, a few helpful rules. There are a number of address endings that indicate the form of thoroughfare: a *straat* is a street; a *laan* is a lane; a *gracht* or *sloot* is a canal, though some of these have been filled in to provide more room for road traffic; a *kade* is a canal-side quay; and a *dijk* is a dike, though in the urban environment this is not always obvious. House numbers are counted from nearest the center of the city, with the Dam as epicenter. Unfortunately postal codes do not adhere to a system that will help you navigate from one neighborhood to another.

THE AMSTERDAM PASS The recently introduced electronic Amsterdam Pass gives you access to the city's main museums, a free canal round trip, free use of public transport and a 25% discount on various attractions and restaurants; savings can amount to over €100. A one-day pass costs €26, two days costs €36 and three days costs €46. The pass comes with a booklet in Dutch, English, French and German. It can be purchased at branches of the VVV (Tourist Information Offices), the GVB (City Transport Company), and through some hotels and museums.

The Nieuwe Zijde: The Eastern Half of the Centrum

A city with a split personality, Amsterdam is both a historic marvel and one of the most youthful metropolises in the world—and you'll get complete servings of both sides of the euro coin in this first, introductory tour. In fact, a full blast of its two-faced persona will be yours simply by walking into Amsterdam's heart (if not soul): the Dam. For, as the very center of the *Centrum,* or center city, this gigantic square has hosted many singular sights: Anabaptists running nude in the name of religious freedom, the coronation of kings and queens, stoned hippies camping out under the shadow of its surrealistically phallic National Monument. The Dam is just one showpiece of the western side of the historic center, known as the Nieuwe Zijde (New Side), a neighborhood just west of the Oude Zijde sector and taking up the area between Damrak (and its Rokin extension) and the Singel canal.

The terms "Old Side" and "New Side" came into being when an expanding Amsterdam was split into two parochials: one around the then more conservative Oude Kerk and the other around Nieuwe Kerk, which attracted the rising merchant class. Although the Old Side always had the highest density of monasteries and nunneries, one event occurred on the New Side's Kalverstraat (Calf Street) that made Amsterdam a major pilgrimage site for more than two centuries—the economic windfall that was fundamental to Amsterdam's rapid growth toward its 17th-century Golden Age. "The Miracle of Amsterdam" occurred on March 15, 1345, when a dying man coughed up the host he had just swallowed during communion. A maid cleaned up the effluence and threw it into a fire, only to discover the next day in the midst of the ashes that the host was still in pristine and overly gracious condition.

As this centuries-old history reveals, the "new side" is far from new. Archaeologists have uncovered buildings that date from the dawn of the 13th century. The New Side's structure and evolution has directly mirrored the Old Side ever since the city's soggy beginnings as two boggy strips on either side of the Amstel River. The Old Side's Oudezijds Voorburgwal ("Old Side's Front of the City Wall") and Oudezijds Achterburgwal ("Old Side's Back of the City Wall"), and the New Side's now paved-over Nieuwezijds Voorburgwal ("New Side") and the Nieuwezijds Achterburgwal (now called Spuistraat), used to be the moats on the inside and outside of the medieval city's wall fortifications. At the center of all is the Dam Square, or *de Plaets* ("the place"), as this space was originally called. Before Centraal Station was built, the Damrak port was essentially the Amstel River, where ships could sail clear up to the Dam area (which then bore a dam across the river) to unload their products and have them weighed before being sent to market. Today, the Damrak has shrunk to toy-size dimensions and is most popular now as the launching pad for glass-roof boats that tour the city canals. But although you'll want to be sure to take one of those tours, the New Side is a fine sector in which to ease into Amsterdam. Compared to the Old Side, or Oude Zijde, the New Side is more sedate, particularly around Spui Square, which has the reputation for being the intellectual heart of the city, since it was where until recently most of the newspapers were based and where still the cafés ring with talk that is often more ambitious than that heard elsewhere in the city.

Numbers in the text correspond to numbers in the margin and on the Exploring Amsterdam: Nieuwe Zijde to the Museum District and the Exploring Amsterdam: Oude Zijde to the Plantage maps.

a good walk

Beginning at **Centraal Station** ❶ ▶, wander straight up the once-watery **Damrak** ❷ while erasing with your mind's eye all the tourist tack and neon that disgrace the formerly epic buildings on the right. No such technique is required on the first prominent building on the left: the former stock exchange, **Beurs van Berlage** ❸, which is considered the most important piece of Dutch architecture from the 20th century. Once you have entered the **Dam** ❹, you will be quick to realize that this freshly scrubbed square—with its centerpiece, the National Monument (which has long attracted the backpacking community to sit beneath its granite shadow)—has been the city's center for centuries. On the right lies the square's most imposing building in both stature and history: the monumental **Het Koninklijk Paleis te Amsterdam** ❺ (Royal Palace), which is flanked to the right by the **Nieuwe Kerk** ❻—the certainly not new "New Church." Less ancient features of the square are **Madame Tussaud Scenerama** ❼ wax museum, the huge and bustling department store Bijenkorf (which appropriately means "beehive"), and the famous diamond outlet Cassans. Ignore the middle-of-the-road walking-and-shopping streets that come out in front of the Royal Palace—the Kalverstraat to the left and its slightly more lowbrow Nieuwendijk to the right—to take the Mozes en Aaronstraat, which runs on the palace's right side. The Neo-Gothic Magna Plaza—the former post office, which has been transformed into a specialty shopping plaza—will force you to take a left. Take the second right, Paleisstraat, but not before admiring the massive load that Atlas is carrying on the top of the Royal Palace's rear, and then perhaps glancing down the Nieuwezijds Voorburgwal, once the country's Fleet Street but now overflowing with bars and cafés that form a magnet to the arty, hip drinking scene.

Then take the first left to walk down Spuistraat. If you see a huge building on the right with a huge punky mural on its facade, you are on the right track: this is the squat Vrankrijk, which has been the focal point of radical politics, music, and cheap beer for decades. Keep going until you get to Rosmarijnsteeg on the left. Proceeding down here and crossing Nieuwezijds Voorburgwal will drop you at the front door of the **Amsterdams Historisch Museum** ❽—certainly one of the city's best museums. If you choose to save it for later, take the alley, Sint Luciensteeg, to its left. Walking onward will connect you to the busiest shopping street of The Netherlands, the previously mentioned Kalverstraat, named after its former function as cattle market. Turn right into the mass of shopping sheep and walk a minute until you get to No. 92, where you can enter the Amsterdams Historisch Museum's courtyard café, "David & Goliath," with its central lime tree, planted for Queen Wilhelmina's coronation. In an adjacent passage across the courtyard is a grand enfilade of 17th-century civic guard portraits, on display here since some were too big to fit into the museum proper.

The next goal is to enter Amsterdam's largest and most ancient *hofje*, or former churchyard almshouse: the tree-filled **Begijnhof** ❾. While this painfully picturesque courtyard with its encircling houses and their pert little gardens is no longer home to nuns, its still purely female residents do enjoy their quiet, and therefore the two entranceways regularly alternate their opening hours to confuse the merely casual (but be warned the hours are getting more and more irregular as some of the residents are battling to close the doors completely—as of press time, the doors were only open between 8–11 AM daily until local courts resolve the issue). If the entrance on the right along the Schutters Gallery's street extension, Gedempte Begijnensloot, is closed, head straight to the **Spui** ❿ Square, following the wall on the right to the right to get to the other arched entranceway. This route was once impossible when this street and square were moats protecting the honor of the Begijnhof's holy residents.

Once you are able to pull yourself away from this delightful part of Amsterdam, exit Spui to the southeast down Voetboogsteeg, whose entrance is immediately recognizable by the Arts and Crafts extravagances gracing the Art Nouveau Helios building (which won its architect, G. A. van Arkel, a bronze medal at the 1900 Paris World Fair) on the left and the more restrained grandeur of the University of Amsterdam's Maagdenhuis on the right (its name, "Virgin House," refers to the orphans who lived here between 1629 and 1953).

Voetboogsteeg (Foot Restraint Alley) will connect you with Heiligeweg (Holy Road), the tiny remains of the Miracle of Amsterdam pilgrimage route that used to follow Leidsestraat and Overtoom out of the city and into Europe. A rather nasty dominatrix type greets you over an arched entranceway whose inscription translates as "wild beasts must be tamed." And indeed, this once led into the Rasphuis (Shaving House) prison, which was quite the tourist attraction in its Golden Age heyday when folks came to watch the prisoners dye themselves black while shaving Brazilian hardwood for the use in paint. Nowadays, tourists might just want to pop through here to enjoy the view from the top of the Kalvertoren shopping complex.

Head south down Heiligeweg toward Koningsplein, an innocent-enough-looking square of sorts that has the sporadic habit of breaking out in riot: once in 1696 to protest the taxing of funerals and once in 1876 when the annual circus was canceled (Amsterdammers sure know how to fight for their rights, don't they?). Turn left down the far side of the

Singel to browse through the floating Flower Market, where you can stock up on bulbs, fresh cut flowers, or (even) peyote home-grow kits.

TIMING Ignoring all the potential interiors, one can walk this route in a half hour, but plan on doing the grand tour and spend at least three or four hours discovering all the sights. De Koninklijk Paleis and the Nieuwe Kerk are known for their variable hours, so calling ahead might ease any potential heartbreak; Beurs van Berlage is closed Monday. If you plan to divert to do some shopping, recall that shops are closed Monday mornings, but rejoice in the fact that the whole of Kalverstraat has recently embraced, after much residual Calvinist procrastination, the concept of "Sunday shopping."

Sights to See

8 **Amsterdams Historisch Museum** (Amsterdam Historical Museum). Any city FodorsChoice that began in the 13th century as a sinking bog of a fishing village to ★ slowly rise to became a marketplace for fishermen and eventually bloomed as the 17th century's powerful trading city must have quite a fascinating story to tell, and this museum does it superbly. Housed in a rambling amalgamation of buildings, the complex had become an orphanage in 1580 after being confiscated during the Altercation from the St. Lucy Convent (which had existed there the previous two centuries). After the departure of the orphans and an extensive renovation, the museum opened in 1975. Economic downswings, French and Nazi occupations, radical politics, and the growth of multiculturalism round out the city's engaging story to the present day. While rich with art, models, and plain old treasures, the museum also employs a lot of state-of-the-art technologies: many will delight in the five different **speaking doll houses** that tell of daily life through the centuries and a "white car" in which you can cruise the city's streets. Budding musicians can even have a go on an old church carillon in one of the building's towers.

On the ground level are the old Boys' and Girls' Courtyards, separated by a loggia. In the boys' section, now the terrace of the **David & Goliath Café**, the rows of wooden lockers once used by the orphans for their meager possessions are adorned with photos and accompanying biographies of some of this city's most prominent 20th-century cultural and artistic heroes. Exiting the opposite end will lead you to the other courtyard, where an immediate left will direct you to the freely accessible atrium, **Schutters Gallery**. This alley—which used to be a narrow canal that separated the boy orphans from the girl orphans—is filled with huge, historic portraits of city militias (some of their red eyes make one suspect that marijuana has always been freely available in this city). ⊠ *Kalverstraat 92 and Nieuwezijds Voorburgwal 357, Nieuwe Zijde* ☎ *020/523–1822* ⊕ *www.ahm.nl* ⌧ *€6* ☉ *Weekdays 10–5, weekends 11–5.*

9 **Begijnhof** (Beguine Court). Here, serenity reigns just a block from the FodorsChoice screeching of trams stopping next to the bustling **Spui** Square. The ★ richly scenic Begijnhof is the tree-filled courtyard of a residential hideaway, built in the 14th century as a conventlike residence for unmarried or widowed laywomen—of which there were many due to the Crusades' efficiency in killing off surplus men—who merely had to follow three simple rules: no hens, no dogs, no men. Rent was paid in the form of caring for the sick and educating the destitute. One resident, Cornelia Arens, so loved this spot that she asked to be buried in the gutter here in 1654—so out of respect, don't tap-dance on the slab of red granite on the walkway on the left side of De Engelse Kerk.

This hof, or almshouse, is typical of many found throughout The Netherlands. At No. 34 is the oldest house in Amsterdam and one of only two remaining wooden houses in the city center. After a series of disastrous fires, laws were passed in the 15th century forbidding the construction of buildings made entirely from timber. On the building's left side there are biblical plaques, which quote scripture and depict scenes from the holy book. The small **Engelse Kerk** (English Church) across from here at No. 48 dates from 1400. To this day, it's unclear why a Scottish Presbyterian church is called the English Church, although it probably has something to do with its having been presented to the Pilgrim Fathers during their brief stay in Amsterdam in 1607 (obviously, the right time: the Altercation of 1578 had seen the church confiscated from the Beguines). Much more recently, its pulpit panels were designed by a young and broke Piet Mondriaan.

Because they were now churchless, the Beguines built the supposedly clandestine **Mirakel-** or **Begijnhof-Kapel** ("Miracle- or Begijn-Chapel"), across the lane at No. 29. Built by the Catholic *bouwmeester* (building master, as the architect-carpenters were called in those days) Philips Vingboons in 1671, it once contained the relics of the Miracle of Amsterdam. However, its stained-glass windows are still here to tell the story. ⊠ *Entrances on the north side of Spui and on Gedempte Begijnensloot opposite Begijnensteeg, Nieuwe Zijde* ⊘ *Mirakel- or Begijnhof-Kapel Mon. 1–6:30, Tues.–Fri. 9–6:30, weekends 9–6.*

❸ **Beurs van Berlage** (Berlage's Stock Exchange). An architectural turning point, completed in 1903, the Stock Exchange is considered Amsterdam's first modern building. In 1874, when the Amsterdam Stock Exchange building on the Dam showed signs of collapse, the city authorities held a competition for the design of a new one. Fortunately the architect who won was caught copying the facade of a French town hall, so the commission was awarded to local boy H. P. Berlage. The building that Berlage came up with proved to be a template for its new century. Gone were all the fripperies and ornamentations of the 19th-century "Neo" styles. The new Beurs, with its simple lines and the influence it had on the Amsterdam School architects who followed Berlage, earned him the reputation of being the "Father of Modern Dutch Architecture."

The building—welcoming and quick to absorb by all—is in fact a political manifesto that preaches the oneness of capital and labor. Built upon 4,880 timber piles, each of the Beurs van berlage's 9 million bricks is meant to represent an individual, who together form a strong and democratic whole. Berlage showed particular respect for the labor unions by exposing their works and accenting the important structural points with natural stone. What details that do exist, many of them designed by Berlage himself, make comment—as the Dutch are so good at—on the follies of greed. Other details of particular interest come courtesy of Jan Toorop (tile tableaux), Antoon Derkinderen (stained glass), and Mendes da Costa (woodwork).

Perhaps intimidated by all the warnings of blind capitalism, the stockbrokers eventually moved to find more reassuringly Brutalist accommodation, and today the Beurs serves as a true Palazzo Publico with concert halls (home to the Dutch Philharmonic Orchestra) and space for exhibitions of architecture and applied arts. The small museum has exhibits about the former stock exchange and its architect and offers access to the view from the lofty clock tower. ⊠ *Damrak 2433–277, Nieuwe Zijde* ☎ *020/624–0141* ⊕ *www.beursvanberlage.nl* ▧ *€5* ⊘ *Tues.–Sun. 11–4.*

MERCHANTS & MASTERPIECES: THE SPLENDOR OF THE BURGHER BAROQUE

MEN IN BLACK? As much as Rembrandt's dour, frowning, and Calvinist portraits of town governors may be the image first conjured up by Holland's Golden Age, it should not be the last. As revealed by historian Simon Schama in his landmark 1987 book, The Embarrassment of Riches: An Interpretation of Dutch Culture in the Golden Age, a closer look at Dutch 17th-century painting shows that Holland was far from a country where people dressed only in black, wore wooden shoes, and interior decoration flowed in a minor key. Rather, befitting the boom economic years of the second half of the 17th century, Vermeer's sunlighted conversation pieces, Gabriel Metsu's music scenes, and Gerard Terborch's tea parties depict settings fitted out with all the fixings of true bourgeois splendor: alabaster columns, Delftware tiles, Turkish carpets, bouquets of Semper Augustus tulips (often as costly as jewels), farthingale chairs, tables inlaid with ivory, Venetian mirrors, ebony-framed paintings, and parrots from India. Strikingly, all this featherbed luxury is still on view today in Amsterdam's historic mansions, such as the Museum Willet-Holthuysen, the Museum Amstelkring, the Bartolotti House, and other grachtenhuis (canal houses).

This Baroque splendor was the result of Amsterdam's transformation into a consumer's paradise in the mid-17th century. Growing fat on the trade of cheese from Friesland, furs from Russia, cattle from Denmark, wine from France, spices from India, and the slave trade from the Java Seas, the rising Dutch burgerij, or burgher class, promptly developed a taste for frills and furbelows. Rose brick gave way to gleaming marble walls; the banketjestukken (breakfast pieces) paintings of the 1620s, often depicting a herring or two and a wineglass, were dropped in favor of the pronkstuk ("showpiece") still life—lobsters and venison set among tall goblets, bowls with strawberries, pewter ware, and silver jugs, all brushed with the sensuality of innuendo.

Civic groups and charitable organizations—not princes and courts— became the standard-bearers of patronage. Not surprisingly, the paintings merchants wanted to hang on their Spanish-leathered walls depicted the realities of daily life: milkmaids, drunkards, henpecked husbands, genteel music lessons, and elegant parties in tea salets (salons)—not muses and madonnas. All the while, preachers did their best to denounce Queen Money from their pulpits: the Dutch had to remember to be Deugdzaam (virtuous) and Deftzig (to act with propriety and reason). Even landscape paintings should be "cozy." In architecture, Mannerist taste for outlandish and overdone ornament—a holdover from the 16th-century Flemish Renaissance— was tempered by a new style of Italian Classicism, which toned down the clutter of design. Woe betide the burgomaster who did not practice moderation. Look at what happened to poor Rembrandt, who had married above his station, bought one of the grandest houses in the city, and decorated it to the nines, only to default on his mortgage and then liquidate his entire estate.

In the end, the "embarrassment of riches" gave Golden Age art its unique luster. Vermeer may essentially show us private individuals wrapped up in their own thoughts, but what enchants us is his wonderful depiction of an interior space, where his brush lovingly delineates everything from the textures of the deep pile of the Utrecht velvet cushion on a chair to the luxurious sheen of a woman's Lyons silk dress, from Delft tile wares to gleaming pewter chandeliers. The 17th-century Dutch may have come down with a case of advanced consumption—the mercantile, not physical, variety—but their art remains all the richer for it.

▶ ❶ **Centraal Station** (Central Station). The main hub of transportation in The Netherlands, this building was designed as a major architectural statement by P. J. H. Cuypers. While sporting many Gothic motifs (including a unique wind vane disguised as a clock in its left tower), it is now considered a landmark of Dutch Neo-Renaissance style. Cuypers must have derived great smugness in having designed the city's other main gateway, the Rijksmuseum, which lies like a mirrored rival on the other side of town. The building of the station required the creation of three artificial islands and the ramming of 8,600 wooden piles to support it. Completed in 1885, it represented the psychological break with the city's seafaring past, as its erection slowly blocked the view to the IJ River. Other controversy arose from all its Gothic detailing, which was considered by uptight Protestants as a tad too Catholic—like Cuypers himself—and hence earned the building the nickname the "French Convent" (similarly, the Rijksmuseum became the "Bishop's Castle"). With more than 1,500 trains passing through it daily, Centraal Station has long learned to live with the guilt. And you should certainly not feel guilty about fighting your way through the buskers and backpackers who litter its doorways. If you have time to kill, perhaps take a return trip on the free ferry to Amsterdam North that departs directly opposite the rear entrance; or check out the rather sci-fi-looking multilevel bicycle parking lot to the right when exiting the front entrance. ⊠ *Stationsplein, Nieuwe Zijde* ☎ *0900/9292 public transport information.*

need a break?

A particularly stylish way to wait for a train is at **1e Klas** (⊠ Platform B, Centraal Station, Nieuwe Zijde ☎ 020/625–0131) whose original Art Nouveau brasserie interior is no longer restricted to first-class passengers and is perfect for a lingering coffee, snack, or full-blown meal accompanied by fine wine. Whatever the hour, it's a fine place to savor the sumptuousness of fin de siècle living.

❹ **Dam** (Dam Square). Home to the Koninklijk Paleis and the Nieuwe Kerk, Amsterdam's official center of town is the Dam, which traces its roots to the 12th century, when wanderers from central Europe came floating in their canoes down the Amstel River and thought to stop to build a dam. A city began to evolve when a market was allowed in 1300, and soon this muddy mound became the focal point of the small settlement of Amstelledamme and the location of the local weigh house. Folks came here to trade, talk, protest, and be executed. Ships once sailed right up to the weigh house, along the Damrak. But in the 19th century the Damrak was filled in to form the street leading to Centraal Station, and King Louis Napoléon had the weigh house demolished in 1808 because it spoiled the view from his bedroom window in the palace across the way. Regardless, the Dam remains the city's true center—which has just been emphasized by the laying of fresh and glistening white cobblestones.

The **National Monument,** a towering white obelisk in the center of the square, was erected in 1956 as memorial to the Dutch victims of World War II; a disconcerting modernist statement, it was designed by the architect J. J. P. Oud with De Stijlian echoes (the architect felt the minimalist De Stijl style was more in keeping with the monument's message). Every year on May 4, it is the national focal point for Remembrance Day, when the queen walks from the adjacent Koninklijk Paleis to the monument to lay flowers. The monument's urns imbedded in its rear contain earth from all the Dutch provinces and former colonies (Indonesia, Suriname, and the Antilles). Oud designed the steps to be welcoming as seating. He was ultimately successful—to the point that the hippie generation used it for sleeping and still today, tourists employ it as a favored rest spot from which to watch the world go by. ⊹ *Follow Damrak south from Centraal Station; Raadhuisstraat leads from Dam to intersect main canals.* ⊠ *Nieuwe Zijde.*

② **Damrak** (Dam Port). This busy street leading up to Centraal Station is now lined with a mostly barbaric assortment of shops, attractions, hotels, and dispensers of greasy food products. It and its extension, Rokin, was in fact once the Amstel River before evolving into the city's inner harbor, bustling with activity, its piers loaded with fish and other cargo on their way to the weigh house at the Dam or to be directly stored in the warehouses. During the 19th century it was filled in, and the only open water that remains is a patch in front of the station that provides mooring for canal tour boats. Besides stopping to admire the Beurs van Berlage, it's usually best to sail through here quickly. ⊠ *Nieuwe Zijde.*

⑤ **Het Koninklijk Paleis te Amsterdam** (Royal Palace, Amsterdam). The Royal
Fodor'sChoice Palace is probably Amsterdam's greatest storyteller. But from the out-
★ side, it is somewhat hard to believe that this gray-stained building—with its aura of loneliness highlighted by the fact that it is one of the city's few freestanding buildings—was once called the "Eighth Wonder of the World" when it was built between 1648 and 1665 as the largest non-religious building on the planet and that it is still used by the royal family for only the highest of state occasions. From the inside, its magnificent interior inspires another brand of disbelief: this palace was actually built as a mere city hall—albeit one for a city, drunk on its cockiness for having created in a mere 100 years the richest and busiest harbor in the world.

The prosperous burghers of the 17th-century Golden Age, wanting something that could boast of their status to all visitors (i.e., rub the noses of monarchs whom they had done without), hired the leading architectural ego of his day, Jacob van Campen, who had traveled to Italy to study the heights of perfection represented by the classical world before the Middle Ages so rudely interrupted. With the commission for building the City Hall, he thought that he finally had the opportunity to create something perfect in its dimensions, spatial relationships, and messages—a veritable sermon in stone. The first problem was to create a surface on the blubbery former riverbed that was solid enough to build on. He used the standard local technique of driving wooden piles down to the solid subsurface—a method that inspired Erasmus to comment that Amsterdammers were the only people he knew who lived on treetops. What was less standard was the sheer total, 13,659—a number that is still pounded permanently into the minds of every Dutch schoolchild by the formula of adding "1" to the beginning and "9" to the end of the number of days of the year.

As the building arose, various relatively trivial compromises had to be imposed, but enough for Campen to give up on the idea of perfection and to leave the rest of the job to his on-site architect, Daniel Stalpaert. Artists and sculptures with such immortal names like Ferdinand Bol, Govert Flinck (both students of Rembrandt whose own sketches were rejected), and Jan Lievens were called in for the decorating. In the building's public entrance hall, known as the **Burgerzaal,** the earth was laid quite literally at one's feet: two maps inlaid in the marble floor show Amsterdam as the center of the world, while the heavens painted above also place the city at the center of the universe. From here, appropriate gods pointed one in the direction of the different rooms whose entranceways had further sculptures to denote their function: hungry rabid rats over the Bankruptcy Chamber, ill-fated Icarus over the Insurance Chamber, a faithful dog looking at its dead master over the Clerks

Chamber, and gruesome scenes of torture over the Sentencing Tribunal. In short: this is a place that practically oozes with symbolism.

During the French occupation of The Netherlands, Louis Napoléon, who had been installed as king in 1808 by his brother Bonaparte, wanted to escape The Hague, where his son had recently died, and decided that this was the building most suitable for a royal palace. Soon the city business was moved to the Prinsenhof (now the Grand Hotel) on Oudezijds Voorburgwal, and the prisoners were transferred to the Rasphuis on Heiligeweg to make room for the wine cellar. To improve his view of Dam Square, he transferred the function of the Waag, the Weighing House, to the one on Nieuwmarkt so that the original one could be destroyed. The ensuing renovation of the interior was actually done quite tastefully, since Campen's 17th-century classicist vision gelled quite nicely with that of 19th-century France. Objects were covered with tapestries or wooden panels rather than removed. The rectilinear French Empire furniture—much of which remains to this day—blended remarkably well with the interior's tight mathematics.

William V's triumphant entrance into the city in December 1813 marked the beginning of a long-standing debate about who actually owned the palace. Matters were not helped by the fact that Amsterdam and the House of Orange had never really gotten along. The Oranges' endless battles for their dynasty did not sit well with the city's more pragmatic attitude of war always being bad for business. However, the city had gotten used to being the country's capital, and when William promised to drop by more often, it was collectively decided that the building would remain a Royal Palace. But, as Geert Mak observed in his definitive book on this building, *De Stadspaleis,* the palace became a symbol of the royal family's absence rather than its presence, with one visitor going so far as to describe the building as a "mummie, wrapped and dried." It was only after World War II that things started to change. While Queen Wilhelmina, returning from her exile in England with a great admiration for Amsterdam's resistance movement, preferred to live in The Hague, she did begin using it for the grandest of state engagements such as the coronation of her daughter Juliana and the decolonization ceremonies for Indonesia. Renovations began to return the interior to its City Hall glory days. And, most importantly perhaps, the locals were allowed in to see things for themselves and admire the 17th-century works of art in their original setting. And so did things pretty much continue under the current Queen Beatrix, who did, however, need a few years to get over her understandable fear of Amsterdam after having her 1966 wedding disrupted by Provos throwing smoke bombs at her wedding carriage and her 1980 coronation derailed by riots on the Dam. ⊠ *Dam, Nieuwe Zijde* ☎ *020/620–4060* ⊕ *www.kon-paleisamsterdam.nl* ⊠ *€4.50* ☉ *Oct.–Dec., Tues.–Thurs. and weekends 12:30–5; July–Sept., daily 11–5; occasionally closed for state events.*

❼ **Madame Tussaud Scenerama.** This branch of the world-famous wax museum, located above the P&C department store, pays its hosting nation ample respect with its depictions of the Hollandwood glitterati, Golden Age names—includes a life-size, 3-D rendering of a painting by Vermeer (but alas, the lighting is dubious)—and even an understandably displaced-looking Piet Mondriaan. Of course, there is also a broad selection of international superstars, including George W. Bush, who is caught actually looking quite stately. Bring your own ironic distance. ⊠ *Dam 20, Nieuwe Zijde* ☎ *020/522–1010* ⊠ *€12* ☉ *Sept.–June, daily 10–5:30; July and Aug., daily 9:30–7:30.*

6 **Nieuwe Kerk** (New Church). Begun in the 14th century, the Nieuwe Kerk is a soaring Late Gothic structure that was never given its spire because the authorities—who were busy obsessing about the building of the "City Palace" next door (Het Koninklijk Paleis)—ran out of money. While the Oude Kerk had the blessing of the Bishop of Utrecht, the Nieuwe Kerk was supported by the local well-to-do merchant class, which resulted in an endless competition between these two parochial districts. While at one point the Oude Kerk led the race with a whopping 38 pulpits against the Nieuwe Kerk's 36, first prize should go to Nieuwe Kerk for its still-existing pulpit sculpted by Albert Vinckenbrinck, which took him 19 years to complete. Other features include the unmarked grave of the poet Vondel, known as the "Dutch Shakespeare," and the extravagantly marked grave of Admiral Ruyter, who daringly sailed his invading fleet up the River Medway in England in the 17th century, to become this country's ultimate naval hero—and who also proved himself to be the ultimate down-to-earth Dutch boy by spending the next day "sweeping his own cabin and feeding his chickens." The Nieuwe Kerk has also been the National Church since 1815, when it began hosting the inauguration ceremony for monarchs. Since this does not occur that often, the church has broadened its appeal by serving as a venue for organ concerts and special—and invariably excellent—exhibitions, which attract a half million visitors a year. These exhibitions have covered everything from Dutch photography to Buddhist Treasures. ⊠ *Dam, Nieuwe Zijde* ☎ *020/628-6909* ⊕ *www.nieuwekerk.nl* ⌧ *Admission varies according to exhibition* ☉ *During exhibitions Sun.–Wed., Fri,. and Sat. 10–6; Thurs. 10–10. In between exhibitions hrs vary.*

10 **Spui** (Spui Square). This beautiful and seemingly relaxed tree-lined square hides a lively and radical recent past. Journalists and the generally well-read have long favored its many cafés, and the Atheneum News Center (No. 14–16) and its enjoining bookstore are quite simply the city's best places to peruse through an international array of literature, magazines, and newspapers. More cultural browsing can be enjoyed on the Spui's book market on Friday and its art market on Sunday.

But it's the innocent-looking statue of a woolen sock–clad boy, the *Lieverdje* ("Little Darling"—local street slang for wild street boys), that formed the focal point for a particularly wacky and inspired social movement that would prove to have a great influence on the yippies in America and the Situationists in France. The Provos—taking their name from their ultimate goal, "to provoke"—arose around the "anti-smoke magician" Robert Jasper Grootveld, who had been hosting absurdist anti-consumerist "happenings" off Leidseplein until the former garage where they were held burned down during a particularly dramatic performance. So in 1964, he moved his show to the Spui around the Lieverdje statue that had auspiciously just been donated to the city by a tobacco multinational. While Grootveld played the clown, anarchist Roel Van Duijn set a more purely political agenda in a Provo newsletter. Increased crowds increased the impatience of police (who were the prime victims of such Provo mind games as endless drug busts that turned up only bales of hay); in their confusion, the police not only became liberal in their use of billy clubs but even ended up confiscating the single white bicycle that the Provos were donating to the city for free use for all in the hopes the city would follow up with others.

Another flurry of provocative activity was unleashed for the 1966 marriage of present-day queen Beatrix with the German, Claus. It was a touchy subject, and paranoia ran high—fueled by published plans of the Provos to taint the city's water supply with LSD to incite the population, and the streets with lion excrement to craze the horses of the Royal Carriage. What ended up happening was watched by millions worldwide on tele vision: a simple smoke bomb temporarily obscured the Royal Carriage from view. When the cloud dispersed, it exposed police showing their billy club expertise; the mayor and the chief of police were fired and the Provos had won another media war. Some of the more dedicated of the Provos, including Van Duijn, actually ended up getting elected into the city government under the banner of the Kabouters ("forest-dwelling dwarfs"), to annoy the State from within. Currently, Van Duijn continues his political career as a member of a mainstream party and Grootveld is happily obsessed with bringing floating-garden islands made of Styrofoam to the canals of Amsterdam. In 2003 after decades of experiments and hundreds of thousands of guilders of city investment, a high-tech version of the "White Bicycle Plan" was finally dismissed as unachievable since they could not find a way to make the bikes "hooligan-resistant." ⊠ *Bounded by Spuistraat and Kalverstraat, Nieuwe Zijde.*

need a break?   Several of the bar-cafés and eateries on Spui Square are good places to take a break, including the ancient **Hoppe** (⊠ Spui 18–20, Nieuwe Zijde ☎ 020/420–4420), which has been serving drinks between woody walls and sandy floors since 1670. Evoking a more rarified bygone era is the **Café Luxembourg** (⊠ Spui 22, Nieuwe Zijde ☎ 020/620–6264). If you just want to eat and run, try **Broodje van Kootje** (⊠ Spui 28, Nieuwe Zijde ☎ 020/623–7451) for a classic Amsterdam *broodje* (sandwich).

City of 400 Bridges: The Western Canal Ring & the Jordaan

One of Amsterdam's greatest pleasures is also one of its simplest: to stroll along the canals. The grand, crescent-shape waterways of the *Grachtengordel* (canal ring), which surround the old center, are made up of Prinsengracht, Keizersgracht, and Herengracht (Prince, King, and Gentlemen canals), all of which are lined with grand gabled houses built for the movers and shakers of the 17th-century Golden Age. Almost equally scenic are the intersecting canals and streets that were originally built to house and provide work space for artisans and workers but are now magnets to the discerning shopper, diner, and drinker. The construction of the canal girdle that began at the dawn of the 17th century proceeded from west to east. This tour covers the first half-completed section between Brouwersgracht and Leidsegracht; some of its principal highlights include the Anne Frank House, the Westerkerk, and Noordermarkt, but many visitors will give pride of place to the gorgeous panoply of canalside mansions.

The area behind this stretch was set aside for houses for workers, many of whom were involved in this immense project, and terrains for some of the city's smellier industries like tanning and brewing. This area— bound by Brouwersgracht, Lijnbaansgracht, Looiersgracht, and Prinsengracht—was to evolve into the city's most singular neighborhood, **Fodor'sChoice** the **Jordaan**. There are various theories on the origins of its name: as ★ the other, more slummy side of the River Jordaan formed by Prinsengracht, or as a mutation of the French word *jardin* (garden), which can be regarded as either a literal reflection of its long-lost richness in gardens (still witnessed by its many streets and canals named after flowers and trees) or simply a sarcastic reference to its once oppressively nonflowery reality (in days of yore, the area had been home to a group of malodorous industries).

In the 1800s, the area became officially pauperized and as such provided a hotbed for the rising socialist and unionist ideas. By the end of the 18th century, things started slowly to improve with the filling in of some of the less aromatic canals and the efforts of community's increased number of social institutions, but its inhabitants maintained a reputation for rebelliousness and community spirit that gave them a special identity, rather like that of London's Cockneys. Until a generation ago, native Jordaaners would call their elders "uncle" or "aunt"—and many still retain the habit of spontaneously breaking out in rousing song. These are a people whose dialect harbors as many words for "drunk" as the Eskimos reputedly have for snow. In the 1950s, the Jordaan identity reached mythical proportions—aided by nationally popular local singers depicting an idealized vision of a poor but always sharing neighborhood—as its residents successfully fought city plans to fill in the remaining canals.

Since the 1980s, the Jordaan has gone steadily upmarket, and now it is one of the trendiest parts of town. Its 1895 population of 80,000, which made it one of the densest in Europe, has declined to a mere 14,000. Today, one has a much better chance of hearing the spicy local dialect in Purmerend or Almere, where much of the original population has moved. But in many ways, the Jordaan will always remain the Jordaan, even though its narrow alley and leafy canals are now lined with quirky specialty shops, excellent restaurants, galleries, and designer boutiques. Add to this equation the area's richness in hofjes and you have a wanderer's paradise.

a good walk

Exit the **Dam** ❹ ☛ on the tiny Eggertstraat—once called Despair Alley when it served as the church graveyard for suicides and the executed—on the right of **Nieuwe Kerk** and turn left onto Gravenstraat (Grave Street), which follows the church's rear walls. Cross the major artery Nieuwezijds Voorburgwal while minding that you do not get grave-bound yourself by a cab or tram at this notoriously dangerous intersection. Enter the narrow Molensteeg and keep going straight to the bridge, Torensluis, over the Singel. If you do stop at one of the charming terraces here, let the knowledge of the bridge's ancient function as a lockup for drunks keep you forging on. Note the bridge's statue of Multituli, the 19th-century writer who questioned Dutch colonial policies, before finally marching straight up Oude Leliestraat. If this early in the tour you have already had a time-out for a brew, you might pay tribute to the former home, to the right at **Singel 140**, of one of the richest men—but generally regarded as "the stupidest"—in Amsterdam, Frans Banning Cocq, who is the central character of Rembrandt's *Night Watch*. This house is an early example of Dutch Renaissance and was built by the noted church builder Hendrick de Keyser.

Oude Leliestraat crosses the Herengracht, where you can turn left to reach No. 168, the gloriously beautiful Bartolottihuis, a part of which houses the **Nederlands Theatermuseum** ⑪ (Netherlands Theater Museum). Return to follow Oude Leliestraat's extension, the lovely Leliegracht, which has some excellent specialist bookstores—not to mention a resident comedian who occasionally provides the canal with a radio-powered "corpse." Be sure to stop and admire the unmissable Greenpeace building on the southwest corner of Keizersgracht (No. 174). This former insurance office—note the painting of the guardian angel near its top beneath its nonfunctional clock (if time is of the essence you can trust the clock belonging to Westerkerk visible to its left)—was built by Gerrit van Arkel and is one of the city's few examples of *Nieuwkunst,* the Dutch version of Art Nouveau architecture. Take a right down Keizersgracht's odd-numbered side, where one can admire a classic Baroque example of the Amsterdam renaissance, Huis met Hoofden (House with Heads), at No. 123. Its heads represent Greek deities and are not, as a local tale has it, the cement-coated skulls of six thieves decapitated by a vigilant but a conflicted maid who ended up marrying the seventh.

Continue straight to goggle at the gables of Keizersgracht, perhaps pausing to graze in the shops to the right and left along Herenstraat and Prinsenstraat, before crossing the bridge over **Brouwersgracht** ⑫, taking a left and crossing back at the next bridge to proceed down the left bank of the Prinsengracht. No. 7 was formerly the location of the clandestine Augustine chapel "De Posthoorn," which was attached by a secret corridor to the still existing café 't Papeneiland, which you can see across the canal on the corner with Brouwersgracht. Also across the canal is the **Noorderkerk** (Northern Church) and its square **Noordermarkt** ⑬, which is host to a variety of markets. Before looping back in that direction over the upcoming bridge—crossing it will denote your official entrance into the Jordaan neighborhood—stop and look, if you can sneak a peak, at the two hofjes Van Brienen (Nos. 85–133, closed to public) and De Zon (Nos. 159–171, open weekdays 10–5), both with plaques telling their stories.

On Noordermarkt, take the Noorderkerkstraat, which runs along the west side of the church to the once watery Lindengracht, host to a food and clothes market every Friday and Saturday. Hang a left and pause at the next intersection to imagine the bridge that once crossed here and hosted the once popular folk sport of eel-pulling. This weekend pursuit involved hanging a slippery eel from a rope tied to the bridge and attempting to yank it off from a tippy boat below. One day in 1885, police tried to untie the rope, and the notorious Eel Riot ensued.

Continuing down Lindengracht will get you to the entrance to the Suykerhoff-hofje at Nos. 149–163 to enjoy a moment of peace in its frighteningly green courtyard, whose houses opened their doors in 1670 to Protestant "daughters and widows" (as long as they behaved and exhibited "a peace-loving humor"). Turn left down 2e Lindendwarsstraat and you can have a straight "locals' walk"—with the street changing names at every block—all the way to Egelantiersgracht. On the way, keep your eyes peeled for the quirky building adornments provided by the Jordaan's artier residents and perhaps poke your head in another hofje, Claes Claesz, at 1e Egelantiersdwarsstraat 3. The ancient bar at the corner on Egelantiersgracht 12 is the scenically set Café t'Smalle, complete with waterside terrace, where Pieter Hoppe began his *jenever* (Dutch gin) distillery in 1780—an event of such global significance that 't Smalle is re-created in Japan's Holland Village in Nagasaki.

Take the shortest of jags to proceed right down Prinsengracht, past No. 158, which was home to Kee Strikker, the woman who broke Vincent van Gogh's heart, while noting the crowds across the canal that are invariably lined up outside the **Anne Frankhuis** (Anne Frank House) ⑭. You may also notice that that side of the canal is about 3 feet higher than the side you are on—only the richer grachtengordel could afford the required sand. You certainly won't miss—and the route to get to—the church tower of Anne's neighbor, **Westerkerk** ⑮, behind which is the square of Westermarkt which is home to both the pink granite slabs that form the **Homomonument** (Monument to the Persecuted Homosexual) ⑯ and a residence of 17th-century ("I think, therefore I am") pundit René Descartes (No. 6) until he allegedly took up with his landlord's young daughter (but this story should be taken with a grain of salt: jealous philosophers can be such gossips after all).

After exploring this Jordaan-defining area—even though officially its on the wrong side of Prinsengracht—cross Rozengracht and proceed down the right bank of Prinsengracht. However, fans of contemporary art might want to break away from the pack and make a small side tour (others should just ignore the rest of this paragraph). Don't cross the street but rather backtrack down Prinsengracht and take the first left up Bloemstraat to **Galerie Fons Welters** (No. 140, open Tuesday–Saturday 1–6) whose bubble entrance built by Atelier van Lieshout denotes the gallery as a great discoverer of both local and international sculptural talents. Taking a side street to the east, crossing Rozengracht (perhaps lingering to track down No. 188, where Rembrandt spent his last poverty-stricken days), and hanging left down Rozenstraat will get you to the **Stedelijk Museum Bureau Amsterdam** (No. 59, 020/422–0471, open Tuesday–Sunday 11–5) which focuses more on local talent than its celebrated mother ship, the Stedelijk Museum. Now take a right down Prinsengracht and a right again onto the nearest side of Lauriergracht to the often edgy **Torch Gallery** (No. 94, 020/626–0284, open Thursday–Saturday 2–6) which has long shown remarkable savvy as an early champion of the soon-to-be established: from local folks like fashion designers Viktor & Rolf and photographer Anton Corbijn to such non-Dutch names like Cindy Sherman and Jake and Dino Chapman. At this point, it's time to return to and proceed right down Prinsengracht.

Take note that the side streets you see across Prinsengracht are part of the Nine Streets specialty shopping—and eating—neighborhood. Docked at the corner of Elandsgracht is the **Woonboatmuseum** ⑰, the House Boat Museum, where one can glean insight into the lives of the city's floating population. If you proceed right up Elandsgracht, you will first pass Johnny Jordaanplein with its bronze busts of Jordaan's revered singers Johnny Jordaan and Tante Leen and accordionist Johnny Meijer who all gained local immortality status with performing songs of lost love and beer in the local bars.

A still existing maze—but one that facilitates the losing of oneself in lost ages of a more kinder and gentler nature—is the rambling **Looiersmarket** (open Saturday–Thursday 11–5), an indoor antiques market, found ahead on the left-hand corner of Elandsgracht with Lijnbaansgracht. There's another very Euro-scenic but more downscale antiques market, **Rommelmarkt** (open daily 11–5), on Elandsgracht's southern parallel, Looiersgracht, at No. 38. From here, you can reconnect with Prinsengracht. While it's not worth taking a right here to see the relatively banal entrance between No. 338 and 340 that once led to a Golden Age pleasure garden complete with mechanical figures of famous people (a Madame Tussaud's of sorts of its day) and a hedge labyrinth, one may pause to ask: What is it about this neighborhood and mazes? However, pipe smokers or folks who just want a whiff of Amsterdam's long and obsessive relationship with tobacco should take this route farther up Prinsengracht to get to the **Pijpenkabinet** ⑱ (Pipe Cabinet).

Others should just head straight over the bridge—which denotes your leaving of the Jordaan and your reentry into the generally more rarified airs of the grachtengordel—and turn left down Prinsengracht's eastern side and then right down Berenstraat into the very browsable heart of the "Nine Streets" specialty shopping area (perhaps checking out those artist-made books at Boekie Woekie at No. 16). Take the first right down Keizersgracht. The 18th-century monolith with the Neoclassic pillars on your right at No. 324 is the **Felix Meritis Cultural Center** ⑲. Farther up at No. 384 are the gates—and only remains of the burned-down Municipal Theater where Vondel premiered his plays—that denote the entrance to the Blakes "designer hotel," a much-touted work of that term's definer, Anouska Hempel. You may want to take a moment here—while being wary of arriving stretch limos—to imagine this stretch of canal as it was during the Golden Age when it was host to the Sunday "Slipper Parade" when the rich strolled back and forth to see and be seen.

Taking the next bridge left, proceed down the gustatory Huidenstraat, with its excellent but sweetly priced pastas and sandwiches of Goodies (No. 9) and decadent chocolates and pastries of Pompadour (No. 12), and take the first right down Herengracht. At Nos. 366–8 is the **Bijbels Museum** ⑳ (Bible Museum) in the midst of a row of houses built by that residential architect to the Golden Age stars, Philip Vingboons, who adorned these creations with bulls-eye windows and an ample harvest of stone fruit. An example of a yet more excessive brand of inspired architecture is the building at No. 380 that now houses the **Nederlands Instituut voor Oorlogs Documentatie** ㉑ (Netherlands Institute for War Documentation) and their 3-km-long (2-mi-long) archive.

To arrive at an optional end point of this tour involves taking the first right down Leidsegracht and then the first left down Keizersgracht where at the corner of Leidsestraat is the designer-friendly Metz & Co. department store. Its glass rooftop showroom was specifically designed in 1933 by *De Stijl* pioneer, Gerrit Rietveld, to highlight functionalist furniture (his own included). It is now a café that affords an epic view of much of your recent wanderings.

TIMING It is difficult to say how long this walk will take as it leads you through areas that invite wandering and the exploration of side streets. At a brisk and determined pace, you can manage the route in about two or three hours. But you could also easily while away an afternoon in Jordaan, or take a leisurely stroll along the Prinsengracht. Allow a minimum of an hour for the Anne Frank House and try to get there early to beat the 10- to 20-minute lines that invariably form by midday.

The best time for canal walks is in late afternoon and early evening— or for you revelers, early in the morning when the darkness gives the water a deep purple color before often becoming shrouded in mist by dawn. If you're planning to go shopping in the Jordaan or the "Nine Streets," remember that shops in The Netherlands are closed Monday morning—however that's the only time that the unmissable Noordermarkt flea market takes place as well as the enjoining textiles market along Westerstraat. With its many restaurants and cafés, the Jordaan is also a prime spot for evening frolicking.

Sights to See

⑭ **Anne Frankhuis** (Anne Frank House). With her diary having sold more than 30 million copies, Anne Frank is by far the most successful and famous author of the 20th century. Small condolence for a girl who died at age 15 in a tragic denouement of a two-year saga now known to countless readers around the world. In the precious pages of *The Diary of Anne Frank* (published in 1947 as *The Annex* by her father after her death) the young Anne kept her sad record of two increasingly fraught years living in secret confinement from the Nazis. Along with the Van Daan family, the Frank family felt the noose tighten, so decided to move into a hidden warren of rooms at the back of this 1635-built canal house.

FodorsChoice
★

Anne Frank was born in Germany in 1929; when she was four her family moved to The Netherlands to escape growing anti-Jewish sentiment. Otto Frank operated a pectin business and decided to stay in his adopted country when the war finally reached The Netherlands in 1940.

In July 1942, the five adults and three children sought refuge in the attic of the annex "backhouse," or *achterhuis*, of Otto's business in the center of Amsterdam, in a hidden warren of rooms screened behind a hinged bookcase. Here, as one of many *onderduikers* (people in hiding) throughout all of Amsterdam, Anne dreamed her dreams, wrote her diary, and pinned up movie-star pictures to her wall (still on view). The van Pelsen family, including their son Peter (van Daan in Anne's journal), along with the dentist Fritz Pfeffer (Dussel) joined them in their cramped quarters. Four trusted employees provided them with food and supplies. In her diary, Anne chronicles the day-to-day life in the house: her longing for a best friend, her crush on Peter, her frustration with her mother, her love for her father, and her annoyance with the petty dentist, Dussel. In August 1944, the Franks were betrayed and the Gestapo invaded their hideaway. All the members of the annex were transported to camps, where Anne and her sister Margot died of typhoid fever in Bergen Belsen a few months before the liberation. Otto Frank was the only survivor of the annex. Miep Gies, one of the friends who helped with the hiding, found Anne's diary after the raid and kept it through the war.

A recent expansion by Benthem Crouwel Architekten, has allowed the recreation of Otto Frank's business in the original house and provided space for more in-depth exhibitions, a bookstore, café, and offices for the employees—which now number 100—of the Anne Frank Foundation. One of the most frequently visited places in the world, this house receives more than 800,000 visitors a year; the wooden stairs behind the swinging bookcase have to be replaced every two years. Anne's diary has now been translated into more than 50 languages, making Anne the international celebrity she always dreamed of being. ⊠ *Prinsengracht 263, Jordaan* ☎ *020/556-7100* ⊕ *www.annefrank.nl* ☒ *€6.50* ⊘ *Sept.–Mar., daily 9–7; Apr.–Aug., daily 9–9.*

⑳ Bijbels Museum (Bible Museum) While this museum does indeed have a massive collection of bibles—as well as exhibits with archaeological finds from the Middle East and models of ancient temples that evoke biblical times—what probably draws more people is the building itself. The two enjoined canal houses (dating from 1662) have had their interiors restored, including incredible 18th-century myth-drenched ceiling paintings from the hands of Jacob de Wit, along with the country's best-preserved 17th-century kitchen. The museum is also currently in midst of efforts geared toward broadening its appeal—such as a "story attic" for children and a modernly landscaped back garden with terraced pools and a "smell cabinet" where one can whiff 16 different biblical essences. ⊠ *Herengracht 366–368, Western Canal Ring* ☎ *020/624-2436* ⊕ *www.bijbelsmuseum.nl* ☒ *€5* ⊘ *Mon.–Sat. 10–5, Sun. 1–5.*

⑫ Brouwersgracht (Brewers Canal). One of the most photographed spots in town, this pretty, tree-lined canal at the northern border of the Jordaan district is bordered by residences and former warehouses of the brewers who traded here in the 17th century when Amsterdam was the "warehouse of the world." Without sacrificing the ancient vibe, most of the buildings have been converted into luxury apartments. Of particular note are the houses at Nos. 188 to 194. The canal is blessed with long views down the main canals and plenty of sunlight, perfect for photo-ops. The Brouwersgracht runs westward from the end of the Singel (a short walk along Prins Hendrikkade from Centraal Station) and forms a cap to the western end of the grachtengordel. ⊠ *Jordaan.*

⑲ Felix Mauritis Cultural Center. If we are to believe its name, "Happiness through Achievement," which is chiseled over its entrance, then this is a very happy building indeed—not to mention an enlightened one, since its Neoclassical architecture arose in the year of the French Revolution, 1789. Felix Meritis was a society whose building housed committees dedicated to the study and promotion of economics, science, painting, music, and literature. Its cupola held an observatory, and its concert hall had the likes of Schumann and Brahms dropping by to tickle the ivories. Political groups and theater companies began calling it home before it settled into its current role as European Center for Art and Science, which hosts a plethora of readings, panels, and discussions with the aim of "connecting cultures." Drop by to pick up a program or to check the hours of its Philosophy Café. ⊠ *Keizersgracht 324, Western Canal Ring* ☎ *020/623–1311* ⊕ *www.felix.meritis.nl* ☉ *Closed to public; café has changeable hrs.*

⑯ Homomonument (Monument to the Persecuted Homosexual). This, the world's first memorial to persecuted gays and lesbians, was designed by Karin Daan, who employed three huge triangles of pinkish granite—representing past, present, and future—to form a larger triangle. On May 4 (Remembrance Day), there are services here commemorating the homosexual victims of World War II, when thousands were killed of the 50,000 sentenced—all of whom were forced to wear pink triangles. Flowers are laid daily for lost friends, especially on the descending triangle that forms a dock of sorts into Keizersgracht. Particularly large mountains of flowers form on December 1 (World AIDS Day). Signs will lead you to the "Pink Point of Presence," one of the stalls along the east side of Westermarkt, which acts as an information point to visiting gays and lesbians. It is open daily noon–6 during tourist season (but by press time may be open year-round). ⊠ *Westermarkt, Jordaan.*

★ Huis met Hoofden (House with Heads). The Greek deities of Apollo, Ceres, Mars, Minerva, Bacchus, and Diana welcome you—or rather, busts of them do—to this famous example of Dutch Neoclassic architecture, one of the grandest double houses of 17th-century Amsterdam. Delightfully graced with pilasters, pillars, and a step gable, the 1622 mansion is attributed to architect Pieter de Keyser, son of the more famed Hendrick. The heads adorn the entry facade and represent classical deities and are not, as a local tale has it, the concrete-coated skulls of six thieves decapitated by a vigilant but conflicted maid who ended up marrying the seventh. The house is now headquarters to the Monumentenzorg—custodian to many of the city's public monuments—and is not open to the public. ⊠ *Keizersgracht 123, Western Canal Ring* ☎ *020/522–4888* ⊕ *www.bmz.amsterdam.nl.*

㉑ Nederlands Instituut voor Oorlogs Documentatie (Netherlands Institute for War Documentation). Established in 1945, this institute has collected vast archives of documents, newspapers, 100,000 photos, and 50,000 books relating to the Occupation of World War II. It is to this institution that Otto Frank donated his daughter's diary. More recently, the institute has expanded its sights to take in the period between World War I and the present with particular emphasis on the former colony of Indonesia. While the institute is essentially not open to the merely curious, it is very welcoming to people doing academic or family-related research. What can be enjoyed by all is the Loire-style château exterior and its rich and obsessive sculptures of frolicking mythical figures. ⊠ *Herengracht 380, Western Canal Ring* ☎ *020/523–3800* ⊕ *www. oorlogsdoc.knaw.nl* ☉ *Weekdays 9–5.*

★ ⑪ Nederlands Theatermuseum (Netherlands Theater Museum). While Amsterdam has several Golden Age house museums, few are as gilded as this one. Currently home to part of the Theater Instituut Nederland

GAY AMSTERDAM

T**HOUGH MANY OF AMSTERDAM'S NATIVE** *inhabitants declare that the Dutch are becoming homomoe (tired of homosexuals), such an opinion is quickly put to rest by the lively and welcoming scene offered to gay and lesbian travelers by Amsterdam. One can feel the city's tolerance in everything from the locals' nonchalant attitude toward public affection to the recent vote to convert the country's registered same-sex partnerships into full-fledged marriages, with divorce guidelines and wider adoption rights. In the early '80s, Amsterdam was quick to cope constructively with the AIDS crisis, and in 1987, it unveiled the Homomonument, a world's first. The COC (or Cultural and Social Center, pronounced say-o-say) of the Nederlandse Vereniging tot Integratie van Homoseksualiteit (Dutch Association for the Integration of Homosexuality), is subsidized by the government and one of the country's largest gay and lesbian rights organizations.*

Roze Zaterdag (Pink Saturday) takes place in a different Netherlands city each June and attracts the most tourists of any gay and lesbian pride event. Since the mid-'90s, Amsterdam has had its own parade early in August, with a boat parade up the Prinsengracht. Every weekend visitors flock to the many gay venues that dot Amsterdam. In Amsterdam, unlike what happens in many other cities, gay establishments do not have covered windows but harbor an open attitude toward anyone. Free maps of gay Amsterdam and other informational leaflets, often bilingual or in English, are available at many venues.

(Netherlands Theater Institute), the **Bartolotti Huis** (No. 170–172) is made up of two spectacular examples of 17th-century Dutch Renaissance houses built by Hendrick de Keyser for a brewer by the name of William van der Huvel (who one day thought to spice up his image by calling himself Guillelmo Bartolotti). The rest of the museum takes up the equally delectable White House (No. 168), built in 1638, and which rates as noted designer Philips Vingboons's first work in Amsterdam (and as such sports the city's oldest neck gable). Its original owner, Michiel Pauw—as one of the initiators of the West Indies Company and the founder of a small settlement on the Hudson River—could easily afford its interior of marble-lined corridors, sweeping monumental staircases, densely rendered plasterwork, and ceiling paintings by Jacob de Wit. All of these attributes have been restored to provide a lush backdrop for exhibitions about the history of theater in all its forms: circus, opera, musical, puppetry, and drama. There are costumes, models of stage sets, and other accessories. There is also an extensive library with archives focused on the theatrical scene in The Netherlands. Its stellar back garden—alone worth the price of admission—is the perfect place to sip a coffee from the café while imagining it as the setting for Baroque-era barbecues. ⊠ *Herengracht 168–170, Western Canal Ring* ☎ *020/551-3300* ⊕ *www.tin.nl* ⊠ *€4.50* ☉ *Tues.–Fri. 11–5, weekends 1–5.*

⓭ **Noordermarkt** (Northern Market). In 1620, city planners envisioned a scheme to build a church for those too lazy to walk to Westerkerk. **Noorderkerk** (Northern Church), designed by Hendrick de Keyser and completed after his death by his son Pieter, was the first Protestant church that featured a new—more democratic—ground plan, which was formed by the Greek cross (four equal arms) with the pulpit in the middle. The building's religious function was dropped whenever the Jordaan locals deemed it necessary to riot for their rights, then becoming headquarters and barracks for the cavalry and infantry. The soberly Calvinist 18th-century interior can viewed on Monday from 10:30 to 12:30, on Saturday from 11 to 1, and during regular Saturday afternoon concert recitals starting at 2.

Until 1688, the surrounding square, Noordermarkt, was a graveyard whose residents were moved to make room for its present—albeit now sporadic—function as a market. The **Maandag Morgen Noordermarkt** (Monday Morning Northern Market), popularly known as the Monday Morning Flea Market, with an enjoining textile market on Westerstraat, is one of the city's most scenic and best-kept secrets. It's also a prime place to see the typically pragmatic sales techniques of the locals in action. All day Saturday (when there's also a more general market along the nearby Lindengracht), there's an organic foods market which often comes supplemented with some more flea-markety stalls of antiques and knicknacks. ⊠ *Bounded by Prinsengracht, Noorderkerkstraat, and Noordermarkt, Jordaan.*

need a break? The city's most cherished slice of apple pie can be had at **Winkel** (⊠ Noordermarkt 43, Jordaan ☎ 020/623–0223). For a funky setting and perhaps an inspired designer sandwich, head to **Finch** (⊠ Noordermarkt 5, Jordaan ☎ 020/626–2461).

⑱ Pijpenkabinet (Pipe Cabinet). Considering Amsterdam's rich history of tobacco trading and its population's long tradition of rolling their own "shag," there should actually be a much larger museum dedicated to this subject. Perhaps this theoretical museum could relate such local facts of how urine-soaked tobacco was hailed as an able aphrodisiac in the 16th century, how "tobacco-smoke enema applicators" were used until the mid-19th-century as the standard method to attempt the reviving of those seemingly drowned in the canals, and how Golden Age painters employed tobacco and its smoke as an able metaphor for the fleeting nature of life. But as things stand, there is only this focused collection of more than 2,000 pipes, which aims to tell the tale of the Western European "sucking"—as the local parlance used to describe it—tradition. You might also want to check out the library or buy a pipe in the Smokiana shop. At press time, the collection was undergoing a renovation. ⊠ *Prinsengracht 488, Western Canal Ring* ☎ *020/421–1779* ⊕ *www.pijpenkabinet.nl* 🖼 *€5* ☉ *Wed.–Sat. noon–6.*

⑮ Westerkerk (Western Church). Built between 1602 and 1631 by the ubiquitous Hendrick de Keyser and presumed the last resting place of Rembrandt, the Dutch Renaissance Westerkerk was the largest Protestant church in the world until Christopher Wren came along with his St. Paul's Cathedral in London. Its tower—endlessly mentioned in Jordaan songs—is topped by a gaudy copy of the crown of the Habsburg emperor Maximilian I (or, rather, to avoid a potential bar brawl, a later model of the crown used by Rudolph II). Maximilian gave Amsterdam the right to use his royal insignia in 1489 in gratitude for help from the city in his struggle for control of the Low Countries, and the crown's "XXX" marking was quickly exploited by the city's merchants as a visiting card of quality. More recently, Amsterdam's notoriety and the phallic nature of the quickly disappearing *Amsterdammertje* parking poles (which bear an XXX logo, a common civic insignia) has led many to speculate that the poles' markings suggest "Triple-X Rated." Now you know differently . . .

The tower rates as the city's highest monument. The tower's gigantic bell (popularly known as the "clock" of this area) rings every half hour but with a different tone to mark the half before the hour. The playing of the church's carillon, which still occurs every Tuesday between noon and one, was often mentioned in the diary of Anne Frank. Another immortal, Rembrandt, lived nearby on Rozengracht 188 during his poverty-stricken last years. He (as well as his son Titus) was buried in the church in an unmarked grave on October 4, 1669. His posthumous reputation inspired some very surreal television three centuries later, when a body was unearthed that was mistakenly thought to be his. While exposed to the glare of the news cameras, the skull turned to dust. Ooopsie. ⊠ *Prinsengracht 281 (corner of Westermarkt), Jordaan* ☎ *020/624–7766* ⊕ *www.westerkerk.nl* ⊘ *Tower June–Sept., Tues., Wed., Fri., and Sat. 2–5; interior Apr.–Sept., weekdays 11–3.*

need a break? Along Westermarkt's southerly side is an excellent fish stall where you can slide a raw herring or some smoked eel down your throat (though there are also less eerily textured options). An equally traditionally Dutch way of keeping eating costs down is to pack one's belly with pancakes. The **Pancake Bakery** (⊠ Prinsengracht 191, Jordaan ☎ 020/625–1333) is one of the best places in Amsterdam to try them, with a menu that offers a near infinite range of topping possibilities—from the sweet to the fruity to the truly belly-gelling powers of cheese and bacon. If you are indeed more thirsty than hungry, head to the one of Amsterdam's historic and smoke-stained "brown" cafés, the **Café Chris** (⊠ Bloemstraat 42, Jordaan ☎ 020/ 624–5942), up on the next corner; it has been pouring beverages since 1624. Its intrinsic coziness is taken to absurd lengths in its tiny men's bathroom, whose cistern's position outside the door means that pranksters can easily shock you out of your reveries with a quick pull of the flusher. Be warned.

⑰ Woonboatmuseum (Houseboat Museum). In Amsterdam nearly 8,000 people (and a whole gaggle of cats at the cat asylum that floats opposite Singel 40—though they may have moved to posher quarters a few boats down from here by now) live on its 2,400 houseboats. This converted 1914-built sailing vessel, the *Hendricka Maria,* provides a glimpse into this unique lifestyle. It almost feels as if you are visiting Grandma—which is also highlighted by the special child-play zone—as you settle into comfy seats to read the information packets. Models and slides help broaden the view. ⊠ *Prinsengracht opposite No. 296, Jordaan* ☎ *020/427– 0750* ⊕ *www.houseboatmuseum.nl* ☑ *€2.50* ⊘ *Mar.–Oct., Wed.–Sun. 11–5; Nov.–Feb., Fri.–Sun. 11–5.*

Van Gogh & Company: The Museum District & Vondelpark

With art, like all good things in life, moderation is the key. The fact remains that you will need to make an exception here, thanks to the efficient fact that Amsterdam's acclaimed density of masterpieces is for the most part concentrated around Museumplein. This sheer quantity of quality can soon render visitors cross-eyed and their other four senses atrophied—thanks to the fact that this square mile offers a remarkably complete lesson in the history of Western art: from the realistic but symbolically obtuse depictions offered by the masters of the Golden Age in the Rijksmuseum, to the artistic revolution of the end of the 19th century when artists—like Van Gogh (and his colleagues on view in the Van Gogh Museum)—had to reinvent the relevance of painting in a photographic age, through to all the ensuing evolutions and revolutions of the 20th century documented in the Stedelijk Museum of Modern Art.

It is therefore fortuitous that this area of the "Old South," built as a very posh residential area for the rich at the end of the 19th century (when Amsterdam was enjoying a second golden age of sorts), harbors both vast expanses of green to neutralize the eyeballs and the city's best up-market shopping opportunities to feed one's baser instincts. And certainly this tour's starting point of the Leidseplein, with its richness in performance and music venues, offers evening entertainment that may soothe any other senses that may feel neglected.

a good walk

We begin in **Leidseplein** ㉒ ▶, which perhaps at first glance comes across as a low-brow start to a tour that will take in some of world's greatest art treasures. But if we ignore the sports bars, the faux Irish pubs, and the side streets filled with tourist-preying eateries, we actually find ourselves in the city's central zone for the performing arts—and this does not include the buskers serenading the terraces. Theatergoers flock here for the offerings at the great **Stadsschouwburg** ㉓ theater while all can also feast their eyes on the adjacent American Hotel and its storybook edifice.

Exit Leidseplein via its southeast extension, the Kleine Gartmanplantsoen, which features bronze lizards in the grass parkette on the left, and the political and cultural center–café, De Balie (No. 10) on the right, beside which are large Greek pillars whose mantle is emblazed with the Latin for "Wise men do not piss in the wind." This is the entrance to Max Euweplein, whose surrounding buildings used to be a prison complex that held Nazi resistors during Occupation (but are now dubiously modernized to confine such commercial ventures as a casino). But the square does have a huge chess set—in tribute to Max Euwe, who as a world champion became the nation's chess hero—and also provides a hasty conduit to the gloriously green Vondelpark, this tour's end point.

But to stay on the culture trail continue down Weteringschans, past the Paradiso, until you see the *Night Watch*'s home, the **Rijksmuseum** ㉔, on the right. Here you may choose to go left down the antiques gallery–rich **Spiegelstraat,** or recall it for later as a handy passage back to the historic center of town. Otherwise, one hopes there will be a violinist or some Mongolian throat-singers on hand to accompany you as you take the acoustically rich arched passage under the museum to reach the freshly revamped **Museumplein** (Museum Square), whose new sense of space is quite at odds with the city's famed crampedness. Visible straight across the wading pool—which can miraculously turn to ice overnight in the heat of summer (thanks to some high-tech wizardry)—is the classical music mecca of the **Concertgebouw** ㉕, cherished by musicians the world over for its superlative acoustics (just imagine if those Mongolian throat-singers could score a gig here). The round titanium-roofed building visible to its right is the new wing of the **Rijksmuseum Vincent Van Gogh** ㉖, whose neighbor is the yet more modern **Stedelijk Museum** ㉗, home to the city's largest collection of contemporary art. From here you can go to the right down Van Baerlestraat to get to the city's green lungs of **Vondelpark** ㉘, perhaps pausing to window-shop along the cross street **PC Hooftstraat,** the nation's poshest high-end designer fashion strip. Film-lovers will be sure to check out the park's **Nederlands Filmmuseum** ㉙, set in a lovely 19th-century pavilion.

TIMING   Merely to walk this tour one needs less than an hour. However, truly to absorb all the art treasures along this route requires an additional two weeks—so you might even bring a sleeping bag. For the less ambitious: spend a couple of hours in the Rijksmuseum and Van Gogh Museum, and then take another hour to bring yourselves up to date in the history of art by wandering through the Stedelijk Modern Art Museum. After seeing infinite representations of light fall, the real thing awaits in Vondelpark—where at just before twilight when it's sunny, one can witness the unique quality of light that has acted as muse for the country's artists for centuries. And attention, shoppers: while PC Hooftstraat offers seven-days-a-week browsing opportunities—with later hours on Thursday—not all its boutiques are open on Sunday and Monday mornings.

Sights to See

★ ㉕ **Concertgebouw** (Concert Building). The Netherlands' premier and globally acclaimed concert hall has been filled since 1892 with the music of the Royal Concertgebouw Orchestra and an endless stream of international artists. With 800,000 visitors per year, it rates as the most visited concert hall in the world. There are two concert halls in the building, the Kleine (Small) and the Grote (Large), the latter being the most acoustically perfect on the planet according to many pundits. You will recognize the building at once, if not by its Viennese classicist facade then by the golden lyre at its peak. Designed by Al van Gendt to be one of Amsterdam's most sumptuous essays in the Neo-Renaissance style, it continues to charm all. The entrance is through the glass extension along the side. There are no tours of the building, so you will need to buy a ticket to a concert to see beyond the broad lobby, or, if you visit on a Wednesday before 12:30, September to June, you can attend a free lunchtime concert. ⊠ *Concertgebouwplein 2–6, Museum District and Vondelpark* ☎ *020/675–4411 24-hr concert schedule and hot line, 020/671–8345 box office* ⊕ *www.concertgebouw.nl.*

> **need a break?**
>
> For Concertgebouw goers, a posh and popular pre- and post-concert dining location is **Bodega Keyzer** (⊠ Van Baerlestraat 96, Museum District and Vondelpark ☎ 020/671–1441), whose French-inspired dishes, old-world interior, and uniformed waiters breathe with an appropriately rarified air.

▶ ㉒ **Leidseplein** (Leidse Square). In medieval times, Leidseplein was the parking lot for horse-drawn carts since they were banned from the city center—an enlightened policy that today's city planners can perhaps learn from. Today, Leidseplein is where tourists come to park their behinds on the terraces and absorb the infinite crowds and buskers. Hence it is somewhat difficult to imagine that this was long a top hangout for artists and intellectuals; more so, between the wars, this was where Communists and Fascists came to clash. After World War II, much bohemian frolicking took place in such still somewhat evocative cafés as Reindeers (Leidseplein 6), the former resistance hangout Eijlders (Korte Leidsedwarsstraat 47), and the one within the impressively Art Deco American Hotel.

The relatively tamer 1950s crowd around the noted CoBrA painters group, like Karel Appel and writers like Harry Mulisch (now the nation's always dandily dressed grand old man of letters), gave way to a younger and yet more radical and wacky crowd at the dawn of the 1960s. "Antismoke magician" Robert Jasper Grootveld started hyping Amsterdam as the "magical center of the universe" and organizing proto-"happenings" from his garage—dubbed the K-Temple ("K" for cancer)—on the Korte Leidsedwarsstraat but eventually moved the show to the Spui to give birth to the more politically motivated Provos. Leidseplein was now left alone to evolve toward its current "international" flavor, but not before going through a "national" stage as the favored spot for football supporters to come celebrate a Dutch victory or exhibit more angry outbursts when they lost. As such, the Leidseplein intellectual aura gave way to mirror the local concept of *pataat cultuur* ("French Fry Culture"). However, the greasy food dispensers of enjoining Leidsestraat are now slowly disappearing to make way for designer-brand outlets. Certainly the **Stadsschouwburg** provides musical, dance, and theatrical performances for the decidedly highbrow (the generally more hip and youthful go a stone's throw away to the **Melkweg** and **Paradiso** clubs).

Architectural buffs should take time to observe the 1925 **bridge** to the south crossing Singelgracht. Its swoopy Amsterdam School style was the work of Piet Kramer (1881–1961), who designed 220 of the city's existing bridges. Armed with this knowledge (and the fact that his later work became slightly more conservative), you can walk the rest of the city and regularly say "Ah, another Kramer . . ." without worrying too much about being labeled a dilettante. ⊠ *Main entrances: Leidsestraat, Weteringschans, and Marnixstraat, Museum District and Vondelpark.*

need a break? Leidseplein and its surrounds are dense with café-break opportunities. The well-read and politically engaged crowd gather around the café **De Balie** (⊠ Kleine Gartmanplantsoen 10, Museum District and Vondelpark ☎ 020/553–5130). The theatrical crowd can be witnessed at **Café Cox** (⊠ Marnixstraat 429, Museum District and Vondelpark ☎ 020/620–7222), part of the Stadsschouwburg building. The lounging American can find a familiar home at **Boom Chicago Lounge** (⊠ Leidseplein 12, Museum District and Vondelpark ☎ 020/530–7300), which also provides a terrace option.

★ ㉙ **Nederlands Filmmuseum.** One of the highlights of Vondelpark is the Netherlands Film Museum, which occupies an elegant 19th-century entertainment pavilion, first opened to the public in 1881 as a café. Here's you'll find on display such historic treasures as Amsterdam's first movie theater, the **Cinema Parisien,** replete with its 1910 Art Deco interior, a film poster collection, and public library, as well as shows every day in its two cinemas, drawing on material from all over the world as well as from its substantial archives (which includes such gems as hand-tinted silent movies). On summer Thursdays, there are free outdoor screenings beginning at dusk. Even if you're not into film, check out the museum's very popular Café Vertigo, whose terrace tables offer grand views of Vondelpark. It's right near the Roemer Visscherstraat entrance. ⊠ *Vondelpark 3, Museum District* ☎ *020/589–1400* ⊕ *www.nfm.nl* ⊡ *Free* ⊙ *Tues.–Fri. 10–5, Sat. 11–5.*

㉔ **Rijksmuseum** (State Museum). The Netherlands' greatest museum, the
Fodor'sChoice Rijksmuseum is home to Rembrandt's *Night Watch,* Vermeer's *The*
★ *Kitchen Maid,* and a near infinite selection of world-famous masterpieces by the likes of Steen, Ruisdael, Brouwers, Hals, Hobbema, Cuyp, Van der Helst, and their Golden Age ilk. This nation's pride (and the information contained herein), however, is soon to be rent by major changes: the Rijksmuseum is set to close between 2004 and 2008 for extensive renovation and rebuilding following the plans of Seville's architect duo Antonio Cruz and Antonio Ortiz. Only the South Wing—which has now through corporate sponsorship been renamed the Philips Wing—will remain reliably open to house a "Best of" selection. However with a new exhibition space in Schiphol Airport (Rijksmuseum Amsterdam Schiphol, Holland Boulevard between piers E and F, 020/653–5036, Monday–Friday 7 AM–8 PM, admission free), and promises of several "roaming" exhibits, visitors can still get an ample dose of Golden Age glory (as long as they call ahead or check the Web site).

Ironically, the Rijksmuseum's fabled collections began life by being housed in the Trippenhuis mansion, an act of French sibling rivalry at the dawn of the 19th-century during French occupation when King Louis wanted to compete with his brother Napoléon's burgeoning Louvre collection. When architect P. J. H. Cuypers came up with the current location's somewhat over-the-top design in the late 1880s, it shocked Calvinist Holland down to its—one imagines—overly starched shorts. Cuypers was persuaded to tone down some of what was thought as excessive (read: Catholic) elements of his Neo-Renaissance decoration and soaring Neo-Gothic lines. During the building's construction, however, he did manage to sneak some of his ideas back in, and the result is a magnificent, turreted building that glitters with gold leaf and is textured with sculpture—a fitting palace for the national art collection.

The Rijksmuseum has more than 150 rooms displaying paintings, sculpture, and objects from both the West and Asia, dating from the 9th through the 19th centuries. The bulk of the collection is of 15th- to 17th-century paintings, mostly Dutch (the Rijksmuseum has the largest concentration of these masters in the world); there are also extensive holdings of drawings and prints from the 15th to the 20th century.

If your time is limited, head directly for the Gallery of Honor on the upper floor, to admire Rembrandt's *Night Watch*, with its central figure, the "stupidest man in Amsterdam," Frans Banningh Cocq. His militia buddies that surround him each paid 100 guilders to be included—quite the sum in those days, so a few of them complained about being lost in all those shadows. It should also be noted that some of these shadows are formed by the daylight coming in through a small window. Daylight? Indeed, the *Night Watch* is actually the *Day Watch*, but it received its name when it was obscured with soot—imagine the restorers' surprise. The rest of this "Best of the Golden Age" hall features other well-known Rembrandt paintings and works by Vermeer, Frans Hals, and other household names—or at least names that you may recognize from wandering the streets of De Pijp neighborhood.

A clockwise progression through the rooms of the adjoining East Wing takes you past works by some of the greatest Dutch painters of the 15th to the 19th century, which will have you walking by: Mannerist renderings of biblical and mythic scenes where gods and goddesses show an almost yogic ability in twisting their limbs; eerily lifelike portraits with the lighting maximized to flatter the paying subject; landscapes that may either be extravagant and fantastical in both subject and style or conversely dull, flat, and essentially lacking everything but sky; Caravaggio-inspired exercises by the painters of the Utrecht School who employed contrast in light and shadow to heighten a sense of drama; straight moralistic paintings of jolly taverns and depraved brothels warning of the dangers of excess; meticulous and shimmering still lifes of flowers, food, and furnishings; cold mathematical renderings of interiors that could be used as architectural blueprints. All of these works prove that the nouveau riche of the Golden Age had a hunger for art that knew no bounds.

Unmissable masterpieces include Vermeer's *The Little Street*—a magical sliver of 17th-century Delft life—and his incomparable *The Love Letter,* in which a well-appointed interior reveals a mistress and her maid caught in the emotional eddies of a recently opened and read billet-doux. Note the calm seascape on the back wall—a quiet sea was seen as a good omen by the Dutch; inner anxieties, however, are present in the mistress' face, so much so that the room's clothes hamper, lace-making pillow, and broom all lie forgotten. Ostensibly, a more sedate missive is being read in Vermeer's *Woman in Blue Reading a Letter,* on view nearby. But is this just a matronly dress or is the woman pregnant and thinking about a missing husband (note the seafaring map)?

The walls of this museum here are virtually wallpapered with other masterpieces by Geertgen tot Sint Jans, the Master of Alkmaar, Cornelis Engebrechtsz, Lucas van Leyden, Jan van Scorel, Joos de Momper, Pieter Aertsen, and Karen van Mander. Especially notable are the group company portraits of Frans Hals, the Caravaggist works by Gerrit van Honthorst, the often funny genre interiors of Jan Steen, the beloved landscapes of Jan van Goyen, Meindert Hobbema, Aelbert Cuyp, Hendrick Averkamp, and Jacob and Salomon van Ruisdael—these artists created the landscape genre and gave us its greatest achievements. Crowning all are the famous Rembrandt works, topped off by the *Night Watch* and the *Jewish Bride* (which Vincent van Gogh would study for hours) plus many other of the master's paintings; also note the many daubs by his pupils, including Gerrit Dou, Nicolaes Maes, and Ferdinand Bol.

The South Wing contains 18th- and 19th-century paintings, costumes, and textiles and the museum's impressive collection of Asian art, which includes some 500 statues of Buddha from all over the Orient. The Rijksmuseum's collection of drawings and prints is far too vast to be displayed completely, and only a small selection is shown in the Print Room at any one time. Here you might catch a glimpse of Italian Renaissance sketches, Rembrandt engravings, or early-19th-century photographs. Elsewhere in the museum you can wander through room after room of antique furniture, silverware, and exquisite porcelain, including Delftware. The 17th-century doll's houses—made not as toys but as showpieces for wealthy merchant families—are especially worth seeing, as is the collection of expressive Art Nouveau furniture.

A particular neglected—and freely accessible—part of this museum is its sculpture- and port-filled gardens formed in the triangle by Hobbemastraat and Jan Luijkenstraat. You can also use the alternative entrance found here when the lines seem too long to its main entrance.

For an institution dedicated to antiquity, the Rijksmuseum has shown a remarkable technical savvy in making its vast collection more accessible via its incredible Web site. From the comfort of your home, you can make a virtual tour, chart out a plan of attack, and absorb vast chunks of background information. The museum has also introduced an "ARIA" (Amsterdam Rijksmuseum Inter-Active) system, which allows a visitor to ask for information—which may include visuals, text, film, and/or sound—on 1,250 objects and then be given directions to find other related objects. These "create-your-own tours" are available in a room directly behind the *Night Watch.* Whether they will still be available here once the massive renovation of the museum is over remains to be seen. ✉ *Stadhouderskade 42, Museum District and Vondelpark* ☎ *020/674–7047* ⊕ *www.rijksmuseum.nl* ✍ *€9 (though the price will be markedly lower if areas are closed during renovation)* ☉ *Daily 10–5.*

need a break?

After walking through miles of art, there's nothing more invigorating than indulging in the fish-protein infusions on offer at the fish stall on the Rijksmuseum's front east side. **Altena** (✉ Jan Luijkenstraat/Stadhouderskade, Museum District and Vondelpark) also has the bonus of a proprietor who will gladly talk you through the finer points of sliding a raw herring down your throat. On Museumplein, one can sit down on the patio of **Cobra Café** (✉ Hobbemastraat 18, Museum District and Vondelpark ☎ 020/470–0111) for a snack from the acclaimed menu, or choose a spot of your own after stocking up at the Albert Heijn supermarket located under the grass slope across from the Concertgebouw.

㉖ **Rijksmuseum Vincent Van Gogh** (Vincent Van Gogh Museum). Opened in
Fodor'sChoice 1973, this remarkable light-infused building, based on a design by famed
★ De Stijl architect Gerrit Rietveld, venerates the short, certainly not sweet, but highly productive career of everyone's favorite tortured 19th-century artist. First things first: Vincent was a Dutch boy and therefore his name is not pronounced like the "Go" in Go-Go Lounge but rather like the "Go" uttered when one is choking on a whole raw herring.

While some of the Van Gogh paintings that are scattered throughout the world's high-art temples are of dubious provenance, this collection's authenticity is indisputable: its roots trace directly back to brother Theo van Gogh, Vincent's artistic and financial supporter. The 200 paintings and 500 drawings on display here can be divided into his five basic periods, the first beginning in 1880 at age 27 after his failure in finding his voice as schoolmaster and lay preacher. These early depictions of Dutch country landscapes and peasants—particularly around the Borinage and Nuenen—were notable for their dark colors and a refusal to romanticize (a stand that perhaps also led in this period to his various failures in romance). The *Potato Eaters* is perhaps his most famous piece from this period.

In 1886, he followed his art-dealing brother Theo to Paris, whose heady atmosphere—and drinking buddies like Paul Signac and Henri de Toulouse-Lautrec—inspired him to new heights of experimentation. While heavily inspired by Japanese woodcuts and their hard contrasts and off-kilter compositions, he also took the Neo-Impressionist obsession with light and color as his own, and his self-portraits (he was the only model he could afford) began to shimmer with expressive lines and dots.

With a broadened palate, he returned to the countryside in 1888 to paint still lifes—including the famous series of *Sunflowers* (originally meant to decorate the walls of a single bedroom)—and portraits of locals around Arles, France. His hopes to begin an artist's colony here with Paul Gauguin were dampened by the onset of psychotic attacks—one of which saw the departure of his ear which, in turn inspired the departure of Gauguin to the South Seas. Recuperating in a mental health clinic in St-Remy from April 1889, he—feverishly, one is quick to assume—produced his most famous landscapes, such as *Irises* and *Wheat field with a Reaper,* whose sheer energy in brushstroke makes the viewer almost feel the area's sweeping winds. In May 1890, Van Gogh moved to the artist's village of Auvers-sur-Oise, where he traded medical advice from Dr. Paul Gachet in exchange for paintings and etching lessons. These highly productive last three months of his life were marred by depression and, on July 27, he shot himself in the chest and died two days later. His last painting, *Wheatfield with Crows,* remains the iconic image of this collection.

The permanent holdings also includes other important 19th-century artists, including those mentioned above, and examples of Japanese woodcuts. In 1999, a new oval extension was opened. Designed by the Japanese architect Kisho Kurokawa and built in a bold combination of titanium and gray-brown stone and connected to the main galleries by an underground walkway, it provides an epic space for a wide range of superbly presented temporary shows of 19th-century art, graphic design, photography, and sculpture. With all this new space, you might be tempted to take a break at the museum's cafeteria-style restaurant. ⊠ *Paulus Potterstraat 7, Museum District and Vondelpark* ☎ *020/ 570–5200* ⊕ *www.vangoghmuseum.nl* ⊠ *€9* ☉ *Daily 10–5.*

㉓ Stadsschouwburg (Municipal Theater). Somehow managing to retain its central dominance on a square given over to neon and advertising, the Stadsschouwburg has been here since 1784 after the original one on Keizersgracht burned down during mid-performance and killed many in the audience—a tragedy that was to be regarded as poetic justice by the more uptight of Calvinists who thought the proceedings there much too decadent. Their God being a vengeful sort, he may have also been responsible for this Stadsschouwburg also burning down on occasion and having to be rebuilt several times before receiving its current Neo-Renaissance facade and lushly Baroque horseshoe interior in 1890. The decades that followed saw the general state of the nation's theater scene descend into staidness until 1968 when, during a performance of the *Tempest,* the actors were showered with tomatoes. Part of a nationwide protest, the "tomato campaign" expressed the discontent with established theater's lack of social engagement. It resulted in more subsidies for newer theater groups—many of which now form the old guard who regularly play here.

While the majority of the programming is in Dutch, it should be said that contemporary Dutch theater is marked by a strong visual—and often hilariously absurdist—sense. And naturally, there is also a constant stream of visiting international theater and dance companies. ⊠ *Leidseplein 26, Museum District and Vondelpark* ☎ *020/624–2311* ⊕ *www. stadsschouwburgamsterdam.nl.*

★ ㉗ Stedelijk Museum (Municipal Museum). Hot and happening modern art of the 21st century and the last has one of the world's most respected homes here at the Stedelijk, which occupies, somewhat paradoxically, a wedding-cake Neo-Renaissance structure first opened in 1895. It's a home that is undergoing renovation, however: beginning in 2004, the museum will be undergoing massive refurbishment and perhaps even the addition—pending the finding of funds—of two new wings by Portuguese architect Alvaro Siza, all of which undoubtedly will disrupt accessibility for several years to come. So it's best to call ahead or check the Web site to avoid disappointment (or to be directed to the many planned exhibitions in temporary spaces).

With roots reaching back to when it began as a heiress's collection that included torturous mental health instruments and a bust of her late husband, the Stedelijk only began to cover its present course after World War II. It now has a collection of paintings, sculpture, drawings, prints, photography, graphic design, applied arts, and new media that numbers 100,000 pieces. While this stunning collection harbors many works by such ancients of modernism as Chagall, Cézanne, Picasso, Monet, Mondriaan, and Malevich, there is a definite emphasis on the post–World War II period: with such local CoBrA boys as Appel and Corneille; American Pop artists as Warhol, Johns, Oldenburg, and Liechtenstein; Abstract Expressionists as De Kooning and Pollock, and contemporary German Expressionists as Polke, Richter, and Baselitz. Still, many head here to find the homegrown masterworks of the De Stijl school, including the amazing *Red Blue Chair* Gerrit Rietveld designed in 1918, and the noted Mondriaan canvases on display, including his 1920 *Composition in Red, Black, Yellow, Blue, and Grey.* When not putting together exhibitions culled from this collection, the staff curates large retrospectives or themed programs of the currently acclaimed. Lately, however, these projects have perhaps become a tad too commercial, for instance, by allowing the queen of The Netherlands to play guest curator, and critics have looked askance. ✉ *Paulus Potterstraat 13, Museum District and Vondelpark* ☎ *020/573–2911* ⊕ *www.stedelijk.nl* ☒ €7 ⊙ *Daily 11–5.*

☾ ㉘ **Vondelpark.** On sunny days, Amsterdam's "Green Lung" is the densest populated section of the city. From all walks of life, Vondelpark becomes *the* place where sun is worshiped, joints are smoked, beer is quaffed, picnics are eaten, bands are grooved to, dogs are walked, balls are kicked, lanes are biked and roller-skated on, children frolic, bongos are bonged, lovers kiss, singles seek. By evening, the park has invariably evolved into one large outdoor café. But the chaos is relatively tame and the appeal now much broader compared to that of the summer of 1973, when more than 100,000 camping youths called it home and airlines like KLM saw bigger profits in advertising tickets to "Hippie Park" instead of its dull surrounds, "Amsterdam."

Such a future was certainly not envisioned in 1865 when Vondelpark was laid out as a 25-acre "Walking and Riding Park" to be enjoyed by the residents of the surrounding affluent neighborhood that was arising around it. It soon expanded to cover some 120 acres. In the process, it was renamed after Joost van den Vondel, the "Dutch Shakespeare." Landscaped in the informal English style, the park is an irregular patchwork of copses, ponds, children's playgrounds, and fields linked by winding pathways. Between June and August, one of the park's focal points is the open-air theater where free concerts, plays, comedy, and children's programs are performed Wednesday–Saturday. Children, when they've grown bored with the many playing facilities, will invariably drag their parents to the llama field for some petting action or go in search of the 400 parrots (apparently the progeny of two escaped pets) that miraculously survive every winter. Plant lovers will follow their noses to the formal and fragrant rose garden. If you do not want to join in on a football game, other forms of specialized exercise are available: at the Amstelveenseweg entrance one can rent in-line skates at the small wooden houses (before perhaps joining the Friday Night Skate crowd who take over the city's streets after meeting in front of the Filmmuseum at 8 PM), while at the van Eeghenstraat entrance one can join the "oriental laughing sessions" every weekday from 8 AM and weekends from 9 AM.

Over the years a range of sculptural and architectural delights have made their appearance in the park. **Picasso** himself donated a sculpture, *The Fish* (which stands in the middle of an overgrown field to deter footballers from using it as a goalpost), to commemorate the park's centenary in 1965. There's an elegant 19th-century bandstand, and the famous **Round Blue Teahouse,** a rare beauty of functionalist Nieuw Bouw architecture, built beside the lake in 1937, which attracts every manner of person to its patio during the day and a more clubby crowd by evening. Here, too, is the city's popular **Nederlands Filmmuseum,** which is ensconced in a pretty 19th-century pavilion and features the popular Vertigo café. ✉ *Stadhouderskade, Museum District and Vondelpark.*

off the
beaten
path

AMSTERDAMSE BOS – The "Amsterdam Woods," the largest of Amsterdam's many parks, covers a total area of 2,210 acres and lies a few miles to the south of the city. This woodland habitat harbors no fewer than 150 tree varieties, but it also has open fields, a boating lake, the Bosbaan rowing course with stadium, and a goat farm. With 137 km (85 mi) of footpaths and 51 km (32 mi) of bicycle paths traversing 50 bridges—many designed in the early 20th-century Amsterdam School style with characteristic redbrick and sculpted stone detailing—it is an easy escape from the city for adults and ideal for children. To get here by bike, cycle through the Vondelpark to its southern tip, then take a left onto the Amstelveenseweg and follow it until you reach the Van Nijenrodeweg. Turn right into the Amsterdamse Bos, and you will find yourself at the stadium end of the Bosbaan rowing course. Buses 170, 171, and 172 take passengers from the Leidseplein to the Van Nijenrodeweg, where you can rent bikes from June to August. Maps and signposting are plentiful throughout the park. At the **Grote Vijver** (Big Pond) you can hire kayaks and rowing boats from April through September. The **Bosmuseum** (⊠ Koenenkade 56, Amstelveen ☏ 020/676–2152) has displays about natural history and the management of the woods, and is open daily 10–5. If you didn't pack your own lunch, the neighboring **Boerderij Meerzicht** (⊠ Koenenkade 56, Amstelveen ☏ 020/679–2744) is a café-restaurant serving sandwiches and traditional Dutch pancakes with a selection of savory and sweet toppings. ⊠ *Amstelveen.*

Beyond the "Golden Bend": The Eastern Canal Ring & De Pijp

Amsterdam's 17th-century Golden Age left behind a tidemark of magnificent buildings to line its picturesque canals. This is most striking along the famous Gouden Bocht (Golden Bend), where elaborate gables, richly decorated facades, finely detailed cornices, colored marbles, and heavy doors created an imposing architecture that suits the bank headquarters of today as well as it did the grandees of yore. This tour takes in such time-burnished marvels, but—to an even greater degree than with the tour of the Western Canal Ring and the Jordaan—this remains a city area of contrasts. Amsterdam's richest stretches of canals, the Eastern Canal Ring, which still glitter with the sumptuous pretensions of a Golden Age past, will be put against the more "street" (albeit quickly gentrifying) realities of the De Pijp district, which reflect Amsterdam's present as an ultimately global village.

In 1660, city planners decided to continue the western half ring of canals that had been arising since 1613 and had already been proven as a prime and scenic living location for the well-heeled. But the mega-well-heeled observed that the allotments there were too narrow and therefore now had an opportunity to buy two adjoining allotments in the east (this excess is the reason why this area is currently much less residential and much more taken over by banks, businesses, and hotels).

De Pijp ("The Pipe"), named for its narrow streets and towering gables, has been destined to be an "up-and-coming" neighborhood pretty much since it was built in the late-19th-century to house working-class families. There's nothing like cheap rent also to attract students, artists, and wacky radicals. This was once a place dense with brothels, where Eduard Jacobs sang his absurd but sharply polemical songs about pimps, prostitutes, and the disenfranchised (thereby laying the groundwork for the typically Dutch form of cabaret that is still popularly practiced by the likes of Freek de Jong and Hans Teeuwen). From his De Pijp grotto, the writer Bordewijk depicted Amsterdam during World War I as a "ramshackle bordello, a wooden shoe made of rock"; Piet Mondriaan began formulating the revolutionary art of De Stijl in an attic studio on Ruysdaelkade (No. 75).

Later, waves of guest workers from Turkey and Morocco and immigrants from the former colonies of Suriname and Indonesia began arriving and were fundamental in revitalizing the area around Albert Cuyp Market—

the largest outdoor market in The Netherlands—with shops, restaurants, and family values. By the 1980s, De Pijp was a true Global Village, with more than 126 nationalities. With a new underground metro line destined—or doomed, depending on whom you talk to—to run through here within the next decade, yet more upmarket investors are now appearing. But regardless, the Pijp remains a prime spot for cheap international eats and the pub-crawling of locals' bars and cafés.

a good walk

The Muntplein, with the Dutch Renaissance **Munt Toren** ③ ▶ (Mint Tower) as its focal point, is chaotic—but for a reason. From here you can enter the floating **Flower Market** to the south, witness the walking-and-shopping **Kalverstraat** to the west, or admire the facade to the north of Hotel de l'Europe (which Hitchcock used as a vertigo inducer in *Foreign Correspondent*).

Some of you may decide first to visit—by taking the road to the right of the tower—the **Torture Museum** (⌧ Singel 449, Eastern Canal Ring ☎ 020/320–6642), with its iron maidens and their ilk. It's open daily 10 AM–11 PM. Most, however, will choose to stick temporarily with the chaos and follow the torturous crowds up Reguliersbreestraat's right side, past Easyeverything—a 24-hour cybercafé whose 650 monitors made it the world's largest for a short time in 2000—and the truly grand **Tuschinski Cinema** ③, a theater that fuses Art Deco with a pure eclectic enthusiasm. For contrast, you might want to glance across the street from here to Nos. 31–33 and admire a classic piece of Functionalist-Constructivist architecture from 1934, which was originally a cinema before failing into the hands of Planet Hollywood. But before deciding that the Dutch are folks with impeccable taste, wait until you witness the neon and touristic atrocities in **Rembrandtplein,** where things have changed a lot since it was the city's butter market. Something has gone terribly wrong here, the first clue of which may be the cheap iron (rather than bronze) statue of a cavalier Rembrandt in its center. But in midst of the infinite middle-of-the-road cafés, clubs, and restaurants, there are some truly classy landmarks: **De Kroon** (No. 17), a shockingly spacious grand café complete with zoological specimens and a balcony, and **Schiller** (No. 26), with its amazing Art Deco interior, which still evokes the bohemian types that used to hang out here.

After loading up on coffee at one of these establishments, exit the square through the enjoining smaller square of Thorbeckeplein (although some of you may first want to divert to the right up the very gay-friendly Reguliersdwarsstraat to pick out a restaurant or nightclub for later). The first canal you come to is Herengracht, and to the right lies the opulent Golden Bend, **Gouden Bocht** ③ with some of the city's most impressive Golden Age residential monuments. However, if you are more interested in looking at the life behind the facades, head left to **Willet-Holthuysen Museum** ③. Then again, if there's a crack in the clouds, you may want to just hurry straight up Reguliersgracht to the intersection with Keizersgracht, where from the bridge an additional 15 bridges can be viewed.

From here hang a right to reach the majestically opulent interiors on display at **Museum van Loon** ③. Its neighbor, No. 676, is a former church that is now dedicated to the worship of modern graphic design; as home to the Baby Society, it sometimes hosts exhibitions, definitely worth a look. Before backtracking east to Reguliersgracht to make the right that will get you to **Amstelveld**, perhaps first pause to observe the Amsterdam School bridge to the west crossing Vijzelstraat.

Approaching the square of Amstelveld, you will see on its first corner a wooden church that now includes the café Kort, with an exceedingly pleasant terrace, which looks across Prinsengracht to "De Duif" (No. 756); it arose in 1796 as one of the first openly Catholic churches after the Altercation in 1578. The curious may want to check if its renovation is complete before taking Kerkstraat, running along Amstelveld's north side, to the east and cross the excellently diverse shopping and eating strip of Utrechtsestraat. Continue until you reach the mighty River Amstel. The skinny bridge that crosses it, **Magere Brug** ㉟, or the "Skinny Bridge," is the most photographed bridge in the city, so click your way to the status quo.

Wandering aimlessly along the Amstel is always a worthwhile occupation. If you are feeling particularly ambitious you can make the 20-minute walk along the river to the south—minding the U-shape jag you have to make to cross Singelgracht—to reach the city archives, **Gemeente Archief** ㊱, with its monumental collection of all things Amsterdam. But if you are more motivated by hunger and/or want to check out Amsterdam's most multicultural neighborhood, **De Pijp,** backtrack down Kerkstraat and turn left down Utrechtsestraat, follow its split to the right, cross the bridge, and take the second right to enter Europe's biggest and busiest day market, **Albert Cuypmarkt** ㊲. Take the walking side street, 1e Sweelinckstraat, to the left toward the green peace of **Sarphatipark** ㊳, on whose opposite end you can connect up with another charming walking and terrace street, 1e Van der Helststraat, which will bring you back down to the market. Heading straight will have you passing through Gerard Douplein with its three funkily mosaiced pillars, past Stichting Dodo (No. 21) on the right (where you can pause to invest in some laughably cheap secondhand Euro-bric-a-brac) before turning left on Daniel Stalpertstraat, which will get you to the Marie Heinekenplein. Turning right on Ferdinand Bol and right again on Stadshouderskade will have you at the front door of the **Heineken Brouwerij** ㊴), a former brewery whose tour remains a must-do for some, a must-avoid for others. But undoubtedly, you've just recently seen a charming spot worthy of partaking in a more relaxed beer. If not, try the many found along the restful, tree-lined, and almost Parisian-flavor Frans Halstraat, which runs as Ferdinand Bolstraat's western parallel. *Proost!*

TIMING If done briskly, this tour can be completed in an hour and a half. Being more of a purely walking, gandering, and following-your-nose tour, there are no major disappointments awaiting you while doing this tour during daylight hours. However, Albert Cuypmarkt is a ghost town on Sunday, and the Museum van Loon does have particularly antisocial hours.

Sights to See

㊲ **Albert Cuypmarkt** (Albert Cuyp Market). As the biggest and busiest street market in Europe, Albert Cuypmarkt—named after a Golden Age painter like the majority of the streets in De Pijp—welcomes 20,000 shoppers daily during the week and double that number on Saturday. While you should come here for all your fresh food, textiles, and sundry other needs, the atmosphere alone makes it worthwhile. With a decades-long waiting list for a permanent booth, things can get dramatic—if not occasionally violent—at 9 every morning on the corner of 1e Sweelinckstraat where the lottery for that day's available temporary spaces take place. ⊠ *Albert Cuypmarkt between Ferdinand Bolstraat and Van Woustraat, De Pijp* ☉ *Mon.–Sat. 9–5.*

need a break? De Pijp offers endless options in the world of global snacking and dining. If you want to keep things cheap and speedy, then try such Surinamese (whose history and geography saw the mixing of Indonesian, Chinese, and Caribbean cookeries) purveyors as **Albine**

(✉ Albert Cuypstraat 69, De Pijp ☎ 020/675–5135). Try the new and remarkably spacious grand café, **De Engel** (✉ Albert Cuypstraat 182, De Pijp ☎ 020/675–0544), where one can linger over a coffee while admiring one's recent market investments. For a flavor of the area's reinvented café culture, check out **Kingfisher** (✉ Ferdinand Bolstraat 23, De Pijp ☎ 020/671–2395), whose stellar kitchen pumps out sandwiches by day and a shockingly inventive and cheap daily special for dinner at night.

🟤 **Gemeente Archief** (Municipal Archives). Established in 1914, this noble institution, which is freely open to the public, is filled with all the archives and collections relevant to Amsterdam. While you won't be able personally to inspect the piece of paper from 1275 by which Floris V extended toll privileges to the then tiny town and thereby initiated its growth toward global dominance, you can do such things as search for your family roots or follow the history of the city's fashion industry. It also holds two city-centric exhibitions per year and harbors an excellent bookstore that sells every available Amster-relevant publication. ✉ *Amsteldijk 67, De Pijp* ☎ *020/572–0202* ⊕ *www.gemeentearchief. amsterdam.nl* ☒ *Free* ⊗ *Mon.–Sat. 11–5.*

🟤 **Gouden Bocht** (Golden Bend). This stretch of the Herengracht—which
Fodor'sChoice indeed bends—between the Vijzelstraat to the Leidsegracht contains some
★ of Amsterdam's most opulent Golden Age architecture and as such provided homes to the financial and political elite of the 17th and 18th centuries. It speaks of the egalitarian tendencies of the Dutch that such excesses arose here on Herengracht (Gentlemen's Canal) as opposed to the yet snootier-sounding Prinsengracht (Princes' Canal) or Keizersgracht (Emperors' Canal). Actually, some of the exteriors may come across at first glance as more modest than overtly opulent and therefore may reflect the Calvinist owners' "Embarrassment of Riches" so well described in Simon Schama's book of the same name. However, embarrassment did not stop them from importing the exterior's construction materials from afar and stuffing the interiors more overtly. In the late 19th century, most of these building were converted into offices for banks and other financial institutions that felt quite comfortable behind the heavy central doors. The most notable addresses here are numbers 475 (designed by Hans Jacob Husly in 1703); 485 (Jean Coulon, 1739); 493 and 527, both in the Louis XVI style (1770); and 284 (Van Brienen House, 1728), another ornate Louis XVI facade. Interestingly, when initially laid out the great canals, including Herengracht, had no trees, making the city look more than ever like a "Venice of the North." With time, elms were planted, in part to allow for their roots to stabilize the canal foundations. ✉ *Bounded by Vijzelstraat and Leidsestraat, Eastern Canal Ring.*

🟤 **Heineken Brouwerij** (Heineken Brewery). Founded by Gerard Heineken in 1864, the Heineken label quickly become one of Amsterdam's (and therefore the world's) most famous beers. As this factory couldn't keep up with the enormous demand (today, most production rolls on in vast plants in The Hague and Den Bosch), it was transformed into a "Heineken Experience," an interactive center that offers tours of the more-than-century-old facilities. Everything from vast copper vats to beer-wagon dray horses is on view, and if you've ever wanted to know what it feels like to be a beer bottle, the virtual reality ride will clue you in. Others may enjoy the option to drink many beers in a very short time (note this tour is open only to visitors over the age of 18). ✉ *Stadhouderskade 78, De Pijp* ☎ *020/523–9666* ⊕ *www.heinekenexperience.com* ☒ *€7.50* ⊗ *Tues.–Sun. 10–6.*

③⑤ **Magere Brug** (Skinny Bridge). Of Amsterdam's 60-plus drawbridges, the Magere is the most famous. Whether or not this is due mainly to its name (which derives from "meager" in Dutch), the legend of its birth—it was purportedly built by two sisters living on opposite sides of the Amstel who wanted an efficient way of sharing that grandest of Dutch traditions, the *gezellig* (socially cozy) mid-morning coffee break—or because it is spectacularly lit with electric lights at night, we can't say. Have your camera ready at all hours, since the bridge is often drawn up to let boats pass by. Many replacements to the original bridge, constructed in 1672, have come and gone, and this, dating to 1969, is but the latest. ⊠ *Between Kerkstraat and Nieuwe Kerkstraat, Eastern Canal Ring.*

▶ ③⓪ **Munt Toren** (Mint Tower). This tower received its name in 1672 when French troops occupied much of the surrounding Republic and Amsterdam was given the right to mint its own coins here for a brief two-year period. While the spire was added by Hendrick de Keyser in 1620, the medieval tower and the enjoining guardhouse were part of a gate in the city's fortifying wall from 1490. The guardhouse, which now houses a Dutch porcelain shop, has a gable stone above its entrance, which portrays two men and a dog in a boat. This is not depicting that founding legend that has Amsterdam arising on the spot where a dog vomited when finally reaching dry land after being lost and sick in a storm with his two masters but rather a symbolic representation of the already formed city: where warrior and merchant bonded by the loyalty—that would be the dog—are sailing toward the future. The tower's carillon of 38 bells was originally installed in 1666 by the famed Hemony Brothers. While it is now automated to play every 15 minutes, a live recital often takes place on Friday between 3 and 4. ⊠ *Muntplein, Eastern Canal Ring.*

★ ③④ **Museum van Loon.** Once home to one of Rembrandt's most successful students, Ferdinand Bol, this twin house, built in 1672 by Adriaan Dortsman, fell into the hands of the Van Loon family in 1886 who lived here until the 1960. After extensive restoration of the house and facade, designed in a sober classicizing mode, the museum opened to depict opulent canal-side living. Along with wonderful period rooms, the house is filled with 80 portraits of the Van Loon family, which follow their history back to the 17th century when one of them helped found the East Indies Company; subjects include paired marriage portraits, and painters include Dirk Santvoort and Cornelis van der Voort. Up the copper staircase—picked out with the initials of Abraham van Hagen and his wife Catharine Trip, who presided over the house in the 1750s—you'll find various salons containing trompe l'oeil paintings known as *witjes,* illusionistic depictions of landscapes and other scenes. Don't miss the real landscape out back: an exquisitely elegant garden of trimmed hedgerows, which forms a lovely repoussoir for the Van Loon coach houses (the family was rich enough to buy back lots just to house their horses), which magisterially adopt the look of Grecian temples. ⊠ *Keizersgracht 672, Eastern Canal Ring* ☎ *020/624–5255* ⊕ *www.museumvanloon.nl* 🎟 *€4.50* ☉ *Fri.–Mon. 11–5.*

③⑧ **Sarphatipark.** This miniature Bois de Boulogne was built by and named after the Jewish jack-of-all-trades and noted city benefactor Samuel Sarphati (1813–66), whose statue deservedly graces the central fountain. This park, whose paths undulate along trees, ponds, and expanses of grass, can be considered a kinder, gentler, and definitely much smaller Vondelpark and as such should be exploited for picnicking—on supplies gathered from the Albert Cuypmarkt—when you are in the neighborhood on sunny days. ⊠ *Bounded by Ceintuurbaan and Sarphatipark, De Pijp.*

THE CROWNING TOUCH:
GABLES & GABLE STONES

THE INFINITE ARRAY OF GABLES of Amsterdam's houses, historic and modern, dominates the city's picture-postcard image and is a carefully preserved asset. The lack of firm land meant that Amsterdam houses were built on narrow, deep plots, and one of the few ways to make a property distinctive was at the top, with a decorative gable. The simplest and earliest form is the spout gable in the shape of an inverted funnel. When houses were still made of wood, this protective front could simply be nailed on. Another early form was the step gable, usually a continuation of the masonry of the facade, which rises to a pinnacle. This form was also used in Flemish architecture, as seen in the Belgian city of Bruges. The neck gable was the next development, a brick frontage in the form of a decorated oblong, hiding the angled roof behind. Bell gables are an elaboration of this, with more elaborate carved stone or decorative moldings. Another eye-catching element is the gable stone. These plaster or stone tablets placed above doors or built into walls were houses' identity tags before house numbers were introduced early in the 19th century. The gable stones are simple reliefs, sometimes brightly painted, which usually depicted the craft or profession of the inhabitants. For example, an apple merchant might have a depiction of Adam and Eve. To see a whole selection of rescued gable stones, pop into the Begijnhof courtyard or go to the St. Luciensteeg entranceway of the Amsterdam Historical Museum.

㉛ Tuschinski Cinema. While officially the architect of this "Prune Cake"—as it was described when it first opened in 1921—was H. L. De Jong, the financial and spiritual force was undoubtedly Abram Icek Tuschinski (1886–1942), a Polish Jew who after World War I decided to a build a theater that was "unique." And since interior designers Pieter de Besten, Jaap Gidding, and Chris Bartels came up with a dizzying and dense mixture of Baroque, Art Nouveau, Amsterdam School, Jugendstil, and Asian influences, it is safe to say that he achieved his goal. Obsessed with details, he became known as "Napoléon of Devil's Triangle" (as the surrounding, then seedy neighborhood was called). While it began as a variety theater welcoming such stars as Marlene Dietrich, it soon became a cinema, and to this day viewing a film from one of the extravagant private balconies remains an unforgettable experience—especially if you order champagne. Sobering note: Tuschinski died in Auschwitz. ✉ *Reguliersbreestraat 26–28, Eastern Canal Ring* ☎ 020/626–2633.

㉝

FodorśChoice
★

Willet-Holthuysen Museum. Few patrician houses are open to the public along the Herengracht, so make a beeline to this mansion to see Grachtengordel (Canal Ring) luxury at its best. In 1895, the widow Mrs. Willet-Holthuysen donated the house and contents—which included her husband's extensive art collection—to the city of Amsterdam. Visitors can wander through this 17th-century canal house, now under the management of Amsterdams Historisch Museum, and discover all its original 18th-century interiors, complete with that era's mod-cons: from ballroom to *cabinet des merveilles* (rarities cabinet). Objets d'art of silverware, glass, and goldsmith's work accent the rooms. The biggest salon is the Blue Room, handsomely decked out in blue Utrecht velvet, a ceiling painted by Jacob de Wit, and porcelain bibelots. Note the gilded staircase, whose walls are painted in faux-marble. You can air out the aura of Dutch luxury by lounging in the French-style garden in the back. For a peek at the Downstairs side to this Upstairs coin, be sure to check out the wonderful kitchen. ⊠ *Herengracht 605, Eastern Canal Ring* ☎ *020/ 523–1822* ⊕ *www.willetholthuysen.nl* 🎟 *€4* ⊙ *Weekdays 10–5, weekends 11–5.*

The Oude Zijde: The Western Half of the Centrum

As the oldest part of Amsterdam, the Oude Zijde (Old Side) has been very old and very Dutch for a long time. It goes to reason, then, that you'll find, in this mirror quadrant to the Nieuwe Zijde, the entire galaxy of Amsterdam here—everything from the archaeological treasures of the Allard Pierson Museum to the famous "Our Lord in the Attic" chapel to, well, acres of bared female flesh. Yes, here within the shadow of the city's oldest church is the most famous Disneyland of Sex in the world: the Red Light District. Within it, most of the city's 13,000 professionals ply their trade and help generate an estimated 1 billion sextrade guilders in revenue per year. While a union, Rode Draad, has been representing sex-for-hire workers since 1984 and the tax man has long finagled a means to take his cut, it's only since 2000 that it has all become perfectly legal—including bordellos, clubs, and sex shops. And pragmatic it is indeed: you may be amazed to find that the area has been grouped according to "predilections" and thereby organized into sections (the turf around the area's ancient heart of the Oude Kerk, for instance, has been staked out by Africans). While ultimately sleazy, especially in the Walletjes ("little walls") area (defined by Oudezijds Voorburgwal and Oudezijds Achterburgwal north of Damstraat and their interconnecting streets), this area is also essentially the oldest and once poshest part of town. Edit out the garish advertising and the sweaty breasts hypnotically sandwiched against the red-neon framed windows, and you have some very pretty buildings indeed. But have no fear: this area is also blessed with the city's Chinatown and large sections—as the vast majority of this tour will attest—of pure, unadulterated old worldness.

But even in the reddest of sections, there is a warm—albeit surreal— sense of community where hard-working and -talking tradespeople, pink rinse–haired grandmothers, frolicking schoolchildren, street-savvy nuns (representing the area's historical richness in religious institutions and former convents), prostitutes, and police all interact, oblivious to the fact that they are not actually living in a small town. The cops, especially, come across as cute and cuddly, often distributing flyers that hype them as being "used to weird things" and offering such canny advice as "parking is not free," "when you feel sick after smoking or eating space cake, drink lots of water with sugar," and "if you visit one of the women, we would like to remind you, they are not always women."

A potential annoyance are the junkies and dealers, but even they provide a unifying bond to the rest of the community by being regarded as a shared annoyance. While a certain alertness is recommended when exploring this area at night by yourself, the area is remarkably safe—there are two basic rules: don't take pictures of prostitutes, and avoid eye contact with dealers. Otherwise just enjoy this dense world of contrasts where sex, religion, history, tourism, dubious coffee shops, food of both the ultimately greasy and posh varieties, and ancient grandeur reign supreme.

a good walk

On exiting Centraal Station you'll see a Catholic church to the left, **Sint Nicolaaskerk** ④ ➤, at which you may want to stop and check the times of its Gregorian chant vesper services in case you get the urge to purge your soul after this tour. In fact, for this tour you should try to take on the easygoing and forgiving nature of St. Nick, who, as the proto-Santa, was patron saint not only to children but also to thieves, prostitutes, and sailors—not to mention the city of Amsterdam. Sailors have long walked by this church on their way to the stress relief traditionally on offer on the **Zeedijk** ㊶. (Perhaps that is why "doing the St. Nicolas" became standard local slang for the engaging in the sex act.) Before turning left onto the Zeedijk, you may want to note that walking straight would connect you with the **Warmoesstraat** or that making a quick right would allow you to pay tribute to that melancholic sailor of jazz notes, Chet Baker, the crooning trumpet player, who made his final decrescendo from a window of the Prins Hendrick Hotel (Prins Hendrikkade 53) in 1988 and where now a brass plaque commemorates this adopted native son and junkie. While walking up the infamous Zeedijk, dart up the side canal Oudezijds Kolk for a gander at the famous landmark **Schreierstoren** ㊷, from where Henry Hudson began his journey that would lead him to New Amsterdam (the island otherwise known as Manhattan).

Zeedijk is capped by the square of **Nieuwmarkt** ㊸, with the evocatively turreted De Waag as its medieval centerpiece. While the religiously named streets to the right, Monnikenstraat and Bloedstraat (Monk and Blood streets), will ironically lead you to the carnal heart of the **Red Light District,** the more culturally inclined should proceed to the opposite side of the square, and head straight up the left side of Kloveniersburgwal to the **Trippenhuis** ㊹, the grand Trip House mansion. At the next intersection, on the southwest corner with Oude Hoogstraat, is the Oost Indische Huis, the former offices of the East India Trading Company, which once smelled of exotic spices but now, as part of the University of Amsterdam, exudes more with the fevered sweat of political science students. You might want to pop into its richly ornate courtyard, accessible via Oude Hoogstraat 24, where sailors once came to sign up for voyages. Continuing straight down Kloveniersburgwal's left bank, cross the first bridge to the right, perhaps pausing to browse through the many excellent English-language books on offer at the Book Exchange (Kloveniersburgwal 58), before proceeding straight down Rusland. For a sense of some traditional religion, make the first right down Oudezijds Achterburgwal to No. 185, the **Spinhuis,** once the location of the Convent of 11,000 Virgins. After circling this building via the small alleys that surround it, return to Rusland and cross the bridge on the right. Proceed straight down Sint Agnietenstraat, where you can make a right down Oudezijds Voorburgwal, following the curved Amsterdam School wall with its myth-drenched sculptures, past the entrance of Café Roux with its Karel Appel mural in its entrance way, and then right into the entrance of the courtyard belonging to the historically dense **Grand Hotel.** Under the name Prinsenhof, this acted as a City Hall between 1652 and 1655 and 1808 and 1988 and has welcomed such illustrious guests as William the Orange.

Backtracking up Oudezijds Voorburgwal—a length known in the 16th century as the "Velvet Canal" for the excessive wealth of its inhabitants— will lead you past the **Universiteitsmuseum de Agnietenkapel** ㊺, or University Museum's Agnieten Chapel. A short jaunt to the left lets you cross another bridge; staying to the left, take the archway almost immediately on the right, which will lead you through sliding glass doors into the covered book market Oudemanhuispoort, where trading has occurred since 1757. After browsing through this now more youth-oriented corridor—this is the heart of the University of Amsterdam—turn right down Kloveniersburgwal, where almost immediately you must choose to turn left over a drawbridge down Staalstraat, a relentlessly scenic specialty-shopping street and favored filming location, which will lead you to **Waterlooplein** ㊻ flea market.

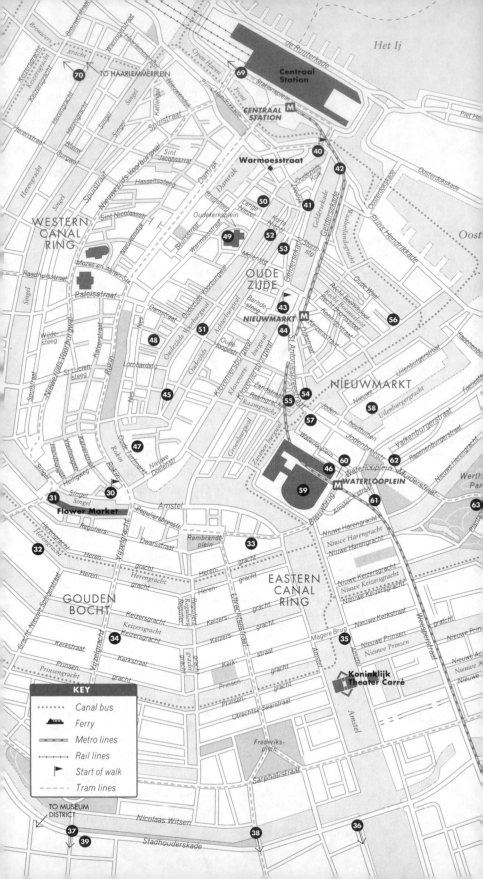

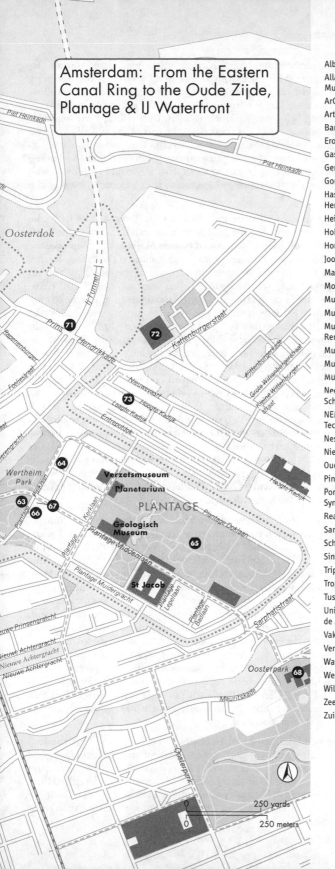

Amsterdam: From the Eastern Canal Ring to the Oude Zijde, Plantage & IJ Waterfront

The second drawbridge you will come across was raised during Occupation to cut off the Jews from the rest of the city. After this northerly diversion head back south and westward the way you came to follow Nieuwe Doelenstraat, at whose entrance on the left is a beige-and-red-brick building belonging to Hotel Doelen. Until 1882, there existed a tower dating from 1481 that was part of a fortification wall to defend the city from potential hoards from Utrecht. This tower also acted as the meeting—and imbibing—place for city soldiers who in 1630 asked Rembrandt to paint a portrait of them that they could employ as wall decoration, a bit of interior enhancement that became known as the *Night Watch*.

Continuing straight past the chic Grand Café Jaren on the left, take the right, before crossing the bridge over the canal, down Oude Turfmarkt past the archaeological **Allard Pierson Museum** ❹. Then take the first right down Langebrugsteeg, to the entrance on the left to the theatrical and the old Spinoza stomping ground of the **Nes** ❹, where on the corner you may want to pause to see what's on offer at the Appenzeller Gallery, a contemporary jewelry and design hot spot. Following the Nes will eventually connect you with the city's main square, the **Dam.** Here, cross the street and take the first alley, Pijlsteeg, to the right running alongside the nearest side of Hotel Krasnapolsky. Between the two sliding glass doors is the entrance, to the left, to the eerily peaceful and green courtyard of Wynand Fockink, where you can stop for a sandwich or a coffee. You may instead choose to pass through the second set of sliding doors to get to its sister establishment, Wynand Fockink Proeflokaal, an ancient "Tasting Local" and distillery (check out those oak caskets through the windows of No. 41) where one can indulge in a startling array of Dutch Courage in preparation for the full dose of Red Light awaiting you at the end of the alley along the Oudezijds Voorburgwal. Turning left down here will have you reaching the reassuringly religious **Oude Kerk** ❹ in no time, beyond which lies the **Museum Amstelkring** ❺ and its celebrated "Our Lord in the Attic" chapel—a must-see for art lovers.

If you want a more leisurely—but no less scholarly—cruise of humanity's darker sides, turn right then immediately left down Oude Doelenstraat to reach Oudezijds Voorburgwal's parallel canal, Oudezijds Achterburgwal, on which you turn left. Sticking to the left bank of this canal will have you passing such unique institutions as the **Hash Marijuana Hemp Museum** ❺; the infamous Casa Rosa nightclub at No. 106-8 (some can't resist posing for a photo in front of the rotating balls of its rather suggestive marble fountain, making sure they include the *krul,* or "curve," a green and aesthetically curved public urinal directly across the canal); and the **Erotic Museum** ❺. If bicycle-powered dildos and other amazing arcana are not your thing, you may forgo the last institution— and the lore-rich erotic "theater," **Bananenbar** ❺, across from it—and take the faithful escape route right before it to the left, Oude Kennissteeg. "Old Friend Alley" will have you praying for your sins at the Oude Kerk in a matter of seconds, although straight beyond which lies the tourist strip of Warmoesstraat.

TIMING   This tour will take two to three hours. If you want to enjoy the Red Light District's namesake lighting, mid- to late afternoon might be a good time to start. Such religious institutions as the Oude Kerk and Museum Amstelkring are closed for services on Sunday morning. The Allard Pierson Museum is closed Monday, and you should also note that the more "fringe" museums start and end their days somewhat later than most public museums.

Sights to See

㊼ Allard Pierson Museum. Once the repository of the nation's gold supply, no less, this former National Bank is now home to other treasures. Behind its stern Neoclassical facade, dynamite helped remove the safes and open up the space for the archaeological collection of the University of Amsterdam in 1934. The museum traces the early development of Western civilization, from the Egyptians to the Romans, and of the Near Eastern cultures (Anatolia, Persia, Palestine) in a series of well-documented displays. While in general it's not exactly a roller-coaster ride, the museum's Egyptian section is particularly well done, with scale models of pyramids, some rather gruesome mummies that look as if they escaped from a B-movie studio lot, and computers that translate your name into hieroglyphics. ⊠ *Oude Turfmarkt 127, Oude Zijde* ☎ *020/525–2556* ⊕ *www.uba.uva.nl/apm* ⊠ *€4.30* ⊙ *Tues.–Fri. 10–5, weekends 1–5.*

㊼ Bananenbar (Banana Bar). Since the 1970s, this ultimately sleazy bar has featured naked barmaids doing tricks "without hands" that use up more than 30 pounds of bananas per evening—impressive, but not exactly something that warrants landmark site status. However, certain events in the 1980s form an "only in Amsterdam" story. The owner at the time realized since Amsterdam had been defined by religious tolerance for centuries that he could circumvent the problems of impending taxation and a lapsed drinking license by registering as a religion. So he decided to recast the bar as the Church of Satan. By 1988, however, when the church was claiming a membership of 40,000, the tax man was finally motivated enough to seek a loophole. Before legal action could be taken, the owner liquidated the businesses and flew to warmer climes. Under a new owner, the bar returned to its sleazy—and taxable—roots. ⊠ *Oudezijds Achterburgwal 137, Oude Zijde.*

㊼ Erotic Museum. "Five floors of highly suggestive trinkets and photos" is probably a better description than "museum." If you're in a when-in-Rome mood, you may want to choose to visit here. Happily, it is all presented rather lightheartedly (although animal lovers should steer clear of the snapshot gallery). Beatles' fans should note that there is an original and satisfyingly suggestive sketch by John Lennon, perhaps rendered when he and Yoko did their weeklong bed-in for peace at the Hilton. Camp fans should note that there is a rich collection dedicated to the leather-clad 1950s muse and proto-dominatrix Betty Page. ⊠ *Oudezijds Achterburgwal 54, Oude Zijde* ☎ *020/624–7303* ⊠ *€5* ⊙ *Sun., Mon., and Thurs. 11 AM–1 AM; Fri. and Sat. 11 AM–2 AM.*

㊼ Hash Marijuana Hemp Museum. One would think that some more effort could have gone into the name of this institution—lateral thinking being one of the positive effects of its subject. But regardless, here's your chance to suck back the 8,000-year history of hemp use. The use of pot as medicine was first recorded in The Netherlands in 1554 as a cure for earaches. By this time, its less potent form, hemp, had long been used—as it would until the late 19th century—as the fiber source for rope and hence was fundamental to the economics of this seafaring town. Besides elucidating certain points in history, a variety of displays educates one on such things as smuggling and joint-rolling techniques. A cultivation zone offers handy hints to the green thumb in your family. And, predictably, there's an endless collection of bongs from around the world. ⊠ *Oudezijds Achterburgwal 148, Oude Zijde* ☎ *020/623–5961* ⊠ *€6* ⊙ *Daily 11–10.*

㊼ Museum Amstelkring ("Our Lord in the Attic" Museum). With its elegant gray-and-white facade and spout gable, this appears to be just another canal house, and on the lower floors it is. The attic, however, of this building contains something unique: the only surviving *schuilkerken* (clandestine church) that dates from the Reformation in Amsterdam, when open worship by Catholics was outlawed. Since the Oude Kerk was then relieved of its original patron, St. Nicholas, when it was de-catholicized, this became the church dedicated to him until the Sint Nico-laaskerk was built. The chapel itself is a triumph of Dutch classicist taste, with magnificent marble columns, gilded capitals, a colored-marble altar, and the *Baptism of Christ* (1716) painting by Jacob de Wit presiding over all. Services and weddings are still offered here, so consider attending a Sunday service in this, one of Amsterdam's most beautiful houses of worship.

The grandeur continues throughout the house, which was renovated by merchant Jan Hartan between 1661 and 1663. Even the kitchen and chaplain bedroom remain furnished in the style of the age, while the drawing room, or *sael,* looks as if it were plucked from a Vermeer paint-ing. With its gold chandelier and Solomonic columns, it's one of the most impressive 17th-century rooms left in Amsterdam. Besides boast-ing other canvases by Thomas de Keyser, Jan Wynants, and Abraham de Vries, the house also displays impressive collections of church sil-ver and sculptures. ⊠ *Oudezijds Voorburgwal 40, Oude Zijde* ☎ *020/ 624–6604* ⊕ *www.museumamstelkring.nl* ⊠ *€6* ☉ *Mon.–Sat. 10–5, Sun. 1–5.*

48 **Nes.** Originating as a boggy walkway along the Amstel River when Am-sterdam was an ever sinking fishing village, the Nes is now a refresh-ingly quiet corridor filled with theaters. At the end of the 14th century, the Nes began evolving into a long strip of monasteries and convents before the Altercation of 1578 (or Protestant takeover) saw their even-tual decline as Amsterdam became more concerned with commercial pur-suits and as it marched toward its Golden Age. The Nes's spiritual life—which had largely made way for tobacco storage and processing—had a slight renaissance when the philosopher Spinoza (1623–77) moved here to escape the derision he was receiving from his own Jewish com-munity for having fused Jewish mysticism with Descartian logic, con-cluding that body and soul were part of the same essence. While the still-existing Frascati theater (Nos. 59–65) began life as a coffeehouse in the 18th century, it was not until the 1880s that the Nes began to bloom with cafés filled with dance, song, and operetta performances; stars often represented the less uptight segment of the Jewish commu-nity. ⊠ *Between Langebrugsteeg and Dam, Oude Zijde.*

need a break?

As to be expected from a theatrical neighborhood, the Nes offers some prime drinking holes, which also offer the option of a lingering meal. Fans of Belgian beer should certainly stop at the patio of **De Brakke Grond** (⊠ Nes 43, Oude Zijde ☎ 020/626–0044), part of the Flemish Cultural Center, to partake in one or two of the dozens of options. Coincidentally, on the "Prayer with End" alley, which runs parallel to Nes's south end, is **Captain Zeppos** (⊠ Gebed Zonder End 5, Oude Zijde ☎ 020/624–2057), which is named after a '60s Belgian TV star; this former cigar factory is soaked with jazzy old-world charm.

43 **Nieuwmarkt** (New Market). Home to the striking Waag gatehouse—where Rembrandt came to watch Professor Tulp in action prior to painting *The Anatomy Lesson*—and also some of the most festive holiday celebra-tions in town, the Nieuwmarkt has been a marketplace since the 15th century. In those days, De Waag—or Sint Antoniespoort (St. Anthony's Port) as it was then known—formed a gateway in the city defenses. It was not until 17th-century expansion that the present form of Nieuw-markt was established and farmers from the province of Noord-Holland began setting up stalls to make it a bustling daily market. The **Kruidenwinkel van Jacob Hooy & Co.** (✉ Kloveniersburgwal 12, Oude Zijde), Amsterdam's oldest medicinal herb and spice shop, and a small row of vegetable stalls are the only vague reminders of those times.

Before the 1796 Civil Liberties Act, when Jews were restricted from most trades, many took up street entertainment and Nieuwmarkt evolved into a favored location for many fairs and circuses complete with acrobat, horse, and freak shows. Nieuwmarkt still maintains these festive roots, especially on Chinese New Year, as the area forms the heart of the city's modestly sized Chinatown (that is, until New China Town, envisioned as a mini-Singapore, arises in the next years to the east of Centraal Station), which extends down Zeedijk and Binnen Bantammerstraat. The community originates from a 1911 seafarers' strike that motivated the hiring of Chinese sailors from England and Hong Kong. Many more came via Suriname after its 1975 independence from Dutch colonial rule. A slightly more curious celebration is the medieval-rooted Hartjes Dag ("Heart Day") in August, which involves that holy trinity of alcohol, firecrackers, and cross-dressing. Suffering a decline in recent decades, it is now experiencing a renaissance since being embraced by the city's ever-growing transvestite population.

The **Waag** (Weighing House) in the center of the square was built in 1488 (as can be attested by the stone tablet emblazoned with MCCC-CLXXXVIII, placed on the small tower facing Geldersekade) and functioned as a city gate, Sint Antoniespoort, until the early 17th century. During those centuries, the gate would be closed at exactly 9:30 PM to keep out not only the bandits but also the poor and the diseased who built shantytowns outside the wall. When the city expanded, it began a second life as a weighing house for incoming products—in particular such heavier goods as tobacco bales, ship artillery and anchors—after a renovation added a tower and covered the inner courtyard. The top floor of the building came to accommodate the municipal militia and several guilds, including the masons who did the evocative decorations that grace each of the towers' entrances. One of its towers housed a teaching hospital for the academy of surgeons of the Surgeons' Guild. The Theatrum Anatomicum (Anatomy Theater) with its cupola tower covered in painted coats of arms (many of which disconcertingly reflect many of the doctors' original trade as barbers), was the first place in The Netherlands to host public dissections. For obvious reasons, these only took place in winter. It was here that Rembrandt sketched Professor Tulp in preparation to paint his great *Anatomy Lesson*. The good professor procured his bodies from those hanged on the southeast side of the Waag. The surgeons must have mourned the coming of the guillotine during the reign of King Louis Napoléon—a time that saw the Waag's importance as weighing house increase when the one on the Dam was cleared to improve the king's view from his palace. Now the building is occupied by a café-restaurant with free Internet service and the **Society for Old and New Media** (⊕ www.waag.org). How things have changed. ✉ *Bounded by Kloveniersburgwal, Geldersekade, and Zeedijk, Oude Zijde.*

need a break?

You may want to sniff out your own favorite among the many café-restaurants that line this square. Many will opt for the historic **In de Waag** (✉ Nieuwmarkt, Oude Zijde ☎ 020/422–7772), which highlights its epic medieval roots with candlelight. An arty and studenty option is **Lokaal 't Loosje** (✉ Nieuwmarkt 32–34, Oude

Zijde ☎ 020/627–2635), which is graced with tile tableaux dating from 1912. Fans of more traditional jazz should check out the legendary **Cotton Club** (✉ Nieuwmarkt 5, Oude Zijde ☎ 020/626–6192), named after its original owner, the Surinamese trumpet player Teddy Cotton.

㊾ Oude Kerk (Old Church). The Oude Kerk is indeed Amsterdam's oldest church and has been surrounded by all the garnishing and offerings of humanity's oldest trade (i.e. prostitution) for the vast majority of its history—a history that has seen it chaotically evolve from single-nave chapel to hall church to a cross basilica. It began as a wooden chapel in 1306 but was built for the ages between 1366 and 1566 (and fully restored between 1955 and 1979) when the whole neighborhood was rife with monasteries and convents.

As a Catholic church dedicated to St. Nicholas (a forgiving sort who was relaxed enough also to offer patronage to salacious sailors and fallen women), it changed denomination during the Reformation when its furnishings were removed by the Iconoclasts—whose arms fortunately could neither reach the 14th-century paintings still visible on its wooden roof (which had already miraculously survived the city fires of 1421 and 1452), nor the Virgin Mary stained-glass windows that had been set in place in 1550. But it did also lose its nickname as the city's "living room" where beggars and the homeless (and, one suspects, those who had squandered their cash in sins of the flesh) could sleep. When it finally settled to become Reformed in the 17th century, it became yet more sober, to be only slightly more balanced with the extravagant placing of its famed Vater-Muller organ. Among its many haphazard side buildings is the Bridal Chamber—whose door wisely warns: "Marry in Haste, Mourn in Leisure"—through which Rembrandt entered to marry Saskia. As it turns out, Saskia was later buried here under the small organ; Rembrandt tried to sell her plot when he was broke. Oude Kerk's haphazard evolution continues unabated: it is now a wholly unique exhibition space for modern art exhibitions and the annual World Press Photo competition. Its carillon gets played every Saturday between 4 and 5. ✉ *Oudekerksplein 23, Oude Zijde* ☎ *020/625–8284* ⊕ *www.oudekerk.nl* 🎫 €4 ⊙ *Mon.–Sat. 11–5, Sun. 1–5.*

★ ㊷ Schreierstoren (Weeping Tower). Famous as the point from which Hendrik Hudson set sail to America, this is Amsterdam's most distinctive fortress tower. Although today this tower's innards host a rather frolicsome marine-theme jazz café, it began its life in 1486 as the end point of the city wall. The term *schreien* suggests the Dutch word for "wailing," and hence the folklore arose that this "Weeping Tower" was where women came to cry when their sailor husbands left for sea and cry again when they did not return (perhaps followed by the short walk to the Red Light District to begin life as a merry widow?). But the word *schreier* actually comes from an Old Dutch word for a "sharp corner"—and, indeed, the building's rounded harbor face, which looks over the old **Oosterdok** (Eastern Dock), forms a sharp corner with its straight street face. A plaque on the building tells you that it was from this location that Henry Hudson set sail on behalf of the Dutch East India Company to find a shorter route to the East Indies. In his failure, he came across Canada's Hudson's Bay in Canada and later—continuing his bad-luck streak—New York harbor and the Hudson River. ✉ *Prins Hendrikkade 94–95, Oude Zijde.*

⊩ ㊵ Sint Nicolaaskerk (St. Nicholas Church). The architect A. C. Bleys designed this church, built in 1887, with its dark and eerie interior as a replacement to all the clandestine Catholic churches that arose during the Protestant times. Following in the footsteps of first Oude Kerk and then Museum Amstelkring's "Our Lord in the Attic" chapel, this church became the third and most likely final (unless those darned Calvinists take over again) Sint Nicolaas church. St. Nick (or Sinter Klaas as he is called here), patron saint of children, thieves, prostitutes, sailors, and the city of Amsterdam, arrived with the Catholic church. The eve of his birthday on December 6 is still celebrated as a mellow family feast where everyone exchanges self-made presents and poems. "Sinter Klaas" mutated when he went to the New World and eventually become drawled out as "Santa Claus"; his day shifted to December 25 to synergize with the feast day of Christ. Although the spirit of gross revenue is making its presence felt in Amsterdam, thanks to the efforts of department stores, Christmas remains a more purely religious holiday here. Note that the church hosts a Gregorian chant vesper service September to June on Sunday at 5. ⊠ *Prins Hendrikkade 76, Oude Zijde* ☎ *020/624–8749* ⌨ *Free* ⊙ *Mon.–Sat. 11–4 (when possible).*

★ ㊹ **Trippenhuis** (Trip House). As family home to the two Trip brothers, who made their fortune in gun dealing during the 17th-century Golden Age, this noted house's buckshot-gray exterior and various armament motifs—including a mortar-shape chimney—are easily explained. But what is most distinctive about this building is that its Corinthian-columned facade actually hides two symmetrical buildings (note the wall that bisects the middle windows), one for each brother. It went on in the 18th century to house both the Rijksmuseum collection and the Royal Dutch Academy of Sciences before the latter became its sole resident. Be sure to look across the canal to No. 26, the door-wide white building topped with golden sphinxes and the date of 1696, which is known as both the "Little Trip House" and the "House of Mr. Trip's Coachman." The story goes that the smarty-pants coachman once remarked that he would be happy with a house as wide as the Trippenhuis door; not to be out smarted, Mr. Trip went on to build just that with the leftover bricks. Or so the story goes; the Little Trip House is actually much bigger than it looks, and its completion date was long after either brother died. ⊠ *Kloveniersburgwal 29, Oude Zijde.*

㊺ **Universiteitsmuseum de Agnietenkapel** (University Museum Agnieten Chapel). One of Amsterdam's only surviving medieval convents, this Gothic chapel was built in the 1470s. However, it has been emphasizing the secular since 1632, when it became part of the original University of Amsterdam, and thereby rates as the country's oldest lecture hall. Imagine bringing an apple to the likes of Vossius and Barlaeus, two greatly celebrated Renaissance scholars who both taught here. The grand interior solemnly sports stained-glass windows, an impressive Renaissance ceiling painting, and more than 40 paintings of humanists, including everyone's favorite, Erasmus. A renovation around 1919 saw the introduction of some elements of the Amsterdam School to its exterior. ⊠ *Oudezijds Voorburgwal 231, Oude Zijde* ☎ *020/525–3339* ⌨ *Free* ⊙ *Mon.–Sat. 9–5.*

Warmoesstraat. This densely touristic strip of hostels, bars, and coffee shops began life as one of the original dikes along the Amstel before evolving into the city's richest shopping street (a sharp contrast to its fallen sister, Zeedijk). Imagine, if you will, the famous 17th-century poet Vondel doing business from his hosiery shop at No. 101 or Mozart's dad trying to unload tickets for his son's concert in the posh bars. It entered a decline in the 17th century when the proprietors forsook their above-store lodgings for the posher ones arising on the canal ring; sailors and their caterers started to fill in the gaps. In the 19th century, it evolved, along with its extension Nes, into the city's primary drinking and frolicking zone. Karl Marx was known to set himself up regularly in a hotel here not only to write in peace but to have the option to ask for a loan from his cousin-in-law, Gerard Philips, founder of that capitalist machine Philips. Thanks to a recent revamp, Warmoesstraat is beginning to lose some of its Sodom and Gomorrah edge. Between the cynical tourist traps, there are some rather hip hangouts like the Hotel Winston; worthwhile specialty stores, such Geels and Co. (No. 67), with its infinite selection of coffees and teas; or the equally complete selection of condoms at the Condomerie Het Gulden Vlies (No. 141)—and even a squatted gallery, the beautifully spacious W139 (No. 139), dedicated to the very outer edges of conceptual art. ⊠ *Between Dam and Nieuwe Brugsteeg, Oude Zijde.*

46 **Waterlooplein.** Before its rezoning, this flea market, named after the famous battle, was a swampy neighborhood, bordered by the Leper and Peat canals, that often took the brunt of an overflowing Amstel River and hence housed only the poorest of Jews. In 1886 it became the daily market for the surrounding Jewish neighborhood—a necessity, since Jews were not allowed to own shops. It became a meeting place whose chaos of wooden carts and general vibrancy disappeared along with the Jewish population during World War II. And yet it still provides a colorful glimpse into Amsterdam's particular brand of pragmatic sales techniques. Its stalls filled with clothes, bongs, discarded electronics, and mountains of Euro-knickknacks can sometimes indeed be a battle—albeit a more than worthwhile one—to negotiate. ⊠ *Waterlooplein, Oude Zijde* ◷ *Weekdays 9–5, Sat. 8:30–5:30.*

41 **Zeedijk.** Few streets have had a longer or more torrid history; until recently known as the Black Hole of Amsterdam (due to its concentration of drug users), the Zeedijk is now on the up and up. As the original dam created to keep the sea at bay, Zeedijk has been around since Amsterdam began life as a fishing hamlet. The building of this dike in 1380 probably represented the first twitchings of democracy in these parts as individual fishing and farming folks were united to make battle with that pesky sea. Less noble democratic forces saw it quickly specialize in the entertaining of sailors—a service it ended up providing for centuries. A more bohemian edge came into the mix last century when it provided a mecca for world-class jazz musicians who came to jam in its small clubs and cafés after their more official gigs in the Concertgebouw. One of the more popular was the still-existing Casablanca (No. 26), which regularly saw the likes of local heroes as Kid Dynamite and Teddy Cotton and more international names as Erroll Garner, Gerry Mulligan, and Count Basie. However, other, more dingy dens began a lucrative sideline in heroin. By the 1970s, the area had become known throughout the country for its concentration of drug traffickers, where the only tourists were those attached to heavily guided "criminal safaris." But recently Zeedijk has gone through a radical gentrification. While certainly not sterile of its past, it's now much easier to accept the stray, dubious-looking character as merely part of the street's scenery as opposed to its definition.

As if to tell a tale of rebirth, the first building on the right is the **Sint Olofskapel** (St. Olaf Church), named after the patron saint of dikes, St. Odulphus. This 17th-century structure sports a life-affirming sculpture: grains growing out of a prone skeleton (verily, in times of yore this is what passed for a positive message). After the Altercation, it began a long history of varying functions. Today, it's a convention hall attached by an underground passage to the Golden Tulip Barbizon Palace Hotel on Prins Hendrikkade.

Across the street at No. 1 is one of only two timbered houses left in the city. It does have stone sides—as law dictated after the great fires of 1421 and 1452, the latter of which destroyed a full three-quarters of the town. Dating from around 1550, **in't Aephen** ("In the Monkeys") provided bedding to destitute sailors if they promised to return from their next voyage with a monkey. It worked: it was soon filled with monkeys and their accompanying lice. And to this day if someone is caught scratching his head, the folk response is "You've been staying with the monkeys." The way each floor sticks slightly more outward than the one below it accounts for the way most of Amsterdam's brick buildings lean forward: they were built aesthetically to follow this line (to ape the wooden architectural forms that preceded). An added bonus was that goods being hoisted into upper floors would not hit the windows. When you walk onward, note the first alley on the right, Sint Olofssteeg, which looks down on the "House on Three Alleys," and the way it goes—for Amsterdam's standards anyway—plummeting downward and hence illustrating Zeedijk's roots as dike.

Café Maandje at No. 65 evokes the 1930s when the first openly gay drinking and dancing dens in the city began popping up here. Its window maintains a shrine to its former proprietor and the spiritual forbearer of lesbian biker babes everywhere: Bet van Beeren (1902–67). While the café opens only on the rarest of occasions, a model of its interior can be viewed at the Amsterdams Historisch Museum. The rest of the street is a quirky mixture of middle-range Asian restaurants, brown cafés with carpeted tables, specialty shops and galleries, and the occasional Chinese medicinal shop. The Chinese community is in full visual effect at the end of the street, where recently the gloriously colorful pagoda-shape **Fo Kuang Shan Buddhist Temple** (No. 118) arose.
⊠ *Oudezijds Kolk (near Centraal Station) to Nieuwmarkt, Oude Zijde.*

> **need a break?** Zeedijk offers some of the best quick snack/meal stops in town. The most revered is auspiciously placed across from the Buddhist Temple: **Nam Kee** (⊠ Zeedijk 111–113, Oude Zijde ☎ 020/624–3470) is a speedy and cheap Chinese spot whose steamed oysters are so sublime that they provided the title and muse for a local author's novel. The ultimate Dutch snack, raw herring, can be enjoyed at the fresh-fish shop **Huijsmans Cock** (⊠ Zeedijk 129, Oude Zijde ☎ 020/624–2070), which also offers much less controversial options for its deliciously nutty whole wheat buns.

East of the Amstel:
From the Jewish Quarter to the Plantage

While Amsterdam has been Calvinist, Protestant, and Catholic for varying chunks of its history, it has been continuously considered a Jerusalem Junior of sorts by migrating populations of Jews from the medieval to the modern era. In fact, the city came to be known as Mokum (the Hebrew word for place), as in *the* place for Jews. And when the Jewish population arrived, so did much of Amsterdam's color and glory. Just witness the legendary diamond trade and feast your eyes upon Rembrandt's *Jewish Bride* in the Rijksmuseum, just one of many canvases the artist painted when, searching for inspiration and Old Testament ambience, he deliberately set up a luxurious household near the heart of the Jewish Quarter.

Since the 15th century, this area has traditionally been considered the district east of the Zwanenburgwal. The Quarter got its start thanks to the Inquisition, which was extremely efficient in motivating many Sephardic Jews to leave Spain in 1492. Over the next hundred years, their descendants slowly found their way to Amsterdam, where they could reestablish a semblance of their traditional lifestyle. The war with Spain inspired the 1597 Union of Utrecht, which, while formulated to protect Protestants from the religious oppression that came with Spanish invasions, essentially meant that all religions were tolerated. This provided a unique experience for the Jews, for here, unlike elsewhere in Europe, they were not forced to wear badges and live in ghettos. They were still, however, restricted—just like all the other non-Calvinists—from joining guilds and being registered as tradesmen. The only exceptions were in the up-and-coming trades where no guild Mafia had arisen, such as diamond cutting and polishing, sugar-refining, silk-weaving, and printing. These slim advantages also helped attract many Yiddish-speaking Ashkenazis Jews from Eastern Europe escaping pogroms. The 17th-century Golden Age and the rise of the capitalist saw the weakening of the hard-core Calvinist grip on daily life, and only the Catholics remained barred from open worship. This accounts for the existence of 17th-century synagogues in the city and not of Catholic churches. Rembrandt came to the neighborhood at this time to take advantage of the proximity of all the "biblical faces" that he could employ in his religious paintings.

But it was only in 1796, inspired by the ideals of the French Revolution, that the guilds were finally banned and equal rights instilled. However, while there were always many rich Jewish merchants, poverty was still the essential lot of most Jews until the end of the 19th century, when the rise of the diamond industry meant the spreading of the community away from the old Jewish Quarter. By 1938, 10% of Amsterdam's population was Jewish and had long ingrained their influence into the city's psyche (however, the charm factor of one instance where core supporters of the Ajax football team have long called and cast themselves as "Jews" was subverted when their archenemies, Rotterdam-supporters, started casting themselves as "Palestinians") and into its slang (the Yiddish word *mazzel,* meaning "luck," remains a standard farewell). What remains much more painfully ingrained in the city's psyche, however, is what happened during the Nazi occupation when the Jewish population was reduced to one-seventh of its size. While there were many examples of bravery and the opening of homes to hide Jews, there are many more—and less often told—stories of collaboration. While the current Jewish population has risen to 20,000, they are now generally dispersed throughout the city, and it is really only the monuments that speak.

Thanks to the devastation of the war and later the demolition to make room for the Stadhuis/Muziektheater (City Hall/Music Theater) and the metro, the neighborhood is marked by a somewhat schizophrenic hodge-podge of the old and new. The enjoining and more residential **Plantage** neighborhood to the east, which began as a sort of recreation park for the rich before houses for them arose in the 19th century, with its wide boulevards offers a more cogent and restful atmosphere.

a good walk

While trying to imagine the original 17th-century housing, walk east up Sint Antoniebreestraat from **Nieuwmarkt** ㊸ ➤, which had been left as a ghost town for years after the Occupation (before experiencing a slight renaissance as a squatters' paradise but then finally getting razed in 1980 to make way for the metro). One ancient exception remains at Sint Antoniebreestraat 69, the Italian Renaissance–style **Pintohuis** ㊺, a magisterial mansion built in the 17th century, with an opulent interior on view (the house is now a public library).

Across the street lies one of the neighborhood's few wholly successful infusions of modernity, the Theo Bosch–designed Pentagon Apartments, where to its right between No. 130 and 132, one can gain access through a skull and crossbones–adorned gateway to the courtyard of the **Zuiderkerk** ⑤⑤, the "Southern Church"; here you can climb its 17th-century tower—certainly one of the most picturesque in all Holland—or see models of Amsterdam's many future building projects. Linger on the bridge where Sint Antoniebreestraat turns into Jodenbreestraat, where to the left beside the disconcertingly crooked café, one can take in the view down Oudeschans toward the harbor. The ancient tower on the left is the **Montelbaanstoren** ⑤⑥, where sailors departed and refugees arrived in small boats that acted as ferries to and from the larger ships anchored in the IJ; this picturesque sight was one of Rembrandt's favorite sketching subjects. Beyond lies a modern green copper building that suggests a sinking *Titanic*: the science and technology museum NEMO (covered in depth in our last neighborhood section, below). Turning around, you see across the street some stairs leading down to the **Waterlooplein** flea market. The first café-outfitted building on the left corner (Jodenbreestraat 2) is marked with the Hebrew date of 5649 (1889) and adorned with caryatids doing Atlas's dirty work. The house that previously stood here was rented to the art dealer Hendrick Uylenburg, who ran a painting school to which a fresh-faced Rembrandt became aligned when newly arrived from Leiden. Rembrandt ended up becoming much more aligned with Uylenburg's niece Saskia; he married her and eventually bought the red-shuttered house next door, today the famous **Museum het Rembrandthuis** ⑤⑦, where he spent his salad days.

Ignore the entrance to the Holland Experience—unless, of course, a certain herb inspires you to take in a 3-D tour of Holland's stereotypes—to the left of Rembrandt's former digs and continue down Jodenbreestraat to take the first left after the brutally modern vastness that houses the Amsterdam Academy of Arts' Dance and Theater School, down Nieuwe Uilenburgerstraat. Along this street one can visit the 1879-established **Gassan Diamonds** ⑤⑧ at No. 173–75, which once hummed with 357 diamond grinders and thereby was a major employer in the neighborhood. Farther down at No. 91, one can admire the facade of a former synagogue that was built in 1766. A straight backtrack will get you to the flea market Waterlooplein. The white building looming ahead is the multitask city hall–music theater, **Muziektheater/Stadhuis** ⑤⑨. After absorbing the surrounding chaos of carpets and stalls filled with vintage clothing and Euro-knickknacks, exit Waterlooplein via its northeast corner, where you can cross the street at the imposing church Moses and Aaronkerk—this structure once had a warehouse facade to disguise its function as a clandestine Catholic church. If this rarely used church could speak it would name-drop the great philosopher Spinoza (for it was built on the location of his birth house) and Liszt (for it hosted a recital of his that he considered his all-time best). More contemporary visions can be gleaned once you cross the street at the modern architecture gallery **ArCam** ⑥⓪, located a few doors to the right of the crosswalk. Continue toward the upcoming bridge, **Blauwbrug**, to admire the view down the Amstel River. The "Blue Bridge," built in 1883, was named after its predecessor, a blue wooden bridge, so don't be distressed if it lacks its namesake color. Disconcerting is the fact that during Nazi occupation it was tangled in barbed wire in order to isolate the Jewish Quarter.

Turning back, take the forking street to the right, Nieuwe Amstelstraat, a walking street where disused tram tracks will tell you that you are at the entrance to a complex of four synagogues that now form the important **Joods Historisch Museum** ⊙ (Jewish Historical Museum). From here cross the street at Mr. Visserplein—named after a Jewish resistance leader (and now sporting a surreal children's playground called Tun-Fun underneath it)—toward the rows of tiny houses that form a square around the **Portugees Israelitische Synagoge** ⊙. On the square, to the right, note the statue of Jonas Daniël Meijerplein. This figure of a husky dock worker, popularly known as *De Dokwerker,* commemorates the February Strike of February 25, 1941, when dock and transport workers protested the first *razzia* ("round-up") of Jews with whom they felt united by common union and socialist ideals that had taken hold in the city in the previous decades. Taking Muiderstraat to the left of the synagogue complex, you will soon see the glass structures of the **Hortus Botanicus** ⊙ botanical gardens. Hang left down Parklaan and right down the former diamond mecca of Henri Polaklaan, which is now home to **Vakbondsmuseum** ⊙, the former headquarters of the Diamond Workers Union. The street ends at the **Artis** ⊙ planetarium-zoo, and if you head left you will come to the World War II resistance tricks on display at the excellent **Verzetsmuseum** ⊙ (Resistance Museum).

Reversing back down Plantage Kerklaan and then making a right after crossing Plantage Middenlaan will get you to the **Hollands Schouwburg** ⊙, a former theater that is now a memorial to the Jews collected there to await transportation to their fate in the concentration camps. Reversing to continue east down Plantage Middenlaan will get you to the Plantage Westermanplantsoen park on the right, where there is a war monument for the artists' resistance movement and superhero Gerrit van der Veen, who led a party to destroy the records of the city's registry office and later managed to escape wounded after an attempt to free resistance prisoners from the complex around Max Euweplein. Betrayal two weeks later led to his arrest at his hiding place. Because he wanted to die standing, he was shot with his stretcher held vertical by friends. Continuing on the same route, you will eventually reach the imposing **Tropenmuseum** ⊙ (Tropics Museum) and the picnicking opportunities available in **Oosterpark**—perhaps after picking up supplies at the very multicultural street market on Dapperstraat.

TIMING To see only the buildings along the main route, block out an hour and a half. Detours to the Tropenmuseum will need an extra 20 minutes' traveling time. Museums along this route need at east a 30-minute visit, though Rembrandthuis, the Jewish Historical Museum, and the Tropenmuseum (whose children's section has very specific visiting times) deserve longer. Also note that the Waterlooplein flea market does not operate on Sunday.

Sights to See

⊙ **ArCam.** "Architecture Centrum Amsterdam" is dedicated to the promotion of something very much in vogue: modern Dutch architecture. Besides exhibitions, this association organizes lectures, forums, and excellent tours—including to the new landmarks arising along the Eastern Docklands and the artificial residential island of Ijburg. For anybody who considers architect-cum-philosopher Rem Koolhaas to be the leading prophet of the 21st century, this is a must. A new and nearby exhibition space, all swoopy and silver, at the corner of Prins Hendrikkade and Rapenburgerstraat should be opening at the corner of Prins Hendrikkade and Rapenburgerstraat by early 2004. ⊠ *Waterlooplein 216, Jewish Quarter and Plantage* ☎ *020/620–4878* ⊕ *www.arcam.nl* ⊡ *Free* ☉ *Tues.–Fri. 1–5.*

☺ ⑥⑤ **Artis** (Amsterdam Zoo). Short for Natura Artis Magistra ("Nature Is the Teacher of the Arts"), Artis was mainland Europe's first zoo and rates as the world's third oldest. Built in the mid-19th century, Artis is a 37-acre park that is home to a natural history museum, a zoo with an aviary, a planetarium, and an aquarium. The aquarium does this coastal country proud, with some 500 species on views in both freshwater and saltwater tanks—the highlight may be its evocative cross section of a canal complete with eels and sunken bicycles. As for the zoo proper, a few of its exhibits are cramped but others are long on inspiration, including the toy ruin, where owls can peer out at you as if on sabbatical from a Hieronymus Bosch painting or, for that matter, a Harry Potter book. A recent expansion, including a new restaurant, has made the zoo bigger and better. In short: it's great for kids of all ages. A special Artis Express canal boat from the Centraal Station is a great alternative to getting here. ⊠ *Plantage Kerklaan 40, Jewish Quarter and Plantage* ☎ *020/523–3400* ⊕ *www.artis.nl* ⊠ *€14* ☉ *Zoo Oct.–May, daily 9–5; June–Sept., daily 9–6; planetarium times vary depending on program.*

⑤⑧ **Gassan Diamonds.** When diamonds were discovered in South Africa in 1869 (which, along with the then recent opening of the North Sea Channel, led to a second golden age of sorts for Amsterdam), there was a near immediate windfall for Amsterdam's Jewish community, where one-third of the employable worked in the diamond trade (increased wages meant that children could stay in school longer and that families could move to fancier neighborhoods). Built in 1879, Gassan Diamonds was once home to the Boas diamond-polishing factory, the largest in the world, where 357 diamond-polishing machines were on permanent hum. Its essential high-techness was in sharp contrast to the poverty in the neighborhood that surrounded it. World War II led to Amsterdam's loss of top position of the world diamond market to Antwerp, who largely retained its lower-paid polishing population. Today, Gassan offers polishing and grading demonstrations and free one-hour tours (for which it is best to book ahead) of the building and its glittering collection of diamonds and jewelry. If you yourself want to glitter, book one of the "diamond and champagne" tours. ⊠ *Nieuwe Uilenburgerstraat 173, Jewish Quarter and Plantage* ☎ *020/622–5333* ⊕ *www.gassandiamonds.nl* ⊠ *Free* ☉ *Daily 9–5.*

⑥⑦ **Hollands Schouwburg** (Holland Theater). Between 1892 and 1941, this was *the* theater for Dutch theatrical performances, which came courtesy of such luminaries as writers Herman Heyermans and Esther de Boer-van Rijk and such singer-entertainers as Louis Davids (the "Little Big Man"). In 1941, the Nazis shortly deemed it a Jewish-only theater before deciding in 1942 to use it as a central gathering point for the deportation of the city's Jews, first to the national gathering point of Westerbork and then to concentration camps in Germany. In the end, somewhere between 60,000 and 80,000 human souls passed through here for this purpose. In 1993, the Jewish Historical Museum renovated it to include a memorial room displaying the 6,700 family names of the 104,000 Dutch Jews deported and murdered and an upstairs exhibition room that tells the story of the Occupation through documents, photographs, and videos. But it is the large and silent courtyard that is perhaps this monument's most effective remembrance. ⊠ *Plantage Middenlaan 24, Jewish Quarter and Plantage* ☎ *020/626–9945* ⊕ *www.jhm.nl* ⊠ *Free* ☉ *Daily 11–4.*

★ ⑥③ **Hortus Botanicus.** This wonderful botanical garden was originally laid out as an herb garden for doctors and pharmacists in 1682 (after existing on another location since 1632) before it began collecting exotic plants from the East India Company's foreign fields of plunder. Today it is a labyrinth of ornamental gardens and greenhouses set to a variety of climates (desert, swamp, tropical, and subtropical) where a total of 8,000 species are represented—including one of the oldest potted plants in the world, a 300-year-old Cycas palm. Its café-terrace is one of the most peaceful in the city, and buying a coffee here is *alone* worth the price of admission. In fact, you can add some historical resonance to your sipping with the knowledge that Hortus harbors the descendants of the first coffee plants of Europe. A Dutch merchant stole it from Ethiopia, presented it to Hortus in 1706, which in turn sent a clipping to a botanist in France, who finally saw to it that further clippings reached their end destination of Brazil . . . where an industry was born. ⊠ *Plantage Middenlaan 2a, Jewish Quarter and Plantage* ☎ *020/625–9021* ⊕ *www.hortus-botanicus.nl* ⊠ *€6* ⊙ *Apr.–Sept., weekdays 9–5, weekends 11–5; Oct.–Mar., weekdays 9–4, weekends 11–4.*

61 Joods Historisch Museum (Jewish Historical Museum). Four Ashkenazis synagogues (or *shuls,* as they are called in Yiddish) dating from the 17th and 18th centuries were skillfully combined with glass-and-steel constructions in 1987 into an impressive museum for documents, paintings, and objects related to the four-century history of the Jewish people in Amsterdam and The Netherlands. World War II plunder saw to it that there are limited objects of a priceless and beautiful nature, but the museum is still rich with a collection of unusual objects ranging from the ceremonial to the domestic, from the antique to the modern. Other permanent exhibitions deal with Jewish identity, religion, and social history. One of the highlights of the collection is the autobiographical art of the Berlin artist Charlotte Solomon (1917–43), who documented her life in 1,000 gouaches accompanied with text and music under the title *Leben? oder Theater?* ("Life? or Theater"). The museum also features a resource center and one of the city's few purely kosher cafés. Whether or not you tour the collections, check out the excellent tours of the Jewish Quarter conducted by this museum. Just outside its doors is the market at Waterlooplein, where the Jewish community once thrived, and which hosts the famous flea market, as lively as it was in the 17th century. The current Jewish community itself exists largely beneath the surface of Amsterdam, many of its constituents placing Dutch identity before Judaism. ⊠ *Jonas Daniël Meijerplein 2–4, Jewish Quarter* ☎ *020/ 626–9945* ⊕ *www.jhm.nl* ⊠ *€6.50* ⊙ *Daily 11–5.*

need a break? While in a refreshingly tourist-free zone, why not check out a friendly local brown café? **Eik & Linde** (⊠ Plantage Middenlaan 22, Plantage ☎ 020/622–5716) is one of the archetypal Amsterdam institutions famed for their brown walls, the result of decades of cigarette and pipe smoking by the patrons. This particular place is noted in recent Jewish history as the radio broadcast location where Ischa Meijer, interviewer extraordinaire, conjoined with his many Jewish guests to confront their own personal stories associated with the Holocaust.

★ **56 Montelbaanstoren** (Montelbaans Tower). Rembrandt loved to sketch this slightly leaning tower, which dates from 1516; in those more perpendicular days, it formed part of the city's defenses against raiding hoards of Gelderlanders. City expansion in 1578 saw it connected until 1578 by a defensive wall with the Sint Antoniespoort (De Waag in Nieuwenmarkt). It is traditionally thought to be the spot where the first Jewish refugees from the Inquisition in Spain and Portugal arrived. It was certainly the ferrying point to the sailing ships anchored in the IJ that were set to depart to the East Indies. In 1606, the ubiquitous Hendrick de

Keyser oversaw the building of a new tower complete with clockworks. But time soon saw the tower leaning toward Pisa, and in 1611 it had to be reset with lots of manpower and ropes on a stronger foundation. Since 1878, it has housed the City Water Office, which maintains the water levels in the canals and engineers the nightly flushing of the entire city waterway system, closing and opening the sluices to change the direction of the flow and cleanse the waters (algae and the use of yacht toilets on houseboats make it a thankless job). ⊠ *Oude Schans 2, Jewish Quarter and Plantage.*

57 Museum het Rembrandthuis (Rembrandt's House). One of Amsterdam's more remarkable relics, this house was bought by Rembrandt, flush with success, for his family and is where he lived and worked between 1639 and 1658. Rembrandt chose this house on what was once the main street of the Jewish Quarter because he felt that he could then experience daily and firsthand the faces he would use in his Old Testament religious paintings. Later Rembrandt lost the house to bankruptcy when he fell from popularity following the death of Saskia, his wife. When he showed a quick recovery—and an open taste for servant girls—after her death, his uncle-in-law, once his greatest champion, became his biggest detractor. Rembrandt's downfall was sealed: he came under attack by the Amsterdam burghers, who refused to accept his liaison with his amour, Hendrickje.

Fodor's Choice
★

A recent expansion allowed the house interior to be restored to its original form—complete with one of Rembrandt's printing presses, his rarities collection, and fully stocked studio (which is now even occasionally used by guest artists). The new gallery wing, complete with shop, café, and information center, is the only place in the world where his graphic work is on permanent display—with 250 of the total of 290 prints that are known to came from his hand, including the magisterial "Hundred Guilder" and the "Three Crosses" prints. Rembrandt was almost more revolutionary in his prints than in his paintings, so this collection deserves respectful homage, if not downright devotion, by printmakers today. ⊠ *Jodenbreestraat 4–6, Jewish Quarter* ☎ *020/520–0400* ⊕ *www.rembrandthuis.nl* ⊠ *€7* ☉ *Mon.–Sat. 10–5, Sun. 1–5.*

need a break?

Beware: the slant of **Café Sluyswacht** (⊠ Jodenbreestraat 1, Jewish Quarter ☎ 020/657611) can end up causing nausea after one too many beers on its patio overlooking Oudeschans. For more stable fare, just across the street from askew Café Sluyswacht are the designer sandwiches at **Dantzig** (⊠ Zwanenburgwal 15, Jewish Quarter ☎ 020/620–9039), to be enjoyed either on its patio looking over Waterlooplein or within its modern interior of mosaics.

59 Muziektheater/Stadhuis (Music Theater/Town Hall). Universally known as the Stopera—not just from the combining of "Stadhuis" (Town Hall) and "Opera" but from the radical opposition expressed during its construction—this brick-and-marble complex when viewed from the south resembles, as a local writer once described it, a "set of dentures." Another writer grumbled that its "two for one" nature was a tad too typical for the bargain-loving Dutch. Discontent with this modern complex began before one stone was in place: what began as a squatter protest against the razing of the 16th- and 17th-century houses in the old Jewish Quarter and around Nieuwmarkt to make way for the metro and this Stopera soon gained neighborhood-wide support. Regardless, the 300 million-guilder building was completed. Perhaps as compensation, it actually boasts an impressive interior architecture complete with stunning acoustics. The Muziektheater is now home base for the Nederlands Opera and the National Ballet and the ballet orchestra. It is also a much-favored stage for other internationally renowned touring companies of both classical and avant-garde tendencies. Tours of the backstage areas are run once a week (Saturday at 3) or by prior arrangement. From September to May, the Boekmanzaal is host to a free Tuesday lunch concert.

City Hall provides a rather odd contrast with its municipal offices and now gay couple–friendly wedding chamber (Dutch marriages all must be performed in the Town Hall, with church weddings optional). Also feel free to wander through the interconnecting lobbies, where there is interesting sculpture on display that frighteningly illustrates Amsterdam's position below sea level. ⊠ *Waterlooplein 22, Jewish Quarter* ☏ *020/ 551–8911* ⊕ *www.stopera.nl* ⛩ *Tours €4.50* ⊙ *Mon.–Sat. 10–6; tours Sat. at 3 or by arrangement.*

★ 🔢 **Pintohuis.** This Italian Renaissance–style house was grandly renovated in 1680 by Jewish refugee Isaac de Pinto, a grandee who escaped the Inquisition in Portugal to come to Amsterdam and become one of the founders of the East India Company. Six towering Italianate pilasters break up the impressive facade, remodeled by Elias Bouwman in the 1670s. The Pintohuis's present function as public library allows easy access to admire its lush and historic interior—in particular its cherub-encrusted ceiling painting by Jacob de Wit, the ubiquitous 17th-century master. The building's history and beauty provided another public service in the early 1970s when it was successfully squatted by activists who were protesting its planned removal to make way for the widening of the street. ⊠ *Sint Antoniebreestraat 69, Jewish Quarter* ☏ *020/624–3184* ⛩ *Free* ⊙ *Mon. and Wed. 2–8, Fri. 2–5, Sat. 11–2.*

🔢 **Portugees Israelitische Synagoge** (Portuguese Israelite Synagogue). With Jerusalem's Temple of Solomon as inspiration, Elias Bouwman and Daniel Stalpaert designed this noted synagogue between 1671 and 1675. Its square brick building within a courtyard formed by brick houses was commissioned by the Sephardic Jewish community that had emigrated via Portugal during the preceding two centuries. On its completion it was the largest synagogue in the world, and its spare, elegantly proportioned wood interior has remained virtually unchanged through the centuries. It is still magically illuminated by candles in two immense candelabra during services. The surrounding buildings that form a square around the synagogue house the world-famous Ets Haim ("Tree of Life") library, one of the oldest in the world, and the winter synagogue for use on those draftier days. ⊠ *Mr. Visserplein 3, Jewish Quarter* ☏ *020/ 624–5351* ⛩ *€5* ⊙ *Apr.–Oct., Sun.–Fri. 10–12:30 and 1–4; Nov.–Mar., Mon.–Thurs. 10–12:30 and 1–4, Fri. 10–12:30 and 1–3, Sun. 10–noon.*

🔢 **Tropenmuseum** (Museum of the Tropics). The country's largest anthropological museum, while honoring The Netherlands' link to Indonesia and the West Indies, does a good job of covering many other non-Western cultures. Its skylighted and tiered interior, rich with wood, marble, and gilt, harbors not only endless pieces of antiquity, art, and musical instruments but also many displays and dioramas depicting everyday life. In the space of a couple hours, one can wander through villages in Java, the Middle East, India, Africa, and Latin America (where you'll also find the city's smallest Internet café, El Cybernetico). There is also a great sunny (that is, if Amsterdam is showing its all too rare tropical side) patio where you can enjoy food from the globe-embracing café.

🔢 Upstairs in the **Kindermuseum** (Children's Museum) children can participate directly in the life of another culture through special programs involving art, dance, song, and sometimes even cookery. Adults may visit the children's section but only under the supervision of a child age

6–12. ✉ *Linnaeusstraat 2, Plantage* ☎ *020/568–8200* 🌐 *www.tropenmuseum.nl* 🎫 *€6.80, Kindermuseum €1.15* 🕒 *Daily 10–5. Kindermuseum activities Wed. at 11, 1:30, and 3:15, weekends at 11:30, 1:30, and 3:15.*

64 **Vakbondsmuseum** (Trade Union Museum). The idea of absorbing the history of Dutch trade unions may perhaps not be enticing to all, but the museum is placed within a monumental building designed by famed architect H. P. Berlage that he himself considered his most successful work. Built in 1900 as headquarters for the Diamond Workers Union (the country's first modern union), Berlage's structure mirrored the architect's noted socialist principles, which he had to suppress in the building of that monument to capitalism, the Beurs van Berlage (Stock Exchange). Climbing the tower will lead you to a view and a small display of Berlage's blueprints. The building's stairwell, Committee Room, and Union Hall remain unchanged, and there are fantastic murals by Richard Roland Holst, stained glass depicting the worker's battle, and many other details that savvily fuse Jugendstil with Arts and Crafts stylings. The exhibitions themselves can actually be enjoyed by all. In particular, there is an excellent collection of posters that show the graphic influence of the Soviet avant garde. And the importance of this union not only for the Jewish community but the worker in general is undeniable. The essentially "third-world" conditions of the times were eased by such now fundamental concepts as the banning of child labor and the instilling of the eight-hour day. ✉ *Henri Polaklaan 9, Plantage* ☎ *020/624–1166* 🌐 *www.deburcht-vakbondsmuseum.nl* 🎫 *€3.40* 🕒 *Tues.–Fri. 11–5, Sun. 1–5.*

66 **Verzetsmuseum** (Museum of the Dutch Resistance). The stirring and suspenseful story of the Dutch resistance to the occupying forces, passive and active, during World War II, is set out here. This museum, which began in another location, was originally set up by resistance members themselves—many of whom were Communist, the only political party at the time to make Nazi resistance part of its platform. Since taking up residence in the Plancius building (whose music-themed facade denotes its history between 1875 and the Occupation as the home to Jewish choir and stage companies), the museum has moved toward embracing all the multimedia gizmos and broadening its vision to take on Dutch collaborators and the plain indifferent. But the highlights remain the original selection of the sneaky gadgets, ingenious hiding techniques, and the bicycle-powered printing presses that pumped out fake ID papers and such now-established publications as *De Parool* ("Password") and *Vrij Nederland* ("Free The Netherlands"), which began as illegal underground newsletters. ✉ *Plantage Kerklaan 61, Plantage* ☎ *020/620–2535* 🌐 *www.verzetsmuseum.org* 🎫 *€3.80* 🕒 *Tues.–Fri. 10–5, weekends noon–5.*

55 **Zuiderkerk** (South Church). Gorgeous enough to have inspired both Sir Christopher Wren and Monet, this famous church was built between 1603 and 1611 by Hendrick de Keyser, one of the most prolific architects of Holland's Golden Age. Legend has it this church hypnotized the great British architect Wren, who went on to build London's St. Paul's Cathedral (which spitefully superceded Keyser's own Westerkerk as the world's largest Protestant church); centuries later, Monet committed the Zuiderkerk to canvas. It was one of the earliest churches built in Amsterdam in the Renaissance style and was the first in the city to be built for the Dutch Reformed Church. The church's hallowed floors—under which three of Rembrandt's children are buried and on which the surplus of corpses were stored during the Hunger Winter of 1945—are now

the reign of the City Planning Office and as such are filled with detailed models of Amsterdam's ambitious future building plans. The church tower—a soaring accumulation of columns, brackets, and balustrades, is one of the most glorious exclamation points in Amsterdam; glorious, too are the panoramic views from its balconies. Its bells are played every Thursday between noon and one. ☒ *Zuiderkerkhof, Jewish Quarter* ☎ *020/689–2565 for tower* ⊕ *www.zuiderkerk.amsterdam.nl* ☒ *Free* ☉ *Church Mon. 11–4; Tues., Wed., and Fri. 9–4; Thurs. 9–8. Tower (tours only) June–Oct., Wed.–Sat. at 2, 3, and 4.*

Along the IJ:
From the Western Islands to the Eastern Docklands

Water: Amsterdam was built on it and the town's riches were created by it as the transport medium to foreign seas of trade (and plunder). Psychologists and certainly Taoists could even theorize that water's fluid and flexible nature was also a fundamental influence in creating the famously pragmatic character traits of the Dutch. The fact remains that this city's historical wealth came via its waterfront, whose waters, the Het IJ, give the waterfront its name, the IJ. And before the building of Centraal Station, this waterfront essentially came into the city's center of the Dam and spread out arterially from there.

Today this true fusion of city with water can only be witnessed to the east and west of Centraal Station. To the west, one finds the artificial islands of Westerlijke Eilanden (Western Islands) built during the Golden Age, as the city was tripling in size, for shipbuilding and product storage. Today, it has a charming "village within the city" feel. To the east, the Eastern Docklands, once a squatters' paradise, are arising as a very modern boardwalk, complete with a wave-shape cruise ship passenger terminal, that is hoped to give the waterfront the same sort of international allure that made Sydney, Australia, such a popular travel destination. In short, this tour takes in both the city's aquatic past and its hopefully shimmering future. This is not to say that Amsterdam as a port is dead in the water. While Rotterdam has long surpassed it as the world's busiest port, Amsterdam and its neighboring ports along the North Sea Canal collectively rank as the 15th busiest port.

a good walk

We find our beginning at **Haarlemmerplein,** a square like Leidseplein in that it began as a parking lot for 17th-century carts. It can be found at the end of the quirky shopping street Haarlemmerdijk (which, together with its westerly extension Haarlemmerweg, began life as the supply road to Haarlem during the Eighty Years' War). If we were to take this route, we would pass the pleasantly green Westerpark, the former gas complex Westergasfabriek (now reinvented as a cultural complex), and the former water-pumping station reinvented as the Amsterdam restaurant. But since this is a seafaring tour and not one of 19th-century industrial monuments, we just pause briefly at the square's imposing **Haarlemmerpoort,** a city gate built for the entrance of King William II on November 27, 1840, before heading north under the elevated train track to take the first right onto Sloterdijkstraat, which has a green slated, modern, and vaguely ship-shaped building on the right by architect Tymen Ploeg (this man seems to have the monopoly on modernizing this ancient neighborhood).

From the narrow wooden bridge going across to Prinsen Eiland, one sees a row of shuttered warehouses (No. 63–73) on the left labeled with their occasionally somewhat odd names (from left to right): Mars, Pants in Waterland, the Golden Head, the Grain Exchange, and the Shellfish. The whole island is worth a circle as you jealously admire all the warehouses reinvented as residences and studio space for artists. The street that intersects the island is called Galgenstraat (Gallow's Street) because of the unobstructed view it once had across the IJ to Volewijk where the executed were strung up to rot. However, instead of crossing the bridge here to Bickers Eiland and perhaps having this image stamped on your brain, exit this island via the bridge on the north side opposite No. 49, a warehouse adorned with its building date of 1629, the contorted face of a man, and a quotation that basically extols "laughter as the best medicine" to explore the most delightful of Amsterdam's little harbor islands, **Realen Eiland** ⑥⑨.

Then cross the bridge to Bickers Eiland, and turn right to walk along Bickersgracht—with its petting zoo and Prinsen Eiland views—to enjoy a very scenic walk to Hendrix Jonkerplein, where you can take the passage under the train track. On exiting, glance to the right to see the huge line of artist and designer studios that are now holding up the rest of the train tracks. Time for a bit of window-shopping perhaps? Window-shopping is certainly still the name of the game if you instead proceed straight down Buiten Oranje and take the left down Haarlemmerdijk. Until less than a decade ago this strip, once a favored home to retired sailors, was a squatters' mecca before evolving into one of the city's more characterful shopping streets and a prime strip of real estate. It is thus ironic that the redbrick **West Indische Huis** ⑦⓪ on the right was the setting for the commissioning of one of the greatest real estate deals in history: buying Manhattan for 60 guilders.

Before crossing the bridge over the Singel, pause to admire across to the right, the dome of the **Ronde Lutherese Kerk** (Round Lutheran Church), a beautiful bit of 17th-century architecture that Van Gogh immortalized in a painting. This bridge also crosses the **Haarlemmersluis** (Haarlemmer Sluice), which is essentially the toilet flusher for the canal ring. Cross the bridge, take an immediate left under the road along the bike and walking paths, and keep as straight as is allowed to get to the harbor behind Centraal Station, that edifice that psychologically broke the view to the city's watery past. Directly opposite its main rear entrance, one may opt to take the free ferry ride across the IJ to Amsterdam Noord.

Returning to the city side of Centraal Station on its east side, take a left down Oosterdokskade. Between the Botel hotel and the floating pagoda-shape Chinese restaurant, Sea Palace, look across the waters to the rather scarily imposing Scheepvaarthuis, regarded as one of the first—and certainly one of the more excessive—examples of the expressive Amsterdam School of architecture.

The post office—or perhaps, by now, construction site—behind you is where New China Town, envisioned as a mini-Singapore of sorts, is arising between 2004 and 2008. By now, you have long espied the modern green copper building that distressingly suggests a sinking ship but is in fact the science and technology museum, **NEMO** ⑦①. Take the shiny silver bridge to get there and find your way up its slanted and easily accessible roof, which offers one of the best views of the city. When your eyes have had their fill, follow the logical way to the **Nederlands Scheepvaartmuseum** ⑦②, but if you want to save this for later, turn right into Kadijkplein, which ends with the entrance to Entrepotdok, once the biggest warehouse complex in Europe but now an example of tasteful re-invention of the historical past into modern dwellings (the entrance between the "Schiedam" and the "Stavoren" will allow you an inside glimpse). Across the canal you can see—and sometimes smell—**Artis Zoo**. When the warehouses end, turn left on the left side of Entrepotdoksluis to find your way to Hoogte Kadijk, where there is the rarely open—but still functioning—shipyard **Museum Werf 't Kromhout** ⑦. If you continue east down Hoogte Kadijk, you will soon find yourself by a windmill that now, as a brewery, pumps out beer: Brouwerij t'IJ, at Funenkade 7, where one can settle in for a fresh beer in its woody- and sandy-floored interior or on its terrace. After this trek, you deserve it.

TIMING This tour involves covering a lot of space, and hence renting a bicycle is heartily recommended—otherwise you may be walking for three or four hours. Alternatively you can attach the Western Dockland part of the tour to that of Jordaan, and the Eastern with a tour of the Jewish Quarter and the Plantage. You should also note that the Scheepvaartmuseum is closed Monday in winter.

Sights to See

⚫ ⑦ **Museum Werf 't Kromhout** (Museum Wharf of the Kromhout). Started by its namesake, a ship's carpenter, in 1757, this is one of Amsterdam's oldest but still functioning shipyards. Almost 300 ships were built here during its most productive period of the last half of the 19th century. During the first part of the 20th century, 't Kromhout produced the diesel engines used by most Dutch canal boats. To this day, old boats are restored here, so expect shuffling your way through wood shavings and succumbing to the smell of tar, diesel, and varnish. Mechanics get particularly excited by the historical collection of 22 old engines. ⊠ *Hoogte Kadijk 147, IJ Waterfront* ☎ *020/627–6777* ⊡ *€3* ☉ *Tues. 10–3.*

⚫ ⑦ **Nederlands Scheepvaartmuseum** (Netherlands Maritime Museum). This was originally built in 1656 as a military depot for the Amsterdam Admiralty after Admiral Tromp refused to salute his British counterparts (thereby sparking a war with those touchy trade competitors). Trading vessels of the East Indies Company (VOC) came here to be outfitted for their journeys, with everything from cannons to hardtack. The VOC was the world's first multinational corporation, and, since it was equipped with its own army, which numbered 11,000 at its height of power, it was essentially a state within a state. During its existence between 1602 and 1798, it built 1,450 ships, made 4,700 profit-making voyages, and employed upwards of 25,000 people at any given time.

Today, this Dutch Classicist building incorporates room after room of displays related to the development and power of both the Dutch East and West Indies companies, as well as the Dutch fishing industry. At any given time there are 1,000 objects—including epic battle paintings, intricate models, bona fide boats, specialized equipment, and obsessively rendered maps—on display from the 250,000-piece collection. Moored alongside the building at the east end of the old Amsterdam Harbor is a replica of the VOC sailing ship *Amsterdam,* which sunk on its maiden voyage off the coast of Hastings in 1749. Fully functional with vast expanses of sail, it generally stays docked for a variety of excellent children's activities. ⊠ *Kattenburgerplein 1, IJ Waterfront* ☎ *020/523–2222* ⊕ *www.scheepvaartmuseum.nl* ⊡ *€7* ☉ *Oct.–May, Tues.–Sun. 10–5; June–Sept., daily 10–5.*

⚫ ⑦ **NEMO Science & Technology Center.** Opened in early 1997, this green copper–clad building, evocative of a ship sinking into the city's boggy surface, was immediately accepted as an architectural landmark. Its architect was no less than Renzo Piano, creator of the Pompidou Centre in Paris. Surrounded by water, the building's colossal volume rises above the entrance to the IJ Tunnel to Amsterdam North. The rooftop café terrace offers a superb panoramic view across the city. But this view can also be enjoyed for free via a staircase on its eastern face and via an elevator just inside the entrance.

The museum recently shortened its name from "NewMetropolis" to NEMO, perhaps in order to exploit that evocative word's use in *The Odyssey*, as the name of Jules Verne's notorious sea captain, and in Winsor McCay's 100-year-old comic strip, *Little Nemo in Slumberland*, which documented a small boy's surreal adventures of discovery whenever he fell asleep. And indeed, this museum is dedicated to imparting the joys of science—past, present, and futuristic—through high-tech, hands-on experience. Children—and the young at heart—have the options of building hydroelectric power stations, constructing a bamboo house, traveling through brains, indulging in dramatic chemistry experiments, playing with a giant domino set, getting charged on static electricity, and even potentially collapsing economies as a global banker. ⊠ *Oosterdok 2, IJ Waterfront* ☎ *0900/919–1100* ⊕ *www.e-nemo.nl* ⊡ *€10* ⊙ *Oct.–May, Tues.–Sun.* 10–5; June–Sept., daily 10–5.

69 Realen Eiland. About a dozen blocks to the west of Centraal Station and due north of the Harlemmerhouttuinen are three off-the-beaten-track islands created from canal landfill back in the 17th century. These Western Islands—known in Dutch as Westelijke eilanden—were then constructed to hold warehouses and now enjoy a quasi-nautical ambience particularly beloved by boaties and other seafaring folk. Most visitors bypass the largest island, Bickers Eiland, jammed as it is with boatyards (and modern apartment buildings) and hew to the west and take the waterside Nieuwe Teruinen for the bridge over to the smallest island, Prinsen Eiland. Forge ahead on its Galgenstraat (Gallows Street—it once framed a vista of the town gallows across the water), then head northward across the wooden drawbridge, to the isle of Realen Eiland. This bridge, Drie Haringbrug, has its name echoed on the gable of the house (Vierwindendwarsstraat 1–3) on its other end on the left: "three herrings" painted silver (perhaps herring storage took place in these parts during days of yore?). Located on the island's eastern shore, the photo-op hereabouts is the waterside **Zandhoek,** a street so named because it used to be the site of the city sand market. Posing for your Nikon is a charming row of 17th-century houses, built by Laurens Reael, a Catholic who became famous for smuggling out treasures from city monasteries before they could be confiscated by authorities. **"De Gouden Reael"** is the name of Reael's own house—quaintly marked with a gold coin on the gable stone—which sits waterside and is now a café, a perfect spot to raise a toast to Reael as you watch boats sail along the Westerdok. ⊠ *Westelijke Eilanden IJ Waterfront, Follow Haarlemmerstraat/ Haarlemmerdijk from Centraal Station and go under the railway tracks at Buiten Oranjestraat or at Haarlemmerplein.*

70 West Indische Huis (West Indies House). These former headquarters of the West Indies Trading Company (WIC) has much historical resonance. The WIC was set up as a means to colonize America and combat Spaniards abroad. While not as sovereign as the VOC, it was essentially given free trading reign of Africa's west coast, America, and all the islands of the West Pacific and New Guinea. In these rooms, the decision was made to buy Manhattan for 60 guilders, the silver was stored that Piet Hein liberated from the Spanish after winning a sea battle in 1628, and the organization was enacted to oversee the export of 70,000 slaves from West Africa to the Caribbean between 1626 and 1680. Now the building is home to local television production companies and a caterer. You can enter its courtyard, with its statue of Peter Stuyvesant, via its side entrance on Herenmarkt. ⊠ *Herenmarkt 93–7, IJ Waterfront.*

WHERE TO EAT

By Steve
Korver

Up until a mere decade or two ago, it seemed that eating in Amsterdam was tinged more with the flavor of Calvinism than with any other taste. Certainly colonialism of the past did much to broaden the puritanical Dutch palate—once in the 19th century when the French occupied Holland and imported their delight for the delicate, then in the 17th century when the Dutch became the occupiers of Indonesia, with its 1,000 islands offering a roller-coaster ride of exotic spices. But often the filling yet unenlightened fare of charred fish or meat, overboiled potato, and limp vegetables remained the standard. Holiday celebrations, of course, allowed the drunken gobbling of whole pheasants. It's little wonder that this splurge-versus-purge philosophy was a favorite subject of Golden Age painters: the skinny were portrayed as holy people of God and the fat as precariously mortal spawn of Satan.

Happily, today the feasting spreads out over the entire year and embraces—thanks to the post–World War II influx of immigrants—every manner of cuisine from all corners of the globe. And international urban eating trends, while perhaps arriving slower in Amsterdam than other places, now make it fairly routine, on a walk through the city, to encounter a sushi shack, a soup shop, a Thai take-out joint, or a hipster lounge. And, as though to compensate for the long drought, many of the city's former industrial- and harbor-related buildings are currently being transformed into distinctive or trendy dining establishments. The term "New Dutch Cuisine" while flaunted for years has only come to have meaning quite recently, thanks to the emergence of young chefs who are finding their inspiration from around the globe—the Dutch are notoriously well-traveled after all—while getting their ingredients from local organic farmers (whose businesses are flourishing thanks to the many recent scares associated with mad cow disease and hormone-engorged poultry). Their creations—think cappuccino-textured pea soup with chanterelles and pancetta, cod smothered in a sauce based on chorizo and fennel, or turbot on a bed of beetroot and nettle leaves—have finally "turned on the style" and succeeded in taking the starch (literally) out of the old mainstays.

While traditional Dutch food only really shines with its advantageous, belly-packing powers in winter, there are two imported-but-"typically" Dutch culinary trips that cannot be missed: the Indonesian *rijsttafel* ("rice table") where dozens of vegetables, meats, and fish each get their own spicy twist as a tiny dish and are then served with rice; and the cheese fondue which the Dutch appropriated from the Swiss probably because it appealed to their "one pot, multiple fork" sense of the democratic. Lunch is a good time to go Dutch and follow the locals into a *bruine kroeg*, one of the cities's famous brown cafés (see the listings under Nightlife, below), or bar to have a *broodje* (sandwich). If you are only out for a cheap snack, there are infinite snack bars where you can buy— sometimes via a heated wall *automaat*—deep-fried meat blobs or french fries that you can have topped with a amazing range of toppings. The many cheap "Suri/Indo/Chin" (or some such combination) snack bars serve a combination of Suriname, Indonesian, and Chinese dishes, and while they are remarkably consistent, it is perhaps advisable to choose a dish that matches the cook's apparent roots.

But probably the best snacks are those that can be purchased at the many fish stalls found on the city's bridges. The prime taste treat is raw *haring*—herring that has been saltwater-cured in vats. This local working person's "sushi" is at its most succulent—and hence, the usual garnishing of onion and pickle is not required—at the start of the fishing season (late May to early June). If this sounds a tad too radical, there's always a selection of battered and fried fishes, *Noordzee garnalen* ("North Sea shrimp," which are tinier, browner, and tastier than most of their brethren) and *gerookte heilbot* (thinly sliced smoked halibut). However, if you decide to go for broke, indulge in *gerookte paling* (smoked freshwater eel), which is rich in both price and calories.

If you're the type who likes to make your own discoveries, here are a few tips to keep in mind. In general, except as a lark, consider the tourist traps around Leidseplein, Rembrandtplein, the Damrak, and the Red Light District as just that. Cheap global eats are concentrated in the De Pijp district. A broad selection of middle-range eateries can be found around Nieuwmarkt, the Jordaan, and Utrechtsestraat. And to find posher purveyors for a true blow-out, head to Reguliersdwarsstraat or the "Nine Streets" (the interconnecting streets of the canal girdle between Raadhuisstraat and Leidsestraat) areas. One thing you should certainly be aware of is the Dutch ritual of eating early; in fact, the vast majority of the city's kitchens close by 10. And since Amsterdam is a casual sort of town, "jacket and tie" means more "if you feel like it" than "required."

WHAT IT COSTS In euros*				
$$$$	**$$$**	**$$**	**$**	**¢**
RESTAURANTS over €30	€22–€30	€15–€22	€10–€15	under €10

*Restaurant prices are per person for a main course only, excluding tax (6% for food and 19% for alcoholic beverages) and service; note that if a restaurant offers only prix-fixe (set-price) meals, it has been given the price category that reflects the full prix-fixe price.

Oude Zijde

The city's "old side" of its historical center, while harboring the the decidedly nonedible neon grotesqueries of the Red Light District, is also host to many bargain Asian restaurants and the fine delicacies of some of Amsterdam's most esteemed eateries.

★ **$$$$** ✕ **Excelsior.** For when only the poshest and most classically elegant will do, take your primped-up selves here. To the tinkling of a grand piano, solicitous waiters, knowledgeable sommeliers, towering dessert trolleys, and preparation carts all waltz together in a setting of towering palms, tall candelabras, and shimmering chandeliers. Even more delicious is the Excelsior's mouthwatering view over the Amstel River toward either the Muntplein on one side or the Music Theater on the other. If you have not already guessed, the kitchen here is traditional French. But the inspired chef, Jean-Jacques Menanteau, also knows some twists, such as a sublime lobster bisque and a grilled turbot with shrimp and Parmesan risotto. The truly adventurous should opt for his fixed-price *menu gastronomique,* which will not only feature seasonal specialties (think truffles) but occasionally also the acclaimed reveries he creates from such untoward meats as liver and kidney. Rest assured, there are another four fixed-priced menus to choose from. ⊠ *Hotel de l'Europe, Nieuwe Doelenstraat 2–8, Oude Zijde* ☎ *020/531–1705* 🏛 *Jacket and tie* ⊟ *AE, DC, MC, V* ☉ *No lunch weekends.*

★ **$$$$** ✕ **Vermeer.** With its milk-white walls, dramatic black-and-white patterned floors, Delft plates, fireplace hearths, and Stern Old Dutch chandeliers, this stately place does conjure up the amber canvases of the great Johannes (if he ever did the decor for a fancy hotel chain, that is). Its very posh vibe, however, suggests that no milkmaid on Earth that will be able

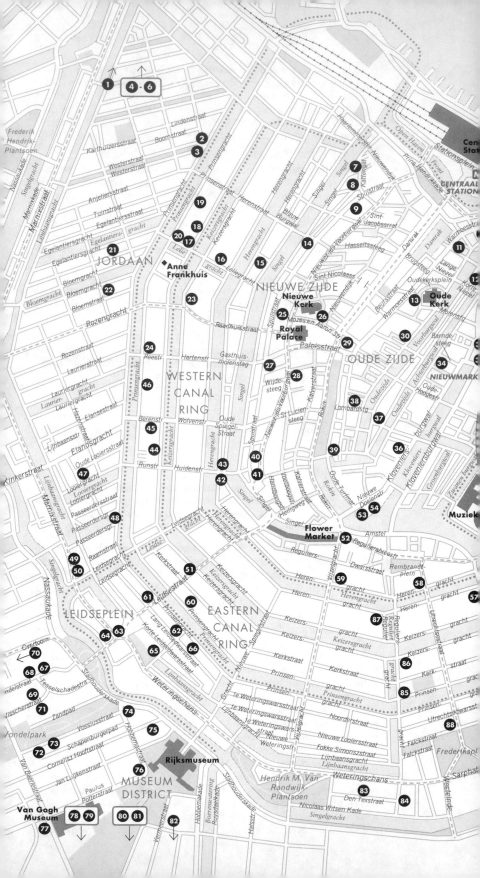

Where to Eat & Stay in Amsterdam

to afford the prices of this restaurant set within the 17th-century wing of the NH Barbizon Palace Hotel. Young chef Pascal Jalaij received a Michelin star a year in the past two years and indeed his creations are cosmic in the way they balance texture and contrast (what this man does with fois gras!). He sums up the current ambitions of local chefs: buying the produce from organic farmers (and going so far as to get his fish from bona fide rod fishermen), building up dishes steeped in classical French, then infusing them with a nouvelle "anything goes as long as it's honest and it works" sensibility. A poached Anjou dove with juniper-berry sauce and a crunchy potato pie, anyone? And of course, an army of waiters are on hand to insure that the service is always impeccable. If you are in feasting mode, opt for Grand Bouffe excess by spending €100 to have a taste of everything on the menu. ⊠ *Prins Hendrikkade 59–72, Oude Zijde* ☎ *020/556–4885* ⊕ *www.restaurantvermeer.nl* ▤ *AE, DC, MC, V* ☉ *Closed Sun. No Sat. lunch.*

$$–$$$ ✕ **Blauw aan de Wal.** In the heart of the Red Light District there is a small alley that leads to this charming oasis, "Blue on the Quay," complete with the innocent chirping of birds. Auspiciously set in a courtyard that once belonged to the Bethanienklooster monastery, this place offers a restful ambience with multiple dining areas (one is no-smoking), each with a unique and serene view. Original wood floors and exposed-brick walls hint at the building's 1625 origins, but white tablecloths, an extensive and inspired wine list, and an open kitchen that employs fresh local ingredients to create Mediterranean-influenced masterworks speak more of an unpretentious and contemporary take on chic. After starting on a cappuccino-textured pea soup with chanterelle mushrooms and pancetta bacon, you may want to indulge in a melt-in-the-mouth cod that has been seductively smothered in a sauce of chorizo and fennel. ⊠ *Oude Zijds Achterburgwal 99, Oude Zijde* ☎ *020/330–2257* ▤ *AE, MC, V* ☉ *Closed Sun. No lunch.*

$$–$$$ ✕ **In de Waag.** The lofty, beamed interior of the historic Waag weigh house has been converted into a grand café and restaurant. While the reading table houses computer terminals with free Internet access, a strict dinner lighting policy of "candles only"—from a huge wooden candelabra no less—helps maintain the building's medieval vibe. The approach is heartily Burgundian with such entrées as baked fillet of salmon with mussels and a creamy sorrel sauce or charcoal-grilled beef with green pepper sauce and a gratin of Emmental cheese. The long wooden tables make this an ideal location for larger groups to eat and if you happen to belong to a party of eight then you should definitely book the spookily evocative "tower room." Daytime hunger pangs are also catered to from 10 AM, when you can enjoy a sandwich, a salad, or a snack on the epic and spacious terrace. ⊠ *Nieuwmarkt 4, Oude Zijde* ☎ *020/422–7772* ▤ *AE, DC, MC, V.*

$–$$ ✕ **De Kooning van Siam.** This Thai restaurant, sitting smack in the middle of the Red Light District, takes delight in the fact that Brad Pitt (who incidentally just went local by buying a home in the Jordaan) once came to visit. It should take more from the fact that it is favored by local Thai residents. Although the beams and wall panels are still visible in this old canal house, the furniture and wall decorations refreshingly dilute the sense of Old Dutchness. Sensitive to wimpier palates, the menu balances such scorchers as stir-fried beef with onion and chili peppers, with milder options such as the chicken and Chinese vegetables with coconut, curry, and basil. ⊠ *Oude Zijds Voorburgwal 42, Oude Zijde* ☎ *020/623–7293* ▤ *AE, DC, MC, V* ☉ *Closed Feb. No lunch.*

★ ¢–$ ✕ **Café Bern.** This dark and woody café, as evocative as a Jan Steen 17th-century interior, has been serving the same cheese fondue for decades and for good reason: it's about perfect, especially if you enhance digestion—and the frolic factor—with plenty of orders from the fully stocked bar. Like the Dutch, you, too, may be inspired to appropriate cheese fondue as your own celebratory meal of choice. ⊠ *Nieuwmarkt 9, Oude Zijde* ☎ *020/622–0034* ⚲ *Reservations essential* ▤ *No credit cards* ♡ *No lunch.*

¢–$ ✕ **Het Gasthuys.** In this bustling and studenty *eetcafé* ("eating cafe") near the university you'll be served handsome portions of traditional Dutch home cooking, choice cuts of meat with simple sauces, fine fries, and piles of mixed salad. Sit at the wood bar or take a table high up in the rafters at the back surrounded by ancient wallpapers. In summer you can watch the passing boats from the enchanting canal-side terrace or anthropologically watch the junkies selling bikes off the nearby bridge. ⊠ *Grimburgwal 7, Oude Zijde* ☎ *020/624–8230* ▤ *No credit cards.*

¢–$ ✕ **Kam Yin.** Representative of the many Suriname snack bars that dot this city, Kam Yin offers this South American country's unique fusion of Caribbean, Chinese, and Indonesian cuisines that arose from its history as a Dutch colony. Perhaps the most popular meal is the *roti,* a flatbread pancake, which comes with lightly curried potatoes and either veg or meat options. If you are only interested in a lunch, try a *broodje pom,* a bun sandwich filled with a remarkably addictive mélange of chicken and root vegetable. Basic, clean, convivial, and noisy, Kam Yin shows extra sensitivity with its speedy service, long hours (daily noon–midnight), and a doggy-bag option. ⊠ *Warmoesstraat 6–8, Oude Zijde* ☎ *020/ 625–3115* ▤ *No credit cards.*

¢ ✕ **Bakkerswinkel van 90s.** This genteel yet unpretentious bakery/tearoom evokes an English country kitchen, one that lovingly prepares and serves breakfasts, high tea, hearty-breaded sandwiches, soups, and the most divine—and dare it be said, most manly—slabs of quiche you will probably ever taste. There's little sense of privacy within their closely clustered wooden tables but this remains a true oasis for those out to indulge in a healthful breakfast or lunch. Not only do they open at 7 AM daily but they also have another handy location, complete with garden patio, in the Museum District (Roelet Hartstraat 68, 020/662–3594). ⊠ *Warmoesstraat 69, Oude Zijde* ☎ *020/489–8000* ▤ *No credit cards* ♡ *Closed Mon. No dinner.*

¢ ✕ **Soup en zo.** Only in the last year, perhaps because *Seinfeld* is still running a few seasons behind here, has the concept of speedy soup purveyors hit Amsterdam. "Soup etc." leads the pack by being particularly speedy (at least between 10 and 7:30 daily) and health conscious. They attempt to make their four daily available soups, which they serve with chunky slices of whole grain breads, from as many organic ingredients as possible and their menu also offers salads and exotic fruit juices imported from Brazil as frozen fruit pulp. Fortified, you can now rush back to wandering for bargains at the Waterlooplein flea market. ⊠ *Jodenbreestraat 94a, Oude Zijde* ☎ *020/422–2243* ▤ *No credit cards.*

Nieuwe Zijde

The historical center's "new side" has the history but none of the neon of the "old side." It's the intellectual heart of Amsterdam and ground central for roaming hipsters who often load up at a restaurant before washing it down with some nightlife in an ancient bar or the latest lounge.

$$$$ ✕ **Supper Club.** The concept is simple but artful. Over the course of an evening, diners casually lounge on white mattresses in a white space while receiving endless courses of food (and drink . . .) marked by irreverent flavor combinations. DJs, VJs, and live performances enhance the club-like, relentlessly hip vibe. Once purely an underground endeavor, the Supper Club is set to go global with a branch already in Rome and more to follow in London, New York City, and Ibiza. Its popularity suggests

that one should really only go in large groups; otherwise you may run the risk of being overwhelmed by one of the same. ☒ *Jonge Roelensteeg 21, Nieuwe Zijde* ☎ *020/638–0513* ⊕ *www.supperclub.nl* ⚑ *Reservations essential* ☰ *AE, DC, MC, V* ☽ *No lunch.*

$$$–$$$$ ✕ **D' Theeboom.** A favorite of the local French business community, this formal, stylish—done up in Art Deco creams and blacks—and honestly priced purveyor of haute cuisine is located behind the Dam in a historic canal-side warehouse. The flavor of, for example, the oven-roasted monkfish with prawns, curry, and grapefruit is particularly enhanced when you take advantage of the sophisticated wine list. Combine this with a sunny day on the terrace and you can definitely settle in for a long and happy linger. ☒ *Singel 210, Nieuwe Zijde* ☎ *020/623–8420* ☰ *AE, DC, MC, V* ☽ *No lunch weekends.*

$$$–$$$$ ✕ **D' Vijff Vlieghen.** The "Five Flies" is a rambling dining institution that takes up five adjoining Golden Age houses. Yet the densely evocative Golden Age vibe—complete with bona fide Rembrandt etchings, wooden *jenever* (Dutch gin) barrels, crystal and armor collections, and an endless array of old-school bric-a-brac—only came into being in 1939. Brass plaques on the chairs, while listing such past visitors as Orson Welles, Walt Disney, and Goldie Hawn, do not tell of its vast popularity—you'll find both business folk clinching a deal in a private nook and busloads of tourists who have dibs on complete sections: book accordingly. You do end up paying extra for the Five Flies vibe thanks to an somewhat overpriced menu of new Dutch cuisine, which emphasizes local, fresh, and often organic ingredients in everything from wild boar to purely vegetarian dishes. Lack of choice is not an issue here: the size of the menu, the set menus, the wine list, and the flavored *jenever* are—like the decor—all of epic proportions. ☒ *Spuistraat 294–302, Nieuwe Zijde* ☎ *020/530–4060* 🏛 *Jacket and tie* ☰ *AE, DC, MC, V* ☽ *No lunch.*

★ $$–$$$$ ✕ **De Poort.** Recently restored in the Old Dutch style (complete with polished woods and ceiling paintings), De Poort—part of the Die Poert van Cleve hotel complex—is, in fact, officially Old Dutch with its roots as a "steak brasserie" stretching back to 1870, when it awed the city as the first place with electric light. By the time you read this, De Poort will have served 6 million of its acclaimed juicy slabs, which come served with a choice of eight different accompaniments. The menu also comes supplemented with other options such as smoked salmon, a traditional pea soup that is thick enough to eat with a fork, and a variety of fish dishes. ☒ *Nieuwezijds Voorburgwal 176–180, Nieuwe Zijde* ☎ *020/622–6429* ☰ *AE, DC, MC, V.*

$$$ ✕ **De Silveren Spieghel.** Despite appearances, this precariously crooked building located near the solid Round Lutheran Church is here to stay. Designed by the ubiquitous Hendrick de Keyser, it has managed to remain standing since 1614, so it should last through your dinner of contemporary Dutch cuisine. In fact, take time to enjoy its famous local specialties, such as succulent lamb from the North Sea island of Texel and honey from Amsterdam's own Vondelpark. There are also expertly prepared fish plates, such as turbot on a bed of beetroot and nettle leaves. Lunch is available by reservation only (phone a day ahead). ☒ *Kattengat 4–6, Nieuwe Zijde* ☎ *020/624–6589* ⚑ *Reservations essential* ☰ *AE, MC, V* ☽ *Closed Sun. No lunch.*

$$–$$$ ✕ **Lucius.** The plain and informal setting may say "bistro," but don't associate that with speedy service. What we have here is infinitely better: one of the best fish restaurants in town, where you can happily linger over such choices as grilled lobster, a deliciously authentic *plateau de fruits de mer* (fruits-of-the-sea platter), or a positively adventurous sea bass served with buckwheat noodles and mushrooms. Find the perfect complement in the intelligent list of wines: it spotlights California but—

attention, oenophiles who think they have heard everything—also sports a Dutch wine from the nation's only vineyard, in Limburg. ⊠ *Spuistraat 247, Nieuwe Zijde* ☎ *020/624–1831* ⚓ *Reservations essential* ▤ *AE, DC, MC, V* ⊗ *No lunch.*

★ **$$-$$$** ✕ **Kantjil en de Tijger.** No folkloric shadow puppets adorn the walls at this unusually large and spacious Indonesian restaurant: the interior is serenely Jugendstil, which provides a refreshing surprise. While you can order à la carte, the menu is based on three different *rijsttafel* (rice tables), with an abundance of meat, fish, and vegetable dishes varying in flavor from coconut-milk sweetness to distressingly spicy. Groups often come here to gel their bellies before a night of drinking in the many bars around the nearby Spui and Nieuwezijds Voorburgwal. ⊠ *Spuistraat 291/293, Nieuwe Zijde* ☎ *020/620–0994* ▤ *AE, DC, MC, V* ⊗ *No lunch.*

★ **$$** ✕ **Haesje Claes.** Groaning with pewter tankards, stained glass, leaded windows, rich historic paneling, Indonesian paisley *fabriks,* and betasseled Victorian lamps, this is a restaurant after any Meinherr Van Tassel's heart. With a menu to match its "Old Holland" menu, Haesje Claes—the name comes from the lady who founded Amsterdam's orphanage in the 16th-century—specializes in packing in busloads of tourists. But all remains happily cheerful. The food, if occasionally overpriced, is actually quite fine: in particular their pea soup and the selection of *stampotten* (mashed dishes that combine potato with a variety of vegetables and/or meats). On cold winter nights, many opt for the *Hotchpotches* (stews) of steamed beef, sausage, and bacon. Still, we give this a star basically for its Pieter de Hooch–worthy interiors. ⊠ *Spuistraat 273, Oude Zijde* ☎ *020/624–9998* ⊕ *www.haesjeclaes. nl* ▤ *AE, MC, V.*

★ **¢-$** ✕ **Café Luxembourg.** One of the city's top grand cafés, Luxembourg has a grand interior and a grand view of a bustling square, both of which are maximized for people-watching. Famous for its brunches, its classic café menu comes equipped with a mighty fine goat cheese salad, dim sum, and excellent Holtkamp *krokets* (indeed: croquettes, these with a shrimp or meat and potato filling). The "reading table" is sensitively packed with both Dutch and international newspapers and mags. ⊠ *Spuistraat 24, Nieuwe Zijde* ☎ *020/620–6264* ▤ *AE, V.*

★ **¢** ✕ **Keuken van 1870.** This former soup kitchen, where sharing tables is still the norm, offers the best and most economic foray into the satiating world of traditional Dutch cooking. As reassuring as a Dutch grandmother, the kitchen serves such warming singularities as *hutspot* (a hotchpotch of potatoes, carrots, and onions), its more free-ranging variant *stamppot* (a hodgepodge of potatoes, greens, and chunks of cured sausage), *erwtensoep* (a sausage-fortified pea soup so thick you could eat it with a toothpick) and naturally a full range of meat, fish, vegetable, and potato plates. After a spell of bad luck—namely bankruptcy—its future is somewhat uncertain (though it is impossible to imagine the city without it) so call ahead to check. ⊠ *Spuistraat 4, Nieuwe Zijde* ☎ *020/ 624–8965* ▤ *AE, MC, V* ⊗ *No lunch weekends.*

Western Canal Ring

The intrinsically posh western stretches of the Grachtengordel canal ring and its intersecting streets constitute a foodie paradise. Meals here, of course, come equipped with the potential for an after-dinner romantic walk to aid the digestion.

$$$$ ✕ **Christophe.** When Algerian-born Frenchman Jean-Christophe Royer opened his canal-side *eettempel* (eating temple) in the 1980s, it was almost immediately lauded for both its William Katz–designed interior, which evokes this artist's acclaimed ballet scenery, and Royer's own culinary vision, which embellishes French haute cuisine with Arabic and

African influences. In short: Christophe's cooking awards are well deserved. The ever-changing menu—always loaded with ample vegetarian options—may include entrées such as ragout of lobster with cocoa beans, pimentos, and coriander or sweetbreads of veal in a sauce of *vin jaune* (a deep golden-color wine from a grape from one very small area in the Jura) with white cabbage and chanterelles. ☒ *Leliegracht 46, Western Canal Ring* ☏ *020/625–0807* ☝ *Reservations essential* 🏛 *Jacket required* ▤ *AE, DC, MC, V* ☉ *Closed Sun. and Mon., 1st wk in Jan., and 2 wks in July and Aug. No lunch.*

$$–$$$ ✕ **De Belhamel.** This restaurant, set on the edge of the Jordaan, is blessed with Art Nouveau detailing and wallpaper that is so darkly evocative of fin-de-siècle living it may inspire a thirst for absinthe and Symbolist poetry. But the views of the Herengracht and the attentive and friendly service help create a more purely romantic setting in which to settle down and enjoy the French-inspired menu, which in winter emphasizes hearty game dishes (venison with a red-wine and shallot sauce) and in summer—when the seating spills out into the street—offers lighter fare with unusual but inspired flavor combinations. ☒ *Brouwersgracht 60, Western Canal Ring* ☏ *020/622–1095* ▤ *AE, MC, V* ☉ *No lunch.*

$$–$$$ ✕ **Van Puffelen.** Dual-natured, the woody and classically ancient Van Puffelen, located on a particularly mellow stretch of canal, offers both a startling array of herbed and spiced *jenevers* as a *proeverij*, or old-fashioned "tasting house," and a huge restaurant section in which to settle the belly. The menu is of modern café variety, but it's the daily special—duck breast with passion-fruit sauce, to name one—that draws the many regulars. Red meat tends to be done rare, so let them know if you prefer medium to well-done. Things can indeed get a tad boisterous here, but one can always escape to the more secluded and intimate mezzanine floor or, in summer, the terrace. Reservations are essential for the restaurant. ☒ *Prinsengracht 375–377, Western Canal Ring* ☏ *020/624–6270* ▤ *AE, DC, MC, V.*

¢–$ ✕ **Pancake Factory.** As a well-honed art form that delicately balances thinness with belly-packing power, one can't really go wrong when going out for Dutch pancakes. But the quaint Pancake Bakery rises above the pack with its medieval vibe, canal-side patio, and a mammoth menu with over 70 choices of sweet and savory toppings. They also do a convincing take on the folk dish of erwtensoep. ☒ *Prinsengracht 191, Western Canal Ring* ☏ *020/625–1333* ▤ *No credit cards.*

¢ ✕ **Lust.** Before you get the wrong idea: "lust" is a much softer word in Dutch and suggests a calmer desire best translated as "appetite." And if you have worked up a lunchy one while wandering the "Nine Streets" specialty shopping area, this is a truly satiating place for healthful club sandwiches, bagels (their tuna spread being particularly sublime), fruit shakes, stir-fries, pastas, and salads. Few leave disappointed from this trendy lunchroom, especially if it included a visit to their wacky washroom. ☒ *Runstraat 13, Western Canal Ring* ☏ *020/626–5791* ▤ *No credit cards* ☉ *No dinner.*

Leidseplein & the Center Canal Ring

Leidse "Square" is the heart of Amsterdam's nightlife. While the connecting streets are packed with middle-of-the-road restaurants, one can still find some culinary treasures.

★ **$$–$$$** ✕ **Blue Pepper.** One of the more widely acclaimed of recent newcomers in town, this blue-tone Indo features the inspired cooking of a chef whose previous restaurant won her a Michelin star. Blue Pepper will undoubtedly follow the same course towards the culinary stars since here you can just sit back and put utter faith in any of the specials of the day (that, unlike most other Indos, does not focus on piling a thousand different dishes on your plate but rather focuses on just a few obsessively prepared ones) or one of their full menus (€45–€55) with bliss as your dessert. Of course, one should heighten the tongue-ballet by heeding more smart advice when ordering a bottle from their savvy selection of wines. So be warned: the price of the mains are deceiving because you will always be inspired to spend more than you planned. ⊠ *Nassaukade 366, Leidseplein* ☎ *020/489–7039* ▭ *DC, MC, V* ☺ *Closed Sun. No lunch.*

$$–$$$ ✕ **Van de Kaart.** This sub-canal-level newcomer with a restful interior blows most starred restaurants out of the water with their savvy and stylish balancing of Mediterranean tastes. Since the menu is in continual flux, cross your fingers that it may include their highly feted shrimp sausages, their octopus with a salad of couscous, basil, and black olives, or their warm polenta cake of goose liver. One can also opt for one of their three surprise menus with matching wines (€34 (+15) for a three-course, €40 (+20) for a four-course, and 45 (+25) for a five-course). ⊠ *Prinsengracht 512sous, Leidseplein* ☎ *020/625–9232* ▭ *AE, DC, MC, V* ☺ *Closed Sun. No lunch.*

$–$$$ ✕ **Café Americain.** Though thousands of buildings in Amsterdam are designated historic monuments, few like the Americain have their *interiors* landmarked as well. And for good reason: it's an Art Deco display of arched ceilings, stained glass, wall paintings, and a huge antique reading table (it's very easy to imagine Mata Hari having her wedding reception here). As a hybrid restaurant-café serving everything from light snacks to full dinners, the food usually rates less "heavenly" than the interior. The coffee and cakes are excellent. ⊠ *American Hotel, Leidsekade 97, Leidseplein* ☎ *020/624–5322* ⌦ *Reservations not accepted* ▭ *AE, DC, MC, V.*

$–$$ ✕ **Walem.** As if ripped from the pages of *Wallpaper* magazine, this sleekly hip and trendy all-day *grand café* serves elegant breakfast and brunch options on crunchy *ciabatta* bread with both cappuccino and champagne on hand to wash it down. Dinnertime is fusion time, as the chefs pack phyllo pastry with Cypriot goat cheese, ginger, and olives; create salads of marinated duck and chicken, crispy greens, and buckwheat noodles; or slather a grilled rib eye with Cajun spices. In summer, you can relax in the formal garden or on the canal-side terrace, and late at night the guest DJs spin hip lounge tunes for neophytes. ⊠ *Keizersgracht 449, Leidseplein* ☎ *020/625–3544* ▭ *AE, MC, V.*

¢–$$ ✕ **De Blonde Hollander** In a setting of wood, candlelight, and Delft blue accents, "The Blond Dutchie" serves up large-portioned and well-practiced interpretations of traditional dishes. In other words: lots of chunky soups, slabs of meat, and hotchpotches of mashed potatoes with vegetables. As bonus local culinary oddity, their kitchen stays open until 11:30 PM on weekends. No reservations accepted. ⊠ *Leidsekruisstraat 28, Leidseplein* ☎ *020/627–0522* ▭ *AE, DC, MC, V* ☺ *No lunch.*

¢–$ ✕ **De Gevulde Koe.** "The Stuffed Cow" is as friendly and socially cozy as its upstairs bar, "The Cow," but it's never so crowded as the skinny kitchen where sardined cooks manage to pump out wonderfully prepared dishes from an ever-changing menu that tends to favor less—strange, considering its name—beef and more fish and ostrich (in truffle sauce!). In short: this is the ultimate in earthy Dutch eating cafés where a yuppie has yet to be sighted. Their menu changes every day but one constant is a daily special priced at a mere €7.95. ⊠ *Marnixstraat 381, Leidseplein* ☎ *020/625–4482* ⊕ *www.cafedekoe.nl* ▭ *AE, DC, MC, V* ☺ *No lunch.*

¢–$ ✕ **Bojo.** There are plenty of mediocre late-night eateries in this touristic zone, but the bambooed Bojo—although not representative of the heights of the Indonesian kitchen—does serve huge portions of enjoy-able food. They have it all, from *saté* (skewered and barbecued meats) snacks to vegetarian *gado-gado* (where raw vegetables are drowned in a spicy peanut sauce) to the monumental rice table where dozens of dif-ferent small side dishes are served. With your belly nicely filled, you could return to your night frolicking, as this place is open until 1:30 AM dur-ing the week and 3:30 AM on the weekend. ⊠ *Lange Leidsedwarsstraat 51, Leidseplein* ☎ *020/620–4989* ▭ *AE, DC, MC* ☺ *No lunch.*

Eastern Canal Ring, Rembrandtplein & De Pijp
The eastern Grachtengordel and the nightclub-rich Rembrandtplein come equipped with some of the city's poshest restaurants. But for a more nonrarified air head to the excellent and economic ethnic eater-ies that dot the more casual De Pijp neighborhood.

★ **$$$–$$$$** ✕ **Breitner.** Whether for romance or the pure enjoyment of fine con-temporary dining, Breitner gets high marks. With a formal interior of rich red carpeting and muted pastel colors, and a view across the Am-stel River that takes in both the Muziektheater–Stadhuis (Music The-ater–City Hall complex) and the grand Carre Theater, Breitner serves French-inspired dishes, many of which pack a flavorful punch. Inspired choices here include a starter of baked quail with goose liver and bacon and entrées such as skate with Indonesian-style vegetables or smoked rib of beef with a sauce of whole-grain mustard and marinated vegeta-bles. Foie gras, fabulous desserts, and an innovative wine list allow one the option to step over into the realm of pure decadence. As to be ex-pected, the service is flawless and the patrons do their share to show re-spect for Breitner's high standards by dressing smartly. ⊠ *Amstel 212, Eastern Canal Ring* ☎ *020/627–7879* ⌂ *Reservations essential* ▭ *AE, DC, MC, V* ☺ *Closed Sun. and Mon. No lunch Sat.*

$$–$$$$ ✕ **Tempo Doeloe.** For decades, this has been a safe and elegant—albeit somewhat cramped—place to indulge in that spicy smorgasbord of the gods, the Indonesian "rice table." Stay alert when the waitstaff point out the hotness of the dishes; otherwise you might stretch your wallet with the downing of gallons of antidotal *witbier* (a sweet local wheat beer). Tempo's more informal neighbor, **Tujuh Maret** (Utrechtsestraat 73, ☎ 020/427–9865), offers a cheaper but no less taste-bud–tantaliz-ing alternative (with takeout as an option). ⊠ *Utrechtsestraat 75, East-ern Canal Ring* ☎ *020/625–6718* ⌂ *Reservations essential* ▭ *AE, DC, MC, V* ☺ *No lunch.*

$$–$$$ ✕ **Inez IPSC.** As the final project of the late and great artist-designer-poet Peter Giele (who had made his name with the famed Amsterdam RoXY nightclub), Club Inez stands as a hip and happening testament to a man who could fuse explosive colors and heavy ornamentation into a curi-ously soothing whole. Add to this a panoramic urban view and food as inspired as the decor and you'll quickly understand its popularity among clubbers, business suits, and food-lovers alike. The "international mod-ern free-style" cookery of chef Michiel van Berge employs the freshest of ingredients and tricks of the flavor trade from around the world. ⊠ *Am-stel 2, Eastern Canal Ring* ☎ *020/639–2899* ⌂ *Reservations essential* ▭ *MC, V* ☺ *Closed Sun. No lunch.*

$–$$$ ✕ **Segugio.** Two local and long respected Italian chefs came together to open this temple to the taste buds. And perhaps as tribute to the an-cient family recipes they brought as their heritage, they even got one of their pappas to stucco the walls Venetian style to give a nice, simple, and spacious feel to the proceedings. In summer you can have aperitifs on the patio and in winter you can request a table by the open fire. No matter what the season, however, foodies will love the full chef five-course menu for €48.50. But even going with one main course, such as the always sublime risotto of the day, or a roasted rabbit hopped up with capers and olives, usually proves fail-safe too. ⊠ *Utrechtsestraat 96, Eastern Canal Ring* ☎ *020/330–1503* ⊕ *www.segugio.nl* ▤ *AE, MC, V.*

Jordaan

As Amsterdam's most colorful and authentic neighborhood, it should not surprise that the Jordaan has some of the most colorful and authentic—whether Italian or Indian—restaurants. Afterwards, you can order your digestive at a friendly local bar.

$–$$ ✕ **Groene Lantaarn.** Traditionally Swiss, cheese fondue has long been the party dish of choice for the Dutch, and this place offers a beautiful old-world setting to enjoy this or another of the many cheese options. The menu documents fondue's evolution and infinite global variants, offering such options as the communal deep-frying of meats to the shared steaming of dim sum. Of fundamental importance: the bar is fully stocked with a variety of grease-cutting agents. ⊠ *Bloemgracht 47, Jordaan* ☎ *020/620–2088* ⚒ *Reservations essential* ▤ *AE, MC, V* ☺ *Closed Mon.–Wed. No lunch.*

★ $$ ✕ **Café de Reiger.** This excellent neighborhood brown café has a long history—reflected in its tile tableaux and century-old fittings—of being packed with boisterous drinkers and diners. The Dutch fare is of the bold and honest meat-potato-vegetable variety, always wonderfully prepared and sometimes even with an occasional adventurous diversion, such as the sea bass tastily swimming in a sauce of fennel and spinach. At lunchtime there is a menu of sandwiches and warm snacks. ⊠ *Nieuwe Leliestraat 34, Jordaan* ☎ *020/624–7426* ⚒ *Reservations essential* ▤ *AE, MC, V.*

★ $$ ✕ **Toscanini.** In the heart of Amsterdam's most authentic neighborhood is a true-blue Florentine cantina, one that is a perennial favorite with professionals and media types alike. The open kitchen, skylighted ceiling, wooden floors and tables, and the ultimately personable service all work to create a sense that you have just stepped into Grandmama's country kitchen. The cooks pride themselves in the creation of any regional dish, but you will undoubtedly find your favorite already listed in the extensive menu. The risottos are profound, the fish dishes sublime, the desserts decadent, plus the wine list is inspired. What more can one ask? ⊠ *Lindengracht 75, Jordaan* ☎ *020/623–2813* ⚒ *Reservations essential* ▤ *AE, DC, MC, V* ☺ *Closed Sun. No lunch.*

$–$$ ✕ **Lorreinen.** There are many nooks and crannies for the romantic-minded to hide in and a general historical ambience that fuses nicely with the evocative square on which it is situated (and where the terrace is set up in summer). The reasonably priced and conscientiously prepared French-based Continental menu usually plays it safe but can also surprise with a thick tuna steak smothered with pesto and served with polenta or a more seasonal dish that stews a venison steak to succulence with the aid of a pear, red wine, and endives. ⊠ *Noordermarkt 42, Jordaan* ☎ *020/624–3689* ▤ *AE, DC, MC, V* ☺ *Closed Tues. No lunch.*

$ ✕ **Tapasbar a La Plancha.** With their tortilla and garlicky gambas both being perfect, Plancha passes the standard tapas test. Indeed all their tapas rate among the best in town. You also quickly realize, as communications invariably break down with the friendly service, they are also the most authentic. This place is very popular with neighborhood locals and so tiny that the bull's head over the bar barely fits, but booking ahead or dropping by during a quieter time during their long hours (till 1 AM on weekdays and till 3 AM on weekends) should have you squashed in no time. ⊠ *1e Looiersdwarsstraat 15, at Looiersgracht, Jordaan* ☎ *020/420–3633* ▤ *MC, V* ☺ *Closed Mon.*

CloseUp
PROOST!: DUTCH BEERS & BREWS

WITH BRANDS SUCH AS HEINEKEN and Grolsch available all around the world, you can be sure that the Dutch know their beers. Although most breweries have moved outside Amsterdam, a cloud of malt and hop vapors occasionally envelops the city in its rich aroma. The Dutch are especially fond of their pils, a light golden lager usually served with a large head. Locals claim their pils tastes better if sipped through the foam, so asking for a top-up may offend. There are stronger beers, usually referred to as bokbier—usually seasonal, they are made with warming spices in winter. In summer, witte bier (white beer) is a refreshing drink, a zesty brew served cool with a twist of lemon. The indigenous liquor of The Netherlands is jenever, a potent gin. Not as bitter as English gin, it is usually drunk neat from small, tall glasses. It comes in varieties from jonge (young gin), with a rough edge, to the more sophisticated oude (mature gin), matured in vats for years. Locals knock back their gin borrel (in one gulp), but beware. When served accompanying a beer it is known as a kopstoot ("headbang"). The name should be taken as a warning to the uninitiated. There are also fruit-flavor gin variants, with currant or lemon juice, for those with a sweeter tooth. Try out Dutch liquors at a proeflokaal or proeverij, an old-fashioned "tasting-house." An after-work phenomenon, most tasting houses close by early evening.

¢ ✕ **Moeders Pot.** "Mother's Pot" does not refer to a beer-swilling matriarch (nor to your mother's lesbian lover as the local parlance would interpret it) but rather to those local old-school home-cooking recipes that deem that each meat, potato, and vegetable should rightly have the life completely fried out of it. But don't be frightened: rarely will you find such mass amounts of staple foods costing less or an interior more charmingly kitsch-addled. And since one man does all the work here, please be sensitive to the fact that he might have to rush off to flip a steak in mid-order. If you want your local cuisine served up quickly and "Cultural," head here. ⊠ *Vinkenstraat 119, Jordaan* ☎ *020/623–7643* ▭ *No credit cards* ☉ *Closed Sun. No lunch.*

Museum District & South Amsterdam
Monuments to culture, acres of lush greenery, and residences for the rich combine to make the areas around Museumplein and Zuid Amsterdam both rich with high-end culinary favorites.

★ $$$–$$$$ ✕ **Le Garage.** A decade ago, this building's industrial roots were erased by the maverick Dutch architect Cees Dam to make room for a brasserie of red plush seating and kaleidoscopically mirrored walls—handy for its clientele of Hollandwood glitterati who like to see and be seen. This is the home of the celebrity "Crazy Chef" Joop Braakhekke, whose busy schedule of TV appearances forces him to leave his "kitchen of the world" to other—ironically more capable—hands. The food is invariably excellent and uses French haute cuisine as the basis on which to embrace the whole world. Particularly sublime is the Flemish *hennepotje,* a starter pâté of chicken, snails, and rabbit, and the Moroccan *pastilla d'anguille* which seals a mélange of duck liver and eel in a thin pastry dough. While champagnes, fine wines, and caviar accent the essential poshness of it all, the daily set lunch menu is actually quite reasonably priced. They now also have a sister establishment, En Pluche (020/471–4695) next door serving "global street foods" and fancy cocktails. ☒ *Ruysdaelstraat 54, Museum District* ☎020/679–7176 ☖ *Reservations essential* ⌂ *Jacket and tie* ▤ *AE, DC, MC, V* ☉ *No lunch weekends.*

★ **$$–$$$** ✕ **Bodega Keyzer.** In the shadow of the golden lyre that tops the Concertgebouw, this institution has been serving musicians and concertgoers alike for almost a century. You can come at almost any hour for a simple drink or a full meal. The appropriately classical, Old Dutch, dimly lit interior—as comfortable as an old shoe—is paneled with dark wood and the tables covered with Oriental carpets. Aside from such relative oddities as *ris de veau* (veal sweetbreads) with orange and green pepper sauce, the tournedos- and schnitzel-rich menu leans toward tradition, with a sole meunière being the house specialty. ☒ *Van Baerlestraat 96, Museum District* ☎ *020/671–1441* ▤ *AE, DC, MC, V.*

$$–$$$ ✕ **Brasserie van Baerle.** If it's Sunday and you want to brunch on the holiest of trinities—blinies, caviar, and champagne—look no further. The simple, elegant modern decor and the professional yet personal service also attracts a business crowd at lunch, as well as late-night diners on an aesthetic roll after attending the nearby Concertgebouw. The imaginative chef also knows how to put on an inspired show with a fusion menu that includes both light and spicy Asian salads and heavier fares such as duck in truffle sauce. There is outdoor dining in good weather. ☒ *Van Baerlestraat 158, Museum District* ☎ *020/679–1532* ▤ *AE, DC, MC, V* ☉ *Closed Sat.*

$$–$$$ ✕ **Sama Sebo.** Taking care that the incendiary level is palatable, this small, busy, and relaxed neighborhood restaurant acts as a good Intro to Indo. Located near Museumplein, Sama Sebo has been dishing out *rijsttafel*, a feast with myriad exotically spiced small dishes, for the last 30 years in an atmosphere characteristically enhanced by rush mats and shadow puppets. There are also simpler dishes such as *bami goreng* (spicy fried noodles with vegetables and meat options) and *nasi goreng* (same, but with the noodles replaced by rice). There's also a bar where you can wait, have a beer, and get to know the regulars. ☒ *P. C. Hooftstraat 27, Museum District* ☎ *020/662–8146* ▤ *AE, DC, MC, V* ☉ *Closed Sun.*

$$–$$$ ✕ **Vakzuid.** This sprawling bar-café-lounge-restaurant is located in the recently reinvented 1928 Olympic Stadium, an architectural monument designed by one of the founders of De Stijl, Jan Wils. Vakzuid (which translates as "Section South," indicating its locale within the stadium complex) fits right in with its contemporary take on the functionally modern. This is indeed a space for all needs: a huge, sunny patio (accessible by water taxi) with plush comfortable seating and parasols; a solo-friendly bar specializing in coffee and designer sandwiches by day and cocktails and sushi by night; a comfortable lounge area with a view over the track field; and a raised restaurant section with an open kitchen and "Wok Bar," serving a fusion of Mediterranean and Asian cookeries. Weekend evenings see Vakzuid transform into something resembling a nightclub, complete with noise, smoke, bouncers, and DJs. Reservations are essential for the restaurant. ☒ *Olympisch Stadion 35, South Amsterdam* ☎ *0900/825–9843* ▤ *AE, DC, MC, V.*

$$ ✕ **Bond.** Bond. Jan Bond. With its golden ceiling above and lush lamps, sofas, and sounds below, Bond is equally double-oh-so-seventies as it is comfortably experimental. Ditto for the menu which darts from rabbit braised to perfection to steak grilled with heirloom mushrooms to fish roasted with corn, wild parsnips, and oranges. Being close to the similarly gilded Concertgebouw, Bond can also be a great location for, say, a post-Rossini martini. Lunchtime sees things a tad more restrained, with choices running more along the lines of club sandwiches and decidedly non-McDonalds-like Caesar salads. ☒ *Valeriusstraat 128b, Museum Quarter and South Amsterdam* ☎ *020/676–4647* ⊟ *No credit cards.*

East of the Amstel

Head away from the historical center and toward this tranquil neighborhood for some of the best meals in town.

★ $$$$ ✕ **De Kas** This 1926-built municipal "greenhouse" (not to be confused with a coffee shop of the same name) must be the ultimate workplace for chefs: they can begin the day picking the best and freshest of homegrown produce before building up an inspired French-based menu around them. For diners it's equally sumptuous, especially since the setting harbors two such very un-Dutch commodities as maximum light and a giddy sense of vertical space. One can also opt for the whole hog on the chef's table which will set you back €102.50 including wine. Reservations are essential since this place was quick to chart high in the culinary orbit when it opened in 2002. ☒ *Kamerlingh Onnelaan 3, East of the Amstel* ☎ *020/462–4562* ⊟ *AE, DC, MC, V* ☺ *Closed Sun. No lunch Sat.*

★ $$$–$$$$ ✕ **La Rive.** The Amstel Inter-Continental's La Rive maintains its long held reputation for celestial cuisine under talented young chef Edwin Kats, whom you can witness in action if you book yourself a seat at the "chef's table." An overall sense of elegance and Amstel River views provide the backdrop to a French-Mediterranean menu that favors only the most luxurious of ingredients. Chubby-walleted epicureans should settle in for one of the three five-course choices on offer, priced €80, €95, and €135. ☒ *Amstel Inter-Continental Hotel, Professor Tulpplein 1, East of the Amstel* ☎ *020/622–6060* ⋔ *Jacket and tie* ⊟ *AE, DC, MC, V.*

★ $$ ✕ **VandeMarkt.** "From the Market" states its intent: to create four choices over three (€32) or four (€42) courses made from the freshest ingredients found at the market that morning. Certainly unique for this neighborhood, the setting is sleek and up-to-the-minute trendy, with simple pine floors and tables contrasting with the eye-arresting walls of bright color blocks. Also accented is the pan-Mediterranean approach, which belies a particular respect for Morocco with the sauces often given substance with nuts and chickpeas. The menu will include anything from a lobster bisque with prawn wonton parcels or a wild duck with a sauce of sage. ☒ *Schollenbrugstraat 8–9, East of the Amstel* ☎ *020/ 468–6958* ⌸ *Reservations essential* ⊟ *AE, DC, MC, V* ☺ *Closed Sun. No lunch.*

★ $–$$ ✕ **Plancius.** With an arty but calming interior of leather walls and primary color accents, Plancius offers a refreshing sense of space after the chaos of the Artis zoo or the cramped exhibits on view at the Resistance Museum. After breakfast and lunch served during the day, evenings see it emerge as a fashionable restaurant with the tables getting packed tighter and the conviviality factor compounded. The superb menu is adventurous, mixing and matching everything from Italian panzarotti to Indian dhal-lentil soup, to fish steaks with teriyaki and tahini sauce. Everything is homemade from scratch, right down to the tapenade. ☒ *Plantage Kerklaan 61a, Plantage* ☎ *020/330–9469* ⊟ *AE, DC, MC, V.*

WHERE TO STAY

By Jonette Stabbert

Amsterdam is a city of hundreds of canals, but its hotels also rack up the numbers; there are more than 300 to choose from. Many are small mom-and-pop operations, best described as pensions, usually found within the 17th-century gabled houses that line the canals or in the residential neighborhoods beyond the center, such as the conveniently situated Museum District. Often decorated with antique furnishings, they capture the charm and flavor of Amsterdam, which can be enhanced by booking a room with a watery vista, so do ask. While many of these rooms are perhaps "cozier" than you are used to, their small size will be usually compensated with friendly, relaxed, and speedy service. The larger hotels, including the expensive international chains, are clustered around Centraal Station, at Dam Square, and near Leidseplein, and one of these—the Amsterdam Hilton—was immortalized (at least for Beatles fans) by John and Yoko's famous "Bed-In" for peace.

Amsterdam being a tourist mecca, reservations are advised at any time of the year and are essential in tulip season (late March–June) and through the summer. Annual conventions also fill the city for weeks in the beginning of September. Some of the hotels are very small and benefit from excellent word-of-mouth, so they book quickly. The Amsterdam tourist office, known as the VVV (Vereniging voor Vreemdelingenverkeer), can book hotel rooms for you in all categories if you arrive without reservations. They charge a small fee per reservation and also receive a commission from the hotel, which has a tendency to drive prices up. The VVV books for everything—including tickets for tours, theater, and concerts—and the offices are ridiculously crowded in summer with all manner of visitors needing same-day booking (and, unfortunately, with an unsavory local crowd of opportunists offering sleazy accommodations to desperate students and backpackers). Off-season travelers, besides bringing an umbrella, should be sure to inquire about the friendlier prices.

The lodgings we list are the current cream of the crop in each price category. We always list the facilities that are available—but we don't specify whether they cost extra: when pricing accommodations, always ask what's included and what costs extra. For instance, although Amsterdam is a biker/pedestrian's paradise, it is a driver's nightmare, and few hotels have parking lots (and if they do, charge accordingly). Most of the pricing includes a VAT (Value Added Tax) of 6% and in some cases the city tax of 5% may be included. Always be sure to ask which of the taxes are included in the pricing. Most hotels operate on the European Plan (with no meals) and some on the Continental Plan (with a Continental breakfast); for the latter, inquire when booking. Price categories are assigned based on the range between their least and most expensive standard double rooms in nonholiday high season, based on the European Plan (with no meals) unless otherwise noted.

WHAT IT COSTS In euros*				
$$$$	$$$	$$	$	¢
HOTELS over €230	€165–€230	€120–€165	€75–€120	under €75

*Prices are for two people in a standard double room in high season, including the 6% VAT (value-added tax).

From the Amstel to the Plantage

Ranging from the Amstel River, running through the southeastern sector of the city center, to the small tranquil neighborhood known as the Plantage, this area is just the place for a relaxed stay. The Hortus Botanicus, Artis Zoo, and the Tropenmuseum dominate the Plantage area; just beyond lies the residential quarters of *Oost* (East) Amsterdam.

★ $$$$ ⊞ **Amstel Inter-Continental.** Welcome to a decidedly old-world vision of heaven and one that rates extra points for its scenic location along the Amstel River. Elegant enough to please a queen, extroverted enough to welcome Madonna, the Rolling Stones, and Michael Jackson, this grand dowager has wowed all onlookers since it opened its doors in 1867. With its palatial five stories, sash windows, and historic roof dormers, this lily was gilded in 1992 with a renovation by Pierre Yves Rochon of Paris, whose emphasis on its long-established grace and elegance made it possible not only to imagine the svelte Audrey Hepburn here but to understand why she became a fixture in this environment. You'll feel like a visiting dignitary when entering the magnificent lobby, a soaring salon covered with wedding-cake stucco trim and replete with a grand double staircase that demands you glide, not walk, down it. The guest rooms are the most spacious in the city (though they shrink considerably on the top floor), and the decor creates the ambience of a home personalized by Oriental rugs, brocade upholstery, Delft lamps, and a color palette of warm tones inspired by Makkum pottery. Fresh tulips are placed in all of the rooms, and the bathrooms spoil guests with showerheads the size of dinner plates. The generous staff-to-guest ratio, the top-notch food—in particular, at the award-winning La Rive restaurant—the riverside terrace, the Amstel Lounge (perfect for drinks), and the endless stream of extra "little touches" (such as yacht service), will make for a truly baronial experience. ⊠ *Professor Tulpplein 1, 1018 GX, Plantage* ☎ *020/622–6060* 🖷 *020/622–5808* ⊕ *www.amsterdam.intercontinental. com* ↯ *55 rooms, 24 suites* & *2 restaurants, room service, in-room data ports, cable TV, indoor pool, health club, bar, dry cleaning, laundry service, business services* ☰ *AE, DC, MC, V* ⑩ *EP.*

$$$ 🏨 **Arena.** This grand complex set in a former 19th-century Roman Catholic orphanage consists of the hotel, a café-restaurant, a patio, a back garden, and a dance club (complete with frescoed walls that reflect its former function as a clandestine church). For those who like spare minimal style the hotel is strikingly austere—as if it were torn from the pages of *Wallpaper* magazine. The lobby is minimalist white, which draws attention to the impressive cast-iron staircase leading to the rooms. The hotel used the hottest young Dutch architects and designers to supervise the recent renovation, which has helped erase the shadow of its past as a youth hostel. Rooms—some of which are split-level to form a lounge area—are painted in white, gray, and mauve tones and are furnished with modernist furniture by Gispen, Eames, and Martin Visser. With all these features, some guests might forget to explore Amsterdam itself. ⊠ *'s-Gravesandestraat 51, 1092 AA, Plantage* ☎ *020/850–2417* 🖷 *020/850–2425* ⊕ *www.hotelarena.nl* ↯ *121 rooms* & *Restaurant, cable TV, bar, dance club; no a/c* ☰ *AE, DC, MC, V* ⑩ *CP.*

$ 🏨 **Fantasia.** Peace and quiet await you in this small, friendly family hotel in a circa-1733 canal house not far from the Plantage. The hotel owner's father was a farmer, which explains the owner's collection of ornamental cows, found everywhere in the hotel. There's a room to suit everyone, from a small attic room (complete with bath) to a family room that sleeps four. ⊠ *Nieuwe Keizersgracht 16, 1018 DR, Plantage* ☎ *020/623– 8259* 🖷 *020/622–3913* ⊕ *www.fantasia-hotel.com* ↯ *19 rooms, 18 with bath* & *Some pets allowed; no a/c, no room TVs* ☰ *AE, MC, V* ☺ *Closed Dec. 16–26 and Jan. 6–Feb. 28* ⑩ *CP.*

★ $ 🏨 **Rembrandt.** Because it is close to the University of Amsterdam, the Artis zoo, Hortus Botanicus, and Tropenmuseum, the Rembrandt hotel is often populated with academics and museum people—so perhaps bring a seriously titled book if you want to gain entry. The rarified air is particularly thick in the remarkable breakfast room: the 18th-century paintings and exquisitely painted woodwork on the ceiling, and the wood paneling and beams carved in and dated 1558, were transported to their current location in the 19th century. Most of the rooms at the back of the hotel facing the garden are quiet. Duplex Room 21, in the front, can accommodate a family of six, and six rooms can house three or four. All rooms are immaculately clean. ⊠ *Plantage Middenlaan 17, 1018 DA, Plantage* ☎ *020/627–2714* 🖷 *020/638–0293* ⊕ *www. hotelrembrandt.nl* 🖙 *16 rooms, 1 suite* ⚭ *Cable TV, library; no a/c* ⊟ *AE, MC, V* ❘⊙❘ *CP.*

The Canal Rings

When in Rome, you know what to do. So, when in Amsterdam, consider opting for a stay in an evocative Grachtengordel (canal ring) lodging with all the Golden Age trimmings. As for neighborhoods, these canal-side hotels are listed as either in the Western Canal Ring, which is northwest of the Golden Bend area, or the Eastern Canal Ring, which is southeast of the Golden Bend area.

★ **\$\$\$\$** 🏨 **Blake's.** Known for her chic London hotels, Anouska Hempel opened this Amsterdam outpost as the city's first "designer" hotel. For discerning travelers, this place has everything—even history: its stone-arch entranceway marks this as the site of the 17th-century Municipal Theater before a fire, occurring tragically in midperformance, literally brought down the house. An 18th-century canal house that replaced it long served as a poorhouse and an orphanage. The structure that then replaced the poorhouse now ranks, with its East-meets-West decor, as one of the city's most elegant buildings. The furnishings are accented with lacquered trunks, mahogany screens, modernist hardwood tables, and cushy cushions in fine fabrics. One suite commands a view of the canal; other rooms overlook a central courtyard and are serenely quiet. The palette of each room exudes a Zen-like calm: gray to blue, terra-cotta to chocolate brown, ruby red to cream. The flow of water in the bathroom sinks acts more like a fountain than a tap. The hotel's exclusive restaurant now offers an acclaimed Asian-Western menu. All the delicious luxury on offer in this hotel is happily accented by the youthful but able service. ⊠ *Keizersgracht 384, 1016 GB, Western Canal Ring* ☎ *020/530–2010* 🖷 *020/530–2030* ⊕ *www.slh.com/blakes* 🖙 *22 rooms, 19 suites* ⚭ *Restaurant, cable TV, in-room data ports, boating, bar, meeting rooms* ⊟ *AE, DC, MC, V* ❘⊙❘ *EP.*

★ **\$\$\$\$** 🏨 **Pulitzer Sheraton.** A clutch of 17th- and 18th-century houses—25 in all—were combined to create this rambling hotel sprinkled with landscaped garden courtyards. It faces the Prinsengracht and the Keizersgracht canals and is just a short walk from both the Dam Square and the Jordaan. The place retains a historic ambience: most guest rooms—which are surprisingly spacious compared with its labyrinth of narrow halls and steep stairs—have beam ceilings and antique stylings. An appropriately historical sound track is provided every half hour when the nearby Westerkerk chimes the time. However, a certain irreverent postmodern quirkiness is occasionally evident by the paintings, belonging to the hotel's own extensive collection, decorating the hallways, rooms, and restaurant (where a "Frans Hals" harbors such time warps as Heineken cans and cell phones). The hotel was completely refurbished in 2000 to increase comfort and convenience—for instance, heated bathroom floors mean that your toes will remain toasty. Other perks, such as a prizewinning wine cellar and a wooden boat for touring, guarantee the Pulitzer its own award: a steady stream of returning guests. Note, there are several lower-priced rooms usually available here. ⊠ *Prinsengracht 315–331, 1016 GZ, Western Canal Ring* ☎ *020/ 523–5235* 🖷 *020/627–6753* ⊕ *www.luxurycollection.com/pulitzer* 🖙 *224 rooms, 6 suites* ⚭ *Restaurant, café, room service, in-room data ports, in-room safes, cable TV, bar, baby-sitting, dry cleaning, laundry service, business services, some pets allowed* ⊟ *AE, DC, MC, V* ❘⊙❘ *EP.*

★ $$$$ ⊞ **Seven One Seven.** Signed with only its house number, "717" is more like an exclusive "home away from home" than a hotel—or would be, if you happened to reside in a classical 19th-century canal-side guest house. Fusing grandeur with tasteful glamour, its designer and former proprietor, Kees van der Valk (who has since retired to warmer climes), was a fashion designer who savvily applied men's suiting fabrics as upholstery for the overstuffed armchairs and sofas. The guest rooms also reflect his discerning eye; set up as minimuseums, they are filled with classical antiquities, framed art, flowers, and objets and candles on tables and fireplace mantels. Each of the splendid suites pays homage to a different composer, artist, or writer. Breakfast can be served in the suites or downstairs in the Stravinsky Room, where coffee, tea, cakes, wine, and beer are available for the asking throughout the day and evening from the discreet but always willing help. There is an extensive DVD selection in the plush library, a setting designed after Sherlock Holmes's own heart. However, literary pursuits are perhaps best enjoyed on the lush back patio. ⊠ *Prinsengracht 717, 1017 JW, Western Canal Ring* ☎ *020/427–0717* 📠 *020/423–0717* ⊕ *www.717hotel.nl* ⟿ *8 suites* ⚹ *In-room data ports, in-room safes, minibars, cable TV* ▤ *AE, DC, MC, V* ⵙ *CP.*

★ $$$ ⊞ **Ambassade.** Ten 17th- and 18th-century houses have been folded into this hotel on the Herengracht near the Spui Square, whose Friday book market might explain the Ambassade's popularity with book-world people: not only did Howard Norman set part of his *Museum Guard* here, but also such renowned surnames as Lessing, Le Carré, Eco, and Rushdie are known regulars. Two lounges—one of which functions as breakfast room—and the library are elegantly decorated with Oriental rugs, chandeliers, clocks, paintings, and antiques. The canal-side rooms are spacious, with large floor-to-ceiling windows and solid, functional furniture. The rooms at the rear are quieter but smaller and darker. Attic rooms have beam ceilings, providing a period atmosphere. In short: there's a room for practically every desire. Service is attentive and friendly, and if by the smallest of chances you do end up getting out of sorts, you can always seek refuge in the flotation tanks. ⊠ *Herengracht 341, 1016 AZ, Western Canal Ring* ☎ *020/555–0222* 📠 *020/555–0277* ⊕ *www.ambassade-hotel.nl* ⟿ *59 rooms, 8 suites, 1 apartment* ⚹ *Room service, in-room safes, cable TV, spa, bar, baby-sitting, dry cleaning, laundry service, business services* ▤ *AE, DC, MC, V* ⵙ *EP.*

★ $$–$$$ ⊞ **Het Canal House.** The owners have put a lot of love and style into this 17th-century (1640) canal-house hotel. It's a beautiful old home with high plaster ceilings, antique furniture, old paintings, and a backyard garden bursting with plants and flowers. Every room is unique—but you can probably count on a grandmotherly quilt on the bed—in both size and decor, and there isn't a television set in sight (although, oddly for this sort of setup, there is an elevator). The elegant chandeliered breakfast room with burled-wood grand piano overlooks the garden, and there is a small bar in the front parlor. Wandering the halls is a treat. ⊠ *Keizersgracht 148, 1015 CX, Western Canal Ring* ☎ *020/622–5182* 📠 *020/624–1317* ⊕ *www.canalhouse.nl* ⟿ *26 rooms* ⚹ *In-room data ports; no a/c, no room TVs* ▤ *AE, DC, MC, V* ⵙ *CP.*

★ $–$$ ⊞ **Prinsengracht Hotel.** With vast town-house windows overlooking the houseboat-graced Prinsengracht Canal, these three 18th-century canal houses are a popular choice. When the weather is fine, it is delightful to breakfast in the hotel's garden. Guests can also choose to stay in the small "house" in the garden, a simple affair that sleeps up to four. Front rooms have a view of the Prinsengracht, and back rooms overlook the garden. A short walk takes you to the Rembrandtplein, the Flower Market, and the main shopping area by the Kalverstraat. ⊠ *Prinsen-*

gracht 1015, 1017 KN, Western Canal Ring ☎ *020/623–7779* 🖷 *020/ 623–8926* ⊕ *www.prinsengrachthotel.nl* ⬥ *33 rooms, 1 garden house* ⑃ *In-room data ports, in-room safes, cable TV, bar; no a/c* ⊟ *AE, DC, MC, V* ⑃ *CP.*

$ 🏨 **Armada.** The Hotel Armada offers a superb canal-side location at the corner of the Utrechtsestraat, an area of excellent shopping and dining. The rooms are simple, and some doubles can be adjusted to accommodate additional guests. Twelve of the rooms have neither bath nor shower but share facilities down the hall. The breakfast room has an aquarium, and—in 17th-century style—small Oriental carpets cover the tables. ✉ *Keizersgracht 713–715, 1017 DX, Eastern Canal Ring* ☎ *020/623–2980* 🖷 *020/623–5829* ⬥ *26 rooms, 14 with bath* ⑃ *Cable TV, bar, some pets allowed* ⊟ *AE, MC, V* ⑃ *CP.*

$ 🏨 **Keizersgracht.** Appealing to youthful and budget-minded travelers, the Hotel Keizersgracht is on its namesake canal within a five-minute walk of Centraal Station. The hotel is very plain, but the staff is friendly and helpful with advice regarding your Holland itinerary. All rooms have private toilets and shower facilities, and there is an elevator. Guests gather in the downstairs bar to socialize, watch TV, and play pool, pinball, or video games. Light meals and snacks can be ordered throughout the day. ✉ *Keizersgracht 15–17, 1015 CC, Western Canal Ring* ☎ *020/625–1364* 🖷 *020/620–7347* ⬥ *26 rooms* ⑃ *Restaurant, bar; no a/c, no room phones, no room TVs* ⊟ *AE, DC, MC, V* ⑃ *EP.*

¢–$ 🏨 **Hegra.** In a 17th-century building on the Herengracht canal, the Hotel Hegra is what the Dutch call *klein maar fijn* (small but good). Rooms are unpretentious but comfortable and the ones in front have a canal view. Not all rooms have private baths. The absence of facilities is offset by the cordiality of the family that runs the hotel, the great location (with a proximity to the Anne Frank House, shopping streets, and the major art museums), not to mention the relatively gentle price tag. ✉ *Herengracht 269, 1016 BJ, Western Canal Ring* ☎ *020/623–7877* 🖷 *020/623–8159* ⬥ *11 rooms, 8 with bath* ⑃ *No a/c, no room phones, no room TVs* ⊟ *AE, DC, MC, V* ⑃ *CP.*

Jordaan

While wandering this most singular of neighborhoods, you may decide it is your most favorite of all—so why not stay in it? The bells from the Westertoren church tower take you back in time. Sleepy little canals and narrow cobblestone streets with lopsided 17th-century houses give the Jordaan a special charm. On the surface, the neighborhood still looks very much as it did when Anne Frank lived here, although behind the weatherworn exteriors it now sports numerous fascinating boutiques and antique shops.

★ $$–$$$ 🏨 **Toren.** The historic setting for the founding of the Free University in the 17th century, this is a perfect example of a canal-side hotel. Occupying two buildings from 1638, the Toren has an evocative garden and offers every modern convenience (such as whirlpool baths in the higher-priced rooms) for both business travelers and honeymooners. A 1999 renovation gained it four-star status, but its service often exceeds even that. Family-run for several generations, the Hotel Toren is in the shadow of the Westerkerk *toren* (Western Church tower) in the Jordaan, but the "toren" is also the family name. There is a beautiful carved wooden and mirrored bar. The unique and charming garden cottage is on call to serve as a delightful bridal suite. ✉ *Keizersgracht 164, 1015 CZ, Jordaan* ☎ *020/622–6033* 🖷 *020/626–9705* ⊕ *www.toren.nl* ⬥ *37 rooms, 2 suites, 1 garden cottage* ⑃ *Room service, in-room data ports, in-room safes, cable TV, bar, some pets allowed* ⊟ *AE, DC, MC, V* ⑃ *EP.*

$$ ⊞ **'t Hotel.** On a romantic canal in the Jordaan, the small and intimate 't Hotel is in an 18th-century house. Because this is a listed monument, they aren't permitted to add an elevator. Those unable to navigate traditional steep and narrow Dutch staircases need not completely despair, as one of the apartments is only three steps down. Rooms are larger than the norm in a hotel this size. Those in the rear are especially quiet, and the top back room has a garden view. Little wonder guests return year after year. Antiques are for sale in a small shop within the hotel. ✉ *Leliegracht 18, 1015 DE, Western Canal Ring* ☎ *020/422–2741* 🖷 *020/626–7873* ⊕ *www.thotel.nl* ⇱ *8 rooms, 1 apartment* ᕕ *In-room data ports, cable TV, some pets allowed; no a/c* ▤ *AE, DC, MC, V* ⏀ *CP.*

★ **$$** ⊞ **Wiechmann.** A favorite with rock musicians—of both the punk (Sex Pistols) and country (Emmy Lou Harris) persuasions—the Wiechmann's main claim to fame is announced by a collection of gold records displayed in the lobby, the pride and joy of the owner, Mr. Boddy, who has run this hotel for 50 years. There are delightful personal touches throughout the lobby and adjoining breakfast room, where Mrs. Boddy's fantastic collection of teapots, toys, and antiques adds a cheerful note. The hotel seems like a maze of hallways leading through three buildings to the guest rooms (which are of wildly varying sizes). It's worth the extra money for the ones with views over the canal. Although the hotel's facilities could use some upgrading, it, along with its owners, is enchanting. ✉ *Prinsengracht 328–330, 1016 HX, Jordaan* ☎ *020/626–3321* 🖷 *020/626–8962* ⊕ *www.hotelwiechmann.nl* ⇱ *38 rooms* ᕕ *In-room data ports, cable TV; no a/c* ▤ *MC, V* ⏀ *CP.*

★ **$** ⊞ **Acacia.** As the Jordaan is Amsterdam's friendliest neighborhood, the small family-run Acacia is a good ambassador for the nabe, thanks to its quiet, clean, and welcoming vibe. The public rooms here are oh-so-cozy and grandmotherly, but you might opt to "go native" and book one of the two self-catering houseboats moored out front. The Acacia is within walking distance of the Anne Frankhuis and the Westertoren church, and is right next door to a typical Jordaan café, noted for its charming *gezelligheid* (coziness), as is, of course, the whole district, full of interesting, quirky shops offering collectibles, handmade jewelry, and antiques. ✉ *Lindengracht 251, 1015 KH, Jordaan* ☎ *020/622–1460* 🖷 *020/638–0748* ⊕ *www.hotelacacia.nl* ⇱ *20 rooms (4 on houseboats), 2 apartments* ᕕ *Cable TV; no a/c* ▤ *MC, V* ⏀ *CP.*

★ **¢–$** ⊞ **Nadia.** Just a few minutes' walk from the Westertoren, Anne Frankhuis and the Royal Palace, this friendly family hotel is in a gorgeous historic building, replete with kiosk corner turret, Art Nouveau-y portals, and redbrick trim. Inside, rooms are white, modern, and casual, and some have adorable views overlooking the canals (sleepers bothered by noise should opt for rooms in the rear) and framed by the building's architectural trim. The breakfast room is idyllic, bathed in a rosy orange glow, topped by a chandelier, with leafy views out the windows. This place enjoys a great location for seeing the sights. ✉ *Raadhuisstraat 51, 1016 DD, Jordaan* ☎ *020/620–1550* 🖷 *020/428–1507* ⊕ *www.nadia.nl* ⇱ *38 rooms* ᕕ *In-room data ports, in-room safes, cable TV; no a/c* ▤ *AE, MC, V* ⏀ *CP.*

Leidseplein

It can be noisy in the city's busiest square, but then again sometimes it pays to be centrally located.

★ **$$$$** ⊞ **Crowne Plaza Amsterdam-American.** Housed in one of the city's most fancifully designed buildings—one that is said to form the missing link between Art Nouveau and the Amsterdam School—the American (the name everyone knows it by) is a beloved Amsterdam landmark. Directly on Leidseplein, this 1902 castlelike structure is an agglomeration of Neo-Gothic turrets, Jugendstil gables, Art Deco stained glass, and an Arts & Crafts clock tower. Gloriously overlooking the Singelgracht canal (one reason why the hotel has its own boat landing), this place is a charmer. As for location, it is in the middle of everything. Guest rooms are sizable, bright, and furnished in a modern Art Deco style, and you have a choice between canal and bustling-square views—the latter option having the bonus of small balconies. The hotel entered the new millennium being upgraded—sort of: readers report some rooms with leaky air-conditioning and dysfunctional heating. The decor at the Café Americain is one of the finest in Amsterdam, with original Art Deco lighting fixtures, and murals from 1930 depicting *A Midsummer Night's Dream*. Newlyweds might want to indulge in the Mata Hari Honeymoon Suite, named after the spy fatale who celebrated her own wedding here. ✉ *Leidsekade 97, 1017 PN, Leidseplein* ☎ *020/556–3000* 🖷 *020/556–3001* ⊕ *www.amsterdam-american.crowneplaza.com* ➣ *174 rooms, 11 suites* ⓑ *Restaurant, room service, in-room data ports, cable TV, gym, sauna, 2 bars, dry cleaning, laundry service, meeting rooms* ▤ *AE, DC, MC, V* ⦿*EP.*

★ **$$$–$$$$** ▦ **Dikker and Thijs Fenice.** "Lavish," "classical," and "cozy" are some of the adjectives typically used to describe this hotel, which has a regal address on the Prinsengracht canal. The hotel, first opened as a shop in 1895, has been renowned for fine dining since its founder, A. W. Dikker, entered into a partnership in 1915 with H. Thijs, who had apprenticed with the famous French chef Escoffier. The busy location—happily, all the majestic sash windows are double-glazed—is convenient to the major shopping areas and one block from the Leidseplein, nightlife center of the city. The Art Deco–style rooms are fully modernized, and the hotel underwent a complete renovation in 2001. Of the upper-price hotels, this is one of the few that includes breakfast in the basic room rate. ✉ *Prinsengracht 444, 1017 KE, Leidseplein* ☎ *020/620–1212* 🖷 *020/625–8986* ⊕ *www.dtfh.nl* ➣ *42 rooms* ⓑ *Restaurant, room service, in-room data ports, cable TV, bar, baby-sitting, laundry service, business services, some pets allowed; no a/c* ▤ *AE, DC, MC, V* ⦿ *CP.*

★ **$$$–$$$$** ▦ **Park.** At first glance, the Park looks like everyone's dream of a grand Netherlandish hotel, topped out by a picturesque pepper-pot tower, its 18th-century building set with regal windows, topped off by a roof aflap with colorful flags, and mirrored charmingly in the Singel River. Then you note that although this stately Amsterdam fixture has one foot in history, the other is firmly entrenched in today, thanks to a 1950s wing, guest rooms done up with Le Meridien's traditional-but-modern luxe (cozy colors, swagged curtains, bright patterned bedspreads), and amenities that business travelers love. If the neon lights of Leideplein's shops, casino, and clubs are around the corner, the sylvan glades of Amsterdam's gorgeous Vondelpark are just across the road, beckoning you to take an early-morning jog. ✉ *Stadhouderskade 25, 1071 ZD, Leidseplein* ☎ *020/671–1222* 🖷 *020/664–9455* ⊕ *www.lemeridien.com* ➣ *181 rooms, 6 suites* ⓑ *Restaurant, cable TV, hair salon, bar, baby-sitting, dry cleaning, laundry service, some pets allowed* ▤ *AE, DC, MC, V* ⦿ *EP.*

$ ▦ **Nicolaas Witsen.** If you're just looking for a place to hang your hat and get a quiet night's sleep, the Nicolaas Witsen is a good choice. Run by the same affable family for two generations, the redbrick-and-white-trim hotel is on a peaceful street within walking distance of the Rijksmuseum and the Heineken Brewery. Windows let in lots of light onto the standard-issue guest rooms, your usual array of white walls, Swedish-wood furniture, and modern bathrooms. The breakfast room is cheery, and there is a family room that sleeps up to four people. ⊠ *Nicolaas Witsenstraat 4, 1017 ZH, Leidseplein* ☎ *020/623–6143* 🖨 *020/ 620–5113* ⊕ *www.hotelnicolaaswitsen.nl* 📠 *29 rooms* ⚒ *In-room data ports, cable TV; no a/c* ⊟ *AE, MC, V* ⦿ *CP.*

Museum District & Vondelpark

If you came to Amsterdam for its reputation as the city of the arts, then convenience and tastes dictate that you book a room in this quarter. With the city's top museums located here—and the priciest shopping area just around the corner—plus the city's sylvan Vondelpark situated just to the west, it is little wonder that this entire area has been colonized by fine hotels.

$$$$ ▦ **Vondel.** On a quiet street next to Vondelpark and very close to the Leidseplein, this hotel is refined and contemporary. The lobby and bar, all beige and light wood, are filled with comfortable suede sofas, sunlight, and flowers. The similarly colored rooms, generous in size, are enhanced with flashes of crimson, while a small garden terrace makes for a verdant oasis. Suites are on the top floor and have large windows that follow the shape of the roof and give you a scenic swoop of the neighborhood. Throughout the hotel are paintings by Amsterdam artist Peter Keizer. The hotel, like the park, gets its name from the 17th-century poet, Joost van den Vondel, and the rooms are named after his poems. A lavish breakfast buffet is available, but is not included in the rate. ⊠ *Vondelstraat 28–30, 1054 GE, Vondelpark* ☎ *020/612–0120* 🖨 *020/685– 4321* ⊕ *www.hotelvondel.nl* 📠 *67 rooms, 3 suites* ⚒ *Room service, in-room data ports, in-room safes, minibars, cable TV, bar, baby-sitting, dry cleaning, laundry service, business services* ⊟ *AE, DC, MC, V* ⦿ *EP.*

★ $$ ▦ **Prinsen.** Architect of the Rijksmuseum and Centraal Station, P. H. H. Cuijpers created several of the city's stateliest landmarks, but he rarely came up with such an adorable edifice as this one, built around 1870. Chalet roof, dormers, bay window, jigsaw trim, Neoclassical columns, and sculpted reliefs of cats (one showing a kitty chasing mice) all enchant the eye. The storybook feeling, sadly, ends with one foot in the door. Although it has been gutted and renovated, however, the Prinsen has lots of cheery and gracious bedrooms. On the ground floor, the yellow breakfast room is made even brighter by opening up on a lovely garden. Set on a quiet street next to the Vondelpark, the hotel makes all its guests very welcome and is particularly gay-friendly. ⊠ *Vondelstraat 36–38, 1054 GE, Vondelpark* ☎ *020/616–2323* 🖨 *020/616– 6112* ⊕ *www.prinsenhotel.demon.nl* 📠 *45 rooms* ⚒ *In-room data ports, in-room safes, cable TV, bar, dry cleaning, laundry service, babysitting, some pets allowed; no a/c* ⊟ *AE, DC, MC, V* ⦿ *CP.*

$–$$ ▦ **Hestia.** Located on a street of extraordinary 19th-century houses, the Hestia is parallel to Vondelpark and close to the Leidseplein. Fitted out with red brick, white trim, and a mansard-cute roof, the Hestia is family-operated, with a helpful and courteous staff, and is the kind of place that reinforces the image of the Dutch as a clean and orderly people. The hotel's breakfast room has a view of the garden, and a large family room has a charming sitting area in a bay window with stained glass, which also overlooks the garden. The rooms are basic, light, and simply modern. Four of the rooms are very small, but so is their cost. Larger rooms can be adjusted to accommodate parties of four or five. ⊠ *Roemer Visscherstraat 7, 1054 EV, Vondelpark* ☎ *020/618–0801* 🖨 *020/685–1382* ⊕ *www.hotel-hestia.nl* 📠 *18 rooms* ⚒ *In-room safes, cable TV, some pets allowed; no a/c* ⊟ *AE, DC, MC, V* ⦿ *CP.*

★ $–$$ 🖭 **Hotel de Filosoof.** Looking for something a little bit different? How about bona fide Amsterdam philosophers, regularly to be found ensconced in this hotel's comfy armchairs. It turns out the Filosoof hosts monthly lectures and discussion evenings for the locals and guests, many of whom are, needless to say, artists, writers, and even thinkers. Even the decorator gets into the act: each of the guest rooms is decorated with a different cultural or ideological motif, from Zen to feminism. There is an Aristotle room furnished in Greek style, with passages from the works of Greek philosophers hung on the walls, and a Goethe room adorned with Faustian texts. Some of the rooms are a little silly—the Walden, for instance, sports some landscape daubs on the wall—but the Spinoza is a total knockout: an homage to Golden Age style, complete with black-and-white floors, 19th-century library lamp, and framed paintings, it is a jewel that fancier hotels in town could well take as a model. Enjoy breakfast, or merely relax, in the large garden. ☒ *Anna van den Vondelstraat 6, 1054 GZ, Vondelpark* ☎ *020/683–3013* 🖷 *020/685–3750* ⊕ *www.hotelfilosoof.nl* ⊠ *38 rooms* ♿ *In-room data ports, cable TV, library; no a/c* ☰ *AE, MC, V* ⍩ *CP.*

★ $–$$ 🖭 **Piet Hein.** Not all chocolates have a gooey center. When in 2003 it came time to refurbish this ornate brick Vondelpark mansion, the owners decided to go for the modern, the light, the airy, the less-is-not-a-bore, and they have gorgeously succeeded. Salons don't come any sleeker than these, thanks to cube-shape chairs, straight-as-an arrow sofas, gleaming Swedish woods, sisal-like carpeting, white-on-white hues, and bright bursts of navy blue, perhaps in homage to Piet Hein, the legendary 17th-century Dutch privateer and vice admiral. Other maritime touches include paintings of sailing ships, navy blue carpets with patterns of seaman's knots, and cozy rooms that make you feel like you're in a ship's cabin. Some bedrooms here are so sprightly done up you will feel 10 years younger. Real color lies outside the windows, as front rooms here have fine views of the park (always in demand—even booking far in advance doesn't guarantee you one of these rooms). Those in the back aren't out of luck, as a garden allures at the rear. Here, too, is a *dépendance* annex with additional rooms. Step out the front door and you are within walking distance of the fashionable P. C. Hooftstraat, the Concertgebouw, and the city's major art museums. And making this place even more popular with the *Wallpaper* crowd are the relatively gentle room rates. ☒ *Vossiusstraat 52–53, 1071 AK, Museum District* ☎ *020/662–7205* 🖷 *020/662–1526* ⊕ *www.hotelpiethein.com* ⊠ *61 rooms* ♿ *In-room data ports, in-room safes, cable TV, bar, dry cleaning, laundry service* ☰ *AE, DC, MC, V* ⍩ *CP.*

★ $–$$ 🖭 **Washington.** This small hotel is set a discreet stone's throw from the Museumplein and often attracts international musicians in town to perform at the nearby Concertgebouw—except perhaps those carrying a cello (there's a steep staircase here). The owners are helpful and will lend from their collection of guidebooks. The breakfast room and lounge are filled with antiques and marvelous brass chandeliers, and the hotel is meticulously polished and sparkling clean. The rooms are simply and charmingly decorated in white and pastel shades. Large windows let in a flood of light. The apartments consist of four rooms and even contain a piano. ☒ *F. van Mierisstraat 10, 1071 RS, Museum District* ☎ *020/679–6754* 🖷 *020/673–4435* ⊕ *www.hotelwashington.nl* ⊠ *17 rooms, 4 apartments* ♿ *Cable TV; no a/c* ☰ *AE, DC, MC, V* ⍩ *CP.*

★ $ 🖭 **Museumzicht.** When they call themselves "Museum View," they mean it: the hotel is directly across the street from the Rijksmuseum. The owner formerly had an antiques shop, so the house is filled with wonderful objects. The breakfast room–lounge is special, with a Murano glass chandelier and Art Deco pottery on the chimney walls. The rooms are simple but delightful, with pastel-striped wallpaper and little etchings. The hotel is on the top floors of the building, and guests must climb a narrow and steep stairway with their luggage to the reception desk and to the rooms—the owners highly recommend traveling light. ⊠ *Jan Luykenstraat 22, 1071 CN, Museum District* ☎ *020/671–2954* 🖷 *020/671–3597* ➯ *14 rooms* ⌂ *In-room data ports; no a/c* ⊟ *MC, V* ⍟ *CP.*

★ $ ⌨ **Quentin England.** The intimate Quentin England is one of a series of adjoining buildings dating from 1884, each of which is built in an architectural style of the country whose name it bears. A connoisseur's delight—adorned with a Tudor gable and five-step gable—the Quentin occupies the England and Netherlands buildings. Rooms are simple and vary greatly in size but are cozy and clean. The tiny breakfast room is particularly enchanting, with flower boxes on the windowsills, dark-wood tables, and fin-de-siècle decorations. Behind the reception desk is a small bar and espresso machine (perhaps on loan from the neighboring Italian building?). The hotel offers tremendous character and attention in place of space and facilities. There is an additional 5% fee for using a credit card. ⊠ *Roemer Visscherstraat 30, 1054 EZ, Vondelpark* ☎ *020/689–2323* 🖷 *020/685–3148* ⊕ *www.quentinhotels.com* ➯ *50 rooms* ⌂ *Cable TV; no a/c* ⊟ *AE, DC, MC, V* ⍟ *EP.*

★ ¢ ⌨ **Flying Pig Palace Hostel.** For those backpackers who like to chill out, have their Simpsons done up in psychedelic pink hair (as a wall mural here attests), and save a load of money, the Pig Palaces—there is one in the city center and another in the posher neighborhood of Vondelpark—are the favored choice of "piggies" everywhere. The Flying Pig Downtown is a bit frantic, so why not opt for the Pig near the park and steps away from the Museum District? The policy is strict: if you're not a backpacker aged 18 to 35, look elsewhere. Not only breakfast and sheets are included in the price, but also free Internet and e-mail service and the use of in-line skates (so lace up and explore the park, or join the once-weekly night skate throughout the city). It gets even better: the downstairs bar claims to serve the cheapest beer in town, and you can cook with other guests in the kitchen. The staff is also comprised of backpackers, and a happy guest provided the paintings on view throughout the hostel. If you're traveling with an amour or don't mind sharing with a friend, the best deal is to book a queen-size bunk bed in one of the dorms. The city center hostel is slightly more expensive, but then it hosts a disco twice a week. ⊠ *Vossiusstraat 46, 1012 GJ, Vondelpark* ☎ *020/400–4187* 🖷 *020/421–0802* ⊕ *www.flyingpig.nl* ➯ *2 rooms, 20 dormitories* ⌂ *Bar; no a/c, no room phones, no room TVs* ⊟ *AE, MC, V* ⍟ *CP* ⊠ *Flying Pig Downtown: Nieuwendijk 100, 1012 MR, Nieuwe Zijde* ☎ *020/420–6822* 🖷 *020/421–0802* ➯ *2 rooms, 20 dormitories, all without bath* ⌂ *Bar; no a/c, no room phones, no room TVs* ⌂ *Reservations not accepted* ⊟ *No credit cards* ⍟ *CP.*

Nieuwe Zijde

If you want to stay in the pulsing aorta of Amsterdam, this is ground zero. Crowds mean you'll have plenty of company in the central area radiating out from the Dam Square.

$$$$ ⌨ **NH Grand Hotel Krasnapolsky.** Competing for prominence with the Royal Palace on Dam Square and Amsterdam's "Hilton" of the 19th century, this was Holland's biggest hotel until the real Hilton came along. For a while this was Holland's best, and you can revisit that gilded age by taking a table in the Kras's soaringly beautiful Wintertuin (Winter Garden), still Amsterdam's loveliest place for luncheon. Sitting in this

masterpiece of 19th-century allure, replete with potted palms, green-house roof, Victorian chandeliers, and buffet tables stocked with cakes and roses, will make you feel like a countess or duke. If only the rest of this 1866 landmark was as sugared. Unfortunately, a mishmash of revamping over the years was done with a progressively penurious attitude toward living space. Last renovated in 2003, the guest rooms—now numbering more than 450—vary greatly in size and tend toward serviceable functionality, somewhat of a disappointment after such a grand beginning. In the end, you can be delighted with your room here (keep in mind, prices are wildly variable and bargains can be had) or chagrined. Abristle with hustle and bustle, this "village on the Dam" can delight those in search of the big city lights. Those in search of peace and tranquility will want to head elsewhere, or just camp out in the glorious Winter Garden. ⊠ *Dam 9, 101 JS, Nieuwe Zijde* ☎ *020/554–9111* 📠 *020/626–570* ⊕ *www.nh-hotels.com* ⇋ *431 rooms, 7 suites, 36 apartments* ⟏ *5 restaurants, in-room data ports, in-room safes, cable TV, hair salon, bar, convention center, some pets allowed* ⊟ *AE, DC, MC, V* ⫯⊙⫯ *EP.*

$$$ 🖭 **Tulip Inn Dam Square.** Just around the corner from the Royal Palace, and right in the very heart of the city, this hotel is a surprising oasis of quiet because of its site on a narrow, pedestrians-only street. Within a half-minute's walking distance, you're immersed in the hustle and bustle of the main shopping center. The Amsterdam School–style building is adorned with storybook-ornate brick and stone trim and a gabled roof, so to view it is to step back in time. Inside, rooms are modern and comfortable with terra-cotta and dark green furnishings. The building once housed a liquor distillery, and you can still enjoy a visit to the tasting house next door. A nice plus here is the hotel's level of service—at times, the staff coddles you. ⊠ *Gravenstraat 12–16, 1012 NM, Nieuwe Zijde* ☎ *020/623–3716* 📠 *020/638–1156* ⊕ *www.tulipinndamsquare.com* ⇋ *34 rooms, 4 suites* ⟏ *In-room data ports, cable TV, bar* ⊟ *AE, DC, MC, V* ⫯⊙⫯ *CP.*

$$ 🖭 **Avenue.** The Avenue Hotel is in several historic buildings, one a listed monument that used to be a warehouse for the United East India Company. The hotel interior underwent renovation in 2000, and the new modernization brings bright and cheerful contemporary style to rooms that are small but comfortable. The large and varied breakfast buffet gets raves from guests. ⊠ *Nieuwezijds Voorburgwal 27, 1012 RD, Nieuwe Zijde* ☎ *020/530–9530* 📠 *020/530–9599* ⊕ *www.avenue-hotel.nl* ⇋ *77 rooms* ⟏ *Room service, cable TV, laundry service, some pets allowed; no a/c* ⊟ *AE, DC, MC, V* ⫯⊙⫯ *CP.*

$$ 🖭 **Rho.** Few hotels have as marvelous a lobby as this one, thanks to the building's origins as a 1910s theater. Jugendstil ornament, tile trim, and etched glass all conjure up the soigné style of the turn of the 20th century. A rich maroon color is carried out in furnishings throughout the hotel, conveying a bit of the music-hall tinkle; guest room furnishings for the most part, however, are modern and standard issue. Happily located on a quiet side street off the Dam Square, the Rho is within walking distance to theaters, nightlife, and shopping. ⊠ *Nes 5–23, 1012 KC, Nieuwe Zijde* ☎ *020/620–7371* 📠 *020/620–7826* ⊕ *www.rhohotel.com* ⇋ *167 rooms* ⟏ *Cable TV, bar, dry cleaning, laundry service, some pets allowed; no a/c* ⊟ *AE, MC, V* ⫯⊙⫯ *CP.*

¢–$$ 🖭 **Asterisk.** A touch of the 19th century still hovers about this very friendly (they love children) hotel. Some guest rooms feature ceiling moldings and chandeliers, and more-modern touches make this a comfy option for all. Major art museums, the Leidseplein, the Flower Market, and the Rembrandtplein are all within walking distance of the hotel, which is on a quiet street. For children, cots and high chairs can be used if requested in advance. Breakfast is included in the price only if you pay cash in advance. ⊠ *Den Texstraat 16, 1017 ZA, Nieuwe Zijde* ☎ *020/ 626–2396* 🖷 *020/638–2790* ⊕ *www.asteriskhotel.nl* 🖘 *40 rooms* ⚒ *In-room safes, cable TV* ▤ *MC, V* ⌾⏀ *EP.*

Oude Zijde

The adjacent Red Light District may cast a less-than-rosy glow, but the Old Side, for the most part, remains the city's poshest and most historical neighborhood.

★ $$$$ 🏨 **Grand Sofitel Demeure Amsterdam.** For captivating elegance, nothing tops the facade of the Grand, a Neoclassical courtyard replete with white sash windows, carved marble pediments, and roof abristle with chimneys and gilded weather vanes. If it all seems unchanged since the days of Rembrandt, that's because this hotel's celebrated city-center site has a long and varied history as far as lodgings go. It started simple in the 14th century as a convent before going poshly secular by becoming a *Prinsenhof* (Prince's Courtyard) in 1578 and welcoming such illustrious guests as William of Orange and Maria de Medici. Today's incarnation, opened in 1992, is one of the city's most deluxe hotels, a suitable home-away-from-home for such guests as Mick Jagger and President Jacques Chirac of France. Once inside, the time machine zooms forward to the 20th century. The lobby and public salons are all fairly sedate, done in champagnes and browns, and accented with marble floors, Jugendstil stained-glass windows, and scattered tapestries. More tranquil, low-key style comes with your key—guest rooms offer eye-soothing scenery, with traditional-luxe furniture, fine fabrics, and quiet hues, plus every manner of business mod con. If you want fireworks, repair to the Café Roux, an oak-and-black-trim Art Deco–ish brasserie supervised by the famed Albert Roux. And try to take a peek at the hotel's Marriage Chamber meeting room and its amazing Jugendstil interior. ⊠ *Oudezijds Voorburgwal 197, 1012 EX, Oude Zijde* ☎ *020/555– 3111* 🖷 *020/555–3222* ⊕ *www.thegrand.nl* 🖘 *160 rooms, 6 suites, 16 apartments* ⚒ *Restaurant, room service, in-room data ports, in-room safes, cable TV, indoor pool, massage, sauna, Turkish bath, bar, babysitting, dry cleaning, laundry service, some pets allowed* ▤ *AE, DC, MC, V* ⌾⏀ *EP.*

★ $$$$ 🏨 **Hotel de l'Europe.** Owned by Freddy Heineken's daughter, this hotel is one of the comeliest tulips on the Amsterdam hotel scene. Quiet, gracious, and plush in both decor and service, this queen has a history extending back to 1638, although its delightful, storybook facade dates only to the 19th century. Overlooking the Amstel River, the Muntplein, and the Flower Market, it may be familiar to those who remember the setting of Hitchcock's *Foreign Correspondent.* The chandeliered lobby leads off to the lounge, aglow with ruby and tangerine hues and glittering with gold-trimmed ceiling coves and blackamoor lamps—the perfect setting in which to perfect the art of high tea (served in full glory here). Guest rooms are furnished with reserved, classical elegance: the city-side rooms are full of warm, rich colors; riverside rooms are in brilliant whites and have French windows to let in floods of light. All rooms have luscious swags of Victorian-style draperies as canopies over the beds. And all this 19th-century sense of splendor is backed up with every 21st-century convenience. The Excelsior restaurant pairs splendid river views with a palacelike interior, complete with enchanting ceiling mural. ⊠ *Nieuwe Doelenstraat 2–8, 1012 CP, Oude Zijde* ☎ *020/ 531–1777* 🖷 *020/531–1778* ⊕ *www.leurope.nl* 🖘 *77 rooms, 23 suites* ⚒ *2 restaurants, room service, in-room data ports, minibars, cable TV,* *indoor pool, gym, hair salon, hot tub, sauna, bar, business services, some pets allowed* ▭ *AE, DC, MC, V* ⊚| *EP.*

$ 🏨 **Vijaya.** As with many 18th-century canal-house hotels, the exterior here is eye-catching—this one has a particularly ornate gable—and the inside is modernized. Comfortably furnished rooms in front have a canal view, but the rooms at the back are quieter. The family room sleeps five. Near Dam Square, the main shopping streets and Centraal Station, you are also just a short tram ride away from the major museums. ✉ *O. Z. Voorburgwal 44, 1012 GE, Oude Zijde* ☎ *020/638–0102* 🖷 *020/ 626–9406* ⊕ *www.hotelvijaya.com* ↪ *30 rooms* ♿ *Cable TV, baby-sitting; no a/c* ▭ *AE, DC, MC, V* ⊚| *CP.*

¢ 🏨 **Stayokay Amsterdam-Stadsdoelen Hostel.** Located in a canal house at the edge of the Red Light district, this hostel is a backpacker's Ritz. Usually filled with young, friendly international travelers, it has a reputation as the most gezellig place to stay in Amsterdam. Some say if you're looking for simple accommodation at a bargain-basement price, you can't do better. The dormitories are immaculate and breakfast and bedsheets included in the price. You can get meals and drinks at the café or do your own cooking in the guest kitchen. Everyone congregates in the lobby to make new friends, watch TV, or use the Internet. ✉ *Kloveniersburgwal 97, 1011 KB, Oude Zijde* ☎ *020/624–6832* 🖷 *020/639–1035* ⊕ *www.stayokay.com* ↪ *10 dormitories, 170 beds* ♿ *Café, laundry facilities; no a/c, no room phones, no room TVs* ▭ *MC, V* ⊚| *CP.*

Rembrandtplein

Rembrandtplein may be a glaring tribute to neon and nightclubs, but its location is close to everything.

★ $–$$$ 🏨 **Seven Bridges.** One of the more famous canal sights in Amsterdam is the lineup of seven consecutive bridges that can be seen gracing Reguliersgracht. This atmosphere-y little retreat takes its name from them as its hotelscape provides some idyllic views of this canal. Set in an 18th-century house in the heart of "Golden Bend" country (yet just a few blocks from Rembrandtplein), this hotel offers uniquely stylish guest rooms, all meticulously decorated with dark woods, Oriental rugs, Art Deco lamps, and marble sinks. The proud owner scouts the antiques stores and auction houses for furnishings, and all have thorough documentation. Handcrafted and inlaid bed frames and tables supplement the antique decorations for a whimsical atmosphere. Top-floor rooms are the smallest and priced accordingly; the first-floor room is practically palatial. No. 5 is a cargo of charm, complete with private terrace. The one catch is that there is no common area or salon, but even here another plus results: breakfast is delivered to your room. Nail down your reservation well in advance. ✉ *Reguliersgracht 31, 1017 LK, Rembrandtplein* ☎ *020/623–1329* ↪ *8 rooms* ♿ *In-room data ports, cable TV; no a/c* ▭ *AE, MC, V* ⊚| *CP.*

$$ 🏨 **Imperial.** The outside of this hotel has a Parisian appearance. It's on a pedestrian-only, tree-lined street with cobblestones and a terraced square. Each room is individually decorated, some masculine, some feminine, and in styles ranging from sedate to cheerful to bold, to appeal to every kind of taste so that each guest feels at home. This is a nonsmoking hotel. Most rooms provide the luxury of a Jacuzzi shower. There is no elevator, and although the stairs are modern (as opposed to steep traditional Dutch staircases), you must walk up at least two flights of them. ✉ *Thorbeckeplein 9, 1017 CS, Rembrandtplein* ☎ *020/ 622–0051* 🖷 *020/624–5836* ⊕ *www.imperial-hotel.com* ↪ *14 rooms* ♿ *In-room data ports, in-room safes, cable TV; no a/c* ▭ *MC, V* ⊚| *CP.*

NIGHTLIFE & THE ARTS

The Arts

By Steve
Korver

Nightlife and the arts have always walked hand in hand—like the most yin and yang of intimate lovers—in this land. One just has to look at the selection of Golden Age paintings by Jan Steen and his colleagues depicting frolicsome bar scenes that grace the walls of the Rijksmuseum to get the idea that there's nothing like a beer after a long day of more noble and artistic pursuits. The organizers of Amsterdam's annual Museum Night suavely tapped into this long legacy and came up with the city's most popular new event to come along in decades. For one night in early November, all the major museums stay open until the wee hours to host a variety of themed parties—tangos under the *Night Watch,* house beats in the Jewish Historical Museum, easy tunes in the Stedelijk, ghost stories for kids in the Bible Museum (to name but a few and, in fact, the relatively sedate of the many often surreal combinations that have occurred).

Although a relatively small city, Amsterdam continues to pack a giant cultural wallop through its numerous venues—from former churches and industrial monuments to the acoustical supremacy of the Concertgebouw—and festivals that invariably feature both homegrown and international talent. While healthy subsidies play a role, it's more the local interest of a culturally inclined people that supports a milieu whose spectrum ranges all the way from the austerely classical to the most outrageously avant-garde. So book that ticket fast. Amsterdam's theater and music season begins in September and runs through June, when the Holland Festival of Performing Arts is held. *What's On in Amsterdam* is a comprehensive, albeit a tad dull, English-language publication distributed by the tourist office that lists art and performing-arts events around the city. Culture hounds are better directed to browse through the many flyers, pamphlets, booklets, and mags—including the Dutch-language but still somewhat decipherable and certainly complete *Uitkrant*—available at the **AUB Ticketshop** (⊠ Leidseplein, at Marnixstraat, Nieuwe Zijde ☎ 0900/0191 [9–9 daily] ⊕ www.aub.nl), open Monday–Saturday 10–6, Thursday until 9. Tickets can also be purchased in person at the tourist information offices through the **VVV Theater Booking Office** (⊠ Stationsplein 10, Centraal Station), open daily 10–5, or at theater box offices. Reserve tickets to performances at the major theaters before your arrival through the AUB Web site or the **National Reservation Center** (⌂ Postbus 404, 2260 AK Leidschendam ☎ 3170/320–2500 ᗑ 070/320–2611).

Film

Have you ever wondered how the Dutch came to speak impeccable English? One of the reasons may be the fact that English films shown in Holland are merely subtitled, not overdubbed—good news for both late-night hotel-TV viewers and city-cinema visitors. While there are cinema programs available or on display at most every bar and café in town, along with the listings in such Dutch-language mags as the free *De Filmkrant* or the "Saturday PS" supplement of *De Parool* newspaper, it may help to have some general information about the scene. Mainstream cinemas are concentrated near the Leidseplein; the largest and most Hollywood blockbuster–oriented is the seven-screen (and monument of functionalist architecture) **City 1–7** (⊠ Kleine Gartmanplantsoen 13–25, Leidseplein ☎ 0900/1458); **Cinecenter** (⊠ Lijnbaansgracht 236, Leidseplein ☎ 020/623–6615), with a sleek modern lounge decor, uses its four screens for the artier and more internationally acclaimed films. If you cannot decide between two films, then choose the one with the best setting, for instance the widely eclectic Art Deco reverie on display at the **Tuschinski** (✉ Reguliersbreestraat 26, Rembrandtplein ☎ 0900/1458), the 1920s ambience of the **Movies** (✉ Haarlemmerdijk 161, Jordaan ☎ 020/624–5790), or the canal-side and popcorn-free **De Uitkijk** (✉ Prinsengracht 452, Leidseplein ☎ 020/623–7460), which also ranks as the city's oldest cinema, having opened in 1913.

Film buffs should definitely pay a visit to the **Nederlands Filmmuseum** (Netherlands Film Museum; ✉ Vondelpark 3, Museum District ☎ 020/589–1400) for its public library and schedule of revivals culled from a collection of more than 35,000 films. It also has occasional special programs that feature outdoor screenings and silent films accompanied by live piano music.

Music

★ There are two auditoriums, large and small, under one roof at The Netherlands' premier concert hall, the **Concertgebouw** (✉ Concertgebouwplein 2–6, Museum District ☎ 020/671–8345 ⊕ www.concertgebouw.nl). Its Viennese Classicist facade surmounted by a golden lyre, this hall draws 800,000 visitors per year, many of whom flock here to enjoy Bach and Beethoven performed under nearly perfect acoustic conditions. In the larger of the two theaters, the **Grote Zaal,** Amsterdam's critically acclaimed **Koninklijk Concertgebouworkest** (Royal Concert Orchestra), whose recordings are in the collections of most self-respecting lovers of classical music, is often joined by international soloists. Their reputation has only grown in the last decade under the baton twirling of conductor Riccardo Chailly who has just passed the honor to the highly regarded Latvian Mariss Jansons. Guest conductors read like a list from the musical heavens: Mstislav Rostropovich, Nikolaus Harnoncourt, and Bernard Haitink. Visiting maestros like these naturally push the prices up but the range remains wide: expect to pay anything between €5 and €100. But throughout July and August, tickets for the Robeco Summer Concerts, which involve high-profile artists and orchestras, are an excellent bargain. The smaller hall, the **Kleine Zaal,** is a venue for chamber music and up-and-coming musicians and which is the usual setting for the free lunchtime concerts on Wednesday at 12:30. The architectural landmark and progenitor of the Amsterdam School, the **Beurs van Berlage** (✉ Damrak 213, Oude Zijde ☎ 020/627–0466) also has two concert halls—including the definitely unique glass-box "diamond-in-space" AGA Zaal—with The Netherlands Philharmonic and The Netherlands Chamber Orchestra as the in-house talent. The **IJsbreker** (✉ Weesperzijde 23, East of Amstel ☎ 020/693–9093), due to move to a new location on the arising new nightlife and culture zone of the Eastern Docklands in late 2004 (call ahead for details around that time), is at the cutting edge of contemporary music and often hosts festivals of international repute.

Many of the city's churches are being exploited by music lovers and players. The former "Pilgrims" hangout, the **Engelse Kerk** (✉ Begijnhof 48, Nieuwe Zijde ☎ 020/624–9665) has weekly concerts of Baroque and classical music which always seek to employ period instruments. The 17th-century **Waalse Kerk** (✉ Oudezijds Achterburgwal 157, Oude Zijde ☎ 070/236–2236) is a small, elegant, and intimate church which once was the Huguenot home base for Amsterdam. Concerts here are organized by the Organisatie Oude Muziek, a group devoted to early music played on period instruments that arranges upwards of 100 concerts in the country each year. Musicians from both The Netherlands and abroad play here on a relatively regular basis.

Skaters, joggers, cyclists, and sun-worshippers gather in Vondelpark each summer to do nothing. However, between late May and September, they're joined by culture vultures, who head to the **Vondelpark Openluchttheater** (⊠ Vondelpark, Museum District ☎ 020/673–1499 ⊕ www. openluchttheater.nlp) for its program of music, theater, and children's events (theatrical events have, in fact, been held in the park since 1865). During the festival, Wednesday offers a lunchtime concert and a mid-afternoon children's show; Thursday nights find a concert on the bandstand; there's a theater show every Friday night; various events (including another theater show) take place on Saturday; and theater events and pop concerts are held on Sunday afternoons.

Opera & Dance

The grand and elegant **Muziektheater** (⊠ Waterlooplein 22, Oude Zijde ☎ 020/551–8911 ⊕ www.muziektheater.nl) seats 1,600 people and hosts international opera, ballet, and orchestra performances throughout the year and is home to **De Nederlandse Opera** (Netherlands National Opera) and **Het Nationale Ballet** (Netherlands National Ballet), whose repertoires embrace both the classical and the 20th century. Muziektheater's huge and flexible stage acts as magnet to directors with a penchant for grand-scale decors, such as Robert Wilson, Willy Decker, and Peter Sellars. Home to the underrated **Nationale Reisopera** (National Travelling Opera) and hosts of the Julidans festival, **Stadsschouwburg** (⊠ Leidseplein 26, Leidseplein ☎ 020/624–2311 ⊕ www. stadsschouwburg.nl) has a wide array of opera and modern dance offerings in an epic setting of gold gilding and red velvet. While more focused on commercial and large-scale musicals, former circus theater **Koninklijk Theater Carre** (⊠ Amstel 115-25, East of Amstel ☎ 020/622–5225) also schedules many acclaimed Eastern Europe companies performing ballet and opera classics.

The relatively small stage of the multimedia center **Melkweg** (⊠ Lijn-baansgracht 234a, Leidseplein ☎ 020/531–8181) brings together both local and international dance names to a more intimate setting. Hosts of the Julidans festival, **Stadsschouwburg** (⊠ Leidseplein 26, Leidseplein ☎020/624–2311 ⊕www.stadsschouwburg.nl) often has a variety of modern dance offerings in an epic setting of gold gilding and red velvet.

Theater

The red-velvet-trimmed **Stadsschouwburg** (⊠ Leidseplein 26, Leidse-plein ☎ 020/624–2311) focuses primarily on Dutch theater but has occasional English and post-language multicultural performances. For lavish, large-scale productions, the place to go is **Koninklijk Theater Carre** (⊠ Amstel 115–125, East of Amstel ☎ 020/622–5225), originally built in the 19th century as permanent home to a circus. Amsterdam's Off-Broadway–type theaters are centered along the Nes, an alley leading off the Dam, and include **Frascati** (⊠ Nes 63, Oude Zijde ☎ 020/623–5723) and **Brakke Grond** (⊠ Nes 45, Oude Zijde ☎ 020/626–6866). **De Engelenbak** (⊠Nes 71, Oude Zijde ☎020/626–3644 ⊕www.engelenbak. nl) is best known for "Open Bak," an open-stage event each Tuesday where virtually anything goes. It's the longest-running theater program in The Netherlands, where everybody gets their 15 minutes of potential fame; arrive at least half an hour before the show starts in order to get a ticket. Otherwise, the best amateur groups in the country perform between Thursday and Saturday.

Alternative "forms" of theater are *very* Amsterdam. The former gas-factory complex **Westergasfabriek** (⊠ Haarlemmerweg 8-10, Amsterdam West ☎ 020/681–3068), now reinvented as a cultural village, employs its singular performance spaces for a variety of shows and festivals that often embrace the more visual, and more avant-garde, of the entertainment spectrum. **Warner en Consorten** (Warner and Company; ⊠ Middenweg 67/D, Amsterdam West ☎ 020/663–2656 ⊕ www.warnerenconsorten. nl), formed in 1993, is an interdisciplinary concept of street theater, where sculpture, dance, physical acting (such as mime), and music collide and challenge the concepts of theater, urban life, and reality. The results are often delightfully, Dada-istially hilarious. Public space is the starting point—streets are analyzed, crowd behavior is studied, passersby are observed. During winter months the company finds abandoned warehouses and factories for venues; in summer, city streets are the "theaters." And if you happen to be in town for the first two weeks of August, don't miss **Parade** (⊠ Martin Luther Kingpark, Amsterdam South ☎ 033/465–4577), a traveling tent city that specializes in quirky performances and a social and carnivalesque ambience.

Nightlife

Fasten your seat belts. Amsterdam's nightlife can have you careening between smoky coffee shops, chic wine bars, mellow jazz joints, laid-back lounges, and clubs either artily—and artfully—intimate or raucous. The bona fide local flavor can perhaps best be tasted in one of the city's ubiquitous brown café–bars—famously called "brown" because of their woody walls and nicotine-stained ceilings (although many have recently let in some light and international styles). Here, both young and old, the mohawked and the merely balding come to relax, rave, and revel in every manner of coffee and alcohol.

The city's nightlife centers mainly on two of its main squares. Leidseplein, rich with cafés and discos that attract younger visitors to the city, also has the city's two major live venues, Melkweg and Paradiso, around the corner. The area around Rembrandtplein, whose cafés fill up with a more local crowd, harbors the trendier nightspots and many of Amsterdam's gay venues (the latter being particularly concentrated along Reguliersdwarsstraat). Warmoesstraat and other streets in the Red Light District provide the spicy setting for the more leather-oriented gay bars and throbbing rock clubs. The lounge phenomenon, while a bit late in arriving, is now in full bloom, offering a kinder, gentler club vibe. Hipsters and those employed in the commercial arts are attracted to the venues concentrated around Nieuwezijds Voorburgwal, but others are springing up throughout the city that invariably have DJs spinning the mellower but latest dance music tunes.

Amsterdam, being one of the most liberal cities in the world, is known for having a tolerant attitude toward prostitution and soft drugs. It is somewhat shocking for first-time visitors to see the world-famous Red Light District and its hundreds of "coffee shops." The soft-drugs trade operates in a less-well-defined fashion, with more gray tones. While it is essentially legal to deal small amounts of marijuana and hashish via the "front door" of a coffee shop, the "back door," through which the product arrives, is linked to the illegal world of the supplier.

Brown Cafés

Coffee and conversation are the two main ingredients of gezelligheid (a socially cozy time) for an Amsterdammer, and perhaps a beer or two (with perhaps a *jenever* added to the mix) as the evening wears on. The best place for these pleasures is a traditional brown café, or *bruine kroeg*. Wood paneling, wooden floors, comfortably worn furniture, and walls and ceilings stained with eons' worth of tobacco smoke give the cafés their name—though today a little artfully stippled paint achieves the same effect. Traditionally, there is no background music, just the hum of chitchat. You can meet up with friends or sit alone, undisturbed for hours, enjoying a cup of coffee and a thorough read of the newspapers and magazines from the pile at hand. The Jordaan district is a particularly happy hunting ground for this phenomenon.

Intensely evocative if out-of-the-way, **Bierbrouwerij 't IJ** (⊠ Funenkade 7, East of Amstel ☎ 020/622–8325), is a microbrewery perched under a windmill and is open Wednesday–Sunday 3–8. Once the tasting house of an old family distillery, **De Admiraal** (⊠ Herengracht 319, Eastern Canal Ring ☎ 020/625–4334) still serves potent liqueurs—many with obscene names. Like many cafés in the Jordaan, **De Prins** (⊠ Prinsengracht 124, Jordaan ☎ 020/624–9382) is blessed with a canal-side patio. **De Reiger** (⊠ Nieuwe Leliestraat 34, Jordaan ☎ 020/624–7426) has a distinctive Jugendstil bar and serves food. If you want to hear the locals sing folk music on Sunday afternoon, stop by **De Twee Zwaantjes** (⊠ Prinsengracht 114, Jordaan ☎ 020/625–2729). A busy, jolly brown café, **In de Wildeman** (⊠ Kolksteeg 3, Nieuwe Zijde ☎ 020/638–2348), attracts a wide range of types and ages. **Nol** (⊠ Westerstraat 109, Jordaan ☎ 020/624–5380) resonates most nights with lusty-lunged, native Jordaaners having the time of their lives. **Rooie Nelis** (⊠ Laurierstraat 101, Jordaan ☎020/624–4167) has kept its traditional Jordaan atmosphere despite the area's tendency toward trendiness. Set with Golden Age chandeliers, leaded glass windows, and the patina of centuries, the gloriously charming **'t Smalle** (⊠ Egelantiersgracht 12, Jordaan ☎ 020/623–9617) is one of Amsterdam's most delightful spots. The after-work crowd always jams the waterside terrace here but opt instead for the historic interior, once home to one of the city's first gin (jenever) distilleries. It is not surprising to learn that a literal copy of this place was created for Nagasaki's Holland Village in Japan. **Wynand Fockink** (⊠ Pijlsteeg 31, Oude Zijde ☎ 020/639–2695) offers similar "tasting" options between 3 and 9 PM daily in a more cramped yet equally evocative locale (and also offers lunch earlier in the day in its atmospheric hidden garden courtyard).

Cabarets

Boom Chicago (⊠ Leidseplein 12, Leidseplein ☎ 020/423–0101 ⊕ www.boomchicago.nl), at the Leidseplein Theater, belongs to a bunch of zany ex-pat Americans who opened their own restaurant-theater to present improvised comedy inspired by life in both Amsterdam and the world; dinner and seating begin at 7, with showtime at 8:15. **Kleine Komedie** (⊠ Amstel 56–58, East of Amstel ☎ 020/624–0534) has for many years been the most vibrant venue for cabaret and comedy (mainly in Dutch). For some straight—and often English—stand-up comedy, check the schedule of **Comedy Café Amsterdam** (⊠ Max Euweplein 43, Leidseplein ☎ 020/638–3971 ⊕ www.comedycafe.nl). **Toomler** (⊠ Breitnerstraat 2, Amsterdam South ☎ 020/670–7400 ⊕ www.toomler.nl) is a popular comedy-club option with often English-friendly programming.

Cocktail Bars & Grand Cafés

Exceedingly popular, the riverside **Café de Jaren** (⊠ Nieuwe Doelenstraat 20, Oude Zijde ☎ 020/625–5771) is a large, airy multilevel bar with a lovely terrace overlooking the Amstel. **Ciel Bleu Bar** (⊠ Hotel Okura, Ferdinand Bolstraat 333, De Pijp ☎ 020/678–7111) has a glass-wall lounge 23 stories high, where you can enjoy the sunsets over Amsterdam and watch the night lights twinkle to life. In the Stopera complex next to the Waterlooplein Market is the lovely **Dantzig** (⊠ Zwanenburgwal 15, Oude Zijde ☎ 020/620–9039). With a view of the Amstel River, it is the perfect location before or after the ballet or opera. **De Kroon** (⊠ Rembrandtplein 17, Rembrandtplein ☎ 020/625–2011) is a grand café with intimate seating arrangements and a U-shape bar surrounding old-style wooden museum cases filled with zoological specimens. The bar attracts a fashionable yuppie clientele in the evenings. **Freddy's** (✉ Hotel de l'Europe, Nieuwe Doelenstraat 2–8, Rembrandtplein ☎ 020/623–4836), cozy and stylish, is a favorite meeting place for businesspeople. Comfy leather chairs and soft lighting give the **Golden Palm Bar** (✉ Grand Hotel Krasnapolsky, Dam 9, Oude Zijde ☎ 020/554–9111) something of the atmosphere of a British gentlemen's club. **Luxembourg** (✉ Spui 22-24, Nieuwe Zijde ☎ 020/620–6264) has an Art Deco–style interior and a glassed-in terrace for people-watching on the Spui Square. One of Rembrandtplein's few redeeming features, **Schiller** (✉ Rembrandtplein 26, Rembrandtplein ☎ 020/624–9846), part of the hotel of the same name, has a faded glory and a real sense of history thanks to a wooden fin-de-siècle interior that other grand cafés would sell their souls for. This remains a favorite with the media crowd. In the afternoon, **Wildschut** (✉ Roelof Hartplein 1-3, Museum District ☎ 020/676–8220), in a 1920s Amsterdam School edifice, is a delightful place for coffee; it's also the place to to meet suited yuppies in the evenings. The terrace is large and has great views for architecture enthusiasts.

Coffee Shops

Generally, the "coffee shops" where marijuana and hashish are smoked are not the most delightful of local places, but the following are among the more acceptable of these establishments. Observers commonly note that one should use caution if indulging, because the available product is very good and those unaccustomed to its high quality may overreact, chemically speaking.

Hidden on a small alley, **Abraxas** (✉ Jonge Roelensteeg 12-14, Nieuwe Zijde ☎ 020/625–5763) supplements its smokeables with a menu of ganja cakes and shakes in an atmosphere that suggest a hip and multilevel home of a family of hobbits. **Barney's** (✉ Haarlemmerstraat 102, Jordaan ☎ 020/625–9761) brings together two stand-alone concepts: a wide variety of smokeables and all-day breakfasts of the world. **Kandinsky** (✉ Rosmarijnsteeg 9, Nieuwe Zijde ☎ 020/624–7023) offers mellow jazz and scrumptious chocolate chip cookies. The clientele at the **Other Side** (✉ Reguliersdwarsstraat 6, Rembrandtplein ☎ 020/625–5141) is primarily gay. **Paradox** (✉ 1e Bloemdwarstraat 2, Jordaan ☎ 020/623–5639), a storefront in the charming Jordaan, is more like a health-food café than a coffee shop. The very popular **De Rokerij** (✉ Lange Leidsedwarsstraat 41, Leidseplein ☎ 020/622–9442) has a magical-grotto feel that requires no extra indulgences to induce a state of giddiness. The mellow **Yo-Yo** (✉ 2e Jan van der Heijdenstraat 79, De Pijp ☎ 020/664–7173) is the quintessential "friendly neighborhood coffee shop" in the heart of the multicultural Pijp.

Dance & Rock Clubs

Arena (✉ 's-Gravensandestraat 51, East of Amstel ☎ 020/694–7444 ⊕ www.hotelarena.nl), part of the Arena hotel complex, is popular for its hip roster of DJs and club nights, which take place in a re-invented former-clandestine church. The huge and popular **Escape** (✉ Rembrandtplein 11–15, Rembrandtplein ☎ 020/622–1111 ⊕ www.escape. nl) can handle 2,500 people dancing under laser lights to DJs spinning techno and its derivatives, with things getting particularly pumped up on the international, star-studded Chemistry evenings. The brand-spanking-new and rather-out-of-the-way **Heineken Music Hall** (✉ Arena Boulevard 590, Amsterdam South-East ☎ 0900/300–1250 ⊕ www. heineken-music-hall.nl), with a capacity for 5,000, offers a sterile but acoustic-rich environment for touring bands that have outgrown the Melkweg and Paradiso. **iT** (✉ Amstelstraat 24, Rembrandtplein ☎ 020/625–

0111 ⊕ www.it.nl), with four bars, special acts, bands, and celebrities, has forsaken its famously gay and extravagant crowds (although they have retained one "Real" night, the third Saturday of every month) for a more "polysexual" and studenty mix.

The legendary **Melkweg** (✉ Lijnbaansgracht 231, Leidseplein ☎ 020/531–8181 ⊕ www.melkweg.nl), or "Milky Way," is named after the building's previous function as a milk factory. It began as a hippie squat in the '60s before savvily evolving with the times and providing a venue for the major trends that followed, from punk to house to world music. Today it's a slickly operated multimedia center equipped with two concert halls, a theater, cinema, gallery, and a café-restaurant. **More** (✉ Rozengracht 133, Jordaan ☎ 020/344–6402 ⊕ www.expectmore.nl) has been attempting to fill the void, with varied success, left by the sadly burned down RoXY club, which had been internationally acclaimed for its theatrical and glamorous crowd who happily grooved to house and techno DJs.If you feel like dancing in a gracious old canal house, head for **Odeon** (✉ Singel 460, Nieuwe Zijde ☎ 020/624–9711 ⊕ www.odeontheater.nl), where hip-hop, R&B, house, and disco get played in different rooms, many of which retain their spectacular painted and stucco ceilings.

The country's most famous concert venue and former church, **Paradiso** (✉ Weteringschans 6-8, Leidseplein ☎ 020/626–4521 ⊕ www.paradiso.nl), known as the "Pop Temple" for its vaulted ceilings and stained glass, began its days as a hippie squat allowed by the local government who hoped it might help empty the Vondel Park (then serving as a crash pad for a generation). To this day, the Paradiso remains an epic venue to witness both music's legends and up-and-comers, regardless of their genre. Amsterdam's relatively new mega-club the **Power Zone** (✉ Daniel Goedkoopstraat 1-3, Museum District ☎ 020/681–8866 ⊕ www.thepowerzone.nl) can pack in over thousands of revelers and often does, thanks to having no door policy and plenty of room for both lounging and dancing to the latest happy house tunes. A favorite with tourists, the **Last Waterhole** (✉ Oudezijds Armsteeg 12, Oude Zijde ☎ 020/624–4814 ⊕ www.lastwaterhole.nl) usually features a blues and rock cover band of usually dubious distinction—but it remains a fun place to trade tales of the road. Pleasure-palace *extraordinaire,* the **Westergasfabriek** (✉ Haarlemmerweg 8-10, Amsterdam West ☎ 020/586–0710 ⊕ www.westergasfabriek.nl), on the historic 19th-century "western gas factory" grounds, originally supplied all of Amsterdam with gas for its street lighting. But when huge gas reserves were discovered north of Holland, it became superfluous, and has since been converted into a multimedia arts complex. The site consists of 13 monumental buildings of various sizes and shapes, which play host to film and theater companies, fashion shows, corporate functions, movie shoots, operas, techno parties and assorted festivals, plus bars, nightclubs, and restaurants.

Gay & Lesbian Bars

Tankards and brass pots hanging from the ceiling in the woody **Amstel Taveerne** (✉ Amstel 54, Rembrandtplein ☎ 020/623–4254) reflects the friendly crowd of Amsterdammers around the bar whose members burst into song whenever the sound system plays an old favorite. **April** (✉ Reguliersdwarsstraat 37, Rembrandtplein ☎ 020/625–9572), which only gets going after 11, has a lounge in the front and a fabulous rotating bar in the back, which management opens when the bar becomes particularly crowded on weekends. April's late-night multilevel bar and disco, **April's Exit** (✉ Reguliersdwarsstraat 42, Rembrandtplein ☎ 020/625–8788) attracts a smart young crowd of gay men and is women-friendly. The always-packed **Soho** (✉ Reguliersdwarsstraat 36, Rembrandtplein ☎ 020/330–4400), is an English-style pub that provides the backdrop to some outrageous flirting. **Getto** (✉ Warmoesstraat, Oude Zijde ☎ 020/421–5151) is an ultimately friendly and pan-sexual lounge-bar that also serves excellent meals. **Le Montmartre** (✉ Halvemaansteeg 17, Rembrandtplein ☎ 020/620–7622) attracts a hip crowd of younger gay men, who stop for a drink and perhaps a sing-along before heading out clubbing. Leather, piercing, and tattoos predominate at the **Web** (✉ Sint Jacobstraat 6, Nieuwe Zijde ☎ 020/623–6758), a local bar.

Amsterdam offers lesbians very few places to meet and party. Women should check at the bars, the gay and lesbian bookstore, or the COC (or Cultural and Social Center of the Nederlandse Vereniging tot Integratie van Homoseksualiteit) for women's parties and events. But there is an official dance club: **You II** (✉ Amstel 178, Rembrandtplein ☎ 020/421–0900) that has tried to fill the void. Amsterdam's best lesbian bar, **Saarein** (✉ Elandsstraat 119, Jordaan ☎ 020/623–4901), has a cozy brown-café atmosphere in the Jordaan and a relatively new "mixed" policy. **Vive-la-Vie** (✉ Amstelstraat 7, Rembrandtplein ☎ 020/624–0114) has a lively bar scene and is both men- and straight-friendly.

Jazz Clubs

In the smoky, jam-packed atmosphere of **Alto** (✉ Korte Leidsedwarsstraat 115, Leidseplein ☎ 020/626–3249), you can hear the top picks of local bands. **Bamboo Bar** (✉ Lange Leidsedwarsstraat 64, Leidseplein ☎ 020/624–3993) has a long bar and cool Latin sounds. At **Bimhuis** (✉ Oude Schans 73–77, Oude Zijde ☎ 020/623–3373), the best-known jazz place in town, you'll find top musicians, including avant-gardists, performing on Friday and Saturday nights, and weeknight jam sessions—call ahead, since they are due to move to the Eastern Docklands at the dawn of 2004. **Bourbon Street Jazz & Blues Club** (✉ Leidsekruisstraat 6–8, Leidseplein ☎ 020/623–3440) presents mainstream blues and jazz to a largely tourist clientele. **Casablanca** (✉ Zeedijk 26, Oude Zijde ☎ 020/625–5685), on the edge of the Red Light District, is an institution in the neighborhood, with jazz during the week and karaoke on weekends. **Café Meander** (✉ Voetboogstraat 3b, Nieuwe Zijde ☎ 020/625–8430) offers a mixed selection of live music, from soul to swing. A pioneer on the up-and-coming nightlife and culture zone of the Eastern Docklands, **Panama** (✉ Oostelijke Handelskade 4, The Waterfront ☎ 020/311–8686 ⊕ www.panama.nl) is a nightclub with a difference: plush and golden interior combined with inspired programming—including everything from tango orchestras to circus acts to big bands unafraid of appropriating contemporary dance beats—that effectively updates a 1920s jazz-club ambience for the 21st century.

Lounges

NZ Lounge (✉ Nieuwezijds Voorburgwal 169, Nieuwe Zijde ☎ no phone) is probably one of the hipper and most "classic" of local lounges, with decor that makes you feel as if you have been transported to N.Y.C. or even Vegas. It changes its name from time to time (originally, it was called the NL Lounge), but the location stays put. A group of artists run **Seymour Likely** (✉ Nieuwezijds Voorburgwal 250, Nieuwe Zijde ☎ 020/627–1427); it was one of the first hip lounges to become the rage and often features funky DJs. **Lux** (✉ Marnixstraat 397, Nieuwe Zijde ☎ 020/422–1412) has a fantastic 1960s decor and an attractive young crowd. Part of the ultimately lounging-oriented Supper Club, the **Supper Club Lounge** (✉ Jongeroelensteeg 21, Nieuwe Zijde ☎ 020/638–0513) is a breathtakingly hip lounge-club with a snooty door policy to match, where you can groove to equally hip tunes or squeeze in around tables in a heavenly white room.

SPORTS & THE OUTDOORS

Beaches

By Steve
Korver

After their long, dreary winter, Amsterdammers count the days until they can hit the beaches at **Zandvoort**, a beach community directly west of the city, beyond Haarlem, where clean beachfront stretches for miles and many of the dunes are open for walking. The train station is close by, and there are lifeguards on duty. Separate areas of the beach are reserved for nudists, though topless bathing is common practice everywhere in The Netherlands. The city's more hip and youthful, however, invariably head to the long line of beach shacks and lounges (complete with DJs) along **Bloemendaal** beach, which can be reached via train taxi (a ticket for which you must buy with your train ticket) from Haarlem Centraal Station.

Participant Sports

Biking

Take a cue from the Amsterdammers and bike your way around the city—it's fun, it's healthful, and it's easy. But keep in mind there are nearly half a million *fiets* (bikes—pronounced feets), so be sure to keep your eyes moving and your bike locked up when you park (there are lots of thefts). Probably one of the more convenient places to rent a bicycle is **Centraal Station** (⊠ Stationsplein 12, 1012 AB, Oude Zijde ☎ 020/624–8391). A longtime favorite is **MacBike, Marnixstraat** (⊠ Marnixstraat 220, 1016 TL, Jordaan ☎ 020/626–6964). **MacBike, Mr Visserplein** (⊠ Mr Visserplein 2, 10111 RD, Jewish Quarter ☎ 020/620–0985) can have you exploring the Plantage and Jewish neighborhood in no time. In the scenic Jordaan, **Frederic** (⊠ Brouwersgracht 78, 1013 GZ, Jordaan ☎ 020/624–5509) is not only friendly but sensitive (because they do not emblazon their bicycles with their name like other bike rental places and hence you are not recognized immediately as a tourist). Expect to pay from €8 per day, plus a deposit of €30–€100 per bicycle. You'll need a passport or other identification. You may just want to ask your hotel for a bike shop most convenient to your neighborhood. For ground rules on biking, *see* Amsterdam on Wheels *in* the Pleasures & Pastimes section of this chapter.

Health Clubs

Several hotels in Amsterdam have fitness facilities for guests, usually including exercise machines, weights, sauna, and whirlpool. **Barry's Fitness Centre** (⊠ Lijnbaansgracht 350, Jordaan ☎ 020/626–1036) has excellent standards when it comes to its equipment, training (by appointment), massages, and sauna. **The Garden** (⊠ Jodenbreestraat 158, 1001 NS, Oude Zijde ☎ 020/626–8772) offers all your physical abuse needs—weights, aerobics, stretching, and calisthenics—while retaining probably the cheapest prices in town. The **Holiday Inn Crowne Plaza** (⊠ Nieuwezijds Voorburgwal 5, Nieuwe Zijde ☎ 020/620–0500) has a large indoor swimming pool. Probably the hippest of all the options, **Shape All-In** (⊠ 2e Hugo de Grootstraat 2–6, 1052 LC, Jordaan ☎ 020/684–5857) is truly "all-in" by supplementing a full array of fitness options with a delightful patio, great food, exotic cocktails, and even DJs after dark—only for those who can resist or want to embrace temptation. Day rates at all of the above are around €12, with extra charges for special services. You may also want to check the Amsterdam Yellow Pages under "Fitnesscentra."

If you're interested in relaxing, sensual (not sexual) activities, plan to spend a delightful fall or winter evening at Amsterdam's most amazing "health club," the **Sauna Deco** (✉ Herengracht 115, 1015 BE, Western Canal Ring ☎ 020/623–8215), an institution for Amsterdam literati and cognoscenti. On entering the canal house designed by Hendrik P. Berlage (in his early "Neoclassical" period), you descend several steps and are dazzled: the interior is truly spectacular with an Art Deco environment salvaged from some historic landmarks, including Paris's Au Bon Marché department store, the Dutch Twentsche Bank, and chairs from the Hotel Suisse. People come here to read, relax, chat—little wonder many guests take up residence for hours. In short: this is the most beautiful sauna in town. Surrender to their Turkish bath and Finnish sauna, bake in their solarium, or revitalize yourself in their cold plunge bath.

Ice-Skating

★ Although utterly and completely obsessed with **ice-skating**, the Dutch rarely get the chance to show off either their famed speed or their distance-skating capabilities—global warming is considered the culprit. Unfortunately, because Amsterdam is not far from the sea, the canals rarely freeze over in the inner city, so head to the Museumplein area to see if they have finally found a steady contractor to run the high-tech pond behind the Rijksmuseum for more than sporadic times. This rink is often artificially induced to freeze and skates are available for rental. On rare occasions, the city canals are solid enough to do a double lutz and the city celebrates appropriately—at various places, stalls are set up to serve hot concoctions and loudspeakers blare Bach. If you can't get to do your Hans Brinker routine on the canals (word to the wise: the ice thaws first along the canal edges and under the bridges), you can also enjoy the Oosterpark pond and the Grote Vijver and Bosbaan in the Amsterdamse Bos park area. The die-hard skater, whatever the season, can head to the outdoor and year-round indoor skating rinks of **Stichting IJscomplex Jaap Eden** ✉ *Radioweg 64* ☎ *020/694–9652* ✉ *Admission €3.70, skate rental from €5 a day.*

Jogging

Sunday morning is about the only time when Amsterdam's city center gets enough of a break from foot, bike, and car traffic to allow for a comfortable jog. Beyond the city near the suburb of Amstelveen, **Amsterdamse Bos** (Amsterdam Woods) is a large, spacious place to run. **Oosterpark** (Eastern Park), behind the Tropenmuseum, and **Vondelpark**, near the art museums, are the only parks within the city proper that do not require having to do endless circuits of the same.

Spectator Sports

Soccer

Soccer is a near obsession with the Dutch, and if you want to impress an Amsterdam host, you would best be advised not only to refer to it as "football" but also to know the current standing of the local team, Ajax (pronounced *eye-*axe), relative to that of its archrivals, Rotterdam's Feyenoord (pronounced *fia*-naut) and Eindhoven's PSV (Philips Sports Vereniging). Making a Dutch friend in this way may be the only method of getting a very scarce ticket. The Dutch soccer season runs from August to June, with a short break in midwinter; matches are played at the **Amsterdam Arena** (✉ Arena A Boulevard 29, Amsterdam South-East ☎ 020/311–1444).

SHOPPING

By Jonette Stabbert

An antique *koekeplank* (cookie mold)? Blue-and-white Delftware? A box of those delicious hard candies called Haagse Hopjes? A pair of hand-painted wooded *klompen* clogs (which the Dutch often nail to the wall and fill with plants)? A cutting-edge vest styled by Viktor & Rolf? A psychedelically hued ski cap from Oilily? Or one of those other delights that have made contemporary Dutch design the darling of high-style fans the world over? Whether you go for Baroque or postmillennium, the variety of goods available here in a continuous parade of boutiques and department stores is one of the major joys of shopping in Amsterdam. Style-setters invariably begin shop-hopping their way through the elegant boutiques of the Grachtengordel (canal ring), where they find a concentration of specialty and fashion shops along the "Nine Streets," or Negen Straatjes. And everybody usually ends up at the year-round outdoor flea market at Waterlooplein, a holdover from the pushcart days in the Jewish Quarter.

While warm and cozy houses with overstuffed chairs, lace curtains, and carpeted floors prevail in most of Holland, modernist architects and furniture designers are popular with the urban population and, of course, with tourist shop-till-they-droppers. Amsterdam has a concentration of international design firms and shops with great contemporary furniture and accessories for the home. In shops around the city, modern European and American classics from Stark and the Eames are interspersed with Dutch designs from the Bauhaus-inspired W. H. Gispen of the 1920s to contemporaries such as Martin Visser, Benno Premsela, Piet Hein Eek, and Henk Stallinga. If you want pure luxe, of course, diamonds have always been an Amsterdammer's best friend. Starting with the Spanish conquest of 1576, many diamond experts fled north, from Antwerp to the Netherlandish capital. Shiploads of raw diamonds from India or Brazil led to a spate of feverish activity, lasting until the cargo was cut and the finished stone sent off, usually to Paris. This stream became a flood when the children of a Dutch farmer living near Hopetown, South Africa, discovered that pebbles in a nearby stream made marvelous toys. Today, some of the best-known diamond dealers still have roots in the city's Jewish Quarter.

Shopping hours in The Netherlands are regulated by law, with one night a week reserved for late shopping. In Amsterdam, department stores and many other shops are closed Monday morning, and stay open Thursday evening (to 9 PM), which is famously known as *koopavonden* ("buying evenings"). Increasingly, following an easing of legislation governing shopping hours, you'll find main branches of major stores in the center of the city open on Sunday afternoon, but note that most stores are shuttered on Sunday. Purchases of €136 or more qualify for a tax refund.

Shopping Districts & Streets

The heart of the city center, or Centrum, **Dam Square** is home to two of Amsterdam's main department stores, the C & A and De Bijenkorf. Beyond the west side of the square sits one of Amsterdam's shopping spectaculars, the **Magna Plaza** (✉ Nieuwezijds Voorburgwal 182, Nieuwe Zijde ⊕ www.magnaplaza.nl). Built inside the city's 19th-century post office—designed by Cornelis Hendrik Peters in "post-office Gothic" (sort of like London's House of Parliament)—this gigantic structure looks like a fairy tale frontispiece. Set behind the Royal Palace, this is now a top place for A-to-Z shopping in a wide variety of distinctive stores, including Villeroy & Boch; Sissy Boy Home and Fashion Decoration; Tolhuysen (soooo cute "Dutch Kitsch," including sailboat-wooden clogs, pottery cows, and porcelain windmills); Ordning & Reda (Swedish paper merchants); fashion boutiques like Björn Borg, Velvet, and Replay; fabulous wooden toys at Pinokkio and kiddie couture at Bam Bam Kinderwinkel. The central Romanesque-columned, three-story atrium is a knockout.

If department stores aren't your speed, head west from the Dam to the ★ heart of the Grachtengordel canal section and explore the **Negen Straatjes** ("The Nine Streets"), nine charming, tiny streets that radiate from behind the Royal Palace. Here, in a sector bordered by Raadhuisstraat and Leidsestraat, specialty and fashion shops are delightfully one-of-a-kind. Heading even farther to the west you enter the chic and funky sector of the **Jordaan,** where generation after generation of experimental designers have set up shop to show their imaginative creations. The small streets radiating from the Elandsgracht and the Rozengracht contain many artistic boutiques selling handmade clothing, collectibles, and quirky gifts. Antiquarian bric-a-brac shops are also in this part of town.

Returning to the Centrum, two popular streets offer something for nearly all tastes and wallets. Stretching to the north from Dam Square and toward Centraal Station is **Nieuwendijk,** a busy pedestrian mall that is good for bargain hunters. To the south of the Dam runs **Kalverstraat,** the city's main pedestrians-only shopping street, where much of Amsterdam does its day-to-day shopping. Here, too, you'll find the imposing **Kalvertoren shopping mall** (⊠ Kalverstraat, near Munt, Nieuwe Zijde), which is a covered shopping mall with a rooftop restaurant with magnificent views of the city. Running parallel to Kalverstraat is the **Rokin,** a main tram route lined with shops offering high-priced trendy fashion, jewelry, accessories, antiques, and even an old-master painting or two. Near the bottom of Kalverstraat's big "C," **Leidsestraat** cuts south to the elegant Museum Quarter. From the Leidsestraat turn east and walk one long canal block to find the **Spiegelkwartier** (Spiegel Quarter), one of Europe's most fabled agglomerations of antiques shops. Antiques always have been a staple item of shopping in Amsterdam, and the array of goods available at any time is broad. There are more than 150 antiques shops scattered throughout the central canal area. The greatest concentration of those offering fine antiques and specialty items, however, is along Nieuwe Spiegelstraat and its continuation, Spiegelgracht. They constitute the main thoroughfare of the Spiegelkwartier, with shops on both sides of the street and canal for five blocks, from the Golden Bend of the Herengracht nearly to the Rijksmuseum. The array of treasures is amazing, from William and Mary armoires to the tiny *spiegels* (mirrors) that gave the quarter its name and were often used, perched from second-story windows, to espy arriving guests. They are still used by a great many homes today!

For possible antiques of the 22nd century, continue east of the Spiegelkwartier several blocks to find **Utrechtsestraat,** which offers a variety of opportunities for the up-to-date home shopper, with stores specializing in kitchen, interior, and design objects. Now head south across the Singel canal to the Museum Quarter, where, a few blocks east of the Rijksmuseum, you'll find the city's posh and prestigious **P. C. Hooftstraat,** generally known as the P. C. Home to chic designer boutiques, this is where diplomats and politicians buy their glad rags. Several blocks to the east, just beyond the Concertgebouw is **Van Baerlestraat,** lined with bookstores specializing in art, music, and language and clothing shops that are smart—but not quite smart enough to have made it to the adjoining P. C. Hooftstraat. To get back to Amsterdam's more democratic roots, continue south to the **De Pijp** neighborhood and exult in its famous Albert Cuypmarkt, a popular-priced playground of stalls that remains a pearl among pearls. Remember if you want to add the very latest stores to the lists below, check out the suggestions in the Holland's high-style monthly glossies, such as *Dutch, Residence, Elegance, Avenue, BLVD,* and the Dutch-language *Elle.*

Department Stores

Perched on the ever-busy Damrak, across the road from the Beurs van Berlage, this representative of the European chain department store **C & A** (⊠ Beurspassage 2 or Damrak 79 [two entrances], Nieuwe Zijde ☎ 0800/022–6768) is a longtime fixture on Amsterdam's shopping landscape. The budget-minded come here for clothing and accessories, while the basement caters to Generation Y and teenagers and their mothers dispute fashion tastes amid disco lighting and music. Far from the lofty heights of Harrods, akin to Bloomingdales, if not as stylish as Paris's Galleries Lafayette, **De Bijenkorf** (⊠ Dam 1, Nieuwe Zijde ☎ 020/621–8080) is the city's best-known department store and the stomping ground of its monied middle classes. It has come far from its save-a-penny-style days and now stocks top international designer lines in interior decoration and clothing, gourmet goodies, the usual repertoire of suitcases, shoes, and appliances, and hipster choices like zebra-stripe pillows or togs by Bang on the Door. You might want to pop into the many branches of **Hema** (⊠ Nieuwendijk 174–176, Nieuwe Zijde ☎ 020/623–4176) that dot this town; it not only provides all your basic needs but has some surprisingly hip designer items, and for the friendliest of prices. With its Paris-style skylights, chandeliers, silently gliding assistants, and coat of arms, the **Maison de Bonneterie** (⊠ Rokin 140–142, Nieuwe Zijde ☎ 020/531–3400) is Amsterdam's most gracious department store. It has basics such as white goods and appliances, but it is most loved for its array of women's fashions. Landmarked by its cupola,

★ the historic and stately **Metz & Company** (⊠ Keizersgracht 455, Eastern Canal Ring ☎ 020/624–8810) has presided over the Grachtengordel since 1908 (but first set up shop elsewhere back in 1740!). Now an outpost of London's famous Liberty store, it carries a range of breathtakingly expensive designer articles from all over the world. Unique leather handbags in bright colors may lure you into the shop—but after purchasing one, will you still have any cash left to keep in it? At the top-floor café you can get the best bird's-eye view of the city.

Street Markets

Few markets compare with Amsterdam's **Waterlooplein** flea market. It is a descendant of the haphazard pushcart trade that gave this part of the city its distinct and lively character in the early part of the 19th century. You're unlikely to find anything of value here, but it's a good spot to look for the secondhand clothing young Amsterdammers favor, and it is a gadget lover's paradise. The flea market is open Monday–Saturday 9:30–5. The **Bloemenmarkt** (Flower Market, along the Singel canal, between Koningsplein and Muntplein) is another of Amsterdam's must-see markets, where flowers and plants are sold from permanently moored barges. The market is open Monday–Saturday 9:30–6 (some flower stalls are open Sunday). On Saturday, the Noordermarkt—which also hosts an old-world evocative flea market on Monday mornings—and Nieuwmarkt host an **organic farmers' market,** with specialist stalls selling essential oils and other new-age fare alongside the oats, pulses, and vegetables. **Sunday art markets** are held in good weather from April to

October on Thorbeckeplein, and from April to November at Spui, which also hosts a **boeken market** on Friday that is a used–and antiquarian-book–browsing paradise. The **Postzegelmarkt** stamp market is held twice a week (Wednesday and Saturday 1–4) by the Spui on Nieuwezijds Voorburgwal.

A favorite with locals is the **Albert Cuypmarkt** (⊠ Albert Cuypstraat between Ferdinand Bolstraat and Van Woustraat, De Pijp). The market, in the heart of De Pijp neighborhood, is replete with stalls overflowing with fresh fish, cheese, poultry, flowers, and a vast selection of hardware and household articles, clothes, bedding, and sundries of all kinds. It's open Monday–Saturday 10–5.

Specialty Stores

Antiques & Golden Age Art

Antiques always have been a staple item of shopping in Amsterdam, and the array of goods available at any time is broad. There are more than 150 antiques shops scattered throughout the central canal area. The greatest concentration of those offering fine antiques and specialty items is in the **Spiegelkwartier** (Spiegel Quarter). **Nieuwe Spiegelstraat** and its continuation, **Spiegelgracht**, constitute the main thoroughfare of the quarter, with shops on both sides of the street and canal for five blocks, from the Golden Bend of the Herengracht nearly to the Rijksmuseum.

For a broad range of vintage and antique furniture, curios, jewelry, clothing, and household items, try **Kunst- & Antiekcentrum De Looier** (⊠ Elandsgracht 109, Jordaan ☎ 020/624–9038), a cooperative housing more than 80 dealers, making it the largest covered art and antiques market in The Netherlands. You wouldn't be the first to get a great buy on an antique doll, a first-edition book, military memorabilia, or even a jeweled trinket. The best days to go are Wednesday, Saturday, or Sunday, when all the vendors, including the *tafeltjesmarkt* (one-day table rentals), are present. You'll find an unusual collection of antique money banks at **Bruno de Vries** (⊠ Elandsgracht 67, Jordaan ☎ 020/620–2437), along with Art Deco and Jugendstil lamps and items from the Amsterdam School. **Galerie Frans Leidelmeyer** (⊠ Nieuwe Spiegelstraat 58, Spiegelkwartier ☎ 020/625–4627) is a good source of top-quality Dutch Art Deco and Jugendstil artifacts, with furniture by H. P. Berlage, Michel de Clerk, and Piet Kramer. For antique European pewter from the 15th to 19th centuries, the authority is **Jan Beekhuizen** (⊠ Nieuwe Spiegelstraat 49, Spiegelkwartier ☎ 020/626–3912). Mr. Beekhuizen also carries antique furniture, antique Delft Blue tiles, and other collectible objects. As you explore the fascinating maze of small rooms at **Odds & Sods** (⊠ 1e Looiersdwarsstraat 11, Jordaan ☎ 020/616–8440), you'll find delightful postwar (1950s–'70s) glass, ceramics, plastics, metalware, and furniture along with Art Deco, Jugendstil, and Amsterdam School designs. Better yet, many affordable small items will fit in a suitcase. The shop is as charming as its owner, who will proudly show you his shop's garden with its artist-made waterfall. In an enormous shop that spans 1,800 square feet, **Prinsheerlijk Antiek** (⊠ Prinsengracht 579, Eastern Canal Ring ☎ 020/638–6623) sells a princely assortment of furniture, bric-a-brac, and chandeliers dating from the early 18th century, as well as unique clock cases, Swedish-style birch-wood furniture, and Dutch hand-painted folk pieces. Many items come from royal families and palaces. It's not unusual to find people admiring the shop windows at **Steensma & Van Der Plas** (⊠ Prinsengracht 272, Jordaan ☎ 020/672–2197), where fine wooden cabinets with myriad drawers are often displayed. The shop is known for functional antique furniture (mainly from England) and pub clocks. You'll also find old leather Chesterfields, club chairs, and imposing oak or mahogany desks.

Books

True to its name, the **American Book Center** (⊠ Kalverstraat 185, Nieuwe Zijde ☎ 020/625–5537) is strongly oriented toward American tastes and expectations. As reputedly the largest English-language book emporium on the Continent, the selection is vast, but the prices are usually higher

★ than you would pay on the other side of the ocean. **Antiquariaat Kok** (⊠ Oude Hoogstraat 14-18, Oude Zijde ☎ 020/623–1191) is an antiquarian heaven, with oodles of treasures on Amsterdam history. Another floor in the store holds one of Amsterdam's largest selections of second-hand books (the best books are always out of print, right?). **Athenaeum Nieuwscentrum** (⊠ Spui 14–16, Nieuwe Zijde ☎ 020/624–2972) has the city's best selection of international magazines and newspapers; its sister bookstore next door offers the latest and greatest in international literature. **Architectura en Natura** (⊠ Leliegracht 22, Jordaan ☎ 020/623–6186) stocks beautiful "coffee-table" art and photography books covering architecture, nature, landscape design, and gardening. Rarely does any one leave the shop empty-handed.

Possibly the largest bookstore in Amsterdam, **De Slegte** (⊠ Kalverstraat 48–52, Nieuwe Zijde ☎ 020/662–4266) is a true haven for book hunters. Every floor stocks tomes in various languages and in every subject (fiction and nonfiction) that you could want. They're particularly known for their large nonfiction section of popular titles at bargain prices, and upstairs floors have a humongous antiquarian book section. Booklovers could spend hours here. The **English Bookshop** (⊠ Lauriergracht 71, Jordaan ☎ 020/626–4230) serves you tea in cozy confines, while recommending reading matter based on your personal tastes. Armchair and other travelers visit **Evenaar Literaire Reisboekhandel** (⊠ Singel 348, Nieuwe Zijde ☎ 020/624–6289) for books covering travel, anthropology, and literary essays. Anything you need to know about foreign cultures you'll discover here.

Oudemanhuis Book Market (⊠ Oudemanhuispoort, Oude Zijde) is a tiny, venerable covered book market in the heart of the University of Amsterdam and has been selling used and antiquarian books, prints, and sheet music for more than a century. Tempting window displays lure passersby into **Premsela** (⊠ Van Baerlestraat 78, Museum District ☎ 020/662–4266), which specializes in art books and stocks many luscious, tempting tomes. **Scheltema** (⊠ Koningsplein 20, Eastern Canal Ring ☎ 020/523–1411) has six floors of books on every imaginable subject with plenty of room for marked-down remainders. It's one of Amsterdam's busiest and best-stocked international bookstores. There is a small café on the first floor. **Waterstone's** (⊠ Kalverstraat 152, Nieuwe Zijde ☎ 020/638–3821) has four floors of English-language books, from children's stories to computer manuals. There's a very large selection of U.K. magazines.

Ceramics & Crystal

You'll find a unique, comprehensive selection of glassware at **Breekbaar** (⊠ Weteringschans 209, Spiegelkwartier ☎ 020/626–1260). For superb porcelain and tiles from before 1800, visit **Frides Laméris** (⊠ Nieuwe Spiegelstraat 55, Spiegelkwartier ☎ 020/626–4066). Fancy a gift fit for a king? Well-oiled shoppers and devout collectors know there is only one address in Amsterdam that can please. **Hogendoorn & Kaufman** (⊠ Rokin 124, Nieuwe Zijde ☎ 020/638–2736) sells the crème de la crème, with the best designs from Baccarat, Lalique, Daum, and Swarovski in crystal; Royal Delft, Makkum, Lladró, Herend and Royal Copenhagen in porcelain; and special designs from Fabergé, Meissen, Mats Jonasson, and others (and with free worldwide shipping too). You're on equal footing with the Russian tsar when you consider a fabulous cobalt blue–and–gold swan egg from Fabergé, while others will covet the Lalique bowl supported by two divinely crafted jugglers or the limited-edition Lalique Deux Coeurs perfume flacon. Some items are much more affordable, including the Royal Delft dish with Dik Bruna's Miffy bunny, personalized with your child's name for under €100. In the glittering interior of **Swarovski** (⊠ Heiligeweg 14, Nieuwe Zijde ☎ 020/618–4108), crystal jewelry, decorative items, and home accessories are for sale. At **'t Winkeltje** (⊠ Prinsengracht 228, Jordaan ☎ 020/625–1352), you'll find a charming jumble of hotel porcelain, glass, and other household collectibles.

Children

★ You may be hypnotized by the magenta-mustache that shop owner Couzijn Simon sports, but it will be his toy treasures here that will make your child as pop-eyed as some of the vintage dolls found at **Couzijn Simon** (⊠ Prinsengracht 578, Eastern Canal Ring ☎ 020/624–7691). The shop is crammed with wonders like an 18th-century rocking horse as finely carved as an 18th-century sculpture; a 4-foot-long wooden ice skate (a former store sign); a 1-inch doll with hinged limbs; vintage trains and collector teddy bears; and porcelain dolls dressed for a costume ball. Some of the toys here even date back to the mid-18th century, which was when this shop first opened as a pharmacy. In the back is a small garden and a cottage, now the atelier of Dutch painter Anton Hoeboeur, whose works are for sale. Your child will feel like a princeling of the House of Orange if he's lucky enough to have a collection of the beau-
★ tifully carved old-fashioned wooden toys on offer at **Pinokkio** (⊠ Nieuwezijds Voorburgwal 182, Nieuwe Zijde ☎ 020/622–8914). Set in the Magna Plaza shopping center, this place is stuffed with Pinocchio figures, step-gabled dollhouses, and other dazzlers. Talk about a perfect gift for that toddler back home: a dollhouse version of a gabled canal house, four "stories" tall. This is just one of the adorable toys available at **De Speelmuis** (⊠ Elandsgracht 58, Jordaan ☎ 020/638–5342 ⊕ www.speelmuis.nl). Check out the unusual hobbyhorses in a host of forms such as bears, ducks, and even motorcycles.

Chocolate

★ Chocoholics, take note. **Arti Choc** (⊠ Koninginneweg 141, Amsterdam Zuid ☎ 020/470–9805) not only sells handmade bonbons, but will also custom design just about anything you could imagine—made from chocolate. Amsterdam's best handmade chocolates come from **Puccini Bomboni** (⊠ Singel 184, Nieuwe Zijde ☎ 020/427–8341 ⊠ Staalstraat 17, Eastern Canal Ring ☎ 020/626–5474), where exotic combinations of chocolate and herbs (such as thyme and pepper) and spices are a specialty. The variety isn't enormous, but there are enough knockouts, including chocolates filled with calvados, Cointreau, rhubarb, and tamarind.

Diamonds & Jewelry

Diamonds are hardly a bargain. But compared to other cities, and thanks to Amsterdam's centuries-old ties to South Africa, they almost fall into that category here. The city's famous factories even allow one-stop shopping. The **Amsterdam Diamond Center** (⊠ Rokin 1–5, Nieuwe Zijde ☎ 020/624–5787) houses several diamond sellers. Set near the Rijks-
★ museum, **Coster Diamonds** (⊠ Paulus Potterstraat 2–4, Museum District ☎ 020/676–2222 ⊕ www.costerdiamonds.com) not only sells jewelry and loose diamonds but gives free demonstrations of diamond cutting

so you can learn all about the "four Cs"—carat, color, clarity, and cut. You can see a replica of the most famous diamond cut in the factory—the Koh-I-Noor, one of the prize gems of the British crown jewels. After your tour, enjoy the petite café here. **Van Moppes Diamonds** (✉ Albert Cuypstraat 2–6, De Pijp ☏ 020/676–1242 ⊕ www.moppesdiamonds. com) has an extensive diamond showroom and offers glimpses into the processes of diamond cutting and polishing.

★ **Bonebakker** (✉ Rokin 88/90, Nieuwe Zijde ☏ 020/623–2294) is one of the city's oldest and finest jewelers and carries an exceptionally wide range of fine watches and silverware. They've been in business since 1792, and Adrian Bonebakker, the founder, was commissioned by King Willem II to design and make the royal crown for the House of Orange. You'll find watches by Patek Philippe, Cartier, Jaeger-leCoultre, Gucci, and Panerai and beautiful silver and gold tableware. Some of the silver designs they produced in the 1920s have been exhibited in Dutch museums, such as the Willet-Holthuysen. **Grimm Sieraden** (✉ Grimburgwal 9, Nieuwe Zijde ☏ 020/622–0501) is savvy about discovering the latest cutting-edge (but wearable) jewelry produced by young designers. The century-old **Schaap and Citroen** (✉ Heiligeweg 36, Nieuwe Zijde ☏ 020/626–6691) is so knowledgeable about jewelry that they even teach students at the butlers' academy how to clean and care for priceless baubles. They carry top brands like Rolex, but you can also find affordable watches and jewelry here.

Gifts & Souvenirs

You can't visit Holland and not buy a pair of *klompen,* can you? Perhaps not what you'd don for clubbing, but wooden shoes are still worn by farmers, fishers, and country folk and are the best footwear for wet and muddy surfaces. They're traditionally worn over a thick pair of *geitenwollen sokken* (goat's wool socks). Located in a former metro sta-
★ tion, **De Klompenboer** (✉ Sint Anthoniesbreestraat 51, Nieuwmarkt ☏ 020/623–0632) sells toys upstairs and klompen downstairs. They no longer make the shoes they sell, but they still hand-paint or wood-burn designs on them and will also do custom orders. They have wooden shoes in the classic bright yellow/orange color, but also in red, blue, and natural wood in sizes to fit feet from two-year-olds to Darling Clementine. Novelty wooden shoe banks and brush holders are also sold, or you can go native and nail your clogs to a wall and fill them with plants. Although souvenir shops are to be found on every other street corner, **Holland Souvenirs Shopping** (✉ Nieuwendijk 226, Dam ☏ 020/624–7252) is distinguished by selling a better class of souvenirs, such as Royal Delft, cuckoo clocks, and automated miniature windmills. Sure, you may find a number of these items elsewhere, but they'll be in cheesy surroundings sometimes just down the aisle from risqué gift items and even drug paraphernalia. You could bring your grandmother to this shop. What better place to buy ice skates than in Holland? Hans Brinker would have loved modern skating emporium **Skatezone** (✉ Ceintuurbaan 57–59, De Pijp ☏ 020/662–2822) which stocks well over 150 models of ice skates and also carries every other kind of skate. There is a large variety of *noren,* the most popular style of skates for adults, but they also have traditional Dutch wooden training skates for children. These have double blades so kids can keep their balance.

Housewares
★ Situated in a canal house, the **Frozen Fountain** (✉ Prinsengracht 629–645, Eastern Canal Ring ☏ 020/622–9375) carries innovative contemporary/futuristic furniture and home accessories from top Dutch designers, such as a pieced wooden *kast* (closet) by Piet Hein Eek, but you'll

also find artistic perfume dispensers, jewelry, and carpets. The store mixes minimalism with chandeliers and Rococo seats. Frozen Fountain's exhibition space showcases the hottest young design talents—names making the headlines are Hutton, Arad, Newsom, Starck, Wanders, and Jongerius. You'll find yourself in a rainbow world at **& Klevering Zuid** (✉ Jacob Obrechtstraat 19a, Amsterdam Zuid ☎ 020/670–3623), thanks to its wide range of tints in porcelain and glass tableware, colorful household accessories, and bright table linens. Top European design brands are all here, including stainless steel cookware from Hackmann, Peugeot pepper mills, lush towels and bathrobes from Van Dijck Sanger, and artistic storage boxes from Galerie Sentou. For an unusual gift, consider their "ironing perfume" from France. The entire harbor district was given a shot in the arm with the five-story showcase for home design, **Pakhuis** (✉ Oostelijke Handelskade 15-17, Eastern Docklands ☎ 020/421–1033). An 1883 warehouse renovated to house more than 30 design boutiques under one roof, it was modernized by the Dutch architectural firm of Meyer and Van Schooten, who added Minimalist glass and stainless steel to the historic ambience. Don't be surprised to find the editors of top home-design magazines browsing here for inspiration, as this is a showcase for the hottest new trends. Catch your breath and enjoy a meal in the Pakhuis café, then turn breathless again at the fantastic view of the IJ through the glass-walled lounge.

Men's Clothing

Gaudi (✉ P. C. Hooftstraat 116, Museum District ☎ 020/679–9319) is a mecca for the trendy and label conscious. **H & M** (✉ Kalverstraat 125-9, Nieuwe Zijde ☎ 020/624–0624) offers remarkably cheap classic and trendy threads. If you've got a small clothing budget, this store will "suit" you. Other good buys here are blazers and casual wear. For European menswear, **Hugo Boss** has four lines available in Amsterdam. The sportswear line is available at **Boss Sport** (✉ P. C. Hooftstraat 112, Museum District ☎ 020/379–5050). Hugo Boss's high-end and trendy design lines for men are available in **Hugo** (✉ P. C. Hooftstraat 140, Museum District ☎ 020/470–2297). **Mulberry Company** (✉ P. C. Hooftstraat 46, Museum District ☎ 020/673–8086) sells stylish fashions from England.

Wives accompany their husbands so they can ogle the staff at **Oger** (✉ P. C. Hooftstraat 75–81, Museum District ☎ 020/676–8695), where the shop clerks look like handsome male runway models and are elegantly attired. You may not match them for looks, but you'll be just as stylish when you leave. **Possen.com** (✉ Van Baerlestraat 38, Museum District ☎ 020/471–2050) uses 3-D body scanning to custom-tailor clothing. You're assured of a perfect fit, and the quality clothing makes this the closest thing to having your own personal designer. **Society Shop** (✉ Van Baerlestraat 20–22, Museum District ☎ 020/664–9281) stocks the classics that Dutch politicians and businessmen like.

Music

Near the Concertgebouw, **Broekmans & Van Poppel** (✉ Van Baerlestraat 92–94, Museum District ☎ 020/675–1653) specializes in recordings, sheet music, and accessories for classical and antiquarian music. There's an antiques-store atmosphere at **Datzzit Verzamel—Muziek en Filmwinkel** (✉ Prinsengracht 306, Eastern Canal Ring ☎ 020/622–1195). The merchandise includes music on 78s, vinyl, and CD as well as film memorabilia. The well-informed staff at **Kuijper Klassiek** (✉ Ferdinand Bolstraat 6, De Pijp ☎ 020/679–4634) offers hard-to-find recordings.The vast **South Miami Plaza** (✉ Albert Cuypstraat 116, De Pijp ☎ 020/662–

2817) has just about every music category, including the Dutch answer to country music, *smartlap*; listening booths are available, too.

Shoes

Located in the Negen Straatjes area, **Antonia Shoes** (✉ Gasthuismolensteeg 18–20, Western Canal Ring ☎ 020/320–9433) offers two stores of hip footwear from top European designers for men and women. Extreme, classic, high heels, flat shoes—if it's available in footwear, they carry it, with handbags to match. There are styles for men, too. **Antonia Shoes** (✉ Gasthuismolensteeg 16, Western Canal Ring ☎ 020/627–2433) sells slippers only. **Jan Jansen** (✉ Rokin 42, Nieuwe Zijde ☎ 020/625–1350) has the crème de la crème of shoes, with gorgeous color combinations and stunning designs. Famed Jansen is an artist/craftsman who designs and makes his special shoes in very small series, but he also has a manufactured line, Jan Jansen Sense, that is carried in shops worldwide. The futuristic interior of **Shoebaloo** (✉ P. C. Hooftstraat 80, Museum District ☎ 020/671–2210) is like being in a disco on a spaceship, and the shoe styles are just as wild, some in neon colors to match the weird lighting in the shop. Just entering the store is an experience you won't soon forget, and you may leave with Day-Glo tiger-striped stilettos. They have other shops around the city. **Smit Bally** (✉ Leidsestraat 41, Eastern Canal Ring ☎ 020/624–8862) sells classically smart shoes for men.

Women's Clothing

Clothing for women and children has never been the same since Willem "Olli" Olsthoorn and his wife, Marieke Olsthoorn, launched Oilily in Alkmaar in 1963. They burst on the fashion scene with colorful, funky, and wildly chic clothing and accessories. They are most famous for their dazzling, nearly psychedelic, colors and patterns that evoke kaleidoscope visions and glass millefleurs. Now a global name, the only shop in the world that showcases the entire collection is **Exclusive Oilily Store** (✉ P. C. Hooftstraat 131–133, Museum District ☎ 020/672–3361), set on Amsterdam's most renowned shopping street. This emporium caters to women and children. Here, you'll find babies' toes are kept toasty in flowered "mini-mukluk" winter booties, their heads kept free from drafts in snug caps with bunny ears. Mothers can color-coordinate their wardrobes to match those of their kids, or mix and match their own distinctive, fun-fashion statements.

In the **Jordaan** neighborhood, generation after generation of experimental designers has set up shop to show its imaginative creations. (Antiques-and used-clothing shops are also in this part of town.) Designer shops stand shoulder to shoulder on **P. C. Hooftstraat,** in the city's Museum Quarter. The chandeliers and marble floors of the elegant interior of **AM** (✉ P. C. Hooftstraat 97, Museum District ☎ 020/662–3588) are a suitable setting for attire by Valentino, Celine, Givenchy, and Missoni. **Boetiek Pauw** (✉ Van Baerlestraat 66 and 72, Museum District ☎ 020/662–6253), which also operates men's and children's shops, is part of a chain that stands out for the quality of both design and craftsmanship of its clothing. Best termed stylishly casual, their clothes look good anywhere, at the office or on a day out. The Dutch minichain **Cora Kemperman** (✉ Leidsestraat 72, Eastern Canal Ring ☎ 020/625–1284) offers architecturally designed clothes that are ageless and elegant. Designer fashions from Jean-Paul Gaultier and Yves Saint Laurent are sold at **Leeser** (✉ P. C. Hooftstraat 117, Museum District ☎ 020/679–5020). Those who really want to make an individual fashion statement pay a visit to **Marlijn** (✉ Govert Flinckstraat 394 hs, De Pijp ☎ 020/671–4742). Move over, Jean-Paul Gaultier—here's a Dutch rival that Madonna hasn't discovered yet, although she's designed for numerous celebrities. If you want to stop traffic or turn heads, Marlijn will design a unique, flamboyant garment for you. The chic Negen Straatjes boutique, **Van Ravenstein** (⊠ Keizersgracht 359, Eastern Canal Ring ☎ 020/639–0067), is the only retail outlet in Holland for Viktor & Rolf ready-to-wear. But don't expect A-bomb fashion—that's seldom seen outside museums and off the catwalk. The design duo also produces smart, beautifully cut clothing that can be worn anywhere, sometimes with three different collars. The shop also carries top Belgian designers such as Martin Margiela and Dries van Noten. For a funky look go to **Sjerpetine** (⊠ 1e van der Helststraat 33, De Pijp ☎ 020/664–1362). The shop is aesthetically organized in a rainbow of colors and patterns. **Edgar Vos** (⊠ P. C. Hooftstraat 136, Museum District ☎ 020/671–2748) is a Dutch designer who caters to women desiring sophisticated, classic, feminine, but never frilly, garments. Hand-beaded and hand-embroidered details on fine silk, wool, and linen make his clothes especially attractive and spotlight the influence of his apprenticeship to Dior and Balmain.

SIDE TRIPS: FOLKLORIC HOLLAND

By Jonette Stabbert

If you want your postcards to come to life, head to the rural districts of the Noord-Holland province. Just to the north of Amsterdam you'll find the Zaanstreek and Waterland areas, home to the famous "folkloric" towns of Zuiderzee, Volendam, and Marken. Here, boys can still be seen wearing Hans Brinker costumes, sleepy little fishing ports are lost in time, replete with wooden fishermen's cottages and towheaded children at play, and canal vistas recall ink sketches by Rembrandt. Just across the amazing Noordzee Kanaal (North Sea Canal)—first built in the late 19th century to be one of Holland's most important commercial trade "highways"—running from behind Amsterdam's Centraal Station to as far as the Kop van Holland (the Top of Holland) and the island of Texel, this part of the country offers a taste of unspoiled rural life and offers lovely options for day trips from Amsterdam.

Numbers in the margin correspond to points of interest on the Side Trips from Amsterdam maps.

Monnickendam

❶ *16 km (10 mi) northeast of Amsterdam. Take Rte. N247.*

Hardly is the salty odor of curing cheese from nearby towns out of the air than the towers of Monnickendam's Grote Kerk (Great Church) and Speeltoren signal our next stop. Every quarter hour, people hasten to the latter, which is the tower of the 18th-century town hall. Instead of bells, a carillon chimes while knights perform a solemn march. Unless they are stuck again. The oldest working carillon (16th century) in the world, this is the centerpiece of the **Museum De Speeltoren,** and its bells still chime musically every 15 minutes. The 5-ton clock was too heavy for the Germans to remove during the World War II occupation, so it was spared being melted down for munitions. Inside, a museum has a permanent exhibit about local historical architecture and findings from architectural "digs." ⊠ *Noordeinde 4* ☎ *0299/652203* 🎫 €4 ⊙ *Easter–June 1, Sat. 11–5, Sun. 1–5; June 2–2nd Sun. in Sept., Tues.–Sat. 11–5, Sun. 1–5.*

Take a moment to stroll down an avenue of dainty gabled houses to the harbor, which is brimming with history. The entire historic center of the Monnickendam is well preserved, with many listed monuments; repairs and new constructions are required to be carried out in the same style.

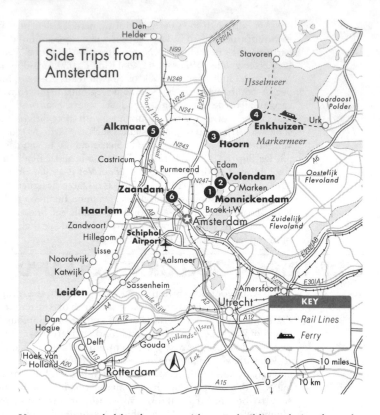

Side Trips from Amsterdam

KEY

⊢──⊣ Rail Lines

🚢 Ferry

0 ──────── 10 miles
0 ──────── 10 km

You are surrounded by the past, with some buildings dating from the 14th century. Monk's Dam was named in 1273 in reference to a medieval monastery that had stood on the site. By the 17th century, the harbor at the edge of the Zuiderzee had great importance; now it is possibly the largest yacht harbor in Europe, yet it still has the feeling of olden times. Virtually every monument has an interesting history, including one house that was a hiding place for Jews during World War II. To enjoy the stories behind every structure, join a **walking tour** (some are free); inquire at the local VVV (Tourist Information Office) or at the Speeltoren.

Where to Eat

$$ ✕ **De Waegh.** Situated in the former *Waeghgebouw*—a 1688 weigh house—this lovely restaurant still has the structure's original scales as part of its decor. Immerse yourself in the past with a view of the harbor, locks, and old inner city while you dine on fine French cuisine for lunch or enjoy dinner by candlelight. The large menu offers so many delicious possibilities you'll be spoiled for choice. ⊠ *Middendam 5-7* ☎ *0299/651241* ⊟ *MC, V* ☺ *Closed Tues.*

Volendam

❷ *4 km (3 mi) northwest of Monnickendam, 18 km (11.5 mi) northeast of Amsterdam. Take Rtes. N247–N517.*

Assuming that other visitors don't block your view, you can stare to your heart's content at the residents of Volendam still wearing traditional costumes immortalized in Dutch dolls the world over. Yes, indeed, they dress this way for real (even cosmopolitan Amsterdammers stop in their tracks when someone from Volendam or Marken visits the city in full gear.) The men wear dark baggy pantaloons fastened with silver guilders instead of buttons, striped vests, and dark jackets with caps. Women wear long dark skirts covered with striped aprons and blouses with elaborately hand-embroidered floral panels. Their coral necklaces and famous winged lace caps complete the picture. Of course, everyone wears *klompen* (wooden shoes). You'll have the most fun in Volendam if you have your photo taken in traditional costume (a real hoot for the folks back home), enjoy a stroll on the dike (or maybe even a swim on one side of it), and explore the narrow streets with their small nostalgic fishermen's cottages. Don't let the many tacky touristy businesses—a room wallpapered with cigar bands?—throughout the main area selling souvenirs put you off; once you head off the beaten track and see the way the native Volendammers live, you'll get to see the "real" unspoiled Volendam. Be sure to sample the region's renowned smoked eels; they're truly delicious.

Learn about Volendam's history at the **Volendams Museum,** which has rooms filled with mannequins adorned with folkloric costumes. ⊠ *Zeestraat 41* ☎ *0299/369258* ⊕ *www.volendams-museum.com* ⊡ *€1.75* ⊙ *Mar.–Dec., daily 10–5.*

Visit a working cheese farm at **Kaasboerderij Alida Hoeve,** where you'll learn how cheese is made and can also purchase various cheeses. ⊠ *Zeddeweg 141* ☎ *0299/365830* ⊡ *Free* ⊙ *Mon.–Sun. 8:30–6.*

Hoorn

❸ *29 km (16 mi) northeast of Volendam, 45 km (27 mi) northeast of Amsterdam. Take Rtes. N247–A7 (E22).*

Although a city with nearly 20,000 residents, Hoorn has many historic nooks and crannies, time-burnished side streets, and a fetching harbor landmarked by the 1532 **Hoofdtoren tower,** now home to a handy restaurant. Hoorn's development was abruptly arrested in the 17th century when England, not limited to flat-bottom boats that could clear the sandbanks of the Zuider Zee, eclipsed Holland in the carrying trade. In a sense the city went to sleep, thus enabling the visitor to step 300 years back in time to an era when Hoorn sent her ships around the world. As the former capital of West-Friesland, Hoorn was an important center for the fleets of the VOC (Dutch East India Company) during the 17th century. William Cornelis Schouten, one of the town's sons, was the first sailor to round the southern cape of America (in 1616), and christened it Cape Hoorn (Cape Horn). Jan Pieterszoon Coen, whose statue lords over the **Rode Steen Square,** founded the city of Batavia in Java, the present-day Jakarta, and governed it from 1617 until his death in 1629. Hoorn's decline was precipitated by the growing naval power of the British during the 18th century and the opening of Noord-Holland's canal linking Amsterdam directly to the North Sea.

The **Westfries Museum** (West Frisian Museum) is housed in the provincial government building dating from 1632, where the delegates from the seven cities of West-Friesland used to meet. The cities are represented by the coats of arms decorating the stunning facade, a testimony to the province's former grandeur. The council chambers are hung with portraits of the region's grandees, and the exhibitions explain the town's maritime history and the exotic finds of its adventurous sailors. ⊠ *Rode Steen 1* ☎ *0229/280028* ⊕ *www.westfriesmuseum.nl* ⊡ *€2.50* ⊙ *Weekdays 11–5, weekends Sun. 2–5.*

Where to Eat

$–$$ ✕ **De Waag.** A monumental building dating from 1609, with wooden beams and the antique weighing equipment still intact, the "Weigh

House" was designed by Hendrick de Keyser. There are soups, salads, and well-filled sandwiches during the day, and at dinnertime you can choose from fish specialties or French cuisine. The terrace affords a stunning view of the towering ornamental facade of the Westfries Museum across the square. *(The Weigh House)* ⊠ *Rode Steen 8* ☎ *0229/215195* 🖃 *AE, MC, V* ⊗ *Closed Tues. Sept.–Apr.*

Enkhuizen

★ ❹ *20 km (13 mi) northeast of Hoorn, 62 km (39 mi) northeast of Amsterdam. Take Rtes. N506 or N302.*

Near the former harbor town of Enkhuizen, about 19 km (12 mi) east of Hoorn, is perhaps the most famous of the "costume villages," the ℭ **Zuiderzeemuseum.** It is one of The Netherlands' most complete outdoor museums, with streets, neighborhoods, and harbors created with historic buildings. There are 130 houses, shops, and workshops where the old crafts are still practiced. To reach the museum you have to take a boat from the main entrance, a romantic way to take a step back in time. Assorted historical treasures here include a 19th-century apothecary, cottages moved from the isle of Urk and the village of Zoutkamp, sail-making and herring shops, picturesque lime kilns from Noord-Holland, and a children's island that takes youngsters back to life in the former fishing village of Marken during the 1930s. The indoor Marine Hall museum houses permanent exhibitions depicting the rich history of the Zuiderzee (now the IJsselmeer) and inhabitants of the area, including traditional costumes and a history of the battle to reclaim the land from the encroachments of the sea. ⊠ *Wierdijk 12–22, Enkhuizen* ☎ *0228/ 351111* 🖃 *€9.50; indoor museum only, €5* ⊗ *Indoor museum daily 10–5; outdoor museum Apr.–Oct., daily 10–5.*

Alkmaar

★ ❺ *45 km (13 mi) southwest of Enkhuizen, 40 km (25 mi) northwest of Amsterdam. Take Rtes. N302–A7/E22–N243–N242.*

As one of the "cheese towns," Alkmaar may be most noted for its traditional cheese market, but it is also worth visiting for its several hundred historical monuments, many windmills, and beautiful medieval courtyards—a concentration of all things Holland. On June 11, 2004, the city will have been on the map for 750 years, but birthday celebrations in the form of special events will go on throughout the year. Town spot- and floodlights will illuminate monuments, gables, and bridges. The town is littered with monuments: the St. Lawrence Church—with its great centuries-old organ and tomb of Count Floris V; the Town Hall, a beautiful Gothic building from 1520; the Remonstraat Church; and the House of the Cannonball (bearing a vestige of Spanish invaders). But the glory of Alkmaar is the **Waaggebouw,** or Weigh House, a 15th-century chapel with a tower added in 1597. As you stand below its ornate step gables, your eye is drawn upward by a labyrinth of receding planes that culminate in the weather vane. If the hour is about to strike, pause to enjoy the chimes and watch the moving figures of mounted knights and trumpeters (the noon hour gets the biggest show). Then climb the tower for a view of the town: canals cross this way and that, and the former ramparts are outlined by gardens often ablaze with flowers. In the distance, windmills turn in the face of a breeze perfumed with the faint scent of the salt sea.

If it is a Friday morning, it won't be easy to tear yourself from the spectacle taking place at your feet. The cheeses arrive at the market by barge (the factory may be as little as half a mile away) and are unloaded by means of a juggling act that would do credit to any circus as the balls are pitched from the barge to barrows that look like stretchers. At this point pairs of colorfully attired men from the Porters' Guild (in existence for 400 years) carry the cheeses away, no mean feat, as the average weight is about 350 pounds per barrow. A "father" directs the activities of the 28 porters, who are divided into four groups, or *veems,* dressed alike in white shirts and trousers but distinguished by blue, red, green, or yellow straw hats. The actual selling of the cheeses takes place in a ring and is consummated by a handclasp that is as binding as a signed contract. The cheese market takes place from the first week in April to the first week in September on Friday mornings from 10 to 12:30. All in all, it may be easier to buy your cheese at a supermarket, but it's nice to remember a world that has a place for pageantry. The local VVV (Tourist Information Office) organizes a walking tour of noteworthy sites. The 1½-hour tour costs €3.50. It starts at 12:30, except in September, when it starts at 11. Tickets can be purchased at the Alkmaar VVV office. If planning to explore on your own, pick up a map from the VVV.

The **Stedelijk Museum Alkmaar** focuses on the history of the region from Alkmaar's "Golden Age"—the 16th and 17th centuries—to the present day. There is an intriguing display of city life shown in detailed miniature dioramas. Paintings depict the Spanish siege of the city, portraits capture noblemen and militia leaders, and other historic artifacts make this a good starting point before exploring Alkmaar itself. ⊠ *Canadaplein 1* ☎ *072/511–0737* ⊠ *€3.40* ☉ *Tues.–Fri. 10–5, weekends 1–5.*

While attending the cheese market, you'll see the cheese being weighed at the Waaggebouw, which is also where the **Dutch Cheese Museum** is located. Cheese has been produced in Noord-Holland for nearly 2,500 years, so it's no wonder Dutch cheese is so good. You'll learn about past and present-day cheese making (farm versus factory). Twenty-four 16th-century panels, painted by women, depict regional costumes from all over Noord-Holland, with some full-size replica outfits on display. ⊠ *Waagplein 2* ☎ *072/511–42 84* ⊠ *€2.50* ☉ *Apr.–Oct., Mon.–Thurs., and Fri. 9–4; Sat. 10–4.*

Zaandam

★ ❻ *31 km (19 mi) southeast of Alkmaar, 16 km (10 mi) northwest of Amsterdam. Take Rte. N203 via Zaanse Schans (Zaandijk).*

During the 17th century Holland was renowned as the leading shipbuilding nation of the world, with Zaandam as its center. One of the many people who came here to learn the craft of shipbuilding was Peter the Great of Russia (whose statue now adorns the Damplein, the town marketplace). Today, modern shipyards stud the area—once immortalized in several canvases by Claude Monet—but set within the Zaanstreek region is a jewel: the **Zaanse Schans,** a living open-air museum. Time appears to stand still, and you can easily immerse yourself in the 17th and 18th centuries. The village, built along the Zaan River, is filled with a great many working windmills and original Zaanse-style green wooden houses. Many have been restored as private homes, but a whole cluster are open to the public, and traditional crafts and businesses are still kept alive. You can see warehouses from the Dutch East India Trading Company and visit the workshop of a clog maker, the shops of a traditional cheese maker, a bakery museum, and the working windmills themselves. Each of these "mini museums" has its own low admission price. The Zaanse Schans presents a terrific skyline when viewed from the water, so avail yourself of the local VVV (Tourist Information Office) canal cruises. A mile or so north of Zaandam you come to Koog aan de Zaan, notable chiefly for the old (1751) **Het Pink windmill**, now a museum devoted to the history and construction of mills. ✉ *Kraaienest, Zaandam* ☎ *075/616–8218* ⊕ *www.zaanseschans.nl* ☞ *Free* ◷ *Daily 8–4.*

Side Trips A to Z

ARRIVING & DEPARTING

By Bus: Many of the larger destinations in this chapter are reached easily (and quickly) by train, but several of the smaller "folkloric" villages, such as **Volendam** and **Monnickendam,** have only bus service connecting to Amsterdam. The **Zuiderzeemuseum** can be reached using a bus from Hoorn.

By Car: To reach the **Zaanse Schans,** you need to navigate the most confusing part of the country's road system, Amsterdam's A10 ring road, from which you take the exit for A8 toward Zaandam. Take the Zaandam exit, and then follow local signs. **Hoorn** is north of Amsterdam just off E22/A7. To reach **Enkhuizen,** take the Hoorn exit from E22/A7 and continue eastward on N302. To reach **Alkmaar** from Amsterdam, take the A8 and A9 north. To get to **Enkhuizen** and its famous Zuiderzeemuseum, follow the A7 via Purmerend and Hoorn, then take the N 302 in the direction of Enkhuizen. ANWB signs direct you to the museum.

By Train: **Koog-Zaandijk** is the station nearest to Zaanse Schans, on the local line from Amsterdam to Alkmaar. The village can be reached on foot in a few minutes. **Local trains** operate once an hour direct from Amsterdam to **Alkmaar, Hoorn, Zandvoort,** and **Enkhuizen.**

By Steam train and ferry: The NS (Dutch Railways) offer a special travel arrangement in which you can visit several folkloric towns: take a train from Amsterdam to Enkhuizen, then travel by museum ferryboat over the IJsselmeer to Medemblik, then ride a museum steam train to Hoorn and return to Amsterdam by train. Call for **national train information** (☎ 0900/9292).

VISITOR INFORMATION

VVV Noord-Holland (✉ Oranjekade 41, 2011 VD Haarlem ☎ 023/531–9413). **VVV West-Friesland** (✉ Veemarkt 4, 1621 JC Hoorn ☎ 0900/403–1055 🖷 0229/215–023). **VVV Zaanstreek/Waterland** (✉ Gedempte Gracht 76, 1506 CJ Zaandam ☎ 075/616–2221 🖷 075/670–5381).

AMSTERDAM A TO Z

To research prices, get advice from other travelers, and book travel arrangements, visit www.fodors.com.

AIRPORTS & TRANSFERS

Set in the suburb of Badhoevedorp, Amsterdam Schiphol Airport is 25 km (15 mi) southeast of the city and has efficient road and rail links. The comprehensive "Helloport" telephone service, charged at €.45 per minute, provides information about flight arrivals and departures as well as all transport and parking facilities.

🖪 Airport Information Amsterdam Schiphol Airport ☎ 0900/0141 ⊕ www.schiphol.nl.

AIRPORT TRANSFER The Schiphol Rail Link operates between the airport and the city 24 hours a day, with service to the central railway station or to stations in the south of the city. The trip takes about 15 minutes and costs €3. Trains leave from the platforms of Schiphol Station, found beneath Schiphol Plaza. They head into the city using one of three routes. The most popular is the NS Schiphollijn, which runs to Centraal Station (with two stops in west Amsterdam). Another route heads to the Amsterdam Zuid/WTC (South/World Trade Center) station in south Amsterdam, while another line heads to the RAI section, near the big convention center. From these south Amsterdam stations, Tram 5 goes to Leidseplein and the Museum Quarter; from RAI, Tram 4 goes to Rembrandtplein. Other than taxis, you may wish to hop aboard a tram or bus to get to your hotel, so go to one of the **Gemeentevervoerbedrifj(GVB) Amsterdam Municipal Transport** booths found in front of the Centraal Station. Here you can find directions, fare information, and schedules.

KLM Shuttle operates a shuttle bus service between Amsterdam Schiphol Airport and major city hotels. The trip takes about half an hour and costs €7.95 one-way. Also, there is a taxi stand directly in front of the arrival hall at Amsterdam Schiphol Airport. All taxis are metered, and the fare will run between €25 and €30 to central Amsterdam. A service charge is included, but small additional tips are not unwelcome.

🗐 Taxis & Shuttles **KLM Shuttle** ☎ 020/649-5651. **Schiphol Rail Link** ☎ 0900/9292.

BIKE TRAVEL

Bicycling is the most convenient way to see Amsterdam. There are bike lanes on all major streets, bike racks in key locations, and special bike parking indentations in the pavement. To rent a bicycle, you'll pay from €6.50 per day, plus a deposit of about €50 per bike, and need a passport or other identification to rent. Never leave your bike unlocked: there is a rapid turnover of stolen bikes no matter what quality or condition. Use a "D" lock, which can't be cut with the average thieves' tools, and lock your bike's frame to something that can't be shifted, like a railing.

🗐 Bike Rentals **Bike City** ✉ Bloemgracht 70 Jordaan ☎ 020/626-3721. **Damstraat Rent-a-Bike** ✉ Damstraat 22 Nieuwe Zijde ☎ 020/625-5029. **MacBike** ✉ Mr. Visserplein 2 Jewish Quarter ☎ 020/620-0985 ✉ Marnixstraat 220 Jordann ☎ 020/626-6964 ✉ Stationsplein 12 Oude Zijde ☎ 020/624-8391.

CAR RENTAL

The major car rental firms have convenient booths at Schiphol Airport, but the airport charges rental companies a fee that is passed on to customers, so you'll get a better deal at downtown locations.

Rates in Amsterdam vary from company to company; daily rates start at approximately €60 for a one-day rental, €160 for a three-day rental, and €320 for a week's rental. This does not include collision insurance, airport fee, or 19% VAT tax. Weekly rates often include unlimited mileage. As standard, cars in Europe are stick shift. An automatic transmission will cost a little extra.

🗐 Major Agencies **Alamo** ☎ 800/462-5266, 0208/750-2800 in the U.K. ⊕ www.alamo.com. **Avis** ☎ 800/230-4898, 800/272-5871 in Canada, 02/9353-9000 in Australia, 0800/655111 in New Zealand, 0870/606-0100 in the U.K. ⊕ www.avis.com. **Budget** ☎ 0144/227-6266 in the U.K. **Dollar** ☎ 800/800-3665, 800/800-6000 in the U.K., where it's affiliated with Sixt, 649/255-0620 in New Zealand ⊕ www.dollar.com. **Hertz** ☎ 800/654-3001, 800/263-0600 in Canada, 0870/844-8844 in the U.K., 03/9698-2555 in Australia, 0800/654321 in New Zealand ⊕ www.hertz.com. **National Car Rental** ☎ 800/227-7368, 020/8745-2800 in the U.K. ⊕ www.nationalcar.com.

🗐 Local Agencies **Avis** ✉ Nassaukade 380, Nieuwe Zijde ☎ 020/683- -6061. **Budget** ✉ Overtoom 121, Vondelpark ☎ 020/604-1349 ⊕ www.budget.com. **Hertz** ✉ Overtoom 333, Vondelpark ☎ 020/612-2441.

CAR TRAVEL

A network of well-maintained superhighways and other roads covers The Netherlands, making car travel convenient. Major European highways leading into Amsterdam from the borders are E19 from western Belgium; E25 from eastern Belgium; and E22, E30, and E35 from Germany. Follow the signs for *Centrum* to reach center city. At rush hour, traffic is dense but not so dense as to become stationary.

EMERGENCIES

The Central Medical Service offers 24-hour medical assistance, including names and hours of pharmacists and dentists. Referrals for doctors and dentists are available through Afdeling Inlichtingen Apotheken, a 24-hour service for all medical assistance, including names and opening hours of pharmacists and dentists; the number is listed below. Academisch Medisch Centrum, Onze Lieve Vrouwe Gasthuis, and VU Ziekenhuis all have emergency rooms.

Police, ambulance, and fire (☎ 112 toll-free 24-hr switchboard for emergencies). The 24-hour help-line service **Afdeling Inlichtingen Apotheken** (☎ 020/694–8709) (*apotheken* means pharmacy) can direct you to your nearest open pharmacy. The **Centraal Doktorsdienst/Atacom** (Medical Center; ☎ 020/592–3434) offers a 24-hour English-speaking help line providing advice about medical symptoms. In the case of minor accidents, phone **directory inquiries** (☎ 0900/8008) to get the number for the outpatients' department at your nearest *ziekenhuis* (hospital). **TBB** (☎ 020/570–9595 or 0900/821–2230) is a 24-hour dental service that refers callers to a dentist (or *tandarts*). Operators can also give details of chemists open outside normal hours. For less urgent police matters, call the **central number** (☎ 0900/8844). The city's **police headquarters** is located at the crossing Marnixstraat/Elandsgracht and can be reached with Tram lines 3, 7, 12, or 17.

MONEY MATTERS

CURRENCY EXCHANGE
GWK/Grenswisselkantoren is a nationwide financial organization specializing in foreign currencies, where travelers can exchange cash and traveler's checks, receive cash against major credit cards, and receive Western Union money transfers. Many of the same services are available at banks, and cash can be exchanged at any post office.

🛂 Exchange Services **International Currency Express** ☎ 888/278–6628 for orders ⊕ www.foreignmoney.com. **GWK (bureau de change)** branches are located near railway stations throughout the country; ☎ 0900/0566. There's an office at **Amsterdam Schiphol Airport** ☎ 020/653–5121. You can find a **GWK** branch in the hall at **Centraal Station,** ☎ 020/627–2731.

TAXIS

Taxi stands are at the major squares and in front of the large hotels. You can also call Taxicentrale, the main dispatching office. Fares are €2.90, plus €1.80 per kilometer (half mile). A 5-km (3-mi) ride will cost about €12.

WATER TAXIS
A water taxi provides a novel, if pricey, means of getting about. Water taxis can be hailed anytime you see one cruising the canals of the city, or called by telephone. The boats are miniature versions of the large sightseeing canal boats, and each carries up to eight passengers. The cost is €75 for a half hour, including pick-up charge, with a charge of €60 per each half-hour period thereafter. The rate is per ride, regardless of the number of passengers.

🛂 Taxi Companies **Taxicentrale** ☎ 020/677–7777 **Water Taxi** ☎ 020/535–6363 ⊕ www.water-taxi.nl.

TOURS

An initiative by the city and the Amsterdam Public Transport Museum offers the opportunity to discover not only the historic inner city but also the harbor and the arising artificial residential islands of Ijburg, in antique trams, buses, and boats.

🖪 Fees & Schedules **Amsterdam Public Transport Museum** ⊠ Haarlemmermeer-station, Amstelveenseweg 264, Amsterdam Zuid ☎ 020/423-1100.

BICYCLE TOURS   From April through October, guided three-hour bike trips through the central area of the city are available through Yellow Bike. Let's Go tours (contact the VVV for further details) takes you out of the city center by train before introducing you to the safer cycling of the surrounding countryside. Its tours include Volendam, Naarden and Muiden, and, in season, a Tulip Tour.

🖪 Fees & Schedules **Let's Go** ⊠ VVV–Amsterdam Tourist Office, Centraal Station, Nieuwe Zijde ⊕ www.lestgo-amsterdam.com. **Yellow Bike** ⊠ Nieuwezijds Kolk 29, Nieuwe Zijde ☎ 020/620-6940 ⊕ www.yellowbike.nl.

BOAT TOURS   The quickest, easiest, and (frankly) most delightful way to get your bearings in Amsterdam is to take a canal-boat cruise. Trips last from 1 to 1½ hours and cover the harbor as well as the main canal district; there is a taped or live commentary available in four languages. Excursion boats leave from *rondvaart* (excursion piers) in various locations in the city every 15 minutes from March to October, and every 30 minutes in winter. Departures are frequent from Prins Hendrikkade near the Central Station, along the Damrak, and along the Rokin (near Muntplein), at Leidseplein, and Stadhouderskade (near the Rijksmuseum). For a tour lasting about an hour, the cost is around €8.50, but the student guides expect a small tip for their multilingual commentary. For a truly romantic view of Amsterdam, opt for one of the special dinner and candlelight cruises offered by some companies, notably Holland International. A candlelight dinner cruise costs upward of €24. Trips for all boat tours can also be booked through the tourist office. Operators of canal cruises include Holland International, Meyers Rondvaarten, Rederij Lovers, Rederij P. Kooij, Rederij Noord/Zuid, and Rederij Plas.

Several boat trips to museums are also available: Canalbus, which makes six stops along two different routes between Centraal Station and the Rijksmuseum, costs €15, including a tickets and/or reductions for museums. Following a longer route is Museumboot Rederij Lovers, which makes seven stops near 20 different museums. The cost is €13.25 for a day ticket that entitles you to a 50% discount on admission to the museums. At Canal-Bike, a pedal boat for four costs €28 per hour.

🖪 Fees & Schedules **Canalbus/Canal-Bike** ⊠ Nieuwe Weteringschans 24, Leidseplein ☎ 020/623-9886. **Holland International** ⊠ Prins Hendrikkade, Centraal Station ☎ 020/622-7788. **Meyers Rondvaarten** ⊠ Damrak 4, Nieuwe Zijde ☎ 020/623-4208. **Museumboot Rederij Lovers** ⊠ Stationsplein 8/Prins Hendrikkade 26, Centraal Station ☎ 020/530-1090. **Rederij Lovers** ⊠ Prins Hendrikkade 26a, Centraal Station ☎ 020/530-1090. **Rederij P. Kooij** ⊠ Rokin, near Spui, Nieuwe Zijde ☎ 020/623-3810. **Rederij Noord/Zuid** ⊠ Stadhouderskade 25, opposite Parkhotel, Leidseplein ☎ 020/679-1370. **Rederij Plas** ⊠ Damrak, quays 1-3, Nieuwe Zijde ☎ 020/624-5406.

BUS TOURS   Afternoon bus tours of the city operate daily. Itineraries vary, and prices range from €15 to €30. A 2½-hour city tour that includes a drive through the suburbs is offered by Key Tours. A 3½-hour tour, focusing on the central city and including a canal-boat cruise, is offered by Lindbergh Excursions. However, it must be said that this city of narrow alleys and canals is not best appreciated from the window of a coach. Also, a number of visitors feel unhappy that part of some tours involves a visit to a diamond factory, where they feel pressured into listening to a sales pitch. The same bus companies operate scenic trips to attractions outside the city.

🎫 Fees & Schedules **Key Tours** ✉ Dam 19, Nieuwe Zijde ☎ 020/623-5051. **Lindbergh Excursions** ✉ Damrak 26, Nieuwe Zijde ☎ 020/622-2766.

WALKING TOURS   The Amsterdam Tourist Board (VVV) maintains lists of personal guides and guided walking and cycling tours for groups in and around Amsterdam and can advise you on making arrangements. You can also contact Guidor–Nederlandse Gidsen Organisatie (Dutch Guides Organization). The costs are from €143 for a half day to €234 for a full day. The tourist office also sells brochures outlining easy-to-follow self-guided theme tours through the central part of the city. Among them are "A Journey of Discovery Through Maritime Amsterdam," "A Walk Through the Jordaan," "Jewish Amsterdam," and "Rembrandt and Amsterdam." Walking tours focusing on art and architecture are organized by Artifex and Archivisie. For walking tours of the Jewish Quarter, contact Joods Historisch Museum. Yellow Bike Tours organizes two-hour walking tours of the Jordaan and the Red Light District.

Probably the best deal in town is Mee in Mokum, which offers walking tours led by retired longtime residents. For a mere €2.50, you are given an entertaining three-hour educational tour of the inner city or the Jordaan, focusing on architecture and surprising facts. The admission fee entitles you to reduced fees to a choice of museums and a reduction in the price of a pancake meal at a nearby restaurant. Tours are held daily and start promptly at 11 AM. You must reserve at least a day in advance.

🎫 Fees & Schedules **Archivisie** ⊕ Postbus 14603, 1001 LC ☎ 020/625-8908. **Artifex** ✉ Herengracht 342, 1016 CG, Central Canal Ring ☎ 020/620-8112. **Arttra Cultureel Org-buro** ✉ Staalstraat 28, 1011 JM, Oude Zijde ☎ 020/625-9303 ⊕ www.arttra.com. **Mee in Mokum** ✉ Hartenstraat 18, Jordaan ☎ 020/625-1390 (call between 1 and 4). **Yellow Bike Tours** ✉ Nieuwezijds Kolk 29, Nieuwe Zijde ☎ 020/620-6940 ⊕ www.yellowbike.nl.

TRAIN TRAVEL

The city has several substations, but all major Dutch national, as well as European international, trains arrive at and depart from Centraal Station. The station also houses the travel information office of NS/Nederlandse Spoorwagen (Netherlands Railways) and its international rail office.

🎫 Train Information **Centraal Station** ☎ 0900/9292 or 0900/9296.

TRANSPORTATION AROUND AMSTERDAM

Everyone's dream of touring Amsterdam is to take a scenic hop on the Canal Bus, or go the two-wheel route with a bike, or just hoof it, as an eager army of bipeds does every year. Indeed, Amsterdam is relatively small as metropolises go and you can virtually connect all the main sites in a five-hour stroll. Happily, however, Amsterdam also has a full-scale bus and tram system—the GVB (city transport company)—that can whisk you from sector to sector, and attraction to attraction, throughout the city. Buses and trams run frequently; schedules and routes are posted at stops. In addition, somewhat surprisingly for this water-bound and centuries-old city, Amsterdam also has a subway, referred to as the metro, with lines running southeast and southwest. Once you understand the fanlike pattern of Amsterdam's geography, you will have an easier time getting around; most trams and buses begin and end their journeys at Centraal Station, sightseeing and shopping are focused at Dam Square and Museumplein, and the arts and nightlife are centered in the areas of Leidseplein, Rembrandtplein, and Waterlooplein. There are usually maps of Amsterdam's full transport network in individual shelters, and diagrams of routes are found on board.

The transit map published by GVB (Gemeentelijk Vervoer Bedrijf/City transport company) is very useful. It's available at the GVB ticket office across from the central railway station or at the VVV tourist information offices next door. It is also reprinted as the center spread in *Day by Day in Amsterdam,* the monthly guide to activities and shopping published by the tourist office. The map shows the locations of all major museums, monuments, theaters, and markets, and it tells you which trams to take to reach them. The GVB also has a very **useful site with transportation information** in English with route maps ⊕ www.gvb.nl. At every bus and tram stop there is a time schedule. Although the bus or tram may not arrive at the exact time listed, the time between arrivals is fairly accurate. You can also discover if the stop is on the route of a night bus. Note that all public transport is smoke-free.

DE OPSTAPPER   A great new public transport option is the *Opstapper,* a transit van that traverses the elegant Prinsengracht—heart of the historic canal sector—between Centraal Station and the Music Theater. For a one-zone stamp on your strippenkaart (see explanation below), you can get on or off anywhere along the Prinsengracht. You can hail it on the street, or get on at its starting point in front of Centraal Station. There are no fixed stops. It passes within walking distance of the Anne Frank House, the Leidseplein, and maybe even your hotel. The buses run ever 10 minutes from 7:30 AM to 6:30 PM. There are eight seats and room for an additional eight standing passengers.

METRO   Amsterdam has a full-fledged subway system, called the metro, but travelers will usually find trams and buses more convenient for getting around, as most metro stops are geared for city residents traveling to the outer suburbs. However, the Amsterdam metro can get you from point A to point C in a quantum leap—for instance, from Centraal Station (at the northern harbor edge of the city) to Amstel Station (a train station at the southeastern area of the city, with connections to many buses and trams)—much faster than a tram, which makes many stops along the way. A strippenkaart is used the same way as for other public transport.

Four metro lines, including the express tram (*sneltram*), serve Amsterdam and the surrounding suburbs. While many stops on the metro will not be of use to the tourist, several stops can prove handy. Nieuwmarkt lets you off near the Red Light District and is near the famous sights of the Oude Zijde area. Waterlooplein is near the eastern edge of the Oude Zijde, stopping at the square where the Stadhuis-Muziektheater is located and offers access to sights of the Jewish Quarter and the Plantage; a walk several blocks to the south leads you to the Eastern Canal Ring and its many historic houses. Wibautstraat is not too far from the Amstel River and provides access to the southern sectors of the city, including De Pijp. Amstel Station is a train station near the Amstel River in the southeastern area of the city, with connections to many buses and trams. Amsterdam Zuid/WTC (South/World Trade Center) is at the southern edge of Amsterdam Zuid (South), and rarely used by any tourists. VU (Vrije Universiteit) is in the suburb of Buitenveldert.
🚆 Train Information **Centraal Station** ☎ 0900/9292 or 0900/9296.

TICKETS &   The same ticket can be used in buses, trams, and metros throughout Holland.
STRIPPENKAART   *Enkele Reis* (single-ride tickets) are valid for one hour only and can be purchased from tram and bus drivers for €1.60. However, it is far more practical to buy a *strippenkaart* (strip ticket) that includes 2

to 45 "strips," or ticket units. The best buy for most visitors is the 15-strip ticket for €6.20. A 45-strip ticket costs €18.30. Although newer trams have ticket control booths, by tradition, Dutch trams and buses work on the honor system: upon boarding, punch your ticket at one of the machines in the rear or center section of the tram or bus. The city is divided into zones, which are indicated on the transit map, and it is important to punch the correct number of zones on your ticket (one for the basic tariff and one for each zone traveled).

When it comes to strippenkaarts, a two- or three-strip ticket can be bought directly from the bus driver. If you buy a ticket in advance, this works out to be much cheaper per journey. You can buy these at railway stations, from post offices, and many bookstores and cigarette kiosks, and they remain valid until there are no more strips left, or for one year from the first stamp.

Amsterdam is divided into zones, and the fare you pay depends on the number of zones you travel through. You can easily travel within one zone (two strips), but to travel across Amsterdam takes you through four (five strips) zones. These zones are displayed on transport maps. Each journey you make costs one strip plus the number of zones you travel through. When you get on a bus, you show the driver your strippenkaart and simply say where your final destination is, or the number of zones you plan to travel through, and let him or her stamp the strips.

In a metro you have to stamp your ticket yourself in the small yellow machines found near the doors, and you can often do this in a tram. Count the number of strips you need, fold your ticket at the bottom of the last strip required, and stamp the final strip in the machine. A stamp on a strip uses that, and the strips above it. If you're staying within the center city Centrum, it's always two zones, so stamp three strips. Two or more people can travel on the same strippenkaart, but the appropriate number of units must be stamped for each person.

The newest trams in Amsterdam (recognizable by their extra-large windows) have ticket control booths in the center of the tram. You may board the tram only there, unless you already have a valid stamp on your ticket, in which case you may board at the front and show your ticket to the driver. On older trams, you can usually board only at the rear, where you will encounter either a ticket controller (*conducteur*) or a stamping machine.

The stamp indicates the zone where the journey started, and the time, and remains valid for one hour, so you can travel within the zones you have stamped until the hour is up.

🏢 **GVB** ✉ Prins Hendrikkade 108-114, Centrum ☎ 0900/9292 🌐 www.gvb.nl/.

VISITOR INFORMATION
The Amsterdam Tourist Board (VVV) has several offices around Amsterdam. The office in Centraal Station is open daily 8-8; the one on Stationsplein, opposite Centraal Station, is open daily 9-5; on Leidseplein, daily 9-5; and at Schiphol Airport, daily 7-10.

🏢 **Amsterdam Tourist Information VVV-Netherlands Board of Tourism** 🌐 www.holland.com/amsterdam ✉ Spoor 2/Platform 2, Centraal Station, Centrum ✉ Stationsplein 10, Central Station ✉ Leidseplein 1, corner Leidsestraat, Leidseplein ✉ Schiphol Airport, Badhoevedorp ☎ 0900/400-4040 €.55 per min weekdays 9-5. Outside office hours, this line has an extensive voice-response program.

METROPOLITAN HOLLAND: ROTTERDAM & THE RANDSTAD (2)

FODOR'S CHOICE

Bollenstreek Route, *for its checkerboards of tulip fields*

Brielle, *redoubt of the legendary Sea Beggars*

Delfshaven, *the last remaining nook of old Rotterdam*

Delft, *to step back 350 years in time to the days of Vermeer*

Gouda, *follow the porters to the town's Cheese Market*

Haarlem, *home to the merrymaking portraits of Frans Hals*

Kasteel de Haar, *a Rothschildian fairy-tale castle*

Kinderdijk, *for 14 of the most beautiful windmills in Holland*

Leiden, *Rembrandt's hometown*

Museum Boijmans van Beuningen, *a Rotterdam treasure*

Rietveld-Schroder House, *Utrecht's modern-art dazzler*

HIGHLY RECOMMENDED

RESTAURANTS De Zwethheul, *Delft*

L'Orage, *Delft*

Parkheuvel, *Rotterdam*

Winkel van Sinkel, *Utrecht*

HOTELS Bridges House, *Delft*

Hotel New York, *Rotterdam*

Grand Hotel Karel V, *Utrecht*

Johannes Vermeer, *Delft*

Nieuw Minerva, *Leiden*

Spaarne 8, *Haarlem*

Many other great sights, restaurants, and hotels enliven this area.
For other favorites, look for the black stars as you read this chapter.

By Charlotte A. R. Vaudrey

Updated by Jonette Stabbert

IN THE PROVINCE OF ZUID-HOLLAND (South Holland), like filings around the end of a magnet, six major urban centers cluster in a horseshoe arc to the west and south of Amsterdam: Haarlem, Leiden, Delft, Gouda, Utrecht, and Rotterdam. Each of these centers has continued to develop, prosper, and grow independently from the capital—so extravagantly that the borders of each community nearly verge on the next. In fact, the whole of South Holland is now dubbed the Randstad ("Border City") because locals consider it one mammoth megalopolis—a movement begun three decades ago, when Leiden began to stretch a hand south to The Hague, and Delft found itself beginning to be compressed between The Hague and Rotterdam. More than 25% of Holland's 15 million residents now live in and around the 10 small- to large-size cities that are within 80 km (50 mi) of the capital. Randstad also means "Edge City," another term the Dutch use to describe the circle formed by the cities of Amsterdam, The Hague, Rotterdam, and Utrecht, since the cities lie on the same geologic ridge at the northwestern edge of the country. Whatever the terminology, this entire region is considered "The West" by young Randstad wannabes waiting for their opportunity to hit the big time.

For that, they first head to Rotterdam, the industrial center of Holland and the world's largest port. The city's quaint statue of Erasmus was long ago overshadowed by some of the most forward-looking architecture to dazzle any European city. When Rotterdam's city center and harbor were completely destroyed in World War II, the authorities decided to start afresh rather than try to reconstruct its former maze of canals. The imposing, futuristic skyline along the banks of the Maas River has been developing since then. Today, say architectural pundits, we have seen the future, and it is Manhattan-on-the-Maas (as locals call it), thanks in large part to the efforts of major figures such as Rem Koolhaas, Eric van Egeraat, and UN Studio. But if Rotterdam is now one of the most vibrant centers of architecture in the world, it is also many other things: a skate city, a harbor city, an artists' haven, a design inspiration, a historical museum center, a jazz lover's dream.

Clearly, Rotterdam is a city that has to remain firmly focused on the present and future—the Nazi bombs of May 1940 took care of its past—but surrounding it is an area that is sublimely history soaked. Within the span of a single day, you can roll the centuries back from Rotterdam's modern glitter to pursue the ghost of Frans Hals through the Golden Age streets of Haarlem; discover the great university and the church of America's Pilgrim Fathers based at Leiden; feast on Gouda, where cheese is but one of the many delicious treats; explore the time-stained town center of Utrecht; and wander through the open-air museum of Delft, which once colored the world with its unique blue. Many other colors are on view in Holland's fabled tulip fields. Every spring, green thumbers everywhere make a pilgrimage to Lisse to view them, the noted tulip garden known as the Keukenhof, and drive the Bollenstreek Route, which takes them through miles of countryside glowing with gorgeous hues and blooms. Though you would miss much of interest if you left Holland after visiting no more than this corner of the country, there is no other region that so well merits your time. Indeed, if it remains an area small enough to drive through in a day, it is interesting enough to take weeks to explore.

Exploring Metropolitan Holland: Rotterdam & the Randstad

The ring that encircles the Randstad incorporates most towns and sights and conveniently makes a circular drive or train trip ideal, avoiding the need for any doubling back. Rotterdam, as the crux in the cultural axis,

If beauty, venerable history, sylvan gardens, majestic cathedrals, and great art are at the top of your list, it can be hard choosing between the towns of the Randstad, that horseshoe arc of urban centers that dot the heartland of Holland. So visit them all: leapfrog from past to future by journeying from Haarlem—earliest center of Dutch art—to Rotterdam, colossus of the waterways and now home to Europe's most daringly modern architecture; travel through an open-air old-master painting by visiting Leiden—birthplace of Rembrandt—and Vermeer's blue-hued Delft; then savor the unique flavors of Utrecht and Gouda, city of cheese, stained glass, and pipes. Welcome to "Holland in a nutshell."

2

There is no need to rent a car to journey through this region, as every location is accessible by public transport. Indeed, for many of the towns covered in this chapter, traffic and parking make car rental somewhat of a headache. Although Kinderdijk, Muiden, and Brielle do not have train stations nearby, all three are on bus routes, which ensures that all visits can be covered by the independent, carless traveler.

Numbers in the text correspond to numbers in the margin and on the Metropolitan Holland, Haarlem, Leiden, Utrecht, and Exploring Rotterdam maps.

**If you have
3 days**

Get an early start from Amsterdam and head west to nearby **Haarlem ①–⑨** ⌐, a Golden Age town made famous by art. Here, you'll find lying in the shadow of a nest of lovely medieval buildings in the heart of this 900-year-old city the Frans Hals Museum, housing many of the roistering and unforgettable portraits of this 17th-century painter. Explore the famous Church of Sint Bavo—adorably framed by a flower market—the history-rich main square, the tapestried Town Hall, and the Renaissance-era Hallen exhibition halls, and end with the great old-master drawings on view at the Teylers Museum. After lunch, set off for 🚊 **Leiden ⑫–㉔**, birthplace of Rembrandt and home base for the Pilgrim Fathers; as home to Holland's greatest university, the city is packed with cosmopolitan hotels, restaurants, and shops, offering a fine place to break your stay. Follow in Rembrandt's footsteps (about all you can do, since nearly all traces of him and his family have vanished hereabouts) and explore the quaint streets. If it's springtime, take the N206 out of town and through the bulb fields to **Lisse ⑪**, heart of Tulip Country and home to the famed Keukenhof Gardens. On your second morning journey south and take your car or tram (20 minutes) to nearby 🚊 **Delft ㉕**, one of the most beautifully preserved historic towns in the country and the place that gave us Delftware and that mysterious master painter Vermeer. Happily, many streets and canals in the Centrum, the historic center, have a once-upon-a-time feel, and you may be tempted to set up your own easel in a minute. There are some patrician mansion-museums to explore here, and you can visit the city's renowned porcelain factory. On your third morning head 23 km (15 mi) southeast to **Rotterdam ㉖–㉛**. Start by going out to Delfshaven, then take a breathless trip around the Dubbelde Palmboom museum as you briskly take in the harbor. On your way back across town walk along the old harbor at Veerhaven, before crossing the Erasmus Bridge to the Kop van Zuid. A great museum is the famous Museum Boijmans van Beuningen, home to some legendary old-master paintings, including Pieter Bruegel the Elder's *Tower of Babel.* Take in Wilhelminaplein and the shops before jumping into a water taxi and crossing the river, this time across to the Oude Haven, where you should have time for the Kijk-Kubus cube houses and Blaak railway station; then hop a train back to Amsterdam.

If you have 6 days Extend the three-day itinerary above by starting with an overnight stay in ⊞ **Rotterdam** ㉖–㉛ ⌐, which will allow you to luxuriate in extra time. You could head to Het Park, an ideal antidote to the city's bustle, and, for a fantastic view, go up the Euromast, or go to the Architecture Institute to learn more about the Kop van Zuid and Blaak districts. In the historic Delfshaven quarter go to the Pilgrim Fathers' church, or explore the Oude Haven. Other museums in the city include specialty collections such as the National School Museum and the city's historical museum, split between exhibitions in the Schielandshuis and De Dubbelde Palmboom. In the Entrepot district you could pick up some shopping in the interior design district, along the marina. Climb on board a warship at the Maritiem Museum. Get into more history at the Schielandshuis, and see photography and art collections at the Witte de With Center for Contemporary Art. As you wander up Westersingel, take in the Sculpture Terrace and the biggest skate park in the city. If you want a mini-escape from urban bustle, visit the enormous Kinderdijk Mills complex, an easy day trip from Rotterdam that you can even visit by boat.

On the way back north, stop off in ⊞ **Gouda** ㊽, famed not only for its cheeses but also for its medieval City Hall and the magnificent stained glass in the Sint Janskerk. Opt to take the train or the A12 to ⊞ **Utrecht** ㊾–㊽, where you can climb the Gothic Domtoren, the highest church tower in The Netherlands, for a panoramic view of the countryside. Back on ground level, you can visit a delightful museum of music boxes, player pianos, and barrel organs. Explore the possibility of an afternoon trip to the **Kasteel de Haar** ㊺, Holland's most spectacular castle extravaganza. Return to Amsterdam either by car or—via Utrecht's railway hub—by train.

---

lies farthest from Amsterdam, 73 km (40 mi) south of the capital, with slightly more to see on the eastern side of the area between the two cities.

As you travel out of Amsterdam, you come first to Muidenslot castle 12 km (7½ mi) from the center of Amsterdam, then to Naarden, a farther 8 km (5 mi). Utrecht is then 30 km (18 mi) south, and Gouda 14 km (9 mi) southwest of Utrecht. Kinderdijk is 12 km (8 mi) directly south of Gouda, and is just 5 km (3 mi) east of Rotterdam. Dordrecht lies 20 km (13 mi) southeast of Rotterdam. Brielle is almost on the coast, 22 km (13½ mi) west of Rotterdam, and Delft is 16 km (10 mi) northwest of Rotterdam, heading toward The Hague. Leiden is 28 km (18 mi) northeast of Delft, and Haarlem is 38 km (24 mi) from Leiden, with the Keukenhof in Lisse almost exactly between. Haarlem is just 10 km (7 mi) west of Amsterdam.

About the Restaurants & Hotels
Although this area of Holland is home to some of the country's most worldly restaurants, keep in mind that bars and Holland's famous, time-stained *bruine kroeg* (brown cafés) also offer house specials usually kept cheap to keep students and young people coming in (look in particular for the *kleine kaart,* or lighter meal menu, usually offered in the bar area). Perennially popular dishes such as saté and pepper steak

never come off the menu. Some bars with restaurants attached have theme nights, so in summer you can expect Javanese nights, with drummers, when the menu takes on Asian influences.

Hotels in the Randstad region range from extensive elegant canal houses, to smaller hotels that create the feeling of living in a comfortable, private residence, to cross-country chains with anonymous decor. Happily, most large towns have one, or even several, deluxe hotels that exceed all expectations. Needless to say, accommodations in Rotterdam—a big convention city—is at a premium, so you should book well in advance. Get in touch with the VVV (tourist offices) of the region you plan to travel to, as they have extensive accommodation listings. They can book reservations for you, according to your specific accommodation requirements. Assume all rooms have air-conditioning, TV, telephones, and private bath, unless otherwise noted.

WHAT IT COSTS In euros*					
	$$$$	**$$$**	**$$**	**$**	**¢**
RESTAURANTS	over €30	€22–€30	€15–€22	€10–€15	under €10
HOTELS	over €230	€165–€230	€120–€165	€75–€120	under €75

*Restaurant prices are per person for a main course only, excluding tax (6% for food and 19% for alcoholic beverages) and service; note that if a restaurant offers only prix-fixe (set-price) meals, it has been given the price category that reflects the full prix-fixe price. Hotel prices are for a standard double room in high season, including the 6% VAT (value-added tax); higher prices (inquire when booking) prevail for any meal plans.

Timing
This part of Holland is at its best in late spring or early autumn. High summer means too many visitors, and touring in winter often puts you at the mercy of the weather (but even in summer, pack your umbrella). For flora lovers, mid- to late April is ideal for a trip around Haarlem and Leiden, as the fields are bright with spring bulbs, although there are plenty of rose gardens in summer months. Many restaurants are closed on Sunday (also Monday); museums tend to close on Monday.

If you're into the arts, you might prefer to schedule your trip to catch one of the area's two world-renowned festivals: the International Film Festival Rotterdam, where 300 noncommercial films are screened in late January and early February, and the Festival Oude Muziek (Festival of Early Music), where 150 concerts are held in venues across Utrecht in late August.

FAR HORIZONS & TULIP FIELDS: HALS'S HAARLEM TO VERMEER'S DELFT

A route south of Amsterdam, running near the coast, takes you through the heart of metropolitan Holland, starting with Haarlem and ending at Rotterdam. Here, great city centers still bear witness to the Golden Age of the 17th century: Haarlem, the only competition to Amsterdam as an art center, thanks to the glories of Sint Bavo's and the celebrated portrait skills of local Frans Hals; Leiden, where a child was baptized and left town two decades later to find fame and riches as Rembrandt van Rijn; and Delft, whose frozen-in-amber scene seems not so distantly removed from that painted in Vermeer's legendary *View of Delft*. Once past the bright lights of these town centers, you'll find the land stretches flat as far as the eye can see, though the coast west of Haarlem and Leiden undulates with long expanses of dunes, many of which are nature reserves. In spring, the farmland between these two towns is legendarily bright with tulips and other blooms. Venture down some unmarked roads and you can still find a storybook Holland of green meadows, hayracks, brimming canals, and—dare we say—a rosy-cheeked child or two. Cows graze in the fields nearly all year-round, and only the distant spires destroy the illusion of a flat infinity leading endlessly onward.

Haarlem

20 km (13 mi) west of Amsterdam, 41 km (26 mi) north of The Hague.

It is just a short hop from the ocean of annual color that is Holland's Bulb Route to this haven of perennial color. For Haarlem's historic center is beautiful, dotted with charming *hofjes* (historic almshouse courtyards), and has a lively population—often the overspill of students who can't find lodgings in Amsterdam or Leiden. The city is also home to fine museums stuffed with art by masters of the Haarlem School, such as the renowned Teylers Museum, and the town center is adorned with the imposing Grote Kerk, often painted by the masters of the Golden Age. All in all, if on occasion eclipsed by Amsterdam, Haarlem is an independent little city in its own right. Plenty of top-quality restaurants and shops cater to well-heeled locals, and people tend to be more friendly than in the downtown districts of Amsterdam. Lying between Amsterdam and the coastal resort of Zandvoort, Haarlem is very close to the dunes and the sea and therefore attracts hordes of beach-going Amsterdammers and Germans every summer. No matter that all traces of Haarlem's origins as a 10th-century settlement on a choppy inland sea have disappeared with the draining of the Haarlemmermeer in the mid-19th century: the town itself hasn't lost its appeal.

If you arrive by train (it's just a 15-minute trip from the capital), take a long look around before you leave the railway station—a fabulous art nouveau building dating from 1908. Head down Jans Weg (to the left of the station as you exit) for several blocks, over the Nieuwe Gracht canal and into the city center, where, farther along on Jans Straat, you ► ❶ hit Haarlem's pulsing heart, the famous **Grote Markt.** Around this great market square the whole of Dutch architecture can be traced in a chain of majestic buildings ranging through the 15th, 16th, 17th, 18th, and 19th centuries. With a smile and a little bravado, you can enter nearly all of them for a quick look. But all eyes are first drawn to the imposing mass of Sint Bavo's.

❷ The Late Gothic Sint Bavo's church, more commonly called the **Grote Kerk,** or Great Church, dominates the square and was built in the 14th century, but severe fire damage in 1328 led to a further 150 years of rebuilding and expansion. St. Bavo was the patron saint of the community. This is the burial place of Frans Hals—a lamp marks his tombstone behind the brass choir screen. Here, too, is buried Laurens Coster, who in 1423 invented printing—sorry, Gutenberg—seemingly because the lovestruck Coster was inspired when carved-bark letters fell into the sand below a tree he was etching with a valentine (a statue of Coster adorns the square outside). The imposing wooden vault shelters a whimsical historic sight. In the north transept, the Dog Whippers' chapel pays tribute to men who ejected snarling dogs from the sacred premises; note the carved capital on the left-hand arch that depicts a man whipping a dog. The church is the home of the Müller organ, on which both Handel and Mozart played (Mozart at age 10). Installed in 1738, and for centuries considered to be the finest in the world, this gilded and gleaming instrument has been meticulously maintained and restored through the years to protect the sound planned by its creator, the master organ

2

Tulipmania You must prepare yourself for a surprise—the landscape of Holland's fabled Tulip Country looks exactly like the color postcards you have seen. In a region set about 36 km (20 mi) south of Amsterdam, in the farmlands around the hub of Lisse, the fields stretch out as far as the eye can see on either side of the roads in a neat checkerboard pattern of brilliant color. The bluest of skies combine with the brilliantly colored living flower quilt to create a dazzling Technicolor world; colors appear clearer and brighter than you've ever experienced them. Little wonder that every spring, buses, bikes, and tours packed with Hollanders and tourists drive down the Bloemen Route, attend the Bulb District Annual Parade (the last Saturday in April), visit the noted Keukenhof Gardens, and generally feast their eyes on the countryside, which looks like a 3-D Van Gogh painting—an unmissable trip for many travelers to Holland.

Art & Artists With exhibitions sporadically circling the globe from New York to London, public interest in the hushed and lucid world of Vermeer's tranquil figures wholly absorbed in their daily tasks has gone through the roof. But it's not only Vermeer to be on the lookout for. Vermeer's fellow Delftian Pieter de Hooch is acknowledged as being part of the movement that resulted in the Delft School. Practically every town or village we take you to in this section has nurtured its own genius, with the town forming the basis of that particular artists' circle or school.

Desiderius Erasmus, the 15th-century scholar, theologian, and humanist, was born in Gouda before moving to Rotterdam, where both a university and a bridge were named in his honor, and he is but one of a whole host of geniuses. For 40 years Muiden Castle, as home to poet and playwright Pieter Hooft, hosted the country's most celebrated circle of literati, the Muiderkring. Leiden was the birthplace of Rembrandt, and Frans Hals and his contemporaries formed the Haarlem School, basing their movement on their hometown. Utrecht, meanwhile, is fiercely proud of enfants terribles of the catwalk Viktor and Rolf, whose clothes hover between visual art and couture, taking a subtle yet witty stand against traditional design. Their provocative yet innovative work has elevated them to such prominence that they are seen as the visionaries of haute couture's future, not just by the city of Utrecht, but by the whole fashion world.

On the Menu It may come as some surprise for travelers to find out that many Dutch restaurants do not serve . . . Dutch food. The old joke that Dutch cuisine is considered an oxymoron is prevalent even among the locals—after all, how can you expect someone to pony up €8 or more for *hutspot*, a traditional and typical Dutch stew of mashed potatoes, carrots, onions, and sausage. This might be just the ticket to get that internal heating system going on a cold winter day, but nouvelle it is not. Thus, many restaurateurs in the metropolitan Holland region choose to specialize in cuisines of other lands. Adding to this preference is the fact that although northern and southern Holland have their own regional specialties, the Randstad does not. Chefs do feature dishes from the border provinces—often with Burgundy overtones— but other regional dishes, such as *bloedworst*, or blood sausage, do not make for four-star dining. Therefore, chefs have turned to French cuisine as their major influence. Other flavors come with a spin: mussels may be poached, or stuffed with anchovies; you might see lasagna but stuffed with cod and salmon. Slowly but surely, these newer-than-nouvelle takes on Dutch food are being increasingly served. If you find grilled perch fillet on the menu, chances are it will be served with couscous and clam ratatouille. Dutch design is not just an affair of architecture and fashion: chefs, too, feel a chicken is so much more when you feed the eye. At stylish restaurants, plates are sometimes beautifully arranged, and gravy is even splashed about with an almost Rembrandtesque élan.

---

builder Christian Müller. Between May and October the official town organists of Haarlem give free weekly or twice-weekly concerts. You may be lucky enough to hear orchestras rehearsing for concerts as you tiptoe through. One thing is clear: there are few places where a Bach prelude or fugue sounds as magisterial. ⊠ *Grote Markt* ☎ *023/533–0877* ▨ €*1.60* ☯ *Apr.–Aug., Mon.–Sat. 10–4; Sept.–Mar., Mon.–Sat. 10–3:30.*

need a break? The spacious **Grand Café Brinkmann** (⊠ Brinkmannpassage 41 ☎ 023/532–3111), adorned with cherubic ceiling paintings, offers baguettes, tacos, and other light snacks. Windows edged with art deco stained glass overlook the Grote Markt and Sint Bavo's church across the square.

❸ On the market square is the 13th-century **Stadhuis,** or Town Hall, originally a hunting lodge belonging to the Count of Holland, who permitted it to be transformed into Haarlem's Town Hall in the 14th century. The large main **Gravenzaal** (Count's Hall) is worth a visit—if you can sneak in between bouts of confetti throwing, as this has a goodly number of bridal parties ascending its steps on a regular basis—to study its collection of 16th-century paintings amassed by the Count of Holland. If you wish to tour the premises, it's best to check or call in advance to get permission, as rooms may be closed for civic functions. ⊠ *Grote Markt 2* ☎ *023/511–3000* ▨ *Free* ☯ *Weekdays 10–4 (when not closed for civic functions).*

❹ Just off the Grote Markt, tucked into a small gabled town building above a shop, is the **Corrie ten Boomhuis** (Corrie ten Boom House) which honors a family of World War II resistance fighters who successfully hid a number of Jewish families before being captured themselves by the Germans in 1944. Most of the Ten Boom family members died in the concentration camps, but Corrie survived and returned to Haarlem to tell the story in her book *The Hiding Place*. The family clock shop is preserved on the street floor, and their living quarters now contain displays, documents, photographs, and memorabilia. Visitors can also see the hiding closet, which the Gestapo never found, although they lived six days in the house hoping to starve out anyone who might be hiding here. The upstairs living quarters are not accessible through the shop, but on the door of No. 19 are meeting instructions, giving the time of the next guided tour. ⊠ *Barteljorisstraat 19* ☎ *023/531–0823* ⊕ *www.corrietenboom. com* ▨ *Free* ☯ *Apr.–Nov., Tues.–Sat. 10–4; Dec.–Mar., Tues.–Sat. 11–3.*

❺ Overlooking the Grote Markt is the **De Hallen,** or The Halls museum complex, whose two buildings—the Vleeshal and the Verweyhal House—contain a variety of artworks, ranging from temporary special exhibitions to a permanent collection of modern art by artists from Haarlem and surrounding areas. A branch of the town's Frans Hals Museum, De

Hallen has an extensive collection, with the works of Dutch impressionists and expressionists, including sculpture, textiles, and ceramics, as well as paintings and graphics. The **Vleeshal** (Meat Market) building is one of the most interesting cultural legacies of the Dutch Renaissance. Externally it is unique, for nowhere in the country is there such a fine sweep of stepped gables that invite you, had you a giant's stride, to clamber up to the pinnacle that almost seems to pierce the scudding clouds. It was built in 1602–03 by Lieven de Key, Haarlem's master builder. The ox heads that look down from the facade are reminders of the building's original function: it was the only place in Haarlem where meat could be sold, and the building was used for that sole purpose until 1840. Today it is used for exhibitions—generally works of modern and contemporary painting, glass, furniture, clocks, and sculpture. Just hope that your visit doesn't coincide with the weather illustrated by Karel Appel in *People in a Storm.* Note the early landscape work by Piet Mondriaan, *Farms in Duivendrecht,* so different from his later De Stijl shapes.

The **Verweyhal Gallery of Modern Art** was built in 1879 as a gentlemen's club, originally named *Trou moet Blijcken* ("Loyalty Needs to Be Proven"). The building now bears the name of native Haarlem artist Kees Verwey, who died in 1995. The Verweyhal is used as an exhibition space for selections from the Frans Hals Museum's enormous collection of modern and contemporary art, providing a range of work from the last century of Dutch art history. In addition to the works of Kees Verwey, the exhibition covers such artists as Jacobus van Looy, Jan Sluijters, Leo Gestel, Herman Kruyder, and Karel Appel. Note, too, a fine collection of contemporary ceramics. ⊠ *Grote Markt 16* ☎ *023/511–5778* ⊕ *www.dehallen.com* ⊠ *€4* ☉ *Tues.–Sat. 11–5, Sun. noon–5.*

Leaving the Grote Markt by the eastern side, take Damstraat over to the river and the **Waag** (Weigh House). Built entirely of stone, and dating to 1598, it was designed by Lieven de Key to weigh goods that ships brought into the city via the Spaarne canal. Head north up the Spaarne embankment to reach the **Teylers Museum**, the best sort of small museum, based on the taste of an eccentric private collector, in this case the 18th-century merchant Pieter Teyler van der Hulst. Founded in 1784, it's the country's oldest museum and has a mixture of exhibits, with fossils and minerals sitting alongside antique scientific instruments. The museum itself is a grand old building with mosaic floors; its major artistic attraction is the legendary collection of drawings and prints by 19th-century masters Michelangelo, Rembrandt, Raphael, and others, based on a collection that once belonged to Queen Christina of Sweden.

Unfortunately, only a few of the drawings are on display at any one time because of their fragility. There is also a collection of coins and medals and even a rare 31-tone Fokker organ. In the beautiful oval library you can use brass parabolic mirrors (dating from 1800) to send the soft ticking of a watch right across the room; the Luminescence Cabinet is stocked with fluorescent and phosphorescent rocks and minerals that glow with extraordinary colors in the dark. Much of the collection is housed in beautiful wooden display cases in the original 18th-century museum building, and the drawing collection is in a discreetly extended modern wing. ⊠ *Spaarne 16* ☎ *023/531–9010* ⊕ *www.teylersmuseum. nl* ⊠ *€5.50* ☉ *Tues.–Sat. 10–5, Sun. noon–5.*

Not far from the Teylers Museum is the **Gravenstenenbrug,** a picturesque drawbridge across the Spaarne. Once you're on the far side of the canal, a short walk takes you to the **Amsterdamse Poort** (Amsterdam Gate), the only remaining city gate, dating from 1400; remains of the city wall can be seen at its base.

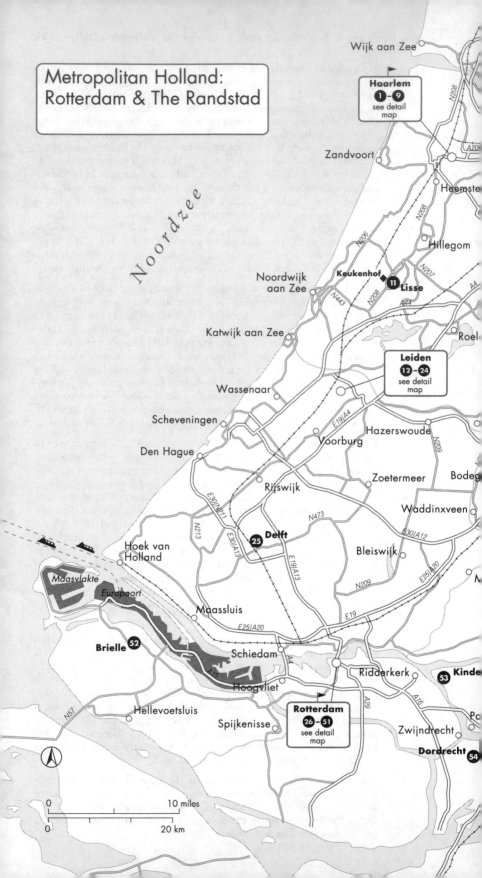

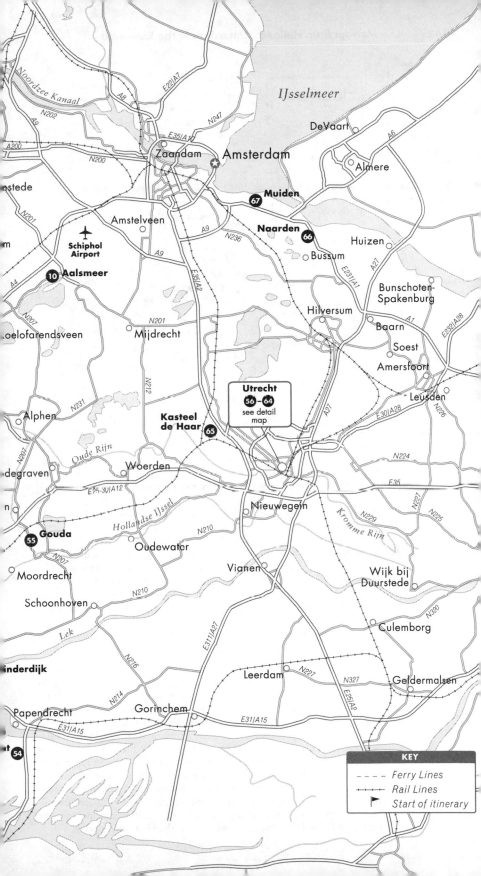

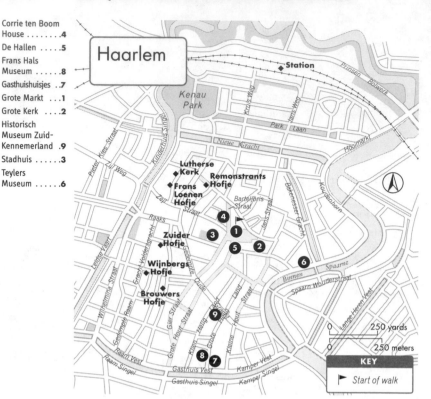

Walking between the Vleeshal and Sint Bavo Kerk, away from the Grote Markt, you come to Warmoestraat—a very different thoroughfare from the street of the same name in Amsterdam. Here in Haarlem it is a quaint cobbled street, not a throbbing neon-lighted avenue. Still, there are shops here, but they cater to the upper end of the market, with designer-wear stores, bespoke jewelers, little specialty shops (note the bead-and-button boutique), and bistros. As you walk down Warmoestraat and

7 its continuations to the Frans Hals Museum, don't miss the **Gasthuishuisjes** on your left-hand side, nearly opposite the museum. This series of houses with identical step gables originally formed part of the St. Elizabeth hospital and was built in 1610. As you walk up Warmoestraat, look at the short posts to restrict cars from parking: the usually rounded tops have been capped with flowerpots, which are filled with geraniums and other brightly colored flowers—just another indication of how locals prize flowers.

8 The **Frans Hals Museum,** set near the River Spaarne (from the Grote Markt, follow Warmoestraat and its continuations, Schagchelstraat and Groot Herlig Land), is named after the celebrated man himself and holds a collection of amazingly virile and lively group portraits by the Golden Age painter; these portraits depict the merrymaking civic guards and congregating regents for which Hals became world famous. The museum is in one of the town's smarter hofjes, in an entire block of almshouses grouped around an attractive garden courtyard, a setting that in itself is a gem of artistry. In the 17th century this was an old men's home, an *Oudemannerhuis.* The cottages now form a sequence of galleries for paintings, period furniture, antique silver, and ceramics. The 17th-century collection of paintings that is the focal point of this museum includes the works of Frans Hals and other masters of the Haarlem School.

You might find yourself overwhelmed by the visual banquet of Hals paintings, but take time to look in all the rooms branching off the main route, festooned with works by other masters. In the first room, you are greeted by a huge triptych commissioned for the visiting Prince of Orange's lodgings in the Prinsenhof. Note, too, the work of Dirk Hals, whose depictions of parties and revelry at musical get-togethers comes as a complete contrast to the more serious portraiture of his famous brother. Some are works with perplexing questions hanging over them, such as the painting where X-rays picked out a second face in the background (experts are not sure whether Hals painted either). But many of the works on display represent Frans Hals at his jovial best—for instance, the *Banquet of the Officers of the Civic Guard of St. Adrian* (1623) or the *Banquet of the Officers of the St. George Militia* (1616), where the artist cunningly allows for the niceties of rank (compositionally, captains are more prominent than sergeants, who are more central than ensigns, and so on down the line) as well as emotional interaction, for Hals was the first to have people gaze and laugh at each other in these grand *schutter* (marksmen) portraits. In many instances, Hals leaves "class portrait" decorum well behind: in a group scene of the *Regentesses of the Old Men's Home* (1664) he appears to have taken revenge on their strict governance, immortalizing the women as a dour and frightening group. Nineteenth-century academicians later criticized Hals for his imprecise handling of details, but remember that Hals was 80 when completing this portrait, and it was his *mouvementé*, nearly proto–Jackson Pollock, way with the brush that has made him the darling of 20th-century artists and art historians.

There is a wide array of works by Haarlem School masters on view, including Hendrick Goltzius, Frans Jansz Post, Judith Leyster, Johannes Verspronck, Pieter Claesz, Willem Heda, Adriaen van Ostade, and Jacob van Ruysdael. But all the works are worthy of this museum, and details are eye-opening: Philips Wouwerman's gorgeous *Landscape with a Horseman* punctuates its dreamy setting with Dutch realism: a dog squatting grossly. As respite from nearly 250 canvases, step into the museum's courtyard—small, lovely, planted with formal-garden baby hedges, of which you hardly get a glimpse as you work your way through the galleries (since most of the blinds are shut against the sunlight to protect the paintings). In one such room, with curtains drawn for extra protection, is **Sara Rothè's Dolls' House**; nearby is an exquisitely crafted miniature version of a merchant's canal house. On leaving, *View of Haarlem* (1655) by Nicolaes Hals, Frans's son, bids you good-bye. Ask whether you can visit the restoration workshop (variable hours), where you can stand behind a glass wall and watch painters work painstakingly on a tiny patch of an old master that will occupy them for months. ⊠ *Groot Herlig Land 62* ☎ *023/511–5775* ⊕ *www.franshalsmuseum. com* ⊠ *€5.40* ☉ *Tues.–Sat. 11–5, Sun. 1–5.*

⑨ Located in the area of the Frans Hals Museum, with two or three small temporary exhibitions a year, the town's history museum, the **Historisch Museum Zuid-Kennemerland** makes the most of its limited resources, offering a decent insight into the history of the city and the surrounding area. Video screenings (in English), models of the city, and touch-screen computers relate stories that take you back in history and will whet children's interests as well. There are lots of fascinating old prints and maps, in addition to quite random exhibits, such as one of the earliest printing presses, dating back to the 17th century. On view here also is a very incisive exhibition on modern Dutch architecture, **ABC Architectuur Centrum Haarlem,** with plans and photographs from around the city of projects already finished and those still in the planning stages

(De Bruijn's Woonhuis is particularly ingenious). ⊠ *Groot Heiligland 47* ☏ *023/542-2427 Historisch Museum* ⌑ *€1.15* ⊙ *Tues.–Sat. noon–5, Sun. 1–5.*

In the lower, southwestern sector of the city, you'll find many of the historic hofjes (almshouse courtyards) that make Haarlem such a pleasant place. In and around Voldersgracht, Gasthuisstraat, Zuiderstraat, and Lange Annastraat, look for the Zuider Hofje, the Hofje van Loo, the Wijnbergs Hofje, and the Brouwershofje. Closer to the Grote Markt are the Remonstrants Hofje, the Luthershofje, and the Frans Loenen Hofje.

Where to Eat & Stay

$$ ✕ **Peter Cuyper.** Situated in a 17th-century mansion that was once a bank, this small but gracious restaurant has a traditional beamed dining room that is brightened with flowers, crisp linens, and light from an enclosed garden (open in summer) filtering through the mullioned windows. Ask for a table with a view over the garden if you've missed out on a table outside. Try a wood dove and mushroom salad with a hazelnut dressing, guinea fowl with wild morel mushroom gravy, or one of the delicious soups and, for dessert, the lemon pie with homemade blackberry ice cream. The restaurant is convenient to both the Frans Hals and the Teyler museums. ⊠ *Kleine Houtstraat 70* ☏ *023/532–0885* ⚖ *Reservations essential* ☐ *AE, DC, MC, V* ⊙ *Closed Sun. and Mon.*

$$ ✕ **XO.** A very funky restaurant-bar, XO has chunky silver graphics, purple-and-gray walls, and oversize but softly lighted lamps. Throw in some fun touches—"king" chairs, complete with claw feet and red cushions; nifty recesses at the bar for extra intimacy; big stone candlesticks—and you've got an alluring setting for lunch and evening edibles. Try the Dutch take on focaccia bread, piled high with Serrano ham, sun-dried tomatoes, and buffalo mozzarella with pesto, and liberally sprinkled with pine nuts and olive oil. You'll find that one serving more than sets you up for an afternoon in the Frans Hals Museum. At night a tapas bar spins into action. ⊠ *Grote Markt 8* ☏ *023/551–1350* ☐ *AE MC, V.*

$–$$ ✕ **De Lachende Javaan.** Stepping into "The Laughing Javanese" off an old Haarlem street that hasn't changed in centuries, you are hit with a flash of color and pungent smells. You can sit upstairs at one of the window tables and look out over the sober gabled houses while eating *kambing saté* (skewers of lamb in soy sauce) and *kipkarbonaade met sambal djeroek* (grilled chicken with a fiery Indonesian sauce), but the menu options are enormous, so you can mix and match, choosing a meal of 12 small dishes if you want. ⊠ *Frankestraat 25–27* ☏ *023/532–8792* ☐ *AE, DC, MC, V* ⊙ *Closed Mon. No lunch.*

¢–$$ ✕ **Pieck.** One of Haarlem's best *eetlokaals* (dining spots), this attracts locals with its long bar, cozy tables, and lovely sun trap of a garden. The menu offers standards but with a twist: try the Popeye Blues Salad—a wild spinach, blue cheese, and bacon number, with creamy mustard dressing for a lighter option—or, for dinner, a butterfish fillet with okra and sugar snaps in a Tuscan dressing. As you'll see, the food makes this restaurant-café very popular, so get here early to snag a table. ⊠ *Warmoestraat 18* ☏ *023/532–6144* ☐ *No credit cards* ⊙ *Closed Sun. No dinner Mon.*

★ $$$$ ▣ **Spaarne 8.** From the outside, no one would guess that behind this town-house facade is an elegant hotel that accommodates only two deluxe suites. Both rooms overlook an immaculate private garden (which contains the city's oldest tree), and each has its own terrace with Philippe Starck chairs. Needless to say, this exclusive 1765 restored hotel, redesigned by Dick Beijer (renowned for his work for Elton John and Sir Terrance Conran), is about superluxury—the fact that it makes a design statement as well is just the topping. Each suite has its own impeccable style and individual decoration, but both offer fancy Egyptian cotton bed linen, chic bath and shower products, and stylish flower arrangements. You can even make this your private house—by taking both suites (and the on-site pantry allows you to dine in as well). When you check in, you'll be offered complimentary champagne, and all further personal drinks are included. It comes as no surprise that the hotel holds an Art Planet culture tourism award and multiple awards for its Web site, which shows off the beautiful rooms to the max. ⊠ *Spaarne 8, 2011 CH* ☎ *023/551–1544* 🖷 *023/534–2602* ⊕ *www.spaarne8.com* ⟳ *2 suites* ✧ *Room service, in-room data ports, cable TV, lounge* ⊟ *AE, DC, MC, V* ⧖ *BP.*

$$$ 🔲 **Golden Tulip Lion d'Or.** This traditional hotel near the railway station has been here since the early 18th century. Thoroughly modernized, it has spacious guest rooms and meeting rooms. A jogging path runs behind the hotel. ⊠ *Kruisweg 34–36, 2011 LC* ☎ *023/532–1750* 🖷 *023/532–9543* ⊕ *www.goldentulip.nl* ⟳ *34 rooms, 4 suites* ✧ *Restaurant, in-room data ports, cable TV, bar, parking (fee), some pets allowed* ⊟ *AE, DC, MC, V* ⧖ *BP.*

¢ 🔲 **Carillon.** This is an old-fashioned hotel with friendly staff, set in the shadow of St. Bavo's across the Grote Markt. The rooms are fresh and comfortable (amply sized but not enormous), though simply furnished. This central location is the selling point—making it a top spot to accommodate a day of exploring and then a night out. There's also a café and bar on the street level, with a nice terrace on the square. ⊠ *Grote Markt 27, 2011 RC* ☎ *023/531–0591* 🖷 *023/531–4909* ⟳ *21 rooms, 14 with bath* ✧ *Restaurant, in-room data ports, cable TV, bar; no a/c* ⊟ *AE, DC, MC, V* ⧖ *CP.*

¢ 🔲 **Faber.** Within walking distance of the beaches of Zandvoort, this is a small family-style hotel with bright, tidy rooms and a summer terrace. It gets booked up very quickly in summer, so if you plan on staying here, make the reservations early on. ⊠ *Kostverlorenstraat 15, 2042 PA Zandvoort* ☎ *023/571–2825* 🖷 *023/571–6886* ⟳ *32 rooms* ✧ *Restaurant, cable TV, bar; no a/c* ⊟ *AE, MC, V* ⧖ *CP.*

Nightlife & the Arts

Haarlem hosts the **International Organ Competition** in even-numbered years during the first week of July, giving people ample opportunity to hear the renowned Müller organ at full throttle.

Haarlem is more than a city of nostalgia, with the **Patronaat** (⊠ Zijlsingel 2 ☎ 023/532–6010) an excellent rock music venue: it's Haarlem's answer to the Melkweg in Amsterdam, though without the really big bands. Bars often metamorphose into busy nightspots, such as **Mickie's** (⊠ Kruisstraat 22 ☎ 023/551–8661), which by day is a mellow, new take on the brown-café theme and moves at night into a full DJ dance scene, with serious lighting rigged up overhead and enormous speakers to ensure the sound is loud.

For lots more bars and cafés head to Lange Veerstraat or the Botor Markt square.

Theo Swagemakers (⊠ Stoofsteeg 6 ☎ 023/532–7761) is one of the latest galleries to open in Haarlem; it displays artwork from Swagemakers (1898–1994) himself, with temporary exhibitions focusing on other artists, and there is a small admission charge. It's open Thursday–Sunday 1–5. Other more commercial art galleries can be found along Koningenstraat. On Frankestraat, look for art nouveau and art deco dealer **Kunsthandel Hermine Guldemond** (⊠ Frankestraat 39 ☎ 023/531–8725).

The Outdoors

BEACHES   **Zandvoort** is only 9 km (5½ mi) from Haarlem and has the area's biggest and best beach, always a favorite for sun-starved Amsterdammers. It can get crowded but is very expansive—if you wander south for ten minutes or so, you can find isolated spots among the dunes; after about 20 minutes, you come to the nude, in places gay, sunbathing beach.

BICYCLING   **De Volkenfietser** (✉ Koningstraat 36, Haarlem ☎ 023/532–5577) has bicycles for rent. You can also rent bicycles from **Peters** (✉ Stationsplein 7, Haarlem ☎ 023/531–7066).

Shopping

The pedestrianized Barteljorisstraat has lots of chic chains, such as Vanilia, Esprit, MEXX, and Street One, as well as a number of streetwear shops for men, such as Man 2 Be. The top end of Kruisstraat has furniture shops, from antiques to designer, and a lot in between. Flowers can be found on Krocht, on the corner junction of Kruisstraat and Barteljorisstraat; the sumptuous displays echo the nearby tulip fields between Haarlem and the Keukenhof.

Aalsmeer

   14 km (9 mi) southeast of Haarlem, 14 km (9 mi) south of Amsterdam, 38 km (24 mi) northeast of The Hague.

At Aalsmeer, about 19 km (12 mi) southwest of Amsterdam near Schiphol Airport, the **Bloemenveiling Aalsmeer** (Aalsmeer Flower Auction) is held five days a week from the predawn hours until mid-morning. The largest flower auction in the world, it has three auction halls operating continuously in a building the size of several football fields. You walk on a catwalk above the rolling four-tier carts that wait to move on tracks past the auctioneers. The buying system is what is called a Dutch auction—the price goes down, not up, on a large "clock" on the wall. The buyers sit lecture-style with buzzers on their desks; the first to register a bid gets the bunch. Note that you can reach the auction hall by taking NZH Bus 172 from the stop opposite the American Hotel near Amsterdam's Leidseplein. ✉ *Legmeerdijk 313, Aalsmeer* ☎ *0297/ 392185* ⊕ *www.aalsmeer.com* 🖼 *€4* ☉ *Weekdays 7:30–11* AM.

Lisse & the Bulb Fields

   15 km (9 ½ mi) southeast of Haarlem, 30 km (19 mi) south of Amsterdam,
Fodor'sChoice   *24 km (15 mi) northeast of The Hague.*
★

How could you visit Holland and not tiptoe through the tulips? Even if you are in Amsterdam for just a couple of days, it is easy to sample one of the best-known aspects of quintessential Holland—the bulb fields, in an area around the town of Lisse, address to the famous Keukenhof Gardens. This flower-growing area to the west of Amsterdam is a modern-day powerhouse of Dutch production techniques, resulting in a blizzard of Dutch flowers falling on every corner of the earth at any time of the year. In spring, the bulb fields blaze with color: great squares and oblongs of red, yellow, and white look like giant Mondriaan paintings laid out on the ground (you're intrigued from the moment you see them from your airplane window). It is a spectacular sight, whether you travel through the fields by bike or bus, or pass by in the train on your way to Leiden. Such great progress has been made in producing new varieties of the main bulb plants that the calendar is no longer quite the tyrant it used to be. In days gone by, it was usually the first week of May that brought optimum tulip viewing. If spring came early, however, the peak of the tulips, hyacinths, and narcissi (many other blooms besides tulips are cultivated in this region) could be as early as the middle of April, with nothing but heaps of discarded blooms left in the fields two weeks later. Everything then depended on the weather during the final critical 10 days after the buds were fully formed. Now with much hardier strains developed, it is no longer such a timely concern. Still, there is a general progression in this part of Holland from crocus from the middle of March, daffodils and narcissi from the end of March to the middle of April, early tulips and hyacinths from the second week of April to the end of the month, and late tulips immediately afterward. An early or late spring can move these approximate dates forward or backward by as much as two weeks. It's good news, then, that most people visit the bulb fields using Amsterdam as their excursion base, so that if the blooms don't cooperate, they can also check out some of the great 17th-century Dutch floral still-life paintings in the Rijksmuseum.

Those paintings, in fact, should be discovered in any event, since they are telling evidence of "tulipmania," the astounding frenzy that broke out in 1630s Holland for the buying and cultivating of the tulip, recently imported from Turkey, which became a sort of 17th-century futures market. The rarest bulbs became more expensive than houses, only to have the whole market crash in due course, taking many fortunes with it. The first tulip bulbs were brought to Holland from Turkey in 1559. The name "tulip" was taken from *tulband,* the Dutch word for "turban," because of the blossom's appearance. In 1625 an offer of Fl 3,000 for two bulbs was turned down, but the speculation in bulbs became a mania during the years 1634–37, as irrational and popular as stock market speculation in the late 1920s, when fortunes were made—and lost—in a single day. One Semper Augustus bloom clocked in at today's equivalent of €4,000—little wonder the great artist of the time, Sir Peter Paul Rubens, was heard to lament that he could afford to buy only one tulip for his wife's birthday. Today, scientists diagnose the condition suffered by the rarest tulips illustrated in that era's books as viruses that caused abnormal (and beautiful) coloring or shape. The most famous aberration is the "black" tulip, which is really darkest purple. This flower was immortalized in Alexandre Dumas's novel *The Black Tulip,* which deals with the saga to develop this strain in the 17th century.

The bulb fields extend from just north of Leiden to the southern limits of Haarlem, but the greatest concentration is limited to the district that begins at Sassenheim and ends between Hillegom and Bennebroek. The apparent artificiality of the sharply defined rectangular fields is not a concession to taste. It is part of the businesslike efficiency of an industry that has made tulip bulbs one of Holland's leading export commodities. It must be remembered that here the bulb, not the flower, is the most important part of the plant. When the flowers are ripe, so to speak, they are cut off, leaving only the green stalks. The children play with the discarded blooms, threading them into garlands that they sell to passing motorists or making floral mosaics with them. If you're really serious about your tulips, be sure to visit the Hortus Botanicus in Leiden—it was here that Carolus Clusius, a leading botanist of the 17th century, promulgated the glamour and glory of this flower, and this garden remains a leading shrine for tulip-philes the world over. Another top destination is the annual **Bloemen Corso** (Bulb District Flower Parade), held on the last Saturday in April, a colorful procession filled with floats and marching bands along a 36 km (20-mi) route that extends from Haarlem to Noordwijk.

Lisse is one of the hubs for the famed Bollenstreek Route (Bulb District Route), more popularly known as the **Bloemen Route.** Day-trippers from

Amsterdam head here by taking the A4 southbound toward Leiden, then the N207 turn for Lisse, if venturing here by car. A quick route by public transport is to take the train from Amsterdam's Centraal Station to Leiden's Centraal Station and from there take bus no. 54, a.k.a. the Keukenhof Express, which travels through Lisse. Other modes of transport are to rent bikes from the train station in Haarlem, or, more comfortably, take Bus 50 or 51 at the rail stations in either Haarlem or Leiden to disembark near a Van Gogh field you want to explore—Hillegom is a top village stop hereabouts. When the bulbs are at their best, they are often "beheaded" (to ensure future growth) by armies of wood-shoed gardeners, who remind us that these bulb fields are private property (so be circumspect about heading down any field lanes). Tour companies and the local VVVs (tourist information offices) also organize walking and bicycle tours, often including a visit to Keukenhof. When you take a walking or bicycle tour, or independently travel one of these ways following a map route, you get to experience the subtle scents in the fields. You'll find roadside flower stalls selling flowers, bulbs, and garlands.

The Bollenstreek was designed as a special itinerary through the heart of the flower-growing region and laid out by the Dutch auto club, ANWB. The route is marked with small blue-and-white signs that read BOLLENSTREEK. It begins in **Oegstgeest,** near Leiden, and circles through **Rijnsburg** (site of one of Holland's three major flower auction houses), where there is a colorful Flower Parade in August. The route extends to the dunes north of **Noordwijk,** a vast, sandy nature reserve almost as big as the bulb district itself. Small canals and pools of water are dotted about in between the dunes, providing a haven for bird life. This is also a popular seaside resort, drawing Dutch, English, and German vacationers who rent rooms from locals. You might want to make a brief stop along the way to see the historic white church in **Noordwijkerhout;** although much of the church has been restored, part of it was a ship that dates from the year 1000. In addition to Noordwijk, the Bulb Route passes through the beach community of **Katwijk** and through **Sassenheim,** where there is an imposing 13th-century ruined castle.

Lisse, the middlemost of the main bulb towns, is noted for its Keukenhof Gardens, but drivers should keep straight ahead to Sassenheim, turning right (west) into the bulb fields at the north edge of town. At Loosterweg, head north again, following the zigs and zags of this country lane as it passes through the very hearts of the fields so overburdened with color. Presently you are back at Lisse again, and follow the signs for Keukenhof.

From the end of March to the end of May the 17-acre **Keukenhof** (Kitchen Garden) park and greenhouse complex, founded in 1950 by Tom van Waveren and other leading bulb growers, is one of the largest living open-air flower exhibitions in the world. As many as 7 million tulip bulbs bloom every spring, either in hothouses (where they may reach a height of nearly 3 feet) or in flower beds along the sides of a charming lake. In the last weeks of April you can catch tulips, daffodils, hyacinths, and narcissi all flowering simultaneously. In addition there are 50,000 square feet of more exotic blooms under glass. Unfortunately, Keukenhof is the creation of the leading Dutch bulb-growing exporters, who use it as a showcase for their latest hybrids. There are many open gardens adorned with colorful flowers (even black tulips) and gaudy frilled varieties. There is also a depressing lack of style—garden after garden has bright floral mosaics, meandering streams, placid pools, too many paved paths, and hordes of people. Any sense of history—Keukenhof's roots extend way back to the 15th century when it was the herbal farm (Keukenhof means "kitchen garden courtyard") of one of Holland's richest ladies, the Countess Jacoba van Beieren—has been obliterated. Tulip time is famous here, but there are special shows on view for every season of the year. In the center of Lisse is a small museum devoted to the history of tulip growing, the **Museum voor de Bloembollenstreek**. For information about rail access to the town of Lisse, log on to ⊕ www.ns.nl or call the main **rail info number** (☎ 0900/9292). ✉ *N207 Lisse* ☎ *0252/ 465555* ⊕ *www.keukenhof.nl* 🎟 *€7.95* ⊘ *Late Mar.–May, daily 8–7:30; early Aug.–mid-Sept., daily 9–6.*

Leiden

35 km (22 mi) south of Haarlem, 45 km (28 mi) south of Amsterdam, 16 km (10 mi) northeast of The Hague.

The town of Leiden owes its first importance to its watery geography— it stands at the junction of two branches of the Rhine—the "Old" and the "New." But as birthplace of Rembrandt and site of the nation's oldest and most prestigious university, Leiden has long continued to play an important part in Dutch history. A place where windmills still rise over the cityscape, Leiden offers the charm of Amsterdam with little of the sleaze. Despite its wealth and historical air, Leiden, it is often said, could not be pompous if it tried.

Cobbled streets, gabled houses, narrow canals overhung with lime trees, and antiques shops give the historic center a tangible feeling of history, and Leiden's university's academic buildings, the historic Waag (Weigh House) and the Burcht fortress, the stately mansions lining the Rapenburg—the most elegant canal in the town—and no fewer than 35 hofjes make it a rewarding place for a stroll. As you walk about, keep a watch for verses painted on lofty gables, a project started some 10 years ago. The proverbs, sayings, and poems now number more than 70, and are in a multitude of languages. Don't keep an eye out for any Rembrandt sightings: although he lived here for 20 years, Rembrandt left almost no trace of his life here—his birthplace was knocked down years ago (marked only by a plaque on a very modern wall). Even his actual birth date (1606 or 1607) is disputed. A Rembrandt "walk" is marked by the absence of any real site, although you can see where his sister Trintje lived and where his brother Adriaen worked as a cobbler.

With a university founded in 1581 (and a list of old boys to boast of, including Descartes, U.S. president John Quincy Adams, and many a Dutch royal), Leiden's appeal is found in the mixture of musty-looking buildings, bicycles, brown cafés, and fresh-faced students, which gives the town zest and energy. Museum lovers will have to be selective. Don't expect the Rijksmuseum, however: windmill history, Japanese artifacts, and Egyptian antiquities are some of the specialties on tap here.

The historic center is marked by the Burcht, an 11th-century mound of earth with a fortification on top to control the confluence of the Old and New Rhine ("De Rijn," whence Rembrandt took his last name), which almost encircle it. Here there may have been a Roman colony, Lugdunum Batavorum, though no one knows for sure. The history of the town has been full enough without insisting on classical origins. The town's finest hour was in the 16th century when the Spanish laid siege after the mayor, in a fashion typical of the age, rejected the surrender terms with a verse from the ancient Roman poet Cato. The siege went on and on, but relief came, incredibly, from the sea. The Dutch fleet sailed overland from lake to lake, breaking another dike every night so that its advance could continue in the morning. On October 3, 1574, the ordeal was over, and the day has been marked by the distribution of loaves of bread and herring on that anniversary ever since. As a reward for its courage and steadfastness, William the Silent offered Leiden the choice between relief from taxes and the establishment of a university. With a sense of realism that has perhaps been overidealized, the rejoicing citizens concluded that tax relief would be only temporary at best, whereas a university would never cease to be an asset. Leiden's professors were soon renowned all over Europe for their learning, their integrity, and their independence—so much so, indeed, that James Boswell, the fun-loving biographer of Dr. Johnson, protested when his father proposed sending him here to study law (he went to Utrecht instead, finding it more to his taste).

a good walk

Just a short stroll from the Stationsplein train station are the first of Leiden's many museums. Heading down Stationsweg, turn right to find the **Rijksmuseum voor Volkenkunde** ⑫ ☞, a museum with myriad marvels of African, Oceanic, Asian, American, and Arctic cultures, including a collection of Japanese artifacts so extensive that people make pilgrimages from Japan to view it. Adjacent, on Binnevest, is Leiden's famous collection of medical curios, the **Museum Boerhaave** ⑬. Continue heading northwest and you'll hit the natural history exhibition, **Naturalis** ⑭, but if you're not a science buff, just head back directly to Stationsweg and continue on to Binnevestgracht to find the **Molenmuseum de Valk** ⑮, which allows you to study the innards of an 18th-century windmill. From here it is just a few blocks to **Stedelijk Museum De Lakenhal** ⑯, a magisterial guildhall of the 17th century, replete with historic halls and a collection of fine old masters by Jan van Goyen, Lucas van Leiden, and other masters. Go east to Turfmarkt and head south over the Bostel bridge and the Rhine River to Breestraat, the narrow bustling street that forms the backbone of the old city. Past the Waslse Kerk looms the **Stadhuis** ⑰ (Town Hall), where you can note a glorious 17th-century facade, all that remains of the original building, destroyed by fire in 1929; one corner of the Town Hall is the historic Waag (Weigh House). A left turn down the street beyond gives you a glimpse of the Korenbeurs Brug, or Cornmarket Bridge, an unusual covered affair from which there are magnificent views, beyond which are the **De Burcht** ⑱ fortification, the 14th-century Hooglandse or St. Pancas church, and the delightful St. Anna Almshouse, the oldest and one of the most beautiful in town.

Backtrack and head southeast, making a turn from the Breestraat to walk uphill to the imposing mass of the **Pieterskerk** ⑲, the oldest house of worship in the city, where Thanksgiving Day services are offered every year by Americans to honor the Pilgrim Fathers who worshipped here. Opposite the church is the **Jan Pesijnhofje** ⑳, an almshouse founded in 1683 by a Delano ancestor of President Franklin Roosevelt. You are already in the student quarter, and the narrow street that continues downhill from the entrance of the almshouse leads across the charming Rapenburg Canal to the famous **Rijksuniversiteit van Leiden** ㉑ (Leiden University) area. Here, Pilgrim aficionados can turn south down the canal to Kaiserstraat to find the small **Het Leidse Amerikaanse Pilgrim Museum** ㉒, or Leiden American Pilgrim Museum. Others will simply make a beeline for the celebrated **Hortus Botanicus** ㉓ (Botanical Garden), which once showcased the greatest display of tulips in the tulip-mad 17th century. After viewing the gardens, continue north along the Rapenburg embankment to the newly renovated **Rijksmuseum van Oudheden** ㉔, which houses the largest archaeological collection in the land; then return several blocks eastward to Breestraat for your well-deserved time-out.

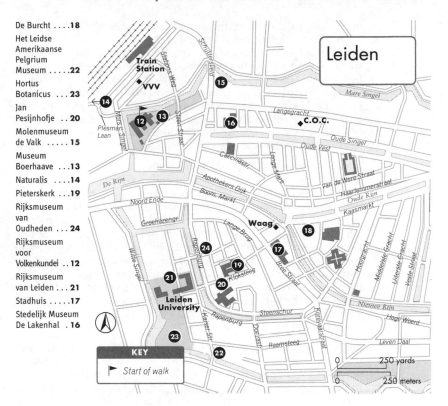

Sights to See

⓲ De Burcht. This medieval fortress, built around AD 1000, is perched high above the town on an ancient artificial mound, providing the best overviews of the city to be had. There is a defiant-looking carved lion at the entrance, with the words "Pugno Pro Patria" ("I fight for the Fatherland") underneath. It isn't a big lion, and it certainly isn't a big fortress, but it was here in 1574 that the town witnessed its finest hour: after a yearlong siege the population had been very close to being starved into submission when William broke down nearby dikes, flooding the ground around Leiden; whether the Spanish were more surprised than scared is not recorded, but it had the desired effect, because they fled as the water approached. William's timely arrival is remembered in the festival-like **Het Onzet van Leiden** (Relief of Leiden), an event celebrated every October, with much eating of *hutspot,* a dark stew, said to be what the starving townspeople fell on when they approached the then-deserted Spanish garrison. ⊠ *Nieuwe Rijn* ✍ *Free.*

⓴ Het Leidse Amerikaanse Pilgrim Museum (Leiden American Pilgrim Museum). This documentation center occupies a small 14th-century house furnished to illustrate what the Pilgrims' daily life was like before they left for the New World. Brief texts and 17th-century engravings tell the story of their extraordinary odyssey. You can get complete information here about the Pilgrim sites throughout the city, notably those at the Pieterskerk. ⊠ *Beschuitsteeg 9* 🕾 *071/512–2413* ⊕ *www.pilgrimhall. org/leidenmuseum.htm* ✍ *€2* ♥ *Wed.–Sat. 1–5.*

★ ㉓ Hortus Botanicus (Botanical Garden). Following the wide Rapenburg canal from the center of town, you reach Leiden University's renowned botanical garden, a leading shrine for tulip lovers the world over. Planted

in 1594, the garden was meant to be a *hortus academicus* and was originally laid out by the greatest botanist of the age, Carolus Clusius, who
had bounced around Europe surveying flowers and writing important
studies for various societies and princely patrons until an offer from the
fledgling University of Leiden brought him north to Holland. It is commonly reported that this garden was the first place that tulip bulbs were
planted in Holland, but this is far from the case. Dutch merchants with
connections to Istanbul had decades before received bulbs as gifts, and
before long they, and scholars like Clusius, were busy dispatching seeds
to all corners of the land.

But it was here in Leiden that Clusius put the cap on a study of tulips,
divining their schools and species, making distinctions between free-grow-
ing ones and hybrid cultivars, and bedding out his garden with wonderful displays of Couleren (single-color) and Marquetrian (multicolor)
tulips, starting the enormous vogue for Rosen, Violetten, Bizarden, and
numerous other species of tulip that came to rage in Holland in the following decades, leading to the Great Tulip Mania of the 1630s. Today,
in addition to seeing the tulip beds of the original design, you can also
find Clusius's garden laid out with extensive rose gardens, shrubs, and
towering trees, as well as an orangery, a Japanese garden, and several
hothouses of orchids and other rarities. ⊠ *Rapenburg 73* ☏ *071/527–
7249* ⊕ *www.leidenuniv.nl/hortus/* ⊠ *€4* ⊙ *Mar. 30–Oct., Mon.–Sun.
10–6; Nov.–Mar. 29, Sun.–Fri. 10–4.*

⑳ Jan Pesijnhofje. This is just one of a number of Leiden's pretty hofjes. Centered on a tranquil garden and founded in the 17th century by a distant
ancestor of President Franklin Delano Roosevelt, it marks the site where
the Reverend John Robinson, spiritual head of the Pilgrims, lived and died
(1625). Robinson had settled in Leiden a decade before his flock arrived
on their *Mayflower* and, unfortunately, fell ill before they departed for
the wilder shores of America. Other Pilgrim sites nearby are the Pieterskerk
and a plaque marking the Pilgrim Press on William Brewster Alley. Many
of the city's hofjes are still used as residential accommodations for the elderly, so if you see a sign that says VERBODEN ("forbidden"), respect their
privacy. Other almshouses can be found at **Coninckshofje** (⊠ Oude Vest
15), **St. Stevenshof** (⊠ Haarlemmerstraat 48–50), and the **Groeneveld-
stichting** (⊠ Oude Vest 41). ⊠ *Pieterskerkhof 21.*

★ ⑮ Molenmuseum de Valk (Windmill Museum of the Falcon). Set not far from
the main train station, this enchanting windmill-turned-museum began
grinding grain in 1743 and is occasionally pressed back into service to
produce whole-wheat flour (which you can purchase at the shop here).
Perfectly preserved living quarters on the ground floor greet you as you
clamber past massive millstones and head up seven stories to the top of
the mill—stop on the way up to step out onto the "reefing stage," the
platform than runs around the outside for a view of the city, where the
gleaming canals remind us that they were once "paved with gold" (as
thoroughfares used to ship the grain made at this windmill, and many
others, to surrounding towns). Most afternoons from April to the end
of September the sails of the windmill are put into operation—get your
camcorders ready. ⊠ *2e Binnenvestgracht 1* ☏ *071/516–5353*
⊕ *http://home.wanadoo.nl/molenmuseum* ⊠ *€2.50* ⊙ *Tues.–Sat. 10–5,
Sun. 1–5.*

⑬ Museum Boerhaave. Housed in the former Caecilia Hospital, this famed
collection allows visitors to study five centuries of scientific and medical research. Highlights include Leeuwenhoek's original microscopes,
early pendulum clocks crafted by Christiaan Huygens, and a recon-

struction of a 17th-century "anatomy theater." ⊠ *Lange St. Agnieten-straat 10* ☎ *071/521–4224* ⊕ *www.museumboerhaave.nl* ⊠ *€3.50* ⊗ *Tues.–Sat. 10–5, Sun. noon–5.*

Naturalis. The latest addition to Leiden's many science-oriented sights is this natural history museum. Displays include full-scale dinosaurs, minerals, and stuffed animals. Look out for a giant 2-foot crab. As a museum that especially appeals to children, there is a dedicated activity center for learning while playing. From the Volkenkunde museum, head northwest on the Plesmanlaan and go under the railway tracks toward the A44; the first road on the right is Darwinweg, and Naturalis is on the Plesmanlaan avenue. ⊠ *Darwinweg 2* ☎ *071/568–7600* ⊠ *€8* ⊗ *Tues.–Sun. 10–6.*

Pieterskerk (St. Peter's Church). Within a stone's throw of the University of Leiden, this noted church is often surrounded by students sunning themselves in the church square. The oldest church in the city, dating from 1428, it is rarely used as a place of worship, because its upkeep became overwhelming in the 1970s. Happily though, it hasn't been abandoned but has diversified into hosting an extraordinary range of events from fashion shows (with a long catwalk stretching the magnificent length of the nave) to student examinations to post-examination graduation balls—indeed, it can even be rented for receptions for a bargain price. But history can be found here—in that corner and in this. The grave of the painter Jan Steen lies on one wall, and somewhere in an unmarked burial chamber Rembrandt's parents sleep on. More important to Americans (who gather here every Thanksgiving Day for a special service), there is a corner devoted to the Pilgrim Fathers—Puritan refugees from English religious persecution—who often worshiped here. They had petitioned the city fathers in 1609 to relocate here from Amsterdam, which they found "torn by the spirit of controversy." Plaques inside and out pay tribute to the Reverend John Robinson, who was spiritual leader to this community of Puritans; his grave is here, because he grew ill before the Pilgrims set out on their momentous journey to the New World. A stroll from the church down Herensteeg can bring you to a house (marked by a plaque) where William Brewster and his Pilgrim Press published the theological writings that clashed so strongly with the dogmas of the Church of England. In the church's Pilgrim display, you'll also find photos of George H. W. Bush making a presentation here from his last visit in homage to his Pilgrim ancestry. ⊠ *Pieterskerkhof* ☎ *071/512–4319* ⊠ *Free* ⊗ *Daily 1:30–4.*

Rijksmuseum van Oudheden (National Museum of Antiquities). Perhaps Leiden's most notable museum, this building houses the largest archaeological collection in Holland. After vast amounts of money were spent, the layout and the thematic grouping of antiquities have been overhauled, making the museum more aesthetically appealing. Collections include pieces from ancient Egypt, the classical world, the Near East, and the Roman Netherlands. Among the 6,000 objects on display, some of the exhibits to look out for include the chillingly ghoulish collection of 13 ancient Egyptian human mummies, monumental Roman portraits, and a complete set of Greek bronze armor from the 4th century BC. As you tour the galleries, you may encounter a "guide from antiquity" who will charmingly provide a "personal" perspective on the objects, which are further placed in context through elaborate scenery, scale models, film footage, and 3-D reconstructions. Temporary exhibitions are always exceptional here and meet the highest scholarly standards. ⊠ *Rapenburg 28* ☎ *071/516–3163* ⊕ *www.rmo.nl* ⊠ *€6, additional charge for temporary exhibitions* ⊗ *Tues.–Fri. 10–5, weekends noon–5.*

need a break?

De Waterlijn (✉ Prinsessekade ☎ 071/512–1279) occupies one of the most attractive spots in town. Just past the end of the Rapenburg canal (which is itself lined with gracious buildings), this strikingly modern, glass-walled café on a moored boat offers views of old boats, gabled houses, and a windmill. The Dutch apple tart will please most.

⑫ **Rijksmuseum voor Volkenkunde** (National Museum of Cultural Anthropology). This is a leading showcase for the cultures of Africa, Oceania, Asia, the Americas, and the Arctic. In particular, the Siebold Collection of Japanese art and artifacts is world-famous. ✉ *Steenstraat 1* ☎ *071/ 516–8800* ⊕ *www.rmv.nl* ▦ *€6.50* ◷ *Tues.–Sun. 10–5.*

㉑ **Rijksuniversiteit van Leiden** (Leiden University). Founded in 1575 in gratitude by William the Silent for Leiden's leading role in the Dutch Revolt against the Spanish, this university became one of the leading meccas of scholastic thought, drawing great thinkers and scientists of the 16th and 17th centuries, including the philosopher René Descartes. Today it is still one of the most respected academic establishments in the country, and the students preserve many time-honored traditions. The old university buildings are not open to the public—except for the celebrated Hortus Botanicus garden—but in the Academic Quarter, between the Rapenburg and Singel canals, students give Leiden a lively atmosphere.

⑰ **Stadhuis** (Town Hall). This was originally built in 1597, but the unattractive brick building you see today dates back to the 1930s, as the first structure was consumed by fire. All that was left was the beautiful front facade, which fortunately you can still see, on Breestraat. At one corner of the Town Hall stands the sturdy 17th-century **Waag** (Weigh House), once the focus of the enormous market square. Streets around here abound in names that end in "markt": Vismarkt (fish) to Botormarkt (butter) to Beestenmarkt (cattle).

★ ⑯ **Stedelijk Museum De Lakenhal** (Lakenhal Museum). Built in 1639 for the city's cloth merchants, this grand structure is adorned with decorations alluding to the manufacture of textiles. Leiden enjoyed a Golden Age of the late 16th and 17th centuries in both textiles and art. It was during this period that the city's artist community was most prolific, spawning three great painters of the time: Rembrandt, Jan van Goyen, and Jan Steen. Although few works by these three artists remain in the city, this collection does have an early Rembrandt, though its rawness comes as quite a surprise to loyal followers. The museum is repository for an impressive collection of paintings, furniture, and silver and pewter pieces, set in the sumptuous surrounds of a 17th-century Cloth Hall, a witness to Leiden's great importance in the wool trade. This is the building where the cloth was inspected and traded, and reconstructed guild rooms, replete with authentic antiques, show where the Guild Governors met. Galleries are hung with paintings by Gerrit Dou, Jan Steen, and Salomon van Ruysdael, as well as a grand collection of the works of Lucas van Leyden (another local boy made good), including his triptych the *Last Judgment*. ✉ *Oude Singel 28–32* ☎ *071/516–5360* ⊕ *www.lakenhal.nl* ▦ *€4* ◷ *Tues.–Fri. 10–5, weekends noon–5.*

Where to Eat & Stay

★ $$–$$$ ✕ **Bistro La Cloche.** This chic, attractive French-Dutch restaurant, just off the Rapenburg canal on the small street leading to St. Peter's Church, is done up in soft pastels, with flowers everywhere. It has a pleasant but small street-side café area and quieter dining upstairs. Try their lovely Dutch lamb with a compote of shallots and Provençale sauce. Leave room for their evergreen dessert specialty, *glace bourguegnonne,* a rich vanilla farm-made ice cream with warm berries, crème de cassis, and crème fraîche. ⊠ *Kloksteeg 3* ☎ *071/512–3053* ⌖ *Reservations essential* ▭ *AE, DC, MC, V* ⊘ *Closed Sun.*

¢–$$ ✕ **Annie's Verjaardag.** This restaurant consists of a low-ceilinged, arched cellar, often full of chatty students, and a water-level canal-side terrace. During the day, there is a modest selection of salads and sandwiches on baguettes, and at least one offering that is more substantial. After 6 you can choose from a fuller menu that includes cheese fondue, grilled trout, and spareribs. ⊠ *Hoogstraat 1a* ☎ *071/512–5737* ⌖ *Reservations not accepted* ▭ *MC, V.*

¢–$$ ✕ **M'n Broer.** Run by a pair of twins, "My Brother" is a cozy brasserie with a brown-café atmosphere. The kitchen serves up such hearty meals as seafood pie and roast duck with port sauce; the portions are generous, and the food is good. ⊠ *Kloksteeg 7* ☎ *071/512–5024* ⌖ *Reservations not accepted* ▭ *MC, V.*

¢–$ ✕ **Pannekoekenhuysje Oudt Leyden.** Besides pancakes, this Dutch-style restaurant has a traditional menu of simple grilled and sautéed meats and fish. It shares a kitchen with its neighbor, Entrekoos. ⊠ *Steenstraat 51* ☎ *071/513–3144* ▭ *AE, MC, V.*

$ **Entrekoos.** This restaurant shares a kitchen with its neighbor, Oudt Leyden, but it has a totally different menu and environment: red-check tablecloths and a relaxed mood. The name is a phonetic Dutch pronunciation of *entrecôtes* (steaks), and a steak dinner, complete with vegetables, costs a mere €10. Vegetarians are not neglected. ⊠ *Steenstraat 49* ☎ *071/ 513–3144* ▭ *AE, MC, V.*

$$$ ▦ **Holiday Inn Leiden.** Just off the secondary highway between Leiden and The Hague and not far from the beaches at Katwijk, this is more a resort than a hotel. There is a vast interior garden lobby, and the decor of the guest rooms carries out the garden theme with bold colors and floral curtains. ⊠ *Haagse Schouwweg 10, 2332 KG* ☎ *071/535–5555* 🖷 *071/535–5553* ⊕ *www.holiday-inn-leiden.com/* ⇥ *200 rooms* ⌖ *Restaurant, in-room data ports, minibars, cable TV, 5 tennis courts, pool, health club, sauna, bar, some pets allowed* ▭ *AE, DC, MC, V* ¶¶ *EP.*

★ $–$$ ▦ **De Doelen.** Placed right on the Rapenburg, the most elegant of Leiden's canals, this hotel is in a patrician mansion, dating from 1638. The communal rooms are gorgeous, wooden-beamed, and robustly decorated—traveling trunks, antique mirrors, and an enormous floral painting atop an ornate mantelpiece are some fetching accents. Guest rooms are comfortable, but it is worth paying more to get one of the deluxe species, on the first floor, which are more spacious, and have prettier, brighter furnishings. ⊠ *Rapenburg 2, 2311 EV* ☎ *071/512–0527* 🖷 *071/512–8453* ⊕ *www.dedoelen.com* ⇥ *16 rooms* ⌖ *In-room data ports, cable TV, some pets allowed; no a/c* ▭ *AE, DC, MC, V* ¶¶ *EP.*

★ $–$$ ▦ **Nieuw Minerva.** Each one of the rooms in this glossy hotel, set in six 16th-century canal houses along De Rijn canal in the old historical center of town, is individually decorated with great flair: one is done in a country-gingham check, another shines with an opulent four-poster in deepest red, and the Delft Blue room is decorated with the town's traditional pottery on the walls. The Keukenhof room has old botanists' prints hanging above the bed. All of this means this place gives you a lot more than the average two-star. ⊠ *Boommarkt 23, 2311 EA* ☎ *071/ 512–6358* 🖷 *071/514–2674* ⊕ *www.nieuwminerva.nl* ⇥ *39 rooms* ⌖ *Restaurant, in-room data ports, cable TV, 2 bars, some pets allowed; no a/c* ▭ *AE, DC, MC, V* ¶¶ *CP.*

$ ▦ **Mayflower.** This hotel, named, of course, after the ship that took the Pilgrim Fathers to Plymouth from Rotterdam, is conveniently located on the Beestenmarkt, one of the main central squares in Leiden (although the site means that the hotel has a fast-food outlet as a near neighbor). The rooms are light and pleasant, but the furnishings are somewhat outdated, with chocolate brown tiles in some bathrooms. It is, however, a scrupulously clean hotel, and boasts friendly service (rarer than you might expect). ⊠ *Beestenmarkt 2, 2312 CC* ☎ *071/514–2641* 🖷 *071/512–8516* 📲 *25 rooms* ₾ *Cable TV; no a/c* 🖃 *AE, DC, MC, V* ⑩ *CP.*

The Outdoors

BEACHES   Leiden's coastal resorts are at **Katwijk** and **Noordwijk**, in the dunes beside the North Sea.

BICYCLING   The place to rent a bicycle in Leiden is the **Fietspoint Oldenburger** (⊠ Stationsplein 3 ☎ 071/512–0068), next to the railroad station. They require a security deposit of €50 and legitimate ID.

CANOEING   A canoe may be the very best way to get a close view of the bulb fields that fill the countryside between Haarlem and Leiden. The **VVV Leiden tourist office** (⊠ Stationsweg 2D ☎ 0900/222–2333 ⊕ www.leiden.nl) has mapped out four different routes of varying lengths through the dune and bulb regions. Ask, too, about the Singel sightseeing route through Leiden's canals and moats.

Shopping

The old city center of Leiden proffers quite a wide variety of shops, with Haarlemmerstraat, which sweeps across the city (from the Beestenmarkt to the Oude Rijn canal) the principal street to head if shopping is high on your agenda. Breestraat, which runs parallel to the Nieuwe Rijn canal, comes in a close second for choice, and the district between Pieterskerk and De Burcht holds the best antiques shops and boutiques. Shops stay open late (until 9) on Thursday *koopavond* (shopping night), and every last Sunday of the month is designated a special shopping day, with the majority of shops open. Leiden's bigger street markets are held in the city center on the Nieuwe Rijn on Wednesday and Saturday 9–6, and at Vijf Meiplein on Tuesday 9–2.

't Spieghel (⊠ Langebrug 91 ☎ 071/512–4958) has the most gorgeous collection of antique French mirrors, most of which date back to the period between 1850 and 1900, and many have gold-leaf or gilded frames. The shop is on the Langebrug (the Long Bridge), which used to be a canal in the 17th century. So many bridges crossed the canal that from a distance it looked like one long bridge, and so it earned its name. **Van Catwijck** (⊠ Langebrug 89a ☎ 071/566–5244), in the former studio of Jacob Swanenburgh—one of Rembrandt's first tutors—has, appropriately, a wide variety of old-master paintings for sale, in addition to 19th- and 20th-century works. **Van Ruiten & Zn.** (⊠ Korte Rapenburg 12 ☎ 071/512–6290) is one of the oldest antiques shops in the city. Manned by three generations of antiquarians, this shop has an extensive collection of antique silver, in addition to gold and silver jewelry. Look for the plaque on the front of the building, which says that Gerrit Dou (1613–75), one of Leiden's great painters, lived here for a short period.

Festivals

Many events and festivals take place in Leiden every year. The highlights include Leiden Jazz Week in January; the 10-day summer festival, the Leiden Lakenfeesten in July, which features music, street theater, and markets across town; and the celebration of the Relief of Leiden October 2–4.

Nightlife & the Arts

The **Groenoord Hallen** (✉ Willem de Zwijyerlaan 2 ☎ 071/521–2521) is Leiden's only concert hall, and is the place to go if you want to catch a band on tour. As Leiden's city theater from 1705, the revamped **Leidse Schouwburg** (✉ Oude Vest 43 ☎ 071/513–1943 ⊕ www. leidseschouwburg.nl) hosts all major plays and performances, as well as dance troupes touring the country. Expect a lively and well-balanced program of serious theater, ballet, stand-up, musicals, concerts, and youth theater. The vast majority of the theater productions are in Dutch.

The **Stadsgehoorzaal** (✉ Breestraat 60 ☎ 071/513–1704 ⊕ www. stadsgehoorzaalleiden.nl) hosts musicians from all backgrounds, ranging from soloists supported by classical orchestras, to cabaret and jazz; this is one of the main venues for the Jazz Week festival. Every Thursday and Sunday jazz musicians from across Holland and beyond gather in a busy bar near De Burcht for aptly named sessions of "Jazz in De Brucht"—for information, contact **Societeit de Burcht** (✉ Burgsteeg 14 ☎ 071/514–2389). Admission is free, but you're advised to hit the bar before the 10 PM kickoff, to be sure of a space to sit or lean.

Evert Castelein (✉ Hooigracht 87, above the Albert Heijn supermarket ☎ 071/512–3583 ✍ €3.50) has come to the fore as one of the most popular dance schools in Leiden, offering ballroom and Latin, in addition to salsa and street dancing. Serious party people shouldn't miss the ballroom and Latin nights, open to all comers, held on the second and fourth Saturday of each month, and the salsa parties held the first Saturday of each month. Partying follows an hour-long workshop (which starts at 8:30).

If you feel like clubbing, head to **In Casa** (✉ Lammermarkt 100 ☎ 071/ 514–4979 ✍ €4), the biggest club in Leiden, with a capacity of more than 1,000. Call in advance to get information about which DJs are playing. Thursday focuses on 1970s and 1980s beats, and Saturday is for 1990s nights. Oddly enough, the club is closed most Fridays. The accommodating DJs at **De Verleiding** (✉ Korte Mare 34 ☎ 071/362–3632) do requests in this intimate club. Friday to Sunday have a chart music vibe, and some Sundays are gay nights (ask in advance). The bar drawing the most hip twentysomethings is **Annie's Verjaardag** (✉ Hoogstraat 1a ☎ 071/512–5737), which adds up to one of Leiden's liveliest central spots.

Delft

★ ㉕   *24 km (14 mi) southwest of Leiden, 14 km (9 mi) southeast of The Hague, 71 km (45 mi) southwest of Amsterdam.*

With time-burnished canals and streets, Delft possesses a peaceful calm that recalls the quieter pace of the Golden Age of the 17th century. Back then the town counted among its citizens the artist Johannes Vermeer, who decided one spring day to paint the city gates and landscape across the Kolk harbor from a house's window on the Schieweg (now the Hooikade). The result was the 1660 *View of Delft* (now the star of the Mauritshuis Museum in The Hague), famously called by Marcel Proust "the most beautiful painting in the world." Spending a few hours in certain parts of Delft, in fact, puts you in the company of Vermeer. Imagine a tiny Amsterdam, canals reduced to dollhouse proportions, narrower bridges, merchants' houses less grand, and you have the essence of Old Delft. But even though the city has one foot firmly planted in the past, another is firmly planted in the present: Delft teems with hip cafés, jazz festivals, and revelers spilling out of bars—all, in fact, when most regional Dutch towns are still in hibernation.

For many travelers, few spots in Holland are as intimate and attractive as this town, whose famous blue-and-white earthenware has gone around the world. Compact and easy to traverse, despite its web of canals, Delft is best explored on foot, although water taxis are available in summer to give you an armchair ride through the heart of town. Many streets in Oude Delft are lined with medieval Gothic and Renaissance houses, and tree-shadowed canals still reflect the same blue sky from which the pottery and tile makers of 350 years ago snatched their matchless color. And at many corners you see a small humpbacked bridge or facade that looks as lovely as Delftware itself.

But Delft has more than painterly charm, for it nearly rivals Leiden for historical import. Great men lived and died here. By the end of the 16th century Prince William of Orange (known as William the Silent) settled in Delft to wage his war against Spanish rule. He never left: in his mansion the founder of the nation was assassinated in 1584 by a spy of the Spanish Duke of Alva and buried with great pomp in the Nieuwe Kerk (New Church). Here, too, is buried Grotius, the great humanist and father of international law. Delft was also home to Anthonie van Leeuwenhoek, who mastered the fledging invention of the microscope and was born the same year as Vermeer, 1632. Vermeer, many people will be interested to know, was just one of many artists who set up shop in Delft. Delft could support so many artists since it had grown fat with the trade in butter, cloth, beer and, in the 17th century, pottery.

The canal waters of Delft didn't always take a smooth course—literally. In the 17th century, the town's canal water became tainted, leading to a decline from 200 breweries to 20. In 1654, the "Thunderclap" leveled one half of the town and killed hundreds (including Carel Fabritius, Rembrandt's most famous student and considered the leading master of the city) when an accident at the town arsenal led to a gunpowder explosion. But Delft quickly rebounded, thanks to the city riches amassed as the headquarters of the Dutch East India Company (whose power can be compared only to Microsoft's today). The porcelains brought back by their traders from the Far East proved irresistible, and in 1645, De Porceleyn Fles started making and exporting the blue-and-white earthenware that was to make the town famous. Civil war in China had dried up the source for porcelains, and Delft potters leaped in and created the blue faience that soon became known as Delft Blue. This technological expertise resulted in the founding of the Technical University of Delft in 1842; today, its 13,000 students give a youthful spin to this historic city.

Everything you might want to see in this compact city is in the old center, where the best views are also to be found. Just across from the train station, walk up Westvest and turn right onto Binnenwatersloot—into the historic city center—to be greeted by a modern, sculptured interpretation of Vermeer's *Melk Meisje* (Milk Maid), in creamy-white stone. There are further sights to look up and around for as you head down the pretty, tree-lined **Oude Delft** canal, which has an abundance of historic gabled houses along its banks and takes the honors for being the first canal dug in the city and probably the first city canal to be dug anywhere in The Netherlands. As you walk around, note the range of facades and ornamental decoration on the buildings. From sober to pretty, there are many different variations. The **Gemeenlandshuis** (⊠ Oude Delft 167) is a spectacular example of 16th-century Gothic and is adorned with brightly painted shields and a coat of arms. The *visbanken* (fish stalls) along the canal were built in 1650, and fish has been sold over the counter here pretty much ever since then.

need a
break?

Kleyweg's Stads-Koffyhuis (✉ Oude Delft 133 ☎ 015/212–4625) looks out over the oldest and one of the most beautiful canals in Delft. Inside, you'll find a *stamtafel,* a large table laid out with newspapers and magazines, where anyone may sit and chat. There are also smaller individual tables where you can enjoy good coffee and delicious pancakes.

Following Oude Delft brings you to the very heart of historic Delft, where you'll find the grouping of the Oude Kerk, the Prinsenhof Museum, and the Museum Lambert van Meerten. The Gothic **Oude Kerk** (Old Church), with its tower 6 feet off kilter, is the last resting place of Vermeer. The tower manages to lean in all directions at once, but then, this is the oldest church in Delft, having been founded in 1200. Building went on until the 15th century, which accounts for the combination of architectural styles, and much of its austere interior dates from the latter part of the works. The tower, dating back to 1350, started leaning in the Middle Ages, and today the tilt to the east is somewhat stabilized by the 3-foot tilt to the north. The tower, whose tilt prevents ascension by visitors, holds the largest carillon bell in The Netherlands; weighing nearly 20,000 pounds, it now is used only on state occasions. ✉ *Heilige Geestkerkhof* ☎ *015/212–3015* ✉ *Combined ticket to Oude Kerk and Nieuwe Kerk €2.50* ☉ *Apr.–Nov., Mon.–Sat. 9–6.*

★ A former dignitary-hosting convent of St. Agatha, **Het Prinsenhof** is directly across the Oude Delft from the Oude Kerk and is celebrated as the residence of Prince William the Silent, beloved as *Het Vader de het Vaderland* (Father of the Country) for his role in the Spanish Revolt and a hero whose tragic end here gave this structure the sobriquet "cradle of Dutch liberty." The complex of buildings was taken over by the government of the new Dutch Republic in 1572 and given to William of Orange for his use as a residence. On July 10, 1583, fevered by monies offered by Philip II of Spain, Bathasar Gerard, a Catholic fanatic, gained admittance to the mansion and succeeded in shooting the prince on the staircase hall, since known as Moordhal (Murder Hall). The fatal bullet holes—the *teychenen derkoogelen*—are still visible (protected by glass) in the stairwell. Today, the imposing structure is a museum, with a 15th-century chapel, a quaint courtyard, and a bevy of elegantly furnished 17th-century rooms filled with antique pottery, silver, tapestries, and House of Orange portraits, along with exhibits on Netherlandish history. ✉ *Sint Agathaplein 1* ☎ *015/260–2358* ⊕ *www.prinsenhof-delft. nl* ✉ *€5* ☉ *Tues.–Sat. 10–5, Sun. 1–5.*

Between the Prinsenhof and the Nusantara Museum is the Agathaplein, a Late Gothic leafy courtyard, built around 1400, which has huge chestnut trees shading an adjacent green, and a somewhat cultivated square, the **Prinsentuin** (Prince's Garden), which, if it's not too busy, is a calming place for a five-minute respite from the city streets.

The **Nusantara Museum** is in the same courtyard as the Prinsenhof Museum. It has a colorful and fascinating collection of costumes and artifacts from the Dutch East Indies—most of it tragically pillaged during the 17th century by members of the Dutch East India Company. This is a rich collection of ethnographic art from Indonesian cultures encompassing Indo-European batik, Javanese statuettes, shields and intricately carved spears, diamond-encrusted daggers from the 18th century, and a beautifully carved tomb. There are displays charting the history of the spice trade. ✉ *Sint Agathaplein 4* ☎ *015/260–2358* ⊕ *www.nusantara-delft.nl* ✉ *€3.50* ☉ *Tues.–Sat. 10–5, Sun. 1–5.*

★ Within the shadow of the Oude Kerk is the **Lambert van Meerten Museum,** a Renaissance-era, canal-side mansion whose gloriously paneled rooms provides a noble setting for antique tiles, tin-glazed earthenware, paintings, and an extensive collection of ebony-veneer furniture. Although much of the works on display are not the original patrician owner's (who lost a fortune when his distillery burned down and he had to auction off everything), the house and some of his collection was bought back by Van Meerten's friends. Note especially the great collection of tiles, whose subjects range from foodstuffs to warships. The gardens here are alluring, with a spherical sundial, two busts, and a stone gateway leading the eye through to the tangled woods beyond. ⊠ *Oude Delft 199* ☎ *015/260–2358* ⊕ *www.lambertvanmeerten-delft.nl* ⊠ *€3.50* ⊙ *Tues.–Sat. 10–5, Sun. 1–5.*

On the Oude Delft, beyond the Lambert van Meerten Museum, is a weather-beaten 13th-century Gothic gate, with ancient-looking stone relief, that leads through to a small courtyard, the **Bagijnhof.** The city sided with the (Protestant) Dutch rebels during the Eighty Years' War, and when the (Catholic) Spanish were driven out in 1572, the city reverted to Protestantism, leaving many Catholic communities in dire straits. One group of women were permitted to stay and practice their religion, but according to a new law, their place of worship had to be very modest: a drab exterior in the Bagijnhof hides their sumptuously Baroque church.

Just to the west of Oude Delft is Phoenixstraat, where you'll find **Molen de Roos** (Rose Windmill), once a flour mill and originally on the town ramparts. The hexagonal base dates back to 1728. The platform encircling the mill about halfway up was restored in 1990. The mill sails get going every Saturday, when you can climb up the rickety stairs to get a view from the platform as the sails swoosh by. ⊠ *Phoenixstraat 111–112* ☎ *015/212–1589* ⊠ *Free* ⊙ *Sat. 10–4, but only when a blue flag is flying from the sails.*

From the Oude Kerk area, head south several blocks to find the **Markt** square, bracketed by two town landmarks, the Stadhuis (Town Hall) and the Nieuwe Kerk. Here, too, are cafés, restaurants, and souvenir shops (most selling imitation Delftware) and, on Thursday, a busy general market. On the Markt you can find the site of Johannes Vermeer's house at No. 52, where the 17th-century painter spent much of his youth. Not far away is a statue of Grotius, or Hugo de Groot, born in Delft in 1583, who was one of Holland's most famous humanists and lawyers.

At the west end of the Markt is the **Stadhuis** (Town Hall), but only the solid 13th-century tower remains from the medieval building. It rises above the surrounding gray-stone edifice, which has bright red shutters and lavish detailing, designed in 1618 by Hendrick de Keyser, certainly one of the most prolific architects of the Golden Age. Inside is a grand staircase and Council Chamber with a famous old map of Delft. You can view the Town Hall interior only by making arrangements through the Delft VVV tourist office, which can also issue you a ticket to visit the torture chamber in Het Steen, the 13th-century tower. ⊠ *Markt 87* ⊙ *Weekdays 10–4.*

Presiding over the Markt is the Late Gothic **Nieuwe Kerk** (New Church), built between 1483 and 1510. More than a century's worth of further Dutch craftsmanship went into its erection, as though its founders knew it would one day be the last resting place of the builder of Holland into a nation, William the Silent, and his descendants of the House of Orange. In 1872 noted architect P. J. H. Cuypers raised the tower up to its current height. No fewer than 22 columns surround the or-

VERMEER: SPHINX OF DELFT

AS ONE OF THE MOST ADORED ARTISTS IN THE WORLD, *Johannes Vermeer (1632–75) has been the subject of blockbuster museum exhibitions, theater pieces (Peter Greenaway's Writing to Vermeer), and best-selling novels (Tracy Chevalier's Girl with a Pearl Earring, transformed in 2003 into a sumptuous movie). He enjoys cultlike popularity, yet his reputation rests on just 35 pictures. Of course, those paintings—ordinary domestic scenes depicting figures caught in an amber light and in fleeting gestures that nearly anticipate cinema—are among the most extraordinary ever created. But Vermeer's glory is of a relatively recent vintage. He died at age 42, worn out by economic woes; at his death, a change in taste for a style of flamboyant art saw his name fall into total obscurity. Only in the mid-19th century did critics rightfully reattribute to him his masterpieces. Yet ever since Proust proclaimed his View of Delft (Mauritshuis, The Hague) "the most beautiful painting in the world," audiences worldwide have been enraptured by Vermeer's spellbinding work.*

Like most artists, Vermeer courted fame, as his legendary Artist in His Studio (Kunsthistoriches Museum, Vienna) reveals. This imposing work (which long hung in his atelier to impress prospective patrons) shows Vermeer sitting at his easel painting a model garbed as Clio, the Muse of History. Her crown of laurels and trumpet, art historians have recently announced, prove that she is, instead, a symbol for fickle Fame. The expected Vermeerian icons—swagged tapestry, gleaming brass chandelier, map of Holland on the wall—are in place, but all eyes first fall on the figure of the artist, whom we see from behind. "This artist who keeps his back to us," as Proust put it, doesn't reveal his face, or little else. Indeed, the more books that are devoted to Vermeer, the less we seem to know of him.

How did he paint scenes of such an incomparable quietude, yet live in a house filled with his 11 children? Why are his early works influenced by Caravaggio, but there is no proof he ever visited Italy? His family was Calvinist, but did he convert when he married a Catholic wife? Did he use a camera obscura box to capture his amazing light effects? In an age fraught with drama—Holland was at war with France—why did he bar the outside world from his paintings? Such questions are difficult to answer, for between baptism and betrothal (a span of 20 years), the archives are totally mute about Vermeer. But we do know that his grandfather was arrested for counterfeiting money and that his father ran the heavily mortgaged inn known as the Mechelen, set on the Voldersgracht just a few paces from Delft's Nieuwe Kerk; his father also sidelined as an art dealer (he needed something to hang on those tavern walls) as did Johannes himself. Vermeer's rich mother-in-law didn't want him to marry her daughter, but the artist won her over. He married Catharina Bolnes and enrolled as the youngest syndic of the Guild of St. Luke—Delft's thriving confraternity of painters—in 1654.

In the end, the only "reality" that matters is the one that Vermeer claustrophobically caught within the four walls of his house—but that unique universe is enough. His ability to transform oil paint into a world is so credible that we even gain an impression of the warmth or chill of the room. His light captures the most transient of effects—you almost find yourself looking around to see where the sunlight has fallen, half expecting it to be dappling your own face. And then there is the telling way Vermeer captures an entire story in a single moment, as in the Glass of Wine (Staatliche Museum, Berlin). A man stands over a woman as she drains her glass, his hand firmly clasping the silver-lipped jug as though intending to refill it—laying the question of his intentions (is he planning to get her tipsy?) open to interpretation. Here, as always, Vermeer keeps us guessing.

nate black marble and alabaster tomb of William of Orange, designed by Hendrick de Keyser and son. Figures of Justice, Liberty, and Valor surround a carving of the prince, at whose feet is shown his small dog, which starved to death after refusing to eat following his owner's death. Below is the Royal Crypt, where 41 members of the House of Orange–Nassau are buried. Throughout the church are paintings, stained-glass windows, and memorabilia associated with the Dutch royal family. There are other mausoleums, most notably that of lawyer-philosopher Hugo de Groot, or Grotius. In summer it is possible to climb the church tower for a view that stretches as far as The Hague and Scheveningen. ⊠ *Markt 2* ☎ *015/212–3025* ☎ *Combined ticket for Oude Kerk and Nieuwe Kerk €2.50, tower €2* ☾ *Apr.–Oct., Mon.–Sat. 9–6; Nov.–Mar., weekdays 11–4, Sat. 11–5.*

At the eastern end of the Markt, you can take Oosteinde south to the twin turrets of the fairy-tale **Oostpoort** (East Gate), the only remaining city gate, dating back to 1400, with the spires added in 1514. Parts of it are a private residence, but you can still walk over the drawbridge. Although it is a short walk out of the center, the effort of getting there is more than rewarded with the view.

From Oostpoort, head east back toward the train station, taking Zuider-straat or hewing instead to the canal bank over to the Zuidwal avenue, which leads to the site of Rotterdamse Poort. Here, at the south end of Oude Delft canal, cross the busy road to overlook the harbor; here is **"Vermeer's View,"** for it was on the far side of this big canal that Vermeer stood when painting his famous cityscape. For a profile of the artist, *see* the Close-Up box "Vermeer: Sphinx of Delft," *above.*

A few blocks north of Zuidwal and not far from the main station is Delft's former armory, the **Legermuseum** (Netherlands Army Museum), which makes an appropriate setting for an impressive military museum. Despite the gentle images of Dutch life, the origins of the Dutch Republic were violent. It took nothing less than the Eighty Years' War (1568–1648) to finally achieve independence from the Spanish crown. In addition to the guns, swords, and other implements of warfare, all periods of Dutch military history are explored in detail, from Roman times to the German occupation during World War II. ⊠ *Korte Geer 1* ☎ *015/215–0500* ☎ *€4.40* ☾ *Weekdays 10–5, weekends 1–5.*

Several blocks north of the Legermuseum is an 18th-century canal-side mansion housing the **Paul Tétar van Elven Museum**, created by a 19th-century painter. The interior is charmingly redolent of Ye Olde Delft, complete with painted ceilings, antiques, and even a reproduction of an artist's atelier done up in the old Dutch style. ⊠ *Koornmarkt 67* ☎ *015/212–4206* ☎ *€2* ☾ *Apr.–Oct., Tues.–Sun. 1–5.*

If you want to purchase Delftware, head south of the city center to **De Porceleyn Fles.** This factory first opened its doors in 1653 and is the only extant pottery works; tours are given through the facility, but you can also potter around by yourself. This is the real McCoy, and there are numerous examples of the town's fabled blue-and-white porcelain ware to tempt all shoppers. ⊠ *Rotterdamseweg 196* ☎ *015/251–2030* ⊕ *www.royaldelft.com* ☎ *€3.50* ☾ *Mon.–Sat. 9–5; Mar.–Oct., also Sun. 9–5. Closed Dec. 25–Jan. 1.*

In addition to De Porceleyn Fles, visitors can also tour **De Delftse Pauw**, which offers a tour through the pottery works to watch painting demonstrations. ⊠ *Delftweg 133* ☎ *015/212–4920* ☎ *Free* ☾ *Apr.–Oct., Mon.–Sun. 9–4:30; Nov.–Mar., weekdays 9–4:30, weekends 11–1.*

Where to Eat & Stay

★ **$$$–$$$$** ✕ **De Zwethheul.** Delft's classiest restaurant is also its best hidden: set a little outside of town, it can easily be reached by cab. In a restored 18th-century building, this award-winner actually began as a humble pancake house. In fine weather, you can eat on a beautiful terrace overlooking the Schie River. Specialties of the house include Bresse chicken ravioli with baked crayfish, trio of lamb in basil sauce, grilled sea bass with langoustines, or risotto with a lobster sauce. The sommelier and his wine list are among the best in Holland. ✉ *Rotterdamseweg 480* ☎ *010/470–4166* ⌕ *Reservations essential* ▭ *AE, DC, MC, V* ⊘ *Closed Mon. No lunch weekends.*

★ **$$$–$$$$** ✕ **L'Orage.** In cool shades of blue, with pristine white linen, Restaurant L'Orage has a sublime aura; as soon as you walk through the door, you anticipate the sensational dining options on offer. It is owned and run by Denmark-born Jannie Munk—Delft's very own prize-winning Lady Chef—who is now reaching out to a wider public thanks to the professional classes she offers in her kitchen. Her architect-husband, Pim Hienkans, was the mastermind behind the look of the place, accented by a huge, hinged glass roof to create an indoors-outdoors feeling. Munk creates delicious fish dishes, many based on recipes from her native country. Sometimes if the kitchen is in the mood, you'll be treated with *amuse-bouches*—three or four of the tastiest dishes on the menu in miniature—to accompany your drinks. Best bet for your main course is the red bass, grilled in its skin and served with risotto and sun-dried tomatoes. ✉ *Oude Delft 111b* ☎ *015/212–3629* ⌕ *Reservations essential* ▭ *AE, DC, MC, V* ⊘ *Closed Mon.*

$$–$$$$ ✕ **Le Vieux Jean.** The tiny, family-run restaurant serves tasty meat-and-potatoes fare as well as good fish dishes such as *kabeljauw* (cod with mustard-sesame sauce). In the adjoining *proeflokaal* (tasting room) you can buy wine and spirits. ✉ *Heilige Geestkerkhof 3* ☎ *015/213–0433* ⌕ *Reservations essential* ▭ *AE, DC, MC, V* ⊘ *Closed Sun. and Mon.*

$ ✕ **De Wijnhaven.** This Delft staple has loyal regulars, drawn by the many terrace tables, music-festival-week songsters, and a mean Indonesian saté. There's a smart restaurant on the first floor, but the bar and mezzanine have plenty to offer, with snacks, a reasonable menu for dinner with the latest tracks on the speakers, and great fries and salads. ✉ *Wijnhaven 22* ☎ *015/214–1460* ▭ *MC, V.*

¢ ✕ **Café Vlaanderen.** Board games keep you entertained on a rainy day inside the extensive café, but sunny skies will make you head for the tables set under leafy lime trees out front on the Beestenmarkt. For a snack lunch, try gazpacho with cucumber, pepper, and croutons. ✉ *Beestenmarkt 16* ☎ *015/213–3311* ▭ *MC, V.*

¢ ✕ **De Nonnerie.** In the arched cellar of the famous Prinsenhof Museum, this luncheon-only tearoom has a sedate, elegant atmosphere. If you can, get a table in the grassy courtyard under an umbrella, and—since you're within the House of Orange—order an Oranjeboom beer to wash down the fine *Delftsche Meesters plaet* (three small sandwiches of pâté, salmon, and Dutch cheese) served here. Entry is via the archway from Oude Delft into the Prinsenhof Museum, down a signposted path beside the gardens. ✉ *St. Agathaplein* ☎ *015/212–1860* ▭ *No credit cards* ⊘ *Closed Sun.*

Other than going through the hotels directly, you can book via the **VVV** tourist office (commission charge). You can also contact **hotels online** (⊕ www.delfthotels.nl).

★ **$–$$$$** ▥ **Bridges House.** The history of this exquisite hotel goes back to Jan Steen—one of the greatest painters of The Hague School—who lived and painted here. As with many other artists revered today, his contemporaries didn't recognize his talent, so he opened an inn and operated a brewery to supplement his income. The current young owner has re-created a patrician's house in his tasteful refurbishment, making this a haven of indulgence on the banks of Delft's oldest canal. Helping to embody the age-old spirit of the city, antiques grace each spacious room, all adorned with extra-long beds with bespoke Pullman mattresses (piled with feather pillows and duvets to ensure a blissful sleep). The bathrooms are luxuriously fitted, with enormous showerheads for a wake-up blast, and all have tubs. The breakfast room overlooks the tree-lined canal; in summer a blue umbrella–shaded barge is moored just alongside, part of a neighboring restaurant. For longer stays you might like to consider one of the apartments. ⊠ *Oude Delft 74, 2611 CD* ☎ *015/212–4036* 🖷 *015/213–3600* ⊕ *www.bridges-house.com* ⊃ *10 rooms, 2 studio apartments* ⟁ *In-room data ports, cable TV; no a/c* ⊟ *MC, V* ❍❙ *BP.*

$$–$$$ 🔲 **Best Western Delft Museumhotel & Residence.** This small hotel is spread through a complex of 11 historic buildings, opposite the Oude Kerk and adjacent to the Prinsenhof Museum. The serious drawback is that the hotel has fallen under an American chain, so the authentic interior has been torn out and replaced by quite a dreary, anonymous standard—you could be anywhere (a great disappointment, given the facades). As if to make amends, the management has cut loose with an over-the-top display of antiques in the public areas. ⊠ *Oude Delft 189, 2611 HD* ☎ *015/215–3070* 🖷 *015/215–3079* ⊕ *www.museumhotel.nl* ⊃ *49 rooms, 2 suites* ⟁ *In-room data ports, in-room safes, minibars; no a/c* ⊟ *AE, DC, MC, V* ❍❙ *EP.*

★ $$ 🔲 **Johannes Vermeer.** It's surprising that no one else thought of it before, but this is the first Delft hotel to pay homage to the town's most famous local son. The buildings of this former cigar factory were completely modernized and turned into a hotel in 2000. You'll be spoiled for choice of views: rooms at the front have a canal view, and rooms at the back have a city view that takes in three churches. In tasteful greens and yellows, the decor is unobtrusive, and the staff are pleasantly friendly. The garden behind the hotel is enclosed but nonetheless a mellow place to have a drink. The restaurant is open only for groups (advance arrangements essential). It's too bad, because the walls of the restaurant are adorned with painted copies of the entire works of Vermeer, with his *Girl with a Pearl Earring* inevitably taking center stage in the grand café area. ⊠ *Molslaan 18-22, 2611 RM* ☎ *015/212–6466* 🖷 *015/213–4835* ⊕ *www.hotelvermeer.nl* ⊃ *24 rooms, 1 suite* ⟁ *In-room data ports, cable TV* ⊟ *AE, DC, MC, V* ❍❙ *BP.*

$ 🔲 **Leeuwenbrug.** Facing one of Delft's canals, this traditional hotel has an Old Dutch–style canal-side lounge. The rooms are large, airy, and contemporary in decor; those in the annex are particularly appealing. ⊠ *Koornmarkt 16, 2611 EE* ☎ *015/214–7741* 🖷 *015/215–9759* ⊕ *www.leeuwenbrug.nl* ⊃ *36 rooms* ⟁ *In-room data ports, cable TV, bar; no a/c* ⊟ *AE, MC, V* ❍❙ *BP.*

★ ¢ 🔲 **B&B Oosteinde.** This small yet friendly bed-and-breakfast is the only one of its kind in the city. Located behind the Beestenmarkt, near the fairy-tale twin towers of the city gate at Oostpoort, this welcoming house will make you feel like a Delft resident, not a visitor. Larger rooms sleep three or four. A minimum stay of two nights is required. There is water in the rooms, but bathroom facilities are shared. ⊠ *Oosteinde 156, 2611 SR* ☎ *015/213–4238* ⊃ *3 rooms with shared bath* ⟁ *Cable TV, some pets allowed; no a/c* ⊟ *No credit cards* ❍❙ *BP.*

Festivals

From February till December, there are annual festivals celebrating music, theater, and comedy. Highlights include the De Konnick Blues Festival in mid-February, held in 20 bars and cafés across the city; Queen's Birthday celebrations in April; canal-side concerts from the end of June through July and August; a week of chamber music during the last week in August at the Prinsenhof; the African Festival in early August; the Delft Jazz and Blues Festival at the end of August; a waiters' race in the Beestenmarkt in early September; and the City of Lights in mid-December. For more details, log on to ⊕ www.vvvdelft.nl or contact the VVV.

The Outdoors

BICYCLING Bike rentals are available at the **railway station** (☎ 015/214–3033), open weekdays 5:45 AM–midnight, weekends 6:30 AM–midnight. Fees run €6–€7.30 per day, with a security deposit of €50. For biking routes through Delft, Delfshaven, and Schiedam, get maps from the VVV.

Nightlife

The most humming nightspot—in fact, the only club (nearly all others are student-only)—in Delft is **Speakers** (✉ Burgwal 45–49 ☎ 015/212–4446 ⊕ www.speakers.nl). Each night there is something different going on. Stand-up comedy, in English as well as Dutch, is usually on Wednesday, with concerts on Thursday; Friday night sees theme night (1970s, for instance); Saturday hosts the techno-beat crowd; and Sunday offers salsa parties. Open regular hours are a restaurant, bar, and sidewalk café.

Shopping

In Delft, Friday until 9 PM is designated*koopavond* (evening shopping). A large weekly market is held every Thursday from 9–5 at Marktplein, with a flower market along the Hippolytusbuurt on Thursday from 9–5. Every Saturday, there is a general market at the Brabanttse Turfmarkt/Burgwal. During Saturdays during summer months, there is a flea market on the canals in the town center and an art market at Heilige Geestkerkhof.

DELFTWARE **De Porceleyn Fles** (✉ Royal Delftware Factory, Rotterdamseweg 196 ☎ 015/251–2030) is home to the popular blue-and-white Delft pottery. The galleries here exhibit famous pieces from throughout Delft's history, and regular demonstrations of molding and painting pottery are given by the artisans. The pottery factories of **De Delftse Pauw** (✉ Delftweg 133 ☎ 015/212–4920), although not as famous as De Porceleyn Fles, produce work of equally high quality. **Atelier de Candelaer** (✉ Kerkstraat 14 ☎ 015/213–1848) makes a convenient stop-off for comparisons of Delftware with other pottery.

ROTTERDAM: COLOSSUS OF THE WATERWAYS

As a city with few remnants of its fabled past, Rotterdam enjoys a future that is perhaps the brightest of all cities in Holland. Gone are the days before World War II when the city fathers would commission a statue of a paint manufacturer but refuse to clear away the grim jungle of its commercial core. On May 14, 1940, the task was done for them by Nazi bombs, which swept away some 30,000 homes, shops, churches, and schools in the course of a few brief hours. To the surprise of those who didn't know the vigor and hardheadedness of the Rotterdam Dutch, a new city of concrete, steel, and glass arose in the 1950s and '60s, phoenixlike, from the ashes of its destruction. And today—with some of the most important buildings of the beginning of the 21st century continuing to rise—some pundits believe that were it not for the devastation of World War II, Rotterdam might never have become the dynamic and influential world port it is today.

Some time ago, Rotterdam ceased to be simply a Dutch city. Thanks to its location on the delta of two great river systems, the Rijn (Rhine) and the Maas (Meuse), and the enormous Europoort and North Sea projects, it has become the largest seaport in the world. Through its harbors—and there are many—pass more tons of shipping each year than through all of France combined. New industry settled in (which the Rotterdammers greatly welcomed: "The question is not how larger a tanker the channel will allow," one executive was quoted, "but rather how deep you want us to dredge it so your ship can get through"), followed by new populations. After the repair of the harbors in 1952, there was an increasing demand for labor, so recruits settled in from Italy, Spain, Greece, Turkey, and Morocco, followed in the 1970s by Cape Verdeans and Netherlands Antilleans. The wealth generated by industry led to new culture and architecture, with the absolute latest in futuristic design now studding the cityscape. Today, Rotterdam and modern architecture are so intrinsically intertwined that the one goes a long way toward defining the other. This architectural renaissance was capped when Rotterdam was named Europe's Cultural Capital in 2001, leading to a yearlong party of exhibitions, theater, music, poetry, and design. Galleries' and museums' profiles were raised, ground was broken for even more modernistic edifices, and art journals hailed "Manhattan-on-the-Maas" as the standard-bearer of architecture of the 21st century and a power station for ideas about the look of tomorrow.

But postmodern architecture is only one of the attractions of the *Maasstad,* or City on the River Mass: the regular traveler will also find much else to satisfy. Visit the urban waterfront along the Maas River and admire the regeneration under way, with varieties of waterside cafés and restaurants. Window-shop through antiques markets. Discover what the Museumpark has to offer, the city's cultural axis running straight down the Westersingel, from Centraal Station to Kop van Zuid. Shop in designer boutiques, or choose to explore Chinese department stores on Westkruiskade. Take a look at avant-garde galleries on Witte de Withstraat, Binnenweg, and Delfshaven. Rappel down the Euromast. Rotterdam has a young, urban culture, with some of the hottest nightlife around—just check out the hipsters at clubs such as Now & Wow. In other words, don't be surprised to learn that techno-rock was born in Rotterdam.

The city divides itself into four main sectors but doesn't really have a central district; for all intents and purposes, that is simply a shopping area these days. The **Kop van Zuid and Entrepot** districts are on the south side of the bridge. Here, famous architects such as Sir Norman Foster and Renzo Piano are designing housing, theaters, and public buildings to complete the area's transformation into a modern and luxurious commercial and residential district. **Delfshaven, Oude Haven,** and **Leuvehaven** are old harbors, but that's just where the comparison stops. In particularly charming Delfshaven you'll find a harbor so narrow it looks like a canal, lined with gabled houses dating back centuries and creating a classic Dutch scene. The Oude Haven, on the other hand, is surrounded by buildings not more than 20 years old, some of which, like the Blaak Rail station and Kijk-Cubus, are among Rotterdam's most photographed buildings. **Museumpark** is known as the cultural heart of the city, because it is home to four museums and bordered by a Sculpture Terrace; you can museum-hop from collections of giant animal skeletons to city history to Golden Age art. (Incidentally, if you plan to visit a lot of museums, it is always worth buying a Museum Jaar Kaart [Museum Year Card], or MJK for short; this pass gives you free entry to more than 440 museums throughout the country for a year and free entry to

15 in Rotterdam, and is available on showing your passport at VVV offices and participating museums for €25.)

Like Amsterdam's, Rotterdam's name is taken from a river—in this case the Rotte, which empties into the Maas at this point. The city's birth extends back to the 10th century, when, despite the constant threat from the sea, a small group of early Rotterdammers settled on the Rotte banks along a small stream running through the boggy, peaty area. The settlement flourished, but it was not until the Golden Age (1550–1650), when Holland was a world power, that the city became a center of trade, home to both the United East India Company and the West India Company. The city's really spectacular growth dates from 1870 when the Nieuwe Waterweg was completed, a 17-km-long (11-mi-long) artificial channel leading directly to the sea.

Along the Waterstad: From the Eastern Docklands to Delfshaven

Men like Erasmus, Grotius, Vermeer, Van Leeuwenhoek, and William the Silent walked the quays of Rotterdam in centuries past, but they would scarcely believe what has become of their harbor town today. They would be thoroughly lost wandering through 21st-century Rotterdam—and so would you: unlike most other cities, it doesn't have a historical city center. If you go to what is called the center of Rotterdam, you'll find yourself in the middle of a very big, rather bland shopping area. Rather, this tour wanders through the harbor-front areas of the city, covering a good amount of ground. Many "sights" on the tour are visual in themselves (you can't enter the buildings), but most buildings and artworks on this route show Rotterdam off in its best designer-cool mode. Many of Rotterdam's museums are included in our second Rotterdam walk.

The Nieuwe Maas River has flowed through Rotterdam for 700 years, dividing the city in two, and acting as the city's lifeline. A continual procession of some 30,000 oceangoing ships and some 130,000 river barges passes through Rotterdam to and from the North Sea. A top option for visitors to the city is boat tours around the harbor, ranging from a hydrofoil called the *Flying Dutchman* to the very popular **Spido boat tours** (✉ Leuvehoofd 5 ☎ 010/275–9988); a variety of water taxis and water buses also operate in the Waterstad (the docks and harbors along the banks of the river). There is also a water-bus link between Rotterdam and Dordrecht, which stops at several places along the way, including Alblasserdam.

a good walk

Begin at "The Kettle"—the train, tram, and metro station, the **Blaak**. The simplest way to get here is take tram No. 1 from the front of Centraal Station, which leaves every 10 minutes, getting off at tram stop Blaak. (You need a *strippenkaart* [strip of tickets]—the cheapest way to make several journeys by bus, tram, or metro—to get to and from the start and finish points of this walk.) The Blaak station gained its nickname from its attention-getting roof, which has steel arches looping overhead. As you walk away from the station, toward the church at the far end of Binnenrotte square, you'll see, to your right, one of Rotterdam's most photographed buildings, the precarious-looking **Blaakse Bos** (Blocks Forest), whose architect, Piet Bloom, intended to create a "forest" with cubic shapes back in 1984.

Head first for the enormous church, the **Sint Laurenskerk** ㉖ ▶, which houses one of the biggest organs in Europe. If you're lucky, your visit may coincide with a rehearsing organist blasting out a tune. Then walk around to the Grote Kerk Plein, the square on the far side of the Bin-

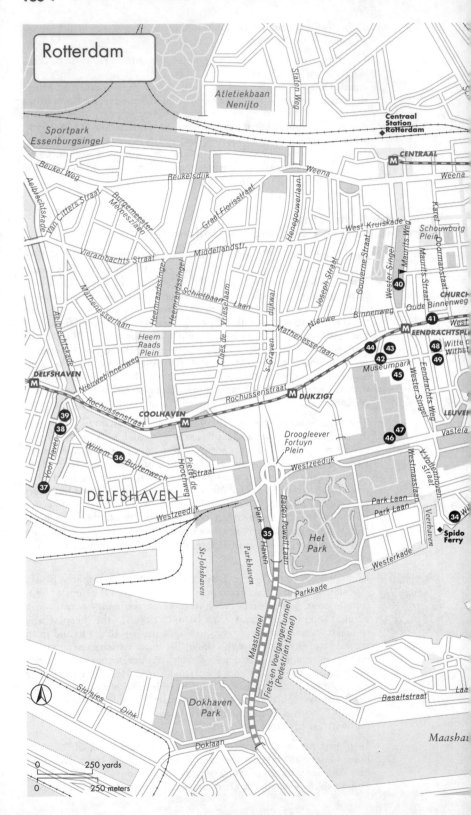

Rotterdam

Atletiekbaan
Nenijto

Stater Weg

Centraal
Station
Rotterdam

Sportpark
Essenburgsingel

M CENTRAAL

Weena

Weena

Beukel Weg

Beukelsdijk

Van Citters Straat

Aelbrechtskade

Burgemeester
Meineszlaan

Graaf Florisstraat

West Kruiskade

Karel Doormanstraat

Schouwburg
Plein

Vierambachts Straat

Middellandstr.

Henegouwerlaan

Wester Singel

Mauritsweg

Maurits-Straat

40

CHURCH

Mathenessserlaan

Heemraadssingel

Heemraadssingel

Schietbaan

Laan

dijkwal

Joseph Straat

Gouverne Straat

Oude Binnenweg

Aelbrechtskade

Heem
Raads
Plein

Claes de Vrieselaan

S. Graven

Nieuwe

Binnenweg

41 West

M EENDRACHTSPL

Nieuwebinnenweg

Mathenesserlaan

44 **43**

48 Witte
withst

42

49

Rochussenstraat

M DIJKZIGT

Museumpark

Wester Singel

45

Eendrachts
Weg

Eendrachtsstraat

LEUVE

Vastela

39

Rochussenstraat

COOLHAVEN

M

Droogleever
Fortuyn
Plein

47

38

Willem

36 Buytenwech

Pieter de Hoochweg

Straat

Westzeedijk

46

Westmaaslaan

37

DELFSHAVEN

Westzeedijk

Park

Haven

Baden-Powell Laan

Park Laan
Park Laan

Vroullenhoven-straat

Veerhaven

34 W

◆ Spido
Ferry

Toon Haven

St-Jobshaven

Parkhaven

Het
Park

Westerkade

Parkkade

Maastunnel

Fiets-en Voetgangertunnel
(Pedestrian tunnel)

35

Basaltstraat

Laa

Sluisjes

Dijk

Dokhaven
Park

Doklaan

Maashai

0   250 yards

0   250 meters

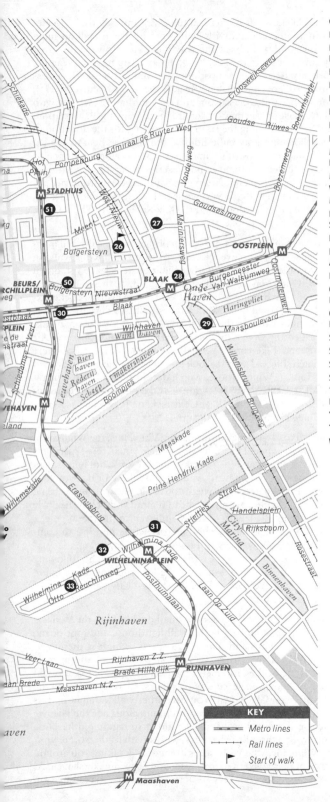

KEY

~~~~~ Metro lines

⊢⊢⊢⊢⊢ Rail lines

▶ Start of walk

nenrotte, where Hendrick de Keyser's statue of Erasmus stands. De Keyser is most famed as an architect, with Delft's ornate Town Hall his main showpiece. Turn and walk back the way you came, toward the gray-and-yellow cube houses to the left. If you fancy a trip to yesteryear, the **Nationaal Schoolmuseum** ㉗ is almost opposite Sint Laurenskerk, across the Binnenrotte square (walk down Librije Steeg to the Nieuwe Markt); here you can sit in a 1920s classroom and try your hand at writing with chalk on slate. Back on the market square, head back to Blaak station, but bear left before reaching the tram stop, making for the direction of Piet Blom's yellow-and-gray cube houses, the Blaakse Bos, to visit, if you must, the one house in this somewhat ugly development open to the public. On your left is a flight of nondescript concrete stairs; at their top, follow the enclosed avenue, marveling at these extraordinarily positioned houses as you walk. If you want to look inside the rather ordinary interior of the cubic domiciles, the **Kijk-Kubus** ㉘, or Show Cube, at No. 70, is open to the public.

This route conveniently acts as a pedestrian bridge over the divided highway below, so when you leave No. 70, turn left and keep walking through this so-called "forest." Another flight of steps leads you down this side to the **Oude Haven**—confusingly named, as there are several old harbors, and worse, there is little left here of the historic docks, except the old boats moored here. Walk left as you leave the cube houses, and you come to the cafés on the waterfront, perfect for a quick break. This area is called the **Openlucht Binnenvaart Museum** ㉙, or Open-Air Maritime Museum. Take your time walking up the harbor side—there are plenty of interesting old boats to look at—to follow the harbor around to the **Witte Huis**, or White House, which dates back to 1898, when it was Europe's first "skyscraper" (you can also take a time-out at the building's ground-floor café, 't Bolwerk, at Geldersekade 1c, which has a great view of the Oude Harbor and Blaak station).

Take the cobbled road running alongside the Witte Huis, the **Wijnhaven.** You never know what might be moored alongside you here—expect tugs and yachts, even a navy warship. You have a short walk, not longer than five minutes along the Wijnhaven, walking past three bridges to your left. This is a real working harbor, where you are likely to see masts being re-varnished, and seagulls cawing overhead remind you of how near the sea you are. Walk up the length of the Wijnhaven to the totem pole, a Native American piece given by the Port of Seattle in 1982 to commemorate the 200th anniversary of Holland-America diplomatic relations. Here at the totem pole at the end of the pier turn right, following the water, toward the enormous statue ahead of you: the tragic figure of Ossip Zadkine's *De Verwoeste Stad* (Destroyed City), a metaphor of the destroyed Rotterdam.

The big building to your left, across the small dockyard, is the **Maritiem Museum Rotterdam** ㉚, complete with small lighthouse and four boats, which children can climb and play in; the prize exhibit is the much-visited *De Buffel* warship. Retrace your steps back to the historic **Regentessbrug** (one of the aforementioned bridges), which is adorned with bronze lions mounted gracefully on pillars. Cross the river on the bridge, and you're on Glashaven. You can either walk straight up this small street to Boompjes, the main road running alongside the Nieuwe Maas ahead, or, if you enjoy wandering along romantic old harbors, you can loop around three little harbors, with a path leading off to your right, along Wijnkade, where old ships are moored, taking you around the waterfront of Bierhaven, Rederijhaven, and Scheepmakershaven. At any point you can make your way back to Glashaven and continue on.

If you are walking around all three harbors, you can walk around only one side of the third, Scheepmakershaven, as you rejoin Glashaven again, and turning to your right, walk up to Boompjes, ("little trees"), which is where three remarkable towers, each a 24-story highrise residential building, create a memorable city skyline. As you walk along Wijnhaven (Wine Harbor), Bierhaven (Beer Harbor), and Scheepmakershaven (Shipbuilders' Harbor), the romantic old boats stand in marked contrast to the modern cityscape. Cross the busy road at the pedestrian crossing and walk to the Nieuwe Maas's waterfront to fully appreciate the vista spread out before you.

To your left stretches the red **Willems Bridge**, linking the north bank with the man-made island, and beyond it, connecting the island to the south bank, the vast green structure of De Hef, an ancient railway bridge. To your right is the enormous pylon of the Erasmus Bridge, which acts as an extension of the Coolsingel road, bringing the heart of Rotterdam straight down onto the Kop van Zuid district, shrouded in new buildings, many laden with interpretations as modernist statements. This is where you are headed next. Turn now toward the Erasmus Bridge, and allow it to draw you nearer. The large pleasure boats docked to your left as you approach the ramp of the locally called Swan Bridge offer waterfront tours. One, the *Spido,* tours the new harbor area and the flood barrier toward the North Sea, and the other, bound for the opposite direction, is a tour that ultimately heads out to the giant windmills at Kinderdijk, via Dordrecht. You'll actually cross a small bridge to get to the Erasmus Brug bridge-ramp, but as it is incorporated into the road, you may not notice it. Built in 1996 at a cost of €160 million, Ben van Berkel's **Erasmus Bridge** is 265 feet long, with a 50-foot-high tower and an angled arm holding the suspension cables that has given it the nickname "The Swan." Take the pedestrian path once over the bridge off to the left-hand side, so you can get the best view of the Kop van Zuid developments on this side.

Stop mid-bridge to take in the view (even in summer, it's breezy here, so you won't stay too long); over to the far right, just on the riverbank in front of the Willems Bridge, note the installation called the Washing Line—a heavy, iron sea chain, with bits of sea junk hanging off it (a controversial piece of "artwork," to say the least). As you begin to descend the far side, keep your eyes peeled to take in the curiosities all along the bank. Nearest the riverbank you can see what looks like a group of massive flattened mushrooms: the **Dynamic Rocks,** actually "seats" for pedestrians. Farther left is the city-specific "artwork" that is the **Tower of Numbers** ㉛, which, along with the nearby Garden of Lost Numbers, comments on past and future Rotterdam.

There is an enormous amount of upscale development to see on the Kop van Zuid, on the Wilhelminapier, and in the rejuvenated district (former warehouses) of the Entrepot—the absolute latest in residential planning, which projects south of the marina. Inevitably, it is the commercial buildings that are the most flamboyant and that attract the most attention, but this tour also passes numerous new and strikingly designed housing developments. As you walk down the ramp onto the Kop van Zuid, turn left onto **Wilhelminakade Walk** down to the river, where you can sit on the Dynamic Rocks and walk up to the Bridgemaster's House, walking over the Garden of Lost Numbers. Cross the extensive paving area, and back on the pedestrian path, follow the road ahead of you as it bends around to the left. Walk over the bridge and continue on until you see an old segment of wall on your left, formerly the Gemeentelijke Handelsinrichtingen, one of Lodewijk Pincoffs's buildings. Continue on under the welcome shade of the trees to the building arching right over the road ahead, the **Poortgebouw**, built in 1879. The former offices of harbor planner Lodewijk Pincoffs, it was supposed to become a legalized brothel in the late 1980s but is now home to a communal group (who host vegetarian meals every Wednesday and Sunday). Walk underneath it and cross the bridge, looking to your right as you do so, as you have an excellent view of the Entrepot haven **City Marina**. On the far side of the bridge, follow the water on your right and head toward the Vijf Werelddelen, the long terrace on the marina dockside.

On the Halfrond, just beyond the terrace of Sinead's café, overlooking the Binnenhaven there is a small, old crane, on four stilts, with a flag hanging off it, dangling, a reminder of the working history of the area. The warehouses have shops on the ground floor and very exclusive apartments on the upper floors. Walk around the U-shape marina, and on Rijksboom, the far side of Vijf Werelddelen, and look across at the sumptuous balconies opening out onto the marina. There are a number of very chic design shops around the City Marina, catering to the apartment dwellers, focusing on interiors and design, along with an international supermarket.

A gallery that houses the **Tram Huis** art center is at the end of Vijf Werelddelen, just off the square behind the City Marina. Walk left across the Handelsplein square to the entrance, on the corner of Rosestraat. Here you'll see a 1998 statue of Lodewijk Pincoffs, the man who originally got the authorities in the 19th century to begin developing the city south of the rivers—a true pioneer of urban planning. From the Zilt café at the end of Rijsboom, the south side of City Marina, there is a stunning view of the modernist stepped Staircase apartment complex. Turn left onto Cargadoorskade, and walk up the terrace of pretty lime-color houses; looking ahead, you can see the Peperklip residential area (literally, "paper clip"), comprising huge circular buildings, with alternating colored squares interspaced with bands of blue that encircle the whole building.

Cross the bridge on your right before reaching the Peperklip housing area. On the far side of the bridge, there are two housing projects: to the left, the Stadstuinen, and to the right, Landtong, the staircase-stepped residential area. Walk left along J. B. Bakemakade through the ritzy housing. Take a right to get a good look around; then on W. G Witteveenplein, take a right again, heading back toward the river and the Erasmus Bridge. Walk straight over Lodewijk Pincoffsweg and up Levie Vorstkade, with a harbor on your left. To your right is the very exclusive stepped Staircase residential area. On the square to your left, you have a good view of the Vijf Werelddelen terrace, but take time to pause at the **Loods 24** installation, on your side of the plaza. This is a group of five of what appear to be enormous swords, stabbed in the ground, with the hilts shielding large lamps. These towering lamps are far more than streetlights: they symbolically refer to 50 years of liberation, memorializing the Jewish lives lost in concentration camps. The name Loods 24 refers to the goods shed on Kop van Zuid, where 12,000 Jewish Rotterdammers were made to gather before their deportation between 1942 and 1945.

Walking straight on from the square, continue in the direction of the Erasmus Bridge. Turn left onto the main road on the harbor front, Stieltjes Straat, and cross the bridge, but instead of heading toward the Erasmus Bridge to the right, go straight to cross Wilhelminakade and go through the big glass doors into the Galleria, to **Wilhelmina Plein**. The metro station is open normal hours, but the Galleria—the link between the station and the new buildings—is open weekdays from early morning to 7 at night only. A soaring-ceilinged glass building, it is worth a stroll to see its mix of glass and manicured brick. If you come on a weekend, when the Galleria is closed, turn right after crossing Wilhelminakade, and walk around the building, making sure to peek in the glass doors to see the massive square beyond.

Then cross the Posthumalaan, looking to your left to see a huge higher-education college, the Ichthus Hogeschool, which has an entirely glazed facade. Ahead of you is the deep red **Nieuw Luxor Theater,** another of Peter Wilson's projects. It is known for the technical wizardry of the interior. The building even has its own jetty. Opposite the Luxor Theater is Italian architect Renzo Piano's famous **Toren op Zuid** ③ office complex. Continue up the Wilhelminakade, passing a converted warehouse, the 't Leidsche Veem, on your left, now a hostel. On your right, at Wilhelminapier 699, is Café Rotterdam, in the former departure hall of the Holland-Amerika Lijn; enormous cruise liners moor alongside the café these days. Almost opposite on your left is the **Las Palmas** ③ workshop, built in 1953, due to be the 2005 home of the Nederlands Fotomuseum. Just up on your right is Sir Norman Foster's Center for Maritime Simulation Training.

A good 10-minute walk up the pier from the Maritime Simulation Center, on the same side of the road, ahead to your right, is the **World Port Center,** taken as the major work of Sir Norman's on the pier and completed in 2000. This 32-story building has a curvaceous facade, looking almost like a sail, swelling as it fills with wind. Sir Norman received the Pritzker Architecture Prize in 1999, an award also made to Renzo Piano and Rem Koolhaas, both of whom have designs on the pier: the former has his Toren op Zuid, and the latter's project is yet to be built, with an estimated completion date of 2006. Rotterdam-born Rem Koolhaas's project **De Rotterdam** is to be built between Piano's Toren op Zuid and Café Rotterdam. Koolhaas's complex is to be enormous, incorporating a massive multiscreen cinema, a hotel, a health center, a swimming pool, shops, and offices on the middle floors and housing on the upper floors. It will be one building but will give the impression of being three separate towers, 8 feet taller than Piano's Toren, and just 3 feet shorter than Sir Norman's World Port Center. The last building currently on the pier is Hotel New York, formerly the Holland-America Line (HAL) headquarters, built in 1901 and renovated and opened as a stylish hotel in 1993. After stopping for a welcome drink in Hotel New York's bar, or on the terrace outside, walk toward the Rijhaven, a harbor on the far side of the pier from the Erasmus Bridge. On the dockside, take a ramp down to a water taxi, denoted by a small sign. Boats ferry passengers across the river regularly every 10 minutes (€2 one-way); most have an open top at the back, where you can get the best view. As you cross over the river to the opposite bank, look to your right for a view of the Erasmus Bridge. Ahead of you to the left is the Euromast, in the middle of Het Park. The boat docks in the pretty **Veerhaven,** an old yacht-filled harbor between two tree-lined quays. Turn to your right as you leave your water taxi, and walk along Willemskade, a renovated riverside street, now amply furnished with benches and trees in pots, making a very pleasant spot for a break. The enormous **Wereld Museum** ③ is on your left, four floors and with impressive exhibitions focusing on non-Western cultures, with excellent audio and video coverage, in addition to exhibits. After visiting the museum, walk back to the Veerhaven, keeping it to your left as you walk right around it. On the corner of Westerstraat is Loos, a top spot for a time-out if you didn't stop at Hotel New York.

Walk the whole way around this small harbor, taking in the picturesque yachts moored up. On the opposite side of the harbor entrance to where you landed in your water taxi is the Westerkade, so walk along this waterfront looking out across the river on your left. You pass several restaurants, the umbrella-shaded tables outside Zeezout, and, farther up, the noted Dewi Sri restaurant. On your right is a park, the biggest in the center of the city, and simply called **Het Park**. It is the place where Rotterdammers head when the weather turns warm. When you reach the park, note that there is a path parallel with the river to your left, but you need to take one of the smaller paths cutting diagonally into the park, keeping the banks of the landscaped canal to your right, as a guide. This takes you in the direction of the Euromast, but make sure you cross in front of the small gardens of De Heuvel, a gorgeous old private house you come to. Cut left in front of the house, over a bridge taking you through a deep green and heavily foliaged grotto. If you're concerned about directions, look up, because you can't miss the **Euromast** ㉟. As soon as you reach a bank, strike left, as you need a footpath bridge over the divided highway ahead. Walking over the bridge takes you directly to the Euromast. You can go up it, for a fantastic panoramic view, and many added attractions; walk around it to the right, and walk up the green park ahead, keeping a harbor, Parkhaven, to your left. If you hear a high-pitched zipping noise, look overhead as a rappeler crazy enough to jump off the main viewing area of the tower plummets over the top with a bungee cord.

At the top of the park harbor, take a left onto Westzeedijk, unfortunately a dreary road but one that leads to **Delfshaven** ㊱. Wait at the first tram stop you come to for a No. 8 tram, traveling in the direction of Delfshaven, to cut the journey to five minutes or so. There is quite an extensive area called Delfshaven, but the next leg of this tour heads for the upper reaches of the Voorhaven, a harbor so small it resembles a canal. On the tram don't get out at Delfshaven but at Schiemond. This drops you at the bottom of the harbor, and if you look back and to your right, you see the windmill that marks the beginning of the last stage of this walk. Although the housing around seems modern, it is just a shield, and the old merchant houses still stand here and about. To get to the mill, walk five minutes around the canal to your right, heading initially in the direction in which the tram departed. Take the first right, a path leading down a flight of steps, and follow the short path as it leads to a road ahead, Middenkous. Branch right, so the windmill is straight ahead of you, across the small harbor. As you round the corner, you are greeted with old historic facades similar to those of other city centers.

In this protected historical landscape, walk along the Voorhaven and marvel at the many old buildings that form an open-air museum. Take time to look at the flat-bow, shallow-bottom Dutch barges in the harbor. If you want to look inside a working mill, the **De Distilleerketel** ㊲ is open on Saturday. Nearby, a fascinating account of Rotterdam's history is found in **De Dubbelde Palmboom Museum** ㊳, or Two Palm Trees Museum, which looks at the city's history as a "junction," with a special emphasis on Delfshaven itself. Next door to the museum is the Dubbelde Palmboom café, another good spot for a break.

From the café, head up the harbor and take the first street on your right, Piet Heijn Straat, named for the 17th-century Delfshaven-born sea hero. He is commemorated with a plaque on the door of the house where he was born, No. 6, and with a statue, found if you walk to the end of this street and go up the two flights of steps opposite: here on Piet Heijn

Plein a raised belvedere with benches has him poised over the Achter Haven (literally, "the harbor behind"). You can see the windmill to your right, behind the houses, and there are yachts moored below, making this a lovely place for a break. Go back to the harbor and turn right. As you continue up Voorhaven, look up to see a big sundial on the facade of the **Oudekerk/Pilgrimvaders Kerk** 39 (Old Church/Pilgrim Father's Church); otherwise you might miss it, as its brickwork front totally melds into the terraces on either side. As the day draws to a close, you could have dinner at any of the charming cafés and restaurants here in Delfshaven. To get back to the center of town, walk to Aelbrechtskolk, and turn left. The tram you need is just down the main road, the Schiedamse Weg—the stop is helpfully called Delfshaven. Tram No. 4 heading in the direction of Centraal Station picks you up here, taking you from this seedy end of Nieuwe Binnenweg to the Westersingel, renowned for its diverse restaurants and bars. The tram turns up the Westersingel to Centraal Station.

TIMING   Not including the time spent in museums, galleries, and vertically commuting up the Euromast, this walk takes approximately 4½ hours—so, in effect, this tour can take an entire day, especially if you allow more time to look at galleries and antiques shops and plan on browsing. Note that most museums in the city are closed on Monday.

Sights to See

37 **De Distilleerketel.** Set in the historic district of Delfshaven, this mill is the only working flour mill in the city. Formerly employed to grind malt to make *jenever* (Dutch gin), the dusty-haired miller now mills grain for specific bakeries in the city, which means it is closed during the week. ✉ *Voorhaven 210, Delfshaven* ☎ *010/477–9181* 💶 €2 ◷ *Sat. 10–4.*

38 **De Dubbelde Palmboom Museum.** Devoted to the history of Rotterdam and its role as an international nexus, this museum traces the city's history from prehistoric times to the current day. The special and very fascinating focus is on how exotic wares imported by the East India Company affected the city. The building itself is literally redolent of history: not only do its heavy beams and brick floors waft you back to yesteryear, but there even seems to be a faint smell of grains, recalling its many years spent as a warehouse.

Ask for the very informative guide in English, as all the labeling is in Dutch. The first floor has some fascinating archaeological finds: one of the spouted ancient jugs, eye-catchingly red striped, has been traced to a town near Cologne, providing proof of trading contacts with the region, as traveling merchants were apparently very active in trading ceramics. One of the prettiest marine tile depictions shows the Maas River with a ship (named the *Rotterdam*), dating to 1697. There is a 1945 replica of a shipping agent's office, which would have been used by a representative of the merchants who used the route regularly, to organize customs and the loading and unloading of goods. ✉ *Voorhaven 12, Delfshaven* ☎ *010/476–1533* ⊕ *www.hmr.rotterdam.nl/* 💶 €2.70 ◷ *Tues.–Fri. 10–5, weekends 1–5.*

★ 36 **Delfshaven.** The last remaining nook of old Rotterdam, an open-air museum with rows of gabled houses lining the historic waterfront, Delfshaven is now an area of trendy galleries, cafés, and restaurants. Walk along the Voorhaven and marvel at the many historic buildings; most of the port area has been reconstructed, with many of its 110 buildings now appearing just as they were when originally built. There are several time-stained streets here, notably Piet Heijn Straat. Piet Heijn was a Delfshaven-born sea hero (1577–1629), who captured a Spanish treasure fleet in 1628. His honor as Fleet Admiral was short-lived, as he was killed in a sea battle the following year. He is commemorated with a plaque on the door of the house where he was born, No. 6, and with a statue, found at the end of the street by the water, on Piet Heijn Plein, where a raised lookout point furnished with benches has him straining eternally toward this harbor, the Achter Haven, which was Delfshaven's first claim to fame.

To compete with the monopoly that Rotterdam had with its harbors, the authorities in Delft requested that the Earl of Aelbrecht (who ruled the area) allow them to have a private connection to the Maas River. The earl granted them permission, and the canal was dug by hand, between 1389 and 1404. This, as its very name attests, was the harbor of Delft, before the surrounding countryside made the entire area an urban settlement. The city made a living out of fishing; then, in the 17th century, riches arrived with the ships that the East India Company was bringing into the country. Here, too, traders of the malt whisky and jenever distilleries did a roaring business. Rotterdam annexed the harbor in 1886, but after the harbor mouth silted up, it was decided in 1972 to make Delfshaven over into a protected historic district.

For historic sights in Delfshaven's environs, check out the working mill of **De Distilleerketel** (open Saturday only), the fascinating **Dubbelde Palmboom Museum** on Rotterdam city history, and the **Oudekerk/ Pilgrimvaders Kerk**. In addition to housing these sights, the district is home to many bars, cafés, galleries, and antiques shops. Note that the affluent quays of pretty, ultraclean Delfshaven are juxtaposed with a vastly different surrounding area, a transition most marked at the top of Aelbrechtskolk, the lane leading off Voorhaven to the main road at the top, the Schiedamse Weg. Here, the litter-strewn, scruffy streets form a depressing sight, as it seems the city council doesn't care about its own residents, seemingly preferring to invest solely in the visitor area. As for locating Delfshaven, the street running alongside the Voorhaven starts off simply as Voorhaven to the south, from the windmill up, and becomes Aelbrechtskolk to the north, near the main road and tram line; Tram 4 connects Delfshaven with the rest of the city. ⊠ *Achterhaven and Voorhaven, Delfshaven.*

③⑤ Euromast. For a great overview of the contrast between Delfshaven and the majority of the city, the Euromast, just a 10-minute walk from Delfshaven, provides a spectacular view of the city and harbor, if you can handle the 600-foot-high vista. Designed by Maaskant in 1960, it was for many years Holland's highest building; when a new medical facility was built for the Erasmus University, an additional 25 feet were added to the tower in six days, restoring it to its premier position. On a clear day, you are supposed to be able to see the coast from the top. The tower not only affords panoramic views of Rotterdam Harbor but also packs in a number of other attractions. The most exciting is the **Space Cabin,** where you experience the sensation of a rocket launch by shooting another 30 feet up the mast. Alternatively, take part in a rappel down (make reservations by calling the number below). The park at the base of the Euromast is where many Rotterdammers spend time when the weather is good. ⊠ *Parkhaven 20, Delfshaven* ☎ *010/436–4811* ⊕ *www. euromast.com* ⊠ *€7.75, rappel €45* ⊗ *Apr.–Sept., daily 10–7; Oct.–Mar., daily 10–5; July and Aug., Tues.–Sat. until 10:30.*

②⑧ Kijk-Kubus (Show Cube). In 1984, architect Piet Bloom made headlines with this eye-popping statement, the **Blaakse Bos** (Blocks Forest), whose "forest" of cubic shapes quickly became a Rotterdam icon. Made of dozens of cubic apartments tilted cater-corner, these startling gray-and-yellow cubes teeter on concrete stilts and are one of Amsterdam's most favored sights for advertising commercials. "Homey" they are not, but most of these houses are occupied. You can visit one, but the interiors are surprisingly ordinary inside. For many visitors, the concept is interesting, but much was lost in the choice of materials. ✉ *Overblaak 70, Meent* ☎ *010/414-2285* 💷 *€1.75* ⊙ *Jan. and Feb., Fri.–Sun. 11–5; rest of year, daily 11–5.*

③③ Las Palmas. Built in 1953, this former workshop center is scheduled to be renovated into a major museum housing the Nederlands Fotomuseum in 2005. International photographs, films, and new media will compose the collections. Programs/collections will be here. Check their Web site for the latest updates. ⊕ *www.laspalmas.nl.*

③⓪ Maritiem Museum Rotterdam. A sea lover's delight, the Maritime Museum is Rotterdam's noted nautical collection. Appropriately perched at the head of the Leuvehaven harbor, it was founded by Prince Hendrik in 1874. Set against the background of modern and historical maritime objects, the seafaring ways of old Rotterdammers make more sense. The first floor is occupied with shipbuilding; on the second floor there are models, steam engines, cranes, and nautical instruments. Of note is the replica of the wooden figurehead of Erasmus from the ship *De Liefde* (Love), which was originally named Erasmus. *De Liefde* was part of a fleet of five merchant ships that attempted to find a new route to India and the Far East in 1598. The others were all lost, but *De Liefde* was the first European ship to reach Japan.

Children have a whole floor dedicated to them, called, no less, "Professor Plons" (Professor Splash), where museum staff are on hand to help with looking through a real periscope, donning a hard hat and taking to the driving seat of a scaled-down crane, and engaging in many other activities dealing with the themes of water and ships. Kids will be gaga over the museum's prize exhibit, the warship *De Buffel,* moored in the harbor outside, dating back to 1868. The ship has been perfectly restored and is fitted out sumptuously, as can be seen in the mahogany-deck captain's cabin. ✉ *Leuvehaven 1, Witte de With* ☎ *010/413–2680* ⊕ *www.maritiemmuseum.nl* 💷 *€3.50* ⊙ *July and Aug., Mon.–Sat. 10–5, Sun. 11–5; Sept.–June, Tues.–Sat. 10–5, Sun. 11–5.*

②⑦ Nationaal Schoolmuseum (National School Museum). In a 1920s classroom you can take a seat at an old desk and try your hand at writing with an ink-dip pen or using chalk on a slate, making for a charming journey back to the good old days. ✉ *Nieuwemarkt 1a, Meent* ☎ *010/404-5425* 💷 *€2.50* ⊙ *Tues.–Sat. 10–5, Sun. 1–5.*

②⑨ Openlucht Binnenvaart Museum. This open-air maritime museum is a dreamy place to wander, looking at all the old Dutch barges moored up in a harbor that used to be reserved for seagoing vessels. Unfortunately, the modern architecture surrounding the pier makes for a rude contrast. This is a harbor that you walk around on your own—there is no guide, no gate, and no admission. ✉ *Oude Haven, Delfshaven* ☎ *010/411-8867.*

③⑨ Oudekerk/Pilgrimvaders Kerk (Pilgrim Fathers' Church). On July 22, 1620, 16 men, 11 women, and 19 children sailed from Delfshaven on the *Speedwell.* Their final destination was America, where they helped found the Plymouth Colony in Massachusetts, New England. Puritan Protestants fleeing England for religious freedom usually went to Amsterdam, but this group, which arrived in 1608, decided to live in Leiden, then 10 years later opted to travel on to the New World by leaving from Rotterdam. On July 20, 1620, they left Leiden by boat, and via Delft they reached Delfshaven, where they spent their last night in Holland. After a sermon from their vicar, John Robinson, in what has since become this church, they boarded the *Speedwell,* sailing to Southampton, England, then left on the *Mayflower* on September 5, reaching Cape Cod 60 days later.

This church was built in 1417 as the Chapel of Sint Anthonius, then extended and restyled in the Late Gothic period. However, in 1761 the ceilings were raised, and the current style dates back to this Regency revamp, when an ornate wooden clock tower was also added. Next to the choir is a vestry from 1819, where you can find a memorial plaque to the Pilgrim Fathers on the wall. The bell tower has a tiny balcony. The church is now owned by the Trust for Old Dutch Churches. ⊠ *Aelbrechtskolk 16, Delfshaven* ☎ *010/482–3041* ⊙ *Sat. 1–4.*

▶ ㉖ **Sint Laurenskerk.** Built between 1449 and 1525, this church is juxtaposed against its modern surroundings. Of the three organs contained inside, the main organ ranks as one of Europe's largest. Hendrick de Keyser's statue of Erasmus in the square was buried in the gardens of the Museum Boijmans van Beuningen during the war and miraculously survived. Guided tours are by appointment only. ⊠ *Grote Kerkplein 3, Sint Laurenskwartier* ☎ *010/413–1494* ⊙ *Tues.–Sat. 10–4.*

㉜ **Toren op Zuid.** An office complex by celebrated modern architect Renzo Piano, this structure houses the head offices of KPN Telecom. Its eye-catching billboard facade glitters with 1,000-odd green lamps flashing on and off, creating images provided by the city of Rotterdam, in addition to images provided by KPN and an art academy. The facade fronting the Erasmus Bridge leans forward by 6 degrees, which is the same as the angle of the bridge's pylon. It is also said that Piano could have been making a humorous reference to his homeland, as the Tower of Pisa leans at the same degree. ⊠ *Wilhelminakade 123, Kop van Zuid.*

㉛ **Tower of Numbers.** Near Piano's Toren op Zuid structure is this creation of Australian architect Peter Wilson. The tower is topped by five LED (light-emitting diodes) boxes, hung from a mast, with digital figures showing, among other things, the time and the world population. This "fluxus" is in contrast to the fixity of the **Garden of Lost Numbers,** found below the yellow bridge-watcher's house designed as a series of numbers set into the pavement. These numbers refer to the city's decommissioned harbor, all of which once were identified by numbers. As Rotterdam has such a heightened awareness of lost identity, these stainless-steel figures serve as a remembrance of things past. ⊠ *Wilhelminakade, Kop van Zuid.*

㉞ **Wereld Museum.** On a corner of rustic Veerhaven, surrounded by old sailing boats moored along modern yachts, this museum is devoted to non-Western cultures, many of which have had a sizable influence on Rotterdam. One of the permanent exhibitions is "Rotterdammers," which explores how the city developed in the 20th century with the arrival of immigrants from around the world. But another attraction is wonderful for children, the **Reispalace** (Travel Palace), a collection of "hotel" rooms of travelers from different countries that they can explore either with museum staff or with parents, learning about other cultures as they visit the room of a "guest" in the "hotel" (who is supposedly out in town): knickknacks spell out the occupant's culture, job, and religion (one, for instance, is for a Moroccan photographer), and children are encouraged to try on clothes, shoes, and hats, and look in bedside tables to see what journals the guest has been reading. Video displays allow the guest to talk about his or her job, home, and friends (in pictures around the room). Result: children explore someone else's culture, seeing what is important to that person, in a "real" context. ⊠ *Willem-skade 25, Kop van Zuid* ☎ *010/270–7172* ⊕ *www.wereldmuseum.rotterdam.nl/* ⊠ €6 ☉ *Tues.–Sun. 10–5.*

The Center City & the Museum Quarter

Sightseeing in Rotterdam automatically divides itself into twin tours: the waterfronts (outlined in the above section) and the city center. Rotterdam's central nexus includes many impressive museums, but you'll find art in unexpected places, such as the Sculpture Terrace near the Centraal Station. Here, too, you'll find two popular parks facing each other across the Westersingel: the Skate Park, Europe's largest—a reminder that Rotterdam is the only city in Holland where the youth population is on the rise—and the cultural heart of Rotterdam, the Museumpark. Architectural wizard Rem Koolhaas designed the Museumpark, an urban garden where you find four of Rotterdam's most dazzling museums. Juxtapose old masters, modern art, and industrial design at the Museum Boijmans van Beuningen; make sense of the city as a development in modern architecture at The Netherlands Architecture Center; explore a spectacular exhibition space that you spiral through in the Kunsthal; and marvel at giant animal skeletons in the Natural History Museum. The park itself is laden with modern and classical sculptures, providing a wealth of opportunities to chill out if an attack of museum feet or gallery gout strikes.

Other delights on tap are the galleries and cafés of Witte de Withstraat and the Center for Contemporary Art and The Netherlands Photography Institute, two outposts for the increasingly hip and hot Dutch avant-garde art scene. A dramatic change of pace awaits at the gorgeous 17th-century mansion, the Schielandshuis, now part of Rotterdam's historical museum. Beyond the Lijnbaan shopping district—radical in its day, it was the progenitor of the American shopping mall—the walk winds up with a visit to Rotterdam city's mayoral offices in the sumptuous 1920s City Hall.

a good walk

Start in front of Centraal Station, with your back to the station. Ahead of you across Stations Plein—the main square in front of the station—is an elegant building, the Millennium Tower. Walk toward it, being careful of the trams, bikes, and taxis. When you reach the tower, go around it, to the right, onto Kruisplein. Continue down the street, which, once separated by a canal, becomes Maurits Weg on the left-hand side and Westersingel on the right. On the left you can look down the road to the Schouwburgplein as you pass, since this is one of the most interesting squares in Rotterdam (you'll return here later at the end of this walk). After crossing over West Kruiskade, about halfway down the road is a long brick terrace along a grassy-banked canal: the **Sculpture Terrace** ⓵ ▶, one of Rotterdam's city council's most celebrated recent projects. Take a seat on a nearby bench and make your own interpretation of masterworks by such sculptors as Rodin and Henri Laurens.

Continue up the Westersingel, crossing to the left-hand side, to turn left onto Westblaak to head to the Skate Park. If you plan to omit this leg, don't take the turn, but continue straight (the walk catches up later on the Westersingel). The **Skate Park** ⓶ is on the central traffic island, so massive screens are in place to prevent motorists from watching daredevil kids jumping off high-sided half pipes. After you've watched (or participated) to your fill, double back to the Westersingel. Turn left and walk up the right-hand side, because your next turn comes up soon.

Being nominated Europe's cultural capital for 2001 helped propel the visitor center into signposting city sights, but the city's famous **Museum Quarter**, with its four major museums and the **Museumpark** ⓷, is barely marked. Make sure you don't miss the turn: look for a nondescript road leading off Westersingel to the right, called Museumpark. Two minutes up the road on the left is the celebrated Musuem Boijmans van Beuningen. You have a chance to visit this colossal gallery shortly, but first continue on to the white house on your right, the **Chabot Museum** ㊸, with works on view by the leading Dutch expressionist painter and sculptor Henk Chabot. When you come out of the Chabot Museum, turn right for one more stop-off before the Boijmans: take the ramp over the fountain to the **Nederlands Architectuurinstituut** ㊹ (or NAi; Netherlands Architecture Institute), paying close attention to the extraordinary sculpture on your left, Auke de Vries's installation, essentially a frame built out of the water, accented with metal spirals. The NAi hosts temporary displays on architecture and interior design in seven exhibition spaces.

Turn to your left, and walk across the open square to the **Museum Boijmans van Beuningen** ㊺, the greatest of all Rotterdam's museums, with a celebrated array of old-master paintings. In the gardens in the back of the museum, there are a number of old and new artworks; Claes Oldenburg's modern *Screw Arch* occupies center position in front of the museum's glass-front café, which is set among eerily black pools. Leaving the museum's gardens, turn right and walk back to the square and head left via the main path through the central gardens of the Museumpark, a project masterminded by design great Rem Koolhaas and his Office for Metropolitan Architecture (OMA). Walking over the bridge lands you neatly on a small square in front of the Kunsthal (on your left) and the Natuurmuseum (on your right).

The **Kunsthal** ㊻ is a huge, warehouse-looking building, which breaks the mold for traditional galleries with its nonsequential spiraling route through rooms. The Kunsthal's café is the perfect spot for a break set under trees and opposite the **Natuurmuseum** ㊼, or Natural History Museum, in a pretty villa with an enormous modern extension. From the Natuurmuseum, walk up the central ramp of the Kunsthal to get up onto the top of the dike and to the Westzeedijk road. Turn left on the dike and walk up to the junction ahead, where a left takes you to the bottom end of Westersingel and what is now Eendrachtsweg. Walk back toward the center of town along this tree-lined street. At the first main junction, the road ahead to the left is Museumpark (which you took earlier), so take the road on the right, Witte de Withstraat, a street renowned for its galleries and fabulous cafés. Stop off at any point along the way, but don't miss the **Nederlands Fotomuseum** ㊽, Holland's Photography Institute. Although it doesn't have any permanent exhibitions, the temporary shows focus on serious talent, crossing the spectrum in styles and themes.

Almost opposite is **TENT Centrum voor Kunst Witte de With** (Witte de With Center for Contemporary Art) ㊾, which showcases both established artists and new talent. Again, exhibitions are on a temporary basis, so you never know which artists you'll encounter. This place doubles as a massive dispenser of information about cultural events, and you can easily find out what's on view in city galleries. The building here is a work of art in itself, with massive crater shapes sculpting the facade. On leaving TENT, turn right and keep walking up the street, which becomes Schilderstraat, just before meeting the larger Schiedamse Dijk. Take a right down this street to have a look at the **Walk of Fame**, where various celebs have made handprints or, more unusually, footprints, framed in the sidewalk.

Next stop is the **Maritiem Museum** ㉚, so when you get to the end of the Walk of Fame, turn and double back, walking right up the Schiedamse Dijk to the junction, where the museum is on your right. If you missed the Maritiem Museum on the our first walk of the waterfront or haven't done that walk yet, take this opportunity to get in the picture by finding out more about Rotterdam's great history of shipbuilding—kids will love the "Professor Splash" floor, with scaled-down, hands-on things such as periscopes, boats, and tubs of water. Just behind the museum is Ossip Zadkine's *Destroyed City* statue, from which you can head to Het Schielandshuis. If you look across the central part of Westblaak, you can see this 17th-century house, but you need to walk back to the junction of Westblaak and Schiedamse Dijk, to the pedestrian crossing by the Maritiem Museum. Cross over, and turn right on the sidewalk to walk up Westblaak; then take your first left onto Korte Hoogstraat, and you'll see **Het Schielandshuis** ⑩, almost engulfed by the skyscrapers towering over it. This brave mansion manages to hold its own; as the only remaining building of the Golden Age in the city, it is appropriate that it now houses Rotterdam's history museum. Among its remarkable exhibits are vintage clothes dating back to the 18th century and the famous Atlas von Stolk collection of old maps.

After visiting the museum, back on Korte Hoogstraat turn left, away from the Maritiem Museum. Take your next left when you reach Beursplein, and go down the steps into the shopping mall, officially called Beurstraverse but nicknamed Koopgoot. Walk under the road and through the other side: this not only gives you a chance to window-shop but is an opportunity to make decide whether you cotton to this Pieter de Bruijn–designed, multiuse complex.

Walk up the steps of the far side, turn right, and walk around the square back to the Coolsingel road. The biggest department store in the city is now on your left-hand side: the Bijenkorf, or "beehive," a name that refers to the patterning of the exterior. Opposite, across the Coolsingel, is the **World Trade Center.** From the Bijenkorf, turn left up the Coolsingel. Look to your right as you walk, where you see the post office and the City Hall, or **Stadhuis** ⑪, the only buildings dating from the 1920s in this area. You can look around part of the interior on weekdays. Cross the road from the Stadhuis to the Stadhuisplein, looking to your right at the fountain at the top of the Coolsingel. There are bars to your right, a hangout for the mid-teen crowd. Down Stadhuisplein, turn left onto Lijnbaan. Following the need to re-create the city center post-1940, town planners decided to go for a completely new approach in their urban design, opening the area to projects such as Lijnbaan, which in 1953 heralded the launch of dedicated shopping precincts, separated from housing. It's aesthetically dull but historically important if you're interested in where the mall concept had its origins. Where the Lijnbaan crosses with Van Oldenbarneveldtstraat, turn right, onto Van Oldenbarneveldtstraat, which is one of the best places to look for designer wear.

Back on the Westersingel/Maurits Weg at the end of Van Oldenbarneveldtstraat, turn right (the station will be ahead of you), then next right, onto Aert van Nesstraat to take you to the **Schouwburgplein.** This whole square was restyled by landscape designer Adriaan Geuze and has quirky features such as street lamps that double as sculptures. The Pathé cinema on the square is said to be a postmodern statement, for it really is an architectural space more than anything else, with its upper cinemas perched on poles, enclosed by transparent walls, a fittingly futuristic touch to conclude this walk through modern Rotterdam. Finish with a well-deserved time-out at Café Floor.

TIMING If you can't rush gallery viewing, you'll need a lot more than the suggested four hours to take in all this walk's museums, let alone some much-needed breaks in museum cafés along the route.

Sights to See

㊸ Chabot Museum. This museum displays the private art collection of leading Dutch expressionist painter and sculptor Henk Chabot, who was active between the two world wars, depicting peasants, market gardeners, and, later, refugees and prisoners. ✉ *Museumpark 11, Museumpark* ☎ *010/436–3713* ⊕ *www.chabotmuseum.nl* ▨ *€5* ⊙ *Tues.–Fri. 11–4:30, Sat. 11–5, Sun. noon–5.*

★ **㊿ Het Schielandshuis.** Staunchly defending its position against the high-rise Robeco Tower and the giant Hollandse Banke Unie surrounding it, this palatial 17th-century mansion is almost engulfed by the modern city. Happily, it holds its own as a part of Rotterdam's historical museum (the other half is the Dubbelde Palmboom in Delfshaven). Built between 1662 and 1665 in Dutch Neoclassical by the Schieland family, it burned down in 1864, but the facade survived, and the interior was carefully restored. Inside are Baroque- and Rococo-style rooms reconstructed from houses in the area, clothing from the 18th century to the present day, and the famous collection of maps, the Atlas von Stolk. Because of the frailty of the paper, only a tiny selection of vintage maps is on display at any one time, usually under a specific theme. The museum's café is in a lovely garden. ✉ *Korte Hoogstraat 31, Centrum* ☎ *010/217–6767* ⊕ *www.hmr.rotterdam.nl* ▨ *€2.70* ⊙ *Tues.–Fri. 10–5, weekends 11–5.*

㊻ Kunsthal. The corrugated exterior of this "art house" sits at one end of the visitor-friendly museum quarter and hosts major temporary exhibitions (an Andy Warhol retrospective is one example). There is not a permanent collection, other than the massive, multistory boxlike center itself, for it was designed by architect-prophet Rem Koolhaas. Some say the design bridging the gap between the Museumpark and the dike is a clever spatial creation; others consider it ugly, pointing to the mix of facades in half glass, half brick, and half corrugated iron, which has led to rusted iron, stained concrete, and long cracks in the central walkway. The steep concrete ramp through the middle of the building, leading pedestrians up, mirrors the route through the galleries, which direct you up and around the exhibition spaces in a spiral. Critics point out elements that are not thought out, such as reaching the top of the gallery to find that the only way down is the route by which you came up. Others decry the glass upper floor, which makes for embarrassment or titillated viewing, depending on which side of the floor/ceiling you are on. The biggest complaint is the lack of elevator, compounded by the hazards of the central ramp, whose steep angle makes this a potential ski slope for wheelchair users. If you just want to look from the outside, the gallery's café, on the more-pleasing-to-the-eye side, is a lovely, tree-shaded spot for a coffee, but face your chair toward the park, not the busy avenue at the top of the dike. As with the Pathé cinema on the Schouwburgplein, this postmodern facade is not representative of the function behind it; rooms here can be adapted to provide any function, from exhibition space to theaters. Such is the way of the future.

A tiny history of Rotterdam-born Rem Koolhaas: after opening his renowned firm, the Office for Metropolitan Architecture (OMA), in 1975, he studied in London and at Cornell University before becoming visiting Fellow at the Institute for Architecture and Urban Studies in New York. While in the city, he wrote his landmark *Delirious New York, a Retroactive Manifesto for Manhattan,* published in 1978. He has been a professor of architecture and urban design at Harvard University since 1995, the same year in which the work of his office was the subject of a retrospective exhibition held in the Museum of Modern Art in New York. Many critics have dubbed him the architectural messiah of the 21st century; whether their prophecy is fulfilled remains to be seen. ✉ *Westzeedijk 341, Museumpark* ☎ *010/440–0301* ⊕ *www.kunsthal. nl* ⛟ €*7.50* ⏲ *Tues.–Sat. 10–5, Sun. 11–5.*

㊺ **Museum Boijmans van Beuningen.** Rotterdam's finest shrine to art, with
Fodor'sChoice treasures ranging from Pieter Bruegel the Elder's 16th-century *Tower*
★ *of Babel* to Mondriaan's extraordinary *Composition in Yellow and Blue,* this museum ranks as one of the greatest painting collections in Europe. If it's not in the same class as Amsterdam's Rijksmuseum or The Hague's Mauritshuis, it ranks a very respectable third. Created more than 150 years ago—when Otto Boijmans unloaded a motley collection of objects on the city, then greatly enhanced by the bequest of Daniel van Beuningen in 1955—it is housed in a stunning building ideally designed to hold the collections of painting, sculpture, ceramics, prints, and furnishings.

The greatest attraction here is the collection of old masters, housed in the first floor of the west wing (pick up a map of the museum at the front desk, as it is very easy to get lost here). This survey of West European art extends from the 14th century to the middle of the 19th century. In particular 15th- and 16th-century art from the northern and southern Netherlands, and 17th-century Dutch painting are well represented, including painters such as Van Eyck, Rubens, and Rembrandt. Highlights include Bruegel's famous *Tower of Babel* (1563), a fascinating depiction of the Genesis 11:1–9 account of how the people of the land of Shinar used brick and lime to construct a city with a tower that would reach up to heaven. The Lord thought otherwise, preventing the builders from completing their task and scattering the peoples of Shinar abroad so that humankind, previously united by a single, common language, became divided into nations no longer able to communicate with each other. Bruegel had visited Rome, and his Tower of Babel is said to have been based on the Colosseum. He has painted the tower as an immense structure occupying almost the entire picture space, although spotted with microscopic figures.

Other notable works include Peter Paul Rubens's *Nereid and Triton* (1636), originally designed for the Torre de la Parada, a hall owned by King Philip IV of Spain. Carel Fabritius's great *Self Portrait* dates from 1650; Fabritius was Rembrandt's most gifted pupil, and this is one of the finest portraits in Dutch art. Jan van Eyck's *Three Marys at the Open Sepulchre* (1425–35) is the only panel by this father of the Early Netherlandish school still in Holland. Another classic on view is the Dutch master Hieronymous Bosch's *Prodigal Son.* The modern art section runs the gamut from Monet to Warhol and beyond, covering the period from 1850 up to the present, with famous works of Monet, Kandinsky, Magritte, and Dalí. German and American art and contemporary sculpture have been recently acquired, and the museum's holdings in contemporary art have become one of the major collections in Holland. In the Decorative Art and Design collection, both precious ornamental objects and everyday utensils dating from medieval times are displayed. The collection includes majolica, tinware, silver, glass, preindustrial utensils, and modern decorative art. The museum has extended this collection to emphasize the importance of industrial design.

In addition to an extensive collection of graphics, the Prints Room displays one of the world's largest collections of drawings. Numerous schools from the Middle Ages to the present day are represented. The collection contains work by such masters as Pisanello, Dürer, Rembrandt, Watteau, and Cézanne.

In the museum café, note the fantastic collection of chairs, each by a different designer. Nearby, more artworks embellish the museum gardens. Renovation of the museum, including the addition of a new pavilion, was completed at the end of 2003. ⊠ *Museumpark 18–20, Museumpark* ☎ *010/441–9400* ⊕ *www.boijmans.nl* ☒ *€7* ⊙ *Tues.–Sat. 10–5, Sun. 11–5.*

㊷ Museumpark. A project masterminded by Rem Koolhaas's Office for Metropolitan Architecture (OMA) in collaboration with French architect Yves Brunier, this modern urban garden is made up of different zones, extending from the Museum Boijmans van Beuningen to the Kunsthal. The "idea" is that each section is screened off from the last and creates a different impression—but each block of the garden isn't as radically different as this theory builds it up to be. The one part you should linger over is just before the bridge, where there is a memorial to city engineer G. J. de Jongh. Various artists had a hand in this, with Chabot responsible for the inscription on the wall and Jaap Gidding designing the beautiful mosaic at the base of the monument, which represents Rotterdam and its surroundings at the end of the 1920s. Sculptor R. Bolle designed the bronze railings, with harbor and street scenes from the period when de Jongh was working in Rotterdam. ⊠ *Museumpark to the north, Westersingel to the east, Westzeedijk to the south, and bounded by a canal on the west side, Museumpark.*

㊻ Natuurmuseum (Natural History Museum). Located in a historic villalike structure together with an enormous glass wing (echoing the hip Kunsthal next door), the Natural History Museum lures in its visitors with glass views of exhibits within, including skeletons of creatures you'll be hard put to identify. As soon as you enter the foyer, you are face-to-face with a mounted scary-hairy gorilla. It doesn't stop there: in the atrium a skeleton of a giraffe stretches as far up as you can crane your own neck. Continue on to be met by a tiger and arching elephant tusks. There is an "ironic" re-creation of a trophy hunter's display, with turtles mounted on a wall, arranged according to size. Children are especially interested in the 10-foot-long skeleton of a sperm whale. ⊠ *Westzeedijk 345, Museumpark* ☎ *010/436–4222* ☒ *€3* ⊙ *Tues.–Sat. 10–5, Sun. 11–5.*

㊹ Nederlands Architectuurinstituut. Fittingly, for a city of exciting modern architecture, Rotterdam is the home of the **NAi,** or The Netherlands Architecture Institute. The striking glass-and-metal building—designed by Rotterdam local Joe Conen in 1993—hosts temporary displays on architecture and interior design in seven exhibition spaces, giving a holistic interpretation of the history and development of architecture, especially the urban design and spatial planning of Rotterdam. Outside, the gallery under the archive section is illuminated at night. ⊠ *Museumpark 25, Museumpark* ☎ *010/440–1200* ⊕ *www.nai.nl* ☒ *€5* ⊙ *Tues.–Sat. 10–5, Sun. 11–5.*

㊽ Nederlands Fotomuseum. Although Holland's Photography Museum doesn't have any permanent exhibits, the changing exhibitions are well worth looking at, and there is an extensive library open during the week for reference. At press time, the museum was scheduled to move in late 2004 to the Las Palmas building in the Kop van Zuid neighborhood, but this may be delayed; check the Web site for information. ⊠ *Witte de Withstraat 63, Witte de With* ☎ *010/213–2011* ⊕ *www.nederlandsfotomuseum. nl* ☒ *€2.30* ⊙ *Tues.–Sun. 11–5.*

▶ **㊵ Sculpture Terrace.** Set along the Westersingel, this outdoor venue exhibits sculptures of the past 100 years, dotting the grassy bank of the canal and creating a sculpture garden. Highlights here include Rodin's headless *L'homme qui marche* (Walking Man), Henri Laurens's *La Grande Musicienne* (The Great Musician), and Umberto Mastroianni's *Gli Amanti* (The Lovers), a fascinating jumble of triangular-shape points. *Westersingel.* ⊠ *Museumpark.*

㊶ Skate Park. If you plan on trying out the largest outdoor skate park in the country, it's best to head here in the morning, when it's not too busy. Rent in-line skates or roller skates for €9 for the day (you need to show a passport and leave a €135 deposit) from Rotterdam Sport Import. ⊠ *Witte de Withstraat 57, Witte de With* ☎ *010/461–0066.*

㊿ Stadhuis (City Hall). At the top of the Coolsingel, this elegant 1920s building is the hallowed seat of the mayor of Rotterdam and is open for guided tours on weekdays. A bronze bust of the architect, Henri Evans, is in the central hall. With the neighboring post-office building, the two early '20s buildings are the sole survivors of their era. ⊠ *Coolsingel 40, Centrum* ☎ *010/417–9111.*

㊾ TENT Centrum voor Kunst Witte de With. The awkwardly named Witte de With Center for Contemporary Art has been shortened to TENT, an apt acronym for showcasing modern art by local artists of the last decade. Shows range from edgy, happening-now issues (such as squatting) to tranquil designs for city gardens. The ground floor is devoted to up-and-coming artists, and the upper floor exhibits established artists' work. Artists also have a workplace to experiment with new projects. All exhibitions are temporary, lasting a maximum of three months, so call ahead to find out about the current show. Every first and third Thursday of the month there is an exciting free evening program. ⊠ *Witte de Withstraat 50, Witte de With* ☎ *010/411–0144 or 010/413–5498* ⊕ *www. cbk.rotterdam.nl/* 🎟 *€2.50* ☉ *Tues.–Sun. 11–6.*

VVV Archicenter. Rotterdam's main information center is also a gallery containing many of the architectural projects that have graced Rotterdam in recent years. Architectural tour maps and leaflets are available here, along with all sorts of information, including background on the many residential housing projects on the outskirts of the city. For lots more information on the city's dynamic and daring future architectural plans, also check out the Infracentrum Rotterdam, at Weena 705. Both these centers nicely supplement the role of the city's tourist office. ⊠ *c/o NAi, Museumpark 25, Museumpark* ☎ *010/205–1500.*

Where to Eat

★ **$$$$** ✕ **Parkheuvel.** Overlooking the Maas, this posh restaurant, run by chef-owner Cees Helder, is said to be popular among the harbor barons, who can oversee their dockside territory from the bay windows of this tastefully modern, semicircular building. Luxuries such as truffles are added to the freshest ingredients, with the day's menu dictated by the availability of the best produce at that morning's markets. Kudos and salaams are offered up by diners to many of the chef's specialties, including the grilled turbot with an anchovy mousse and crispy potatoes. ⊠ *Heuvellaan 21, Centrum* ☎ *010/436–0766* ⚔ *Reservations essential* 🖃 *AE, DC, MC, V* ☉ *Closed Sun. No lunch Sat.*

$$$–$$$$ ✕ **De Engel.** The international kitchen of this former town house has created a loyal following, who flock here for excellent food, a sash-window view over the Westersingel, and intimate setting (tables are very close together). The very friendly staff are more than helpful with their recommendations, as are your next-table neighbors. For a special taste treat, try the truffle soup. Note that this is not the same establishment as Grand Café Engels, on the Stationsplein, which is much more mainstream. ✉ *Eendrachtsweg 19, Centrum* ☎ *010/413–8256* ⚐ *Reservations essential* ▬ *AE, MC, V* ⊙ *Closed Sun.*

$$$ ✗ **Brancatelli.** Around the windblown environs of the Erasmus Bridge you can find several eateries specializing in Mediterranean cuisine, Brancatelli being the best. "Kitsch" is the word that springs to mind when you spot the large glass animals on every table; add a piano programmed to a recording, and you are going to either laugh or cringe. If you feel a smile tickling, then the (very) pink table settings won't be too much, either. The friendly staff really play on being Italian, making, as they say, "a nice evening" of it, especially for groups. The menu is not confined solely to Italian dishes, but a typical five-course menu is usually fish based. Even if the price pushes up your expectations, the presentation and sheer quality of the dishes justify the cost. ✉ *Boompjes 264, Centrum* ☎ *010/411–4151* ⚐ *Reservations essential* ▬ *AE, DC, MC, V* ⊙ *No lunch weekends.*

$$$ ✗ **Zinc.** This restaurant is wildly popular—just don't ask us why. It is usually so packed, conversation must be carried on at sonic-boom levels, and tables are very close to each other. The staff's attention can't be faulted as they chirpily refill and replenish water, bread, and butter without even being asked. The food, however, can be a disappointment, with some dishes both overcooked and poorly presented. Critics cluck over the open kitchen, where some standards seem worrisomely low. That said, this is a leading Rotterdam-scene arena and hipsters will really enjoy the party. Funny, though, that there is no bar. ✉ *Calandstraat 12a, Scheepvaartkwartier* ☎ *010/436–6579* ⚐ *Reservations essential* ▬ *No credit cards* ⊙ *Closed Mon. No lunch.*

$$–$$$ ✗ **Asian Glories** Reputed to be the city's best Cantonese restaurant, Asian Glories serves lunches, dinners, and Sunday brunches in a tasteful modern Asian interior or outdoors on its terrace. It's hard to choose what is most delicious; their dim sum, fresh oysters, mussels in black bean sauce, and Peking Duck consistently get raves from fussy eaters. Leave room for an exotic dessert such as ice cream with rice and red bean sauce. ✉ *Leeuwenstraat 15, Centrum* ☎ *010/411–7107* ▬ *AE, DC, MC, V* ⊙ *Closed Wed.*

$$–$$$ ✗ **Dewi Sri.** This restaurant has rijsttafel to dream about, with creative takes on traditional Indonesian dishes. Choose from a multitude of tantalizing options from Indonesian, Javanese, and Sumatran menus. Some diners may find the mock wood carvings a little heavy, given the subtle flavors of the food being served. The large restaurant upstairs could feel quite empty midweek, but the staff are incredibly polite, appearing discreetly at your table just as soon as you feel the need to ask for something. All in all, this probably has the best Indonesian food in Rotterdam, so don't let the decor faze you. ✉ *Westerkade 20–21, Scheepvaartkwartier* ☎ *010/436–0263* ▬ *AE, DC, MC, V* ⊙ *No lunch weekends.*

$$–$$$ ✗ **Loos.** In the grand style of Rotterdam's cafés, Loos has a range of international magazines and newspapers on its reading racks, and in a fun gesture, six clocks with different time zones decorate one wall. You enter and see what looks like a forest of tables, but this trompe-l'oeil effect is largely caused by a wall-size mirror. Palms create privacy between tables and add to a feeling of outdoor dining. The tables are laid with linen, and the menu selection is precisely detailed. All these nicities add up. As for the food, some dishes are excellent: clear fennel and tarragon soup with truffle tortellini; cod and Serrano ham saltimbocca, served with saffron rice and a sesame vinaigrette; peach and almond pie with tonka bean ice cream and crème fraîche. If you want to eat less luxuriously, try the bar menu—but you will miss out. ✉ *Westplein 1, Scheepvaartkwartier* ☎ *010/411–7723* ▬ *AE, MC, V.*

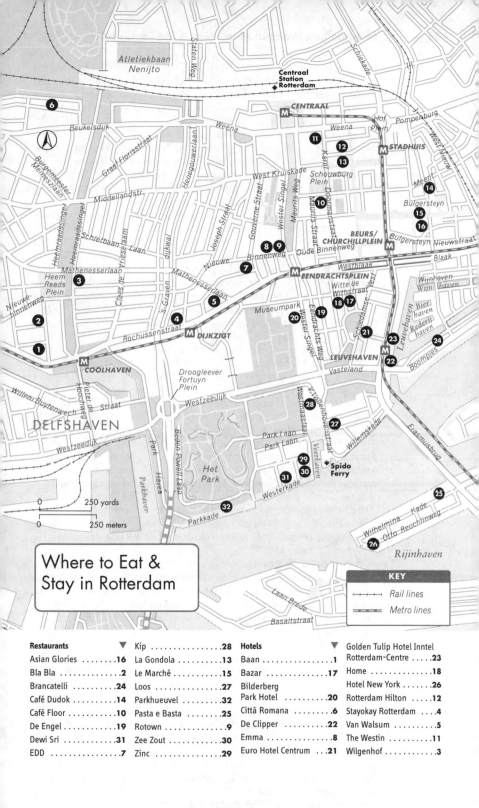

Where to Eat & Stay in Rotterdam

Restaurants ▼
Asian Glories 16
Bla Bla 2
Brancatelli 24
Café Dudok 14
Café Floor 10
De Engel 19
Dewi Sri 31
EDD 7
Kip 28
La Gondola 13
Le Marché 15
Loos 27
Parkhueuvel 32
Pasta e Basta 25
Rotown 9
Zee Zout 30
Zinc 29

Hotels ▼
Baan 1
Bazar 17
Bilderberg
Park Hotel 20
Città Romana 6
De Clipper 22
Emma 8
Euro Hotel Centrum ...21
Golden Tulip Hotel Inntel
Rotterdam-Centre 23
Home 18
Hotel New York 26
Rotterdam Hilton 12
Stayokay Rotterdam ...4
Van Walsum 5
The Westin 11
Wilgenhof 3

$$–$$$ ✕ **Zee Zout.** On the corner of an elegant, riverfront terrace, around the corner from the old Veerhaven moored with old sailing ships, this charming restaurant mirrors the freshness of its sea-based menu in crisp linen tablecloths and its spotlessly clean open kitchen, where watching the staff work whets your appetite. A large fish mosaic on the wall looks out across the river to the floodlighted Erasmus Bridge; a window awning adds to the romance of the view. Try the monkfish, accompanied by ravioli filled with Portobello mushrooms and truffles, or the lobster tempura with soy potato and curried cabbage salad. ⊠ *Westerkade 11b, Scheepvaartkwartier* ☎ *010/436–5049* ⚭ *Reservations essential* ▤ *AE, DC, MC, V* ⊙ *Closed Sun. and Mon.*

★ **$–$$$** ✕ **Kip.** With dark wooden floors, flickering candelabras, pretty jars of olive oil, and a big fireplace, Kip offers traditional, comfortable atmosphere in spades. The kitchen, however, is far from conservative. There's much more than chicken on the menu, in spite of the name, although the most popular dish is chicken breast (from a special Dutch breed) with truffles. Try the fried IJsselmeer eel with shallots, bacon, and syrup, or the grilled perch fillet with couscous and clam ratatouille. The menu must work, because this spot is always very busy. ⊠ *Van Vollenhovenstraat 25, Scheepvaartkwartier* ☎ *010/346–9923* ⚭ *Reservations essential* ▤ *AE, DC, MC, V* ⊙ *No lunch.*

$$ ✕ **Bla Bla.** This is an excellent vegetarian option. There is always a choice of four main dishes, and the menu changes often. They try to offer a good variety of cuisine from all over the world. A lively atmosphere makes it fun to eat here, and since this place gets very crowded, make sure you're having dinner on the early side to get the freshest ingredients—and a seat. ⊠ *Piet Heynsplein 35, Delfshaven* ☎ *010/477–4448* ▤ *V* ⊙ *Closed Mon. and Tues. No lunch.*

$$ ✕ **Café Floor.** Adjacent to the Stadsschouwburg (Municipal Theater), Café Floor doesn't look too inviting from the outside, but it's home to local and international regulars, artsy students, and culture-bound diners heading for a play or concert. The kitchen produces excellent food but gets busy, so be prepared to be patient if you go late-ish on a Saturday. The delicious passion-fruit cheesecake comes from Café Dudok's kitchen. The beautiful garden and accompanying birdsong from the local fauna make this a restful stop. ⊠ *Schouwburgplein 28, Centrum* ☎ *010/ 404–5288* ▤ *AE, MC, V.*

$$ ✕ **Pasta e Basta.** With singers crooning arias around you, this can be a fun place to eat, but it can get very noisy and crowded, so is not a good venue for a romantic evening out. The dishes are simple but good, served on designer-oversize plates. Everything is made from organic ingredients, and they claim it is all low in cholesterol. ⊠ *Vijf Werelddelen 1, Kop van Zui* ☎ *010/290–8080* ▤ *AE, MC, V* ⊙ *Closed Mon. and Tues. No lunch.*

$–$$ ✕ **Café Dudok.** Lofty ceilings, former warehouse, long reading tables stacked with international magazines and papers—little wonder this place attracts an artsy crowd. At its most mellow, this spot is perfect for a lazy afternoon treat of delicious homemade pastries, but you can come here for breakfast, lunch, high tea, dinner, or even a snack after midnight. They also offer a small selection for vegetarians. Since it's terribly crowded at times, you should get here unfashionably early. At all hours, service can be more than just a little snooty—a surprise in usually friendly Rotterdam—but the trouble is that this place is too successful for its own good. Still, don't let that put you off from coming here, as there's nowhere else like it in Rotterdam. ⊠ *Meent 88, Centrum* ☎ *010/433–3102* ▤ *AE, DC, MC, V.*

$–$$ ✕ **EDD.** Recently opened EDD, or "Eat, Drink, Dance," is one of Rotterdam's more stylish calling cards, complete with a "this century" ambience—funky plastic chairs and pony-skin rugs—and a bar that hums with the mid-twenties-plus crowd. The continent-crossing menu features superfresh produce. It is reasonably priced to boot, so better reserve a table or you'll be disappointed. ⊠ *Nieuwebinnenweg 153, Centrum* ☎ *010/436–4474* ⌕ *Dinner reservations essential* ▭ *AE, MC, V* ⊙ *Closed Mon. No lunch Sat.–Sun.*

$–$$ ✕ **La Gondola.** Although not entirely patronized by suits—there's a photo wall that reads like a history of modern pop music—this restaurant does have a feeling of hotel overspill, with the Hilton right across the road and a "safe" traditional Italian menu range. The dishes are basic Italian staples but prepared well. There are quirky twists—zucchini soup, or spaghetti with eggplant and bell peppers. The food is delicious, and reasonably priced, considering the central location. ⊠ *Kruiskade 6, Centrum* ☎ *010/411–4284* ▭ *AE, DC, MC, V* ⊙ *No lunch weekends.*

¢–$ ✕ **Rotown.** This venue is more celebrated for its funky bar than for its restaurant proper. A buzz fills the dining area, a spillover from the crowd up front. The menu is quite extensive, but the staff doesn't write down your order, so expect an informal, slapdash approach (if you're very unlucky, courses could even come in the wrong order, and a main course, brought out too early, will be reheated and returned later). But if you like a stylish, party-hearty atmosphere (bands often play at the bar), this could be worth it. ⊠ *Nieuwebinnenweg 19, Centrum* ☎ *010/436–2669* ▭ *AE, DC, MC, V for dinner only.*

¢ ✕ **Le Marché.** The V&D department store has a market stall with a nice luncheon option: a tempting variety of reasonably priced sandwiches. On the top floor the self-serve café La Place transforms the roof into a sunny terrace in summer. ⊠ *Hoogstraat 185, Centrum* ▭ *No credit cards* ⊙ *Closed Sun.*

Where to Stay

★ $$$$ ▦ **The Westin.** The only five-star hotel in the city is on the first 14 floors of the new Millennium tower, smack opposite Centraal Station. Although this is primarily a business hotel, the slick service of this landmark draws celebrity guests, such as pop and rock stars who perform at Rotterdam's celebrated Ahoy concert theater, Robbie Williams and Lionel Richie among the most recent. With regal purple corridors leading to light, bright spacious rooms—each fitted out with a luxuriously huge bed, topped with a 10-layer mattress and sumptuous snowy-white linen—it will be hard not to feel like a member of the glitterati yourself. The panorama across town makes the extra rates for rooms from the fourth floor up more than worthwhile, with many looking out over the Erasmus Bridge and the skyline (both dramatically floodlighted after dark). In the Lighthouse restaurant, chef Fred Smits serves superb nouvelle cuisine. Try the Irish Black Angus beefsteak served with tiger prawns or the fried brill fish fillet with anchovy risotto and smoked emperor salmon, accompanied by crispy ham and salsify. In keeping with the spirit of Rotterdam, the decor has a maritime theme; even the bar is in the form of a ship's prow. Fans adore the four-course afternoon high tea. There's a glass-covered skywalk to De Doelen concert and business center on the Stadsschouwburgplein, so on concert nights make the most of the Lighthouse's special dining offers to see just how good the chef really is. ⊠ *Weena 686, 3012 CN, Centrum* ☎*010/430–2000* ⊟*010/430–2001* ⊕ *www.westin.nl* ⊷ *213 rooms* ⌕ *Restaurant, in-room data ports, in-room safes, minibars, cable TV, health club, bar, laundry service, some pets allowed* ▭ *AE, DC, MC, V* ⊙| *EP.*

$$$–$$$$ ▦ **Bilderberg Park Hotel.** Although this hotel welcomes you with a town-house facade dramatically yoked to a metallic skyscraper, its interior is fairly unexciting, both in terms of style and appearance. Rooms are decorated in traditional English style; higher-priced rooms are more modern looking. However, it does offer a wide spectrum of top-brass services. The Restaurant 70 serves a fusion of new style–global–traditional cuisine in the classical surroundings of the old wing of the hotel. Just a few minutes' walk from the Museum Boijmans van Beuningen, this spot is centrally located. Another plus is the staff, which offers the sort of apparently effortless, unobtrusive attention to your every need that makes a stay here very pleasant. ⊠ *Westersingel 70, 3015 LB, Centrum* ☎ *010/436–3611* 🖷 *010/436–4212* ⊕ *www.bilderberg.nl* 🖙 *187 rooms, 2 suites* ⚴ *Restaurant, in-room data ports, minibars, cable TV, sauna, bar, laundry service, health club, some pets allowed* 🗖 *AE, DC, MC, V* 🍴 *EP.*

$$–$$$$ 🖭 **Rotterdam Hilton.** During the International Film Festival at the end of January, this hotel often hosts some of the notable participants, thanks in part to its top facilities, a number of suites, meeting rooms, and luxury appointments and amenities. A major plus is its location, right in the middle of downtown. Since it does tend to appeal to visitors who want a name they can rely on, it can also get filled with tour groups. ⊠ *Weena 10, 3012 CM, Centrum* ☎ *010/710–8000* 🖷 *010/710–8080* ⊕ *www.rotterdam.hilton.com* 🖙 *246 rooms, 8 suites* ⚴ *In-room data ports, minibars, cable TV, health club, hair salon, bar, lounge, laundry service, some pets allowed* 🗖 *AE, DC, MC, V* 🍴 *EP.*

$$$ 🖭 **Città Romana.** You generally don't think of resorts when you think of Rotterdam, but this vast place is considered a pleasant retreat set a half hour from the center city. More than 200 charming thatch-roof, gable-window cottages are stylishly furnished (although we could do without those mock orange columns in the public areas). Located 10 minutes' drive from the North Sea and 5 minutes' walk from a local lake, Haringvliet, its villas come fully furnished and even have chairs and sun beds for the gardens. The living room is complete with open kitchen, and most villas have two bathrooms. ⊠ *Parkweg 1, 3221 LV Hellevoet-sluis,* ☎ *0181/334455* 🖷 *0181/334433* ⊕ *www.cittaromana.com* 🖙 *263 villas* ⚴ *Restaurant, café, pool, gym, parking (fee)* 🗖 *MC, V.*

$$–$$$ 🖭 **Euro Hotel Centrum.** Despite the businessy, anonymous name, this is a comfortable, modern hotel with lots of flowers and plants, so the overall feeling is spruce and well cared for. They have family rooms, in case you're traveling with children. This place is particularly handy for Museumpark and strolls along the Westersingel. Enjoy the buffet breakfast before setting out. ⊠ *Baan 14–20, 3011 CB, Centrum* ☎ *010/214–1922* 🖷 *010/214–0187* ⊕ *www.eurohotelcentrum.nl* 🖙 *53 rooms, 2 suites* ⚴ *In-room data ports, cable TV, bar; no a/c* 🗖 *AE, MC, V* 🍴 *CP.*

$$–$$$ 🖭 **Golden Tulip Hotel Inntel Rotterdam-Centre.** The majority of the rooms in this modern high-rise, built at the opening to the Leuvehaven inner harbor, have water views. All 149 guest rooms are simply but tastefully decorated, wearing a designer-look edge. The conservatory-style breakfast room overlooks a terrace for true relaxation. Hotel guests can use two neighboring restaurants, then add dinner to the hotel bill. The staff are incredibly friendly and make all effort to make your stay pleasant, especially if you are a returning guest. The top-floor restaurant, Le Papillon, has long-reaching views across the Maas, as do the rooftop health club and swimming pool. ⊠ *Leuvehaven 80, 3011 EA, Centrum* ☎ *010/413–4139* 🖷 *010/413–3222* ⊕ *www.hotelinntel.com* 🖙 *149 rooms* ⚴ *Restaurant, café, minibars, pool, health club* 🗖 *AE, DC, MC, V* 🍴 *EP.*

★ $–$$$ 🖭 **Hotel New York.** Rotterdam is very much a commercial harbor city, with hotels aimed primarily at the business trade; the Hotel New York, a converted shipping office from the first part of the 20th century, is a particularly atmospheric exception. The twin towers rising over the water of the Nieuwe Maas, across from the city center, were known to Rotterdammers for decades as the headquarters of the Holland-America Line, before being renovated and opened as a hotel. Rooms are individually decorated, with high ceilings contrasting with the modern decor, so it's not just the view that boosts the price. The enormous restaurant (which seats 400) somehow maintains an intimate café atmosphere, although those in the know delight in the afternoon tea served here but don't stay for dinner. An oyster bar, tea salon, and water taxi are also amenities to enjoy at the Hotel New York. ✉ *Koninginnenhoofd 1, 3072 AD, Kop van Zuid* ☎ *010/439–0500* 🖷 *010/484–2701* ⊕ *www. hotelnewyork.nl* ⇨ *71 rooms, 1 penthouse apartment* ♿ *Restaurant, room service, in-room data ports, cable TV; no a/c* ☰ *AE, DC, MC, V* ⊙ *EP.*

$–$$ 🏨 **Van Walsum.** On a residential boulevard within walking distance of the Museum Boijmans van Beuningen and major attractions, the Van Walsum is not far from the Euromast. The gregarious owner proudly restores and re-equips his rooms, floor by floor, on a continuously rotating basis, with the always-modern decor of each floor determined by that year's best buys in furniture, carpeting, and bathroom tiles. There is a bar-lounge and a small restaurant that has a summer garden extension. ✉ *Mathenesserlaan 199–201, 3014 HC, Centrum* ☎ *010/436–3275* 🖷 *010/436–4410* ⊕ *www.hotelvanwalsum.nl* ⇨ *29 rooms, 3 apartments* ♿ *Restaurant, cable TV, Internet, bar, parking (fee); no a/c* ☰ *AE, DC, MC, V* ⊙ *CP.*

$–$$ 🏨 **Wilgenhof.** This charming place near the city zoo offers themed rooms, along with some simply decorated nooks. Sleep in a traditional Dutch bed box, a wine cellar, or in a jail cell–theme room, if you don't mind paying almost double for the spacious privilege. Because a bar and restaurant are attached, you won't have to leave the hotel for a drink. ✉ *Heemraadssingel 92–94, 3021 DE, Blijdorp* ☎ *010/425–4892* 🖷 *010/ 477–2611* ⇨ *40 rooms* ♿ *Restaurant, bar* ☰ *AE, MC, V.*

¢–$$ 🏨 **Home.** Located on the liveliest street in town, five minutes from the Museumpark, this hotel is right in the middle of Rotterdam's best dining, shopping, and nightlife. When you're back at the hotel, incredibly helpful staff are on hand for recommendations and assistance, making this a pad you really want to come back to. The rate drops by 50% if you stay longer than 30 days—and plenty of people do, as en-suite kitchenettes and sitting areas in each room make this a popular choice for longer stays. ✉ *Witte de Withstraat 38, 3012 BR, Witte de With* ☎ *010/ 414–2150* 🖷 *010/414–1690* ⇨ *80 rooms* ♿ *Kitchenettes, cable TV; no room phones* ☰ *AE, MC, V* ⊙ *EP.*

$ 🏨 **Bazar.** The well-traveled owner has created havens from his wanderings, with hot, deep colors evoking Turkey and Morocco throughout the rooms on the second floor, and motifs conjuring up Africa on the third and South America on the fourth floor. (The first floor houses the reception area.) Although there is an elevator, it goes only to the third floor. The restaurant of the same name on the ground floor has, needless to say, a very international menu. The location on the young, busy Witte de Withstraat draws a nicely "in" crowd to both hotel and restaurant. ✉ *Witte de Withstraat 16, 3012 BP, Witte de With* ☎ *010/206–5151* 🖷 *010/206–5159* ⇨ *18 rooms* ♿ *Restaurant, in-room data ports, minibars, cable TV, some pets allowed* ☰ *AE, DC, MC, V* ⊙ *CP.*

$ 🏨 **Emma.** At this hotel on social, busy Nieuwe Binnenweg, plenty of shops and nightspots are conveniently close; the nearest sidewalk café is right outside the hotel. This is the third generation of the Orsini family seeing to the comfort of the hotel's guests. Furnishings are modern, and there is an elevator. Staffed by a friendly and approachable team, this place offers special rates for groups and those staying longer. ⊠ *Nieuwe Binnenweg 6, 3015 BA, Centrum* ☎ *010/436–5533* 🖷 *010/436–7658* ⊕ *www.hotelemma.nl* ⤳ *24 rooms* ↳ *In-room data ports, minibars, cable TV, lounge, some pets allowed; no a/c* ▭ *AE, DC, MC, V* ¶◎¶ *CP.*

¢–$ ▦ **Baan.** This is a comfortable family-run hotel on the Coolsingel, overlooking the canal, and only five minutes from the waterside at Delfshaven. All the rooms are getting a face-lift in 2004. ⊠ *Rochussenstraat 345, 3023 DH, Centrum* ☎ *010/477–0555* 🖷 *010/476–9450* ⊕ *www. hotelbaan.nl* ⤳ *14 rooms* ▭ *AE, MC, V* ¶◎¶ *CP.*

¢ ▦ **De Clipper.** Perhaps the most unusual way to spend a night in Rotterdam is on a boat moored in one of the harbors in the center of the city. Because the skipper here can also take you off on sailing trips (book way in advance for this), you'll find that sometimes this hotel is literally missing. This is really a floating hostel: the rooms are shared in twos and fours—the cost is per person—so come in a group if you don't fancy mixing it up. ⊠ *Scheepmakershaven, Centrum* ☎ *06/5331–4244* ⊕ *www.hostelboat.com* ⤳ *8 rooms.* ▭ *MC, V* ¶◎¶ *CP.*

¢ ▦ **Stayokay Rotterdam.** If you're running on a budget, this modern hostel right in the middle of the city, between Delfshaven and the Museumpark, is just the ticket. Dorms are shared with three, five, or seven others, and you can use a fully equipped kitchen. If you're booking way in advance, you might be lucky and get one of the double rooms, best for extra privacy, where you have your own en-suite facilities. ⊠ *Rochussenstraat 107–109, 3015 EH, Centrum* ☎ *010/436–5763* 🖷 *010/436–5569* ⊕ *www.stayokay.com* ⤳ *2 rooms for 2 people, 20 shared dorm rooms* ↳ *Kitchen, data ports, bar, laundry facilities; no a/c* ▭ *MC, V* ¶◎¶ *CP.*

Nightlife & the Arts

The Arts

Rotterdam's arts calendar extends throughout the year. You can book tickets and find out what's on around town through the local tourist information office, the VVV. **VVV Rotterdam** (⊠ Coolsingel 67, Centrum, 3012 AC ☎ 0900/403–4065).

DANCE Rotterdam's resident modern dance company, **Scapino Ballet,** has the reputation of being one of the most formidably talented troupes in the country. It performs at **Rotterdamse Schouwburg** (⊠ Schouwburgplein 25, Centrum ☎ 010/404–4111 ⊕ www.scapinoballet.nl). The Scapino works regularly with guest choreographers, such as universally acclaimed Krisztina de Châtel. For more modern productions, look out for performances by the Rotterdamse Dansgroep, a contemporary dance group.

FILM Partly because of the annual avant-garde **International Film Festival Rotterdam,** held in late January–early February, there is a lot of general interest in film in this city—as a result, you have many screens to choose from. The **Pathé** (⊠ Schouwburgplein 101, Centrum ☎ 0900/1458) is the place to head for blockbusters. A film theater with a special program is the **Theater Lantaren/Venster** (⊠ Gouvernestraat 129–133, Centrum ☎ 010/277–2277), which shows art films in addition to hosting small-scale dance and theater performances. There's an open-air cinema at the Museumpark in September.

MUSIC Rotterdam's renowned concert orchestra is the excellent **Rotterdam Philharmonic Orchestra,** which performs at the large concert hall **De Doelen** (⊠ Schouwburgplein 50, Centrum ☎ 010/217–1707 ⊕ www.rpho.nl). Attracting 400,000 visitors a year, the orchestra is known for its adventurous range of music—this troupe can not only play Beethoven but has also tackled the score from the film *Jurassic Park.*

THEATER   The leading theater company of Rotterdam is **RO Theatergroup,** which performs at its own theater, **RO Theater** (✉ William Boothlaan 8, Meent ☎ 010/404–6888); the RO Theatergroup's subsidiary venue is the **Rotterdamse Schouwburg** (✉ Schouwburgplein 25, Centrum ☎ 010/404–4111). The majority of RO Theater's productions are in Dutch, as are, unfortunately, Onafhankelijk Toneel's, the city's other leader in the field. Cabaret and musicals in Rotterdam are performed at the two Luxor theaters, both of which offer many English-speaking performances. The **Luxor Theater** (✉ Kruiskade 10, Centrum ☎ 010/484–3333) features flamenco and other dance performances, mime artists, and musicals. The **Nieuwe Luxor Theater** (✉ Posthumalaan 1, Kop van Zuid ☎ 010/484–3333) has 1,500 seats, specifically to cater to major stage musicals and other popular events. The theater, one of The Netherlands' largest, was designed by Australian architect Peter Wilson and has a marvelous view of Rotterdam's harbor and skyline. Rotterdam's cultural climate facilitates the staging of productions from many semiprofessional groups, such as Turkish folk dance, classical Indian dance, and Capoeira Brazilian martial art troupes. The **Theater Zuidplein** (✉ Zuidplein 60–64, Charlois ☎ 010/203–0203) is particularly well known for its multicultural program.

Nightlife

To get your bearings and find your way around the party scene, look out for glossy party fliers in cafés, record stores, and clothes shops selling clubbing gear. The best nights tend to be Thursday to Saturday, 11 PM to 5 AM. Most venues have a clubbing floor, with DJs working the crowd and more ambient rooms for smoking or just plain relaxing. From hard-core techno—whose birthplace was right here in Rotterdam—to early-hour chill-out cafés, there is a wide gamut of nighttime entertainment. Innovation is the name of the game—just take a look at the city's 1980s elektro band Kiem, famed for using a drum kit created from used parts of an abandoned ship in the harbor. West Kruiskade (also known as China Town) is the place to go if you want lively bars and music from around the world. Nieuwe Binnenweg and Witte de Withstraat have many busy late-night cafés and clubs. Oude Haven is particularly popular with students, and the Schouwburgplein is favored by visitors to the nearby theaters and cinemas. Stadshuisplein has a number of pretty tacky discos and bars. The Kop van Zuid district is still developing, but there are one or two bars worth visiting.

CAFÉS   **Breakaway** (✉ Karel Doormanstraat 1, near Centraal Station, Centrum ☎ 010/233–0922) is busy, with a young international crowd, and the nearest you'll get to a Dutch take on an American bar. **Café Rotterdam** (✉ Wilhelminakade 699, Kop van Zuid ☎ 010/290–8440) is on the Wilhelminakade in the up-and-coming Kop van Zuid district, between the architectural designs of Sir Norman Foster and Renzo Piano. This former shipping terminal designed by Bakema is now a massive meeting center, with a large café and fantastic view of the white Erasmus Bridge. **De Consul** (✉ Westersingel 28B, Museumpark ☎ 010/436–3323) offers movies, as well as new age and pop music. With two floors, music drifts through the place from the bar upstairs. **De Schouw** (✉ Witte de Withstraat 80, Witte de With ☎ 010/412–4253), an erstwhile brown café and former journalists' haunt, is now a trendy brown bar with a mix of artists and students. **Hallo** (✉ Stadhuisplein 41, Meent ☎ 010/414–6400) attracts a late-night, chill-out crowd; with a well-stocked bar and an intimate dance floor the wide-ranging music gets people taking to the floor.

CLUBS   Three floors and one of the best live music lineups make **Nighttown** (✉ West Kruiskade 26–28, Centrum ☎ 010/436–1210 💳 €11.35–€18, €1.80

membership fee required) *the* place to be in Rotterdam. If you can't get tickets for the big-band nights, make sure you catch the after-event party, definitely not to be missed. Music ranges from hip-hop to drum and bass, funk, techno, and pop. The adjoining café Fresh Up has very mellow music Thursday night, with R&B till late. **Now & Wow** (⊠ Graansilo, Maashaven ZZ 2, Rotterdam Zuid/Maashaven ☎ 010/477–1074 ⊕ www.now-wow.com) is the wildest addition to the clubbing scene in Rotterdam. It's in a warehouse by metro station Maashaven. On Saturday night, a weekly MTC Party (Music Takes Control) pushes the envelope for excess. In a former pedestrian tunnel, the **Blauwe Vis** (⊠ Weena-Zuid 33, Centrum ☎ 010/213–4243), or Blue Fish, is a seafood restaurant until the late hours, when the mood changes and the music really kicks in with soul, jazz, and funk. The long, narrow **Club Vibes** (⊠ Westersingel 50A, Museumpark ☎ 010/436–6389) has a friendly staff who chat at the bar to early punters—this is another place you shouldn't arrive at before 1:30 AM. Music is mostly 1970s and 1980s, with some more mainstream 1990s nights. **Rotown** (⊠ Nieuwe Binnenweg 19, Museumpark ☎ 010/436–2669), a high-style restaurant, has new-talent bands playing on Saturday night.

GAY & LESBIAN BARS
Very much part of the late-night scene, **Gay Palace** (⊠ Schiedamsesingel 139, Centrum ☎ 010/414–1486) attracts crowds of young gay and lesbian Rotterdammers to its large dance floor. **Club Vibes** (⊠ Westersingel 50, Museumpark ☎ 010/436–6389) hosts gay-only nights on Sunday.

JAZZ
In August the **Heineken Jazz Festival** (☎ 010/413–3972) fills Rotterdam's streets and cafés with music and bopping youth. **Dizzy** (⊠ 's-Gravendijkswal 127–129, 's-Gravendijkwal ☎ 010/477–3014 ⊕ www.dizzy.nl) is *the* jazz café if you appreciate live performances. A big terrace out back hosts both Dutch and international musicians every Tuesday and Sunday. The café also serves good, reasonably priced food. Come early if you want a seat. Concerts and jamming sessions are free.

POP & ROCK
For mega-events, choose between the **Ahoy,** which holds pop concerts and large-scale operas, and **De Kuip,** Rotterdam's major football stadium, which boasts of its Bob Dylan, Rolling Stones, and U2 concerts. Tickets for both venues sell out very quickly, but De Kuip has a better sound system. Despite being able to seat more than 51,000 people, concerts at **De Kuip/Feyenoord Stadion** (⊠ Van Zandvlietplein 1, Kop van Zuid ☎ 010/492–9444 or 010/482–4843) usually sell out. **Ahoy** (⊠ Ahoyweg 10, Zuidplein ☎ 010/293–3300) hosts major pop concerts for icons such as Santana and Ozzy Osbourne, but also hosts classical philharmonic orchestras and top jazz performers.

Sports & the Outdoors

Participant Sports & Outdoor Activities

BICYCLING
You can rent bicycles in Rotterdam from the **Rijwiel Shop** (⊠ Stationsplein 1, Centrum ☎ 010/412–6220).

JOGGING, RIDING, ROWING, SAILING, SURFING & SWIMMING
All the parks in the city have jogging routes, and you can ride a horse in the **Kralingse Bos** (Kralingse Wood), with its stables—take Bus 38 from Centraal Station to Corroswijk and get out at the last stop. The wood has a big lake, the **Kralingse Plas,** which is a favorite place for windsurfing, sailing, or just swimming. It even has a sandy beach. Surfers, sailors, rowers, and swimmers head out to the **Zevenhuizer Plas** when the weather gets really hot—take Bus 175, and stop at Wollefoppenweg in Oude Verlaat. There is also a lake and beach here.

MARATHON
Since the first **Rotterdam Marathon,** run in May 1981, there is now a 10-km (6-mi) amateur event. Largely because of its flat route, it is one of

the fastest marathons in the world. If you want to take part, pick up an application form from the VVV.

Spectator Sports

BASEBALL   Every two years the international **World Port Baseball tournament** is held in the Neptunus Family Stadium; the next tournament will be held in 2005. ⊠ *Neptunus Familiestadion, Abraham van Stolkweg 31, Blijdorp.*

SOCCER   Rotterdam has three professional "football" clubs, the biggest being Feyenoord; Their home stadium is **Feyenoord Stadion** (⊠ Van Zandvlietplein 1, Kop van Zuid ☎ 010/482–4843 or 010/492–9444). If football is a passion, take a guided tour around the stadium, popularly called "De Kuip."

TENNIS   The ABN-AMRO sponsors the **World Tennis Tournament** (☎ 0900/235–2469 ⊕ www.abnamrowtt.nl), a top Rotterdam event on the championship circuit, attracting world-class tennis players and more than 85,000 spectators every February to the Ahoy Stadium.

Shopping

Rotterdam is the number one shopping city in the south of Holland. Its famous Lijnbaan and Beurstraverse shopping centers, as well as the surrounding areas, offer a dazzling variety of shops and department stores. Rotterdam is where the shopping mall was born: the opening of the Lijnbaan—which dissects the pedestrianized area between the Stadhuis and the Schouwburg plein in the center of the city—in 1953 heralded the launch of dedicated shopping precincts (that is, separated from housing). It continues to be a commercial success, although you'll find the buildings very dull aesthetically. Here you'll find many of the biggest chains in Holland, such as Mango, MEXX, Morgan, Invito, and Sacha.

The archways and fountains of the Beurstraverse—at the bottom of the Coolsingel, near the Stadhuis—make this newer, pedestrianized area more pleasing to walk around. It is now one of the most expensive places to rent shop space, and like most other unusual buildings in Rotterdam has a nickname: Koopgoot, which can be taken to mean "shopping channel" (if you like it) and "shopping gutter" (if you don't). The majority of the stores are chains, with branches of Bennetton, Sting, Zara, Dockers, the Body Shop, and Esprit. The two main department stores have entrances on the lower-street level: Hema and the more luxurious Bijenkorf. Van Oldenbarneveldtstraat and Nieuwe Binnenweg are the places to shop if you want something different. There is a huge variety of alternative fashion to be found here.

Department Stores

De Bijenkorf (⊠ Coolsingel 105, Centrum ☎ 010/282–3700) is a favorite department store, designed by Marcel Breuer (the great Bauhaus architect) with an exterior that looks like its name, a beehive. The best department store in Rotterdam, it covers four floors. There's a good range of clothing and shoes from both designers and the store's own label, plus a selection of cosmetics and perfume on the ground floor, with a Chill Out department on the same floor geared toward street- and club-wear; here, on some Saturdays a DJ keeps it mellow, and you can even get a haircut at in-store Kinki Kappers. What De Bijenkorf is well known for is its excellent household-goods line, ranging from lights and furniture to sumptuous fabrics and rugs. Check out the second-floor restaurant with its view out over the Coolsingel and Naum Gabo's sculpture *Constructie.* For less expensive wares, head to **Hema** (⊠ Beursplein 2, Centrum ☎ 010/282–9900), popular with the ever-practical Dutch, who appreciate quality goods at low prices. Tools, cosmetics, and undergarments are the best buys here. Slightly more upmarket than Hema is **V&D** (✉ Hoogstraat 185, Centrum ☎ 0900/235–8363), great for household goods, stationery, and other everyday necessities. Rest your tired tootsies and admire the city view from the rooftop restaurant, La Place, where you can indulge in a wide selection of snacks and full meals.

Indoor Markets

In a former warehouse, the **Konmar** (✉ De Vijf Werelddelen 33, Vrij Entrepot bldg., Kop van Zuid ☎ 010/290–9988) is the city's largest supermarket, with an abundance of food from around the world.

Shopping Districts & Streets

Exclusive shops and boutiques can be found in areas such as the Entrepotgebied, Delfshaven, Witte de Withstraat, Nieuwe and Oude Binnenweg, and Van Oldenbarneveldtstraat. West Kruiskade and its vicinity offer a wide assortment of multicultural products in the many Chinese, Suriname, Mediterranean, and Arabic shops. The shops in the city center are open every Sunday afternoon, and late-night shopping—until 9— in Rotterdam is every Friday.

Specialty Stores

There are numerous specialty stores across town, and depending on what you are looking for, you should be able to find it somewhere.

ANTIQUES   Look on both sides of the **Voorhaven** in Delfshaven, and along **Aelbrechtskolk,** also in Delfshaven, for the best antiques. On Sunday head to the **Schiedamsdijk,** where you can expect to find a market that specializes in antiques and old books, open noon–5.

ART GALLERIES   Many galleries provide the opportunity both to look at art and to buy it. These can be found especially along the Westersingel and in the Museumpark area. The top gallery address is With de Withstraat, lined with numerous cafés, making it an ideal street to spend some time window-shopping.

Mama Showroom for Media and Moving Art (✉ Witte de Withstraat 29–31, Witte de With ☎ 010/433–0695 or 010/233–1313 ⊕ www.mamamedia.nl) encourages the collaboration of emerging, experimental artists. If you're looking for new, exciting, and innovative art with high standards, you'll find it here. Some of the work will shock, some will make you laugh out loud in delight, but all of it is art-critic-worthy. Consider film- and video-based art by the Dutch Galleon of Mayhem or the inflatable sculptures by a group of "artoonists," including a giant rabbit by Florentijn Hofman. The gallery is open Wednesday to Sunday 1–6.

BOOKS   **Donner Boeken** (✉ Lijnbaan 150, Centrum ☎ 010/413–2070) is the biggest bookstore in Rotterdam. Its 10 floors include an excellent range of English-language books, which are distributed throughout the shop under specific headings.

DESIGN   **Regalo** (✉ Beurstraverse 115, Centrum ☎ 010/213–0871) sells quirky products and fun things from Alessi and other great design signatures. The owner builds her collection around her regular customers' tastes. Serious collectors go mad at **Beljon** (✉ Oude Binnenweg 102, Centrum ☎ 010/2282–7539 ⊕ www.beljon.com), which stocks new and secondhand retro-style furniture. The self-styled "mini-department store" carries avant-garde jewelry and footwear as well as clothing for men and women from Danish design label Bruuns Bazaar. More like a museum of modern art and home furnishings than a mere gallery, the **Galerie ECCE** (✉ Witte de Withstraat 17a–19a, Witte de With ☎ 010/413–9770) has an exclusive collection of ultramodern furniture, lamps, and glassware from Dutch and European designers and offers a custom-design service. You'll find a variety of smaller unique design items, suitable for gifts, such as coasters and wall sconces. The gallery has a new exhibition of paintings and sculpture every two months, and also specializes in the production of trompe l'oeil wall paintings. **Dille & Kamille** (⊠ Korte Hoogstraat 22, Centrum ☏ 010/411–3338) is a fantastic store for anyone interested in cooking. From herbs to sturdy wooden spoons to recipe books, this is a browser's heaven. It is one of the few shops in The Netherlands that still carries traditional Dutch household items, such as a huge water kettle to make tea for 25, a nutmeg mill, or a *zeepklopper,* a device that holds a bar of soap and can whip up bubbles—a forerunner to liquid dish-washing detergent. You should also walk through the **Entrepot Harbor design district,** alongside the marina at Kop van Zuid, where there are several interior-design stores.

FASHION For fashion suggestions, start with **Sister Moon** (⊠ Nieuwe Binnenweg 89b, Centrum ☏ 010/436–1508), which has a small collection of exclusive hip clothing for men and women in the party scene; part of the boutique is devoted to trendy secondhand togs. **Rigter** (⊠ Oude Binnenweg 129, Centrum ☏ 010/413–3282) has fabulous men's shoes, from its own brand to Dutch shoe king Van Bommel, making this a must-stop for a pair of funky, original street-wear. Graffiti artists favor **Urban Unit** (⊠ Nieuwe Binnenweg 63b, Centrum ☏ 010/436–3825), loving the look of the men's sneakers and street-wear on sale (while stocking up on spray cans and other graffiti supplies). On Van Oldenbarneveldtstraat the prices rise as the stores get more label based. **Van Dijk** (⊠ Van Oldenbarneveldtstraat 105, Centrum ☏ 010/411–2644) stocks Costume National and Helmut Lang, and the owner, Wendela, has two of her own design labels. You can find trendy shoes, bags, and accessories here and have plenty of room to try on clothes in the *paskamers* (fitting rooms) Where there's fashion, there's music: keep in mind that Holland's largest concentration of international record stores can be found on the Nieuwe Binnenweg, ranging from techno to ambient, rock to Latin and African.

Street Markets

The expansive **Binnenrotteplein,** between Laurenskerk and Blaak railway station, is home to one of the largest street markets in the country, every Tuesday and Saturday from 9 to 5, Friday from noon to 5. Among the 520 stalls you can find a flea market, book market, household items, used goods, food, fish, clothes, and flowers. From April to December, a fun shopping market with 200 stands is held on Sunday from noon to 5. There are often special attractions for children, and you can chill out on the terrace.

Brielle

 22 km (14 mi) west of Rotterdam.

A popular side trip from Rotterdam, the town of Brielle is famous as the redoubt of the legendary Sea Beggars and, as such, remains a historic haven worth persevering past Rotterdam's industrial harbors to reach. Look out for the wind turbines that herald your approach to the coast. Upon arrival, you'll find that the narrow lanes weaving through Brielle are relatively traffic free, meaning it is a town made for exploring on foot; its restored fortress girdle makes a walk around the ramparts equally possible. By car from Rotterdam head west, following signs for the Hoek van Holland on the A15, then the N15, until Brielle is signposted. By public transport from Rotterdam Centraal, take the metro to Spikanesse; then take Bus 100 or 103.

Brielle prospered throughout the Middle Ages, owing to its location on the Goote River, near the mouth of the Maas River, which provided direct access to the sea. When the Goote silted up, Brielle lost the source of its wealth; the town was on the brink of drifting into obscurity when the provinces of The Netherlands revolted against Spanish rule. Protestant rebels (called *Geuzen*—beggars—by the Spanish) led the 1568 uprising, launching pirate attacks and seizing Spanish galleons. On April 1, 1572, the Sea Beggars unexpectedly converged outside Brielle with 5,000 men in 36 boats. They broke into the Spanish garrison, overwhelming them so totally that their victory inspired the Dutch people to renew their efforts to oust the Spanish.

The annual **Liberation Day** (Bevrijdingsdag in Dutch) festivities commemorating Brielle's release are not to be missed. Every year on April 1, the locals turn back the clock to 1572 to commemorate the liberation from the Spanish, filling the streets with straw and selling traditional crafts from stalls across town. Locals dress as Spaniards and Sea Beggars to reenact Brielle's liberation, battering down the town gates complete with cannon and musket fire and hand-to-hand fighting. Inevitably, the Spanish lose and their leaders are paraded through the streets in wooden cages. The day ends in a celebration worthy of the Middle Ages, with the mass consumption of spit-roasted meat and goblets of wine.

Today, Brielle makes a good open-air museum, with its narrow streets and grassy-banked fortifications, not to mention the numerous historic monuments. The imposing 15th-century **Sint Catharijnekerk** (St. Catherine's church) has witnessed a substantial part of Dutch royal history. In 1688, Mary Stuart waved good-bye from the church tower to her departing husband, William III, who was soon to become king of England. From the top, 318 steps up, you can see the Maas River and Rotterdam harbor. Local heroes from the Liberation Day battles are immortalized in stained-glass windows. ⊠ *Sint Catharijneplein* ☎ *0181/475475* ⊕ *www.catharijnekerk.nl* ⊠ €1 ⊘ *June–Sept., daily 1–4:30; July and Aug., Sat. 11–4:30, Sun. services only.*

The **Historisch Museum Den Briel** (Brielle Historical Museum) is in a 17th-century former town jail on the third floor; the voice of a "17th-century prisoner" addresses you (in Dutch) via a loudspeaker. Among historical retellings of Brielle's liberation are paintings by local artists and a re-created medieval marketplace on the ground floor. ⊠ *Markt 1* ☎ *0181/ 475475* ⊕ *www.historischmuseumdenbriel.nl* ⊠ €2 ⊘ *Apr.–Oct., Tues.–Fri. 10–5, Sat. 10–4, Sun. noon–4; Nov.–Mar., Tues.–Sat. 10–4.*

At the end of the Voorstraat are some noted centuries-old **Asyplein Hofjes** (almshouses), ornamented with a sculpted sea nymph that, surrounded by roses and ornamental trees, looks eternally in the direction from which the rebels came to liberate the town from the Spanish in the 16th century.

When the weather's good, tables from **De Hoofdwacht** (⊠ Markt 7), the largest bar on the central markt, spill across the square. Don't miss the ornate bell tower on top of the former Town Hall opposite, which now houses the Brielle VVV and the Historical Museum. The tightly packed buildings provide shelter from winds whipping off the nearby Brielse Meer (Brielle Lake), making the café into an ideal break stop.

Where to Eat & Stay

$–$$ ✕ **Pablo.** At this Indonesian restaurant the menu changes regularly, with the *Pablootjes* (little specials) always well worth trying. ⊠ *Voorstraat 87–91* ☎ *0181/412960* ⊟ *AE* ⊘ *Closed Mon.*

¢–$$ ✗ **La Plu.** Situated on a traffic-free shopping street, this trendy black, white, and red eetcafé serves everything from pizzas to steaks and doesn't neglect vegetarians. Good eats, reasonable prices, and a garden terrace make this a popular spot. ⊠ *Voorstraat 41* ☎ *0181/415230* ▭ *V* ⊙ *Closed Mon. and Tues.*

$–$$ ✗⌑ **Hotel De Zalm.** A very popular town-house hotel catering to smart business visitors from the nearby docks during the week, De Zalm offers special rates during the weekend. The inspired restaurant (closed Sunday) makes the absolute most of Brielle's location, offering an extensive range of North Sea fish; savor *zeetong* (sole) with chunky Belgian chips and salad for lunch or opt for a lightly baked monkfish in leek sauce for dinner. ⊠ *Voorstraat 4, 3132 BJ* ☎ *0181/413–388* ⌂ *0181/417712* ↵ *37 rooms* ♿ *Cable TV, in-room data ports* ▭ *AE, DC, MC, V* ❏❘ *BP.*

Festivals

On the second Saturday in June, **Street Theater** takes over Brielle when miming mummers prance about the streets. The last Sunday in July sees the **Brielle Blues,** a popular open-air event that brings floods of music lovers to town.

Kinderdijk

★ ➄ *55 km (32 mi) southwest of Amsterdam.*

Once you leave the urban center of Rotterdam behind, you quickly find yourself in rural surroundings, with meadows, greenhouses, and farmhouses. In one such area, in the Alblasserwaard—a polder enclosed by the Rivers Noord and Lek—you come across the Kinderdijk Windmills, traditionally one of the most famous tourist sights in Holland. Its description so often gets mutated to sound saccharine sweet that many visitors discount a visit, mistakenly thinking it must be faux. The name (which means "child's dike") comes from a legend that probably has a lot to do with its chocolate-boxy aura: a baby was washed up here in a cradle after the great floods of 1421, with a cat sitting on its tummy to keep them both from tumbling out. Nevertheless, the sight of 19 mills under sail is magnificently, romantically impressive. The mills loom large, even in the distance partly because they are: eight of the mills are among the largest in the world. They line Het Nieuwe Waterschap in pairs, each facing another on opposite banks.

The 19 windmills date back to the 18th century, and the site is on the UNESCO world cultural heritage list. The mills enable the Dutch to live on reclaimed riverbeds. Water had to be drained from the land, and 150 years ago 10,000 windmills were in operation across the country. In 1740, 19 mills were built in the meadows of Kinderdijk, to drain the excess water from the Alblasserwaard polders, below sea level. The mill sails harnessed the energy of the wind to scoop up the water. Electrical pumping stations have now taken over water management, but the majority of mills operate at certain times—for the delight of tourists. The mills are open in rotation, so there is always one interior to visit during opening hours. Looking around the inside of a mill provides a fascinating insight into how the millers and their families lived. Tours can be taken of the mechanical workings if you want to get a closer look.

The mills are under sail from 2 to 5 on the first Saturday in May and June, then every Saturday in July and August. Throughout the second week in September the mills are illuminated at night, really pulling out the tourist stops. You can walk around the mills whenever you like; the opening times given below refer to visiting the interior of the mill. From

Amsterdam, 55 km (33 mi) southwest, the mills are just to the north-east of the town. By public transport, leave from Amsterdam Centraal Station to Utrecht, and then take Bus 154 (end destination Rotterdam). From Rotterdam Centraal, take the metro to Rotterdam Zuidplein, then Bus 154 (end destination Utrecht). ⊠ *Molenkade, Kinderdijk* ☎ *078/691–5179* ☝ *Interior of mill €1.50* ⊙ *Interior Apr.–Sept., daily 9:30–5:30.*

Where to Stay

There are just a few restaurants in Kinderdijk, so you might consider bringing a picnic if the weather is good.

¢ 🏨 **Hotel Kinderdijk.** To the west of Kinderdijk is this unremarkable lit-tle hotel. It's nice enough, especially if you want to witness sunrise or sunset over the mills. ⊠ *W. Kinderdijk 361, 2953 XV Alblasserdam* ☎ *078/691–2425* 🖷 *078/691–5071* ➱ *12 rooms* ♿ *Cable TV, some pets allowed; no a/c, no room phones* ⊟ *AE, MC, V* ⦿ *CP.*

The Outdoors

From May to October you can join a guided tour and take a half-hour boat trip out to see the mills using the **Rederij Vos and Zn. lines** (☎ 078/ 691–5179), based off Molenkade in Kinderdijk, which run these tours daily 10–5.

COMPLETING THE RANDSTAD ARC

Continuing the circuit starting from Amsterdam and extending from Haar-lem to Delft and on to Rotterdam, any grand tour of central Holland should head back northwest past the famous town of Gouda to the province of Utrecht. Although this is the smallest province in the coun-try, it has such a variety of geographical features for the visitor that it has often been called "Holland in a nutshell." It is in this area that the late Queen Juliana chose to live, so that she could bring up her four daugh-ters in peaceful and unspoiled home life. True, they lived in a palace, but Soestdijk Palace is also a home, just as Holland's ruler was both queen and mother. Utrecht is now a bustling modern town, but it is studded with some impressive relics of history, including the Dom Tower of the "church that isn't there." Northward lies the garden district of Gooiland, a tranquil overture to the nearby bustle of Amsterdam and such sump-tuous treasures as the Kasteel de Haar, home to the Barons van Zuylen.

Dordrecht

54 *23 km (15 mi) southeast of Rotterdam.*

Claiming to be the oldest town in the province of Zuid Holland, Dor-drecht lies just east of the main road leading south to Antwerp and Brus-sels. Thanks to its location in the midst of a tangle of Rhine and Maas waterways, it was once among the most important towns in Holland. Fortified in 1271, it was badly damaged by the St. Elizabeth flood of 1421, an event recalled by a stained-glass window in the town's Grote Kerk.

Today the city is a mix of old and new. Much of it is given over to ship-building and yachting facilities, but the old sector is worth visiting along the riverfront (indeed, the best view of the city is from the oppo-site, north bank) and in the streets leading back to the Voorstraat. Dom-inating the scene is the imposing mass of the 15th-century **Grote Kerk/ Onze Lieve Vrouwekerk** (Great Church/Our Lady Church), whose tower is a good 6 feet off the vertical and whose chancel bends left to sym-bolize the head of Christ inclining toward his left shoulder. A window pictures the 1421 disaster, and the huge 2,600-pipe organ has a 10-second echo. The interior is astonishing in its whiteness, accented by a mahogany sounding board and a bronze screen (which used to be kept brilliantly polished by the local schoolchildren). It was in this church that the Protestant synod met in 1618 to settle the controversy between Arminius and Gomaurus, two professors of theology at Leiden. The outcome was Prince Maurits's choosing for Gomaurus, who believed in a less strict Calvinism. From the church, follow the Voorstraat (on the far side of the canal), with old houses at every turn, to the Groenmarkt, where at No. 31 you'll find the city's oldest house (1550). ⊠ *Lange Geldersekade 2* ☎ *078/614–4660* 🎫 *Contribution requested* ⊙ *Apr.–Oct., Tues.–Sat. 10:30–4:30, Sun. noon–4; Nov. and Dec., 1st and 3rd Sat. of the month noon–4.*

★ To the west of the Grote Kerk, on the quay of the Nieuwe Haven (New Harbor) is the **Museum Mr Simon van Gijn.** This lavish 18th-century house was occupied from 1864 to 1922 by art collector Simon van Gijn, who left his home and collection to the city. There are magnificent period rooms on view, along with—up the stairs in the attic—the childless banker's extensive antique toy collection. ⊠ *Nieuwe Haven 29–30* ☎ *078/639–8200* 🎫 *€5* ⊙ *Tues.–Sun. 11–5.*

Stroll up the tree-lined Steegoversloot in the town center (which runs from the Spuihaven harbor-canal to the Wijnhaven harbor-canal) to have a surreptitious peek into the working artists' and potters' studios, many of which are open to the public. Keep your eyes peeled for a narrow lane leading off in the direction of **Het Hof** (The Court), originally an Augustian monastery but rebuilt in the 16th century after a fire. In the Statenzaal, a video presentation takes you back to the meeting of the First Assembly of the Seven Provinces. Cloister gardens offer an island of calm. Leave the Hof via the west entrance; here on Hofstraat, take time to look at the extraordinary terrace, probably the closest thing you'll see to gingerbread-biscuit houses, each with individual decoration that, in a pinch, could be colored icing. ⊠ *Het Hof* ☎ *078/613–4626* 🎫 *Free* ⊙ *Tues.–Sat. 1–5.*

The leading sight on Museumstraat is the **Dordrechts Museum,** stuffed with many paintings, drawings, and prints by Netherlandish artists, especially native son and fabled landscape artist Albert Cuyp and, to boot, works by his father, Jacob. Star names here include Ferdinand Bol and Nicolaes Maes—famed as pupils of Rembrandt. The collection extends to the 20th century, and there are some important works on view by Karel Appel. ⊠ *Museumstraat 40* ☎ *078/648–2148* 🎫 *€5* ⊙ *Tues.–Sun. 11–5.*

On the Maas side of the Maartensgaat harbor is the statuesque **Catharijnepoort** (Catherine's Gate), one of two medieval town gates, which takes you through the city walls to a wharf and dates from 1652. At the far end of the Wolwevershaven you come to the **Groothoofdspoort,** the much larger and extensively decorated city gate. This one leads out onto a vast jetty. It was originally built between 1440 and 1450, but what you see now is a Renaissance fill-in around the medieval archway. Nonetheless, the colorful display of shields and balconied tower certainly make it worth the walk. Through the gate you stand overlooking the exact confluence of the Oude Maas, the Noord, and the Merwede rivers—often touted as one of the best river prospects in all the land.

Where to Eat & Stay

$ ✕ **Comme Çi–Comme Ça.** Choose your restaurant carefully, especially around honeypot areas like the Groothoofdspoort, as some places rely more on their location, trading it for a decent menu, interior, and staff attitude. Happily, for casual dining and reasonable prices, this restaurant has no rival. The terrace looks out on the harbor, and even when indoors, you have the feeling you're dining on a boat. The food isn't adventurous—mainly steaks and fish dishes—but their accompaniments are interesting, such as a pine-nut sauce. The friendly chef is more than flexible, creating special menus for large groups on request. ⊠ *Groothoofd 8* ☎ *078/613–0616* ☰ *AE, DC, MC, V.*

$–$$ ⊞ **Hotel Dordrecht.** Opposite Dordrecht's historic harbor, this large town-house hotel provides comfortable rooms with tasteful interiors and slick service that is hard to beat, especially given the price range of the four-poster beds with hot tub en suite. An in-house chef serves dinner. ⊠ *Achterhakkers 72, 3311 JA* ☎ *078/613–6011* 🖨 *078/613–7470* ➷ *21 rooms* ♿ *Restaurant, in-room data ports, minibars, cable TV, bar, some pets allowed* ☰ *AE, DC, MC, V.*

Festivals & Markets
Dordrecht's historic setting lends itself to cultural events. The Italian opera **Belcanto Festival** is held in Het Hof in late summer, and **Jazz Days** floods the city with more music lovers. **Dordt in Stoom** is a biannual, three-day event that attracts steam power enthusiasts. The annual **Antiquarian Book Market** is held in early July, and a **Christmas Market** in December (check with VVV for time, location, and ticket details for individual events).

Sports & the Outdoors
Take a **Waterrondje Dordt** (☎ 078/613–0094) or a canal tour, of Dordrecht on board a launch through the harbors. Tours start on the hour from the Wijnbrug and last an hour. Buy tickets from the booth at the door of the restaurant De Stroper, next to the tour boat's docking area; tours are offered mid-April to the end of May and September to October, daily 2–5; June to August, 11–5, with tickets costing €5. About 5 km (3 mi) outside the city center is the **Biesbosch**, an enormous marshlands area with meadows and reed lands, intersected by rivers and streams. Swim in one of the natural pools, or bike on cycle tracks that rollerbladers can also use; between the mountain-bike tracks there's even a golf course. Hire canoes or join a boat trip along one of the navigable rivers, from the Biesbosch Visitor Center. There is no adequate public transport to the Biesbosch from Dordrecht, though Bus 5 can take you to within 45 minutes' walk of the **Biesbosch Centrum Dordrecht.** ⊠ *Baanhoekweg 53, 3313 LP* ☎ *078/630–5353* ⊕ *www.dordt.nl/ biesboschcentrum* ⊗ *Visitor Center year-round Tues.-Sunday 9–5; May–June Mon.1–5; July–Aug. Mon. 9–5.*

You can rent bikes right next to the station, from **Zwaan** (⊠ Stationsplein 6 ☎ 078/635–6830).

Shopping
Dordrecht is known for its antiques shops, many of them situated along the Voorstraat (where, in 1877, Vincent van Gogh is said to have worked for a few months in a bookshop). As you walk up toward the Groothoofd area, prices tend to drop as shops have a more secondhand, rummage-sale appearance. Late-night shopping is on Thursday, and shops are open on the last Sunday of the month.

Gouda

55 *53 km (33 mi) southwest of Amsterdam, 13 km (8 mi) southeast of Rotterdam.*

There is more to Gouda than the rich cheese that made it famous (pronounced *howdah* and not *goo*-da). A walk through the town is a lesson in Dutch history: a clock on the east side of the Gothic Town Hall tells the story of its founding in July 1272. When the clock strikes, every half hour, figures representing spectators and standard-bearers emerge from the clock's castle door. After the chimes ring out, a miniature Count Floris appears and hands a charter to a town official. The city's most famous son was the medieval philosopher Erasmus, the offspring of a local priest—so they say; some historians say Erasmus may have been conceived in Gouda, but he was actually born in Rotterdam. Gouda took full advantage of its commercial rights, prospering on its trade in beer, then diversifying into pipe making and ceramics—by about 1750 about half the population worked in the pottery industry.

According to popular myth, in winter Rotterdammers would undertake a challenge to skate up to Gouda on frozen canals, buy a pipe, and skate home without breaking the fragile stem. Gouda's candles are another city classic: the industry didn't become dominant until the mid-19th century, but it's honored in the 20,000-plus candles used to illuminate the square during the annual Christmas tree ceremony, **Gouda bij Kerstlicht,** or Gouda by Candlelight. This lovely event is held sometime in mid-December, and it's a memorable occasion to see all the electric lights in the town turned off, with flickering candles the only illumination. Over the centuries, periods of prosperity were followed by economic collapse, particularly under French occupation in the 1790s. By the early 19th century, once-rich Gouda had become synonymous with "beggar." But the industrial revolution restored its fortunes, and one of the world's largest multinationals, Unilever, actually started off making candles and soap here.

One of the quaintest of all town halls in Holland is Gouda's hyper-Gothic **Stadhuis,** built in 1450 and now the focal point of the market square. With its icicle-like spires, pretty shutters, and melodious carillon, it's the ultimate photo-op: no wonder couples flock here for weddings. Inside are ornately carved marble fireplaces and 17th-century tapestries in the **Trouwzaal** (Marriage Room); if you head up to the exhibition space on the first floor, you have the history of the city traced through drawings, photographs, and maps. As you walk around to the main entrance on the southwest side, don't miss the northeast facade. You'll notice locals in the know walking up the left-hand side of the double staircase at the entrance, because convicted criminals used the right-hand one on their way to the gallows. ⊠ *Markt 1* ☎ *0182/588475* ◷ *Weekdays 10–4, Sat. 11–3.*

The **De Waag** (Weigh House) is behind the Stadhuis in a building built in 1668. In case you can't guess what it was used for, the enormous gable stone shows cheeses being weighed. Today this is a **Kaasexposeum** (Cheese Museum), with interactive presentations about dairy products and cheeses. The café even serves fresh buttermilk. Downstairs, on one of the original scales, an attendant weighs young visitors and quotes their weight in an equivalent number of cheeses. ⊠ *Markt 35–36* ☎ *0182/ 529996* ◷ *€2* ◷ *Tues.–Sun. 1–5.*

★ **Sint Janskerk** (St. John's church), called the Grote Kerk (Great Church), is the longest in Holland and has memorable stained-glass windows, which some connoisseurs rank right up there with those of Chartres for delicacy of color and boldness of design. Most of the building dates from the late 15th century; very little has changed since the tower was finished in 1600. The stained glass dates mostly from the 16th century. Miraculously, the windows survived the Protestant iconoclasts, the French revolutionaries, and World War II. Altogether, the church contains 70 stained-glass windows, some as high as 60 feet. In addition to depicting John the Baptist and Christ, they portray Philip II, the King of

Spain, and Mary Tudor, the Queen of England. The most recent window was created in 1947 as an expression of joy at the liberation of The Netherlands from German occupation. The magnificent organ dates from the early 18th century and is still played every week between April and September. On Sunday, the church is open only to worshippers. ⊠ *Achter de Kerk 16* ☎ *0182/512684* 🎫 *€1.90* ⊘ *Mar.–Oct., Mon.–Sat. 9–5; Nov.–Feb., Mon.–Sat. 10–4.*

★ The **Museum Het Catharina Gasthuis** (Catharina Hospital Museum) is housed in the Catharina Hospital, which was founded in 1302. In the 17th century the front was replaced with a classical facade, most probably the work of Pieter Post, who also built the Weigh House. The museum's collections cover nearly every aspect of life in Gouda: 16th-century altarpieces from the church, antique toys, a reconstructed 17th-century pharmacy, kitchen, and classroom; paintings by artists of the Barbizon and Hague schools; a fine work by Jan Steen, *The Quack*; and applied arts from the 16th to the 20th century. ⊠ *Oosthaven 9* ☎ *0182/588434* 🎫 *€3.60* ⊘ *Mon.–Sat. 10–5, Sun. noon–5.*

The **Stedelijk Museum De Moriaan** (Blackamoor Municipal Museum) houses collections of pottery and clay pipes in a Late Gothic building that was originally a sugar refinery and later belonged to a company selling spices and tobacco. Gouda's pipe industry was started 300 years ago by British soldiers who were stationed in Holland as mercenaries in the pay of Prince Maurits. In their spare time they began fashioning little clay pipes of various shapes and styles, and soon the locals began to fashion them, leading to Gouda's becoming the country's leading pipe and ceramic producer. The figure above the door with the pipe in its mouth is a "Moriaan" (Blackamoor), which was also the company name. Gouda pottery was famous in the 19th century, and the floral earthenware on display represents some of the finest work by Gouda craftsmen, manufactured by companies such as the Royal Earthenware Factory, Goedewaagen, and Zenith. Ultimately, cheaper imitations took over the market. As for pipes, look for the so-called "mystery" pipes: new, they were pure white, but as they turned brown through use, a pattern appeared on the bowl. If you buy an example today, just what the design will be the buyer never knows in advance. ⊠ *Westhaven 29* ☎ *0182/588444* 🎫 *Combined ticket with St. Catharina Gasthuis €3.60* ⊘ *Mon.–Sat. 10–5, Sun. noon–5.*

Where to Eat & Stay

$$–$$$ ✕ **L'Etoile.** Despite the French name, this restaurant is a blend of all things Mediterranean. The interior has warm, natural tints, and intimate corners for tête-à-tête dinners. Specialty of the house is a tart made with marinated smoked salmon. For a unique twist on an old favorite, try a dessert of crème brûlée made with lemongrass. The roof garden has a good canal view. ⊠ *Blekerssingel 1* ☎ *0182/512253* 🍴 *AE, MC, V* ⊘ *Closed Sun. and Mon. No lunch Sat.*

$$ ✕ **Buiten Eten & Drinken.** The name means "eat and drink outdoors" and refers to the large garden at the back of the restaurant, where you can enjoy dining under the stars when the weather permits. There's lots of room indoors, too, where a local artist has painted the four seasons on the walls. Enjoy the duck confit with a *salade chaud* (warm salad) or let the English chef spoil you with a bread-and-butter pudding. There's a good selection of wines from all over the world. ⊠ *Oosthaven 23* ☎ *0182/524884* 🍴 *AE, MC, V* ⊘ *Closed Mon. No lunch.*

$–$$ ✕ **Tapas.** Spanish tapas bars are springing up all over Holland. This one scores high on quality and hospitality. The interior is unpretentious, with cozy tables and candlelight. Friendly staff serve the tapas, those delectable small appetizers that hail from Spain, in two rounds: first, warm ones, then a cold selection. You can also opt for a main dish. Be sure to leave room for the delicious chocolate cake. On weekends, you're treated to live music from flamenco guitarists and Gypsy King wannabes. ⊠ *Lange Groenendaal 57* ☎ *0182/523035* ⊟ *AE, DC, MC, V.*

¢ ⌑ **De Utrechtse Dom.** This friendly hotel, a block or two behind Sint Jans, is run by a family who live just next door, making this a homey option. This was originally a coach house—and thereby hangs a tale: traders from Utrecht would stable their horses here while doing business in the town, but what money they made was invariably spent on beer. That meant no money left for bed, so they came to sleep with their horses on the floor. Over time, the "stables" became a hotel. ⊠ *Geuzenstraat 6, 2801 XV* ☎ *0182/528833* 🖷 *0182/549534* ⊕ *www.hotelgouda.nl* ⊋ *14 rooms* ⚴ *Minibars, cable TV, some pets allowed; no a/c, no room phones* ⊟ *AE, DC, MC, V* ⱺ *CP.*

Shopping

Although the first thing you think of buying in Gouda is cheese, the town also has a thriving trade in crafts. It's also well known for its candles and claims to produce a large percentage of Holland's "Delft" blue. Gouda also has its own ceramic style, which incorporates richer colors. In its heyday, Gouda also supplied much of the country with soap and *stroop wafels* (syrup waffles).

CHEESE MARKETS Every Thursday morning, from June through August, farmers and porters (cheese carriers) dress in traditional costume to go through the ritual of a **Kaase Markt** (Cheese Market) beside the Waag, mainly for the benefit of tourists, since Gouda is the best-known type of Dutch cheese. Expect Goudse "locals" to play on their heritage: outside De Waag a porter, dressed in yellow clogs, with a yoke across his shoulders, greets visitors as they approach. This is probably the best place to buy cheese if you want to shop in open-air style; it is usually sold as *Jongekaas* (mild cheese), *Oudekaas* (mature cheese), or *Belegen* (medium ripe). There are many thatched-roof *kaasboerderijen* (cheese farms) near Gouda, several of which are on the picturesque River Vlist. If you're driving through, look out for signs reading *kaas te koop* (cheese for sale), since this indicates a farm shop where you may be able to look behind the scenes as well as buy freshly made Gouda. If you are using public transport, the VVV organizes excursions and short bicycle rides to nearby dairy farms where you can follow the whole process from cow to cheese counter. At press time, Holland was recovering from an outbreak of foot-and-mouth disease, so contact the local VVV for information about which farms you can visit without risk of spreading the disease.

PIPES & At Peperstraat 76 you can see the enormously moustached Adrie Mo-
CERAMICS erings making pipes in the traditional way. Just wander into his open studio, **Adrie Moerings Pottenbakkerij en Pijpenmakerij** (⊠ Peperstraat 76 ☎ 0182/512842), or Adrie Moerings Pottery Kiln and Pipe Maker, and watch him throw a pot or demonstrate pipe making. He is perhaps the last man in Holland who still makes clay pipes professionally. His pottery is on sale at the back of the shop.

Festivals & Concerts

Gouda by Candlelight is a Christmas staple, held in mid-December. All the electric lights in the market are switched off, and the windows in the Stadhuis and surrounding houses are decorated with candles and with an enormous Christmas tree taking center stage. Not as faux as it sounds, you get really carried away on the Christmassy spirit of the event. The Catharina Gasthuis and Sint Janskerk host monthly **Chamber Music Concerts,** which alternate between the two venues. Buy tickets up to an hour before the classical recitals start.

The Outdoors

BICYCLING   Gouda is compact enough to explore on foot, but a bicycle makes it easy to tour the rich dairy region that surrounds it. **Rijwielshop Gouda** (✉ Stationsplein 10 ☎ 0182/519751), next to the train station, rents bikes.

Utrecht

58 km (36 mi) northeast of Rotterdam, 40 km (25 mi) southeast of Amsterdam.

Birthplace of the 16th-century pope Adrian VI, the only Dutch pope, Utrecht has been a powerful bishopric since the 7th century and is still a major religious center and home to Holland's largest university. It was here that the Dutch Republic was established in 1579 with the signing of the Union of Utrecht. Today, Utrecht has so many curiosities, high-gabled houses, fascinating water gates, hip shops, artsy cafés, and winding canals that the traveler can almost forgive the city for being one of the busiest and most modern in Holland. Happily, the central core of Utrecht remains redolent with history, particularly along the Oudegracht (Old Canal), which winds through the central shopping district (to the east of the station shopping complex). Utrecht's storybook cityscape was long dominated by its famous 365-foot-high tower of the Cathedral, known as the Domtoren. But the tall Holiday Inn and the modern Hoog Catharijne complex have now joined the Dom in the skies, and this combination of two differing worlds at such close quarters sums up the contrasts to be seen everywhere these days in Holland. Indeed, if you arrive by train, you might be forgiven for thinking that Utrecht is one enormous covered shopping mall, since the station is now incorporated into this warren of 200-plus shops and that big blot on the horizon, the Hoog Catharijne. You can get lost in that mall maze for a day, but if you follow signs for *Centrum* (town center) through the shopping precinct and keep walking with determination, you will eventually come out on Achter Clarenburg in the historic center.

First settled by Romans, Utrecht achieved its first glory in the 16th century, when the religious power of the town was made manifest in the building of four churches at points of an enormous imaginary cross, with Utrecht's **Dom** (cathedral) in the center. The soaring tower of "the cathedral that is missing" on the skyline will direct you to the center of the action. Once, before the Union of Utrecht was signed and the Protestants took the reins of power, the city skyline was punctured by more than 40 church spires.

▶ ⑤⑥   The **Oudegracht,** the long central canal—which suffers a confusing name change at several points en route through the city—is unique in Holland, for its esplanade has upper and lower levels, with shops and galleries opening onto the street level, and restaurants and cafés opening onto the walkway that is just above water level of the city's unique sunken canals (the sinking water level centuries ago led to the excavation of a lower story).

Make your way to the central Domplein, where you'll find the **RonDom,** a one-stop cultural and historical information center for the historic quarter, where you can buy tickets for almost everything as well as book a guided tour or barge trip. There is an excellent range and display of free leaflets, to which you should help yourself (they usually prove more informative than the counter service at the VVV). ✉ *Domplein 9* ☎ *030/ 233–3036* 🖷 *030/230–0108* ⊕ *www.utrecht-museumkwartier.nl.*

☾ ⑤⑦   Two or three blocks to the east of the Domplein is the supercharming **Rijksmuseum van Speelklok tot Pierement,** or National Musical Box and

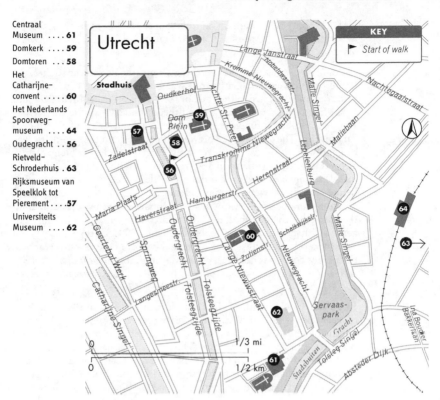

Street Organ Museum, housed in an old church. The Music Factory occupies budding musicians, and a large collection of automated musical instruments taken from the 15th to the 19th century absorbs adults—and soundproofing ensures no conflict of interests. Wander by yourself, or wait for a tour (also in English), for only on these are the dazzling automata put into play, and you can marvel at an ancient furry rabbit popping up out of a cabbage and beating time with its ears to the music, along with many other delights. Fittingly for Holland, the development of the barrel organ—still the bane of shoppers on many busy streets—is charted from the Renaissance onward in a gleaming white interior. In the center of the church, the children's Music Factory has displays of historical instruments hardy enough for three-year-olds to try—they will have a go at it on percussion instruments, bicycle bells, and harps. There are also interactive stands where children can shout into voice distorters, or watch themselves on a TV screen as they sing. To find the museum, follow the Oudegracht to Steenweg and look for the signs. ✉ *Buurkerkhof 10* ☎ *030/231-2789* ⊕ *www.museumspeelklok.nl* 🎫 *€6* ⊙ *Tues.–Sat. 10–5, Sun. noon–5; guided tours every hr.*

Soaring lancet windows add to the impression of majestic height of the famous tower of "the cathedral that is missing," the 14th-century **Domtoren** (Cathedral tower). The sole remnant of an enormous house of worship that was destroyed by a storm late in the 17th century (the outline of its nave can still be seen in the paving squares of the Domplein), it is more than 367 feet high. Not only is it the highest tower in the country, but its more than 50 bells make it the largest musical instrument in Holland. The tower is so big that city buses drive through an arch at its base. You can climb the tower, but make sure you feel up to the 465 steps. The panoramic view is worth the blisters, though, for it stretches

40 km (25 mi) to Amsterdam on a clear day. ⊠ *Domplein* ☎ *030/233–3036* ✉ *€6.80* ⊙ *Mon.–Sat. 10–5, Sun. noon–5; view by tour only; last tour at 4.*

59 Holding its own against the imposing Domtoren across the square, the grand Gothic **Domkerk** (Cathedral) was built during the 13th and 14th centuries and designed in the style of the Tournai Cathedral in Belgium. It has five chapels radiating around the ambulatory of the chancel, as well as a number of funerary monuments, including that of a 14th-century bishop. The entire space between the tower and the Domkerk was originally occupied by the nave of the huge cathedral, which was destroyed in a freak tornado in 1674 and not rebuilt. Many other buildings were damaged, and the exhibition inside Domkerk shows interesting before-and-after sketches. Today only the chancel and tower remain, separated by an open space, now a sunny square edged by a road. Behind the chancel is the **Pandhof,** a 15th-century cloister with a formal herb garden with medicinal herbs, replanted in the 1960s. If you're lucky you'll come upon classical musicians, making the most of the wondrous acoustics. A free concert is held every Saturday at 3:30. ⊠ *Domplein* ☎ *030/ 231–0403* ✉ *Free; guided tours €3* ⊙ *May–Sept., weekdays 10–5, Sat. 10–3:30, Sun. 2–4; Oct.–Apr., weekdays 11–4.*

60 Just a few blocks south of the Domplein brings you to **Het Catharijne-convent** (Convent of St. Catherine), a vast and comprehensive museum of religious history and sacred art that occupies a former convent near the Nieuwe Gracht (New Canal). There are magnificent altarpieces, ecclesiastical vestments, beautifully illustrated manuscripts, sculptures, and paintings—including works by Rembrandt and Frans Hals. Note the painting of a silvery-bearded God, by Pieter de Grebber (1640), where God is "just as you imagine him," holding what appears to be a crystal ball, inviting Jesus to sit at his right hand, in a cherub-bedecked chair. Temporary exhibitions here are scholarly and first-rate. Cross the first-story walkway to get a great view of the cloister gardens. Unfortunately, the labeling of exhibits is all in Dutch, so if you don't know your religious history, you'll be in the dark. ⊠ *Lange Nieuwestraat 38* ☎ *030/231–7296* ⊕ *www.catharijneconvent.nl* ✉ *€6* ⊙ *Tues.–Fri. 10–5, weekends 11–5.*

61 South by several blocks of the Het Catharijneconvent is the **Centraal Museum,** which brought in a number of hot Dutch designers to work on its renovation. "Central" is the word to describe this place's collection, since it ranges from a 10th-century boat to a Viktor and Rolf A-Bomb coat, from Golden Age paintings to minimalist home furnishings. Karijn de Kooning's work on the spatial layout and wall colors cannily encourages you to view these collections from different angles—shapes cut out of the wall open up to give you new perspectives. From a multitude of options you choose your own path through the museum, up spiral staircases, along underpasses, and in glass elevators.

Depending on the theme of the current temporary exhibitions, you might be lucky enough to see some of the museum's substantial Viktor and Rolf collection. In the main building don't miss **Petronella de la Court's Dolls' House** (1690), with 28 dolls all dressed in contemporary fashion. Adorning its walls are real miniature paintings by 17th-century masters such as Willem van Mieris and Gerard de Lairesse. Of course, the museum has its own extraordinary collection of Golden Age art, including Abraham Bloemaert's sublime *Adoration of the Magi* (1624), and artists from the Utrecht school such as Van Bronkhorst, as well as later Dutch painters, with particularly good pieces by Ad Dekkers and modern-day artist Marlene Dumas. Across the square, modern-art lovers will make a beeline for the **Gerrit Rietveld Wing,** focused on the most famous of all De Stijl architects and designers. There is a reconstruction of his studio and lots of original Rietveld furniture.

Visitors have access to the garden, where paths are cut through the long grass, creating a wonderful meadowy feel; when you sit outside you are transported right back to the days of Napoléon, when the complex's stables held his cavalry. The museum's depot service offers artwork not exhibited to the public for a private viewing for €20. Put in your request an hour before viewing during the week, and at weekends, request before 3 on the preceding Friday. ⊠ *Nicolaaskerkhof 10* ☎ *030/236–2362* ⊕ *www.centraalmuseum.nl* ⌨ *€8* ⊙ *Tues.–Sun. 11–5.*

☝ ⑥② The **Universiteits Museum** (University Museum), set on the way to the Centraal Museum, on the same street as the Convent of St. Catherine, deals with both the history of Utrecht University and the fields of science. The first thing to grab your attention is the building itself: international architects visit specially to look at Koen van Velsen's square building and his garden "boxes," since he has said, "Things are collected in boxes." A glassed-in corridor runs the length of the building, giving an immense feeling of space and height.

One collection, bought by William I and donated to the museum, verges on the ghoulish: skulls, anatomical models, and preserved "things" in jars; medical ethics would prevent many of these exhibits from being preserved now, most notably embryos, which only increases their fascination for youngsters. On the third floor kids can have a field day as the museum turns up its hands-on approach to the max. In the Youth Lab children put on mini–lab coats to do experiments and play with optical illusions (with assistants patrolling the floor to provide guidance and assistance on Wednesday, Saturday, and Sunday afternoons). A former orangery is now a garden-fronted café. You are strongly encouraged to ask for a guided tour, not just because labeling is mainly in Dutch but also because the guides are particularly proficient in illuminating the history of each collection. ⊠ *Lange Nieuwestraat 106* ☎ *030/253–8008* ⌨ *€4* ⊙ *Tues.–Sun. 11–5.*

★ ⑥③ The **Rietveld-Schroderhuis** (Rietveld-Schroder House) exemplifies several key principles of the De Stijl movement that affected not only art but also modern architecture, furniture design, and even typography in the early part of the 20th century. The house was designed for the Schroder family by Gerrit Rietveld, one of the leading architects of De Stijl, who has many objects on view in Utrecht's Centraal Museum. The open plan, the direct communion with nature from every room, and the use of neutral white or gray on large surfaces, with primary colors to identify linear details, are typical De Stijl characteristics. Rietveld is best known outside Holland for his "Red-Blue-Yellow" chair design. The house is just a few blocks away from the Centraal Museum. From the central train station in Utrecht you can take Bus 4 to the Hoogstraat area. ⊠ *Prins Hendriklaan 50* ☎ *030/236–2310* ⌨ *€16 (includes guided tour)* ⊙ *By appointment only Tues.–Sat. 11–4:30.*

⑥④ **Het Nederlands Spoorwegmuseum** (Netherlands Train Museum), just beyond the city wall, is in a converted 19th-century train station and holds a buffed and shiny collection of more than 60 locomotives, trams, and carriages, from the earliest days of steam and horse-drawn trams to sleek electric trains. Visitors can drive on an intercity train simulator, and children get to ride the *Jumbo Express.* ⊠ *Maliebaanstation 16* ☎ *030/230–6206* ⌨ *€8* ⊙ *Tues.–Fri. 10–5, weekends 11:30–5.*

Utrecht is a day-tripper's paradise, as it is in the very center of a super-abundant region of castles, moated great houses, forests, and arboretums. To the northwest of the city are the estates of the Van Zuylen family—Slot Zuylen and Kasteel de Haar. Although those palaces remain at the top of the list, also check out the gorgeous gardens, concerts, and art exhibitions at **Kasteel Groeneveld** (Groeneveld Castle; ⊠ Groeneveld 2, Baarn ☎ 035/542–0446), just northeast of Utrecht. To the south of the city is Doorn, which has several places of delight. Stroll in the beautiful **Arboretum von Gimborn** (⊠ Vossensteinsesteeg 8, Doorn ☎ 030/253–5177). Doorn's most fabled attraction is the **Kasteel Huis Doorn** (⊠ Doorn Castle, Langbroekerweg 10, Doorn ☎ 034/342–1020), where you can see how royalty lived at the turn of the 20th century. This was also somewhat notoriously the last home of the deposed German kaiser William II from 1920 to 1941; Hitler ordered the kaiser's state funeral to be held here.

Where to Eat & Stay

Utrecht hotel rooms are much in demand, since the city is a business and college center—so always book as far in advance as you can. A useful aid can be the **Utrecht Hotel Service** (☎ 030/236–4822 🖷 030/236–4842 ⊕ www.hotelsupportutrecht.nl).

$$$ ✕ **Het Grachtenhuys.** There is the feeling of being in a gracious home at this canal-house restaurant overlooking the fashionable New Canal. The young owners offer a choice of four- or five-course menus of French-influenced Dutch cuisine classics. Tempting selections might include rabbit fillet with a puree of various nuts, or truffle and potato soup with smoked eel. ⊠ *Nieuwegracht 33* ☎ *030/231–7494* ⚑ *Reservations essential* ▭ *AE, DC, MC, V* ☉ *No lunch.*

$$–$$$ ✕ **Polman's Huis.** This grand café of the old school is a Utrecht institution. Its Jugendstil–art deco interior is authentic. Other reasons to find your way to Polman's are its relaxing atmosphere and range of meal choices, from a simple quiche to a steamed fish dinner, from a kitchen that uses Mediterranean influences. ⊠ *Keistraat 2* ☎ *030/231–3368* ▭ *MC, V.*

$–$$ ✕ **Café le Journal.** This spot has the widest terrace so catches the most sun (when there is sun to be had) of the cafés along Winkenburgstraat and Neude. Large trees soften the view across the square, so this is a prime place for lazy weekend afternoons. Inside, a large central reading table is spread with magazines and newspapers, and floor-to-ceiling framed pictures make you feel you're in Italy. The menu is excellent and wide ranging. Although the café is relatively big, there is no feeling of being processed when you come here, thanks to the charming staff. Even when it is busy, you can linger over a *koffie verkerd* (café au lait) as long as you want. ⊠ *Neude 32* ☎ *030/236–4839* ▭ *No credit cards.*

$–$$ ✕ **De Zakkendrager.** Students, concertgoers from the nearby Vredenburg Music Center, and fashionable young locals come here for generous grills smothered in sauces, with an unusually large vegetarian range. The atmosphere is even better—the restaurant is cozy, friendly, and informal. Outside, in the tiny walled garden, a 175-year-old beech tree towers over all. ⊠ *Zakkendragerssteeg 22–26* ☎ *030/231–7578* ▭ *AE, DC, MC, V* ☉ *Closed Sun. and Mon.*

★ ¢–$$ ✕ **Winkel van Sinkel.** This Neoclassical *paleis* (palace) started out in the 18th century as Holland's first department store, then a century later went on to host the Nederlands Filmfestival before becoming Utrecht's foremost social hot spot. Fronted with columns and cast-iron statues of women, it conjures up images of Grecian luxe and abundance. The enormous statues were produced in England in the mid-19th century and shipped over, but they were too heavy for the crane that unloaded them, which collapsed, thereby earning the ladies the nickname "the fallen women" (alternatively, "the English whores"). Funky aluminum chairs and tables overlook the canal Aan de Werf; if the terrace is packed, head inside to have a tasty lunch or dinner (with an extensive vegetarian selection) in the fantastic, high-ceilinged Grote Zaal. If you fancy eating after-hours, the Nachtrestaurant serves tapas and southern Mediterranean cuisine until late, and ClubRisk kicks in late every weekend. Sunday afternoons feature Mediterranean music, games, and cocktails, in the Nachtrestaurant. Almost each night of the week features a monthly event, from salsa to open discussions and Latino nights. Check out the Web site for more details. ⊠ *Oudegracht 158; Nachtrestaurant entry via an de Werf* ☎ *030/230–3036, 030/230–3036 Nachtrestaurant* ⊕ *www. dewinkelvansinkel.nl* 🖃 *No credit cards* ⊘ *Closed Mon.*

$ ✕ **Eet Café de Poort.** This place is on Ledig Erf, one of Utrecht's small squares, which become hives of energy and filled with huge shade umbrellas when the sun comes out. This café's tables spill over the bridge, so you can sit overlooking canal-side gardens. On the far side of the plaza black-and-white squares are painted onto the pavement, carrying out a popular chess theme from the surrounding cafés. ⊠ *Tolsteegbarrière 2* ☎ *030/231–4572* 🖃 *No credit cards.*

★ **$$$$** ✕🏨 **Grand Hotel Karel V.** This former military hospital and restored 11th-century convent has been transformed into Utrecht's most luxurious hotel. The Garden Wing is a separate building surrounded by extensive gardens but lacks the historic aura of the main building, where Napoléon's brother Louis once resided. Canopied guest bedrooms are comfortably large, if the terra-cotta and gold furnishings are a bit overdone. Accent pieces are very new and yet not modern, and enormously heavy curtains are roped back to reveal almost floor-to-ceiling sash windows. The sumptuous dining room glitters with opulent metallic murals, and designer-oversize vases—a regal setting for the excellent fare. A lighter-eating alternative is the Brasserie Goede Louisa, where you can be served in the gardens or courtyard, if the weather is fine; note the afternoon tea and garden barbecue menus. ⊠ *Geertebolwerk 1, 3511 XA* ☎ *030/ 233–7555* 🖨 *030/233–7500* ⊕ *www.karelv.nl* ⤚ *70 rooms, 21 suites* ⚖ *Restaurant, café, in-room data ports, minibars, cable TV, health club, bar, some pets allowed* 🖃 *AE, DC, MC, V* ⦿ *EP.*

$–$$$ 🏨 **Malie Hotel.** Located on a tree-lined avenue behind a stylish 19th-century facade, this classically designed hotel is both modern and attractive. Guest rooms are brightly decorated, though simply furnished. The breakfast room overlooks a pretty garden, which guests have access to, and the bar-lounge doubles as a small art gallery. ⊠ *Maliestraat 2–4, 3581 SL* ☎ *030/231–6424* 🖨 *030/234–0661* ⊕ *www.hampshirehotels. nl* ⤚ *45 rooms* ⚖ *Cable TV, bar, Internet* 🖃 *AE, MC, V* ⦿ *CP.*

$ 🏨 **Hotel Ouwi.** A convivial family hotel, this is just off one of the main transit routes to the city center. The rooms are tight and simple in furnishings and decor, but they're very clean and tidy. ⊠ *F. C. Dondersstraat 12, 3572 JH* ☎ *030/271–6303* 🖨 *030/271–4619* ⤚ *30 rooms* ⚖ *In-room data ports, cable TV, some pets allowed; no a/c, no room phones* 🖃 *AE, DC, MC, V* ⦿ *CP.*

¢ 🏨 **Stayokay Hostel Bunnik.** Backpackers and travelers on a budget can find a bargain bunk in shared dorms just outside Utrecht, only 10 minutes from town by bus. ⊠ *Rhijnauwenselaan 14, 3981 HH, Bunnik* ☎ *030/656–1277* 🖨 *030/657–1065* ⊕ *www.stayokay.com* ⤚ *24 dorm rooms of 2, 4, 6, 8, or 12 beds* ⚖ *Restaurant, bar, Internet; no a/c, no room phones* 🖃 *AE, V* ⦿ *CP.*

Nightlife & the Arts

THE ARTS In Utrecht you can find dance on the programs of **Stadsschouwburg** (⊠ Lucas Bolwerk 24 ☎ 030/232–4125), which has a major performance hall as well as the Blauwe Zaal (Blue Room) for small productions. The annual **Spring Dance** festival brings international performers to town in June, with the biggest events usually on the big squares in the center of town, the Neude.

The **Vredenburg Muziek Centrum** (⊠ Vredenburgpassage 77 ☎ 030/231–4544 box office, 030/286–2286 information ⊕ www.vredenburg.nl) is the biggest venue in Utrecht for classical and pop concerts, but is usually closed in July. Utrecht's **Festival Oude Muziek** (☎ 030/230–3838 ⊕ www.oudemuziek.nl), or Festival of Early Music, in late summer each year is immensely popular, selling out rapidly. Note the full programs of concerts in Utrecht's many fine churches, including the **Dom** (☎ 030/231–0403), **Sint Peter's church** (☎ 030/231–1485), and **St. Catharine's church** (☎ 030/231–4030 or 030/231–8526).

Visiting opera companies and talented local musicians keep up a high standard at the **Stadsschouwburg** (⊠ Lucas Bolwerk 24 ☎ 030/232–4125).

The annual mid- to late-September **Film Festival** is a seriously taken review of the past year of Dutch productions held in Winkel van Sinkel café and cinemas around town.

NIGHTLIFE Utrecht's students strike a lively note at cafés around the center, more during the week than over weekends. Larger cafés such as the **Winkel van Sinkel** and **Oudaen** are gathering spots for all ages. **Polman's Huis** attracts a lively crowd of students and thirtysomethings. **ClubRisk** (⊠ Oudegracht 158 ☎ 030/230–3030) is what Winkel van Sinkel's Saturday "serious fun" night is called (trading on its catchphrase *van tango tot house* [from tango to house]) to pack both floors with frenetic clubbers. In-house and guest DJs flock from across Europe to host RealHouse-Music nights. **Axl Roach Club** (⊠ Stadhuisbrug 3 ☎ 030/231–7271) is the place in town for R&B fans. The entrance is down a flight of stone steps to the quay on Aan der Werf; here in the cellars of the Stadhuis top DJs spin the night away. **Trianon Union Salsa** (⊠ Oudegracht 252 ☎ 030/231–6939) is a fast-growing salsa club that organizes great dance events—on some nights there are salsa classes earlier in the evening before the party starts. There are also demonstrations, dance lessons, and workshops on offer at the center, as well as Spanish- and Portuguese-language lessons. **De Roze Wolk** (⊠ Oudegracht 45 ☎ 030/232–2066) is a mellow gay and lesbian bar with a friendly atmosphere and a canal-side dance space in the cellar. Every March heralds the start of the blues season, with a weekend in the Vredenburg Center, and the annual **Blues Festival** takes place in early June, in venues across town. Late April sees the start of the jazz season, with a weekend session in the Vredenburg.

Sports & the Outdoors

BICYCLING You can rent a bike from **Rijwiel Shop** (⊠ Centraal Station Utrecht ☎ 030/231–57802). **Co van Beek** (⊠ Springweg 14–16 ☎ 030/231–9933) is a popular option. Water ski–bikes can be found at **Canal Bike** (⊠ Oudegracht, opposite the back of City Hall ☎ 020/626–5574 (head office in Amsterdam).

SPORTS COMPLEX The sports center **De Vechtsebanen** (⊠ Mississippidreef 151 ☎ 030/262–7878) offers bowling, badminton, volleyball, squash, curling, and a number of other sports; there is a small running track, as well as both indoor and outdoor tennis courts and ice-skating rinks.

Kasteel de Haar

65 *10 km (7 mi) northwest of Utrecht.*

Fodor's Choice
★ The spectacular **Kasteel de Haar** (Haar Castle) is not only the largest castle in The Netherlands, it is also the most sumptuously furnished. Thanks to the fortuitous way the Barons van Zuylen had of marrying Rothschilds, their family home grew into an Neo-Gothic extravaganza replete with moat, fairy-tale spires, and machicolated towers. The castle was first built back in 1165, but several renovations and many millions later, the family greatly expanded the house under the eye of P. J. H. Cuypers, famous designer of Amsterdam's Centraal Station and Rijksmuseum in 1892. Inside the kasteel, there are acres of tapestries, medieval iron chandeliers, and the requisite ancestral portraits snootily studying you as you wander through chivalric halls so opulent and vast they could be opera sets. One portrait is of Belle van Zuylen, one of Holland's most noted 18th-century writers; you can visit her home, **Slot Zuylen** (⊠ Zuylen Castle, Tournooiveld 1, Oud Zuilen ☎ 030/244–0255) on the outskirts of Utrecht on your way to the Kasteel de Haar; Slot Zuylen can be seen only on weekend afternoon guided tours.

At de Haar, be sure to explore the magnificent gardens and park, dotted with romantic paths, fanciful statues, and little bridges. As was the wont of aristo owners in the 19th century, entire villages were relocated to expand their estate parks, and, in this case, Haarzuilens was reconstructed a mile from the castle. Designed in 1898 around a village square, all of its cottages have red-and-white doors and shutters, reflecting the armorial colors of the Van Zuylen family. Every year in September, the village fun fair is kicked off by the current baron to the accompaniment of a fireworks display. As for the castle itself, you can view its grand interiors only on a guided tour, which leaves on the hour and is given only in Dutch. No matter, the objects of beauty on view here can be understood in any language. Once you explore this enchanted domain, you'll easily understand why Marie-Hélène van Zuylen, who grew up here, went on to become Baroness Guy de Rothschild, the late-20th-century's "Queen of Paris," famous for her grand houses and costume balls. Directions for car travelers are given on the castle Web site. For public transport, take Bus 127 from Utrecht Centraal Station, direction Breukelen/Kockengen, until the Brink stop in Haarzuilen, which is a 15-minute walk from the castle. You can also train it to Vleuten station and then take a taxi. ⊠ *Kasteellaan 1, near Haarzuilen* ☎ *030/ 677–8515* ⊕ *www.kasteeldehaar.nl* 🎫 *€7.50* ⊗ *Mar. 17–May 31, Tues.–Thurs., 1–3, weekends 1–4; June, Tues.–Sun. 1–4; July–Sept. 4, Tues.–Fri. 11–4, weekends noon–4:30; Oct. 4–Oct. 31, Tues.–Thurs. 1–3, weekends 1–4; Nov.1–Nov. 23, Sun. 1–4; Dec. 26, noon–4:30, Jan. 2–Mar. 16, Sun. 1–4.* ⊠ *Kasteellaan 1, near Haarzuilen* ☎ *030/677–3804* ⊕ *www.kasteeldehaar.nl* 🎫 *€7.50* ⊗ *Mar. 15–May, Tues.–Thurs. and weekends 1–5; June, Tues.–Sat. 1–5; July–Sept. 4, Tues.–Fri. 11–5, weekends noon–5; Oct. 4–Oct. 31, Tues.–Thurs. and weekends 1–5; Jan.–Mar. 14, Sun. 1–5.*

Naarden

66 *30 km (19 mi) northeast of Utrecht, 20 km (12 mi) southeast of Amsterdam.*

The idyllic town of Naarden was the scene of one of the most horrific moments in Dutch history. In 1572, near the beginning of the war for Dutch independence from Spain, Spanish troops massacred the townspeople, as an example to other Dutch rebels, and burned everything but the Gothic church, which is still standing. The event is depicted on a small stone carving above the doorway of the **Spaanse Huys** (Spanish House; ⊠ Turfpoortstraat). In the 17th century, Naarden erected a massive and complex series of fortifications with a double moat, based on the principles of the French military architect Vauban. The new defenses had to take artillery into account, so the high stone walls of the Middle Ages became a thing of the past. Instead, low walls were pushed far out into the countryside with arrowhead-shape bastions and moats. Remarkably, these fortifications remained part of Holland's defenses until World War II. Even today, the only three entrances to Naarden are across a moat.

The three main streets meet at the **Grote Kerk** (Great Church). The highlight of Naarden's Late Gothic church is its painted wooden ceiling, portraying scenes from the Old and New Testaments. The choir screen is one of the finest in Holland. The church itself hosts exhibitions and is famous for its Easter-season concerts of such sacred music as Bach's *St. Matthew Passion* (which always sells out). For the best possible view of Naarden and its star-shape ramparts, join a guided tour and climb the tower. ⊠ *Marktstraat* ☎ *035/694–2836* ▣ *€2 (includes tour), tower €1.80* ☉ *Grote Kerk mid-May–mid-Sept., daily 1–4; tower May–Sept., Wed.–Sun. 2–3.*

The **Stadhuis** (Town Hall), with its double set of step gables, is a classic piece of Holland Renaissance–style architecture. It is still in use by the city council and for weddings and cultural events. ⊠ *Marktstraat 22,* ☎ *035/695–7811* ▣ *Free* ☉ *Mon.–Sat. 1:30–4:30.*

Naarden's history is a bit hazy, since most of the town records were destroyed during regional skirmishes, one of which saw Count Floris acquire the town through conquest in 1280. All battles led Naarden to becoming one of the best-preserved fortified towns in northern Europe; the defenses date back to 1560 and were in active service as recently as 1926. All is explained in the **Vestingmuseum** (Fortification Museum), located partly underground in the Turfpoortbastion (Peat Gate Bastion), which actually forms the ramparts. In addition to enjoying exhibits and a video, for an additional fee you can take a boat trip out to the middle of the moat to get an impression of what it must have been like to attack the ramparts from the moat. ⊠ *Westwalstraat 6* ☎ *035/694–5459* ▣ *€4.50 (plus €1.80 for boat trip)* ☉ *Mar.–May, Sept., and Oct., Tues.–Fri. 10:30–5, weekends noon–5; June–Aug., weekdays 10:30–5, weekends noon–5.*

Where to Eat & Stay

★ **$$$–$$$$** ✕ **Paul Fagel at Het Arsenaal.** Past and future come together here in a high-concept renovation of a 17th-century arsenal masterminded by Jan des Bouvrie, who is to Holland what Philippe Starck is to France. In fact, adjoining the restaurant here is a shop (☎ 035/694–1144) filled with Bouvrie designs. As for the kitchen, another mastermind holds the reins—Paul Fagel, just one of a talented family of culinary whiz kids. His menu changes every three weeks, but dishes as succulent as oven-roasted lamb usually find their way onto the daily specials. All in all, it's an exceptional spot. ⊠ *Kooltjesbuurt 1* ☎ *035/694–9148* ⊕ *www.paulfagel.nl* ☰ *AE, DC, MC, V* ☉ *No lunch weekends.*

★ **¢–$$$** ✕▥ **Poorters.** Located in a former shipping exchange, this meticulously maintained, sash-windowed spot has terraces along its length and width that scenically overlook Naarden's inner moat. Adjacent to a café is Poorters's gleaming restaurant, cheerily done in bright reds and eggshell whites and proffering a fairly stylish menu. Upstairs are five guest rooms, making Poorters the only hotel actually in Naarden's old fortified town. Antiques shops, museums, the 17th-century Town Hall, and the 14th-century St. Vitus church are just a quick jaunt from the front door. ✉ *Marktstraat 66, 1411 EB* ☎ *035/694–4868* 📠 *035/694–4868* ⊕ *www.poorters.nl* 🛏 *5 rooms* ♨ *Restaurant, café, cable TV, bar; no a/c, no room phones* ⊟ *MC, V* ⅩⅠ *CP.*

The Arts

More than an exhibition, Naarden's biannual themed **Photography Festival** (⊙ weekdays 11–5, Sat. 11–6, Sun. noon–6), running from the end of May until mid-June every other year, plays host to a nice array of photos taken by national and international lenses. The next fair will be in 2005. The admission price for the last fair was €10, although many of the exhibits are always free.

Muiden

⑥⑦ 8 km (4½ mi) northeast of Naarden, 12 km (7½ mi) southeast of Amsterdam.

The route into this rather petite village takes you to a narrow tree-lined avenue where you think you have entered a miniature regality—an excellent preparation for a visit to **Rijksmuseum Muidenslot,** or Muiden Castle, another contender for that honorific, the largest castle in Holland.

This certainly is one of Holland's most history-soaked abodes, home to several celebrated Dutch figures, with several notable Dutch events taking place in this medieval fortress. That history begins with Floris V, Count of Holland, who in 1280 had a stone fortress built strategically here at the mouth of the River Vecht, then the main route to Utrecht, which was the principal center of commerce in northern Holland. Unfortunately, greed got the better of the count and he instituted a toll to be paid by all vessels passing through on his stretch of the estuary. His scheme irked the locals, and in short order, Floris was captured while out hunting in 1296, imprisoned in his own castle, then brutally murdered. In a further act of vengeance the castle and surrounding buildings were destroyed by a warring bishop from Mechelen.

A vision out of a fairy-tale storybook, the castle you see today was rebuilt on the remains of Floris's original home, almost a century later, in 1370. The 17th-century furnishings you see as you tour the castle may seem out of context, but they originate from its most famous occupant, poet Pieter Corneliszoon Hooft (1581–1647), who was Muiden's *drost* (bailiff) and summered here from 1609 to 1674, filling it with Baroque-era treasures to amuse his *Muiderkring* (literary circle)—the country's most famous gathering of Dutch intellectuals. You can see the desk where Hooft wrote his poems, standing up. The rooms have other curiosities, such as an enclosed family box bed, where children slept underneath in drawers and adults slept sitting up (the cord pulled open a vent when it all got a bit too close).

The castle is also an ideal place for a stroll, with an herb garden, plum orchard, and paths running right around the moat. There are guided tours of the gardens, scheduled on the first Saturday of each month, starting at 11. There are also falconry demonstration days at the castle, which take you right back in time to the days of Count Floris. It's not surprising to find that of its 120,000 visitors a year, 35,000 are children, and guides provide animated group tours specifically geared toward children, with activities. If your kids are interested, ask about joining an international school tour, where the guide takes the children through in English. Visitors must be accompanied by a guide. Guided tours leave on the hour. Call ahead to confirm times for tours in English. By public transport, take Bus 136 (two an hour) from Amstel Station in Amsterdam. ⊠ *Herengracht 1* 🕾 *0294/261325* ⊕ *www.muiderslot.nl* 🔳 *€5* ☉ *Apr.–Oct., weekdays 10–5, weekends 1–5; Nov.–Mar., weekdays 1–5.*

need a break?

Take a beer outside at the **Café Ome Ko** (⊠ Herengracht 71 🕾 0294/261330) to sit at one of the many tables on the River Vecht with the calming—and unusual, in Holland—sound of whooshing water, thanks to the nearby lock gates. Basically, only beverages are served here, but dessert will be your vista of Muiden Castle in the distance as you look up the river.

Where to Eat

$$–$$$ ✕ **De Doelen.** To really appreciate the setting of this restaurant, come here for lunch, not dinner, so you can sit under lime trees and eat overlooking the rural canal lock and small harbor, filled with yachts. With the entire menu stuffed with temptations such as crispy, baked sole, you'll be hard-pressed to stop yourself from coming back for dinner, too. ⊠ *Sluis 1* 🕾 *0294/263200* 🖃 *AE, DC, MC, V.*

METROPOLITAN HOLLAND A TO Z

To research prices, get advice from other travelers, and book travel arrangements, visit www.fodors.com.

AIRPORTS

Amsterdam Schiphol Airport is 25 km (15 mi) southeast of Rotterdam and has efficient road and rail links. The comprehensive "Helloport" telephone service, charged at €.45 per minute, provides information about flight arrivals and departures as well as all transport and parking facilities. **Rotterdam Airport,** 17 km (10 mi) northwest of Rotterdam, is the biggest of the regional airports, providing a daily service to a number of European cities. However, to reach the airport from Rotterdam you need to take a bus or taxi, as there are no rail links. If you take a taxi, expect to pay around €20.

🚺 Airport Information **Amsterdam Schiphol Airport** 🕾 0900/0141. **Rotterdam Airport** 🕾 010/446-3444.

BIKE TRAVEL

In this flat land, a bicycle is an ideal means of getting around, and cities have safe cycle lanes on busy roads. Bikes can be rented at outlets near most railway stations, called **Rijwiel** shops, or by contacting local rental centers found in the regional (Rotterdam, etc.) *Gouden Gids* (Yellow Pages), under *Fietsen en Bromfietsen.*

BOAT TRAVEL

If you are traveling to the United Kingdom, there are two daily Stena line crossings between the Hoek van Holland—the main port for ferries and boats heading to England—to Harwich, on the fast car ferry, taking approximately three hours. The overnight crossing takes about seven hours. These ferry crossings can be booked at the international travel window in large railway stations. The PO North Sea Ferries run an overnight crossing between the Europoort in Rotterdam and Hull, England, which takes about 14 hours.

🚺 Boat Information **PO North Sea Ferries** ⊠ Beneluxhaven, Havennummer 5805, Rotterdam/Europoort 🕾 020/201-3333 ⊕ www.ponsf.com/index/ **Stena** ⊠ Hoek van Holland Terminal, Stationsweg 10, Hoek van Holland 🕾 0174/315-800, 0900/8123 reservations (10¢ per minute) 📠 0174/389389 ⊕ www.stenaline.nl/.

CAR RENTALS

Auto-verhuur (car rental) in Holland is best for exploring the center, north, or east of the country, but is to be avoided in the heavily urbanized northwest, the Randstad, where the public transport infrastructure is excellent. If you do decide to tempt fate, there are several agencies available in Rotterdam.

🚗 **Car Rental Agencies Avis** ✉ Marconistraat 1a, Rotterdam ☎ 010/433-2233 ✉ Rotterdam Airport ☎ 010/298-2424. **Budget** ✉ Rotterdam Airport ☎ 010/437-8622 ✉ Abraham van Stolkweg 96, Rotterdam ☎ 010/415-1833. **Europcar** ✉ Tandwielstr 2, Rotterdam ☎ 010/423-2022 ✉ Rotterdam Airport ☎ 0900/1576.

CAR TRAVEL

Using a car in the Randstad, with the complexity of one-way streets in city centers, makes driving a real headache, let alone the added burdens of parking and expense. In addition, there is also the consideration of traffic, especially around rush hour, when driving between Haarlem and Delft can take up to three times longer than traveling by train. If you decide to travel by car, you can reach Rotterdam directly from Amsterdam by taking E19 via Amsterdam Schiphol Airport. The city is bounded by the A20 on the northern outskirts, the A16 on the east, the A15 on the south, and the A4 on the west. N5/A5 goes to Haarlem from Amsterdam (from there N208 leads through the bulb district to Leiden); to reach Leiden and Delft directly from Amsterdam, take E19 via Amsterdam Schiphol Airport; to continue to Utrecht from Rotterdam, take A15 and then the A27, or to reach Utrecht directly from Amsterdam, take E25. Take E30/A12 from The Hague to Utrecht to bypass the congestion of Rotterdam.

EMERGENCIES

Pharmacies stay open late on a rotating basis. Call one of the numbers listed below for addresses on a given night.

🚗 **Emergency Services National Emergency Alarm Number** for police, fire, and ambulance ☎ 112.

🚗 **Hospitals Delft** ✉ Reinier de Graaf Gasthuis, Reinier De Graafweg 3-11 ☎ 015/260-3060. **Haarlem** ✉ Spaarne Ziekenhuis, Van Heythuijzenweg 1 ☎ 023/514-1516. **Leiden** ✉ Academisch Ziekenhuis Leiden, Rijnsburgerweg 10 ☎ 071/526-9111. **Rotterdam** ✉ Erasmus MC, Dr. Molewaterplein 40-50 ☎ 010/463-9222. **Utrecht** ✉ Universitair Medisch Centrum Utrecht, Heidelberglaan 100 ☎ 030/250-9111.

TAXIS

Taxis are available at railway stations, at major hotels, and, in larger cities, at taxi stands in key locations. You can also order a taxi by using the telephone numbers below. Expect to pay approximately €27 for a 30-minute journey between Rotterdam and Delft.

When you buy your train ticket from a station office, you can buy a *trein-taxi* (taxis that operate out of train stations) ticket from some smaller stations for a standard €3.80 per person, per ride. It doesn't matter where you're going, so long as it's within the city limits. The fare is so cheap because it's shared—but with waiting time at a guaranteed maximum of 10 minutes following your call, you won't be hanging around long. Trein-taxis are ideal for getting to sights on the outskirts of smaller towns. Call one of the numbers below to order a taxi in metropolitan Holland, but for trein-taxis, simply go to the ticket window at the smaller train station; note that not all small towns have this service.

🚗 **Taxi Companies Delft** ☎ 015/361-3030. **Haarlem** ☎ 023/515-5555. **Leiden** ☎ 071/521-2144. **Rotterdam** ☎ 010/462-6060 or 010/425-7000. **Utrecht** ☎ 030/230-0400.

TOURS

The best way to see Rotterdam's waterfront is by boat; **Spido Harbor Tours** offers excursions lasting from just over an hour to a full day. In Delft, Dordrecht, Kinderdijk, Leiden, Rotterdam, and Utrecht guided sightseeing boat tours allow you to explore the cities. Ask at the local VVV office, in the towns you would like to tour for the latest departure information and routes. In Leiden, **Groene Hart Cruises** runs 3½-hour boat trips, including a windmill cruise, Tuesday–Thursday and Sunday summer afternoons from the *haven* (harbor) at 1 PM, going across the Braassemer Lake and the Kager lakes; the fare is €12. In Utrecht, opt for one of the many guided tours operated by the **RonDom**, a one-stop cultural and historical information center for the museum quarter, where you can buy tickets for almost everything as well as book a guided tour, or barge trip.

🚩 **Fees & Schedules Avifauna** ☎ 0172/487575. **Jaap Slingerland** ☎ 071/541-3183. **Ron-Dom** ✉ Domplein 9 ☎ 030/233-3036. **Spido Harbor Tours** ✉ Willemsplein 85 ☎ 010/413-5400. **Utrecht Tourist Office** ✉ Vredenburg 90 ☎ 06/3403-4805.

TRAIN TRAVEL

Getting about by rail is the ideal means of intercity transport in the metropolitan area. Trains are fast, frequent, clean, and reliable, and stations in all towns are centrally located, usually within walking distance of major sights. All international and intercity trains from Brussels and Paris stop in Rotterdam Centraal. From here connections can be taken to travel directly to Delft (15 minutes northwest), Leiden (35 minutes northwest), and Haarlem (55 minutes northwest), on a twice-hourly *sneltrain* (express train) in the direction of Amsterdam. Intercity trains to Amsterdam traveling via Schiphol also stop in Leiden, but not Delft or Haarlem. To go to Gouda (20–25 minutes northeast) take a *snel-* or *stoptrein* (local train) in the direction of Amsterdam, Arnhem, Nijmegen, or Utrecht. Intercities heading to Arnhem, Nijmegen, and Enschede also stop in Utrecht, where the faster trains shorten the journey time (35–50 minutes northwest). Seat reservations aren't permitted.

When traveling around the metropolitan area, a sneltrain leaves Amsterdam twice an hour for Haarlem, which also stops in Leiden, Delft, Rotterdam, and Dordrecht. From Rotterdam, a sneltrain leaves twice an hour for Gouda and Utrecht. For Muiden and Naarden, take a train to Amsterdam Amstel (in the city suburbs), then take Bus 136, which stops in Muiden and Naarden. For Naarden, you can also take a train from Amsterdam Centraal to Naarden-Bussum, then a 20-minute walk to Naarden. Returning to Amsterdam, you can take Bus 136, or the *treintaxi* (☎ 035/693-5756).

🚩 **Train Information Intercity** ☎ 0900/9292. **Rotterdam Centraal** ☎ 0900/9292. **Trein-Taxi** ☎ 035/693-5756.

TRANSPORTATION AROUND METROPOLITAN HOLLAND

In combination with trains, the efficient system of buses and trams in the metropolitan area will easily take care of most of your transportation needs. Bus service is available in all cities in this region, and trams run between Delft and The Hague, in Rotterdam, and in Utrecht. Trams operate within Rotterdam, and between Delft and The Hague; buses offer services across the Randstad to certain smaller towns served only by secondary rail connections. Bus lanes are shared only with taxis, meaning they remain uncongested, ensuring that you travel more swiftly than the rest of the traffic in rush hour.

Rotterdam also has a subway, referred to as the metro, with only two lines (east to west and north to south) that extend into the suburbs and cross in the city center for easy transfers. All three options are excellent for transport within the city.

The same ticket can be used in buses, trams, and metros Holland-wide. Called a *strippenkaart* (strip ticket), a two- or three-strip ticket can be bought directly from the bus driver. If you buy a ticket in advance, this works out much cheaper per journey: a 15-strip ticket is €6.20 and a 45-strip ticket costs €18.30. You can buy these at railway stations, from post offices, and from many bookshops and cigarette kiosks, and they remain valid until there are no further strips left, or for one year from the first stamp. *See* Tickets, *in* Getting Around by Bus, Tram, and Metro *in* Smart Travel Tips for how to use the strippenkaart.

🚊 Public Transportation Information ☎ 0900/9292.

VISITOR INFORMATION
Each *VVV* (tourist board) across the country has information principally on its own town and region. Contact the VVV of the area you plan to travel to, and ask directly for information, as there is no one central office; information lines cost €.70 per minute.

🚊 Tourist Information **VVV Brielle** ✉ Markt 1 ☎ 0181/475475.**Touristen Informatie Punt Delft** ✉ De Hippolytusbuurt 4, 2611 HN ☎ 0900/515-1555.**VVV Dordrecht** ✉ Stationsweg 1, 3311 JW ☎ 078/632-2440. **VVV Gouda** ✉ Markt 27, 2801 JJ ☎ 0900/4683-2888. **VVV Haarlem** ✉ Stationsplein 1, 2011 LR ☎ 0900/616-1600. **VVV Kinderdijk (c/o Alblasserdam)** ✉ Cortgene 2 (inside city hall) ☎ 078/692-1355. **VVV Leiden** ✉ Stationsplein 2D, 2312 AV ☎ 0900/222-2333. **VVV Muiden** (⇨ VVV Naarden). **VVV Naarden** ✉ Adriaan Dortsmanplein 1b ☎ 035/694-2836. **VVV Rotterdam** ✉ Coolsingel 67, 3012 AC ☎ 0900/403-4065. **VVV Utrecht** ✉ Vinkenburgstraat 19, 3512 AA ☎ 0900/128-8732.

THE HAGUE

3

FODOR'S CHOICE

The Binnenhof, *a castle fit for knights in shining armor*
Escher in Het Paleis Museum, *for its dazzling optical illusions*
Haags Gemeentemuseum, *for its great Mondriaans*
Madurodam, *Holland magically built on a scale of 1:25*
Mauritshuis, *home to Vermeer's Girl with a Pearl Earring*
Museum Bredius, *a connoisseur's delight*
Museum Mesdag, *a gilded 19th-century art collection*
Scheveningen, *the Dutch seaside resort par excellence*
Vredespaleis, *housing the Peace Palace and Courts of Justice*

HIGHLY RECOMMENDED

RESTAURANTS Dudok Brasserie
Garoeda
It Rains Fishes
Le Haricot Vert
Marc Smeets
Pláto

HOTELS Des Indes Inter-Continental
Kurhaus, *Scheveningen*
Parkhotel Den Haag
Savelberg, *Voorburg*

Other great sights, restaurants, and hotels enliven this area. For other favorites, look for the black stars as you read this chapter.

By Anna
Lambert

Updated by
Anne
Hodgkinson

IT'S ALL TOO EASY, AT FIRST GLANCE, TO SEE THE HAGUE as nothing more than Amsterdam's prissy maiden aunt. And its status as Holland's seat of government, its role as a diplomatic capital, plus its worldwide reputation as a center of legislative excellence (the town is home to the International Court of Justice) doesn't do much to contradict its staid and serious image. Those who experience Den Haag—to use the Dutch name—up close and personal, however, will be won over not only by its elegance but by its unexpected quirkiness. This is a place that embodies the clichés and contradictions of Dutch living, embracing both minimalism and flamboyance, exuberance and restraint. Here you'll find narrow, winding streets and wide-open places (how many other major urban centers can boast 26 parks?), with the latest in cutting-edge architecture sitting equally comfortably beside 17th-century mansions resplendent with frescoes, ornate spun-sugar plasterwork, and glittering chandeliers. And a trek through its premier art galleries blends old masters from the Dutch 17th-century Golden Age with contemporary works in a fascinating *hutspot* stew of fine arts.

As befits such a multifaceted city, The Hague has more than one name. It's known to the French as La Haye, whereas its official Dutch name is 's-Gravenhage, literally, "the Count's Hedge." This harks back to the early 13th century, when the Count of Holland's hunting lodge was based in a small woodland village called Die Haghe—and Den Haag is the location still favored by the Dutch in conversation today. In 1248, Count Willem II built a larger house; the noted Knights' Hall, or Ridderzaal, was added in 1280; and gradually Den Haag became the focus of more and more government functions. Throughout the 17th and 18th centuries, The Hague was the seat of government for the United Provinces, but only with the Napoléonic occupation (the French entered the city in 1795) did the town receive a full civic charter, bestowed upon it by Bonaparte's brother, Louis. Between 1814 and 1831, The Hague shared political-capital status with Brussels—a less-than-happy power split, with parliaments meeting alternately in the two cities. By 1814, both government and court had returned to The Hague, although the title of capital city stayed with Amsterdam. In 1899 the first international conference for the suppression of war was held at The Hague, leading to the Permanent Court of Arbitration and the building of the Peace Palace (1913). Today, The Hague is home to the reigning monarch, Queen Beatrix, and visitors can enjoy the many buildings that are a testament to her family's history. Royal residences include the beautiful cream-color Noordeinde Palace (the setting for the crown prince's 2001 royal engagement announcement and closed to the public), Lange Voorhout Palace (currently a museum), and Huis ten Bosch, the private home of the queen herself.

As an adjunct—or maybe an antidote—to so much history and tradition, The Hague has plenty of sybaritic tricks up its sleeve. Discerning diners can enjoy everything from pancakes to kangaroo steaks, and shop-till-you-droppers can indulge themselves in both classy department stores and the most idiosyncratic of designer boutiques. And should you by any chance find The Hague's pace a little too refined, a little too gracious, there's always the fishing port and seaside town of Scheveningen just up the road, which couldn't offer a greater contrast. Almost seamlessly connected to The Hague and nicknamed "our national bathing place," the town boasts all the bright lights, glitz, and occasional tackiness that you'd expect of a traditional vacation mecca. If you fancy a flutter at the casino tables or a spot of fishing or a dip in the stupendously icy North Sea (now that *is* really something to write home about), this is the place to visit.

Exploring The Hague

For a city that sees so much political, legal, and diplomatic action, The Hague can seem surprisingly quiet, thus a delight to those who want to escape the crowds. It may be home to around 450,000 people and see a steady influx of visitors, but even on a Saturday you're unlikely to find yourself joined cheek-by-jowl with an infinitude of other people. It's precisely this sense of peace that helps make visitors feel they can get to know The Hague well, and in a relatively short space of time. Because it's a compact city, you can easily cover most of the key sights—the medieval complex of the Binnenhof, the masterpiece-filled Mauritshuis, and the nearby lovely streets of Lange Voorhout, Denneweg, and Noordeinde—on foot from the Centraal Station. Most of the modern venues—the wide-ranging municipal Gemeentemuseum, the miniature version of Holland that is the Madurodam, the science-orientated Museon and Omniversum—are to the north of town. The Hague's predictably efficient bus and tram network can take you there, and on to Scheveningen, with frequent departures from either station; a tram from the center of town will do likewise. The transport lines you need to look for are as follows: for the Gemeentemuseum, Omniversum, Museon, and GEM/Museum of Photography, Tram No. 17 or Bus No. 4 from Centraal Station, or Tram No. 10 from Hollands Spoor station; for Madurodam, Tram No. 1 from either station.

About the Restaurants & Hotels

Even the pickiest diner should find something that appeals in The Hague. For a good selection of a restaurant's fare, opt for a set, prix-fixe menu. This will give you three, four, or even five courses, sometimes including appropriate wine servings, for a bargain price (indeed, in spite of all the government limousines purring around here, restaurant tabs will prove considerably cheaper than you might expect). As in other towns in Holland, you won't have to dress up to chow down—the tone remains relaxed despite the city's upmarket reputation. Local diners usually start their evening meal around 7 PM, not the 5:30–6 start experienced elsewhere. In general, it's always wise to reserve in advance, although if you arrive early without a prior booking, you may nevertheless be seated.

With more than 20 million visitors a year, The Hague needs to have plenty of spare beds available. The daily round of international business, though, means that hotels quickly fill up with conference delegates, diplomats, and visiting lawyers, so rooms at the better places need to be booked well in advance of a planned visit. When it comes to sleeping in style, The Hague boasts one of the grandest traditional hotels in the country, the Des Indes hotel—dripping with crystal chandeliers and stuffed with both antiques and a history of famous guests, including everyone from glamorous Dutch spy Mata Hari to crooner Bing Crosby. Five-star pampering is what you can expect here. Elsewhere, hotel accommodations can be a little on the bland side; The Hague's smaller, family-run bed-and-breakfast facilities will offer homey, more individual surroundings. Luxurious or cozy, most places offer a considerably gentler price tag that you might expect from this ostensibly pricey region. Assume all rooms have air-conditioning, TV, telephones, and private bath, unless otherwise noted.

An audience with The Hague—Holland's Queen of Cities—may well exceed all expectations. For a start, there's her Vermeers at the exquisite Mauritshuis, the fairy-tale Binnenhof, and very modern Gemeentemuseum. With her cobbled streets, proper avenues, and cinnamon-and-coffee-scented cafés, The Hague has one side that's undeniably traditional, but don't call her an anachronism. With a finger firmly on the pulse of the 21st century, she's proved herself a fine patron of the arts, an upholder of international justice at her Peace Palace, and—in her seaside resort of Scheveningen—an undisputed good-time gal. In spirit, then, The Hague is the very essence of the modern urban monarch; spend a few days here and pledge your undying allegiance.

Other than side trips out of town to Scheveningen, The Hague is custombuilt for the eager army of bipeds who discover it every year. A walk through the town—since it isn't too large, it's never an overly aerobic one—exercises the spirit as well as the limbs, because, of course, you'll be seeing Vermeers along with noted government ministries.

Numbers in the text correspond to numbers in the margin and on The Hague map.

If you have 1 day

Begin with a gentle tour of the **Binnenhof** ❷—the time-burnished, governmental complex that remains the heart of town. Arrive as soon as it opens up (10 AM), and even if the weather's not great, a palpable mistiness might still be hanging over these 13th-century courtyards, halls, and palace buildings. From here, move around the corner to the exquisite **Mauritshuis** ❸—home of such wonders as Vermeer's *View of Delft* and his even more magical *Girl with a Pearl Earring*; if you feel pushed for time, ask for the free brochure "The Highlights of the Mauritshuis in 45 Minutes." Ready for lunch? Walk through dignified Lange Voorhout and head for one of the cafés on Denneweg, where a "doorstep" (one of those notorious Dutch sandwiches where the slices of bread are so thick that they're best described thus) stuffed with tarragon chicken or grilled steak washed down with a cold beer should keep you going for an hour or two. Take half an hour or so to explore some of Denneweg's delightful boutiques, and then head for the **Haags Gemeentemuseum** ⓬, repository of fine modern art, ranging from Monet to Appel, and including the world's largest collection of Mondriaans. If you can drag yourself away before 4 PM, it's worth your while to dive into the next-door science-oriented **Museon** ❿, a model of Dutch modernity. State-of-the-art interactive exhibits make for a fascinating, if whirlwind, visit. If you want to continue to wander through the 17th-century Golden Age, forget about the Museon and blissfully set your sights on the treasure troves of the **Museum Mesdag** ❾, the **Museum Bredius** ❻, and the **Schilderijengalerij Prins Willem V** ⓱ (Prince William V Painting Gallery), three magnificent art collections housed in stately interiors worthy of a king or connoisseur. In the evening, treat yourself to a cocktail at the gilded Des Indes hotel, and then head for supper at one of the restaurants on quiet Molenstraat, such as Le Haricot Vert.

If you have 3 days

With more time at your disposal, you can afford to do things at a less frenetic pace. On Day 1, concentrate on the **Binnenhof** ❷ and the **Mauritshuis** ❸; then head for the intimate **Schilderijengalerij Prins Willem V** ⓱, whose walls are almost literally wallpapered with paintings collected by the Stadholder Prince in the late 18th century. For something totally different, the **Gevangenpoort Museum** ⑯ just next door has a collection of instruments of torture that will make you appreciate living in the 21st century. Then do a little leisurely shopping—window or otherwise—in the nearby Noordeinde area, or head off in the opposite direction for Denneweg. On your second day, lose yourself among the Mondriaans at the **Haags Gemeentemuseum** ⑫ before enjoying lunch in the light-filled restaurant there; then spend plenty of time at the science **Museon** ⑩ next door. Finally, round off your day with an awe-inspiring film experience at the **Omniversum** ⑪. Here, thanks to the place's vast semidomed screen, you'll feel not so much that you're watching a wildlife movie as that you're actually *in* it. Shift down a cultural gear or two on Day 3 with a trip to the seaside resort of **Scheveningen** ⑲. Dabble your toes in the water, walk around the old village, and enjoy either a soothing visit to the Sculptures by the Sea exhibit or, as an antidote to artistic overload, a massage at the Vitalizee spa. For lunch, try herring from a stall, or indulge in an afternoon tea in the splendidly painted hall of the Kurhaus Hotel. Head back to The Hague in the evening and catch a performance by either the Nederlands Dans Theater at the Lucent, or the city's resident orchestra at Dr. Anton Philipszaal next door.

If you have
5 days

For a totally different view of Scheveningen, visit the **Panorama Mesdag** ⑮ on Day 4; a vast cylindrical work by artists of The Hague School, it shows the old fishing village as it was in 1880. Then, if the weather's fine, grab a picnic and head out east to glorious **Clingendael** ⑱, whose beautiful gardens are packed with flowers and unusual shrubs. Alternatively, if sunshine proves nonexistent, a trip to the Duinrell theme park could be order; in its renewed Tikibad water world, you can enjoy indoor chutes and slides in tropical temperatures, whatever the weather. On the final day of your trip, discover the giant within you at Madurodam—where the best of Netherlandish architecture is collected in one place, and all on a scale of 1:25. En route back into town, stop off at the **Vredespaleis** ⑧, or Peace Palace (open weekdays only), to learn more about the work of the International Court of Justice and to admire the magnificent surroundings created courtesy of philanthropist Andrew Carnegie.

WHAT IT COSTS In euros*				
$$$$	$$$	$$	$	¢
RESTAURANTS over €30	€22–€30	€15–€22	€10–€15	under €10
HOTELS over €230	€165–€230	€120–€165	€75–€120	under €75

*Restaurant prices are per person for a main course only, excluding tax (6% for food and 19% for alcoholic beverages) and service; note that if a restaurant offers only prix-fixe (set-price) meals, it has been given the price category that reflects the full prix-fixe price. Hotel prices are for a standard double room in high season, including the 6% VAT (value-added tax); higher prices (inquire when booking) prevail for any meal plans.

Timing

Done at a pace that will allow you to soak up The Hague's historical atmosphere, a minimal tour around the city center Centrum alone should take you about two hours. If you take time to visit all the sights en route, you're looking at as much as a day. At the very least, allow

30 minutes for each site you choose to visit (some people would spend their lives at the Mauritshuis).

Before you start out, bear a couple of things in mind. First, as in all other Dutch cities, both walking surfaces and the weather can change at short notice; if you're going to be on your feet all day, make sure you're equipped with both an umbrella and sturdy walking shoes. Second, despite The Hague's international status, museums and galleries usually close by 5 PM, so don't plan any early evening art visitations without careful checking. Many sites are also closed Monday, so plan accordingly. Finally, it's a good idea to double-check bus and tram lines with an up-to-date map; in 2004 the city center was undergoing some massive renovation (expected to continue at least until 2005), and not only have some transit lines been rerouted or eliminated, but a couple of streets have disappeared entirely.

THE CENTRUM: HEART OF THE HAGUE

The Hague's center is crammed with the best the city has to offer in terms of art, history, and architecture. An exploration of a relatively small area will take you through busy thoroughfares and quiet backstreets, into the famed Mauritshuis Museum and past the bourgeois homes of the 17th century. If you want to explore the political hub of The Netherlands, you can do so at the Binnenhof, home to the famous Ridderzaal (Knights' Hall) and the Houses of Parliament. Or, if you want a little peace and quiet, turn onto the leafy Lange Voorhout and stroll through what in the 19th century was the place to see and be seen. (This is the street Queen Beatrix takes to get to services in the Kloosterkerk at the corner.) Just off the Lange Voorhout is the Denneweg, whose book- and antique shops and fashion boutiques combine the quaint and the cutting-edge in just a few blocks. Wandering streets like these, you'll understand immediately how The Hague earned its reputation for elegance, restraint, and charm.

a good walk

Heading out the west exit of the Centraal train station (by track No. 1), cross the tram tracks and proceed into the pedestrian street, which turns out to be a covered plaza that is actually the inside of an office complex (a good introduction to the Dutch obsession with efficient use of space). Continue straight down a long block to a prime example of The Hague's innovative municipal architecture: the gleaming white **Stadhuis Atrium ❶ ▶**, which, completed in 1995, combines town hall and library. Locals refer to it as either the White Swan or, less affectionately, the Ice Palace, and opinion is divided as to which epithet is the more appropriate. From here, cross straight over Kalvermarkt and into little Bagijnestraat. Follow the pedestrianized alley past the back of some restaurants and into Lange Poten. Again, follow the road around to the left via noisy Hofweg until you reach the government complex of the **Binnenhof ❷**, home of the legendary Knights' Hall, or Ridderzaal. As you enter via its Grenadier's Gate, the place might look like something that's been preserved in metaphorical aspic, but as the heartbeat of Dutch politics, the Binnenhof couldn't be more relevant and contemporary. The distinctive fountain, complete with its skinny gargoyles and gilded statue (King Willem II), is in fact far more modern than it looks, as it was built in 1885 and is a Neo-Gothic creation. Once you've headed right to take a look at the Knights' Hall, exit via the arched, cream-color gatehouse. This will bring you to the front of the perfectly proportioned **Mauritshuis ❸**, where you can feast your eyes on no fewer than 15 Rembrandts and 3 Vermeers, among many other treasures.

For a perfect time-out, head to the restful lake, the **Hof Vijver ④**, behind the museum. From here, walk along Korte Vijverberg with its horse-chestnut trees and to the **Haags Historisch Museum ⑤** (Hague Historical Museum), where you can explore seven centuries of the city's history. Walk on a little way until you reach busy Tournoor Veld; if you cross over and turn left here, you'll come to the **Museum Bredius ⑥** on Lange Vijverberg; bearing right on Tournooiveld will bring you to elegant, tree-lined Lange Voorhout, dominated by the stately Des Indes hotel and the badly designed U.S. Embassy. Adjacent to this is **Escher in Het Paleis ⑦**, an 18th-century former palace that now is a museum housing the eye-crossing works of artist M. C. Escher. Take the road between the two—Vos in Tuinstraat—leading into Denneweg. Head all the way up this lovely street, pausing to be diverted by the gorgeous art and antiques shops and to take a good look at the buildings, some with art nouveau detailing and pretty tiled entrances. When the street ends, turn left and walk along Mauritskade, with the gardens of the 19th-century villas overlooking the water on the other side of the road. Soon, you'll arrive at busy Parkstraat and, as you look to your right on crossing it, you'll notice Plein 1813, with its monument commemorating the end of Napoléonic occupation.

Should you want to make a lengthy detour, the **Vredespaleis ⑧**, or Peace Palace, and the lushly beautiful 19th-century **Museum Mesdag ⑨** are situated in the direction behind the Plein, and beyond them is the Statenkwartier district, which harbors four of the city's museums: the science-oriented **Museon ⑩**; the **Omniversum ⑪**, home of the IMAX theater; the famous modern art collection of the **Haags Gemeentemuseum ⑫**; and the **GEM Museum of Contemporary Art/Museum of Photography ⑬**. It's a good hike to the Statenkwartier museums, but if you choose to walk, you can either view many of the stately embassies en route along the Tobias Asserlaan and Johan de Wittlaan, or take a slightly longer walk along the Scheveningseweg through the Scheveningse Bosjes (the woods between The Hague and Scheveningen), turning left on the Adriaan Goekooplaan. If, on the other hand, you want to save your feet, catch a tram (No. 17) at the Vredespaleis and get off at Statenplein. If none of this detour appeals to you, just continue down Mauritskade for some time until you reach Noordeinde. Directly on the opposite side of Mauritskade is Zeestraat, where both the **Museum voor Communicatie ⑭**, or Communication Museum, and the evocative **Panorama Mesdag ⑮** are situated. If you don't fancy a detour to check these two out, keep on heading down into Noordeinde, where you can't miss the elegant Royal Palace on your right (the statue in front of it is of Prince William of Orange). Keep on for several more side streets; then turn left onto the pleasant Plaats, where you've earned a cold beer at Café Juliana. Finally, from Plaats, turn right into Buitenhof, and you'll see both the **Gevangenpoort Museum ⑯**, notorious for its torture collection, and the charming painting collection of the **Schilderijengalerij Prins Willem V ⑰** almost immediately, giving you a choice of either the barbaric or the sublime as a final stop. As a coda, you might consider escaping to the sylvan glades of the park known as the **Clingendael ⑱**.

What to See

② Binnenhof and the Ridderzaal (Inner Court and the Knights' Hall). The
Fodor'sChoice governmental heart of The Netherlands, the complex of the Binnenhof
★ (or Inner Court) is in the very center of town yet tranquilly set apart from it thanks to the charming Hof Vijver (court lake). Although much of the day-to-day governing of the country goes on here in its legislative halls, the setting of the Binnenhof is anything but prosaic. All its pomp and decorum come into full play every third Tuesday of Septem-

On the Menu Dutch cuisine has a deserved reputation for being of the starchy, protein-packed variety. The term "hearty meal" could have been devised specifically for the nation, and Netherlanders enjoy plenty of stomach-lining insulation in the form of thick stews and mashed root vegetables (the Dutch love to squish their food: in one survey, no fewer than 62% of respondents admitted to mashing their food from time to time). In The Hague, too, you can indulge in all of the classic Dutch delicacies. Enjoy herring courtesy of a roadside stall, not forgetting that there is an art to doing so: pick your fish up by its tail (it'll be surrounded by half-moons of aromatic, vinegary onions), dangle the morsel into your mouth, then knock it back with a good slug of the *jenever* (Dutch gin) that you'll have decanted into your hip flask at the start of the day. And should your blood-sugar level feel like it's sinking, pavement pounders can turn to another local delicacy: *Haagse hopjes,* the coffee-flavor hard candies created at the end of the 18th century to assuage the cravings of a Baron Hop and still sucked today throughout The Netherlands. But Eurocrats, diplomats, and lawyers tend to demand more substantial culinary fare, and The Hague can certainly satisfy the most exacting of palates. From French haute cuisine to Tex-Mex, you'll be able to sample it here, and, as you'd expect of a town that is only a stone's throw from the seaside, the *fruits de mer* seafood platters are of the very freshest variety. Meanwhile, The Hague's Indonesian restaurants are second to none, which is understandable given that the place is considered the hometown of The Netherlands' Indonesian population. By all means, have a *rijsttafel* (rice table) blowout.

Vermeer & Company It's no wonder Hagenaars, or the locals, are crazy about art. In the Mauritshuis alone, the city possesses one of the world's finest small galleries. Pride of place, of course, goes to Vermeer's sublime *Girl with a Pearl Earring,* a painting that has inspired Tracy Chevalier's eponymous and best-selling novel—as well as the 2003 filmed version starring Scarlett Johansson and Colin Firth—and everyone's constant speculation (who exactly was this Dutch "Mona Lisa"?). And the size of the collection—just 883 works, of which around 333 are on show at any time—only adds to its accessibility and charm. Those who love art galleries will come here anyway, but those who usually have to be dragged may find themselves profoundly converted upon arrival, especially if they visit the collections set in three magisterial historic houses. The Museum Mesdag is a sumptuous time capsule back to the age of the 19th-century Dutch aesthete. The Museum Bredius has walls hung with the "little" old masters of the 17th century. The Schilderijengalerij Prins Willem V is a princely collection housed in a spectacular picture *kabinet* gallery. Meanwhile in The Hague's Gemeentemuseum, there's an outstanding collection of 19th- and 20th-century works, including the world's largest collection of Piet Mondriaan's works, and paintings by artists of The Hague School. This was a group who took their inspiration from the coast and reclaimed land near the city, so, as you'd expect, their oeuvre features low, silvery skies and plenty of beach scenes. Key names in the movement include the Maris brothers (Jacob, Matthijs, and Willem), Jan Hendrik Weissenbruch, and Johannes Bosboom. Their work can also be seen at the Museum Mesdag.

3

Festivals & All That Jazz

What is it about Hagenaars and festivals? Any excuse, and they'll arrange one. Every year, visitors and locals alike can share in a variety of unusual events that—in some cases quite literally—provide The Hague with more than a little color. For a start, there's the North Sea Jazz festival, held over three days in July at The Netherlands Congress Centre in The Hague. It's the brainchild of Dutch jazz promoter Paul Acket, who, at the inaugural jazz festival of 1976, managed to pull in performers of the caliber of Sarah Vaughan, Count Basie, Dizzy Gillespie, and Stan Getz. Over the ensuing decades the events grew in strength, and it's now a happening of international proportions. Then, centered on Scheveningen, there are two other great summer festivals, the first of which is the International Sand Sculpture Competition. Forget bucket-and-spade-constructed castles; the entries are on a giant scale, and of the highest order of art. Teams from around the world compete to create fantastic beasts, vast palaces, and mythological gods; at night the sculptures are romantically floodlighted. Finally, in August, there's the Scheveningen Summer Fireworks Festival—four consecutive nights of glorious Catherine wheels and diadems bursting skyward from the shore. Join the throng along the pier and boulevard, or, for the best vantage point, book passage on a boat and do your oohing and aahing from the sea. For more details on these two festivals, contact the VVV (☎ 015/215–7756), or go to the web site (⊕ www.northseajazz.nl) for more information on the North Sea Jazz Festival.

---

ber, when you will see Queen Beatrix driven in a golden coach to the 13th-century Ridderzaal, or Knights' Hall, to open the new session of Parliament. Her cortege passes through much of the city, coming and going, in a display of color and ceremony that has few equals in Holland. The Binnenhof makes a suitable backdrop. For many centuries the court of the Counts of Holland, it is now a complex of buildings from a spectrum of different eras.

As you enter, the former castle of the Earls of Holland, complete with twin turrets, dominates. This was originally built by Count Floris V and became a meeting hall for the Knights of the Order of the Golden Fleece, one of the most regal societies of the Middle Ages. Its medieval towers recall an era when architects were as much concerned with defense as shelter, its shape suggesting more of a church than a castle. Inside, the Great Hall has seen several transformations. Today, it is adorned with vast beams spanning a width of 59 feet, flags of the 12 Dutch provinces, a vast rose window bearing the coats of arms of the major Dutch cities, and a sense of history. Note the carved heads positioned near the beams; when the hall served as a court, judges would tell the accused to fess up, otherwise these "eavesdroppers" would have words with the heavenly powers. In 1900, the hall was restored to its original 13th-century glory, and it now looks much as it would have when built for the counts as a venue for their feasts and revelries. In 1904, Queen Wilhelmina opened Parliament here for the first time; since that time the hall has been referred to as the Knights' Hall. It continues to play a key role in Dutch legislative life.

The Binnenhof also incorporates the halls used by the First and Second Chambers of the States General (equivalent to the U.S. Senate and House of Representatives). Visitors can wander freely around the open outer courtyard, but entrance to the Knights' Hall and either the First or Second Chamber is by guided tour only. In the atmospheric reception area below the Knights' Hall there's a free exhibition detailing the political history of the Low Countries. ⊠ *Binnenhof 8a* ☎ *070/364–6144* 🖾 *€4.55* ☉ *Mon.–Sat. 10–4, though some areas, including the Knights' Hall, may be closed when government meetings are taking place.*

⑱ Clingendael. More than 123 acres of beautiful grounds, the Clingendael park includes a Japanese garden (open May to June) that dates from 1896. The rest of the park has magnificent plantings of rhododendrons and azaleas, a glorious sight when in bloom. ⊠ *Van Alkemadelaan* 🖾 *Free* ☉ *Daily 9–sundown.*

☺ **❼ Escher in Het Paleis Museum** (Escher Museum). First known as the Lange
Fodor'sChoice Voorhout Palace, this lovely building was originally the residence of Car-
★ oline of Nassau, daughter of Prince Willem IV. In 1765, Mozart gave a concert for her here. Later, the intimately scaled house became Queen Emma's winter residence, then the official Hague reception chamber for the queens Wilhelmina, Juliana, and Beatrix. But in 2001, it was transformed into a museum devoted to the Dutch graphic artist M. C. Escher (1892–1972), whose prints and engravings of unforgettable images—roofs becoming floors, water flowing upward, fish transformed into birds—became world-famous in the 1960s and 1970s. Replete with ever-repeating Baroque pillars, Palladian portals, and parallel horizons, the perspectival tricks of Maurits Cornelis Escher presage the "virtual reality" games and worlds of today. Fittingly, the museum now features an Escher Experience where you don a helmet and join 30 other passengers through a 360-degree trip into his unique world. Concave and convex, radical metamorphoses, and dazzling optical illusions are on view in the impressive selection of his prints (including the famed *Day and Night* and *Ascending and Descending*), mirrors make children big and adults small, and there are rooms that are Escher prints blown up to the nth power. A family ticket for €20 makes this an even more attractive museum for kids. ⊠ *74 Lange Voorhout* ☎ *070/362–4061* ⊕ *www.escherinhetpaleis.nl* 🖾 *€7.50* ☉ *Tues.–Sun. 11–5.*

⑬ GEM Museum of Contemporary Art/Museum of Photography. These small museums, both opened in 2002, occupy an elegant 1962 annex first constructed as part of the Haags Gemeentemuseum. Now thoroughly renovated and state-of-the-art, their movable walls and multimedia facilities showcase the latest in cutting-edge art and photography. About six temporary exhibitions are mounted every year, highlighting international trends in contemporary video, painting, sculpture, performance art, film, and digital art. For instance, the GEM recently hosted shows devoted to Raymond Pettibon and Hans op de Beeck. Additional pluses are evening open hours and the eye-catching Gember café (open until midnight), which is replete with dazzling "moderne" lighting fixtures. The café is perched over the water-lily-covered Gemeentemuseum pond—if you're lucky, you'll enjoy gazing at one of The Hague's ubiquitous herons (the city's emblem) posing on the pond as you enjoy your cappuccino. ⊠ *Stadhouderslaan 43* ☎ *070/338–1133 GEM, 070/338–1144 Museum of Photography* ⊕ *www.gem-online.nl or www.fotomuseumdenhaag.nl* 🖾 *€5 (good for both museums)* ☉ *Tues.–Sun. 2–10.*

⑯ Gevangenpoort Museum (Prison's Gate Museum). Now a museum showcasing enough instruments of inhumanity to satisfy any criminologist, the Gevangenpoort, or Prison's Gate, was originally a gatehouse to the local duke's castle, then converted to a prison around 1420. In 1882, it opened in its current incarnation as both a monument to its own past and a national museum displaying apparatuses of punishment. After a slide presentation, the guided tour will take you through the torture chamber, the women's section, and the area where the rich were once imprisoned. For those who are interested in seeing such things as a branding iron with The Hague's coat of arms, the Gevangenpoort Museum offers a fascinating, if chilling, experience. Don't be surprised if your guide pulls a few stunts on you. ⊠ *33 Buitenhof* ☎ *070/346–0861* 📷 *€3.60* ⊙ *Tues.–Fri. 11–5, weekends noon–5. Guided tours only, every hr on the hr and preceded by a slide presentation.*

⑫ Haags Gemeentemuseum (Hague Municipal Museum). Designed by H.
Fodor'sChoice P. Berlage (the grand old master of modern Dutch architecture), com-
★ pleted in 1935, and restored from 1996 to 1998, the Gemeentemuseum is considered one of the finest examples of 20th-century museum architecture. Although its collection ranges from A to Z—sumptuous period rooms highlighting Golden Age silver, Greek and Chinese pottery, a celebrated group of historic musical instruments, and paintings by Johann Jongkind, Claude Monet, and Vincent van Gogh—it is best known as the home of the world's largest collection of works by Piet Mondriaan (1872–1944), the greatest artist of the Dutch De Stijl movement. The group is particularly strong in his early works, those breathlessly beautiful watercolors of chrysanthemums, and bleak Holland landscapes, although the crowning masterpiece of the collection (and widely considered one of the landmarks of modern art), the artist's *Victory Boogie Woogie*—an iconic work, begun in 1942 but left unfinished at the artist's death, with the signature black-and-white grid interspersed with blocks of primary color—arrived only in 1998, when The Netherlands Institute for Cultural Heritage controversially paid 80 million guilders for the work (until then American-owned). In doing so, it ensured the homecoming of the last work to be painted by Dutch art's most pioneering son.

In addition to more than 150 works by Mondriaan, there are around 50 drawings by Karel Appel, one of the founders of the revolutionary CoBrA group (its name is a combination of the first letters of Danish, Belgian, and Dutch capital cities). "I paint like a barbarian in a barbarous age," Appel once said; see if you think the same sentiments apply to his drawings. Elsewhere in the museum are paintings by artists of The Hague School. As far as the decorative arts are concerned, there's a magnificent display of traditional silverware, plus old glass, ceramics, Dutch and Chinese porcelain, and a dollhouse with real doll-size Delft Blue chinaware. The museum's Costume Gallery contains no fewer than 55,000 items (although not all are on display at one time!), providing endless inspiration for dedicated students of fashion. ⊠ *Stadhouderslaan 41* ☎ *070/338–1111* ⊕ *www.gemeentemuseum.nl* 📷 *€7* ⊙ *Tues.–Sun. 11–5.*

★ ❺ Haags Historisch Museum (Hague Historical Museum). One of the series of museums that encircle the Hof Vijver lake, The Hague Historical Museum is housed in the Sebastiaansdoelen, a magnificent Classical-Baroque mansion dating from 1636 built to house the Civic Guard of St. Sebastian. Worthy of a visit in itself, this mansion holds collections that offer an in-depth look at The Hague's past. Treasures here include Jan van Goyen's enormous 17th-century panoramic painting of the city, a collection of medieval church silver, a gem of a doll's house from 1910, and the dreamy views out the windows over the Hof Vijver lake and the greensward of the Lange Voorhout. ⊠ *7 Korte Vijverberg* ☎ *070/364–6940* ⊕ *www.haagshistorischmuseum.nl* 📷 *€3.60* ⊙ *Tues.–Fri. 11–5, weekends noon–5.*

❹ Hof Vijver (Court Lake). Beside the Binnenhof, this long, rectangular reflecting pool—the venerable remains of a medieval moat—comes complete with tall fountains and a row of pink-blossomed, horse-chestnut trees. Today, the lake is spectacularly surrounded by some of The Hague's most elegant historic buildings and museums.

③ **Mauritshuis.** Home to the enigmatic gaze of the Dutch "Mona Lisa"—
Fodor'sChoice Vermeer's *Girl with a Pearl Earring*—and several other of the most re-
★ produced paintings in the world, the Mauritshuis is one of the greatest art museums in Europe. Here, in only a dozen rooms, is one of the richest feasts of Dutch art anywhere: 14 Rembrandts (including the *Anatomy Lesson*), 10 Jan Steens, and 3 Vermeers, with his incomparable *View of Delft* taking pride of place. As an added treat, the building itself is worthy of a 17th-century master's brush: a cream-color mansion tucked into a corner behind the Parliament complex and overlooking the Hof Vijver court lake. It was built to a strictly Classical design around 1640 for one Johan Maurits, Count of Nassau-Siegen and governor-general of Dutch Brazil, and the pair behind its creation, Jacob van Campen and Pieter Post, were the two most important Dutch architects of their era.

Visitors enter at basement level, where there are cloakrooms and an excellent book and gift shop. To reach what is called the ground floor, you ascend one flight. Such is the quality of this collection that even comparatively minor paintings are real jewels. Case in point: Hendrick Avercamp's charming *Winter Scene* of 1610, where you can search out, among the tiny figures, a bared buttock or two, a drowning couple, and, in the foreground, a dandy. Also on this ground floor are Rubens's *Assumption of the Virgin* and Holbein's portrait of *Robert Cheseman*.

Ascend yet another flight for the greatest treasures—some of the finest paintings of Holland's 17th-century Golden Age. Among the Rembrandts on display are no fewer than four self-portraits covering a 40-year span of his life, from a smooth-cheeked adolescent to a weary, resigned old man about to die. Here, too, is Rembrandt's *Anatomy Lesson,* painted when he was only 26, showing a group of eight surgeons around a cadaver. If the subject, commissioned by the Amsterdam Medical Society, is startling, the arrangement of the group into a harmonious composition represents a historic advance in 17th-century portraiture, a precursor of the vast *Night Watch* in Amsterdam's Rijksmuseum.

Don't miss local boy Paulus Potter's vast canvas *The Bull,* complete with steaming cow dung; the 7-by-11-foot painting leaves nothing to be said on the subject of beef on the hoof, and the artist (1625–54) never surpassed it during his brief 29 years of life. Other masters you'll meet here include Franz Hals, Carel Fabritius, Gerard Dou, Adrien van Ostade, Rusydael, Hobbema, Gabriel Metsu, and, of course, Johannes Vermeer (1632–75). The rediscovery of his *View of Delft* in the late 19th century all but assured the refound fame of Vermeer (Marcel Proust left his famous cork-lined room for one of the last times in his life to see this painting when it was on view in Paris); note the disturbing shadows Vermeer casts across the waterside buildings in his painting, which serve to emphasize the golden accents falling on the church spire of Delft's Nieuwe Kerk. In the same room is Vermeer's most haunting work, *Girl with a Pearl Earring,* which inspired Tracy Chevalier's 1999 best-selling novel. A novel may be the only way to understand this sphinxlike lady, as historians have never determined who she is. Some think it is Maria, the eldest of Vermeer's 11 children; the novel sets out that it is Vermeer's maid. Considering the complete lack of ostentatious dress and iconographic symbols, the latter could be a real possibility. No matter who it is, the picture has a glowing light and an immediacy that make it one of the loveliest portraits ever painted.

For something completely different, look to the works of Jan Steen (1626–79), who portrayed the daily life of ordinary people in The Netherlands of the 17th century. His painting *The Way You Hear It Is the Way You Sing It* is particularly telling. All in all, as in other museums, you can spend hours here; unlike with other collections, however, you'll waste no time on second-rate works. ⊠ *Korte Vijverberg 8* ☎ *070/302–3435* ⊕ *www.mauritshuis.nl* ☒ *€7* ⊙ *Tues.–Sat. 10–5, Sun. 11–5.*

🐣 ⑩ **Museon.** With lots of hands-on, interactive displays, this bills itself as "the most fun-packed popular science museum in The Netherlands." Permanent exhibitions center on the origins of the universe and evolution, with three themes: Earth, Our Home; Between Man and the Stars; and Ecos, an environmental show. The frequent special exhibitions here are always engagingly presented, with archaeological and intercultural subjects the common themes, plus there are children's workshops on Wednesday and Sunday afternoons (book in advance). The Museon is conveniently next door to the Gemeentemuseum, so you can easily combine a visit to both. ⊠ *Stadhouderslaan 41* ☎ *070/338–1338* ⊕ *www.museon.nl* ☒ *€6* ⊙ *Tues.–Fri. 10–5, weekends noon–5.*

⑥ **Museum Bredius.** Housed in an 18th-century patrician mansion, the col-
Fodor'sChoice lection of traveler and art connoisseur Abraham Bredius (1855–1946)
★ supports the argument that private collections are often the most delightful. It includes works by the likes of Cuyp and Jan Steen, as well as nearly 200 paintings by Dutch "little masters"—whose art Bredius trumpeted—of the period, all held together by the thread of a personal vision. Once curator of the Mauritshuis, Bredius was the first art historian who began to question the authenticity of Rembrandt canvases (there were zillions of them in the 19th century), setting into motion the enormous seismic quake of connoisseurship that, today, has reduced the master's oeuvre to fewer than 1,000 works. The house itself, overlooking the north side of the Hof Vijver (court lake), makes a quaint setting for the paintings. Salons are fitted out with Neoclassical moldings and armoires stuffed with Delft porcelains and important silverware, but the main show remains the art on the walls. ⊠ *Lange Vijverberg 14* ☎ *070/362–0729* ⊕ *www.museumbredius.nl* ☒ *€4.55* ⊙ *Tues.–Sun. noon–5.*

⑨ **Museum Mesdag.** Enter the beauteous world of a 19th-century Dutch con-
Fodor'sChoice noisseur, aesthetic, and art collector with one step into this often over-
★ looked treasure-house, nearly wallpapered with grand paintings, glittering frames, and exquisite period fabrics and tapestries. The former town house of noted 19th-century Dutch painter H. W. Mesdag, famed for his vast Panorama Mesdag (*see below*), it was left by the artist as a repository for his collection of works from The Hague School, together with French 19th-century paintings from the Barbizon School, including works by Delacroix, Corot, and Millet, which heavily influenced the style of The Hague School masters such as Josef Israels, Anton Mauve, Willem Maris, and, of course, H. W. Mesdag. He was best known for painting seascapes and the life of fisherfolk in the nearby village of Scheveningen, and served as a relentless ambassador for The Hague School, traveling around the world and bringing back some impressive objets d'art from Japan. Stay a while in these silk-lined rooms—note the collection of 19th-century Dutch ceramics—and you can easily visualize the sumptuous gatherings the artist and his wife, Sientje (also a painter), hosted for the leading Netherlandish art society of its day, Pulchri. Small temporary exhibitions devoted to 19th-century art are often mounted by the museum. ⊠ *7F Laan van Meerdervoort* ☎ *070/364–6940* ⊕ *www.museummesdag.nl* ☒ *€3.65* ⊙ *Tues.–Sat. 10–5, Sun. 1–5.*

♨ ⑭ **Museum voor Communicatie** (Communication Museum). Ultramodern and with lots of space, light, and activities, the Communication Museum looks at the ways in which people have gotten in touch with one another over the years, from carrier pigeon to postal service. There's a Eureka exhibit designed for children between 8 and 12 that allows them to experiment with faxes and computers. Much of the signage is in Dutch, although English-speaking audio guides are available. ⊠ *80–82 Zeestraat* ☎ *070/330–7500* ⊕ *www.muscom.nl* ⊠ *€6* ⊙ *Weekdays 10–5, weekends noon–5.*

⑪ **Omniversum.** The IMAX theater shows a rotating program of film spectaculars, including several with nature-based and futuristic themes, on a screen that is six stories high. Like the GEM/Museum of Photography around the corner, it's one of the few Hague museums open in the evenings. ⊠ *Pres. Kennedylaan 5* ☎ *070/354–5454* ⊕ *www.omniversum. nl* ⊠ *€8.80* ⊙ *Box office–showings hourly Mon. noon–7; Tues. and Wed. 10–7; Thurs.–Sun. 10–9.*

★ ⑮ **Panorama Mesdag.** Long before TV was capable of reproducing reality, painted panoramas gave viewers the chance to immerse themselves in another world. The *Panorama Mesdag,* painted in 1880 by the renowned marine artist Hendrik Willem Mesdag and a team that included his wife, Sientje Mesdag-van Houtenback, is one of the largest and finest surviving examples of the genre. A truly spectacular, nearly Cineramic vision, it offers a sweeping view of the kind of scene so beloved by The Hague School's artists: the sea, the dunes of Holland, and the picturesque fishing village of Scheveningen. To enhance the effect of the painting, you are first led through a narrow, dark passage, then up a spiral staircase, and finally onto a "sand dune" viewing platform. That's when the painting first hits you. To the west is The Hague, detailed so perfectly that old-time residents can identify particular houses. So lifelike is the 45-foot-high panorama that encompasses you in its 400-foot circumference that it's hard to resist the temptation to step across the guardrail onto the dune and stride down to the water's edge. Elsewhere, the rooms that lead to the *Panorama* house a good collection of oil paintings and watercolors by Mr. and Mrs. Mesdag, as well as temporary exhibitions. A few blocks away is the painter's house, now the Mesdag Museum. ⊠ *65 Zeestraat* ☎ *070/364–4544* ⊕ *www.panoramamesdag. com* ⊠ *€4* ⊙ *Mon.–Sat. 10–5, Sun. noon–5.*

★ ⑰ **Schilderijengalerij Prins Willem V** (Prince William V Painting Gallery). One of the last remaining Dutch art *kabinets,* this princely gallery is lined with tier upon tier of old-master paintings, inimitably hung in 18th-century *touche-touche* fashion (there's nary an inch between each painting). In 1773, Willem V created this new gallery in his palace, to which the citizenry were invited three days each week, thus earning it a reputation as The Netherlands' first public museum (until then, most collections were seen only by special appointment). Although the cream of the collection was moved eventually to the Mauritshuis across the Hof Vijver lake, many fetching works remain here. The long, narrow room has fine Louis XVI stucco ceilings embellished with motifs from the world of art and architecture but nevertheless exudes an intimate, homey atmosphere, as if a friend who just happened to own a collection that included works by Jan Steen, Paulus Potter, and Rembrandt had asked you over to see them. ⊠ *Buitenhof 35* ☎ *070/362–4444* ⊕ *www.mauritshuis.nl* ⊠ *€1.50 (free with entry to Mauritshuis)* ⊙ *Tues.–Sun. 11–4.*

▶ ❶ **Stadhuis Atrium** (Town Hall). Completed in 1995, Richard Meier's Neo-Modernist complex, comprising the Town Hall, Central Library,

234 <

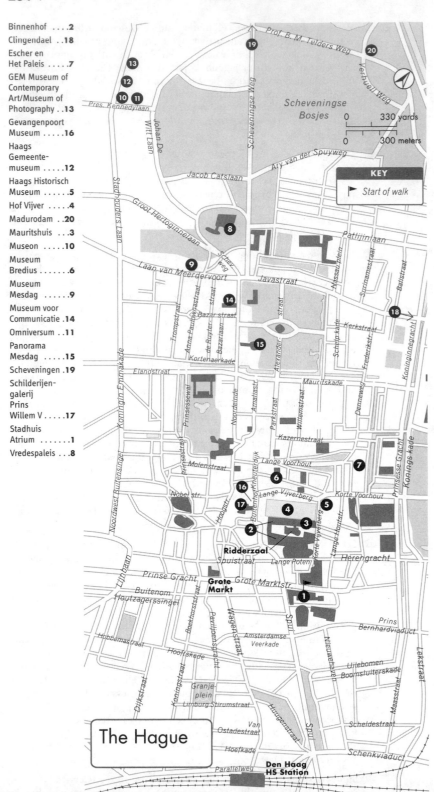

The Hague

and Municipal Record Office, is an awe-inspiring creation in aluminum, glass, and white epoxy resin. Inside, it takes an elevator ride to the 11th floor to powerfully hit a visitor with a sense of scale of the vast Atrium. What also makes the place so mesmeric is the American architect's attention to mathematical relationships; every aspect of the design, including, apparently, the pointing between the tiles, is based on measurements that are multiples of 17.73 inches. Meier has endeavored to show the building, both literally and metaphorically, in its best light. "The clouds in The Hague are incredible," he says. "When the sun breaks through, it's often like a beautiful painting. The natural light in the Town Hall is a reflection of that light, and this is what you experience when you walk through the building." ⊠ *Spui 70* ☎ *070/353–3099* ⬚ *Free* ☉ *Mon.–Sat. 7–7.*

❽ **Vredespaleis** (Peace Palace). Facing the world across a broad lawn, this **FodorśChoice** building houses the International Court of Justice plus a 500,000-volume law library. The court was initiated in 1899 by Czar Nicolas II of ★ Russia, who invited 26 nations to meet in The Hague to set up a permanent world court of arbitration. The current building was constructed in 1903 with a $1.5 million gift from the Scottish-American industrialist Andrew Carnegie. Built in Flemish style, its red-and-gray granite and brick pile has become a local landmark. Gifts from each of the participating nations embellish the interior, with examples of their national craftsmanship in the form of statuary, stained-glass windows, gates, doors, and clocks. Cases can be heard here only with the consent of both parties; comparatively few litigations are heard here these days, although some still make headlines, such as the famous trial of Slobodan Milosevic. ⊠ *Carnegieplein 2* ☎ *070/320–4137* ⬚ *€3.50* ☉ *Weekdays 10–4; guided tours at 10, 11, 2, 3, and 4.*

WHERE TO EAT & STAY

★ **$$$–$$$$** ✕ **Marc Smeets.** Hotel restaurants may not have the bona fides of a eatery with its own address but that is an academic question here at one of The Hague's top culinary temples. The decor is luxe and stylish, thanks to shimmering chandeliers, creamy white walls, mirrors, and gigantic red-orange banquettes. The fireworks happen in this peaceful cocoon when the food arrives. Thanks to owner and chef Marc Smeets' winning ways, his more-than-nouvelle combinations often dazzle the tongue, as you'll find savoring his wild duck prepared with thyme and cinnamon, risotto of pearl barley and caramelized apples, with a date gravy, or his thermidor of Canadian lobster, or his potato-bacon salad with grilled scallops, duck liver, and vinaigrette of apple, or his oven-cooked pheasant with sauerkraut and pancetta bacon. It is all as dee-scrumptious as it sounds. ⊠ *Buitenhof 39* ☎ *070/363–7930* ⊕ *www.marcsmeets. nl* ⬚ *AE, DC, MC, V* ☉ *Closed Sun.*

★ **$$–$$$$** ✕ **Pláto.** Ravishingly festooned with gilded mirrors, candles, passementerie-trimmed lamps, and flowers, this restaurant attracts a hip and relaxed crowd. The emphasis is on international cuisine, with dishes ranging from risotto to sushi to ostrich fillet served with a creamy Roquefort and herb sauce. If you feel like splurging, splash out for the blinis and sevruga caviar, accompanied—of course—by champagne. ⊠ *Frederikstraat 32* ☎ *070/363–6744* ⊕ *www.cosmosnet.info/restaurantplato* ⬚ *AE, DC, MC, V.*

★ **$$–$$$$** ✕ **Zo uit de Zee.** The name means "fresh from the sea" so the emphasis in the kitchen here is just that. There are plenty of oysters and scallops to start off with, followed by, say, a wonderful grilled sea bream with a lemongrass sauce. Set on a quiet canal parallel to the Denneweg,

Zo uit de Zee's decor balances white stucco with brickwork and touches of red stained glass in the windows, with colorful fish artwork adorning the walls. The atmosphere is convivial without being boisterous. Desserts highlight the seasonal; a typical fall lineup relies on lots of pears and nuts. ⊠ *Hooikade 14* ☏ *070/346–2603* ☱ *AE, MC, V.*

$$$ ✕ **Restaurant Julien.** A glamorous Belle Epoque interior, lush with Tiffany-style chandeliers and ornate mirrors, echoes an equally decadent menu. Choose from veal stew with truffled potato puree, or a less-traditional green lasagna layered with sweetbreads and scampi. Julien prides itself on an extensive wine list, and the house dessert, a trio of crème brûlées, is recommended. ⊠ *Vos in Tuinstraat 2a* ☏ *070/365–8602* ⊕ *www.julien.nl* ☱ *AE, DC, MC, V* ☉ *Closed Sun.*

★ **$$–$$$** ✕ **It Rains Fishes.** Crown Prince Willem Alexander has been known to pop in here, so you know it must be good. A gleaming eggshell, ivory, and mirrored jewel box, It Rains Fishes is run by a team of five international chefs, whose predominantly aquatic specialties combine Thai, Malaysian, Indonesian, and French flavors. Its name, taken from a Thai folktale of fishes jumping from the river after a heavy rainfall, finds a few echoes in the restaurant's decor, with the occasional painted fish leaping around on the ceiling and walls. Specialties include local pike with wild spinach, homemade venison ham stuffed with mushroom-chestnut potato salad, Welsh beef, and Brittany oysters. For an unorthodox but totally winning dessert, choose the Thai basil and chocolate sorbet. Additional pluses are outdoor dining in good weather and valet parking. ⊠ *Noordeinde 123* ☏ *070/365–2598* ⊕ *www.itrainsfishes.nl* ☱ *AE, DC, MC, V* ☉ *No lunch Sat.*

$$–$$$ ✕ **Fouquet.** For a taste of Provence and the warm south, Fouquet fits the bill, with its mix of French and Mediterranean-style cuisine. Its interior decor, warmed by terra-cotta frescoed walls, may be more reminiscent of Italy than France, but that's merely hair-splitting. Imaginative, well-priced dishes include mussel-and-spinach-stuffed squid, baked sea bass with rosemary-olive vinaigrette, and duck breast served with a lavender-and-fig sauce. If you've any room left, fill it with a spoonful or two of creamy pistachio parfait. In summer, make the most of the pretty, parasol-bedecked terrace for a perfect alfresco meal. ⊠ *Javastraat 31a* ☏ *070/360–6273* ⊕ *www.fouquet.nl* ☱ *AE, DC, MC, V* ☉ *No lunch.*

★ **$–$$$** ✕ **Le Haricot Vert.** In a 17th-century building that once housed the staff of the nearby Noordeinde palace, Le Haricot Vert is a popular haunt for locals who come to enjoy good food in an intimate, candlelighted atmosphere. Surrounding a grouping of simple wooden tables, every possible wall surface is hung with china, sections of stained glass, pictures, and mirrors, and the overall effect is one of beguiling, romantic clutter. Dishes such as tuna with a Provençale sauce and lamb cutlets served with a rich wine gravy combine Dutch simplicity with French flair. The menu changes seasonally, so it's safe to expect irresistible asparagus in spring and game in winter. ⊠ *Molenstraat 9a–11* ☏ *070/365–2278* ☱ *AE, MC, V* ☉ *No lunch Sun.–Wed.*

★ **$$** ✕ **Garoeda.** Named after a golden eagle in Indonesian mythology, a symbol of happiness and friendship, Garoeda is something of an institution among Hagenaars, many of whom consider it the best Indonesian spot in town. Established in 1949 and spread over five floors, the restaurant is decorated with appropriate art and lush plants to give it a unique "colonial" atmosphere. Waiters are dressed in traditional costume and are more than happy to advise patrons new to the Indonesian dining experience. ⊠ *Kneuterdijk 18a* ☏ *070/346–5319* ☱ *AE, DC, MC, V.*

★ **$–$$** ✕ **Dudok Brasserie.** These days, Dudok is *the* in place in The Hague, because it's ideal for people-of-every-stripe-watching, from politicians debating over a beer, to the *jeunesse d'orée* toying with their salads, to pensioners tucking into an afternoon tea of cream cakes and salmon sandwiches. The vast granite-and-metal interior looks like a cross between a 1930s railway station and an ultracontemporary factory, and besides the countless small tables and roomy bar area, there's a communal central table and a packed magazine rack to keep solo diners busy. The menu combines international dishes—carpaccio of beef, steaks, and grilled chicken—with traditional Dutch fare such as mustard soup (surprisingly mild and flavorsome) and sausage with cabbage. Additional pluses include a terrace for outdoor dining and a 1:30 AM closing on Saturday. ⊠ *Hofweg 1A* ☎ *070/890–0100* ⊕ *www.dudok.nl* ⊟ *AE, DC, MC, V.*

$–$$ ✕ **Juliana's.** Sit outside and watch the world go by, or opt for the interior, which combines French-Victorian-style fitted-wood seating and mirrors with a very Dutch fresco featuring a map of old Den Haag. Food here is of the substantial, international variety—everything from steak to baked scampi to tapas. ⊠ *Plaats 11* ☎ *070/365–0235* ⊕ *www.julianas.nl* ⊟ *AE, DC, MC, V.*

$–$$ ✕ **Sapphire Tower Restaurant.** Recommended by no less an expert than the concierge from the magisterial Des Indes hotel, the Sapphire is behind the Centraal Station, set above an apartment tower, and thus can claim to be The Hague's highest restaurant. The spectacular views it offers over the city are equaled by the great Chinese food (though some say the portions could be bigger); live music on Saturday and a sophisticated cocktail bar also make the place worth visiting. ⊠ *Jan van Rieheekstraat 571* ☎ *070/383–6767* ⊕ *www.sapphire.nl* ⊟ *AE, MC, V.*

★ $–$$ ✕ **'T Goude Hooft.** Magnificently dating from 1423 but rebuilt in 1660, the oldest restaurant in The Hague has a well-preserved interior, with plenty of wooden beams, brass chandeliers, and "antique" furniture all richly redolent of the Dutch Golden Age. In warm weather, the large terrace overlooking the market square makes a pleasant spot in which to enjoy a drink and a platter of *bitterballen*. (What are these croquettes made of? No one will tell you, but they are basically stuffed with finely ground meat, then deep-fried.) For something more substantial, try the wine-enriched beef stew. ⊠ *Dagelijkse Groenmarkt 13* ☎ *070/346–9713* ⊟ *MC, V.*

¢–$ ✕ **Barbagallo.** Although he specializes in takeout for busy professionals and closes at 8:30 (Saturday at 7), Mr. Barbagallo has a few tables in his tiny Molenstraat eatery (and, on sunny days, a few more outside) that are well worth snagging. Mouthwatering pastas and baked dishes such as stuffed zucchini can be ordered by the portion for an early sit-down dinner or a picnic on the beach. ⊠ *Molenstraat 30* ☎ *070/362–8580* ⊟ *No credit cards* ☺ *Closed Sun. and Mon.*

¢–$ ✕ **Eetlokaal Lokanta.** Don't let the colorful floral oilcloth on the tables, the giant-size tomato-paste can holding your silverware, or your gilded Kleenex-box napkin holder fool you into thinking this restaurant is only about funky decor. Cheery staff serve a delicious combination of Greek, Turkish, and Moroccan dishes while making you feel welcome. Try the *imam beyildi* (Turkish for "the imam fainted"), which is a yummy eggplant stuffed with a spicy meat mixture. Because Lokanta is a bit less expensive than some of the other places on the street, it fills up fast, so get there early if you can. ⊠ *Buitenhof 4* ☎ *070/392–0870* ⊟ *MC, V* ☺ *No lunch Sun.*

¢–$ ✕ **Greve.** Take your place at one of the long trestle tables, then enjoy the warmed pumpernickel brought to you while perusing the menu. Opt for the mouthwatering delight of grilled swordfish with guacamole or the hearty chicken soup thick with fresh vegetables—perhaps even both? You'll need to make your mind up fairly quickly, as service in this chatty, communal, and informal eatery is surprisingly speedy. Greve has both a restaurant and a café section. ⊠ *Torenstraat 138* ☎ *070/360–3919* ▤ *AE, DC, MC, V (restaurant only)* ◎ *Closed Sun. and Mon.*

★ **$$$$** ✕▦ **Des Indes Inter-Continental.** A stately grande dame of the hotel world and once a 19th-century mansion built principally for grand balls and entertainment, the Des Indes has a graciousness that makes it one of the world's special hotels. Stay here and you'll be following in the footsteps of Empress Josephine of France, Theodore Roosevelt, and the legendary ballerina Anna Pavlova (who, sorry to note, died here, after contracting pneumonia while on her travels). In the very center of The Hague, surrounded by all the important buildings—the Parliament, embassies, ministries, the best shops—the Des Indes sits on one of the city's most prestigious squares. The interior is a harmonious blend of Belle Epoque elements: marble fluted columns, brocaded walls, a good deal of gilding, and luxurious and ample bedrooms with all the best facilities—there are even Jacuzzis in some of them (although not Belle Epoque ones). Note that renovations are scheduled for many rooms during 2004. The former inner courtyard is now a towering reception area leading to the superb formal dining room—all crystal and linen—called Le Restaurant. On offer here is ambitious French-Mediterranean cuisine; chef Van-Beusekom changes the Menu Royal every week, so dishes are always seasonal. A favorite is grilled lobster served with herbs and a typically Dutch garlic biscuit, but there are also some dishes that bring Holland's East Indian past to mind. After all, this hotel isn't called Des Indes for nothing. ⊠ *Lange Voorhout 54–56, 2514 EG* ☎ *070/361–2345* 🖷 *070/345–1721* ⊕ *www.desindes.com* ⟳ *92 rooms, 6 suites* ⚱ *Restaurant, minibars, cable TV, parking (fee), no-smoking rooms; no a/c* ▤ *AE, DC, MC, V* ⦿ *EP.*

★ **$$–$$$$** ✕▦ **Savelberg.** In the ancient village of Voorburg—just to the southeast of the city in a leafy suburb—and surrounded by woods, Savelberg offers restful accommodation and exceptional dining in a prizewinning restaurant. The hotel is country-house style: a lovingly restored 18th-century mansion with 14 bedrooms, plenty of antique mahogany furniture, and beautiful paintings. Here, honeymooners and pleasure seekers can rub shoulders with visitors from the international political scene. At dinnertime (the restaurant is closed Sunday and Monday) if you enjoy being at the heart of the action, choose to sit at the special chef's table in a corner of the vast kitchen, which gives a bird's-eye view of chef Henk Savelberg and his team at work. Specialties include Salade Van Kreeft "Savelberg," where the lobster is cracked and shelled, then combined with haricot beans, truffles, artichokes, and goose liver at table side. Or try grilled turbot with white asparagus with lamsoren (a special seaweed that grows only where sea and river meet, it comes from nearby Oosterschelde). ⊠ *Oosteinde 14, 2271 EH Voorburg* ☎ *070/387–2081* 🖷 *070/387–7715* ⊕ *www.restauranthotelsavelberg.nl* ⟳ *14 rooms* ⚱ *Restaurant, bar, parking, some pets allowed; no a/c* ▤ *AE, DC, MC, V* ⦿ *EP.*

$–$$$ ✕▦ **Corona.** Created from what were once three 17th-century homes, the Hotel Corona is conveniently located across from the central and historic Binnenhof complex, near the Mauritshuis and Museum Bredius, and—how convenient—at the edge of the shopping district. Relatively few rooms, decorated in warm pastels and with chintz curtains, help to create a cozy feel. If you don't have the energy to venture beyond its confines after a day of sightseeing, you can eat very well at its award-winning Corona restaurant, Marc Smeets. Though its interior style is a little on the corporate side, the atmosphere is elegant but relaxed, and you can dine by the light of candles and crystal chandeliers. French-style dishes include Dutch shrimps served with a compote of tomatoes, sirloin steak with eggplant and wild mushrooms, and dark-chocolate pie.

If you don't want to go whole hog, settle for simple salads, hearty soups, and sandwiches at the hotel's Brasserie Buitenhof. ☒ *Buitenhof 39–42, 2513 AH* ☎ *070/363–7930* 🖷 *070/361–5785* ⊕ *www.corona. nl* ⬙ *36 rooms, 17 with bath* ⟂ *2 restaurants, minibars, bar, parking (fee), some pets allowed; no a/c* ⊟ *AE, DC, MC, V* ⎁ *EP.*

$$$$ ⊞ **Sofitel.** From the outside, it may look like a black-and-white Rubik's Cube, but inside the emphasis is firmly on luxury and comfort. Rooms are decorated in creams and terra-cotta, and the in-house restaurant relies on Dutch old masters for its artistic theme. The bartender in the colorful bar, with checkerboard flooring, can mix you a mean tequila sunrise. ☒ *Koningin Julianaplein 35, 2595 AA* ☎ *070/381–4901* 🖷 *070/ 382–5927* ⊕ *www.sofitel.nl* ⬙ *143 rooms* ⟂ *Restaurant, bar, parking (fee)* ⊟ *AE, DC, MC, V* ⎁ *EP.*

★ $$$ ⊞ **Parkhotel Den Haag.** Situated in lovely Molenstraat, a boutique- and café-busy street with a bohemian feel, the Parkhotel has been sheltering visitors since 1912. The building still exults in plenty of art nouveau detailing; architecture buffs won't want to miss its fabulous five-story brick-and-stone stairway, for example. Today, friendly staff plus light, airy rooms complete with all the modern conveniences (including snazzy bathrooms) add to its charms. ☒ *Molenstraat 53, 2513 BJ* ☎ *070/362– 4371* 🖷 *070/361–4525* ⊕ *www.parkhoteldenhaag.nl* ⬙ *114 rooms* ⟂ *Restaurant, bar, parking (fee); no a/c* ⊟ *AE, DC, MC, V* ⎁ *BP.*

$$–$$$ ⊞ **Novotel.** It's a case of "Lights, camera, action!" in this Novotel, housed as it is in what was once a cinema. Its interior designers have cleverly capitalized on this former life, with the entrance foyer and lounge atmospherically decorated with movie posters, cameras, and directors' chairs. It all helps to create a sense of individuality in what might otherwise be just another bland chain hotel. The guest rooms, safely decorated in shades of peach and blue, aren't quite as interesting, but what they lack in imagination they more than make up for in cleanliness and modern conveniences. And the Novotel's location is ideal for shopping and sightseeing. ☒ *Hofweg 5–7, 2511 AA* ☎ *070/364–8846* 🖷 *070/ 356–2889* ⊕ *www.accorhotels.nl* ⬙ *106 rooms* ⟂ *Restaurant, bar, parking (fee); no a/c* ⊟ *AE, DC, MC, V* ⎁ *EP.*

$ ⊞ **Delta.** With its light interior, pale woods, and frosted-glass-and-metal detailing, the Delta is the closest The Hague gets to a boutique-style hotel. The light-filled breakfast area has fresh flowers on each table; bedrooms are small and white, with contemporary furniture and walk-in-style shower rooms. A helter-skelter spiral staircase and no elevator means this isn't a place for the infirm, but its location—north of the center yet within walking distance of Denneweg—is still pretty appealing. ☒ *Anna Paulownastraat 8, 2518 BE* ☎ *070/362–4999* 🖷 *070/345–4440* ⬙ *11 rooms* ⟂ *Minibars; no a/c* ⊟ *AE, DC, MC, V* ⎁ *BP.*

$ ⊞ **Petit.** On a residential boulevard between the Peace Palace and The Hague Municipal Museum, this quiet, family-style brick hotel is operated by a young couple. Bright and simply furnished and with period stained-glass accents, it has a pleasant, wood-paneled bar-lounge in which you can relax. There's also a minuscule but pretty garden area just outside the front door. ☒ *Groot Hertoginnelaan 42, 2517 EH* ☎ *070/346–5500* 🖷 *070/346–3257* ⬙ *20 rooms* ⟂ *Bar; no a/c* ⊟ *AE, DC, MC, V* ⎁ *BP.*

$ ⊞ **Sebel.** The friendly owners of this hotel have expanded into two buildings between the city center and the Peace Palace. Tidy and comfortable, the rooms are large and have high ceilings and tall windows for lots of light and air. ☒ *Zoutmanstraat 40, 2518 GR* ☎ *070/345–9200* 🖷 *070/345–5855* ⊕ *www.hotelsebel.nl* ⬙ *27 rooms* ⟂ *Bar, parking (fee); no a/c* ⊟ *AE, DC, MC, V* ⎁ *BP.*

¢–$ ▦ **Staten.** Away from the bustling town center, the small and quiet Staten is conveniently close to the Gemeentemuseum/Museon complex and the North Sea Jazz Festival and set on a somewhat high-end shopping street in the chic Statenkwartier district. You can have your breakfast on a pleasant geranium-festooned balcony if weather permits. ⊠ *Frederik Hendriklaan 299, 2582 CE* ☎ *070/354–3943* 🖷 *070/331– 7042* ⊕ *www.statenhotel.nl* ⊄ *10 rooms, 8 with bath* ☖ *No a/c* ⊟ *MC, V* ¶○¶ *BP.*

¢ ▦ **Aristo.** The Aristo's owners take pride in having run a clean if simple establishment for more than 40 years. Just a half block from the bustling Hollands Spoor station, they manage to maintain an old-fashioned family-hotel atmosphere. There are only a few rooms on each floor, so it never feels too noisy. All rooms here share assorted bathrooms. ⊠ *Stationsweg 164–166, 2515 BS* ☎ *070/389–0847* 🖷 *070/389–0847* ⊄ *11 rooms without bath* ☖ *Bar, parking (fee); no a/c, no room phones, no room TVs* ⊟ *No credit cards* ¶○¶ *BP.*

¢ ▦ **Stayokay.** Stayokay is one of the leading hostel chains in Holland, and this one enjoys a location close to both of The Hague's train stations. Besides the 10 double rooms, there are rooms for three to eight. Rooms here are fitted out with two to eight beds (all twins—even some bunk beds!). Clean, modern, and light, the hostel is in a renovated former warehouse and has a deck on the water plus a library, Internet stations, and pool table for when you just can't sightsee any more. ⊠ *Scheepmakersstraat 27, 2515 VA* ☎ *070/315–7888* 🖷 *070/315– 7877* ⊕ *www.stayokay.com/denhaag* ⊄ *10 rooms (doubles), 6 dormitory rooms without bath* ☖ *Restaurant, bar, parking (fee); no a/c, no room phones, no room TVs* ⊟ *No credit cards* ¶○¶ *BP.*

NIGHTLIFE & THE ARTS

The Arts

The Hague has a thriving cultural life—you only have to look at the gleaming Spui arts complex of theaters for proof. The resident orchestra and ballet company are so popular throughout The Netherlands that it is nearly essential that you make your reservations before you arrive in town if you want to be sure of a ticket. And if you do catch a show, you'll note an unusual phenomenon from the otherwise normally reserved Dutch: the standing ovation. For some mysterious reason, this response seems to be given with far greater frequency than in other countries. For information on cultural events, call the **Uit information** (⊠ Uitpost Den Haag ☎ 070/363–3833 weekdays 9–5) in The Hague. In addition, you can pick up the monthly *Info: Den Haag, Scheveningen en Kijkduin (Day to Day Tourist Information)*, which lists (in Dutch) what's going on in major theaters in that area, with English copy describing major events.

Dance

The **Nederlands Danstheater** (⊠ Spuiplein ☎ 070/360–4930) is the national modern dance company and makes its home at the Lucent Dance Theatre, the world's only theater built exclusively for dance performances. It has an international reputation for groundbreaking productions, which might cause a run on tickets.

Film

A trip to the cinema in The Netherlands is always an event. American movies are subtitled rather than dubbed, seats are comfy, and often you can take drinks and snacks in with you. Be warned, though, that just when you're becoming absorbed in the movie, a *pauze* will strike. This is the vital 15-minute interval, when smokers, prohibited from puffing in front of the screen, can leave for their necessary fix. In The Hague, **Cinematheek Haags Filmhuis** (⊠ Spui 191 ☎ 070/365–6030) shows independent, sometimes avant-garde movies. Mainstream movie theaters include the **Babylon Filmtheater** (⊠ Koningin Julianaplein 30 ☎ 070/347–1656) and **Pathé Buitenhof** (⊠ Buitenhof 20 ☎ 0900/1458). Or try **Pathé Scheveningen** (⊠ Kurhausweg 2, Scheveningen ☎ 0900/1458).

Music

The Hague's **Residentie Orkest** has an excellent worldwide reputation and performs at **Dr. Anton Philipszaal** (⊠ Houtmarkt 17 ☎ 070/360–9810 ⊕ www.residentieorkest.nl) and **Nederlands Congresgebouw** (⊠ Churchillplein 10 ☎ 070/354–8000).

Theater

De Appel company has a lively, experimental approach to theater and performs at its own **Appeltheater** (⊠ Duinstraat 6–8 ☎ 070/350–2200). Mainstream Dutch theater is presented by the national theater company **Het Nationale Toneel**, which performs at the **Royal Schouwburg** (⊠ Korte Voorhout 3 ☎ 0900/345–6789).

For an outing with children, visit **Kooman's Poppentheater** (⊠ Frankenstraat 66 ☎ 070/355–9305), which performs musical shows with puppets every Wednesday and Saturday. Advance booking is recommended.

Musicals, including occasional world tours from Broadway, can be seen at **Nederlands Congresgebouw** (⊠ Churchillplein 10 ☎ 070/354–8000). The **Circustheater** (⊠ Circusstraat 4 ☎ 070/415–7600), in the adjoining beach resort community of Scheveningen, puts on many productions of popular musicals, mostly in Dutch.

Nightlife

Though The Hague seems fairly quiet at night, don't be fooled. Behind the reserved facade are plenty of clubs and bars tucked away, often in the city's tiny backstreets. If you like your nightlife of the pumpingly loud variety, you'd best hop on a tram out to Scheveningen.

The latest local and international bands can be heard at **Het Paard** (⊠ Prinsengracht 10 ☎ 070/363–7949), where you can also dance and watch multimedia shows. A planned expansion due to be completed in 2004 also includes a cinema. The huge **Marathon** (⊠ Wijndaelerweg 3 ☎ 070/368–0324) offers a wide variety of music and attracts a young, energetic crowd.

Tapperij Le Duc (⊠ Noordeinde 137 ☎ 070/364–2394) has a delightful old-world ambience, with lots of wood, tiles, and a magnificent fireplace. For what many say is the best pint of Guinness in town, head for **O'-Casey's Irish Pub** (⊠ Noordeinde 140 ☎ 070/363–0698). **De Paap** (⊠ Papestraat 32 ☎ 070/365–2002) has live music most nights and a cozy, welcoming atmosphere. The beer's cheap, too. To enjoy an aperitif in an upmarket setting and surrounded by the great and the good of The Hague, a trip to **Bodega de Posthoorn** (⊠ Lange Voorhout 39a ☎ 070/360–4906) is a must. You can have light meals, here, too. **Frenz** (⊠ Kazernestraat 106 ☎ 070/363–6657) is a lively gay outpost for both sexes. **Stairs** (⊠ Nieuwe Schoolstraat 11 ☎ 070/364–8191), gay-oriented (but women are welcome), is friendly and relaxed.

SPORTS & THE OUTDOORS

Participant Sports

Bicycling

You can rent bicycles in The Hague at the **Centraal Station** (✉ Koningin Julianaplein 10 ☎ 070/385–3235). If they're all booked, try the bike parking garage at **Hollands Spoor Station** (☎ 070/389–0830). In Scheveningen, bikes can be rented at **Du Nord Rijwielen** (✉ Keizerstraat 27–29 ☎ 070/355–4060).

Ice-Skating

Twirl—or trip—away to your heart's content at **Uithof Schaatscentrum** (☎ 070/329–9991), which has both indoor and outdoor facilities.

Spectator Sports

Horse Racing

Near The Hague, **Duindigt Racecourse** (✉ Waalsdorperlaan 29, Wassenaar ☎ 070/324–4427) is one of two racetracks in The Netherlands (the other is in Hilversum, between Utrecht and Amsterdam). The racing season runs from mid-March to mid-November and includes both flat and trotting races with betting. Races are held on Wednesday and Sunday.

SHOPPING

There is a plethora of intimate, idiosyncratic specialty boutiques to explore in The Hague, and in the larger department stores you can kid yourself that you're there only to admire the architecture—several are housed in period gems. With its historic and artistic connections, the city's art and antiques trade has naturally developed a strong reputation, and you can certainly find treasure here. Despite the Dutch reputation for thrift, haggling for antiques isn't "done." That said, you can almost always secure some kind of discount if you offer to pay in cash.

Department Stores

De Bijenkorf (✉ Wagenstraat 32 [entrance on Grote Markstraat] ☎ 070/426–2700) is Holland's premier department-store chain. It has a reputation for combining class with accessibility and is excellent for cutting-edge homeware, fashion accessories, and clothing basics. Do look, too, at the building's period detailing: the stained-glass windows, carvings, and original flooring that adorn the sweeping stairway on the left of the store. The artistic feel even extends to the free gift wrap; ask the counter person if he or she can spare some of the chic black-and-white paper that graphic artist M. S. Escher designed for the Bijenkorf in 1933.

Hema (✉ Grote Markstraat 57 ☎ 070/365–9844) is next door to its big sister De Bijenkorf (the stores are owned by the same group). If you've forgotten to pack something vital, from pajamas to sunscreen, this is where you'll find a replacement. Goods are well made and well priced.

The **Maison de Bonneterie** (✉ Gravenstraat 2 ☎ 070/330–5300) is The Hague's most exclusive department store—and it's got the "By Royal Appointment" labels to prove it. Built in 1913 and with an enormous central atrium, it's a glittering mixture of glass and light. On Maison de Bonneterie's four floors you'll find everything from Ralph Lauren shirts to wax candles.

Shopping Streets

Denneweg, Frederikstraat, and Noordeinde are the main areas for antiques shops, galleries, and homeware boutiques. For other quirky, one-of-a-kind gift shops, try Molenstraat and Papestraat, two of The Hague's most atmospheric streets. You'll find small chain stores in the pretty, light-filled Hague Passage (Spuistraat 26), dating from 1882–85, The Netherlands' last remaining period shopping mall. In the maze of little streets behind the Passage there are more fashion and homeware boutiques, and on Saturday you can shop to the accompaniment of a barrel organ. Between the Venestraat and Nieuwstraat is the charmingly named Haagsche Bluf (the name is akin to the "hot air" coming out of Washington, D.C.) pedestrian mall, featuring mainly clothing chain stores. For department stores, head for Grote Markstraat. Increasingly in the center of town, you'll find larger stores open on Sunday. Late shopping in The Hague is on Thursday—shops close around 9. Many shops take a half day or don't open at all on Monday.

Specialty Stores

Antiques & Fine Art

There are so many reputable antiques and art specialists on Noordeinde and Denneweg that a trip down either street is sure to prove fruitful. **Smelik Stokking** (✉ Noordeinde 101–150 ☎ 070/364–0767) specializes in contemporary art, welcomes browsers, and has a pretty sculpture garden full of unusual pieces. **Voorhuis Kunst en Antiek** (✉ Noordeinde 88 ☎ 070/392–4138) has a suit of armor positioned outside its door that seems to demand that shoppers enter. Inside, various rooms are filled with seemingly every style of furniture, dating from the 17th century onward. **Limburg Antiques** (✉ Denneweg 55 ☎ 070/345–5103) sells antique tiles, clocks, and china as well as larger pieces, all beautifully displayed. **Fred Spoor** (✉ Denneweg 68 ☎ 070/346–0149) has a wide selection of pewterware, plus elegant brass candle sconces, tables, and chairs—family heirlooms just crying out for a new home.

Books & Prints

M. Heeneman (✉ Prinsestraat 47 ☎ 070/364–4748) is a respected dealer who specializes in Dutch antiquarian prints, maps, and architectural renderings. Staff in this small shop are happy to advise customers, and purchases are wrapped in beautiful paper that depicts a fantasy old Dutch town. **J Wennekes en Zn** (✉ Denneweg 25c ☎ 070/365–9141) sells antique prints of faded tulips and ancient maps of Den Haag and is a great place for browsing. You'll always be able to buy English-language newspapers at the city's train stations, but otherwise the centrally located **Verwijs** (✉ Hoogstraat 17 ☎ 070/311–4848), one of a chain of bookstores, sells a good range of English-language magazines and books. **Van Stockum** (✉ Noordeinde 62 ☎ 070/365–9938) stocks a supply of U.S. newspapers and books. **A. Houtschild** (✉ Papestraat 13 ☎ 070/346–7949) has a broad selection of books, including great coffee-table art titles.

Clothing

Both men and women can find classics with a twist in natural linens, cottons, and wools at **Hoogeweegen Rouwers** (✉ Noordeinde 23 ☎ 070/365–7473); stock includes VICRI and Etro. The service is as timeless as the clothes—it's the sort of place where purchases are carefully wrapped in tissue paper. For handmade men's shirts, visit the diplomats' favorite supplier, **FG Van den Heuvel** (✉ Hoge Nieuwstraat 36 ☎ 070/346–0887), in business since 1882. If you've admired the whimsical turnout of Dutch kids, you'll love **Careltje** (✉ Frederikstraat 70 ☎ 070/

310–6423), with clothes for younger children and babies, including pretty shoes and hats, swimwear, and those requisite three-quarter-length baggy trousers.

Crystal, China & Homeware

Ninaber van Eyben (⊠ Hoogstraat 5 ☎ 070/365–5321) sells the classic Dutch lifestyle look—antique-finish globes, silverware, and traditional blue-and-white china. There's plenty of room to look around without fear of breaking anything. To see the cutting-edge side of contemporary Dutch homeware, visit **Steitner & Bloos** (⊠ Molenstraat 39 ☎ 070/360–5170). You'll find steel bathroom accessories, geometrically shaped lights, and sofas, tables, and chairs designed along clean, graphic lines.

Foodstuffs

For tea, coffee, and jam try the charming **Betjeman and Barton** (⊠ Frederikstraat 3 ☎ 070/362–3435). You'll also find elegant tea caddies and spongeware teapots from Amsterdam here. For picnic provisions for an outing to Scheveningen, **Laura Traiteur** (⊠ Frederikstraat 52 ☎ 070/364–2775) has plenty of mouthwatering goodies, including stuffed avocados, grilled chicken, and designer breads.

Gifts, Souvenirs & Jewelry

Tucked away from the crowds is **Emma** (⊠ Molenstraat 22 ☎ 070/345–7027), a tiny, very feminine store complete with whitewashed walls and a wooden floor. The owner specializes in silver plate and costume jewelry, much imported from Paris and Berlin. She also stocks a small range of fabulous chandeliers, sometimes in unusual colors such as purple. If you want to try your hand at making Dutch-style goodies once you're home, **De Heksenketel** (⊠ Denneweg 67 ☎ 070/365–0197) is a kitchenware shop selling a range of inexpensive cookie cutters and wooden molds, featuring gingerbread-style men in traditional dress and, of course, windmills. **H. Sinnema** (⊠ Passage 14 ☎ 070/346–3904) sells every kind of souvenir, from tulip-form pens to T-shirts of the "I Love Holland" variety to Delft china clogs. The tiny, family-run store **Loose** (⊠ Papestraat 3 ☎ 070/346–0404) is a toy shop for grown-ups. Glass cabinets are filled with rolling pins, pots, and pans no bigger than a fingernail just perfect for dollhouse enthusiasts. Meanwhile there are also larger wooden toys, a wonderful selection of old Dutch books and albums, and, in the rear of the store, a wide range of old prints. **Meander** (⊠ Passage 7 ☎ 070/427–7672) should appeal to those who like ornate, old-fashioned gifts. It's a modern store, but the feel is decidedly that of a bygone era. You'll find tea caddies and hatboxes here, as well as china trinkets and scented soaps. The store also sells modern-style items for children, including jaunty floral aprons and squishy-soft toys. If you want to make your own gifts or kill some time with older kids, a good place to visit is the funky DIY-jewelry store **Bija** (⊠ Prinsestraat 60 ☎ 070/362–8186). You can choose delicate beads—candylike glass ones, metallic baubles, or fake pearls—then join the others at the big table and string them into pretty necklaces and earrings. Customers at **Backers & Zoon** (⊠ Noordeinde 58 ☎ 070/346–6422) receive the sort of personal, attentive service one would expect from an old-fashioned family jeweler. There's a sophisticated stock of pieces, including signet rings, diamond rings, and Fabergé-style accessories. Prices are not for the fainthearted. For contemporary jewelry with a young-at-heart feel, pay a visit to **Goudsmid Trudith** (⊠ Spekstraat 4 ☎ 070/427–1622), which sells chunky, tactile pieces studded with semiprecious stones. **Papier Damen** (⊠ 186 Noordeinde ☎ 070/360–0166) sells exquisite handmade papers and gift wrap, as well as covered notebooks.

Street Markets

The main traditional street market (an organic farmer's market at that) in The Hague is generally held outside the **Grote Kerk** on Wednesday from 11 to 6. From the beginning of May until the end of October on Thursday and Sunday, there's an antiques market on **Lange Voorhout**. Wandering through the stalls on a fine day, perhaps to the accompaniment of a nearby street musician, makes for a lovely experience, plus there's a seasonal alfresco café where you can order coffee and apple cake. From January to April and October through December, on Thursday there's an antiques market on the **Plein**; check with the VVV for details.

SIDE TRIP: SCHEVENINGEN

⓳
Fodor'sChoice
★

The Dutch have been building seaside homes at **Scheveningen** since the 17th century, but it wasn't until Jacob Pronk opened the first bathing resort in 1818 that the town really took off as a vacation resort. Today, many visitors come here for more racy pleasures: the casino and the clubs, the music that pumps out from the seafront restaurants, and the general sense that Scheveningen is where the action is. But of course there are less hectic pastimes to pursue: a walk on the promenade, a potter down the pier, a selection of health and beauty treatments, or maybe a deep-sea fishing trip. If you visit the town on a Sunday, don't miss the opportunity to walk to the old village near the harbors (there are three inner harbors, added in succession as Scheveningen's fishing industry grew)—you might still see some of the older local women wearing traditional dress, complete with shawls and distinctive white caps. And the town's famous and grand old lady, the **Kurhaus Hotel,** is certainly well worth a visit, if only to enjoy a cup of tea while marveling at the magnificent dome and painted ceilings of its Kurzaal restaurant.

Feeling lucky? Blackjack, poker, and the roulette wheel await at the **Holland Casino**; afterward, you can blow any winnings at the in-house bar, brasserie, and restaurant. You have to be over 18 to attend. ⊠ *Kurhausweg 1* 🕾 *070/306–7777* ⊕ *www.hollandcasino.nl* 🖼 *€3.50* 🕔 *Daily 1:30* PM*–3* AM.

In the **Scheveningen Sea Life Centre** you will encounter hundreds of exotic sea creatures, from starfish to stingrays. The imaginative design of this aquarium includes a transparent tunnel, 30 feet long, where sharks swim above your head. ⊠ *Strandweg 13* 🕾 *070/354–2100* ⊕ *www.sealife. nl* 🖼 *€9.50* 🕔 *Sept.–June, daily 10–6; July and Aug., daily 10–8.*

June is the time to visit **Westbroek Park,** when its 20,000 rosebushes are in magnificent bloom. The scent in the air is fabulous. ⊠ *Kapelweg* 🖼 *Free* 🕔 *Daily 9–1 hr before sunset.*

The **Vitalizee Spa Baths** offer an opportunity for nonstop pampering. Besides the sun beds, saunas, and baths here, you can splurge for a facial or massage. Pop in for just a day, or arrange a longer program. ⊠ *Strandweg 13f* 🕾 *070/416–6500* ⊕ *www.vitalizee.nl* 🖼 *Varies with treatment* 🕔 *Daily 10* AM*–11:30* PM.

Take a step back in time at the **Scheveningen Museum.** Located in a former school, it tells the fascinating story of Scheveningen's role both as fishing village and seaside resort. ⊠ *Nepunusstraat 92* 🕾 *070/350–0830* ⊕ *www.museumscheveningen.nl* 🖼 *€3.40* 🕔 *Tues.–Sat. 11–5, Sun. 1–5.*

Statistically, the Dutch are the tallest people in Europe, and never must they be more aware of their size than when they visit **Madurodam**. Set in a sprawling "village" with pathways, tram tracks, and railway station, every important building of The Netherlands is reproduced here, on a scale of 1:25. Many aspects of Dutch life ancient and modern can be found here: medieval knights joust in the courtyard of Gouda's magnificent town hall; windmills turn; the famous cheese-weighing rite is carried out in Alkmaar; a fire in the harbor is extinguished; the awe-inspiring Delta Works storm surge barrier (constructed after the disastrous flooding of 1953) holds the ocean at bay; and planes land on the newest runway at Schiphol Airport, which requires them to taxi over a highway. The world's longest miniature railway is here, too. There are also two restaurants, a picnic area and a playground, and the entire exhibit is surrounded by gardens. The sunset hour provides a fairy-tale experience as some 50,000 lights are turned on in the houses. In July and August there is also an after-dark sound-and-light presentation, free to park visitors. ⊠ *George Maduroplein 1* ☎ *070/416–2400* ⊕ *www.madurodam.nl* ⊠ *€11* ☉ *Sept.–Mar., daily 9–6; Apr.–June, daily 9–8; July and Aug., daily 9 AM–10 PM.*

When Scheveningen's frenetic pace becomes too demanding, step into the **Beelden aan Zee Museum** (Sculptures by the Sea Museum). Situated both next to and under the pretty Pavilion von Weid, it's an oasis of calm where you can explore the unique Scholten-Miltenburg sculpture collection, whose highlights include a 230-foot-long etched glass wall. ⊠ *Hartevelstraat 1* ☎ *070/358–5857* ⊠ *€5* ☉ *Tues.–Sun. 11–5.*

The Pier at Scheveningen dates from 1901, but was extensively restored in 2000. Today, you can simply enjoy the view under cover of glass, or take part in more energetic activities, including a "Sling Shot" that will catapult you skyward via an elasticized rope. The 984-foot-long promenade deck is on two levels: a top deck that's exposed to the sun and wind, and a glass-protected inside deck. The transparency of the entire structure offers marvelous views of sun, sea, and sandy beaches. ⊠ *Strandweg.*

off the beaten path

DUINRELL THEME PARK – Set in the woods and dunes of nearby Wassenaar, the Duinrell theme park has rides, slides, and a fairyland for kids, as well as the tropical Tikibad indoor pool center. You can also rent a bungalow. To get there via public transport, take Bus No. 43 or No. 90 from The Hague. ⊠ *Duinrell 1, Wassenaar* ☎ *070/515–5255* ⊕ *www.duinrell.nl* ⊠ *€15* ☉ *Apr. 7–Oct. 28, daily 10–10; Tikibad is also open Oct. 28–Jan. 3.*

Where to Eat & Stay

★ **$$$$** ✕ **Restaurant Seinpost.** The perfect place to eat seafood is, of course, over-looking the sea—something you can do in magnificent style at this much-acclaimed restaurant. In a nautical atmosphere (think glass, pale wood, and seashell accessories), begin your fishy feast with smoked eel served on a blini and accompanied by a tangle of cucumber spaghetti. Then take your pick from one of seven different types of oyster (yes, there really are that many), or perhaps you'd prefer turbot served with morels gathered from the sand dunes of Scheveningen. Dutch specialties include new herring, and the cheeses that have ripened in the restaurant's own cellar. ⊠ *Zeekant 60* ☎ *070/355–5250* ⊕ *www.seinpost.nl* ⊟ *AE, DC, MC, V.*

★ **$$$$** ✕⊞ **Kurhaus.** Holding the prime position at the center of the beach at Scheveningen, this vast hotel first opened its doors in 1885. Since then, it has enjoyed a rich history. Just 14 months after its initial opening, it was almost completely destroyed by fire (allegedly started by a maid accompanying the Heineken brewing family on their vacation). The Kurhaus was restored, and phoenixlike, was up and running again by June 1887. Since then, guests have included Winston Churchill, Marlene Dietrich, and Luciano Pavarotti. Today it is fully modernized. Now engulfed on the street side by shops and apartments, it still has its famous turn-of-the-20th-century profile from the amusement pier, and you can dine on a buffet supper (with dancing on Friday) in the magnificent Kurzaal with its fancifully painted, coffered ceiling high overhead. The guest rooms are grand and opulently decorated in a variety of modern and traditional styles. In addition, guests can make use of the adjoining *Kuur Thermen Vitalizee* center with its saunas, plunge rooms, and herbal baths. ⊠ *Gevers Deynootplein 30, 2586 CK* ☎ *070/416–2636* 🖶 *070/416–2646* ⊕ *www.kurhaus.nl* ⇨ *245 rooms, 10 suites* ♦ *2 restaurants, minibars, gym, bar, parking (fee), some pets allowed, nosmoking rooms* ⊟ *AE, DC, MC, V* ⎮⊙⎮ *EP.*

$ 🖭 **City Hotel.** Just off the beach in Scheveningen, this small, spanking-clean, brightly decorated, and very friendly family hotel spreads through several houses. It's on a main street leading to the waterfront. ⊠ *Renbaanstraat 1–3 and 17–23 2586 EW* ☎ *070/355–7966* 🖶 *070/354–0503* ⇨ *28 rooms, 14 with bath* ♦ *Restaurant, bar, parking (fee); no a/c* ⊟ *AE, DC, MC, V* ⎮⊙⎮ *BP.*

Nightlife & the Arts

Film
The top house in town is **Pathé Scheveningen** (⊠ Kurhausweg 2 ☎ 0900/1458).

Theater
Musicals and live entertainment are often on tap at **Circustheater** (⊠ Circusstraat 4 ☎ 070/415–7600).

Sports & the Outdoors

Beaches
The beach at **Scheveningen** is one of the most popular in the country and has a boardwalk and amusement pier as well as numerous cafés and sunbathing terraces.

Bicycling
In Scheveningen, the place to go for bike rentals is **Du Nord Rijwielen** (⊠ Keizerstraat 27–29 ☎ 070/355–4060).

Sea Fishing
To try your hand at deep-sea fishing, a popular Scheveningen pursuit, contact **Sportviscentrum Trip** (⊠ Dr. Lelykade 3 ☎ 070/354–1122).

THE HAGUE A TO Z

To research prices, get advice from other travelers, and book travel arrangements, visit www.fodors.com.

AIRPORTS & TRANSFERS
Amsterdam Schiphol Airport is half an hour by train from The Hague. Its comprehensive telephone service, charged at €.10 per minute, provides information about flight arrivals and departures, as well as all transport and parking facilities (press No. 2 for English).

🛪 Airport Information **Amsterdam Schiphol Airport** ☎ 0900/0141.

BICYCLE TRAVEL

Bicycles can be rented at railway stations or by contacting local rental facilities. With plenty of cycle lanes, The Hague is as safe for cyclists as anywhere else in The Netherlands.

CAR RENTAL

For car travel beyond The Hague, arrange a rental from Avis. Europcar is a popular option.

🔃 Major Agencies **Avis** ✉ Theresiastraat 216 ☎ 070/385-0698. **Europcar** ✉ De Savornin Lohmanplein 5 ☎ 070/361-9191.

CAR TRAVEL

To reach The Hague directly from Amsterdam, take E19 via Amsterdam Schiphol Airport. To reach the city from Utrecht, take the A12. Once you're approaching the city, follow the signs for the central parking route. This is an extremely helpful ring road that covers the many inexpensive parking lots within the city center.

EMERGENCIES

Pharmacies stay open late on a rotating basis; call for addresses on a given night. Tourist Assistance Service is an organization serving foreign tourists who've fallen victim to crime or been involved in an accident; it's open seven days a week.

🔃 Emergency Services **National Emergency Alarm Number** for police, fire, and ambulance ☎ 112.

🔃 Hospital **The Hague** ✉ Bronovolaan 5 ☎ 070/312-4141.

🔃 Hot Line **Tourist Assistance Service** ☎ 070/424-4000.

🔃 Late-Night Pharmacies **Late-Night Pharmacy Information** ☎ 070/345-1000.

MONEY MATTERS

CURRENCY EXCHANGE It's possible to change money at all of the larger banks, including ABN Amro and RaboBank.

TAXIS

Taxis are available at the railway stations. Alternatively, to get one to collect you from your location, try one of the taxi firms recommended by the VVV: HTMC, ATC Taxi, or Baantax.

🔃 Taxi Companies **ATC Taxi** ☎ 070/317-8877. **Baantax** ☎ 070/350-4924. **HTMC** ☎ 070/390-7722.

TOURS

A Royal Tour that takes in the palaces and administrative buildings associated with Queen Beatrix operates April–September; the cost is €26.50 per person. The VVV also arranges a variety of tours covering everything from royalty to architecture. Or you can purchase booklets that will allow you to follow a walking tour at your own pace. The VVV does tours and has brochures for them, as well as tickets, at the VVV offices.

🔃 Fees & Schedules **Day Trips Department, Den Haag Marketing** ☎ 070/338-5816.

TRAIN TRAVEL

There are two railway stations in The Hague: one is in the central business district, the **Station Hollands Spoor** (✉ Stationsweg). The other station, **Centraal Station** (✉ Koningin Julianaplein), is in the residential area. Trains from Amsterdam run directly to both the Centraal and Hollands Spoor stations, but the Centraal stop is an end stop, whereas the HS stop is a through destination and is used as a stop for trains to and from Amsterdam, Delft, and Rotterdam. Travel from Hollands Spoor to these cities is more often by Intercity (express) train and will not involve a transfer.

🔃 Train Information **Intercity Express Trains** ☎ 0900/9292.

TRANSPORTATION AROUND THE HAGUE

More than 30 buses and tram lines in The Hague whisk travelers all over the city. Most of the sights in the town center are within a 15-minute walk from either of the city's two train stations, but Tram lines Nos. 3 and 17 cover many of the sights and Tram No. 10 will get you to the Statenkwartier museums. For information on specific lines, ask at the HTM offices in The Hague's stations, or at offices listed below. Meanwhile, for information on public transport (trains, buses, trams, and ferries) nationwide, call the information line listed below from anywhere in the country.

🚺 HTM ✉ Wagenstraat 35 ☎ 070/390-7722 ✉ Venestraat 9 ☎ 070/390-7722. **Public Transportation Information** ☎ 0900/9292.

VISITOR INFORMATION

Stichting Promotie Den Haag/VVV Kantoor Babylon (The Hague Information Office) is open January–May and September–December, Monday–Saturday 10–5; June–August, Monday–Saturday 10–5, Sunday, 11–5. VVV City Mondial on the Wagenstraat is open Tuesday–Saturday 10–5. VVV Scheveningen is open Monday–Sunday, hours vary.

🚺 Tourist Information Stichting Promotie Den Haag/VVV Kantoor Babylon ✉ Koningin Julianaplein 30, Babylon shopping center ☎ 0900/340-3505. **VVV City Mondial** ✉ Wagenstraat 193 ☎ 070/402-3336.**VVV Scheveningen** ✉ Gevers Deynootweg 1134 ☎ 0900/340-3505.

WHERE TO STAY

HOTELS If you arrive in The Hague without a room, the reservations department of The Hague Visitors and Convention Bureau should be able to help you. It's open weekdays 8:30–5. Alternatively, head for the VVV outside Centraal Station.

🚺 Reserving a Room The Hague Visitors and Convention Bureau ☎ 070/338-5815 ⊕ www.denhaag.com.

THE BORDER PROVINCES & MAASTRICHT

4

FODOR'S CHOICE

Breda, *famed for its Brabant Gothic castle and church*
De Efteling, *the Dutch answer to Disney World*
Heusden, *a fetching town with 11 centuries of history*
Maastricht, *the posh city home to the European Fine Art Fair*
Middelburg, *with its venerable town hall and abbey*
's-Hertogenbosch, *birthplace of Hieronymus Bosch*
Stedelijk van Abbemuseum, *a modern-art mecca in Eindhoven*
Thorn, *one of the area's famed "White Villages"*
Valkenburg, *for caves, castles, and the "Dutch Alps"*
Veere, *a pretty town with Scottish Stuart roots*

HIGHLY RECOMMENDED

RESTAURANTS Château Neercanne, *Maastricht*
In Den Verdwaalde Koogel, *Heusden*
Manoir Inter Scaldes, *Yerseke*
Prinses Juliana, *Valkenburg*
Toine Hermsen, *Maastricht*

HOTELS Botticelli, *Maastricht*
Campveerse Toren, *Veere*
Hotel Château St. Gerlach, *Valkenburg*
Hotel Mercure De Draak, *Bergen op Zoom*
Langoed De Hertgang, *Bergen op Zoom*

Many other great sights, restaurants, and hotels enliven this region.
For other favorites, look for the black stars as you read this chapter.

By Anna
Lambert

Updated by
Derek
Brookman

THE REGION BORDERING BELGIUM AND GERMANY south of the heavily urbanized Randstad region, is considered by many Dutch to be like "another country." Northern Calvinists find their Catholic southern cousins (with their softly accented singsong speech and ebullient mannerisms) almost a breed apart. In fact, the shared heritage of religion, architecture, food, and lifestyle makes Brussels as appealing as Amsterdam to the people of the southern provinces. The Catholic Dutch are more gregarious and outspoken than their northern counterparts; they also pursue the good life of food, drink, and conviviality with more gusto, and less guilt, than their Calvinist-influenced countrymen who live "above the Great Rivers."

Little wonder, then, that a trip "down south" means a change of gear, a chance to relax and indulge in life's finer pleasures. In fact, when Amsterdammers want to spend a weekend eating well and being pampered in elegant hotels, they think first of the southern provinces of their own country, where some of the most delectable culinary delights await. You can take your pick from fresh Zeeland shellfish or the gastronomically assured French kitchens of Maastricht—for throughout the region there are restaurants of exceptional quality. Meanwhile, Limburg's castles often harbor luxurious hotels, several of which are far more special than much that's to be found in the big Randstad cities.

Not only is the way of life utterly different here, but so is the countryside, as billiard-table flatness gives way to gentle hills—many of them adorned with castles and grand manor houses. If you've been missing wide-open spaces during your time in The Netherlands, you'll get your fill of them here. On the whole, there's little untamed greenery left in The Netherlands, so it pays to explore what there is when the opportunity presents itself. Limburg, in particular, has glorious natural scenery. Here, at last, you'll be able to stroll on quiet footpaths, and romp through fields, woods, and meadows without seeing anything more intrusive than a local out walking the dog or a painter trying to outdo Meindert Hobbema.

Study the map and you'll see that the three southern provinces zigzag their way along the long border between The Netherlands and Belgium from the North Sea coast to the German frontier. In most Dutch provinces the sea presses in to the land, constantly striving to win a foothold, but Zeeland (Sea Land), to the contrary, pushes out into the water, invading the invader's territory and looking for trouble—a collection of flat, open, and windswept islands and peninsulas, known for their agriculture and shellfish. Noord Brabant, also known simply as Brabant, is a wooded and water-laced industrial area bordered on both east and north by the River Maas. Limburg is a region of hills and half-timbered farmhouses that extends along the River Maas deep into the south and can be variously described: perhaps it is hanging on to The Netherlands like a reluctant child to its mother's skirts, eager to go its own way; maybe it is like a waggling finger pointing to the rolling Ardennes and the warmer sun farther south; it could even be called the mark of Dutch stubbornness determined to keep Germany separate from Belgium, no matter the inconvenience or danger to itself. Here, the capital city of Maastricht remains a mecca of sophistication, its antiques shops and famous fine art fair drawing merchants and millionaires from around the world. With its excellent museums, glorious treasure-filled churches, and the sheer quality of life that it offers, it is a must-do destination.

The region's other major towns, such as Den Bosch, Breda, and Middelburg, also offer plenty of attractions, both cultural and social. Cathedrals and churches hereabouts are particularly impressive, and the paved squares and busy sidewalk cafés offer a chance to relax as well as opportunities for people-watching. Dotted throughout the entire southern region are other historic and picturesque towns, such as Veere and Thorn, with their museums and 17th-century architecture—all perfect for a memorable day or two of escape and exploration.

Exploring the Border Provinces & Maastricht

Zeeland, in the southwestern part of The Netherlands, is almost entirely taken up by sprawling estuaries. Travel in this area is of necessity often circuitous, along many bridges and dikes. But the experience is a rewarding one, with a plethora of spectacularly wide, sandy beaches and endless dunes that cry out to be explored on two legs or two wheels. As you head eastward, the gently undulating heath land is punctuated by historic towns such as Breda and altogether more modern attractions like the award-winning Efteling theme park. Further north, toward the river Maas, you can discover little gems like the beautifully preserved fortress town of Heusden and charming 's-Hertogenbosch. By the time you hit the province of Limburg in the south, the hilly terrain and distinct whiff of southern European *bonne vie* could fool you into thinking you'd already left the country. But you haven't—and don't dare to until you've visited Maastricht, a gastronome's delight with more cultural diversions than you can shake a stick at. The border provinces are spread out, so allow yourself plenty of time to really get a feel for the area. If you're not keen on byways and side trips, concentrate on the eastern and western extremes of the region—Zeeland and Maastricht.

About the Restaurants & Hotels

You'll enjoy your food in the border provinces—the locals certainly do. With its proximity to the coast, Zeeland is a great place to try all manner of former ocean dwellers, including oysters, mussels, and lobsters. But the real culinary hub of the region is Limburg, where the influence of neighboring cuisines is all too apparent in the frying pans of the local chefs. You may pay slightly more to fill your belly in Limburg, but you certainly won't regret it. Anyplace in the border provinces worth its salt will be busy from Thursday through Sunday, and without a reservation you'll often find yourself with your nose pressed forlornly against the wrong side of a restaurant window.

Accommodations in this area of The Netherlands range from Old Dutch cozy through modern European cosmopolitan to over-the-top luxe. There are attractive family-run hotels in canal houses and historic buildings, smart international chain hotels, and historic castles and manor houses that have been converted into sumptuous resorts, many with golf courses and award-winning restaurants. Standards are consistently high, and it is repeatedly said that you'll be more comfortable (in more stylish surroundings) here than in any other region in Holland. Behind a 17th-century facade, rooms may come equipped with all modern conveniences. And because the Dutch are so interested in interior design and home comforts, even many smaller hotels and family-owned inns are lovingly decorated, and the guest rooms may well have individual TVs. Assume all rooms have air-conditioning, TV, telephones, and private bath, unless otherwise noted.

4

The Netherlands' southern region is a beguiling mix of sounds, sights, and tastes that often proves the exception to the Dutch rule. First, Zeeland—a province characterized by a love-hate relationship with the sea—provides centuries-old shelter, not to mention mouthwatering sustenance, in its picturesque towns of Veere and Middelburg. In Brabant, there's cobbled, gabled Breda, plus Den Bosch with its soaring cathedral and irresistible chocolate pastries. Just when it all seems too much of a fairy tale, along comes the city of Eindhoven to shed a little light—it's the birthplace of the modern electric bulb. Finally, as the Limburg grass grows ever greener, there's cosmopolitan Maastricht, where feasting and the arts top the bill. Because the southern provinces cover a particularly extensive area, this is one part of the country where it may well pay to rent a car. But if you prefer not to drive, you can happily still reach all the major sites by train or bus. By supplementing these modes of transportation with a rented bike, or your feet when going off the beaten track, you'll have both town and country well covered—especially if you follow these suggested grand tours.

Numbers in the text correspond to numbers in the margin and on the Border Provinces and Maastricht maps.

If you have 3 days

If you have three days, sticking closely to 🔲 **Maastricht** ❶❼–❸❹ ⌐ means you can fully explore both the city and the glorious Limburg scenery. It is possible to cover a lot of ground in only three days provided you do a good deal of driving and are willing to treat some of the sites as whistle-stops. At this pace, you'll be pretty exhausted by the end of your tour, but it'll be worth it. So—presuming you've come down south from Amsterdam way—begin with tiny **Heusden** ❶❷ in North Brabant, an ancient fortified town that's the epitome of picture-postcard prettiness. In the afternoon, head for the province's capital, **'s-Hertogenbosch** ❶❶, whose magical cathedral, 17th-century houses, and excellent museum will give you an in-depth impression of the past, and particularly of the historic Dutch Golden Age. Take time to sample a fabled pastry, the chocolate-drenched *Bossche bol,* whose sugar content should be enough to fuel you onward. Leave in the early evening for the drive toward the North Sea coast, perhaps stopping over in 🔲 **Bergen Op Zoom** ❼. On Day 2, head for Neeltje Jans Island and the Waterland Neeltje Jans Delta Expo—the massive dam and flood barrier that, together with its accompanying exhibition, eloquently conveys The Netherlands' long, hard struggle with the sea. Spend the morning here, and then head south for 🔲 **Veere** ❸, once an important seaport and still rightfully considered one of The Netherlands' prettiest towns.

If you're planning on spending the night in Maastricht, be warned that, depending on road conditions and inclement weather, the drive there from Veere could take up to three hours, so allow time for the journey (a drive via Belgium is by far the quickest route). For a truly relaxing night in Limburg's capital, book yourself into the small and personal Hotel Botticelli, or, if a little pampering is in order, in the Château St. Gerlach with its superlative French restaurant, just outside town in Valkenburg. Spend the next day marveling at Maastricht's many treasures (St. Servaas basilica is a must) and soaking up the café-society atmosphere. Eat early in town (the grilled meat and fish specialties at Sagittarius are particularly tasty); then, in the cool of the evening, work off the after-effects with a trip to the nearby village of Hontem—a walk or bike ride through its surrounding countryside, with its fields and wildflowers, should ensure a deep, fresh-air-induced sleep on your final night.

If you have 5 days

Five days will allow you to take things at a more leisurely pace. On Day 2 of your itinerary, add a quick north coast visit to **Domburg** ❷, where the braver souls in your party can dip a toe into the sea. Then, after visiting **Veere** ❸, travel on to spend the second night in 🔲 **Eindhoven** ⓭, home of the first Philips lightbulb factory and still today Holland's high-tech headquarters. Here you'll find the recently reopened Van Abbemuseum, one of Europe's most remarkable collections of contemporary art. Alternatively, travel farther south to **Thorn** ⓮, an ancient "White Village" whose impressive abbey church allows for great photo opportunities. Spend your last two days exploring the cobbled streets and churches of 🔲 **Maastricht** ⓱–㉞, being sure to carve out visits to the Bonnefanten museum and the chilly but fascinating marl caves of Sint Pieter; the guided, lamplighted tour through its mysterious passages could leave you feeling like something of a pioneer.

If you have 9 days

Because The Netherlands is such a small country, a whole nine days at your disposal will allow you to explore many more of the pleasures of the southern provinces and Maastricht. Extend your five-day itinerary with more in-depth sightseeing, adding a few more stop-offs along the way. After 🔲 **Heusden** ⓲ ▶ and 🔲 **'s-Hertogenbosch** ⓫ on Day 1, use Day 2 to give smaller visitors a treat with a trip to De Efteling, the fairy-tale amusement park that seems to have something to delight everyone. In the evening, opt to stay the night in 🔲 **Breda** ❽. Spend Day 3 on some low-key exploration of the town. In style, Breda is rather like a smaller version of 's-Hertogenbosch, but its grand Grote Markt (the main setting for Carnival festivities), lovingly restored church, and tiny, hidden Begijnhof ensure a thoroughly appealing atmosphere. Day 4 should see you beside the sea—follow your visit to that magnificent work of hydraulic engineering, the Waterland Neeltje Jans Delta Expo, with a seafront walk at **Domburg** ❷. For lunch, head to **Veere** ❸ and 't Waepen van Veere; then, with no need to hurry, pay a visit to the Museum De Schotse Huizen. Day 5 should find you in **Eindhoven** ⓭, perhaps visiting the DAF museum if you're a car lover, or the open-air museum, where you could try Iron Age or medieval activities such as spinning and wood whittling. Stay the night in the city, and then spend Day 6 traveling to **Maastricht** ⓱–㉞ via the "White Village" of **Thorn** ⓮ with its 10th-century abbey church. Days 7 to 9 will allow you to shift down a gear as you make a leisurely tour of Maastricht. Take a complete break from culture while resting your weary limbs at the Valkenburg spa. You'll feel so reenergized after indulging in a few of its wide range of treatments that you may even feel like starting the whole trip all over again.

WHAT IT COSTS In euros*				
$$$$	**$$$**	**$$**	**$**	**¢**
RESTAURANTS over €30	€22–€30	€15–€22	€10–€15	under €10
HOTELS over €230	€165–€230	€120–€165	€75–€120	under €75

*Restaurant prices are per person for a main course only, excluding tax (6% for food and 19% for alcoholic beverages) and service; note that if a restaurant offers only prix-fixe (set-price) meals, it has been given the price category that reflects the full prix-fixe price. Hotel prices are for a standard double room in high season, including the 6% VAT (value-added tax); higher prices (inquire when booking) prevail for any meal plans.

Timing

So far as timing your visit is concerned, late spring and fall are the ideal seasons. You can never count on the weather, though; even in high summer, a single day can bring not just sunshine but also hail and rain. If you can't stand crowds, it's best to avoid the Easter holiday, and the months of July and August. In late spring, the days get longer and more golden and the weather can be balmy. Fall days can be particularly glorious, when the bronze-leaf Limburg woods really come into their own. That said, there are some busy times that you won't want to avoid: the region is at its liveliest at Carnival time (usually in mid-February), and gourmets visit in summer to make the most of the asparagus season (early May to June 24). The mussel season (mid-October to April) usually starts off with parties in village squares around Zeeland, where you'll find steaming cauldrons full of as many of these tasty shellfish critters as you can eat.

ZEELAND: THE LAND OF THE SEA

On the fingerlike peninsulas and islands of the province of Zeeland you are never more than a few miles from a major body of water; never more than a few inches above sea level, either, if above it at all: floods have put this province almost completely under water on several occasions, most recently in 1953. Once one of the wealthiest and most important of the Dutch provinces, the entire area was known for its seafaring and trading skills. The province capital of Middelburg boasted its own East India Company, and the Scottish wool trade was centered on Veere. The province's coat of arms shows a lion rising from the sea, and its Latin motto means "I struggle and I survive," words that were to prove all too apposite in the 20th century.

Zeeland suffered terribly during World War II. The Germans bombed the capital of Middelburg and nearly destroyed its Town Hall and 12th-century abbey. Toward the end of the war, the Allies demolished the Walcheren dikes as a means of flooding the island, in the hope of flushing out the Nazis. Repair work began on them in the winter of 1944, but it took another year and a half before the last hole in Zeeland's dikes was repaired. Sadly, when the famous storm of 1953 struck, the dikes weren't sufficiently strong to withstand its force. Today, new and stronger dikes, dams, and bridges connect Zeeland's four chief islands and peninsulas (Schouwen Duiveland, Noord-Beveland, Walcheren, and Zuid-Beveland), guarding against the possibility of the sea's reclaiming the land again.

There's a delightful sense of the past in this area of The Netherlands—historic towns such as Zierikzee, Veere, and Middelburg boast Gothic architecture, 17th-century merchants' houses, and town halls bedecked with towers, turrets, and carillons. Old traditions are honored, with some local women in Walcheren still wearing lace caps, old-fashioned buttoned-up shirtwaists, and black-and-white skirts, many of them appearing in force on a Middelburg market day. But no one could say that Zeeland is frozen in a time warp: it can't afford to be. The Delta Works dam and flood barrier provides state-of-the-art protection against the elements (and the Delta Expo lets you discover how this was accomplished), and Vlissingen is a model of the bustling modern ferry terminal.

Zierikzee

❶ *67 km (40 mi) southwest of Rotterdam.*

Traveling south from Rotterdam across the islands and frail peninsulas, following A29 to N59, will bring you to the chief center of Schouwen Duiveland: the small, old city of Zierikzee, a yachting port with an attractive Old Harbor (where 17th- and 18th-century houses still line the quaysides), cobblestone streets, three historic gateways—the Nobelpoort (15th century), the Noordhavenpoort (with a facade dating to 1559), and the Zuidhavenpoort (15th century)—and a canal connecting it to the open waters of the Oosterschelde. It stands in the midst of typical Dutch imagery: busy tillers of the soil, black-and-white cattle, distant windmills, broad green fields, and neat rows of plants and flowers. At the harbor end of the canal are high sea walls, and rising above them is the four-spired tower of one of Zierikzee's medieval gateways. Founded in 849, Zierikzee is reputed to be the best-preserved town in The Netherlands. Because of its strategic location as well as its ability to supply two much-needed commodities, salt and madder, for making red dye, the town enjoyed considerable prosperity from the Middle Ages onward. Zierikzee's most spectacular attraction is the great clock tower of the cathedral, **Sint Lievens Monstertoren,** begun in 1454 but never completed (when it reached a height of 199 feet, the townspeople ran out of money). The rest of the cathedral was destroyed by fire in 1872. Nearby, look out for the unusual onion-shape dome topping the wooden tower of the **Stadhuis** (Town Hall); it dates from 1550. At its peak is a statue of every seaman's favorite, the sea god Neptune. Inside the building is a small municipal museum, the **Gemeentemuseum,** whose treasures include ship models, silver, local costumes, and a room decorated with traditional tiles made in the area. The intricately constructed ceiling in the Harquebusiers' Hall is worth careful examination. ☒ *Meelstraat 608* ☎ *0111/454409* ☒ *€2* ☉ *Mon.–Sat. 10–5, Sun. noon–5.*

★ ☾ **Waterland Neeltje Jans** offers a firsthand tour of the most important achievement of Dutch hydraulic engineering. The Delta Works, a massive dam and flood barrier that closed up the sea arms, is most impressive, plus there are exhibits documenting the 2,000-year history of the Dutch people's struggle with the sea. Films and slide shows, working scale models, and displays of materials give a comprehensive overview of dikes, dams, and underwater supports. The visit includes a boat trip in good weather. There is also a water playground with all kinds of interesting aquatic-based contraptions, a storm surge barrier one can stand on, a new futuristic-style whale pavilion, and even a hurricane simulator. ☒ *Eiland Neeltje Jans, Burgh-Haamstede (6 km/4 mi south of Burgh-Haamstede on the N57)* ☎ *0111/652702* ⊕ *www.neeltjejans.nl* ☒ *€12.50* ☉ *Apr.–Oct., daily 10–5:30; Nov.–Mar., Wed.–Sun. 10–5.*

en route From Zierikzee, continue on N59 west to Serooskerke and then turn south onto N57 across the **Oosterscheldekering** dam. This dramatic ride may be restricted at times of high winds; the North Sea to one side, the Oosterschelde bay to the other, and the looming storm-surge

Carnival

Carnival There is no way around it: to understand Carnaval (to use the Dutch spelling) you must experience it. In a last fling of pre-Lenten indulgence, the Catholics of the south set their controls to full blast. In the four days before the onset of Lent, business in the south comes to a virtual halt as residents concentrate on the one thing on everyone's mind: partying. Visitors are made especially welcome, whirled up into the action in no time at all. The feasting aspect of the festivities comes as less of a surprise if we bear in mind the root of the word "carnival": it springs from the old Italian *carnelevare,* or "a removing of meat," referring to the Lenten need to cleanse the home of excess food, allowing for one last, larder-emptying feast before the start of the 40-day fast. But Carnival is not just about eating and drinking, although there's plenty of that, but also about music and merrymaking, pageantry and parades. Preparations for the festivities begin months in advance, including, in November, the election of a "Prince of Carnival." He is given the arduous task of leading the revels throughout the four days before Ash Wednesday.

Then there are the costumes: when the parade passes by, expect to see a plethora of fairy-tale characters, local heroes, orange-painted faces, and psychedelic-color wigs. Costumes often take the form of humanlike bananas, potatoes, and hams that somehow manage to elbow their way down tiny local sidewalks along with the flowing crowd, to reappear later cavorting at the all-night parties. Maastricht's Carnival is generally held to be the most lively of the region, with a main parade, a special children's parade, plus a contest to select the best brass bands. A fair number of Carnival aficionados consider Den Bosch's festivities a better version; the town is smaller and, being farther from the borders, seems to offer a more authentically Dutch experience. You may not get much sleep if you're visiting during Carnival time, but you are sure to eat well if you join the revelers on the street putting away hot-cakes and *nonnevotten* (deep-fried dough balls) to ward off the cold. And intrepid travelers will be sure to make plenty of friends—although they may not be able to recall their names if they're nursing a hangover the next morning.

On the Menu

On the Menu Dutch foodies know that "south of the rivers" they'll find some of the best food in the country—from the fat, succulent oysters and mussels of Zeeland to the French- and German-influenced cuisine of Limburg (around Maastricht), such as *Limburg vlaai,* a delicious custard and fruit tart. The region's white asparagus (Limburg produces 80% of the crop that's devoured by a grateful Dutch nation) and its earthy cave mushrooms are superb and serve as both ingredients and inspiration for those master chefs in their hillside château-restaurants. Just like the landscape, dishes in this area differ considerably from those elsewhere. In some parts of The Netherlands, food is viewed primarily as fuel, whereas mealtimes in the south are treated with appreciation and respect. Because of the Franco-Germanic influence, you'll find that people generally eat later here; expect to dine around 8 PM, though you would also be welcomed from 6:30 PM on. As elsewhere, the three-, four-, and five-course all-inclusive menus offer excellent value and give you a chance to sample local specialties.

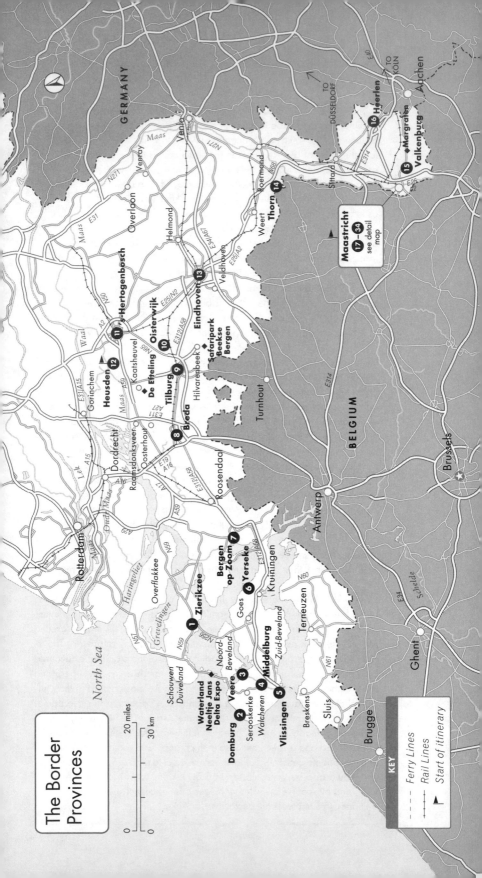

barriers beside the road remind you that it requires massive constructions of steel and concrete to resist the forces of the sea.

Domburg

❷ *42 km (26 mi) southwest of Zierikzee, 16 km (10 mi) west of Middelburg.*

Domburg is the oldest seaside resort in Zeeland, and the special quality of its light has proved a magnet for artists. Early in the 19th century, Jan Toorop built a pavilion here as an exhibition space for the work of his followers, including Piet Mondriaan. Today this has been reconstructed as the **Museum Domburg,** where there's a range of changing exhibitions by local artists, past and present. ✉ *Oostsraat 10a* ☎ *0118/584618* ✑ *€2.25* ✆ *Apr.–early Nov., Tues.–Sun. 1–5.*

During Domburg's heyday in the 19th century, Europe's doctors prescribed sea baths as a cure for everything from apathy to thrombosis, with the first bathing pavilion opening here in 1837. Today, the North Sea winds and chilly water temperatures are still a bracing form of therapy. Unfortunately, the beach is situated quite near major sea lanes—swim too far out and you risk colliding with a cargo ship. Beach pavilions offer glass-enclosed sunbathing areas, cafés, and changing rooms that can be rented by the day or half day. You can also rent a *windscherm,* a colored tarp that serves as a windbreak.

Veere

❸ *15 km (9 mi) east of Domburg, 7 km (4 mi) north of Middelburg, 106*
Fodor's Choice *km (67 mi) southwest of Rotterdam.*
★

One of the prettiest small towns in The Netherlands, Veere is well worth a few hours' stopover to explore its quiet streets and admire its elegant architecture. A village of 2,000 (compared with 20,000 in the 16th century) and now the principal sailing port of the Veerse Meer (Veerse Lake), created when they closed off the estuary with a dike), the town was an important seaport during the 16th century, with a busy trade in such items as wool, linen, and salt. Reach Veere by crossing both the Oosterscheldekering and the Veersegatdam dams and then following the dike road.

Veere's Gothic **Stadhuis** (Town Hall), built of sandstone and begun in 1474, has a fairy-tale facade that harks back to the town's glory days. It is decorated with statues (all extensively restored in the 1930s) commemorating Veere's former lords and ladies, notably members of the Van Borselen family. The building has a minaret-style Renaissance tower, added in 1599, that contains a 48-bell carillon. The whole thing seems unexpectedly grand for the sleepy village of today. Inside is one of The Netherlands' oldest formal audience chambers, resplendent with portraits and Gobelin tapestries and displaying a silver goblet given to Count Maximilian of Burgundy in 1546 by Emperor Charles V. Maximilian, who left it as a gift when he came to inspect the town cistern. ✉ *Markt 5* ☎ *No phone* ✑ *€1.75* ✆ *June–Sept., Mon.–Sat. noon–5.*

The **Museum De Schotse Huizen** (The Scots' Houses Museum) stands beside 16th-century buildings, which face the town's small inner harbor, that were once the offices and warehouses of Scottish wool merchants. Highly ornate, the buildings are named Het Lammetje (The Little Lamb) and De Struys (The Ostrich); you'll know which is which by studying the facade stones. Inside is a collection of local costumes, porcelain, furniture (don't miss the Zeeland "star cabinet" inlaid with star shapes in ivory and wood), household items, and paintings. It's all delightfully old-world Dutch: the blue-and-white tiled fireplace, high ceilings, and exposed brickwork may make visitors feel like they've stepped into a Vermeer painting. ☒ *Kaai 25–27, Veere* 🕾 *0118/501744* ⊕ *www. deschotsehuizen.nl* 🖭 €3 ⊙ *Mon.–Sat. noon–5, Sun. 1–5.*

The massive **Grote Kerk** (Great Church), also known as Onze Lieve Vrouwekerk (Our Beloved Lady's Church), dates from the 14th century and has had a turbulent history. In 1686 its interior was destroyed by fire, and in the 19th century Napoléon requisitioned it as a barracks and hospital, which also didn't help. Its lofty, though incomplete, tower offers great views. Just next to the church is the pretty **municipal fountain** or town cistern, another Gothic structure, built by order of Maximilian of Burgundy, in 1551, to collect rainwater falling from the church roof, which was needed by the wool merchants to conduct their flourishing trade. 🕾 *0118/501829* 🖭 €2.50 ⊙ *Apr.–Sept., Mon.–Sat. 11–5, Sun. 1–5.*

When the dam between Walcheren and Noord-Beveland was finished in 1961, Veere was no longer a seaport, and instead found itself separated from the sea. So Veere is now on the shore of the Veerse Meer, 26 km (16 mi) long and one of the largest lakes in Holland. In the past two decades this lake has developed into a major water-sports center in which every form of aquatic activity is practiced.

Where to Eat & Stay

★ **$–$$$** ╳🖭 **Campveerse Toren Hotel & Restaurant.** Down on the quay, this fabled redoubt is landmarked by its spectacular 15th-century tower, a former gunpowder magazine and part of what were once Veere's city wall fortifications. Overlooking the water and a tiny jetty, replete with bobbing boats, the brick tower—now home to the hotel restaurant—has lovely stepped gables and enjoys a great history: William of Orange and his bride Charlotte of Bourbon feasted here in 1575; Prince Rainier and Princess Grace of Monaco visited more recently. Today you can enjoy servings of fresh local oysters, smoked eel, or grilled lamb. Whereas the public salons are accented with antiques, most guest rooms are simple but comfortable; several are in the massive 17th-century stone hall adjacent to the Campveerse Toren tower, two are in the tower themselves, and others are in quaint two-story houses, one of which, the t'Sternje, has two luxurious deluxe apartments that offer fabulous views over the harbor and Veerse Meer. ☒ *Kaai 2 4351 AG* 🕾 *0118/ 501291* 🖷 *0118/501695* ⊕ *www.campveersetoren.nl* ⌂ *Reservations essential* 🖙 *10 rooms* ⚭ *Restaurant, some pets allowed; no a/c* ▤ *AE, DC, MC, V* ¶⊙l *MAP.*

¢**–$$** ╳🖭 **'t Waepen van Veere.** The family-run hotel-restaurant just a couple of doors from the towering city hall often blows its trumpet about its fine restaurant, which offers a full-blast Menu Gourmand, serves fine renditions of Zeeland-style fish soup, grilled sole, and asparagus in season, and comes replete with the usual nouvelle trimmings, such as a scallopy *"cappuccino" de coquilles St-Jacques* and lobster with chanterelles and truffles. Good-value rooms, complete with TVs and bath, are simply decorated with dark-wood contemporary furniture, white walls, and cream curtains. A special gastronomic three-day weekend food-and-board plan is offered. ☒ *Markt 23–27, 4351 AG* 🕾 *0118/501231* 🖷 *0118/ 506009* ⊕ *www.waepenvanveere.nl* ⌂ *Reservations essential* 🖙 *6 rooms* ⚭ *Restaurant, some pets allowed; no a/c* ▤ *AE, MC, V* ⊙ *Closed Jan.–mid-Feb. and on Mon. and Tues. in late Feb., Mar., Nov., and Dec.* ¶⊙l *MAP.*

Sports & the Outdoors

SAILING The lakes and dams of Zeeland are great sailing territory, and there's much fun to be had yachting between the area's attractive small harbors. **Rederij Dijkhuizen** (✉ Campveerse Toren ☎ 0118/419367) organizes trips from the pier behind the Campveerse Toren. You can tour the Veerse Meer, with an optional excursion to Haringvreter, or get off at Kamperland (bikes permitted on board). Tickets are available on the boat or from the VVV, and start at €2. To arrange a day on the water in Zeeland, contact **Jachtwerf Oostwatering** (✉ Polredijk 13 B, Veere ☎ 0118/501665); **Jachtwerf Wolphaartsdijk** (✉ Zandkreekweg 5, Wolphaartsdijk ☎ 0113/581562);**Marina Veere B.V.** (✉ Kanaalweg wz 5, Veere ☎ 0118/501223); or **WSVW en RYCB** (✉ Wolphaartsdijk ☎ 0118/586103).

Middelburg

❹ *9 km (5 mi) southwest of Veere, 97 km (60 mi) west of Breda.*

Fodor's Choice ★ Middelburg, the ancient capital of the province of Zeeland, has one great advantage that has helped ensure its safety in this water-dominated area: it is on the rise of a slight incline. The town was an important trading post in early times, beginning with cloth and French wine imports, followed by the presence of the Dutch East and West India companies during the 17th century. Today it is a bustling, friendly town that—despite severe bombing during World War II—preserves many impressive monuments. Thanks to its excellent Abdij complex, visitors can enjoy all kinds of exhibitions, from displays on local history and a fossilized mammoth to a costume hall and a collection of contemporary art. All in all, Middelburg is a particularly fascinating Dutch city. The only way to enjoy it is to walk around, for hidden away in the old stronghold called the **Binnenhof**, or Inner Town, are many splendid examples of old architecture—note the Blauwpoort (Blue Gateway), the Kuiperspoort (Cooper's Gate), the Koepoort (Cow Gate), and Vis Markt (Fish Market) in a picturesque square—plus placid canals reflecting former glory.

A testimony to Middelburg's past grandeur, the elaborately decorated **Stadhuis** (Town Hall) stands resplendent on the market square. Begun in the mid-15th century and said to have been inspired by the Stadhuis in Brussels, it is a showpiece of southern-Dutch Gothic architecture. The building was designed as a grand home for the town's prestigious cloth guild. It is adorned with statues of past counts and countesses of Zeeland; much of the facade, however, is not authentic, having been added as part of an overenthusiastic 19th-century restoration. Inside, the most impressive room is the austere Vleeshal (Meat Market), which is now used for exhibitions. To see the rest of the building's 17th-century furniture and tapestries, you will need to join a guided tour. The tours are normally in Dutch and German, but if you ask nicely, most guides will offer some commentary in English, too. ✉ *Markt* ☎ *0118/675450* 💰 *€3.50* 🕙 *Mar.–Oct., Mon.–Sat. 10–5, Sun. noon–5.*

The heart of Middelburg is the 12th-century **Abdij** (Abbey Complex), which incorporates three churches, countless provincial government offices (Zeeland's local government meets here on a monthly basis), the Roosevelt Studiecentrum (a major research library), the provincial cultural and historical museum, and a tall tower that overlooks the city and surrounding countryside. Although it was badly damaged in World War II, the entire complex has been faithfully reconstructed. This is the only abbey complex within a city center in The Netherlands. **Onze Lieve Vrouwe Abdij** (Our Beloved Lady Abbey) was founded in 1150 as a Premonstratensian abbey and served as a monastery until 1574. There's a sweet-smelling herb garden in the courtyard and a 100,000-year-old Zeeland mammoth to admire. You can also visit the cloisters, regional government halls, and the crypt. ⊠ *Abdij 9* ☎ *0118/616616* ☒ *€2* ☉ *Apr.–Nov., Mon.–Sat. 10–6, Sun. noon–6.*

The **Zeeuws Museum** (Zeeland Museum) is closed until 2005 for renovation, though it will be hosting temporary exhibitions (see the Web site for the latest information). When the permanent collection is once again on show, you'll be able to see famous tapestries illustrating major sea battles of the 16th century fought between the Dutch and Spain. The varied collection will also include a "curiosity cabinet," some of the country's most impressive presentations of historic costumes, presentations on life in Zeeland from the Middle Ages up to the 20th century, and canvases by Mondriaan and Toorop. To determine when (and if) the museum will reopen by late 2005, call the phone number or check the Web site. ⊠ *Abdij* ☎ *0118/653060* ⊕ *www.zeeuwsmuseum.nl.*

Of particular interest to American visitors to Zeeland is the **Roosevelt Studiecentrum** (Roosevelt Study Center), whose exhibition hall has a permanent display on the life and times of the Roosevelts. There are often temporary photo exhibitions as well. Theodore Roosevelt and Franklin Delano Roosevelt were descendants of a Zeeland family; the purpose of this center is to make known the historical links between the United States and The Netherlands and particularly to publicize the role of the United States in Europe during the 20th century. ⊠ *Abdij 9* ☎ *0118/ 631590* ⊕ *www.roosevelt.nl* ☒ *Free* ☉ *Apr.–Oct., weekdays 11–12:30 and 1:30–4:30.*

You can climb the 207 steps to the top of the octagonal **"Lange Jan" Abdijtoren** ("Long John" Abbey Tower), which is attached to the Choral Church of the Abbey Complex. The stone tower, 280 feet high, was constructed in the 14th century and is topped with an onion-shape dome from the 18th century. This is a landmark that's visible not only throughout the town but throughout most of Walcheren. There are carillon concerts on Thursday for an hour beginning midday, and more often during July and August. ⊠ *Abdij* ☎ *0118/675335* ☒ *€2.70* ☉ *Apr.–Oct., Mon.–Sat. 10–5, Sun. noon–5.*

Buildings and landmarks typical of the Middelburg region have been
☾ duplicated in one-twentieth actual size in **Miniatuur Walcheren** (Miniature Walcheren), a miniature city within a garden that is home to 1,400 bonsai trees and approximately 300 different types of plants. The skillfully made models include houses, churches, and windmills, and a reconstruction of Veerse Lake replete with motorized boats. Trees and plants are executed on a tiny scale, along with traveling buses, trains, and barges. ⊠ *Koepoortlaan 1, Molenwater* ☎ *0118/612525* ☒ *€8* ☉ *Apr.–June, daily 10–6; July and Aug., daily 10–7; Sept. and Oct., daily 10–6.*

Where to Eat & Stay

$$$–$$$$ ✕ **Het Groot Paradys.** Facing the market square in a house that dates from the mid-16th century, this renowned and intimate restaurant retains a traditional town-house decor, crowned by shining chandeliers. Head chef Ferdie Dolk serves up predominantly French cuisine with a definite emphasis on local ingredients. Seafood lovers are in for a treat and oyster lovers should consider taking up residence. The wine list sees renowned French labels nestle side-by-side with an impressive selection from Australia and New Zealand. Fresh-baked breads are the pride of the kitchen. ⊠ *Damplein 13* ☎ *0118/651200* ⚭ *Reservations essential* ▭ *AE, DC, MC, V* ☉ *Closed Sun. and Mon. No lunch Sat.*

$$$ ✕ **Nummer 7.** Under the same ownership as the more famous Het Groot Paradys, this restaurant has a finesse all its own in a relaxed setting of pale-yellow walls and marble tables. It is not every day you can eat a three-course meal with generous portions of North Sea crab salad, Zeeland pork with truffle sauce, and white chocolate mousse for €22.50. ⊠ *Rotterdamsekaai 7* ☎ *0118/627077* ⊟ *AE, DC, MC, V* ⊘ *Closed Mon. No lunch.*

$–$$ ✕ **De Vriendschap.** The split-level interior successfully blends dark brown girders with soft orange lighting and organic elements such as bamboo screens and lobster pots. Starters include Japanese-influenced raw fish (warn your nose in advance of the horseradish source), and there is a wide variety of seafood-based main courses. ⊠ *Markt 75* ☎ *0118/ 628989* ⊟ *AE, MC, V.*

$–$$ ▥ **Le Beau Rivage.** This attractive hotel occupies a gabled turn-of-the-20th-century canal-side brick building near the city center. The rooms are comfortable and decorated in pale colors with modern prints on the walls; the management is efficient and friendly. ⊠ *Loskade 19, 4331 HW* ☎ *0118/638060* ☎ *0118/629673* ⤳ *9 rooms, 1 suite* ❦ *No a/c* ⊟ *AE, MC, V* ⦿ *CP.*

Nightlife

De Mug (⊠ Vlasmarkt 56) has a warm, inviting atmosphere and a wide selection of beer, plus you can eat here, too. There's live jazz on the last Tuesday of each month. **Rockdesert** (⊠ Damplein 20) attracts a young and very lively clientele; it's great if you like your music loud and throbbing.

Sports & the Outdoors

BEACHES In the vicinity of Middelburg, you will find the best beaches at **Domburg, Kouderkerke, Oostkapelle, Vrouwenpolder/Serooskerke, Westkapelle,** and **Zoutelande;** all have beach houses to rent, and all but Vrouwenpolder/ Serooskerke have beach pavilions.

BICYCLING You can rent bicycles from **Stationsrij|wielstalling** (⊠ Kanaalweg 22 ☎ 0118/612178).

BOATING In central Middelburg, you can take an open-top boat to explore the town's canals. These leave from **Lange Viele bridge** (⊠ Achter de Houttuinen 39 ☎ 0118/643272 ⊕ www.rondvaartmiddelburg.nl) mid-May to mid-September (Mon.–Sat. 11–5, Sun. noon–4); and April and October (Mon.–Sat. 11–4). The ticket price is €5.

TOURNAMENT In Molenwater in Middelburg, there's a **tilting at the ring,** or *rigrijderij,* event every July and August, all good medieval-style fun. Times vary, so check with the VVV.

Shopping

Middelburg's **fruit market** is held on Saturday. The **summer antiques and curiosities market** is at the Vismarkt from mid-June through August, Thursday 9–4. Late shopping is on Thursday.

Vlissingen

❺ *12 km (5 mi) south of Middelburg.*

Also known as Flushing, this major port and ferry terminal at the mouth of the Scheldt has long played a key role in The Netherlands' naval history: it was from here that Philip II finally embarked for Spain back in 1559. Meanwhile, between 1585 and 1616, the town was "lent" to the English as insurance against costs incurred by the Earl of Leicester when preserving the United Provinces after William II's murder. Heavily damaged by bombing in World War II, Vlissingen also suffered badly dur-

CloseUp
SEA SURGE: THE FLOOD OF 1953

O N THE NIGHT OF JANUARY 31, 1953, *a storm blew up that was to prove a disaster for The Netherlands and see its landscape altered forever. Dangerously high tides were forecast for Rotterdam, Willemstad, and Bergen op Zoom that arrived with dire consequences: by morning, 1,855 Dutch people had drowned and hundreds more were left homeless. Proving woefully inadequate, 48 km (32 mi) of dikes burst, with another 139 km (92 mi) suffering extensive damage, resulting in widespread flooding. The Dutch Red Cross Organization began a collection of clothing, food, and blankets, and by Monday, February 2, a fund of Fl 2 million (€ 900,000) had been established. Meanwhile, planes, helicopters, and land forces continued to evacuate victims and mounted an intense program of air-dropping food and life rafts onto villages and visible islands of dry ground.*

The vast scale of the disaster and the sense of tragedy that followed led, in 1958, to the creation of the Delta Act, a plan allowing the construction of a network of barriers that would close off the estuaries toward the southwest of the region. Today, only the New Waterway and the Westerschelde remain open to facilitate ships' access to Rotterdam and Antwerp. The Oosterschelde (Eastern Scheldt) basin can be closed off by an enormous storm-surge barrier consisting of 62 steel gates. On October 4, 1986, Queen Beatrix led a ceremony opening the storm surge barrier, thereby marking the official completion of the Delta Expo.

ing the disastrous flood of 1953. Today, the town is known as an industrial center and for its naval shipyards and college. Facing the Scheldt River and high above the water is Vlissingen's great boulevard, successively called De Ruyter, Bankert, and Evertsen, after famous Dutch sea captains; at the south end is a wide terrace called the Rotonde, and nearby is tranquil Bellamy Park.

☚ At the 1823 **Maritiem Attractiecentrum Het Arsenaal** (The Arsenal), visitors learn about life at sea in a theme park–like environment. Imaginative, hands-on displays include a pirates' cave and a mini-reconstruction of the *Titanic*'s final moments. A climb up the watchtower offers panoramic views across Zeeland, Belgium, and the Westerschelde. ⊠ *Arsenaalplein 1* ☎ *0118/415400* ☒ *€9.50* ☼ *Feb.–June and Sept.–Dec., daily 10–7; July and Aug., daily 10–8.*

Opened in 2002, the **Zeeuws maritiem muZEEum** (Mu-Sea-Um) charts the rich maritime history of Zeeland. Housed in several buildings, some dating from the 16th and 18th centuries yet interconnected by wholly appropriate modern architecture, it has at its heart an expertly-restored Golden Age mansion dating from 1641. The museum lets you get acquainted with the fascinating struggle between the locals and the sea through themes such as Adventure, Water, Work, and Glory. Locals will point with pride to the exhibits on MIchael de Ruyter (1607–76), Vlissingen's most famous son. As a Dutch admiral he distinguished himself during the third war against the English in the early 1670s. There are also exhibits detailing the town's involvement with the Dutch East India Company. Children have been taken into consideration as well, with special informative games, computer presentations, and even a treasure hunt. ⊠ *Nieuwendijk 11* ☎ *0118/412498* ⊕ *www.muzeeum.nl* ☒ *€6* ☼ *Weekdays 10–5, weekends 1–5.*

In quieter days of yore, Vlissingen was known as a particularly pleasant place; newcomers, the story went, "woke up unconscious," for the air is heavy and soft and the sea air most conducive to slumber. The many ships that pass here en route to Antwerp are not asleep, however, for it is here that the sea pilots hand over control to river pilots. You can watch this happening from the Boulevard de Ruyter, named after the 17th-century admiral who has his statue here.

Where to Stay

$$-$$$ 🏨 **Grand Hotel Arion.** For an excellent view over the sea, this decade-old hotel has clean rooms furnished in a palette of soft colors and with modern furniture. There's a lively bar area, too. ⊠ *266 Blvd. Bankert, 4382 AC* 🕾 *0118/410502* 🖷 *0118/416362* ⊕ *www.hotelarion.nl* ⟋ *68 rooms* ♿ *Restaurant, some minibars, bar, some pets allowed; no a/c* ⊟ *AE, DC, MC, V* ⫶⦶⫶ *MAP.*

Yerseke

❻ *33 km (18 mi) northeast of Vlissingen, 35 km (22 mi) northeast of Middelburg.*

The small fishing port of Yerseke is the oyster nursery of Europe. Lobster boats dock at the piers along the waterfront; the beds that nurture some of the finest, sweetest, and most flavorful oysters and mussels in the world lie in pits below the seawalls. In the small buildings on the docks shellfish are sorted and packed for shipment. On the third Saturday of August, Yerseke celebrates with a **Mosseldag** (mussel festival). There are special tours around the oyster beds during the season (mid-September–April) and regular tours of the Oosterschelde (the eastern area of seawater around the Yerseke region) departing from Julianahaven.

Where to Eat & Stay

Zeeland-style cooking often pairs delicately poached fish with a generous bath of rich, wine-based sauce. One particularly delicious way in which mussels are prepared is by baking them with *Zeeuws spek* (Zeeland grilled bacon) and caramelized onions. The fresh oysters are usually consumed raw.

★ **$$$$** ✕ **Nolet's Restaurant Het Reymerswale.** Yerseke's best and most expensive restaurant is run by the Nolet family. The restaurant interior doubles as a museum on Reymerswaele, with many excavated exhibits from the village that gave the world the famous Flemish painter Marinus van Reymerswaele but was unfortunately overrun by the sea some 500 years ago. The beamed second-floor dining room overlooking the water is spacious and graciously decorated. It has a comfortable lounge area with a fireplace and a summer porch in back. There is also an impressively large aquarium, whose inhabitants are apparently not destined for the end of your fork, although the sight of this fishy prison will dismay enough animal lovers. The menu's focus is on seafood, classically prepared to the finest French standards. Grilled turbot or sea bass in basil sauce with sun-dried tomatoes are specialties of the house. From April to July you can also satisfy your lobster cravings. ⊠ *Burgemeester Sinkelaan 5* 🕾 *0113/571642* ♿ *Reservations essential* ⊟ *AE, DC, MC, V* ⊘ *Closed Jan., 2 wks in mid-May, and Tues. and Wed.*

$$-$$$ ✕ **Nolet's Vistro.** The name of this bistro-style annex next to Nolet's Restaurant (they share the same kitchen) alludes to the emphasis on seafood; *vis* is Dutch for fish. This spot has a less formal setting and less emphasis on creativity and presentation, but the lobsters, crabs, oysters, mussels, and fish are just as fresh. ⊠ *Burgemeester Sinkelaan 6* 🕾 *0113/572101* ♿ *Reservations essential* ⊟ *AE, DC, MC, V.*

$–$$ ✗ **Nolet.** This simple and traditional restaurant is run by another branch of the Nolet family and offers crustaceans, bivalves, and fish prepared Zeeland style, poached, baked, or grilled. ⊠ *Lepelstraat 7* ☎ *0113/571309* ☰ *AE, MC.*

★ **$$$** ✗🍴 **Manoir Inter Scaldes.** Seven kilometers (4 mi) south of Yerseke is the simple farm town of Kruiningen, a firm fixture on the culinary map for many, many years. Master chef and local boy Jannis Brevet has picked up a string of awards and accolades for his luxurious concoctions at previous restaurants in Germany and The Netherlands. People come from far and wide—some even by helicopter—to feast on delights such as local oysters served with cardamom potato cream, followed by scallops with truffles and smooth cauliflower mousseline, and rounded off with curd cheese soufflé accompanied by lemon and bourbon vanilla. The bright conservatory restaurant looks out onto lush English-style gardens with hedgerows and impressive floral arrangements. For lucky diners who want to stay overnight, there is a luxuriously appointed, Relais & Châteaux 12-room *manoir* on the premises, in a beautiful building on the far side of the restaurant's garden—a long, two-story house brimming with sash windows and "thatched" coves. For dining (restaurant closed Monday and Tuesday), reservations are essential, as are jacket and tie. ⊠ *Zandweg 2, 4416 NA Kruiningen* ☎ *0113/381753* 🖶 *0113/ 381763* ⊕ *www.relaischateaux.com* ⇗ *12 rooms* ᴒ *Restaurant, minibars, helipad, some pets allowed* ☰ *AE, DC, MC, V* ⭐ *FAP.*

NOORD BRABANT

Once upon a time—1190 to 1430, to be precise—Brabant was an independent duchy; in fact, the area didn't officially join The Netherlands until the Treaty of Münster in 1648. Perhaps this historic separateness goes some way toward explaining the region's markedly individual feel. Despite the intimate appeal of many of its towns, it's one of the largest provinces in the country and has the delightful old city of 's-Hertogenbosch as its capital, home to a magnificent cathedral, an excellent museum, and plenty of well-preserved 17th-century houses. Other interesting towns include photogenic Breda and Tilburg; the latter is not expansively appealing, but it has an absorbing textile museum and the fabulous De Pont exhibition space. Bustling Eindhoven, meanwhile, testifies to the success of 20th-century Dutch industry, linked as it is to the Philips lightbulb. The stunning new Van Abbemuseum houses an extraordinary collection of contemporary art. There is also a lively open-air museum focusing on life in the Iron Age and Middle Ages. Aesthetic purists, be warned: with all that industry, Eindhoven cannot really be described as a pretty place. But in the North Brabant region as a whole, you can enjoy plenty of lighthearted pleasures: in particular, De Efteling, a fairy-tale theme park planned with typically Dutch efficiency and imagination, is one of most popular places in The Netherlands, packed at all times with visitors young and old.

Bergen op Zoom

❼ *36 km (22 mi) east of Yerseke, 40 km (25 mi) west of Breda.*

Bergen op Zoom enjoyed its heyday in the Middle Ages, when it was the site of two large annual fairs. With an old port that was once connected to the Oosterschelde, the town had a solid reputation for hardiness: twice it withstood Spanish sieges, first in 1588, then again in 1622. These days, it comes fully into its own at Carnival time, with the town's festivities regarded as some of the liveliest in the region.

If you appreciate truly splendid interiors, you won't be disappointed by ★ the **Markiezenhof**, a grand house built in the 15th and 16th centuries by the Keldermans, a notable Mechelen-based family firm of architects, for the marquises of Bergen. The place stayed in the family until 1795 and has been restored. The Louis XIV, Louis XV, and Louis XVI rooms are lavishly decorated with crystal chandeliers, plasterwork ceilings, parquet flooring, and fine oil paintings. In the great hall, you can't fail to notice the vast carved chimneypiece with its representation of St. Christopher. On the second floor, the emphasis is on displays on the general history of Bergen op Zoom, plus old toys, prints, and carpets. ⊠ *Steenbergsestraat 8* ☎ *0164/242930* ⊕ *www.markiezenhof.nl* 🖼 €5 ⊙ *Apr.–Sept., Tues.–Sun. 11–5; Oct.–Mar., Tues.–Sun. 2–5.*

Where to Stay

★ **$-$$$** 🏨 **Hotel Mercure De Draak.** Simply bursting with history, magnificent halls, and stylish guest rooms, the De Draak began life as an inn way back in 1397, so it can claim to be The Netherlands' oldest hotel. In that very year, a fire destroyed the entire town except for this structure, which, in the 19th century, was taken over by the church fathers and expanded into a presbytery for the successive deans of Bergen op Zoom (the town church is just beyond the hotel courtyard). Today, Het Wapen van Henegouwen and three other historic buildings, St. Joris, De Draak, and De Borse, make up the hotel complex, which is headlined by its Great Hall and Markiezen Hall, spectacular set-pieces that still look ready to welcome the 17th-century burgomasters of Rembrandt (and, today, often host corporate conferences). Guest quarters, on the other hand, have been ravishingly updated, with a mix of old and new—beamed ceilings, bright white walls, Swedish woods, fine antique Dutch cupboards, strikingly modern prints and photographs. Most rooms are large, and some even feature modern conveniences such as air-conditioning. De Draak is *the* place to stay during Carnival, so if you're looking for a bed for that time, book well in advance. ⊠ *Grote Markt 36, 4611 NT* ☎ *0164/252050* ☎ *0164/257001* ⊕ *www.hoteldedraak.com* 🛏 *56 rooms, 20 suites* ঌ *Restaurant, some minibars, bar, meeting rooms, some pets allowed; no a/c in some rooms* ▤ *AE, DC, MC, V* ⊙ *Closed Christmas wk* ⧖ *MAP.*

★ **¢** 🏨 **Landgoed De Hertgang.** For car-trippers, this is a delightful place to stay just outside Bergen op Zoom. It's a private family home with five large, tastefully converted rooms, featuring luxuries such as TVs, toiletries, some double washbasins, and deep baths. The house may be large, but the place is cozy even in winter. Excellent breakfasts include pastries and ham and cheese, but it's the garden that's a particular delight; enormous, and perfect for exploring, it contains sculptures by various Dutch artists as well as peacocks ambling about the lawn. ⊠ *Klaverblokken 18, 4661 HJ Halsteren* ☎ *0164/683801* ☎ *0164/687934* ⊕ *www.hertgang.nl* 🛏 *5 rooms* ঌ *Some pets allowed; no a/c in some rooms, no TV in some rooms* ▤ *No credit cards* ⧖ *CP.*

Breda

❽ *96 km (60 mi) east of Middelburg, 147 km (93 mi) northwest of* **Fodor'sChoice** *Maastricht.* ★

Historically known as "the Baronie," Breda—a name familiar to art aficionados because of *The Surrender of Breda,* the masterpiece painted by the great 17th-century Spanish painter Velázquez—lies on the main road between Rotterdam and Antwerp and at the junction of several railway lines. Dwarfed by its Gothic-Brabantine Grote Kerk and threaded by pedestrian streets lined with pleasant houses, the city had its first glory days during the 16th and 17th centuries, when it was the seat of the powerful Counts of Nassau, ancestors of the current Dutch royal family. It was also the site of some of Holland's biggest brewers, so much so that it was believed local average daily consumption was among the highest in Holland. However, as the VVV is keen to assure visitors, the people in those times could hold far more of their liquor (thanks to less alcoholic content) without ill effect than we can today—so we shouldn't have visions about an entire city ambling about intoxicated. Today, this small city (with a population around 126,000), dotted with parks, maintains a quiet, medieval charm that belies its more modern role as a major manufacturing center.

Heart of the city, the imposing 15th- and 16th-century **Grote Kerk** (Great Church), built in the French-influenced Brabant Gothic style in brick and sandstone, was the family church of the House of Orange–Nassau. William of Orange's first wife and child are buried here, as are several of his ancestors. After a recent three-year restoration, the splendor of its architecture is once again evident, as is the magnificence of the blue-and-gold-painted 18th-century organ and the triptych painted by the noted 16th-century master Jan van Scorel. In the choir stalls, note several remarkable carvings, one featuring a motorcycle, that depict aspects of the town's experience during the Second World War. The beautiful church tower, visible from wherever you are in Breda, is 318 feet high and was originally home to watchmen, whose job it was to toll the bells if they spotted fire in the town, and to sound a horn to mark each new hour; you can climb the tower's 275 steps. ⊠ *Kerkplein* ☎ *076/521–8267* 🖃 *€1.75* 🕙 *Mon.–Sat. 10–5, Sun. 1–5.*

Just behind the Grote Kerk is the Grote Markt; pride of place on this central market square is Breda's **Stadhuis** (Town Hall), built in 1767. It counts among its treasures a copy of the celebrated Velázquez painting of the surrender of Breda to the Spanish commander Spinola in 1625, today one of the greatest paintings in Madrid's Prado, where it is known as *Las Lanzas*, in reference to the multitude of bristling lances in this stirring canvas. ⊠ *Grote Markt 19* ☎ *076/529–3000* 🕙 *Wed.–Sat. 10:30–5, Sun. and Tues. 1–5.*

need a break?

A good selection of restaurants and cafés surrounds the Grote Markt. **De Drie Gezusters** (⊠ Grote Markt 45–49 ☎ 076/515–2105 ⊕ www.driegezusters-breda.nl), next to the Great Church, is a traditional high-ceiling café with a clientele of all ages. Alternatively, if you need cooling down, the **Ijssalon Toetie Froetie** (⊠ Grote Markt 21 ☎ 076/521–1436), or Tootie-Fruitie Ice Cream Salon, has an appealing '50s-diner interior, with lots of mirrors, glass, and marble. Sit down for a sundae, or take a delicious vanilla or chocolate ice-cream cone away with you.

The entrance to the **Begijnhof** (Beguine Court) is several blocks from the Grote Markt, along Catherinastraat, marked by the austere **Waalse Kerk** (Walloon Church). A home for unmarried or widowed laywomen who dedicate their lives to prayer and charitable works, a Begijnhof takes its name from the Beguines who live there, and they in turn take their name from their beige-color robes. This Begijnhof was occupied until 1990. Its peaceful and attractive courtyard is one of only two remaining cloisters of this type in The Netherlands (the other is in Amsterdam). A formally laid out fragrant herb garden occupies the center of the court. ⊠ *Catherinastraat 83a* ☎ *076/541–1303 Walloon Church information.*

Just beyond the Begijnhof is the main city park, the **Stadspark Valkenburg** (Valkenburg Park), dating from 1350 and named after the falconry house in the forest, part of the castle grounds, where the birds were trained for hawking. The area was redesigned in the 17th century as an elaborate French-style garden by the Counts of Nassau. The Renaissance-inspired **Kasteel van Breda** (Breda Castle) was built by Count Hendrik III of Nassau around 1536, on the former site of a castle dating from 1300. One of its most famous occupants was Charles II, who promulgated his Declaration of Breda (1660) from here to announce his terms for ascending the throne of England. In 1667, the Treaty of Breda was signed here; one of its results was that the Dutch colony of Nieuw Amsterdam was given to the English. The castle sits majestically beyond the moat and now houses the KMA (Royal Military Academy). Today, the castle can be visited only on the city walks organized by the VVV in summer. It is not far from the railroad station. It is also the memorable site for the annual August National Tattoo festival of military bands. ⊠ *Kasteelplein* ☎ *0900/522–2444 local VVV office.*

To the west of the Kasteel van Breda, on Cingelstraat, is the **Spanjaardsgat** (Spanish Gate), which was built by order of Henrik III around 1530 in an effort to improve the drainage of the castle moats. Legend has it that the liberation of Breda from the Spaniards took place on this very spot, though historians consider this far-fetched. On Shrove Tuesday in 1590, the story goes, as the Spaniards were partying, one Adriaan van Bergen is said to have steered his rickety old peat barge into the city. Stashed away under the peat were a band of soldiers who emerged and succeeded in overwhelming the tipsy Spaniards.

Where to Eat & Stay

★ **$$$–$$$$** ✕ **Wolfslaar.** In a beautiful, 17th-century manor house whose grand windows flood it with light, chef Maarten Camps offers a French-inspired seasonal menu. Imaginative combinations include grilled halibut with asparagus, and dessert puddings are tops—try the white chocolate mousse served with seasonal fruit that somehow manages to be both decadent and light at the same time. On Sunday you can enjoy lighter fare—salads and pastries—out on the spacious terrace, a lovely setting when the weather is fine. Often host to corporate events, Wolfslaar also offers cooking classes (check the Web site). ⊠ *Wolfslaardreef 100* ☎ *076/560–8080* ⊕ *www.wolfslaar.com* ▤ *AE, DC, MC, V* ☉ *Closed Mon. No dinner Fri.*

$–$$ ✕ **Restaurant Charelli.** Run by a young, enthusiastic chef and decorated in a low-key manner with simple wooden tables and mosaics, Charelli serves particularly good salad dishes; try the goat cheese or chicken versions. Outside, there's a pretty plant-filled garden where you can enjoy your choice when the weather is fine. ⊠ *Coothplein 35* ☎ *076/522–4039* ⊕ *www.charelli.nl* ▤ *AE, MC, V* ☉ *Closed Mon.*

$$ ▥ **Mercure.** Next to the railway station in a building that formerly housed the offices of the telephone company, this member of the French hotel chain is a straightforward business hotel with a no-nonsense approach to decorating. Still, rooms are spacious, and the staff exhibit a certain degree of Gallic charm. ⊠ *Stationsplein 14 4811 BB* ☎ *076/522–0200* 🖷 *076/521–4967* ⊕ *www.mercure.nl* ⌑ *36 rooms, 4 suites* ♨ *Restaurant, minibars, bar, meeting rooms, some pets allowed* ▤ *AE, DC, MC, V* ⎮⎺⎮ *MAP.*

$ ▥ **De Klok.** This small hotel is a busy and friendly part of the lively market square of Breda. There is a café on the street in summer, and a bar and restaurant occupy the lobby. Double rooms are generously sized, and beds have *dekbedden* (comforters) to keep you warm. Baths may have shower or tub; some quads are available. ⊠ *Grote Markt 26–28*

4811 BB ☎ 076/521–4082 🖷 076/514–3463 ⊕ www.hotel-de-klok.nl
↝ 22 rooms, 15 with bath ♿ Restaurant, bar, some pets allowed; no
a/c ▭ DC, MC, V ⎮◎⎮ MAP.

Nightlife & the Arts

The **Holland Casino Breda** (✉ Kloosterplein 20 ☎ 076/525–1100 ⊕ www.
hollandcasino.nl) is the largest casino in Europe, and is housed in a former monastery: the previous occupants must be spinning in their tombs.
You can play blackjack, roulette, and other favorites.

For a week in late August every year, the air in Breda fills with the sounds
of the National Tattoo—a great festival with military and civilian marching bands from around Europe. Complete with spectacular lighting effects and the theatrical setting of Breda Castle's forecourt, the **Nationale
Taptoe** (✉ Postbus 90002, 4800 PA, Breda ☎ 076/522–0519) is truly a
drum-thumping, baton-twirling occasion to remember.

The Outdoors

BICYCLING   To rent a bicycle, contact **Rijwielstalling NS** (✉ Stationsplein 16–20
☎ 076/521–0501).

Shopping

Breda has a general market open Tuesday–Friday, as well as a market
for secondhand goods on Wednesday, at Grote Markt. Late shopping
is on Thursday.

Tilburg

❾   24 km (15 mi) east of Breda, 125 km (79 mi) east of Middelburg.

In terms of population—about 183,000 inhabitants—Tilburg is one of
Holland's largest towns. The town has a rich industrial heritage, having made its fortune through textiles. In the 1870s, there were 125 woolen
mills in the area, employing more than 4,500 people. Today, Tilburg's
main industries are technological (photographic equipment, high-tech
printing, and so on). Although not particularly photogenic, the town's
backstreets are worth exploring for some pretty examples of art nouveau–era architecture; a number of houses with stained glass are still
standing in streets such as Molenstraat and Lange Nieuwestraat, but
they do need to be sought out.

Just past Wilheminapark, about 20 minutes' walk from the city center,
is the **Nederlands Textielmuseum.** Housed—appropriately enough—in a
converted textile factory, it tells visitors the complete story of the Dutch
textile industry. A functioning 1906 steam engine is just one of a number of machines on view that totally revolutionized the industry. In addition, there are experts on hand to display skills such as weaving and
spinning, and you can see fabrics from around the world, as well as an
interesting collection of Dutch household textiles. Before leaving, pick
up a silk scarf or linen tea towel as a souvenir from the museum's gift
shop. ✉ Goirkestraat 96 ☎ 013/536–7475 ⊕ www.textielmuseum.nl
🎟 €5.50 ☉ Tues.–Fri. 10–5, weekends noon–5.

Northwest of the railway station you'll find the pride and joy of Tilburg's
citizens: **De Pont** is a magnificent gallery set up in the name of local busi-
nessman Jan de Pont, who left a legacy upon his death in 1987 to fund
a foundation for the promotion of contemporary art. A former woolen
mill was converted into a vast, light-filled exhibition space, with an especially impressive central hall. Artists on display here often include such
contemporary, cutting-edge masters as Anish Kapoor, Jan Dibbets, and
Guido Geelen. Smaller wool-processing sheds are now used for temporary exhibitions and, every two years, De Pont's large walled garden is

offered as "a room without a roof" to a different artist, who can then use it for special projects and presentations. De Pont also has a well-stocked bookshop and a very relaxing café. ⊠ *Wilheminapark 1* ☎ *013/543–8300* ⊕ *www.depont.nl* 🖾 *€3.50* ⊘ *Tues.–Sun. 11–5.*

Even sober adults are turned into wide-eyed, joy-filled children by ☺ **De Efteling,** once crowned "best amusement park in the world." Located FodorsChoice just north of Tilburg, this enormous fairy-tale park offers a wealth of ★ rides and amusements, but to call some of these treats just that misses the mark. Yes, you'll find all manner of mechanical thrill-inducing contraptions, from imitation bobsleigh runs to a giant swinging pirate ship, but the real jewels here are to be found in the "Enchanted Forest"—a bona fide domain of trees and plants adorned with fanciful and witty dioramas by Dutch artist Anton Pieck that depict classic fairy tales. Here, you'll see Sleeping Beauty's chest heave as she breathes and be surprised by elves and goblins galore. Attractions are pitched at all levels: the adventure maze with its wobbly bridges and hidden water spouts thrills kids barely old enough to demand "Again! Again!" The Vogel Rok rollercoaster, on the other hand, is enclosed in a darkened dome and has the potential to embarrass even the sturdiest of adults when, on leaving, they recognize the look of blank terror on their faces, as caught on photos snapped at a particularly G-force inducing corner. The charm of De Efteling is compounded by its laid-back feel. From the air it looks more like a forest than a theme park, and it certainly isn't over-commercial; you can even take your own food and drink in. One of The Netherlands' most popular attractions, it lures large crowds most of the time and especially in July and August, so plan to arrive as early as possible. Luckily, entertainers are on hand to keep you amused as you line up for the various rides. ⊠ *Kaatsheuvel* ☎ *0416/288111* ⊕ *www.efteling.nl* 🖾 *€22* ⊘ *Apr.–mid-July and Sept. and Oct., daily 10–6; mid-July–Aug., Sun.–Fri. 10–9, Sat. 10–midnight.*

The Netherlands gets immeasurably more exotic just southeast of ☺ Tilburg, where the **Safaripark Beekse Bergen** is home to hundreds of animals from Africa, Asia, South America, Australia, and Europe. There are lions, cheetahs, giraffes, zebras, kangaroos, and much more. Ride a safari bus or take your own car, although going on foot (perfectly safe!) gets you much closer, particularly to the elephants and monkeys. There is also a safari boat that lets you see the animals from the water. **Speelland** (Playland), strategically located next to the main entrance, is ideal for children who didn't use up all their energy on safari. A broad assortment of slides, swings, climbing frames, water attractions, and adventure possibilities should have them snoring soundly on the journey back to your lodgings. ⊠ *Beekse Bergen 1, Hilvarenbeek* ☎ *013/549–1200* ⊕ *www.beeksebergen.nl* 🖾 *€13.50 (€15.40 combined with Speelland)* ⊘ *Dec. and Jan., daily 10–3:30; Nov. and Feb., daily 10–4; Mar.–June and Sept. and Oct., daily 10–4:30; July and Aug., daily 10–5:30.*

Where to Stay

★ $$–$$$$ 🏨 **Golden Tulip Efteling Hotel.** If you plan to stay late at the storybook realms of De Efteling, there is an on-site hotel whose fairy-tale-castle design, spacious rooms, and modern conveniences echo those of the theme park. In fact, there are even themed rooms, so you can opt, for example, to sleep in canopy beds under a briar roof in the Sleeping Beauty suite (don't prick your hand on the spinning wheel!); get crowned when you book the Royal Suite, replete with thrones and enchanting wood-timbered sloping roofs; or, for 1950s-style diehards, find yourself sleeping in a vintage Chevrolet that's been converted into a bed. As you would expect, the place is extremely child-friendly, with lots of play areas and reduced portions available at mealtimes. The Hoffelijke Heraut (Happy Messenger) restaurant is gracious and pretty and offers a floor show where a countess arrives to audition members of the audience in a talent-show hunt. ⊠ *Horst 31, 5171 RA Kaatsheuvel* ☎ *0416/287111* ⊜ *0416/ 281515* ⊕ *www.efteling.nl* ➳ *120 rooms* ⚭ *Restaurant, some minibars, bar, shops, baby-sitting, parking, some pets allowed; no a/c in some rooms* ⊟ *AE, DC, MC, V* ⏀ *MAP.*

The Arts

Tilburg's main theater complex, the **Stadsschouwburg** (⊠ Louis Bouwmeesterplein 1 ☎ 013/543–2220), is an important venue for theater, opera, and dance troupes. The Schouwburg en Concertzaal (playhouse and concert hall) has an experimental program that embraces everything from classical opera to Dutch modern dance, plus there are occasional visits from overseas troupes. The arts complex also includes a film house and a relaxed café.

Oisterwijk

⑩ *13 km (8 mi) northeast of Tilburg, 28 km (18 mi) east of Breda, 39 km (25 mi) northwest of Eindhoven.*

Oisterwijk is a wooded community and resort town perfect for a quiet day in the country or a weekend getaway. There's a charming central square planted with lime trees (originally as a route for bridal parties) and a bird sanctuary with a number of exotic species.

Where to Eat & Stay

★ **$$–$$$** ✕⊡ **Hotel Restaurant De Swaen.** This very plush French-Victorian town hotel, on a tree-shaded square, has a shallow front porch with rocking chairs that is used as a café in summer; there is also a patio terrace. The crystal-chandeliered restaurant, overlooking an elegant formal garden behind the hotel, serves excellent French cuisine. There is also a bistro with a large outdoor dining area that serves less expensive, more traditionally Dutch choices. The Swaen's hotel rooms are luxuriously gracious; baths are marble. ⊠ *De Lind 47, 5061 HT* ☎ *013/523–3233* ⊜ *013/528–5860* ⊕ *www.hoteldeswaen.nl* ➳ *21 rooms* ⚭ *Restaurant, minibars, bar, some pets allowed* ⊟ *AE, MC, V* ⏀ *MAP.*

's-Hertogenbosch (Den Bosch)

⑪ *18 km (11 mi) northeast of Oisterwijk, 23 km (14 mi) northeast of Tilburg,*
Fodor'sChoice *45 km (28 mi) east of Breda, 123 km (77 mi) northwest of Maastricht.*
★

The hometown of that celebrated painter Hieronymus Bosch, 's-Hertogenbosch has considerable charms (although few reminders of its native son, other than his statue in the Markt square), a particularly lively city scene during Carnival, and a cathedral crawling with appropriately devilish gargoyles. The name 's-Hertogenbosch means "The Duke's Woods" in Dutch, and although that is the official name of this medieval city, the name you will hear more commonly is Den Bosch (pronounced "den boss"), "The Woods." Not much remains of the woods for which it was named, the forests having long since been replaced by marshes and residential and industrial development. Start by crossing straight over the road opposite the station entrance and over the bridge (this city is picturesquely threaded by canals), and head down and right, following the signs for the museum and cathedral along Visstraat. Around Molenstraat, you'll find yourself in the old Uilenberg district, filled with elegant backstreets graced by well-preserved 17th-century mansions that now house shops and restaurants. Take Karrenstraat and continue east to the

Markt square and the main tourist office in **De Moriaan,** the city's oldest house, to get information about lesser-known sights in the city. These include the Het Provinciehuis, with a modern art collection; the Museum Slager, with a group of 19th-century paintings; and Het Zwanenbroedershuis, the headquarters of the Illustrious Brotherhood of Our Dear Lady, a philanthropic group whose members included Hieronymus Bosch and whose historic house still contains some impressive antiques, many of which relate to church music, a society specialty.

need a break?

There is a very special sweet treat in store for you in 's-Hertogenbosch: a *Bossche bol* is a ball-shape cream-puff pastry, filled with whipped cream, dipped in dark chocolate, and served chilled. **Patisserie Jan de Groot** (✉ Stationsweg 24), on the road leading from the railway station, makes the best in town and serves light lunches, too.

★ From the Markt it's a short stroll to the only cathedral in The Netherlands. With spidery Late Gothic windows and a noble Romanesque tower, the magnificent **Sint Janskathedraal** (St. John's Cathedral) stands out as Den Bosch's principal attraction. Built between 1380 and 1520 in the Brabant Gothic style and abundantly decorated with statuary, grotesques, and sculptural detail, it is a cruciform, five-aisle basilica with numerous side chapels around the apse. Its nave is supported by double flying buttresses that are unique in The Netherlands. But the most famous feature is the army of little stone figures swarming over the flying buttresses and up the steep copings in a frantic effort either to escape the grasps of the demon-gargoyles or to reach heaven as quickly as possible. We don't know what Hieronymus Bosch (1450–1516)—whose 15th-century canvases filled with devils, pitchforks, roasting bodies, and grotesque semihuman monsters marked him as a Surrealist before the word was invented—thought of them, but visiting German artist Albrecht Dürer was enamored with their exuberant charm. Inside there are several treasures, including a fine carved 16th-century Altar of the Passion, but head for the chapel on the northeast side of the church built by the Illustrious Brotherhood of Our Dear Lady. Bosch was once a member of this confraternity, and the grisaille murals in situ have sometimes been attributed to him (more likely, his students). Bosch came from a family of artists, and his ribald paintings, giant altarpieces, and anecdotal genre scenes (his pictures of daily life, such as cripples and card-conjurers, were among the first ever painted) all made him a celebrated figure throughout Europe; in the coming two centuries, every great king or court had to have their Bosch, whether it was simply a tapestry knockoff of a picture or an actual, and extremely rare, painting (it is now thought there are only 30 of his paintings in the world, a figure agreed upon by scholars who put together the major Bosch retrospective held recently in Rotterdam). The large square on the south flank of the church is called the Parade. ✉ *Parade* ☎ *073/613–9740* ✉ *Free* ◷ *Mon.–Sat. 10–5, Sun. 1–5.*

From the cathedral and the Parade square head southwest via Lange Putstraat and Waterstraat to the **Noordbrabants Museum** (North Brabant Museum), one of the foremost provincial museums in the country. If by any chance you miss the signs directing you to it, you'll recognize it by the enormous bronze dog, just waiting to be patted, that sits in the museum's driveway. The exhibits are housed in the imposing former residence of the provincial governor. Inside, in the light, bright, and imaginatively converted interior, you'll find historical, archaeological, and cultural exhibits related to the history of Brabant, as well as an outstanding art collection. This includes many particularly fine examples of Dutch floral painting, with most of the 17th- and 18th-century floral masters on view, plus works by Brabant artists of various periods. ⊠ *Verwersstraat 41, from Parade, follow Lange Putstraat to Verwersstraat and turn left* ☎ *073/ 687–7800* ⊕ *www.noordbrabantsmuseum.nl* ⤢ *€5.70* ⊙ *Daily 10–5.*

One of the nicest places to spend time in 's-Hertogenbosch is on the water, with a **boat trip along the city canals** (☎ 073/631–2048 ⊕ www. rederijwolthuis.nl), passing under low bridges and overhanging trees. Options range from sailing all the way to Heusden, to taking a cultural tour around 's-Hertogenbosch, to going on an arty tour that takes you through the pretty Binnendieze area, where artists have placed various sculptures along the banks of the Groote Stroom.

Ⓒ Located approximately 12 km (8 mi) east of s'Hertogenbosch, **Het Land van Ooit** (Ever Land) is an intimate theme park set in woodland where children are deemed to be in charge. A whole army of wandering minstrels, entertainers, and costumed lackeys ceremoniously greet all little half-pints to emphasize the point. A knight's tournament, shows in numerous theaters, assorted "giants," a haunted mansion, a pretty-in-pink mansion, plus plenty of small-scale attractions should keep the kids—particularly younger ones—delighted all day. ⊠ *Parklaan 40, Drunen* ☎ *0416/377775* ⊕ *www.ooit.nl* ⤢ *€16.50* ⊙ *Mid-Apr.–Sept., daily 10–5.*

Where to Eat & Stay

There are plenty of good, ambience-rich restaurants in Den Bosch, though hotels are a little more on the bland side.

★ **$$$$** ✕ **Chalet Royal.** For a mouthwatering definition of French cuisine this spacious, refined restaurant is hard to beat—as devotees from all over The Netherlands will tell you. Set in a charming, turn-of-the-20th-century Brabant villa—with an open fire to warm winter evenings—the restaurant is noted for its lobster with truffle sauce, roast wild duck, and a trio of desserts including the imaginative rhubarb and star anise sorbet. There's an enormous wine list, an appropriate calling card for the extensive wine cellar below your feet. Opting for a food-and-wine arrangement could see you starting off with duck salad complemented by a light, fruity 1994 Nederburg Prelude, with your main course of pheasant and wild mushrooms accentuated by an aromatic California cabernet sauvignon. You can round off your meal with a selection of fine French cheeses and don't forget to enjoy the delicious Brabant Gothic decor touches. ⊠ *Wilhelminaplein 1* ☎ *073/613–5771* ⊕ *www.alliance.nl/ chalet-royal/* ⊟ *AE, DC, MC, V* ⊙ *Closed Sun. and Mon.*

$–$$ ✕ **Pilkington's.** In the shadow of the St. Jans tower, this informal restaurant has a British touch, with such old-fashioned favorites as shepherd's pie on the menu. But there's also grilled veal, fresh fish, and all manner of other delights. In good weather the walled garden, covered with climbing roses, is a must. You can also stop off here just for coffee and cake. ⊠ *Torenstraat 5* ☎ *073/612–2923* ⊕ *www.pilkingtons. nl* ⊟ *AE, DC, MC, V.*

$$ ✕ Golden Tulip Hotel Central. More than just a typical full-service business hotel, the Hotel Central has a family-run atmosphere, especially reflected in the warmth of the service. The rooms have a modern, tailored look. The restaurant, De Leeuwenborgh, with a separate entrance on the square, is intimate and graciously appointed. Its mirrors are etched with images of the city's important buildings, and the menu is traditional and French. ⊠ *Markt 51–57, 5211 JW* ☎ *073/692–6926* 🖷 *073/614–5699* ⊕ *www.hotel-central.nl* ⤥ *124 rooms, 3 suites* ♿ *Restaurant, minibars, bar, meeting rooms, some pets allowed; no a/c* ⊟ *AE, DC, MC, V* ⦿ *EP.*

¢ 🖭 **Het Tuynhuys.** If you've got a car, delightfully unorthodox accommodations await in Den Dungen, just 7 km (4 mi) southeast of Den Bosch: a rustic-style self-contained little cottage, set in the garden of a private house, with a spacious sitting-dining area, two beds, a shower, and a kitchenette. Het Tuynhuys (or the Garden House) is decorated in restful blue, with some antique furniture, plus pictures and ornaments picked up by the owners on their travels abroad. It's not luxurious, but it is charming—and in the morning, breakfast is brought to your door. ⊠ *Brinkhoeve, Grinsel 74, 5721 TL Den Dungen* ☎ *073/644–3732* 🖶 *073/594–4059* ⊕ *www.sbkbb.nl* ⤵ *1 cottage* ♨ *No a/c* ⊟ *No credit cards.*

Nightlife & the Arts

Once a week, 's-Hertogenbosch offers back-to-back **carillon recitals** from two sets of bells. The Town Hall bells play every Wednesday morning from 10 to 11, followed by another carillon concert from the cathedral from 11:30 to 12:30.

King's (⊠ Vughterstraat 99a ☎ 073/613–4479) is open late, plays loud music, and attracts a boisterous but good-natured crowd. Sporty types and young businesspeople frequent **Silva Ducis** (⊠ Parade 6–7 ☎ 073/613–0405), an elegant grand café that looks out onto the most attractive square in town. There is a wide range of beer to choose from and jazz or classical music in the background.

The Outdoors

You can rent bicycles at **Cyclepoint** (⊠ Hoek Zuid-Willemsvaart-Hinthamereinde ☎ 073/613–9020) or **Stationsfietsstalling** (⊠ Stationsplein 22 ☎ 073/613–4737 or 073/613–4033).

Shopping

There is a large general market every Wednesday and Saturday on the market square. Equestrian lovers may be interested in the sale of horses that takes place every Thursday from 7:30 to noon in the Brabanthallen. Late shopping is on Thursday.

The shop of the **North Brabant Museum** (⊠ Verwersstraat 41 ☎ 073/687–7800) offers an exceptional collection of art books covering many periods and styles of Dutch and international art.

For quirky gifts, **Favfallino** (⊠ Putstraat 10 ☎ 073/614–0481) sells everything from drink coasters to mugs and pepper pots, all in zingy colors. Next door to Favfallino is **Wolvers Porselein** (⊠ Putstraat 6 ☎ 073/613–2444), which specializes in wafer-thin art pottery; you'll want to buy it, but the question is, will you be able to get it home in one piece?

Heusden

▶ ⑫ *17 km (11 mi) northwest of s'-Hertogenbosch.*

Fodor'sChoice
★

Fronting the River Maas, the little town of Heusden is a must-visit stop. There are no specific buildings or museums to see, but the entire town radiates a very special atmosphere, composed as it is of a windmill, a harbor, little cobbled streets, perfectly restored buildings, and history—and no less than 11 centuries of it. Best of all, Heusden is a perfect place to explore on foot; in fact, visitors are asked to leave their cars in designated lots outside the town center.

The Heusden story is a stirring one. Its strategic importance and heavy fortifications led the counts of Holland and Gelderland to battle the Dukes of Brabant over its possession; it later became a major defense post against the Spaniards in the Dutch war of independence (1568–1648). Between 1794 and 1813, the town was occupied by the French, after which it fell into a long economic decline. Heusden suffered greatly in the Second World War: before the Nazi forces retreated from the advancing Allies in November 1944, they blew up the medieval tower of Sint Catharijne Kerk together with the city hall, killing the 134 townspeople hiding in its cellar. With modernization looming after the war, it was proposed that Heusden's remaining buildings be razed and replaced with high-rise apartment blocks. The local population put up a fierce resistance, and in the 1960s the Dutch government decreed that the place should become a national historic monument, not as a museum but as a living town. Since 1968, the equivalent of $75 million has been spent on the town's restoration, and the result—full of character and charm without being faux—is a hit with both the 1,500 residents and Heusden's 300,000 annual visitors.

A physically undemanding stroll around the town makes for a fascinating and extremely pleasant afternoon. The **Kasteel** (close to Johannes van Brabanstraat in the outer town) and its ramparts are on the former site of a large, four-sided, 12th-century stone fortress topped by a huge, eight-sided tower with enormously thick walls. Though its original purpose was defensive, its downfall came with a later incarnation as a powder magazine (when lightning struck the tower in 1680, the fortress blew up—together with about a quarter of Heusden's other buildings). The ramparts were modified in 1581 by Jacob Kempt, one of Europe's leading defense experts, on the orders of William of Orange. The result—completed in 1613—was a system admired throughout Europe: to protect the city from attack, eight bulwarks and ramparts were erected in conjunction with a series of brick tunnels through which defending militia could enter and exit the inner city; these were once protected by the small triangular islands known as *ravelijnen*, which are still visible. Kempt's system succeeded in protecting Heusden until the French occupation of 1794. ✉ *Johan van Brabantstraat.*

The **Vismarkt** (fish market, facing the Stadshaven, inner town) operated until 1900; salmon and sturgeon were the specialties. At the far end of the marketplace, look out for the columned **Visbank**, or "Fish Bank," where fish were laid out, built in 1796 during the French occupation, to connect the marketplace with the inner harbor. To the right of the Visbank is a reproduction of the old customhouse (currently home to a wine wholesaler), where duty was collected on goods that had arrived via the harbor.

Built over a range of periods, beginning around 1200, the **Sint Catharijne Kerk** (Catherine Church) and the **Gouverneurs Huis** (Governor's House) became the center for Protestant worship when Heusden pledged its loyalty to William of Orange in 1578. The Governor's House was built originally as part of the church complex, to be a home for its pastor, around 1592; later in the mid-17th century it was taken over by the military governor. Today, it is a public building used for local events, so you might be able to take a peek around if the doors are open. Sint Catharijne Kerk dates from around 1210, and its treasures include a glorious rib-vaulted roof, an ancient clock dating from the mid-14th century, and the ornate tomb of Johan Baron von Friesheim, a commander-governor of Heusden who died in 1733. ✉ *Putterstraat* ☽ *Mon.–Sat. 10–5, Sun. 1–5.*

need a break? Rest your feet over a cup of tea and one of a vast selection of cakes at **Bertels** (✉ Botermark 3 ☎ 0416/661237), a tea and coffeehouse that is something of a Heusden institution. The banana-cream tarts are highly recommended.

Where to Eat & Stay

★ **$–$$$** ✕⌨ **In Den Verdwaalde Koogel.** This elegant hotel-restaurant (the name translates as the "Stray Bullet," a reference to a leftover from World War II that's still visible in the hotel's exterior) boasts a beautiful, stepgabled facade that dates from the 17th century. Inside, things are equally attractive with just 13 rooms, each individually decorated in its own classic style and with restored original features such as exposed brickwork. The restaurant is regarded as the best in town, with delicious local pork dishes especially worth sampling, and plenty of choice regarding the type of wine you wish as accompaniment. The surroundings are extremely convivial, with exposed ceiling beams and a large fireplace. In fine weather, you can sit outside on the terrace, placing yourself in the very heart of Heusden. ✉ *Vismarkt 1, 5256 BC* ☎ *0416/661933* 🖶 *0416/ 661295* 🛏 *13 rooms* ⚘ *Restaurant, minibars, some pets allowed; no a/c* ▤ *MC, V* ⦿ *FAP.*

Eindhoven

⓭ *38 km (24 mi) southeast of Heusden, 38 km (24 mi) south of 's-Hertogenbosch, 125 km (79 mi) north of Maastricht.*

"The Town That Anton Built," Eindhoven was founded by that great Dutch industrialist and visionary Anton Philips, who died in 1951. A century ago, Eindhoven was a village of 6,500 souls who thought it a real adventure to journey to any of the neighboring boroughs. Today, all those villages have been swallowed up in one of the most remarkable cities in Holland, with more than 200,000 inhabitants, and the center of an industry that has literally illuminated the world, starting in 1891 when Eindhoven's first lightbulb factory opened. Philips may have moved its headquarters office to Amsterdam, but the Eindhoven region is still home to Europe's third-largest concentration of high-tech companies, after Paris and Munich. Since the bombings of World War II, there is no longer any traditional, historic center to explore, but there are interesting examples of contemporary architecture throughout the city. Instead of the usual doses of aesthetic beauty, expect to find a technically innovative center with an exceptional museum of modern art, the unusual DAF car museum, and an open-air historical museum where you can really get your hands dirty.

Situated on the east side of Eindhoven's vast central square, the Lichtplein (the light square), there's an interesting example of early-20th-century industrial architecture. Known to locals as the "White Lady," this complex of buildings, originally constructed for the Philips company, includes the **Philips Lichttoren** (Philips Light Tower), built in 1921 as the factory where the longevity of the bulbs' filaments could be tested. It was once Eindhoven's most prominent building, and is still one of the city's best-known landmarks. Outside the tower, there's a statue known as "the little lightbulb maker" commemorating the women who made the first lightbulbs. ✉ *Emmasingel 12* ☎ *040/296–2937.*

If you're keen to learn more about Eindhoven's Philips connection, you can visit the **Philips Gloeilampenfabriekje** (Philips Lightbulb Factory; ✉ Emmasingel 31 ☎ 040/297–9106), which opened in 1891; it's just a stone's throw from the "White Lady," with tours only by reservation. Die-hard Philips aficionados will want to make the trip to the western outskirts of the city, where they'll find the **Philips Museum.** On view are industrial artifacts dating from 1890 to 1960, from old-fashioned wireless sets to—you guessed it—lightbulbs. ✉ *Looyenbeemdstraat 14* ☎ *040/272–3308* ⊕ *www.philipsmuseumeindhoven.nl* 🖃 *€3* ☉ *Mon.–Wed. 9–3, Thurs.–Sun. by appointment only.*

Close to the Town Hall on the fringe of the city center, the revamped

Fodor'sChoice **Stedelijk van Abbemuseum** (Municipal Van Abbe Museum) houses an ex-
★ traordinary collection of modern and contemporary art. The collection
began in 1936 as the simple wish of a local cigar maker, Henri van Abbe,
to be able to visit a museum in his own town. On January 17, 2003, H.
M. Queen Beatrix inaugurated the museum's new extension, which is
striking even from the outside; its angled walls, with their gray mosaic-
style finish, offer a refreshing counterpoint to the attractive brickwork
of the original building. Inside, depending on which tenth of the museum's own collection is on display, you can see examples of every
major trend of the last hundred years.

The small but first-rate Cubist collection includes pieces by Picasso, Mondriaan, and Chagall, and chances are you won't find a richer offering
of Russian avant-garde art anywhere in the world outside Russia. There
are also plenty of three-dimensional works on display, from a disori-
enting balloon-headed gossiping couple to Moholy Nagy's mechanical
Light-Room-Modulator, to the latest names being dropped in New
York City, including Lawrence Weiner and Matt Mulican. The new building itself is also an integral part of the exhibition. Standing on the top
floor looking down at the intriguing way in which balconies, walkways,
and walls bisect, you could almost be gazing into a real-life M. C. Escher drawing. The new 80-foot-high tower also serves as a canvas, since
Douglas Gordon has decorated its walls with phrases and snatches of
conversation printed at various points between floor and ceiling. Inside,
Marten van Severen, a noted Belgian designer, has graced the interiors
with high-style Minimalist accents. The Van Abbemuseum also boasts
one of the most comprehensive art libraries in the country. ⊠ *Bilderdi-
jklaan 10* ☎ *040/238–1000* ⊕ *www.vanabbemuseum.nl* ⊠ *€8.50*
☉ *Tues.–Sun. 11–5.*

Ⓒ The **Historisch Openluchtmuseum** (Historical Open-Air Museum), just
past Eindhoven's central ring road in a leafy waterside area of Genneper
Park, is one of those educational but entertaining experiences that the
Dutch do so well. Find out what it was like to live in a village, here called
"Eversham," during the Iron Age (the period between 750 and 50 BC)
or in medieval times (AD 500–1600) in a city called "Endehoven" as volunteers in appropriate costume busy themselves in and around their
dwellings, happy to answer any questions you might have about ancient
life. And you can join in, too, if the idea grabs you—there is bread to
be baked (and sampled) and wool to be spun, and there are animals to
be looked after, and old bones to be shaped into tools, toys, and weapons.
⊠ *Boutenslaan 161b* ☎ *040/252–2281* ⊕ *www.historisch-
openluchtmuseum-eindhoven.nl* ⊠ *€6.50* ☉ *Daily 10–5.*

To the east of the center, the **DAF Museum,** a tribute to Holland's best-
known and best-loved vehicle, will delight car buffs. The museum is housed
in the restored brewery where, in 1928, Hub van Doorne started his car
factory. The DAF car has acquired something of a cult status, not just
in The Netherlands but throughout Europe. In February 1958, Hub's
dream to produce a luxury-quality car that everyone could afford became reality when the first DAF car was launched at the Amsterdam
motor show. It was small, economical to run, could carry four people,
and—most revolutionary of all—was ultraeasy to drive, thanks to Van
Doorne's innovative "Variomatic" gear-change system. Many thousands were produced, but DAF eventually fell from favor; the last DAF-
stamped car was produced in 1975, after which Volvo took over the
company. Today, DAF revivalists have ensured a newfound status for

the boxy little numbers, with collectors competing to possess their easy-driving power and chunky design. ⊠ *Tongelresestraat 27* ☎ *040/244–4364* ⊕ *www.dafmuseum.nl* 🖃 *€6* ⊙ *Tues.–Sun. 10–5.*

Housed inside the beautiful Steentjeskerk church, **Museum Kempenland** highlights the cultural history of Eindhoven and the surrounding area. In the cool brick-and-marble interior, everything from local paintings to photography and sculpture is on view, providing a pleasant enough way to spend a hour or so. ⊠ *Sint Antoniusstraat 5–7* ☎ *040/252–9093* ⊕ *www.museumkempenland.nl* 🖃 *€2.50* ⊙ *Tues.–Sun. 1–5.*

For a look at cutting-edge 20th-century architecture, go to **Het Witte Dorp** ("White Village"; ⊠ at Geldropseweg and Sint Jorislaan): 264 white houses with red roofs, designed by functionalist architect W. M. Dudok. The entire housing scheme, now a listed monument, was funded by a private housing association and built between 1937 and 1974.

Where to Eat & Stay

$$$–$$$$ ✕ **De Karpendonkse Hoeve.** In this light-filled, classy restaurant—it's found its way to more than one list of Holland's finest—chef Peter Koehn produces classic dishes with a twist. Terrine of foie gras in a Sauternes jelly, prime roast beef, and lobster soup are some signature dishes. The finesse and care to details is ever apparent, as you'll note when you see the restaurant initials stamped on every pat of butter. ⊠ *Sumatralaan 3* ☎ *040/281–3663* ⚲ *Reservations essential* ☐ *AE, DC, MC, V* ⊙ *Closed Sun. No lunch Sat.*

$–$$ ✕ **Grand Café Berlage.** This spacious Art Deco brasserie has a street-side terrace and a large, attractive garden replete with plenty of trees and parasols for cooling down after all your exertions. The lunch menu is extensive; take your pick from well-filled baguettes, inventive salads, and sturdier fare like pasta with oyster mushrooms or chunky hamburgers dressed in bacon. ⊠ *Kleine Berge 16* ☎ *040/245–7481* ☐ *AE, MC, V.*

$ ✕ **Plaza Futura.** Set in a "cultural center," this restaurant serves an eclectic range of inexpensive dishes. The culinary world tour includes Moroccan-style perch, pork in a Mexican sauce, and a weekly offering whose country of origin often coincides with that of a film being shown at the art cinema upstairs (paired with a theater where the emphasis is on less mainstream productions). Wet your whistle at the bar, with its arty, semi-refurbished factory feel, or on the large street-side sitting area lined by boulders and complete with its own fake "art" telegraph poles. On Tuesday and Friday evenings in July and August, films are projected on a large screen outside. ⊠ *Leenderweg 65* ☎ *040/294–6840* ⊕ *www. plazafutura.nl* ☐ *AE, MC, V* ⊙ *No lunch.*

$–$$$ 🛏 **Mandarin Park Plaza Hotel.** The Mandarin is unique in that it was designed to meet East Asian standards of service. Its decor includes small bridges spanning water gardens, used as footpaths through the lobby. Its several restaurants are all Asian in theme and cuisine: one serves fine Chinese specialties, another offers a range of Indonesian and Asian dishes, and the third is a Japanese steak house. The French influence is felt via a Parisian coffee shop. ⊠ *Geldropseweg 17, 5611 SC* ☎ *040/ 212–5055* 🖷 *040/212–1555* ⊕ *www.parkplazaeurope.com* ⤙ *102 rooms, 6 suites* ⚲ *3 restaurants, minibars, indoor pool, 2 saunas, meeting rooms, parking (fee), no-smoking rooms* ☐ *AE, DC, MC, V* ⏀ *MAP.*

¢ 🛏 **De Bengel.** This hotel is located in a former merchant's house on the Wilhelminaplein, a lively and attractive market square close to the center of town and the perfect destination for a summer evening beer or two. The De Bengel offers no-nonsense, well-maintained guest rooms, the pick of which look out over the square. The wood-paneled café downstairs is run by the same owner; and is an ideal destination for a nightcap. ✉ *Wilhelminaplein 9, 5611 HE* ☎ *040/244–0752* 🖷 *040/245–4229* ⊕ *www.debengel.com* ➘ *15 rooms* ⚭ *Restaurant, bar; no a/c* ▤ *AE, MC, V* ⦿ *CP.*

Sports
Eindhoven's soccer team **PSV** (Philips Sport Vereniging) is one of the top three in the country and plays September–May at **PSV-stadion Eindhoven** (✉ Frederiklaan 101A ☎ 040/250–5505 ⊕ www.psv.nl).

LIMBURG

If you want to feel you're really getting away from it all, Limburg, The Netherlands' most southerly province, is the place to go—one of the few areas where you can take a walk without hearing a background hum of traffic or stumbling across a group of modern homes. This is *echt landscap*—real countryside. Archaeologists reckon that as early as 750 BC Roman soldiers had settled here, attracted to the strategically important crossing point at the Maas, and from then on visitors have been flocking to enjoy both its natural and man-made pleasures.

You'll find yourself in ideal vacation terrain. Not only does the gently hilly countryside with its woods and rivers mean that outdoor types can pursue a whole range of activities, from cycling to kayaking, but urbanites can make the most of Maastricht's historical and culinary offerings. In between there are pretty villages, more Roman ruins, and, in Valkenburg, some 21st-century pleasures (theme parks, a spa, and a casino)—in short, something to keep everyone happy. There are plenty of places to stay, from campsites to first-class hotels, but don't underestimate Limburg's popularity; it's such a convenient destination, not just for the Dutch but for the Belgians and the Germans, too, that at times its best-known towns become even busier than Amsterdam. To be sure of a bed or a table, book well in advance.

Thorn

⑭ *46 km (28 mi) southeast of Eindhoven.*

Fodor'sChoice
★

As you travel south toward the bustling metropolis of Maastricht, this town is worth a quick stop. Thorn may have been named by a pre-Christian sect whose god was named Thor. Today, it's also known as a "white village" because of its abundance of white-painted 18th-century houses. A less familiar term is "the musical village" because of the number of musical societies here (on a fine day, you may even be able to hear a local group practicing as you tour the backstreets). The 10th-century **abbey church** was built by Count Ansfried, whose uncle was the Archbishop of Trier. He himself later entered the church, becoming Bishop of Utrecht, and was given land grants and the right to create his own principality as a reward for his faithful service to Otto I. Ansfried and his wife, Hilsondis, founded two religious orders in Thorn, one for men and one for women, installing their daughter as the first abbess.

Inside Thorn's beautiful **Stifskerk** (abbey church) all is light and space. The church has been remodeled throughout the centuries following the architectural fads of the day. In the 12th century it was Romanesque in style; toward the end of the 13th century it was rebuilt in Gothic style, and in the 16th century, Baroque elements such as the Priests' and Noblewomens' Choirs were added. The church also possesses an outstanding Baroque-era altar.

Valkenburg

⑮
40 km (25 mi) south of Thorn, 16 km (10 mi) east of Maastricht,

Those who think Holland is monstrously flat should visit Valkenburg, whose district is known as the Dutch Alps. Even though imagination is needed to agree, its steep, 1,000-foot-high hills are at least some justification. You won't have to tax your imagination, however, when confronted with the city's marvels, which include natural wonders and a storybook amusement park. As Limburg's chief tourist center, Valkenburg attracts Dutch, Belgian, and German visitors throughout the year, and much of the time it is crowded to excess. Crowds aside, though, it's worth a visit for its caves and its castle (walking shoes and sweaters recommended), and the spa and the casino provide a welcome respite for those who've had their fill of high culture and Mother Earth. Younger visitors, too, will appreciate the town, with the thrills and spills of bobsled rides, various fun fairs, and the amusement park known as the **Sprookjesbos** (Fairy-tale Woods) on offer.

The ruins of the **Kasteelvalkenburg** make for a fascinating walk that offers wonderful views over the Geul Valley. The castle was destroyed in 1672 on the orders of William III after he had vanquished its French occupiers. It remains under restoration, and you can combine a visit here with a tour of the **Fluwelengrot** cave, another by-product of the region's marlstone-quarrying industry. Its dank atmosphere is enhanced with wall paintings, sculptures, and even bats. A secret passageway leads to the castle. You can also see signatures of American soldiers who hid here during World War II. ⊠ *Daalhemerweg 27* ☎ *043/609–0110* ⊕ *www.kasteelvalkenburg.nl* ☑ *€5.90 (castle and cave)* ⊙ *Daily 10–5.*

If you're not completely caved in by your visit to the Fluwelengrot, your next stop might be the **Gemeentegrot** (town caves), which you can explore courtesy of a minitrain. Some of the fossils on view are more than 100 million years old. There's also a rather magical underground lake, which, with its ghostly, greenish light, looks almost phosphorescent. ⊠ *Cauberg 4* ☎ *043/601–2271* ⊕ *www.gemeentegrot.nl* ☑ *€4* ⊙ *Daily 10–4.*

At the **Sprookjesbos** (Fairy-tale Woods) theme park, the young—and the young at heart—can enjoy an encounter with some 16 fairy-tale stars, including Snow White and the Seven Dwarfs and Little Red Riding Hood. There's a cheap and cheerful family restaurant, but the bad and the ugly might prefer to eat at the Wild West Saloon. Afterward, listen to the sounds of the water organ while majestic fountains play, or explore a couple of playgrounds packed with enough slides and swings to exhaust even the most energetic of toddlers. You might even embark on the special swinging Pirate Ship—just make sure everyone has digested lunch before you set sail. ⊠ *Oude Valkenburgerweg* ☎ *043/601–2985* ⊕ *www.sprookjesbos.nl* ☑ *€7* ⊙ *Apr.–mid-Sept., Mon.–Sat. 10–5, Sun. 10–6.*

One of the special treats to be had in Valkenburg is at **Thermae 2000**, a decadently luxurious hill spa that offers a complete range of services, including indoor and outdoor spring-fed pools, a sauna, a steam bath, yoga/meditation, hydro-gymnastics, aerobics, sports massage, herbal and mud baths, and more. Fees vary with treatments ⊠ *Cauberg 27* ☎ *043/609–2000* ⊕ *www.thermae.nl* ⊙ *Daily 9* AM–11 PM.

Where to Eat & Stay

★ **$$$$** ✕⊞ **Hotel Château St. Gerlach.** Located in an old tenant farm on the Château St. Gerlach estate, this gorgeous hotel offers accommodations that range from plush, Provençal-style rooms with swagged drapes, antique furniture, and fine paintings, to simpler but still-luxurious rooms that make a feature of the building's rustic past, with exposed beams and open brickwork. Guests can tackle a variety of activities if they wish, from painting to music, plus there's a Roman-style swimming pool and sauna where you can try a Kneipp herbal treatment. The St. Gerlach is the sort of unstuffy place where they'll lend you a pair of gum boots if you want to go walking in the nearby countryside. Families will be delighted to know that children are welcomed here; the staff will arrange for a baby-sitter for you if necessary. But that's not all. The in-house restaurant, **Les Trois Corbeaux,** attracts gourmands who come to feast on dishes such as marinated scallops with lime cream served with a savarin of couscous and lobster meat, partridge with sauerkraut and smoked sausage, and chocolate mille-feuille with lavender and orange. Be warned: with such tempting largess at hand, your only problem if you stay at St. Gerlach may be finding the will to venture beyond its gates. ⊠ *Joseph Corneli Allée 1, 6301 KK* ☎ *043/608–8888* 🖷 *043/604–2883* ⊕ *www. stgerlach.com* 🛏 *58 rooms* ♿ *Restaurant, minibars, pool, sauna, baby-sitting, some pets allowed; no a/c in some rooms* 🗏 *AE, DC, MC, V* ❍| *MAP.*

★ **$$–$$$$** ✕🏠 **Prinses Juliana.** The classic French haute cuisine served here has been recognized internationally for more than 10 years. Members of the Dutch royal family and many foreign dignitaries have tended their appetites here. The decor is elegant in an unadorned way so you can pay attention to the food, which might be roast saddle of venison or poached oysters. For less formal dining in warm weather, there is a relaxing terrace. If you want to stay overnight, the suite-style rooms are bright, spacious, and as elegant as the hotel. ⊠ *Broekhem 11, 6301 HD* ☎ *043/ 601–2244* 🖷 *043/601–4405* ⊕ *www.juliana.nl* 🛏 *25 rooms* ♿ *Restaurant, minibars; no a/c* 🗏 *AE, DC, MC, V* ❍| *MAP.*

Nightlife
The **Holland Casino Valkenburg** (⊠ Odapark ☎ 076/525–1100 ⊕ www. hollandcasino.nl) offers blackjack, roulette, and Punto Banco in chic surroundings.

Heerlen

 14 km (9 mi) northeast of Valkenburg, 26 km (16 mi) northeast of Maastricht.

Although it shares an ancient Roman past with Maastricht, Heerlen—the second-largest city of the province—has an appeal at first glance less distinctly felt. In the absence of any obvious monuments, it comes across as simply a hardworking, average Limburg town, whose recent wealth was founded on coal. But the discovery in 1940 of the ancient foundations of a large, elaborate bathhouse established the historic importance of Coriovallum (as Heerlen was once known) as a meeting place for the Roman troops stationed in this northern outpost and, needless to say, placed Heerlen on the tourist radar. After extensive excavations in the 1960s and '70s, the entire area is now on display for history-loving visitors, many of whom will enjoy the town's highly reputed restaurants and hotels.

Now enclosed in a large, glass-encircled building, the **Thermenmuseum** (Baths Museum) has catwalks over a perfectly preserved Roman bath complex. Built around the beginning of the 2nd century AD, the *thermae* (baths) incorporated open-air sports fields, a large swimming pool, shops, restaurants, and the enclosed bathhouse complex, which included a large dressing room, the hot-air sweating room, and a series of baths (warm, lukewarm, cold, and immersion). The museum's sound-

and-light show documents one Lucius the Potter's first visit to the baths. In the museum hall, a series of lively models and reconstructions give the visitor an idea of what it was like to live and work in the Roman trading center of Coriovallum. ⊠ *Coriovallumstraat 9* ☎ *045/560–5100* ⊕ *www.thermenmuseum.nl* 🎟 *€3.50* ⊙ *Daily 10–5.*

From the 14th to the 20th century, **Kasteel Hoensbroek** (Hoensbroek Castle) belonged to the same family, who added on bits here and there as the years went by. Nowadays, it is open to the public as the largest and best preserved of the castles in South Limburg. You can see sections dating from the 14th century and products of various architectural styles, including Baroque and Maasland-Renaissance. There are several sparsely but appropriately furnished rooms and various small galleries that show temporary exhibitions. ⊠ *Klinkertstraat 118, 5 km (3 mi) northwest of Heerlen city center* ☎ *045/522–7272* ⊕ *www.kasteelhoensbroek.nl* 🎟 *€4.50* ⊙ *Daily 10–5:30.*

Where to Eat & Stay

$$–$$$ ✕ **De Boterbloem.** An ambitious young chef, Leon Winthagen, runs this restaurant gem (it has only 13 tables). Specialties include bouillon with mussels and Provençal-style leg of lamb. There are three- and four-course fixed-price menus. ⊠ *Laanderstraat 27* ☎ *045/571–4241* 🔥 *Reservations essential* ☰ *AE, DC, MC, V* ⊙ *Closed Sun. and Mon., 2 wks in Feb., and 2 wks in Aug.*

★ **$$–$$$$** ✕🔲 **Kasteel Erenstein.** An elegant 14th-century moated château set in a sprawling park, this spot is rightly known for its restaurant, whose menu and wine cellar are French. The dining area is adorned with voluminous chandeliers and a couple of very regal-looking portraits, but the atmosphere is anything but stuffy and exclusive: the staff pride themselves on the easy-going bistro-style atmosphere, so leave your bow tie and cummerbund in your suitcase. Across the road, a traditional whitewashed Limburg farmstead houses the luxury hotel. Many rooms have beamed ceilings, and some are bi-level and skylighted; others have rooftop balconies. As with the restaurant, there is a completely unpretentious vibe about the place despite its inherent grandeur. ⊠ *Oud Erensteinerweg 6, 6468 PC, 8 km (5 mi) east of Heerlen* ☎ *045/546–1333* ⊕ *www. chateauhotels.nl* 📠 *045/546–0748* 🛏 *44 rooms* ♢ *Restaurant, minibars, bar, some pets allowed; no a/c* ☰ *AE, DC, MC, V* 🍽 *MAP.*

★ **$$–$$$** ✕🔲 **Kasteel Geulzicht.** Set amid gentle hills near the village of Houthem-St. Gerlach, this 19th-century fantasia of a Renaissance castle is a Disney-like vision, truly bristling with machicolations, stepped gables, and a looming tower. Inside, period rooms allure with historic keynotes, including a magnificent ceiling painting in the main salon, fireplaces wainscotted with tiles and set below Gobelin tapestry, flocked wallpapers, chandeliers, and Neo-Gothic chairs, all of which thankfully add a *gezelligheid* (congenial and welcoming) appeal to these vast and sometimes daunting salons. Despite their grand appearance and sumptuous entrance hall, the hotel has a cozy, family-run atmosphere, and the guest rooms (some occupying the castle turrets and tower) are made for mortals, not legendary knights. A few antiques adorn these rooms, but they are mostly modern and pleasant. Because the entire estate is open only to hotel guests, you can often enjoy the flagstone garden terrace all to yourself. ⊠ *Vogelzangweg 2, 6325 PN Berg en Terblijt, 6 km (4 mi) east of Maastricht, 3 km (2 mi) from Thermae 2000 Spa* ☎ *043/604–0432* 📠 *043/604–2011* ⊕ *www.kasteelgeulzicht.nl* 🛏 *11 rooms, 1 suite* ♢ *Restaurant, minibars, bar, some pets allowed; no a/c* ☰ *AE, DC, MC, V* 🍽 *MAP.*

★ **$$–$$$** ✕🔲 **Kasteel Wittem.** This fairy-tale castle-hotel, with its duck-filled moat, spindle-roof tower, and series of peekaboo dormers dotting the roof, is human in scale. Since AD 1100 it has been a citadel, an abbey, the home to the Knights Scavandrie, a barony created by Emperor Charles V, and a base once used by William the Silent to defeat the Spaniards in the 16th century. The family that has owned it for more than 35 years welcomes you to a comfortable environment furnished in vintage Dutch. The intimate dining room, offering French cuisine, has towering windows open to views of gardens and fields. There is a summer terrace beside the moat. ⊠ *Wittemer Allée 3, 6286 AA Wittem/ Limburg, 15 km (9 mi) east of Maastricht, 14 km (9 mi) south of Heerlen* ☎ *043/450–1208* 🖨 *043/450–1260* ⊕ *www.kasteelwittem.nl* ⤳ *12 rooms* ⟁ *Restaurant; no a/c* ⊟ *AE, DC, MC, V* ⟊ *MAP.*

MAASTRICHT

Fodor'sChoice ★ The Dutch have an ongoing love affair with Maastricht—22 km (15 mi) southeast of Heerlen, 207 km (130 mi) southeast of Amsterdam, and 25 km (16 mi) west of Aachen (Germany)—and once you've been there, it's easy to understand why. Yet Netherlanders will be the first to tell you, perhaps paradoxically, that the city is just so . . . un-Dutch. Randstad dwellers up in the far west point enviously to the legacy of Maastricht's years of Burgundian rule, resulting in the Burgundian *levensstijl* (lifestyle). This is best defined as a capacity for seizing the moment, enjoying life to the fullest, and indulging all the senses—witness the local diet. Not for Maastricht's residents a bowl of *erwtensoep* (pea soup) and a *broodje* (sandwich); more likely, you'll find them tucking into a juicy steak and a good bottle of wine, followed by a generous piece of patisserie.

It's little wonder that, in their ebullient lifestyle, Maastricht dwellers seem to have more in common with southern Europeans than with their cool, northern cousins. One major fact may explain why: as the oldest city in The Netherlands, Maastricht enjoys a history that goes back all the way to the Romans, who founded the city more than 2,500 years ago. Maastricht takes its name from the Latin *Mosae Trajectum*—the point where the Maas River could be crossed. The initial walled Roman settlement was abandoned at the end of the 4th century. From then until circa 722, the place became a bishop's see, with St. Servatius (whose cyclopean church still graces the city) and St. Hubert the first and last bishops, respectively. By 1202, Maastricht was being ruled jointly by the Duke of Brabant and the Prince-Bishop of Liège, an arrangement that prevailed until 1795.

As the river's crossing point, Maastricht has always been strategically significant, and both the Spanish and French have laid siege to it in their time. When the city fell to the French in 1673, among the casualties was D'Artagnan, the inspiration behind the character of the same name in Alexandre Dumas's novel *The Three Musketeers*, who was fatally wounded while rescuing John Churchill (later Duke of Marlborough and an ancestor of Winston Churchill). For his deeds, Dumas is remembered with a statue in Maastricht's Waldeckpark. Later, during the occupation of 1795, the French forces made Maastricht the capital of a French province, the Department of the Lower Meuse. After Napoléon was routed at Waterloo, and the subsequent unification between Belgium and The Netherlands came to an end, Maastricht, miraculously, remained in Dutch control. It may be a miracle that the city has remained Dutch—probably because the dignity of its capitalship has weighed heavily upon its hoary head.

With its reputation as a crossroads between Germanic and Latin cultures, Maastricht was an appropriate venue for the signing of the famous treaty of 1992, which regulated the affairs of the European Union and heralded the birth of the euro. Today, wedged somewhat hesitantly between Belgium and Germany, Maastricht retains an intriguing mixture of three languages (Dutch, French, and German) and a variety of traditions. Small but quintessentially European, the city's lighthearted lifestyle, meticulous attention to service, and exceptionally fine, French-influenced cuisine continue to delight visitors, many of whom arrive for the city's many events such as the spectacular Maastricht Art Fair or the Preuvenemint, a sumptuous gastronomic festival where you can sample the delights of more than 35 restaurants at stalls set up on the Vrijthof, to the backdrop of live music. So, anyone who likes to feel that they've experienced northern European life at its best will definitely want to spend a few days here.

Exploring Maastricht

Maastricht's charm, coupled with its border location, makes one thing inevitable: an influx of incomers in the thousands. On high church days and holidays you may find yourself unable to move freely in the streets, let alone find a seat at a café. At off-peak times, however (early spring, fall, and winter), tourists with a sense of adventure can still escape the worst of the crowds by scampering down tiny side streets and mazelike alleyways, to emerge once more into the hustle and bustle of the town's major squares. It's a relatively small city, but should your sense of direction by any chance fail, you can always rely on the soaring red tower of Sint Janskerk to help reestablish your bearings. Restaurants are spread far and wide, although there is a higher-than-average concentration around the Vrijthof and Onze Lieve Vrouwplein, the most beguiling of all Maastricht's squares. For exclusive designer clothes and jewelry, head for the exclusive Stokstraat quarter and its side streets. And make sure your credit card is fully charged! Most of the action in town takes place on the Maas's western bank in a lively city sector known as the Wyck, replete with many cafés and interior design shops. Maastricht's newer neighborhoods, the Bonnefanten museum, and the railway station are all within walking distance on the eastern side.

Concerning other methods of transport, there seem to be fewer bicycles here than in other Dutch cities, possibly because of Maastricht's compactness and undulating topography. What you will find, though, are plenty of relaxing but less orthodox means of travel, courtesy of the VVV. These include bright-red step-scooters that teenagers and exhibitionists will love, and three-wheeler Tuk-Tuks: quirky, Thai-style vehicles powered by electricity. Meanwhile, for a unique view of the city, not to mention a cooling alternative to sidewalks teeming with humanity, a trip on a cruiser down the wide Maas River should prove both edifying and soothing to the soul.

a good walk

Begin on the east side of town at the **Bonnefantenmuseum** ⑰ ⌐, a striking building designed by the architect Aldo Rossi, featuring an end tower shaped like the top of an old-fashioned space rocket. Inside, a jewel-like collection of religious sculptures, Renaissance oil paintings, and genre paintings by the likes of Brueghel are complemented by large-scale contemporary artworks and installation pieces. When you've had your fill, head out with the museum behind you and the river to your left. It will be clear from the river traffic that the Maas is still one of Maastricht's major arteries: you'll see sand-laden barges, houseboats complete with clothes-strewn washing lines, and pleasure cruisers full of tourists, all gently making their way up and down the river.

Farther on, cross over **Sint Servaasbrug** ⑱, built between 1280 and 1298 and one of the oldest bridges in The Netherlands, pausing to admire the views it offers of the town center's skyline. Head straight on down Maastrichtse Brugstraat, and turn right into busy Kleine Straat. Here, you'll find the VVV (tourist office), housed in the impressively ancient-looking **Dinghuis** ⑲, originally a courthouse dating from the turn of the 15th century. Very nearby on Jodenstraat is **De Historische Drukkerij** ⑳, a venerable printing shop, and a few blocks to the west is the enchanting **Poppen Museum** ㉑, or Doll Museum. Several blocks north is the **Stadhuis** ㉒, on the Markt square, adorned with the noted statue of '**Moosewief** ㉓. The walk from the VVV into shop-lined Grote Staat will shortly bring you onto the **Vrijthof** ㉔ square and Maastricht at its liveliest. On the square itself, look out for the colonnaded Military Guard House (Militaire Hoofdwacht), an elegant 18th-century building of gray Namur stone from which the city's borders were once controlled. To the left of the square you'll also see the russet-color **Museum Spaans Gouvernement** ㉕ (Spanish Government Museum), with its period interiors and Renaissance-style arcade in the courtyard. Keep an eye out for the gable stones adorning the buildings around the square; often elaborately decorated, they show the name of the house and the year it was built. A particularly fine example is at No. 15, "In den Ouden Vogelstruys" ("In the Old Ostrich").

On the square, head to the far left up Henric van Veldeke Plein, and at this point you'll almost certainly want to make a couple of stops. First, take the trip up the lofty tower of **Sint Janskerk** ㉖ and admire the breathtaking views; then immerse yourself in the Gothic splendors on offer next door, courtesy of **Sint Servaasbasiliek** ㉗, and its glittering St. Servatius' Treasury. Then it's back down Veldekeplein (don't miss the magnificent residential 17th-century mansion on your right) and across Vijthof onto Bredestraat. Head on past Honstraat on your right, and take the next right onto **Onze Lieve Vrouweplein** ㉘. If you've wondered before what Netherlanders mean when they talk about Maastricht's "French feel," you'll understand now: this leafy square, filled with little tables and strung with fairy lights, retains an intimate, Provençal-style atmosphere even when packed, and those who come here to relax over a bottle of wine with friends certainly seem full of joie de vivre. Just to the northeast are two notable sites that bear witness to the ancient Roman history of the town: **Op de Thermen** ㉙ and **Derlon Cellar** ㉚.

But providing a compelling backdrop to all the action is the magnificent, twin-towered **Onze Lieve Vrouwebasiliek** ㉛, or Basilica of Our Beloved Lady. Dating to before the year 1000, it is the oldest church in Maastricht and formed the hub of the Liège governership before the city's walls were constructed in 1229. Savor the stillness of its incense-scented interior before you take the side road bearing to the right as you look at the church, and head on past street cafés and the right-hand turn onto Sint Benardusstraat, taking you up to the city wall. With the river in front of you, walk up the steps onto Onze Lieve Vrouwewal, constructed some time after 1229 as part of the first medieval city wall. Today it's crowned with balconied period residences, jaunty in spring with red geraniums, and some with interesting gated entrances worth noting. End your walk with a visit to the **Helpoort** ㉜, the gatehouse at the bottom of the wall's steps, formerly part of the wall itself, which houses a little museum full of Maastricht lore. If you feel the need to fortify yourself, now would be a good time to head back toward Onze Lieve Vrouweplein for a glass of Limburg wine or a local beer. But if you have energy left to do more exploring, head southwest of the city center to the **Natuurhistorisch Museum** ㉝, with its lovely botanic gardens, then con-

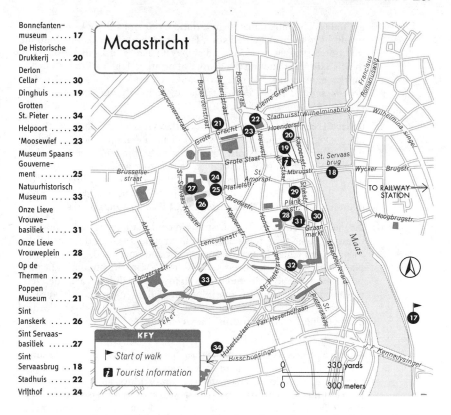

tinue southward to tunnel back to the ancient past in the evocative **Grotten Sint Pieter ③④**.

TIMING   For the walk only, allow about 1¾ hours, but if you take in all the sights and detours and use it as the springboard for tangential explorations, it could easily take the full day. Bear in mind that, like most other places in The Netherlands, many museums and shops are closed Monday.

Sights to See

► ★ ⑰   **Bonnefantenmuseum** (Bonnefanten Museum). Set on the east bank of the Maas, this E-shape building with its lofty tower was designed by the famed Italian architect Aldo Rossi. Its spacious, light-filled interior makes this a worthy home for Limburg's excellent provincial museum. Here, diversity is the order of the day: not only are there displays on the archaeological history of the province, but there is an art collection with gems from 13th- to 15th-century Romanesque and Gothic Mosan sculpture of the Maas region; 14th- to 16th-century Italian paintings; and 16th- to 18th-century paintings of the South Netherlands, including works by Jan Brueghel and Pieter Brueghel the Younger. An intriguing and intelligently selected exhibition of contemporary art includes work by many important Dutch painters of the late 20th century, several of them from Limburg. Artists represented include LeWitt, Signer, Kounellis, and Mangold. A changing array of temporary exhibitions and installation pieces means that there is something to suit every taste, and there's a good café in the tower, should you need to take time out from the heady world of high art. ⊠ *Avenue Ceramique 250* ☎ *043/329–0190* ⊕ *www.bonnefanten.nl* ☑ *€7* ☉ *Tues.–Sun. 11–5.*

⑳   **De Historische Drukkerij.** You may end up with inky fingers at this period printing shop, a stone's throw from the tourist office and still in use today. The shop dates from around 1900 and still looks much as it would have then. A guided tour, lasting an hour, reveals much about traditional typesetting skills and shows ancient presses in action, plus there's a display detailing the history of printing. It all makes for a lively, quirky excursion. ⊠ *Jodenstraat 22* ☎ *043/321–6376* ⊕ *www.drukmuseum.nl* ⊠ *€2.50 guided tour* ⊙ *Mar.–July and Sept.–Nov., tour Fri. at 1:45, Sat. at 1:45 and 3.*

㉚ Derlon Cellar. Before builders began work on this hotel, Maastricht's city archaeologist made an extensive survey of its chosen site. The earth yielded up fascinating artifacts and examples of architecture from the 2nd through the 4th century, including a 3rd-century well and a section from a pre-Roman cobblestone road, all of which have been preserved beneath the hotel. Display cabinets and panels contain additional information and finds. ⊠ *Plankstraat 21* ⊠ *Free* ⊙ *Sun. noon–4.*

⑲ Dinghuis. The city's VVV tourist board couldn't have found a more interesting home than this edifice, built around 1470 as the seat of the former Lord Chief Justice of Maastricht and once used as a prison by Napoléon. It's been restored several times. Note the building's beautiful stone gable and timbered side wall toward its Jodenstraat side. Venture inside if you want to have a look at its dark, cozy interior—just be prepared to face plenty of other tourists, who'll be busy picking up leaflets and booking their hotel rooms. ⊠ *Kleine Straat 1* ⊠ *Free* ⊙ *Weekdays 9–6, Sat. 9–5.*

㉞ Grotten Sint Pieter (Caves of St. Peter). A warm sweater and sturdy shoes are essential gear as you head off for an experience that will mark you as an intrepid explorer. These man-made corridors, approximately 200 km (124 mi) of chambers and passageways, carved deep into the limestone hills, have yielded building stone since Roman times. In some areas the mining was so extensive that the ceiling is nearly 40 feet high; this means that graffiti left by the Romans are now far above your head, although the signatures of such visitors as Napoléon can still be seen. And there are almost as many anecdotes regarding the caves' history as there are chambers; the tale of how Rembrandt's *Night Watch* was hidden here during World War II is just one example, or you could ask to hear the creepy story of the four 17th-century monks who lost their way when the thread they were using as a guideline failed. Because the caves are complex, dark, and chilly you can visit them only with a guide, and you may be asked to carry a gas lamp—your only light source once inside. Be aware that your guide will speak only the dominant language of the group he or she is accompanying. Check when buying your tickets—if you're in a predominantly Dutch group, for example, it would be best to pick up an English-language guidebook, or plan your July/August visit around the early afternoon English-language tours. ⊠ *Grotten Noord (Northern System), Luikerweg 71, Zonneberg Caves, Slavante 1 (near Enci Cement Works)* ☎ *043/325–2121* ⊠ *€3.25* ⊙ *July and Aug., English-language tours at 1:45 daily.*

㉜ Helpoort (City Gate). The Netherlands' oldest remaining city gate lies at the end of the first medieval rampart wall, dating from 1229. The small museum inside gives the lowdown on its history, and as you leave you'll go through a gate, which would originally have been fitted with a portcullis. The projecting parapet above the gateway had a special use in times of battle: its floor had special openings through which the enemy could be bombarded. ⊠ *Bottom of steps at end of Onze Lieve Vrouwewal* ☎ *043/325–7833* ⊠ *Donation appreciated* ⊙ *Easter–Oct., daily 1:30–4:30.*

㉓ **'Moosewief** (Greengrocer's Wife). The jolly statue of a roly-poly woman carrying a basket of vegetables stands on one side of the **Grote Markt** (market square). Keep your eyes open, too, for the flame-carrying bronze statue of Jan Pieter Minckelers (by Bart van Hove), who, appropriately enough, invented the gaslight. Wednesday and Friday are market days in Maastricht, and the square is chockablock with stalls and stands offering fruits, vegetables, meats, household items, and fish (Friday). Business here was conducted in three currencies (Dutch, Belgian, and German) until the arrival of the euro, and deals are still done in four languages (Dutch, French, German, and English).

㉕ **Museum Spaans Gouvernement** (Spanish Government Museum). Housed in a lovely red-front mansion dating from the 16th century (it was originally built as a chapter house), this was the home of the Duke of Brabant from the end of the 14th century. Today, the museum is a feast of opulent detailing: crystal chandeliers, fine period furniture, and ornate wall frescos are all to be found here. In the Renaissance-style courtyard, carved medallions depict Charles V, Isabelle of Portugal, and Philip II, all of whom stayed in the house at one time or another. Interior-design fans can admire rooms decorated in the authentic Liège style of the mid-18th-century, as well as silver, porcelain, and paintings from the large Wagner–de Wit collection. ⊠ *Vrijthof 18* ☏ *043/321–1327* ⊕ *www. museumspaansgouvernement.nl* ▧ *€2.50* ☉ *Tues.–Sun. 1–5.*

㉝ **Natuurhistorisch Museum** (Natural History Museum). With some 550,000 natural objects covering 11,000 species of life, the Natural History Museum is one of the largest of its kind in The Netherlands. Plenty of interactive displays, audiovisual explanations, and computers to tinker with mean that no one could charge the museum with a dated outlook. Marvel at the museum's collection of gemstones, or—if the weather's fine— enjoy the sights and smells of its lush **botanical gardens.** Here, laid out in a variety of beds and terraces, is a collection of rare and common plants native to the Limburg region. The lush grounds make it hard to believe you're in the heart of the city. ⊠ *De Bosquetplein 6–7* ☏ *043/350–5490* ⊕ *www.nhmaastricht.nl* ▧ *€3.10* ☉ *Weekdays 10–5, weekends 2–5.*

㉛ **Onze Lieve Vrouwebasiliek** (Our Beloved Lady Basilica). Maastricht's oldest monument (recent excavations reveal) was erected atop an ancient Roman temple. The Westwork, a massive flat facade in Romanesque style that is topped with two round turrets, is the oldest part of the structure, dating from the 11th and 12th centuries. Inside is a two-story apse with a double row of columns and a half-dome roof. You'll also find two crypts, both dating from the Romanesque period, and restful 16th-century cloisters. Though the treasure house here isn't as spectacular as the one at St. Servatius, there's still plenty to relish, including capes, copes, and tapestries rich with detail (look out for the Levite tapestry of St. Lambertus, Maastricht's last bishop), ivories, statues, silver, and other ecclesiastical relics. ⊠ *Onze Lieve Vrouweplein* ☏ *043/321–3255* ⊕ *www.sterr-der-zee.nl* ▧ *Church free, treasure chamber €1.75* ☉ *Easter–Oct., Mon.–Sat. 11–5, Sun. 1–5.*

㉘ **Onze Lieve Vrouweplein** (Our Beloved Lady Square). The basilica of the same name opens out onto this tree-shaded, intimate square—one of Maastricht's most atmospheric spots.

㉙ **Op de Thermen.** This small residential square, discovered in 1840, was once the site of a Roman villa and baths. It hints at the Roman heritage that lies deep beneath the surface of Maastricht. Recently laid paving stones indicate the outline of the ancient buildings—red for a 1st-century house with under-floor heating, gray for a 2nd-century bathhouse, and white for a 4th-century bathhouse. ⊠ *Between Luikerweg and Stokstraat.*

🌀 ㉑ **Poppen Museum** (Doll Museum). Children and adults alike will love this permanent exhibition of all kinds of toys, dating from 1780 to 1950. As well as teddy bears, windup monkeys, and china dolls, also on view are all the appropriate accessories to make their little lives complete—umbrellas, handbags, and outfits, plus tiny furniture and the grandest of miniature dinner services. And should the unsilenceable cry "I want one of those!" go up from any tykes, rest assured there's also a small in-house store selling toys and replicas, proceeds from which are donated to a worthy cause. ⊠ *Grote Gracht 41* 🕾 *043/326–0123* ⊕ *www. poppenmuseum.maastricht.waarnaartoe.nl* 🎫 *€3.50* ⊙ *Thurs. and Sat. 11–4.*

㉖ **Sint Janskerk** (St. John's Church). Beautiful in its simplicity, this 14th-century Gothic church has been in the possession of the Dutch Reformed Church since 1633. In its stark white interior you'll find murals and fine sculpted corbels depicting the 12 disciples, a carved pulpit by Coenrad Pierkens dating from 1780, plus a wonderfully mellow-sounding organ. The tall, red tower of the church offers panoramic views of the city; your voluntary donation goes toward its upkeep. ⊠ *Vrijthof (enter Henric van Veldekeplein)* 🕾 *043/347–8880* ⊕ *http://home.hccnet.nl/jef.schuit/ welkom.html* 🎫 *Church free, donation appreciated; tower €1.15* ⊙ *Easter–Oct., Mon.–Sat. 11–4.*

★ ㉗ **Sint Servaasbasiliek** (St. Servatius Basilica). Beneath the magnificent and historic 7th-century church lie the bones of its namesake, the 4th-century saint whose choice of Maastricht as the location for his see stimulated the development of the city after the departure of the Romans in 402. The basilica's recent restoration included using the bright paint colors of the original interior design. The focal points of the church are the richly carved 13th-century **Berg Portal** and the **Schatkamer van Sint Servaas** (Treasure Chamber of St. Servatius) in the 12th-century chapel. This extraordinary collection of treasures dates from 827 and contains religious relics (some of them donated by Charlemagne) and exquisitely wrought liturgical objects. The most important item in the collection is the 12th-century Noodkist, an elaborately decorated, gold-plated oak chest, adorned with gold and silver figures and containing the bones and relics of St. Servatius and other local bishops. For a simpler strain of beauty, investigate the musty lower crypt, where ancient excavations create a strong sense of the past. ⊠ *Vrijthof* 🕾 *043/325–7878* ⊕ *www. sintservaas.nl* 🎫 *€2.50* ⊙ *Nov.–Mar., Sun. 12:30–5; Apr.–June and Sept. and Oct., daily 10–5; July and Aug., daily 10–6.*

⑱ **Sint Servaasbrug** (St. Servatius Bridge). The span crosses the Maas between the old and new parts of town and offers the best views of the old city. Built solidly of gray Namur stone in the late 13th century to replace an earlier, nine-arched wooden version, it is one of the oldest bridges in The Netherlands. ⊠ *Maasboulevard, Wycker Brugstraat.*

㉒ **Stadhuis** (Town Hall). Maastricht's civic building stands imposingly at one end of the large market square. Designed in 1662 by the architect Pieter Post—he of Mauritshuis (The Hague) fame—it's a proud testament to burgher prosperity, filled with fine tapestries, stucco, and paintings. The sumptuous entrance hall with its moldings and painted ceiling is open to the public. The tower dates from 1684 and houses a carillon of 49 bells—listen for them between 3:30 and 4:15 PM if you're in the neighborhood on a Saturday. ⊠ *Markt 78* 🕾 *043/350–5050* 🎫 *Free* ⊙ *Weekdays 8:30–12:30 and 2–5:30.*

Stokstraat. Now a fashionable street lined with galleries and boutiques, Stokstraat was the heart of the original Roman settlement of Maastricht.

㉔ **Vrijthof.** Each February, this enormous square explodes with the festivities of Carnival. It is also the location for the taste-bud-tantalizing Preuvenemint, which takes place toward the end of August). Ringed with restaurants, grand cafés, dance clubs, and traditional pubs, it is the major public gathering place of Maastricht, year-round. It is studded with some interesting statues that glitter in the sunlight—and a pretty fountain that you can cool your hands in when the weather gets hot.

need a break? A cheerful place to stop any time of day is the plant-filled **Café Britannique** (✉ Vrijthof 6 ☎ 043/321–8691). It serves breakfast (with champagne if you like) as well as simple light meals throughout the day, and drinks, including a house beer, until midnight.

Where to Eat & Stay

With more award-winning restaurants than any other place in The Netherlands, Maastricht will erase any negative feelings you may have harbored about Dutch cuisine. You'll notice the difference not only in taste and finesse but in the quality of service here. The snail-like service encountered in other parts of The Netherlands is nonexistent in Maastricht, where restaurant staffs are usually highly attentive; many are students at or graduates of the city's renowned hotel school. But quality comes at a price, and meal prices here can be higher than elsewhere in the region. Still, you won't mind paying those extra euros for local delicacies such as earthy, rich, cave-grown mushrooms; seasonal asparagus (white and sweet, rather than green and acidic); and creamy but whiffy Rommedoe cheese. Diners are sometimes surprised to learn that they can also quaff a selection of high-quality local white wines as well as enjoy the French-style cuisine and delicious patisseries for which the city is famed. The Apostelhoeve vineyard, for example, is the oldest wine growing estate in The Netherlands and produces four dry, fruity whites made from Müller Thurgau, Auxerrois, Riesling, and Pinot Gris grapes, each well worth sampling.

When it comes to finding a bed for the night, many Netherlanders claim that you'll find the country's best and best-value hotels in Maastricht, especially in its range of boutique hotels. Although you won't see Zen-like minimalist design (with the Hotel Bergère a notable exception), or many in-house restaurants—what's the point when there are so many excellent eateries to choose from?—what you will find are plenty of intimate, unusual places, some with as few as six rooms, lovingly furnished in classic style.

★ **$$$$** ✗ **Château Neercanne.** Built in 1698 as a pleasure dome for one of Maastricht's military governors, this spot—comfortably distant from the crowds of central Maastricht—is extremely special. No wonder Queen Beatrix chose it as the venue for her state banquet with Europe's leaders during the Maastricht summit of 1991 (you can still see the guests' signatures on the ceiling of the château's caves). Still the only terraced kasteel in The Netherlands, the château was built in 1698 by Baron Daniël de Dopff. Both château and grounds were extensively restored from the 1950s to the 1980s. There are a variety of dining spaces here—some exclusively available for group bookings—but anyone can enjoy the pretty restaurant known as L' Auberge, with its glorious views over the terraces. Outstanding dishes include creamy spinach soup with smoked eel, and chocolate *delice* with vanilla cream and a cointreau sauce. The finest of wines are stored in the château's caves. On a Sunday, you can come here simply for patisserie and coffee (no other comestibles are offered that day). Anytime, you can walk off any excess calories in the magnificent Baroque-style garden (today landmarked by UNESCO), created in the Louis XIV style by de Dorff and overlooking the Jekervallei valley, which is home to the area's finest vineyards, including that of Neercanne itself. ⊠ *Cannerweg 800* ☎ *043/325–1359* ⊕ *www.neercanne. com* ♨ *Reservations essential* ⊟ *AE, DC, MC, V* ⊗ *Closed Mon. No dinner Sat.*

$$$$ ✕ **Mediterraneo.** Given Maastricht's plethora of fine French restaurants, a visit to Mediterraneo—an Italian spot that enjoys an excellent reputation throughout The Netherlands—makes a refreshing change. Decor is rustic and warm, with tiles, mirrors, and plenty of plants. Deceptively simple-sounding dishes packed full of Tuscan flavors include homemade ravioli with potato and truffle filling, a salad of arugula and shrimp, and turbot cooked with tomato and basil. Naturally, a bottle of 1993 Barolo should help you appreciate the experience even more. ⊠ *Rechtstraat 73* ☎ *043/325–5037* ♨ *Reservations essential* ⊟ *AE, DC, MC, V* ⊗ *Closed Sun.*

$$$$ ✕ **'t Pakhoes.** Clever use has been made of an old brick warehouse (which began life as an ammunition magazine centuries ago) to create this four-story restaurant, each floor having a different atmosphere. Begin your "tour" with an aperitif on the ground floor, and then work your way up through the building for successive courses. Or, in summer, you can simply settle down to dine in the shade provided by an umbrella and the surrounding lush foliage with a perch over the banks of the Meuse. The food of chef's Guidy Wolfs has a French-Belgian slant; the lamb cutlets with sage and fresh garlic are cooked to rosy perfection, and blow the diet in style with the fresh lobster salad, nicely rejuvenated with a creamy mango and curry sauce. ⊠ *Waterpoort 4–6* ☎ *043/325–7000* ♨ *Reservations essential* ⊟ *AE, DC, MC, V* ⊗ *Closed Sun. Lunch by prior arrangement only.*

★ **$$$–$$$$** ✕ **Petit Bonheur.** In its original incarnation around 1700, the Petit Bonheur was a farm located just inside the city walls. Today it is like a little sliver of Provence transported into the heart of Maastricht. Try and get a table in the secluded cobbled courtyard to dine below a canopy of grapevines in the summer or underneath a retractable roof once winter sets in. You might even be able to sample an aperitif in the hemispherical cellar, where dusty wine bottles abound and a filled-in well bears testimony to many occupations of the city; locals used to hide their valuables here. The food is heavily influenced by French and Belgian cuisines. You can get the ball rolling with a roll of smoked wild boar and forest mushrooms, and follow it up with fillet of venison smothered in a blackcurrant sauce. ⊠ *Achter de Molens 2* ☎ *043/321–5109* ⊕ *www. petitbonheur.nl* ♨ *Reservations essential* ⊟ *AE, MC, V* ⊗ *No lunch.*

★ **$$$–$$$$** ✕ **Toine Hermsen.** Despite receiving significant culinary honors, Toine is not a pretentious place. It is, however, unashamedly elegant: think crystal, crisp white napery, and gleaming silverware. But it's the food that dominates. A menu might begin with carpaccio of salmon with lemon-dill sauce and move on to Bresse duck with tomato confit, bell peppers, and potatoes in Provençale sauce; for dessert perhaps almond phyllo pastry with cherry filling and vanilla ice cream and champagne sauce. There are fixed-price menus for three, four, and five courses. ⊠ *Sint Bernardusstraat 2–4* ☎ *043/325–8400* ♨ *Reservations essential* ⓜ *Jacket and tie* ⊟ *AE, DC, MC, V* ⊗ *Closed Sun. No lunch Sat. and Mon.*

$$$ ✕ **Roxy's.** Wicker chairs, a wood-beamed ceiling, and wooden tables add a laid-back atmosphere to Roxy's, located just a stone's throw from the Vrijthof. This is a reliable outpost for meat lovers, who can tuck into a grilled beefsteak served with a tarragon and mustard sauce, or perhaps lamb served with a fresh mint and garden pea puree. ⊠ *Kruisherengang 4* ☎ *043/321–1219* ⚛ *Reservations essential* ▭ *AE, DC, MC, V* ☯ *Closed Tues. Lunch by prior arrangement only.*

$$$ ✕ **'t Hegske.** This romantic spot is near Sint Amorsplein off Vrijthof. Window boxes full of flowering plants decorate the street side, and there is a bubbling fountain in the interior courtyard. The warmth of half-timbered walls, hanging baskets, and antique collectibles here and there adds to the intimacy. The kitchen is open, the cuisine classic French. ⊠ *Heggenstraat 3a* ☎ *043/325–1762* ⚛ *Reservations essential* ▭ *AE, DC, MC, V* ☯ *No lunch.*

$$–$$$ ✕ **La Ville.** During the day you can take your pick of delicious salads and light meals. In the evening the friendly and enthusiastic staff serve hearty, French-influenced cuisine, such as filet mignon with shallots and red wine sauce. The restaurant is on Maastricht's prettiest square and has tables under the trees in good weather. ⊠ *Onze Lieve Vrouweplein 28* ☎ *043/321–9889* ⚛ *Reservations essential* ▭ *AE, DC, MC, V* ☯ *Closed Tues. Nov.–Apr. No lunch.*

$$–$$$ ✕ **Sagittarius.** You'll find it hard to resist the aroma of garlic butter and freshly grilled seafood that invariably wafts from this narrow little restaurant. The young staff manage to be both friendly and solicitous without being overbearing. Food flavors here are rich, robust, and redolent of southern France. Start with grilled sardines or a warm goat-cheese salad, then move on to lobster served with a cream, garlic, and red peppercorn sauce or perhaps duck confit if you fancy a change from seafood. ⊠ *Bredestraat 7* ☎ *043/321–1492* ⚛ *Reservations essential* ▭ *AE, DC, MC* ☯ *Closed Sun.–Tues.*

$–$$ ✕ **Gio's Cucina Casalinga.** White linen tablecloths, candles, a dark oak floor, and an overabundance of deep red roses create an intimate and elegant backdrop for some excellent yet unpretentious Italian cuisine (the restaurant's name means Gio's "Homey Kitchen"). You can fill yourself up adequately with pizza or pasta for less than €10, but you'd be selling yourself short. Choose a set menu and watch your table fill up with enormous homemade ravioli, king prawn dishes, anchovies on toast overlaid with long rasps of Parmesan, and exquisitely crunchy vegetables prepared with enough garlic to destroy the entire vampire population of Europe. Gio himself ambles amiably around, chatting with the clientele, while a battalion of Italians in the kitchen below—including the 73-year-old Gina—help prepare the food. ⊠ *Vrijthof 29* ☎ *043/325–6275* ▭ *AE, DC, MC, V* ☯ *Closed Mon.*

¢–$$ ✕ **De Blindgender.** Not far from Onze Lieve Vrouweplein, De Blindgender is a particularly warm and cheerful eating pub with large windows looking onto the street. The tables are plain and unadorned, the service is relaxed, and the menu has a good selection of fish dishes, including salmon cooked with sesame seeds. ⊠ *Koestraat 3* ☎ *043/325–0619* ⚛ *Reservations not accepted* ▭ *MC, V.*

¢–$ ✕ **Café Charlemagne.** A perfect place for those who want hearty fare in the center of town, Café Charlemagne is just opposite the Onze Lieve Vrouwe Basilica. The darkish interior hews to the traditional style, brightened with plenty of knickknacks and a gargantuan chandelier (but not much light). In summer, when tables spill out onto the outside square, the place comes alive. Choose from steak or the simply fried cod or even an Indonesian saté. In the warm months, the goat-cheese salad is a good option. ⊠ *Onze Lieve Vrouweplein 24* ☎ *043/321–9373* ▭ *DC, MC, V.*

$–$$ ✕▣ **Kasteel Elsloo.** This grand 6th-century manor house, with its own park and botanical garden, was once the property of one of Limburg's leading families and the scene of many a glittering occasion, including the 19th-century wedding of a daughter of the family to the Prince of Monaco. Guest rooms are spacious and restfully decorated in creams and pastels. Adjacent to the mustard-yellow bar, topped off by country-style chandeliers, the restaurant has a palatial manor-house feel to it, thanks to its soaring, spectacular stone vaults; the kitchen is traditional French, serving such dishes as beef with onion confit and port sauce. ⊠ *Maasberg 1, 6181 GV Elsloo, 10 km (6 mi) northeast of Maastricht* ☎ *046/437-7666* 🖨 *046/437-7570* ⊕ *www.kasteelelsloo. nl* 🔊 *26 rooms, 1 suite* ⚅ *Restaurant, bar, some pets allowed; no a/c* 🖃 *AE, DC, MC, V* ⎮◎⎮ *MAP.*

¢   ✕🖃 **Maison du Chene.** Located close to the action, this long-established hotel (almost 150 years old) allows you to step out right out the front door on to the Markt market square. The interior is simple, with cream-color walls, tile floors, and a long antique wooden table at the front. The adjoining restaurant serves a variety of fish and meat dishes, including a tempting cod in saffron sauce. ⊠ *Boschstraat 104–106, 6211 AZ* ☎ *043/ 321-3523* 🖨 *043/325-8082* ⊕ *www.maastrichthotel.com* 🔊 *24 rooms, 18 with bath* ⚅ *Restaurant* 🖃 *AE, DC, MC, V* ⎮◎⎮ *MAP.*

$$–$$$$ 🖭 **Derlon Maastricht.** The relaxed and quiet elegance of Onze Lieve Vrouweplein is perfectly reflected in this small luxury hotel. Guest rooms are graciously sized and decorated in relaxing sand-and-seashell tones, and each has a distinct work of art, most often a contemporary painting. The rooms face either the medieval side street or, if you are especially fortunate, the tree-filled square. A unique feature of this hotel is a private museum in the cellar, with exhibits ranging from the 1st century BC to the 15th century AD. There is a gratifying personal quality to the service, especially in the elegant restaurant. ⊠ *Onze Lieve Vrouweplein 6, 6211 HD* ☎ *043/321-6770* 🖨 *043/325-1933* ⊕ *www.hotels. nl/maastricht/derlon/* 🔊 *42 rooms, 1 suite* ⚅ *Restaurant, minibars, shops, meeting room, some pets allowed* 🖃 *AE, DC, MC, V* ⎮◎⎮ *MAP.*

$–$$$ 🖭 **Hotel Bergère.** As part of the Design Hotels group, the emphasis here is not only on service but on aesthetics—if cutting-edge modernism is your thing, you'll appreciate its combination of clean lines and cool woods. Features include "La Byb" (an in-house library where you'll find international books, magazines, and newspapers), a state-of the-art fitness center offering great views of Maastricht's skyline, a designer florist and gift shop, and water beds in some rooms. ⊠ *Stationsstraat 40 6221 BR* ☎ *043/328-2525* 🖨 *043/328-2526* ⊕ *www.la-bergere.com* 🔊 *70 rooms* ⚅ *Gym, shop, parking (fee); no a/c* 🖃 *AE, DC, MC, V* ⎮◎⎮ *EP.*

★ ¢–$$$ 🖭 **Hotel Botticelli.** Billing its philosophy as "the simple art of living," the Hotel Botticelli doesn't disappoint. Two buildings dating from the 18th century and originally built for a local wine merchant have been lovingly converted into a quiet and spacious hotel (opened 1997). Decorwise, the place takes its inspiration from Italy, with warm colors and a number of Renaissance-style sculptures scattered here and there. Each room has been individually decorated using paint effects such as stippling, sponging, and trompe l'oeil—but, like the furnishings, the overall effect is classily understated. And wherever possible, the hotel's original features have been retained, so you may stay in a room with a beamed ceiling, or an antique chimney breast. The central courtyard separating the two buildings is the perfect place to relax with a drink after a day spent sightseeing. The Botticelli's location—in a street just around the corner from Sint Janskerk and the Vrijthof—couldn't be better. ⊠ *Papenstraat 11, 6211 LG* ☎ *043/352-6300* 🖨 *043/352-6336* ⊕ *www.botticellihotel.com* 🔊 *18 rooms* ⚅ *Minibars, bars* 🖃 *AE, DC, MC, V* ⎮◎⎮ *CP.*

$–$$ 🖭 **Best Western Hotel Du Casque.** Smack-dab in the center of old Maastricht, this hotel has a tradition that dates back to a 15th-century inn, although today's building is a modern postwar structure. Some rooms overlook the Vrijthof square, and there's direct access to a steak house with a terrace fronting the square. ✉ *Helmstraat 14, 6211 TA* ☎ *043/321–4343* 🖷 *043/325–5155* ⊕ *www.hotelducasque.nl* ↙ *27 rooms* ♨ *Minibars, parking (fee), some pets allowed; no a/c* ⊟ *AE, DC, MC, V* ⦿I *CP.*

$ 🏨 **Dis.** This tiny hotel has an unusual location: a historic building above an art gallery that bears the same name. Guest rooms are clean, spacious, and bright with white cotton bed linen, some antique furniture, and wooden beams. Contemporary art from the gallery lends splashes of color to the walls. Downstairs, enjoy breakfast among the paintings and plants while admiring the ceiling and the ancient archways. ✉ *Tafelstraat 28 6211 JD* ☎ *043/321–5479* 🖷 *043/325–7026* ⊕ *www.hoteldis.nl* ↙ *6 rooms* ♨ *Minibars; no a/c* ⊟ *AE, MC, V* ⦿I *CP.*

★ $ 🏨 **Hotel d'Orangerie.** Situated in a building that dates from 1752, this is a delightful, intimate little hotel with just 22 rooms, 9 of which have views over the river. The decor combines country-house coziness with contemporary touches, translating to period-style lamps and desks, plus comfortable beds with padded headboards and modern, marble-clad bathrooms. The breakfast room boasts a marble fireplace, chandeliers, and pretty frescoed walls, and on sunny days, you can enjoy your croissant on the tiny grottolike terrace behind the breakfast room. ✉ *Kleine Gracht 4, 6211 CB* ☎ *043/326–1111* 🖷 *043/326–1287* ⊕ *www.hotel-orangerie.nl* ↙ *22 rooms* ♨ *Minibars, bar, parking (fee), some pets allowed; no a/c* ⊟ *AE, DC, MC* ⦿I *CP.*

¢ 🏨 **De Poshoorn.** Conveniently situated between the railway station and the Old Town, the De Poshoorn has smallish rooms, but they are spotlessly clean and brightly decorated. The hotel is above an ambience-rich café with a friendly clientele, and service is attentive and efficient. ✉ *Stationsstraat 47 6211 BN* ☎ *043/321–7334* 🖷 *043/321–0747* ⊕ *www.poshoorn.nl* ↙ *11 rooms* ♨ *No a/c* ⊟ *AE, DC, MC, V* ⦿I *CP.*

Nightlife & the Arts

Maastricht enjoys a thriving multicultural arts scene, which attracts world-class performers from all over Europe. Its status as a student town ensures a particularly lively nightlife, so you'll always be able to find some sort of evening entertainment here. For information on what is going on during your visit, check *Maandagenda,* a monthly calendar you will find around town, or *Uit in Maastricht,* published biweekly by the VVV tourist office.

The Arts

BRASS BANDS Maastricht is home to more than 30 music groups that give concerts throughout the summer, often in the city's major squares. Check with the VVV for details.

CARILLON CONCERTS In summer the air rings with a series of evening concerts played by carillonneurs on various church bells of the city, and throughout the year there are midday concerts every Saturday from 3:30 to 4:15 from the cheerful 43-bell carillon atop the Town Hall in the market square.

CARNIVAL The Catholic heritage of the southern provinces of The Netherlands is most dramatically felt during the days preceding Ash Wednesday. The public celebration of Carnival survives in its full bloom of conviviality and relative recklessness in Maastricht, with parades, parties, and fancy dress.

CINEMA A movie is always a good option for an evening's entertainment, simply because the majority of English-language films shown here are subtitled rather than dubbed. Maastricht's cinemas include the atmospheric **Palace Cinema** (✉ Wycker Brugstraat 1 ☎ 043/321–5662), the large **Minvera** (✉ Wilhelminsingel 39 ☎ 043/325–3565 ⊕ www.minervabioscopen.nl), and the arty **Ciné-K** (✉ Sint Bernardusstraat 13 ☎ 043/321–6525).

CLASSICAL MUSIC In Maastricht, the **Limburgse Symfonie Orkest** (Limburg Symphony Orchestra) is the leading regional orchestra (⊕ www.lso.nl). It performs at the **Theater aan Het Vrijthof** (✉ Vrijthof 47 ☎ 043/350–5555); the box office is open Monday–Saturday 11–4. Maastricht has a thriving and talented student and amateur music scene. Performances are at both the **Kumulus Auditorium** (✉ Sint Maartenspoort 2 ☎ 043/350–5669) and the **Theatre Kumulus** (✉ Herbenusstraat 89 ☎ 043/350–5664 ⊕ www.kumulus.nl).

In July and August, Maastricht's great churches make magnificent settings for organ recitals, which usually take place on Tuesday evenings and Sunday afternoons. Contact **Pro Organo Maastricht** (✉ Jekerschans 75 ☎ 043/321–0890) for more details.

THEATER The main theater of Maastricht, the **Theater aan Het Vrijthof** (Theater at Vrijthof; ✉ Vrijthof 47 ☎ 043/350–5555 ⊕ www.theateraanhetvrijthof.nl) has a reputation for exciting programming that extends beyond the city limits. Top-quality national and international companies perform here. The **Het Vervolg Theater** (✉ Plein 1992–15 ☎ 043/350–7171 ⊕ www.hetvervolg.nl) stages experimental and esoteric work.

Nightlife

CAFÉS In the heart of the city, with a terrace that hums with life on summer evenings, **De Lanteern** (✉ Onze Lieve Vrouweplein 26 ☎ 043/321–4326) attracts everyone from tourists to the corner shopkeeper. A special pub to visit is the very old **In den Ouden Vogelstruys** (✉ Vrijthof 15 ☎ 043/321–4888), first mentioned in town records of the 13th century. It has remained virtually unchanged since 1730 (except, of course, for the modern conveniences of electricity and beer on tap). Named for a type of potbellied gin bottle, **Sjinkerij De Bóbbel** (✉ Wolfstraat 32 ☎ 043/321–7413) is a traditional Maastricht pub with an atmosphere to match—well worth visiting if you've time. Informal yet understatedly elegant, it's the sort of place that produces the buzz of good conversation. It has sand on the floor, simple wooden chairs, and marble-top tables—and a good choice of beers.

A spacious but exceptionally friendly bar, tucked away down a Maastricht side street, is **Café Steine Brök** (✉ Heidenstraat 7 ☎ 043/321–2372). If the weather's fine, the few tables outside its doors are a terrific sun trap, and it's a good place to sit and read a book or watch the world go by.

On the opposite side of the River Maas from the city center, **Cafe Zondag** (✉ Heidenstraat 7 ☎ 043/321–2372) is a bright, airy place with large windows and an easy-on-the-eye gray/beige interior. It is a relaxing place for snacks during the day and very popular in the evenings. Tables outside allow you a ringside view of the constant stream of people moving between the railway station and city center.

DANCE CLUBS The somewhat utilitarian interior of **De Kadans** (✉ Kesselskade 62 ☎ 043/321–1937) regularly comes alive during midweek salsa nights or at the weekends. It is generally open until 2 AM Sunday–Tuesday, and to 5 AM Wednesday–Saturday. **Night Live** (✉ Kesselskade 43 ☎ 0900/202–0158) is extremely popular with those with plenty of energy to burn and attracts performances from top DJs. It is open Wednesday–Saturday, and you can bop 'til you drop from 10 PM to 5 in the morning.

GAY BARS **La Ferme** (✉ Rechtstraat 29 ☎ 043/321–8928), with a light show and the latest music, is a vortex of South Netherlands gay life. Near the railway station, and decorated with Dutch Rail flotsam and jetsam, **La Gare** (✉ Spoorweglaan 6 ☎ 043/325–9090) has a long bar, a tiny dance floor, and chatty customers.

The Outdoors

Ballooning

On a late spring or summer evening, you'll often see colorful hot-air balloons floating gently over Maastricht. Providing the ultimate high, they allow a bird's-eye view of the Limburg countryside, including the point where The Netherlands, Germany, and Belgium meet. The **VVV** can arrange trips for you—contact one of its offices for details.

Beaches

For a spot of beach living away from the sea, you could visit the **Dagstrand Oost-Maarland** (✉ Oosterweg 5, between Maastricht and Eijsden ☎ 043/409–4441 ⊕ www.dagstrand.nl), on the east bank of a lake just south of Maastricht. You can swim, surf, and canoe, plus there's miniature golf and a beach pavilion with cafés.

Bicycling

Rent bicycles at the **Railway Station** (✉ Stationsplein ☎ 043/321–1100).

Shopping

If you're after luxury goods, high-quality gifts, or antiques, Maastricht is the place where you'll find them. Shopping here is a delight, with plenty of distinctive small boutiques to satisfy both window-shoppers and those with money to burn. The larger chain stores are concentrated in the pedestrian cross streets that connect and surround the three main squares of the city. **Maastrichter Brugstraat** takes you into the network of intriguing shopping streets from the Sint Servaasbrug. **Maastrichter Smedenstraat** and **Plankstraat** are lined with exclusive shops, with Wolfstraat and the exceptionally fashionable Stokstraat intersecting both of them. In the other direction, Kleine Staat and Grote Staat lead to **Vrijthof**, with a mixed bag of shopping opportunities. Off Grote Staat is a trio of small shopping streets—Spilstraat, Nieuwestraat, and Muntstraat—that end at the Markt. Off Helmstraat is a shopping square, **W. C. Entre Deux.** Late-night shopping is on Thursday.

Maastricht has a tri-country general market in front of the Town Hall on Wednesday and Friday mornings, and there's a flea market opposite the railway station on Saturday. Thursday sees the farmers' market arrive—also on Stationsstraat—where the range of cheese, jams, and honeys are worth exploring.

Antiques, Prints & Paintings

Each year Maastricht's MECC Congress and Exhibition Hall is the site of the **European Fine Art Fair** (⌖ European Fine Art Foundation, Box 1035, 5200 BA 's-Hertogenbosch ☎ 073/614–5165 ⊕ www.tefaf.com) for 10 days beginning in mid-March. Major dealers and the most famous collectors around for antiques and fine arts from all over Europe have made this *the* international show for top-quality, big-ticket (we're talking $35 million Rembrandts), drop-dead name paintings, and objets d'art. Billionaires and art lovers flock here to see the special treasures saved up for this show in old-master paintings, drawings, and prints; furniture and objects; and textiles, tapestries, and rugs. There are also music programs and lectures.

Every March, the Maastricht Art Fair transforms the city from an easy-going, fine-living, understated kind of place to a magnet for the world's wealthiest, most glamorous art and antiques lovers. The fair takes place within the unprepossessing Maastricht Exhibition and Congress Centre (MECC) and has been running annually since 1987. Tickets to the event cost €42.50 for two, though the price includes an appropriately glossy catalog. Despite its size (around 200 dealers take part, with visitor numbers passing 66,000), it's an event that, from the beginning, has maintained exceptionally high standards. This is partly because of the vetting procedure each antique must undergo before it can be approved for exhibition. For two days before the fair opens, a team of experts examines items to weed out any pieces of dubious authenticity.

Of those items that pass the test, the best known and most sought after are probably the old-master paintings of the Renaissance to Baroque eras. Approximately 60% of important 17th-century Dutch and Flemish art on the market at any one time can evidently be found at this event. In recent years, the Maastricht Art Fair also has worked hard to increase its reputation as a hunting ground for 19th- and 20th-century art, with Picassos, Cézannes, and Modiglianis heating up the action. Annual sales are measured in hundreds of millions of dollars, not surprising when you realize that the show draws from the ranks of museum curators to dedicated connoisseurs to moneyed collectors. They know that if it's an early Rembrandt they're after, or perhaps a diamond-and-emerald Cartier necklace, or an 18th-century French drawing room, complete with furniture and walls, the Maastricht Art Fair is the place to look for it. For exact dates, times, and prices of the next Maastricht Art Fair, contact the European Fine Art Fair Foundation.

Gerard Delsing (✉ Sint Pieterstraat 28 ☎ 043/325–7987 ⊕ www. antiquesmaastricht.nl) is young, enthusiastic, and always on the lookout for unusual pieces from the 17th and 18th centuries. His shop, closed Monday and Tuesday, holds everything from period sculptures and burnished walnut bureaus to tiny figurines.

Maaslands Antiquariat (✉ Stokstraat 20 ☎ 043/325–0510 ⊕ www. maaslands.nl) is a very smart shop with an excellent reputation—and prices to match. It specializes in prints, maps, and books relating to the 17th-century provinces of the Low Countries and also stocks a range of engravings and lithographs dating from later periods. Staff will help you track down exactly what you're looking for.

Robert Noortman (✉ Vrijthof 49 ☎ 043/321–6745 ⊕ www.noortman. com) is famed as the man who offered a $35.6 million Rembrandt portrait of an elderly lady for sale at the Maastricht Art Fair, and his firm has provided works of art to such venerable institutions as the Rijksmuseum, the Metropolitan Museum of Art in New York City, and the Tel Aviv Museum. His glorious Vrijthof gallery is in an old mansion whose walls are bejeweled with great 17th-century Dutch paintings. Who knows what you might find on a visit here—another Rembrandt, perhaps? (In fact, yes; Noortman was also the purchaser of a $9 million Rembrandt portrait of a man—let's hope one of them sells soon for Noortman's sake.) One thing's for sure, though—anything on sale here certainly won't be going for a song.

Children
De Winkel van Nijntje (✉ Maastrichter Smedenstraat 2 ☎ 043/326–0326) delights toddlers of all ages who are fans of Dick Bruna's cheeky

rabbit Miffy (or Nijntje—a diminutive of *konijn*, Dutch for "rabbit"), who has been making fans the world over since 1955. Here you can find every kind of Miffy item, from the original Dutch storybooks plus English-language translations to Miffy bubble bath, rucksacks, toys, and crockery—all emblazoned with images of Bruna's simple, colorful character and her friends.

Clothes & Fashion Accessories

Clio (⊠ Sint Amorsplein 11 ☎ 043/325–0802) seems a world away from Maastricht's crowds, thanks to its cool, shady interior; on display are Swiss watches, bold modern jewelry, unisex scents, and leather handbags in every imaginable shape and color.

Elle & Lune (⊠ Sint Amorsplein 8 ☎ 043/321–4969), in a small center-city square, sells exquisite, elegant lace-trimmed lingerie; La Perla negligées and nightgowns; and classic swimsuits. Colors range from timeless black and white to ice-cream pastels.

Galerie Amarna (⊠ Stokstraat 9 ☎ 043/325–5471) features one-of-a-kind women's wear in floaty chiffons, plus quirky hats. The use of color and pattern is sure to be a talking point back home, and with such lightweight fabrics, whatever you buy won't take up much room in your suitcase.

Food & Provisions

Adriaan (⊠ Sint Pieterstraat 36 ☎ 043/325–8865) has shelves stacked with delicious concoctions: ocher-color mustards, ruby-red jams and jellies, mayonnaise, marmalades, and chutneys. You can even see them being concocted in the back kitchen—irresistible.

Joosten (⊠ Wycker Brugstraat 43 ☎ 043/321–4464) is the source where you can stock up on local white wines and cheeses (and sample the latter before you buy). The waxy white goat cheese is a fine choice, as of course is the Rommedoe—a richly pungent cheese not often found outside the province of Limburg—and both make perfect picnic fare.

Gifts & Housewares

Boutique Elizabeth (⊠ Sporenstraat 18 ☎ 043/325–5869) allures shoppers with a checkerboard floor, plenty of space, and a fountain gently playing at the back of the store, all of which add character to Elizabeth's furniture and furnishings. The mix here features everything from period cupboards and antique school satchels to modern bridge sets, cushions, and wrought-iron clothes hooks. It's a great place for browsing.

Frissen Pieters (⊠ Stokstraat 49 ☎ 043/321–2277) is a gorgeous, light-filled florist where the blooms are of the old-world variety: think languidly drooping roses and sweet-scented stock in chintz colors. Elegant home accessories here include silver wine coolers with leather handles, creamy china, chandeliers, and crystal.

Gaia (⊠ Bredestraat 22 ☎ 043/350–0478) offers very chic and very now goodies. East meets West in this colorful but cool housewares shop where you'll find crackle-glazed plates, woven throws in jewel tones, candles, and incense holders; the staff is welcoming and enthusiastic, whether you buy or not.

Gay Jongen (⊠ Rechtstraat 59 ☎ 043/321–6824) is the place to head for state-of-the-art, exotic accessories and furniture, especially for the bathroom and kitchen. You'll find pared-down china, cutting-edge cutlery, and intriguing accoutrements.

THE BORDER PROVINCES & MAASTRICHT A TO Z

To research prices, get advice from other travelers, and book travel arrangements, visit www.fodors.com.

AIR TRAVEL

Once you're actually in The Netherlands, there is absolutely no need to take internal flights; the country is simply too small to warrant it. Instead, travel from north to south via train, bus, or car.

CARRIERS In addition to regular flights to Eindhoven and Maastricht from Amsterdam, KLM City Hopper operates a service direct from London Heathrow to Eindhoven. An additional service to Eindhoven from the United Kingdom is scheduled by Ryan Air from London Stanstead.
🖪 Airlines & Contacts **KLM City Hopper** ☎ 020/474-7747. **Ryan Air** ⊕ www.ryanair. com.

AIRPORTS

There are airports in Eindhoven and Maastricht. In addition to regular flights to both cities from Amsterdam, **KLM City Hopper** (☎ 020/474–7747) operates a service direct from London Heathrow to Eindhoven. Ryan Air (⊕ www.ryanair.com) connects Eindhoven to London Stanstead.
🖪 Airport Information **Eindhoven Airport Luchthaven** ⊠ Weg 25, 5657 AA ☎ 040/ 291-9818. **Maastricht Aachen Airport** ⊠ Vliegveldweg 90,, 6199 AD ⊕ Box 8081, 6199 ZG ☎ 043/358-9898.

BUS TRAVEL

Local and regional buses leave from and return to the Dutch railway stations, but bus travel can be slow. The public transportation number and Web site for the entire country is listed below. Operators can also give you information about local bus routes.
🖪 Bus Information **Public transportation number** ☎ 0900/9292 ⊕ www.9292ov.nl.

CAR RENTAL

In Maastricht, you can rent a car from the national Interrentcar (and motorbike) service. An agency at the Maastricht Airport is Idem.
🖪 Local Agencies **Idem** ⊠ Maastricht Aachen Airport ☎ 043/364-5430. **Sixt Autoverhuur** ⊠ Spoorweglaan 18, 6221 BS Maastricht ☎ 043/321-6163.

CAR TRAVEL

To reach Zeeland take E19 from Amsterdam to Rotterdam and pick up A29 south; connect with N59 west to Zierikzee and N256 across the Zeelandbrug bridge to Goes, where you can pick up E312/A58 west to Middelburg, capital of Zeeland province.

To reach the provinces of Brabant and Limburg, take E25/A2 from Amsterdam south through Utrecht. Pick up A27 south to Breda, or stay on E25 through 's-Hertogenbosch to reach Eindhoven and other points south. To travel from Zeeland across to Maastricht, it is far quicker to travel via Antwerp (in Belgium), taking the A4 and then the E313.

EMERGENCIES

🖪 Emergency Services **National Emergency Alarm Number** for police, fire, or ambulance ☎ 112.
🖪 Hospitals **Breda** ☎ 076/595-1000. **Eindhoven** ☎ 040/239-9111. **'s-Hertogenbosch** ☎ 0411/634000. **Maastricht** ☎ 043/387-6543. **Middelburg** ☎ 0118/425000.

MONEY MATTERS

CURRENCY EXCHANGE In the area, you can change money at any of the major banks (ABN Amro or RaboBank, for example), and also in the larger hotels.

TAXIS

If you are not traveling under your own steam, you will need to hire a taxi to get to some of the more distant castles. To summon a taxi, call the number listed below for each respective city.

🔢 Taxi Companies **Breda** ☎ 076/522-2111. **Eindhoven** ☎ 040/252-5252. **'s-Hertogenbosch** ☎ 073/631-2900. **Maastricht** ☎ 043/347-7777. **Middelburg** ☎ 0118/412600.

TOURS

The Maastricht Tourist Office offers a 1- to 1½-hour guided tour of the city for €3.25. Tours of the province are available through Touring Car Bedrijf Van Fraassen.

🔢 Fees & Schedules **Maastricht Tourist Office** ✉ Kleine Staat 1 ☎ 043/325-2121. **Touring Car Bedrijf Van Fraassen** ✉ President Rooseveltlaan 768 ☎ 0118/419220.

BOAT TOURS For cruises on the River Maas, contact Stiphout Tours and Trips. Fares start at €5.75.

🔢 Fees & Schedules **Stiphout Tours and Trips** ✉ Maasboulevard 81, 6211 JW Maastricht ☎ 043/351-5300 ⊕ www.stiphout.nl.

WALKING TOURS The Middelburg Tourist Office occasionally offers guided walking tours (1¼ hours, daily Apr.–Oct.) for €4.50 per person.

🔢 Fees & Schedules **Middelburg Tourist Office** ✉ Markt 65a ☎ 0118/659900.

TRAIN TRAVEL

There are frequent Intercity express trains from Amsterdam direct to 's-Hertogenbosch, Eindhoven, Middelburg, or Maastricht. To reach Breda by train, it is necessary to connect either in Roosendaal or 's-Hertogenbosch. There is also an Intercity train line that crosses the country, west to east within the Border Provinces, twice each hour. From Breda there is frequent service direct to Eindhoven, for connections to Maastricht. As always in The Netherlands, traveling by train between cities is fast and efficient.

🔢 Train Information **Intercity** ☎ 0900/9292 ⊕ www.ns.nl.

VISITOR INFORMATION

🔢 Tourist Information To access the Web sites for each town and city listed below, log on to ⊕ www.vvv(town name).nl. **VVV Breda** ✉ Willemstraat 17-19, 4811 AJ ☎ 0900/522-2444. **VVV Eindhoven** ✉ Stationsplein 17, 5611 AC ☎ 0900/112-2363 or 040/297-9100. **VVV 's-Hertogenbosch** ✉ Markt 77, 5211 JX ☎ 073/613-9629. **VVV Heusden** ✉ Pelsestraat 17, 5256 AT ☎ 0416/662100. **VVV Maastricht** ✉ Het Dinghuis, Kleine Staat 1, 6211 ED ☎ 043/325-2121 🖨 043/321-3746. **Tourist Shop Middelburg** ✉ Markt 65c, 4331 LK ☎ 0118/674300. **VVV Tilburg** ✉ Stadhuisplein 132 ☎ 0900/202-0815. **VVV Vaals** ✉ Maastrichterln 73a ☎ 0900/9798. **VVV Veere-Vrouwenpolder** ✉ Oudestraat 28, 4351 AV ☎ 0118/501365. **VVV Vlissingen** ✉ Oude Markt 3, 4381 ER ☎ 0118/422190. **VVV Yerseke** ✉ Kerkplein 1 ☎ 0113/571864. **VVV Zierikzee** ✉ Nieuw Haven 7 ☎ 0111/412450.

THE GREEN HEART

5

FODOR'S CHOICE

Amersfoort, *a medieval jewel of a town*

Arnhem, *home to World War II's "bridge too far"*

Bronkhorst, *the tiniest town in The Netherlands*

Deventer, *a Hanseatic center cloaked in the Middle Ages*

De Hoge Veluwe, *an Edenic preserve near Otterlo*

De Librije, *this Zwolle spot is perhaps Holland's best restaurant*

Giethoorn, *a verdant, miniature version of Venice*

Kampen, *is that Rapunzel atop the town tower?*

Kröller-Müller Museum, *nearly wallpapered with Van Goghs*

Paleis Het Loo, *the most beautiful palace in Holland*

Staphorst, *a famed Dutch picture-village*

HIGHLY RECOMMENDED

RESTAURANTS De Librije, *Zwolle*

Eethuis Bij de Stadsmuur, *Amersfoort*

Kasteel Doorwerth, *Arnhem*

HOTELS Château de Havixhorst, *Staphorst*

De Keizerskroon Bilderberg, *Apeldoorn*

Herberg de Gouden Leeuw, *Bronkhorst*

Logies de Tabaksplant, *Amersfoort*

Molendal, *Arnhem*

*Many other great sights, restaurants, and hotels enliven this region.
For other favorites, look for the black stars as you read this chapter.*

By Shirley J. S. Agudo

Updated by Shirley J. S. Agudo and Carol Conover

LIKE A MYSTERY PACKAGE THAT REVEALS A SERIES of ever smaller, ever more intriguing boxes, the wooded heart of The Netherlands is an unfolding treasure, its great national park acting as the wrappings. Pumped with contrasts that will take your breath away, the region popularly known as the Green Heart lies precociously still amid the hinterland set between Amsterdam in the west and Germany in the east. Everyone from the ancient Romans to the Hanseatic League and medieval marketeers have beheld this region's glory, which extends over the middle provinces of Gelderland and Overijssel, along with the bordering town of Amersfoort. Throughout various times in history, many of these groups have taken advantage of the region's position as a strategic trade artery. A prime target amid war-torn Europe, its undying legacy has left a scarred but well-preserved testimony to the inimitable Dutch prescription for land reclamation, recovery, and reuse. Armed with vast areas of unspoiled towns and villages still pulsing with ageless traditions in a pristine yet more rugged terrain than its neighboring provinces, the Green Heart is the elixir sure to satisfy any pangs of nostalgic wanderlust.

The provinces of Overijssel and Gelderland, and the Green Heart's adopted daughter, Amersfoort—too green and medieval not to include here—are a minestrone of spices in this garden soup of a region. Start with the woodlands, dunes, and heath of the Veluwe core with its national parks and palaces, plus a priceless art museum buried deep in the forest. Blend in an outlying rim of towns steeped in a strong brew of history, ranging from Staphorst with its rigid, ingrained beliefs and customs reminiscent of the Amish, to the Hanseatic cluster of former market towns. Garnish with the punter's paradise of Giethoorn, complete with its Venetian playground of canals providing the only means of transport through a village of thatched-roof cottages; Zutphen's famous medieval library (where the books are still chained to their ancient lecterns); the "Operation Market Garden" spot where the famous World War II Battle of Arnhem took place; and the seemingly misplaced Charles Dickens museum in teeny-tiny Bronkhorst—the smallest official town in The Netherlands, a mere whisper of cobbled streets in a china-cup brim.

To better understand this area's recipe for success, remember that 700 years before the advent of the European Common Market or the European Union, there was an association of northern European trading cities called the Hanseatic League. It began as a pact among itinerant merchants to travel together for mutual safety, but in time it became an alliance of more than 150 towns and cities scattered over the Continent. Among the important members of that league were the Dutch cities of Zwolle, Kampen, Deventer, and Zutphen along the River IJssel. Their beat lives on in the well-endowed mansions, churches, and monuments from that period, historic reminders of a bygone period of wealth and prosperity. Go back as far as you can on the low country's time line and you begin with the Roman settlement in Nijmegen and the surrounding area, a precursor of fortune and fame. Eventually, Dutch royals also chose this area as a fitting place for hunt and home because of its natural beauty and abundance of game. A veritable stockpot of à la carte pleasures and pastimes, the Green Heart offers a 2,000-year-old menu of delicacies begging to be served again and again.

Exploring the Green Heart

While the Ranstad may be the pulse of Holland, the Green Heart, in all its throbbing glory, is the impulsive, natural beauty. Only a deep breath away, it lures you with open spaces and open arms. Heathland, forests, wetland farms, a sprawling national park and a royal garden akin to that of Versailles make this a perfect area in which to let your hair down. The Rivers IJssel and Rhine wend their way through towns where castles and medieval market squares mark time in a slower beat than in the more heavily populated west, the rhythm of life here being hushed, undulating, and restorative.

Gelderland, the largest province and central core of Holland, lies southwest of its fraternal twin, the province of Overijssel, and is home to the combined splendor of the Hoge Veluwe National Park and the Royal Forest, a dazzling oasis of peace carved by a regal preference for this area. Although biking and hiking are popular all over the Green Heart, the Hoge Veluwe is particularly suited for such excursions and appeals to the outdoorsman in everyone. Farther east, arranged in an arc that stretches from north to south, is Overijssel and its historic Hanseatic towns and Arnhem, scene of the famous World War II battle of September 1944.

About the Restaurants & Hotels

Fortunately, those traveling to the Green Heart will appreciate the somewhat braver cuisine than is typically to be found throughout the quieter areas of Holland. Whereas Dutch cooking seems to inspire only the Dutch themselves, "the national menu," if you will, whereby each restaurant seems to have the same basic choices, can begin to bore even the most tolerant tourist. The Green Heart, however, seems to offer more gusto with at least a selection of local wild game on the menu. If you do prefer simple fare, the cafés or *eetcafés* ("eating cafés") as they were, offer a step up from the snack bars one finds on many corners, with French-bread (*stokbrood*) sandwiches at lunchtime and reasonably priced, standard but hearty meals in the evenings. Outdoor cafés are abundant and welcome, considering the surrounding scenery to enjoy. Hours are in keeping with general guidelines across Holland that dictate early-evening meals hovering around 6 PM in marked contrast to the significantly later dinner hours of their European neighbors.

From moat-fronted castles to campsites, from city mansions to country inns to woodland cottages, the Green Heart has something to suit every whim and budget. Camping is popular, particularly in and around the Hoge Veluwe National Park, and the local VVV information offices can provide you with an endless list of choices. Rather than staying in a town, you might opt for one of the village hotels—some are simple, others have a country-house atmosphere, but many have a special charm and relaxing sense of isolation. Do not assume that all rooms have air-conditioning, but you can normally count on TV and telephones unless otherwise noted.

WHAT IT COSTS In euros*				
	$$$$	**$$$**	**$$**	**$**	**¢**
RESTAURANTS	over €30	€22–€30	€15–€22	€10–€15	under €10
HOTELS	over €230	€165–€230	€120–€165	€75–€120	under €75

*Restaurant prices are per person for a main course only, excluding tax (6% for food and 19% for alcoholic beverages) and service; note that if a restaurant offers only prix-fixe (set-price) meals, it has been given the price category that reflects the full prix-fixe price. Hotel prices are for a standard double room in high season, including the 6% VAT (value-added tax); higher prices (inquire when booking) prevail for any meal plans.

Timing

Fall is an ideal time to visit this region, because not only do the restaurants offer all sorts of delicious game dishes, but the scenery of the Hoge Veluwe is then spectacular. Stretches of the park were especially planted

Poised center stage, the Green Heart, with its distinctive topography, beats to an altogether different drummer from the rest of the motherland. Here one finds a visible concerto of forests primeval, heaths and moors with a Roman bearing, a medieval second act, and a contemporary cadence. Harmoniously, it blends Hanseatic strains, war-torn turbulence, and princely pursuits into a melody where the past is made accessible. With leading lures such as Holland's greatest park reserve, De Hoge Veluwe—home to the Kröller-Müller Museum's Van Goghs—Apeldoorn's magisterial Het Loo Palace, and the medieval enclave of Amersfoort, it's little wonder you'll fall in love with this region, heart and soul.

5

Roughly an hour or so from Amsterdam, the provinces of Gelderland and Overijssel lend themselves perfectly to exploration starting out from that city. If quieter surroundings suit you better, consider making Amersfoort your base. It is central to the entire country. You can combine a Hanseatic tour with a wilderness expedition through the Hoge Veluwe, with stops at various points of interest along the perimeter.

Numbers in the text correspond to numbers in the margin and on the Amersfoort and The Green Heart maps.

If you have 3 days Short escapes should include a visit to **Otterlo/De Hoge Veluwe National Park** ⑲ ▶ and its Kröller-Müller Museum—a private ode to Dutch painter Vincent van Gogh and friends in a spectacular setting in the forest—which can easily fill an entire day, especially if you include time for a brief bike excursion on one of their 1,000 white bikes. Allow another day to explore at least one of the Hanseatic towns—such as **Zutphen** ⑳, **Zwolle** ⑬, **Kampen** ⑯, **Deventer** ⑰, or **Nijmegen** ㉓—and another day to visit the palace of Het Loo in **Apeldoorn** ⑱, a royal retreat in the Royal Forest. Or, if war history intrigues you, venture to **Arnhem** ㉒, where one of the most famous battles of World War II took place.

If you have 5 days After hitting the highlights of the three-day itinerary, allow time to visit one or more of the other Hanseatic towns—such as **Kampen** ⑯, **Zwolle** ⑬, **Deventer** ⑰, **Zutphen** ⑳, or **Nijmegen** ㉓—and then choose one of the smaller villages: **Bronkhorst** ㉑, the smallest town in the country and a self-contained national monument piping with local artisans; **Giethoorn** ⑮, the "Venice of the North," where the mode of transport is via canals instead of streets; or **Staphorst** ⑭, a time warp of a village where the locals still wear traditional costume. Alternatively, you may wish to spend time in **Amersfoort** ❶–⑫, a medieval enclave and one of our favorite picks, either en route to or returning from the other destinations, as it is the closest to an Amsterdam base.

with trees that make a brilliant mosaic of gold, crimson, and orange in autumn. Summer and spring are equally good times to visit but Gelderland is an extremely popular vacation area among the Dutch themselves so expect lots of company if you tour during the peak months of July and August. In spring, cherry, apple, and pear trees are at their peak and

May is a fine time to visit the Open Air Museum at Arnhem. Winter can be a bit dreary, but you will at least have all the dreariness to yourself.

AMERSFOORT: GATEWAY FROM UTRECHT

Fodor'sChoice
★

Get thee to Amersfoort, a medieval town pulsing with Middle Ages blood in the western artery surrounding the Green Heart. Officially part of the province of Utrecht, Amersfoort begs to cross the line, like a knight in shining armor with dual loyalties. Poised for battle with its fortress gates and double-ringed canal—the only such vein in all of Europe—it is a highly walkable town with winding, cobblestone streets, parts of which are closed to traffic, where you can almost hear the clack of hooves of jousting horses.

Before you set out to explore the town—about 50 km (32 mi) from Amsterdam—be sure to pick up a copy of the VVV information office's indispensable walking guide "Amersfoort . . . Best Experienced on Foot" (€2.25) in both Dutch and English, featuring Piet Mondriaan's birthplace; Amersfoort's famous carillon school; unique wallhouses (built into and out of the old city wall); a dashing museum chiseled out of the medieval foundation, with a nearby 14th-century hospice where history literally comes alive each summer; a modern art museum housed in a church where homage is paid to a living artist; and the local brewery.

▶ ❶ Salvaged by someone's grace, the most prominent tower in Amersfoort, **Onze Lieve Vrouwetoren** (Tower of Our Lady), is a 328-foot masterpiece thrusting against the sky; the once-adjoined church blew up in 1787 during its days as an ammunition depot when sparks from a soldier's knife ignited its contents. Seventeen people were killed, but the tower, which marks the exact epicenter of The Netherlands, remained intact. ⊠ *Lieve Vrouwekerkhof* ☉ *July and Aug., Tues.–Fri. 10–5, weekends noon–5; or by special appointment through the VVV.*

❷ Fast-forward to a living Dutch modern artist who, rare enough, already has a museum in his honor, the **Armando Museum**, which, even rarer, is housed in an early-19th-century Neoclassical church, **De Elleboogkerk.** Known for his diverse talents as a painter, sculptor, writer, film and theater director, and violinist, Armando (b. 1929), as he is simply known, draws upon the war years he spent growing up near the Amersfoort internment camp as the basis for much of his work. There is a free guided tour every third Sunday of each month at 2:30 with entrance ticket. ⊠ *Langegracht 36, 3800 AR* ☎ *033/461–4088* 🖼 *€3.40* ☉ *Tues.–Fri. 11–5, weekends noon–5.*

need a break?

If the time of day is right (open Thurs.–Sat. 1–7) and you're hankering for a beer, why not go to the source—directly across from the De Nederlandse Beiaardschool (Dutch Carilloneur's School) is **De Drie Ringen brewery** (The Three Rings; ⊠ Kleine Spui 18 ☎ 033/465–6575), a little spout of a place where you can freely sample the wares, the most popular of which is the Blond beer, one of six types produced here. At the **Stadscafé** (⊠ Stadhuisplein 7 ☎ 033/469–5718), breakfast, lunch, and light dinner salads and pastas are tossed up with a sprinkling of jazz, classical, or Motown music in a well-lighted restaurant-cum-gallery.

❸ Pity that they have no originals (which are mostly in the Gemeentemuseum in The Hague), but the birthplace of Dutch artist Piet Mondriaan (1872–1944), **Het Mondriaanhuis,** now a museum about his life and work with an exact replica of his famed studio in Paris, is worth seeing

5

Once Upon a Village For the traveler seeking a dichotomy of pleasures away from the madding crowd of Amsterdam, the Green Heart wrestles up a yin and yang of poignant and pretty. No other area in Holland dares to grab your attention and focus it as equally on the pain of history as it does on painfully picturesque villages. On balance, it's possible, given a short amount of time, to feast on the World War II history branded on this area as easily as it is to wrap your arms around some of Holland's most sensual, melt-in-your-mouth villages. Pulling your heartstrings in both directions, the dilemma is which to see first—the plethora of memorials, monuments, and museums devoted to the horrors of war and the costs of freedom (for the WWII buff, perhaps the best known of the historic sites are in and around Arnhem, including the Airborne Museum Hartenstein and the Rhine Bridge), or the panting, prepossessing villages and towns prickling the area. Between Bronkhorst, officially the smallest town in Holland; Giethoorn, a fairy-tale version of Venice; Staphorst, a time warp; Amersfoort with its medieval bodice; and Zutphen chained to its medieval books, who needs fantasy—or the rest of Holland, for that matter?

On the Menu With the Royal Game Reserve in the north and the fruit- and vegetable-growing region to the east, the restaurants of the Green Heart are well supplied with abundant, high-quality ingredients from their own backyard. Although the main game season is fall, clever restaurateurs manage to find something for almost every month; some even go hunting themselves. Braised hare is a specialty, and the local boar and venison are delicious, as is the pheasant. Sampling local game is a must, whether prepared as a family-style stew in a simple restaurant or as the culinary creation of one of the area's top chefs. Top it off with the wintertime pleasures of *Glüwein*, a hot-mulled wine that has made inroads from neighboring Germany, and a thick, hearty bowl of unmistakably Dutch pea soup (*erwtensoep*), and you'll be ready for your own hunt.

Wild Life The core of the Green Heart, as its name implies, is verdant and lush, thereby lending itself to a unique concentration of wildlife, particularly in the National Park area of the Veluwe between Apeldoorn and Arnhem. Countless red and roe deer, mouflons (wild sheep), wild boar, and a variety of small animals are visible in grazing pastures and fields, affording good game observation in the park, with De Hoge Veluwe being the most visitor-friendly area, thanks to its tailor-made lookout towers. According to the visitor center there—which can provide you with suggested game-watching tactics and mapped-out posts—the best time of day to catch the big game is late afternoon or early evening when the animals leave their cover in search of food. With October being mating time for the mouflons, it's a good time to hazard a surreptitious peek as the rams fight over the ewes, slamming their distinctive curled horns against each other in battle.

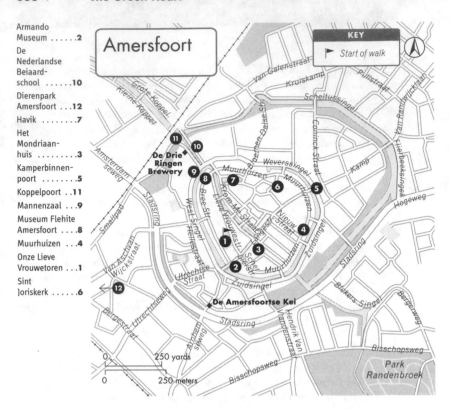

if you're intrigued by his cubist/Neo-Plasticist work. There is a gift and coffee shop on-site. ⊠ *Kortegracht 11, 3811 KG* ☎ *033/462–0180* 🖃 *€3* ⊙ *Tues.–Fri. 10–5, weekends 2–5.*

❹ Unique to Amersfoort are the **Muurhuizen** (wallhouses), some of medieval origin, built along the foundation of the original inner-city wall and, indeed, from its very rubble, as the wall itself was demolished in the 15th century for outward expansion of the town. Walk around the entire perimeter until you reach **Tinnenburg** at No. 25, a former merchant's house and cotton-spinning site mentioned in a 1414 document, where you can see in the masonry how the house was attached to the fortress gate. (Take a discreet peek at another old merchant's mansion across the canal at Zuidsingel 38; built around 1780, this "house with the purple windows" once served as the temporary residence of William V and his wife, Wilhelmina, of Prussia and is now, strangely enough, the domain of seven fortunate nuns, who dislike gawkers.)

❺ Heralding you to enter, the **Kamperbinnenpoort,** the last remaining part of the ancient inner-city wall, leads to the 21st-century version of former market stalls—a thoroughfare of modern-day shops sentried along Langestraat and its side street, Krommestraat, and farther on to the Varkensmarkt (Pig Market) and Utrechtsestraat. Late-night shopping is on Thursday evening until 9.

❻ Dating from the 12th century, **Sint Joriskerk** (St. George's Church) and its immediate environs take center stage in the oldest inhabited area of Amersfoort. The chapel was altered and expanded over the centuries until it achieved its current form, a three-hall church, in the 16th century. Besides religious services, there are concerts and living-history enactments here as well. The **hof** or courtyard surrounding the church offers its own concerto of sorts as it resonates with the sounds of summer from the outdoor cafés, festival music, street performers, and a market humming with activity on Friday mornings and Saturday year-round. Completing the score, the chimes on the adjacent 16th-century weigh house play on the hour and the wooden doors below eject a mechanized St. George slaying the dragon, a constant reminder of days of yore.

7 The **Havik,** a charming old merchant and artisan area, was Amersfoort's original harbor until the Koppelpoort replaced it. The former **Beer Brewers' Guild** at No. 35 looks strikingly like the redbrick gabled house in Dutch artist Johannes Vermeer's street scene that he painted in Delft. The narrow house at No. 33 was once a passageway to the hof, the administrative center of this crossroads.

8 Couched canal-side in three splendidly gabled Muurhuizen, or wallhouses, (circa 1500) is the **Museum Flehite Amersfoort** of local artifacts and art relating to the history of the region, including a medieval prison door; a beam and post from which people were hanged during the Middle Ages and on up to the end of the 18th century; and the Vanitas painting by Matthias Withoos (1627–1703). ☒ *Westsingel 50, 3811BC* ☎ *033/ 461–9987* ⊕ *www.museumflehite.nl* 🎫 *€4* ☉ *Tues.–Fri. 11–5, weekends 1–5.*

9 Part of the **Museum Flehite Amersfoort,** and located across the street, is the men's ward, or **Mannenzaal,** of the St. Pieters en Bloklandsgasthuis (Hospice), originally established in the 14th century and in use until the beginning of the 20th century, and containing no fewer than 22 cupboard beds or *bedsteden* where otherwise homeless men slept, two in a bed, until 1838. Adjacent to the chapel, this ward, which appears as it did from the 16th century until 1907, is the scene for a dramatic living-history forum in July and August whereby local volunteers reenact life in the ward as if they were back in the early 1900s. Pose any question and they will respond as if they were in that time frame, making for an ear- and eye-opening experience for young and old. ☒ *Westsingel 47, 3811 BC* ☎ *033/472–0669* 🎫 *Free with admission to Flehite Museum* ☉ *Tues.–Fri. 11–5, weekends 1–5.*

If you've been hearing bells, you're not imagining things, as the **Tower of Our Lady** is home to not one but two carillons and seven swinging bells, 100 bells in total, whose glorious tones resound every 15 minutes and *al concerto virtuoso* (Thursday from 8 to 9 PM, Friday from 10 to 11 AM, and Saturday from 1 to 2 and 4 to 5 PM). Take a seat in an outdoor café and be swept away by concerts of students from the world-**10** famous **De Nederlandse Beiaardschool** (Dutch Carilloneurs' School), one of only two in the world devoted to the art of the carillon. ☒ *Grote Spui 11, 3811 GA* ☎ *033/475–2638* ⊕ *www.hku.nl* ☉ *Tours by appointment.*

11 The **Koppelpoort** is uniquely both a land and water gate predating 1427. Part of the outer defensive wall, the north side of the port, retains its wooden annex where boiling tar and oil were dropped on the heads of would-be intruders. Guards stationed above on precarious platforms would raise a flag to alert the guard on the Onze-Lieve-Vrouwetoren, who in turn raised a flag to alert the other ports surrounding the city. Amersfoort was thus protected. If you want to see the two tread wheels inside, you can arrange a tour through the VVV.

🐾 **12** Every kid's dream zoo come true, the **Dierenpark Amersfoort** (Animal Park) features an Ancient Village and the chance to come face to face with lions, tigers, and bears. ☒ *Barchman Wuytierslaan 224, 3819 AC* ☎ *033/422–7100* ⊕ *www.amersfoort-zoo.nl* 🎫 *€14.50* ☉ *Daily 9–5, Apr.–Oct. until 6.*

Where to Eat & Stay

★ $$ ✗ **Eethuis Bij de Stadsmuur.** Aptly named, this "Eatery by the City Wall" is indeed near remnants of the old city wall, in a building dating from 1485. The cuisine may be French, but the Delft chandeliers keep you mindful of where you are. The food is so good, and the creamy yellow dining room so restful, that you may be reluctant to go anywhere else the following night. The service is impeccable and personable. ⊠ *Kamp 88* ☎ *033/475–6096* ☰ *MC, V.*

$–$$ ✗ **Bistro in den Vollen Pot.** Just follow your nose and the unmissable Tower of Our Lady to this very popular bistro with "a full pot" of Dutch/French food, a truly *gezillig* (cozy) place. ⊠ *Lieve Vrouwekerkhof 8–10* ☎ *033/ 463–2329* ⚹ *Reservations essential* ☰ *AE, DC, MC, V.*

$–$$ ✗ **The Far East.** This spot offers Asian cooking at its best, with a mouthwatering menu spotlighting China's many provinces with dishes that are often a feast for the eyes. ⊠ *Kamp 74* ☎ *033/472–5021* ☰ *AE, DC, MC, V* ☉ *Closed Tues.*

$–$$ ✗ **Mama Roux.** In a picture-window-perfect location overlooking the hof marketplace, this is a great place to have lunch during bustling market days. Mama makes a great house salad with cheese and nuts, and the best cappuccino in town, served with *Tante Kaatje* ("Aunt Kate")—a side glass of coffee liqueur and a dollop of cream. ⊠ *Hof 9* ☎ *033/462– 0023* ☰ *No credit cards* ☉ *Closed Mon.*

¢–$ ✗ **San Giorgio.** An Italian restaurant in a 14th-century abbey . . . that'za San Giorgio, pure heaven on earth. Blend in some arias sung by live singers (Monday only, October–March, reservations essential) and presto, you have their special "Mangia alla Classica," offered at a fixed-price menu (€40). ⊠ *Krommestraat 44* ☎ *033/461–5685* ☰ *AE, DC, MC, V* ☉ *Closed Wed. Oct.–Apr.*

$$ ⊡ **Best Western Berghotel Amersfoort.** Perched atop Amersfoort's highest point, this hotel—only a 15-minute walk from the station, a 20-minute walk to the center of town, and a 5-minute drive to the local zoo—previously catered to the rich and famous of Holland as a deluxe hotel that not only accommodated VIPs, but came complete with a stable for their horses as well. Today it caters to you with its indoor pool, solarium, and free sauna, and all the in-room amenities you expect, even if you show up saddleless. ⊠ *Utrechtseweg 225, 3818 EG* ☎ *033/422–4222* ⊟ *033/465–0505* ⊕ *www.berghotel.nl* ⤳ *90 rooms* ⚭ *Restaurant, minibars, cable TV, indoor pool, sauna, bicycles, 2 bars, some pets allowed; no a/c* ☰ *AE, DC, MC, V* ⅋◎ *BP.*

$$ ⊡ **Tulip Inn Amersfoort.** Reposing in a wooded area just a 10-minute bike ride to the old city center and a 5-minute drive to the local zoo, this one-level hotel is part of a chain of well-respected inns throughout the country. ⊠ *Stichtse Rotonde 11, 3818 GV* ☎ *033/462–0054* ⊟ *033/461– 9281* ⊕ *www.tulipinnamersfoort.nl* ⤳ *74 rooms* ⚭ *Restaurant, cable TV, bar; no a/c* ☰ *AE, DC, MC, V* ◎ *BP.*

¢–$ ⊡ **Logement De Gaaper.** A fitting remedy for weary travelers, this former pharmacy from the 1860s is now a recently renovated hotel with original beams and elements from what happens to be the oldest brick house in Amersfoort, dating from 1250. Easy to spot on the main hof marketplace, the hotel is landmarked by its wooden model of De Gaaper's (literally, "the gaper's") Head, a traditional symbol of a pharmacy. (Open mouth, insert pill?) ⊠ *Hof 39, 3811 CK* ☎ *033/453–1795* ⊟ *033/453–1796* ⊕ *www.degaaper.nl* ⤳ *11 rooms* ⚭ *In-room data ports, minibars, cable TV; no a/c* ☰ *V* ⅋◎ *BP.*

★ ¢–$ ⊡ **Logies de Tabaksplant.** By far the best value and the best location for exploring Amersfoort is Mieke and Theo's bed-and-breakfast, one of 350 declared monuments in town, built between 1600 and 1650 by a rich tobacco grower (and hence the name, "Tobacco Plant Lodging").

A breath away from the Kamperbinnenpoort gate and the heart of the shopping area, this completely modernized facility offers in-room coffee/tea-making facilities, high-tech refrigerators, and a choice of rooms with or without bathrooms and kitchens. Room No. 21 sports a Jacuzzi and breakfast in bed for the recently married or discriminating duo. Don't hesitate on this one too long; it books up quickly. ⊠ *Coninckstraat 15, 3811WD* ☎ *033/472–9797* 🖷 *033/470–0756* ⊕ *www.tabaksplant.nl* ⬑ *17 rooms, 5 apartments* ♿ *In-room data ports, cable TV, some pets allowed; no a/c* ⊟ *No credit cards* ⍟ *BP.*

Nightlife & the Arts

Het Filmhuis (The Filmhouse; ⊠ Groenmarkt 8 ☎ 033/465–5550) is a hip, casual place in grand café style, with light music on Sunday in winter and a band outside in the square every Saturday in summer. Have a convivial dram and a game of billiards in one of the oldest bars in Amersfoort, **Onder de Linde** (Under the Linden Tree; ⊠ Appelmarkt 16 ☎ 033/461–4203), a 1530 building with a bar established under that name since 1775. A popular option is **In den Grooten Slock** (⊠ Zevenhuizen 1 ☎ 033/461–3239), with original fittings and furnishings. The 1930s-style, one and only jazz café in town, **Lazy Louis Jazz Café** (⊠ Arnhemsestraat 1–3 ☎ 033/461–3638) serves lunch and dinner.

The Outdoors

In July and August, 45-minute canal-boat rides with narration are conducted by **Watorlijn** (⊕ www.amersfoort-rondvaarten.nl) at Krommestraat 5. **Eemlijn** (⊕ www.eemlijn.nl) boat trips on the Eem River where you can hop on or off with or without your bike. The boat alights on the Kleine Koppel between Brabantsestraat and Geldersestraat and takes about eight hours for the round-trip. For a shorter experience hop off in Soest, Baarn, Eemdijk, or Spakenburg, and return by bike. There is no service from November to April. Contact the VVV office (☎ 033/463–2804) for details.

OVERIJSSEL PROVINCE

The garden party of The Netherlands, the province of Overijssel or "the land beyond the IJssel" River is a backyard scene set with a centerpiece of parks, nature reserves, forests, wetlands, and more rolling terrain than its northern and western neighbors. Imposing castles and historic towns hark back to medieval days in this realm, where the ancient tradition of storytelling lives on. From peat to punters, it's home turf to a diverse slice of Dutch culture and hospitality, with everything from Hanseatic towns to a Dutch version of Venice and a microculture that appears frozen in a time warp.

Zwolle

⑬ *41 km (26 mi) north of Apeldoorn, 87 km (54 mi) east of Amsterdam, 68 km (43 mi) northeast of Amersfoort.*

Seen from the air, Zwolle, founded in 800 and the provincial capital of the province of Overijssel, is really a star-shape island surrounded by a ring of canals flanked by the IJssel and Vecht rivers, a shiningly strategic location for an important depot of trade between The Netherlands and Germany during the time of the Hanseatic League. Religious philosopher Thomas à Kempis lived here in the early 1400s when he wrote his influential work *Imitation of Christ,* and Dutch painter Gerard Terborch (1617–81) was born here. Today it is a university town flickering with nightlife, and home not only to an impressive museum housed in a city mansion but to what many regard as the best restaurant in The Netherlands, *De Librije*. Sweet on sweets, Zwolle is also known for its candies and for shortbread fingers with chocolate tips (*blauwvingers*, translated "blue fingers.") The VVV office's "Town Walk" brochure in English, for those with time to explore, provides a great route for seeing Zwolle. Ask them about the wooden shoe (*klompen*) canoes for hire as well—great photo-ops for your album.

Confined within the towers of the castlelike **Sassenpoort** (Saxon gate), for centuries a prison and the only one of the original town gates of 1406 left standing, is an exhibit of Zwolle's deep-rooted history. The cannon in front dates from around 1580, and a chiming clock completes the fantasy. ⊠ *Sassenstraat* ☎ *038/421–6626* 🖼 *€.45* ◷ *Wed.–Fri. 2–5, weekends noon–5.*

The **Grote Kerkplein** is the main square of Zwolle and the site of the Gothic Stadhuis (Town Hall). There is also a charming shop, **Zwollse Balletjes Huis** (⊠ Grote Kerkplein 13 ☎ 038/421–8815) that sells the local sweet specialty, *Zwollse balletjes* (fruit-and-spice-flavor hard candies in the shape of little cushions). The Gothic **Sint Michaelskerk** (St. Michael's Church), which dates from 1370–1446 and contains a magnificent 18th-century organ with 4,000 pipes, made by the Schnitger brothers from Hamburg, is the final resting place of the 17th-century genre painter Gerard Terborch, Zwolle's native son. ⊠ *Grote Kerkplein.*

Pause before you go inside the **Stedelijk Museum Zwolle** (Zwolle Municipal Museum) to note the imposing 16th-century city mansion next to the contemporary museum entrance, for this is, in fact, the main reason for being here. It *is,* indeed, the crux of the museum, a remarkable period house with a wainscoted living/dining room featuring works of art by Hendrick Avercamp and Zwolle natives Gerard Terborch and Hendrick Ten Oever, and every nostalgic woman's dream kitchen complete with floor-to-ceiling tiles, scullery, linen press—and the imaginary chief cook and bottle washer, all exemplifying the lifestyle of the prosperous family once resident here. Changing exhibits on three floors of the modern side of the museum are accessible by way of a central glass staircase and fire escape–like stairs on the last, rather hidden, stretch. (Hints: Be sure to go all the way up to Rooms 8–11 of the mansion, and later, to step outside via the coffee shop to see the Vermeerian back of the mansion.) ⊠ *Melkmarkt 41, 8001 BC* ☎ *038/421–4650* ⊕ *www. musuemzwolle.nl* 🖼 *€3.50* ◷ *Tues.–Sat. 10–5, Sun. 1–5.*

off the beaten path

ANTON PIECK MUSEUM – About 6 km (4 mi) southwest of Zwolle, like a chocolate box begging to be opened, the Pieck Museum (⊠ Achterstraat 46–48, Hattem ☎ 038/444–2192 ⊕ www. antonpieckmuseum-hattem.nl 🖼 €3 ◷ May–Nov., Mon.–Sat. 10–5; July and Aug. also open Sun. 1–5; Dec.–Apr., Tues.–Sat. 10–5) is your chance for an intimate glimpse of the work of one of the more famed early-20th-century illustrators of Grimm's fairy tales. A delectable courtyard entrance lets you enter a miniworld of 17th-century houses, adorned with requisite windmill, gift shop, and rooms filled with vintage editions and the artist's creations. From Zwolle, take a train taxi or bus (No. 90) to Hattem-Centrum.

Where to Eat & Stay

$$$–$$$$
Fodor'sChoice
★

✕ **De Librije.** Housed in the stunning, beamed former library of a 15th-century monastery, owner-chef Jonnie Boer's restaurant is lined with accolades, searing his reputation as one of the country's best chefs, if not Holland's crème de la crème. With creativity extraordinaire, he has mastered what he calls "Cuisine Pure," based on fresh, locally produced

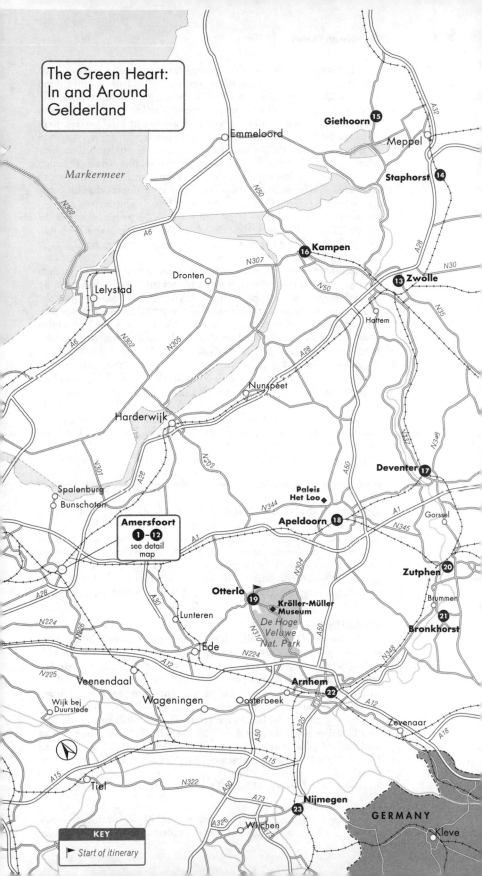

The Green Heart:
In and Around
Gelderland

Markermeer

Emmeloord

Giethoorn **15**

Meppel

Staphorst **14**

Kampen **16**

Dronten

Zwolle **13**

Lelystad

Hattem

Nunspeet

Harderwijk

Spalenburg
Bunschoten

Deventer **17**

Paleis
Het Loo

Amersfoort
1 – **12**
see detail
map

Apeldoorn **18**

Gorssel

Zutphen **20**

Otterlo **19**

Kröller-Müller
Museum

*De Hoge
Veluwe
Nat. Park*

Brummen

Lunteren

Bronkhorst **21**

Ede

Veenendaal

Wageningen

Oosterbeek

Arnhem **22**

Zevenaar

Wijk bej
Duurstede

Tiel

Wichen

Nijmegen
23

GERMANY

Kleve

ingredients such as nettles, water mint, wild mushrooms, and even cat-tails (the plant version), and all manner of local fishes from in and around his native Giethoorn, all about which he's written a delightful cookbook, *Purer.* One signature dish is the sublime *polderduif,* wild pigeon from the surrounding water lands, served with a sauce of local berries. Reg-ular De Librije followers insist on the pike perch with apple syrup and Riesling wine sauce, the scallops with vanilla, Giethoorn lamb, duck liver lollies (yes, duck liver on a stick), and turbot with Jabugo ham, although we'd defy you to find anything blasé on Jonnie's menu, right down to the homemade lavender mayonnaise. Cross your fingers that his crepe soufflé with preserved Gieten blueberries in brandy and sautéed apple— his mother's own recipe—is on the menu. ⊠ *Broerenkerkplein 13* ☎ *038/421–2083* ⊕ *www.delibrije.nl* ⚓ *Reservations essential* ☐ *AE, DC, MC, V* ⊙ *Closed Sun. and Mon., 3 wks in summer, and 2 wks at Christmas. No lunch Tues. or Sat.*

$$ ✕ **Restaurant Poppe.** Any restaurant daring enough to have the kitchen greet you as you enter through former blacksmith stalls and wind up being classy to boot is a spot with confident panache. Sidestepping the atmosphere, the food is a full dressage of everything from duck liver pâté with grapes and figs to ostrich. You'll feel like you're riding high at this showstopper. ⊠ *Luttekestraat 66* ☎ *038/421–3050* ⊕ *www.restaurant-poppe.nl* ☐ *AE, DC, MC, V* ⊙ *Closed Mon. No lunch weekends.*

★ ¢–$ ✕ **La Bodega Tapas Bar.** More than a place to drink, this authentically Spanish bar with a chef who hails from San Sebastian is a great place to dabble in those savory treats called tapas. Specialties include *cala-mares* (squid), *gambas a la plancha* (grilled shrimp), tortilla *española* (potato and egg omelet), *salpicón de mariscos* (seafood salad), paella (the Spanish national dish of rice, chicken, and seafood), Manchego cheese, and chocolate *con churros* (hot chocolate with long sugar doughnuts). Can't decide? Go for the combo plate with eight different hot and cold tapas. The Spanish mainland is further represented by fine sherries, wines, and music. ⊠ *Bethlehemskerkplein 36* ☎ *038/422–9139* ☐ *AE, MC, V.*

$–$$$ ⊞ **Bilderberg Grand Hotel Wientjes.** The grande dame of Zwolle where every whim is catered to, this stately former mayor's residence is con-venient to both the train station and the city center and exudes modern comfort. Among special features are bike rentals with a picnic hamper provided by the chef. ⊠ *Stationsweg 7, 8011 CZ* ☎ *038/425–4254* 🖷 *038/425–4260* ⊕ *www.bilderberg.nl* ⟿ *56 rooms, 1 suite* ⚲ *2 restaurants, minibars, cable TV, bar, some pets allowed; no a/c* ☐ *AE, DC, MC, V* ¶⊙l *EP.*

Nightlife

As a university town, Zwolle offers a variety of heady nightlife. A fa-vorite for party animals is **De Bommel Café** (⊠ Jufferenwal 19b ☎ 038/421–1759), where dancing has even been spotted on top of the bar. **Eet-café De Casteleyn** (⊠ Kamperstraat 33 ☎ 038/421–8099) powers along with hard-driving music and servers who entertain the crowds. **Grand Café De Harmonie** (⊠ Grote Markt 13a ☎ 038/422–0019) is billed as the largest grand café in The Netherlands, with easy-listening music. **Tap-perij De Joffer** (⊠ Jufferenwal 5–7 ☎ 038/422–5223) is a bulwark of students and housed in a 1738 monument. **Café Roots** (⊠ Grote Markt 13b ☎ 038/421–6318) is a basement dance venue with American over-tones and a surprise every Friday night. For beer tasting at its best, **'t Proeflokaal van Zwolle** (⊠ Blijmarkt 3 ☎ 038/421–7808) is a top place.

The Outdoors

CANOEING In summertime it's not only possible, but highly pleasurable, to canoe on the waterways in and around Zwolle. **Vadesto Kanocentrum** (⊠ Veenrand 5, 8051 DW Hattem 🖼 038/444–5428) at the Potgietersingel rents canoes. The VVV sells canoeing maps.

Shopping

A great shopping route that ends in decadence is to start at the Grote Markt and head down Diezerstraat. Note the crooked gabled building at the corner of this intersection, now a nut shop, and a bit farther down, the scary druggist above the entrance of No. 14, now a women's clothing store retaining some of the old pharmacy interior. At the end of this long street, near the bridge and the old city wall, is your shop-till-you-drop reward: 42 different flavors of artificial-color-free ice cream, three of them without sugar, at the **IJssalon Salute** (✉ Diezerstraat 121 🖼 038/423–7566). There's usually a run on *croccantino* ice cream made with almonds in caramelized sugar. Market days in Zwolle are Friday morning and Saturday. Late shopping is on Thursday until 9.

Staphorst

⑭ *57 km (37 mi) north of Apeldoorn, 25 km (16 mi) north of Zwolle.*

Fodor'sChoice
★

Staphorst and the twin neighboring towns, Rouveen and IJhorst, win the time-warp prize, yet their sternly religious, fiercely independent Calvinist-cum-Dutch-reformed-Protestants want no accolades. In fact, they want no attention at all, and will shamelessly shun the shutterbugs who insist on photographing them in their traditional black costumes with colorful floral overlays, and matching skullcaps. Be content to snap their thatched farmhouses trimmed with blue (to ward off evil), green (youth), and white (purity) accents. Of the 15,000 people in the three villages, approximately 1,800 women and children still wear the local garb; only about 40 men, the youngest of whom is 75 at this writing, still dress all in black, particularly on Sunday when families go not once, but twice, to church. You can attend the services, but be forewarned— they last about two hours each, seemingly made all the longer by psalms sung in a *very* slow, exaggerated drone. Women must wear a dress or skirt, stockings, and a head covering of some kind to be admitted.

Amish they are not. Staphorstians do believe in conveniences such as electricity, and they do drive cars. They have, however, espoused some rather strong beliefs until the not-so-distant past, such as prohibiting childhood immunizations (dismissed only since the 1970s when the government required certain inoculations) and, perhaps the most paradoxical of all, the "open bedroom window" policy, by which unmarried daughters' bedrooms were purposely outfitted with easy window access so male suitors could slip into the room and under the sheets, as it were, of the shuttered cupboard beds called *bedsteden*. The rest is history. It wasn't until a local official banned this so-called *"queesten"* (quest) practice in 1920 and forbade "making love in the window" that bars were installed on the culprit windows, an example of which can be seen, ★ along with the inviting bedsteden, at the **Gemeentelijke Museumboerderij** (Museum Farm), the real McCoy. Coffee and sweets are available. ✉ *Gemeenteweg 67, 7951 CE* 🖼 *0522/462526* 🖼 *€2* 🕐 *Apr.–Oct., Mon.–Sat. 10–5.*

Where to Eat & Stay

$$–$$$ ✕ **Het Boerengerecht.** The decor here is nearly more delicious than the food, thanks to a Staphorst period room, where you can actually dine amid the venerable beams, Delft tiles, and elaborately painted wood. If the crab soup (*kreeftensoep*) with aniseed is on the menu, postpone your next destination; it's that good—and the homemade bread rivals it. ✉ *Mid-*

denwolderweg 2, 7951 EC ☎ *0522/461967* 🖷 *0522/461166* ▭ *MC*
⊘ *Closed Sun. and Mon.*

★ **$$–$$$** ✕▣ **Chateau de Havixhorst.** Both storks and gentry have landed at this
18th-century haven of manorial tranquility, ideal for some regal R&R
with just the right infusion of fuss. Be one with nature (you can rent a
bike for €11.50 per day) while perched, like the nesting and highly discriminating storks on the roof, in a moated castle (now a National Monument) with king-size designer rooms and up-to-date bathrooms. Once
upon a time, Havixhorst was the most important residence in the
province of Drenthe, just over the border from Staphorst, and lorded
over by the wealthy and powerful Vos van Steenwijk family. Only since
1980 has the Wijland family turned it into a romantic hotel and highly
respected restaurant (open for lunch Tuesday–Friday only by reservation; dinner Tuesday–Saturday). Children can roam the woods, catch
creepy-crawlies in the moat, and visit the local stork sanctuary, De
Lokkerij, just a five-minute walk through the forest. Breakfast is served
to order, and the homemade jams complete the exquisite experience. Go
on, enter this realm . . . you only live once. ⊠ *Schiphorsterweg 34–36,
7966 AC De Schiphorst* ☎ *0522/441487* 🖷 *0522/441489* ⊕ *www.
dehavixhorst.nl* ↩ *8 rooms* ♿ *Restaurant, lounge; no a/c* ▭ *AE, DC,
MC, V* ⊠ *EP.*

Giethoorn

🕒 *18 km (11 mi) north of Zwolle, 111 km (72 mi) east of Amsterdam, 25*
Fodor's Choice *km (16 mi) northwest of Staphorst.*
★

Vying for first-place prize in photogenicity (some cynics might say photo
infamy), Giethoorn is a verdant, miniature version of Venice—an irresistible punter's paradise where not only residents and tourists but
cows, horses, milk cans, and bridal parties are transported on canals in
this roadless matrix of waterways crisscrossed by wooden footbridges
lighted at night. Flanked by a profusion of thatched-roof cottages, the
village makes you wonder whether you're in Hansel and Gretel's garden or Alice in Wonderland's fantasy.

The reality is that Giethoorn was settled around 1230 by a group of flag-
ellants escaping religious persecution, making their living by digging peat
(turf that was dried and used for fuel). The village owes its name to the
countless number of wild goat horns they found here, presumably from
the beasts buried by the floods that frequently plagued the area.

In winter, this unparalleled beauty turns into a skating scene straight
out of a 17th-century Avercamp snowscape. Indeed, the "Holland-
Venice" ice-skating tour (as it is aptly dubbed because of its Venetian-
like backdrop), which begins here in ferociously frigid winters, is a
sight to behold. In spring and summer, the narrow transport canals, excavated by manual labor as late as 1924, swell with punts—long flat-
bottomed boats propelled with poles—and whisper-quiet motorboats
(charging about €5 for an hour's cruise). Do-it-yourselfers can rent wa-
tercraft of varying types. On the last Saturday evening of each August,
illuminated gondolas bedecked with flowers parade in a **Gondelvaart**.
There's also a jazz and blues festival every mid-to-late August. (Because
it's hidden from the main road and inaccessible to cars, the best way to
reach the charming core of Giethoorn is to turn off Beulakerweg at the
sign for "Centrum-Dorp" [Center-Village], follow the "P" sign to the
parking area, and walk a short distance to the Binnenpad thoroughfare.)

★ 🕒 For a look back in time, the farmhouse museum **'t Olde Maat Uus** (The
Old Maat Family House) provides a richly detailed portrait of life and

work in 1800s Giethoorn. Among the household treasures are examples of bedsteden (Dutch cupboard beds), a 100-year-old incubator for babies, a posture board for children deemed "less than straight," an early outhouse named Uussie, and a thatching exhibit. At one point a family of 13 lived within these four walls, so have your kids try to figure out where they all slept. ⊠ *Binnenpad 52, 8355 BT* ☎ *0521/362244* ⊠ €3 ☉ *Easter–Oct., Mon.–Sat. 11–5, Sun. noon–5; Nov.–Easter, Sun. noon–5.*

Where to Eat & Stay

$$$ ✕ **De Lindenhof.** Something to write home about is owner-chef/rising star Martin Kruithof's famous fare served in a farmhouse setting just outside the main village—including the Dutch eel he smokes on an open fire in the lovely garden. (Come on, try it . . . you need *something* to write about on that postcard.) ⊠ *Beulakerweg 77* ☎ *0521/361444* 🍴 *Reservations essential* ▤ *AE, DC, MC, V* ☉ *Closed Thurs., 2 wks in Mar., 2 wks in Oct.; lunch by special arrangement only.*

$$ ✕ **'t Achterhuus.** For the best lunch or dinner in the main village of Giethoorn, plant yourself at this thatched-roof, converted farmhouse restaurant with an outdoor terrace facing the canal. After dining, a guide will take you on a canal cruise on one of their boats (€3.40 per hour). ⊠ *Ds. T.O. Hylkemaweg 43* ☎ *0521/361674* ⊕ *www.achterhuus.nl* ▤ *AE, MC, V* ☉ *Closed Tues. and Wed. Oct.–Feb.*

¢ 🏠 **Fam. Heida B&B.** In quiet repose, this B&B is canal-side and just off the footpath. Choose between the main house or the separate quarters, which just happens to be the smallest house in Giethoorn. Surrounding gardens add a bountiful splash of color. Note that bathrooms are shared in the main house accommodations. ⊠ *Zuiderpad 18, 8355 CA* ☎ *0521/361117* 🛏 *4 rooms in main house without bath, separate house sleeps 3* ♻ *No a/c, no room phones, no room TVs* ▤ *No credit cards* ❑ *BP.*

¢ 🏠 **Mol/Groenewegen.** Smack-dab in the heart of charm central, this simple but spartan B&B wins hands down for location. Although inaccessible by car, parking is not far away. Bicycles, canoes, kayaks, and punts are available for rent. ⊠ *Binnenpad 28, 8355 BR* ☎ *0521/361359* 🛏 *0521/362567* ⊕ *www.molgroenewegen.nl* 🛏 *5 rooms* ♻ *Cable TV; no a/c, no room phones* ▤ *AE, MC, V* ☉ *Closed Nov.–Mar.* ❑ *BP.*

Shopping

You can lose track of time in **Het Winkeltje** (⊠ Ds. T.O. Hylkemaweg 32, on the right as you come from the parking area, before you reach 't Achterhuus restaurant and 't Olde Maat Uus museum ☎ 0521/362269); "The Little Shop" is a rabbit warren crammed with antiques and small collectibles, including a wide range of kitchenware and linens.

Kampen

⑯ *14 km (9 mi) northwest of Zwolle, 103 km (64 mi) northeast of*
Fodor'sChoice *Amsterdam.*
★

Kampen is a schizophrenic puff of smoke along the IJssel River where cigar manufacturing took over in the 1820s after a phlegmatic hiatus following its Hanseatic heyday as a herring hub. Once the viceroy in the pack, Kampen's wealth dried up when the harbor silted up near the end of the Middle Ages. As if preserved in amber, however, the town boasts nearly 500 historic monuments outlined by the remaining 3 of its 21 phantom city gates. Sunday, when Kampen turns into a veritable ghost town, is the ideal time for a city walk to view the rich display of *gevelstenen* (façade stones). You can pick up a map (€1.59) of the route at the Stedelijk Museum Kampen in advance (as it is not open Sunday). A visit to Kampen, where one of the longest cigars in the world exists, makes for a good day trip that can be combined with a family outing to **Six Flags Holland** amusement park (☎ 032/132–9999 ⊕ www.sixflagsholland.nl) in nearby Dronten, billed as the "Roller Coaster Capital of Europe," where you can stay in one of 141 bungalows.

The best view of the ancient skyline is from the **Stadsbrug** (Town Bridge) across the river. From there you can take a medieval circuit past the defensive city gates: stroll down the waterfront to the **Koornmarktspoort** (Grain Market Gate) on IJsselkade, recognizable by its two 14th-century towers. Peek into the **Sint Nikolaskerk** (Church of St. Nicholas) on the Koornmarkt, then cross over to the old moat and Ebbingstraat where **Cellebroederspoort** (Cloister Brothers Gate) still stands; farther north on Ebbingstraat is the **Broederpoort** (Brother Gate).

Rapunzel has reputedly been sighted overlooking the onion-shape tower on the 14th-century **Oude Raadhuis,** where statues on its gabled facade depict Charlemagne, Alexander the Great, and less martial figures representing Moderation, Fidelity, Justice, and Love. Inside, the *Schepenzaal,* the oak-lined and timber-vaulted Magistrates' Hall with its elaborately carved chimneypiece, is a stunning example of a medieval courtroom. Unfortunately, this jewel is now closed for renovation through 2005. ⊠ *Oudestraat 133, 8261 CL* ☎ *038/331–7361.*

The **Stedelijk Museum Kampen** (Kampen Municipal Museum) occupies a perfectly preserved Gothic merchant's house where, in addition to minting your own Kampen coins from an original mold, you can see exhibits on local history and industry, such as eel fishing and cigar making. ⊠ *Oudestraat 158, 8260 GA* ☎ *038/331–7361* 🎫 *€2.20* ☉ *Mid-Sept.–mid-June, Tues.–Sat. 11–12:30 and 1:30–5; mid-June–mid-Sept., Tues.–Sat. 11–5, Sun. 1–5.*

See the 15-foot-long cigar, reputedly one of the longest in the world (the Cubans claim to have the longest) at the **Kampen Tabakmuseum.** ⊠ *Botermarkt 3, 8261 GR* ☎ *038/332–5353* 🎫 *€1.20* ☉ *Apr.–Nov., Thurs.–Sat. 11–5; Dec.–Mar., by appointment.*

Where to Eat & Stay

★ **\$\$** ✕ **Restaurant d'Olde Vismark.** Talk about romance! Chef Ron Wesseler began his international career in a bakery, made five trips around the world as a ship manager with the Holland America line, and disembarked in Kampen after sailing down the Rhine. Come enjoy his fish specialties or vegetarian delights with views of the IJssel River (you were expecting the Mediterranean?) and fantasize about his past, unless yours was more exciting. Desserts served in a cloud of mist and surprise menus are part of the draw, so reservations are highly recommended. ⊠ *IJsselkade 45* ☎ *038/331–3490* ⊟ *AE, DC, MC, V.*

¢ 🏠 **De Stadsboerderij.** Built in the 17th–20th centuries, this former "City Farm" was the real McCoy until the 1980s. Renovations have modernized the structure, but many original features have been retained. If being boxed in, literally, appeals to you, ask for the large bedroom with two original box or cupboard beds built into the wall, Dutch-style. After all, there's something to be said for cozy. Likewise, former stalls have been transformed into a living room. If you can't sleep, count the black and white tiles, not sheep, that date from the early 1600s. It's a five-minute walk or taxi ride from the central train station. ⊠ *Groenestraat 148–150, 8261 VL* ☎ *038/333–0678* ⊕ *www.stadsboerderij.nl* 🛏 *2 rooms* ⚒ *Cable TV, some pets allowed; no a/c, no room phones* ⊟ *No credit cards* ⦿⊨ *EP.*

Deventer

⑰ *39 km (24 mi) south of Zwolle, 16 km (10 mi) east of Apeldoorn, 107*
Fodor'sChoice *km (67 mi) east of Amsterdam.*
★

Meticulously medieval Deventer, one of the oldest towns in The Netherlands, is paved with holy grails and cornerstones of thought. It was founded late in the 8th century by an English cleric named Lebuinus, whose mission in life was to convert the Saxons to Christianity, and by the 9th century it was a prosperous port and a powerful bishopric. But it was also a center of learning and printing, which was the medium used to disseminate the thoughts of scholars such as Thomas à Kempis, Erasmus, and, in the 17th century, French philosopher René Descartes, as well as Pope Adrian VI, all of whom made their home here at various times. Be sure to pick up two brochures at the local VVV: "Deventer, A Hospitable Hanseatic City" and "Town Walk," both in English, which will guide you past the oldest brick house in the country on Sandrasteeg, dating from 1100. True to its roots, there is an annual medieval fair held here on Ascension Day in May, harking back to Deventer's role as one of the largest marketplaces in the Middle Ages.

Undergoing restoration until late 2004, Deventer's late Gothic **Waag** (Weigh House), begun in 1528, is a stately testament to the city's Hanseatic past. Inside, an exhibition on town history, from prehistoric times to the present day, includes The Netherlands' oldest bicycle, the spindly *Vélociède*, built in 1870. ⊠ *Brink 56, 7411 BV* ☎ *0570/693780* 🖼 *€2.30* ☉ *Opening in late 2004 after restoration.*

Ⓒ Two huge medieval houses barely contain the **Speelgoed-en Blikmuseum** (Toys and Tin Museum), an enchanting collection of toys dating from the Middle Ages to the 20th century. There are dolls, puppets, and tin soldiers galore, and an exceptional collection of mechanical toys and electric trains. In the museum's darkroom you can see a 17th-century magic lantern and a host of other optical playthings. ⊠ *Brink 47, 7411 BV* ☎ *0570/693786* 🖼 *€3.30* ☉ *Tues.–Sat. 10–5, Sun. 1–5.*

Cobbled streets and crooked gables lead to the 13th-century Romanesque Gothic **Bergkerk** (Church on the Mountain), with pleasing views down medieval side streets (Bergstraat and Roggestraat are particularly evocative.) ⊠ *Bergkerkplein* ☉ *Open for expositions.*

The **Lebuinuskerk** (St. Lebuinus's Church), a huge stone cross-basilica, built in the 10th century on the site of Lebuinus's small wooden church, has some fine 16th-century murals and a 700-year-old floor. Hanging in the 15th-century tower is the oldest extant carillon made by the Hemony brothers, who in the 17th century were the most celebrated bell makers in the world. The tower can be climbed in summer months for a wide view of the town; the carillon is played at least twice a week. ⊠ *Grote Kerkhof* 🖼 *Free* ☉ *Mar.–Oct., Mon.–Sat. 11–5; Nov.–Feb., Mon.–Sat. 11–4.*

Where to Stay

★ $ 🏨 **Huis Nieuw Rande.** On the outskirts of town this country-manor hotel sits on 380 acres of woodland surrounded by Shetland ponies, undulating streams, and a garden landscaped by Jan Zocher, famed for the Vondelpark in Amsterdam. Largely devoid of televisions and the like, it's a writer's paradise, but even those without a poem in their soul will fall for the seclusion and tranquility offered here. Request the Rosendael room in the main house—a princely room with a priceless view of the surrounding countryside, replete with ponies and peace—or for a family or group affair of 8–10 people, rent the Klein (Little) Rande, a private cottage by the woods complete with all the amenities, including two baths, kitchen, and living/dining room, as well as a TV and CD player for the uninspired. ⊠ *Schapenzandweg 3, 7431 PZ Diepenveen* ☏ *0570/ 593666* 🕮 *0570/593667* ⊕ *www.huisnieuwrande.nl* ☞ *7 rooms in main house, 1 cottage* ₺ *No a/c, no room phones* ▤ *MC, V* ⑩ *BP.*

Shopping

Friday and Saturday are market days in Deventer, when the Brink, or main square, is crowded with fresh-produce stalls and a few antiques dealers. On the first Sunday in August the largest **book market** in The Netherlands stretches for 3 km (2 mi) along the IJssel River.

GELDERLAND PROVINCE & DE HOGE VELUWE

The riches of Gelderland, the largest province of The Netherlands, are hugely evident. Even its name—*geld,* meaning "money"—refers to the region's wealthy aristocracy. Royalty recognized its appeal when they chose this wooded province for their palatial residence, Paleis Het Loo, discriminatingly placing it in the very midst of the forest, the perfect ground for their hunting pursuits. And as with the province of Overijssel, the Hanseatic League seconded it, so central were the two provinces for trade routes and burgeoning markets. But even earlier than that, at the beginning of the first millennium, Romans had established a holding here, making their city of Nijmegen, where they settled, the oldest city in The Netherlands (although Maastricht in the very southeast corner of the country makes the same claim). The lavish guildhalls, churches, castles, and private estates in this area are a result of the area's ensuing prosperity and popularity as a naturally beautiful, strategic location between the port of Rotterdam in the west and Germany in the east.

Central to Gelderland's appeal is the Veluwe, which, despite the unfortunate translation of its name as "badland" (referring to its infertility as farmland), is the largest expanse of natural beauty in northwestern Europe. A true hinterland of heaths, moors, dunes, and untouched forests above sea level and therefore protected from saltwater floods, it offers a wealth of recreational opportunities concentrated around hiking and biking just north of the Rhine River. Inhabited by wild game, a large portion of the Veluwe is a protected national park, De Hoge Veluwe, which fills much of the triangle formed by the three main cities of the Green Heart: Arnhem, known for its World War II battle; Apeldoorn, where Het Loo Palace is located; and Amersfoort, the medieval lady of the pack.

Apeldoorn

⑱ *16 km (10 mi) southwest of Deventer, 44 km (28 mi) east of Amersfoort, 89 km (56 mi) east of Amsterdam.*

Though not much of an attraction in itself except for the old town center situated around the Raadhuisplein, the small city of Apeldoorn is the gateway to the Royal Forest and the Hoge Veluwe National Park, the latter an absolute must on your itinerary. But before you give it up for naught, there's a palatial reason to come to this neck of the woods: the recently occupied royal palace of **Het Loo,** the Dutch version of Versailles. Conveniently, there are other attractions in the immediate area, particularly for families, that make it an all-round, regal choice. Although we concentrate here on the city and the palace, the sights included in the Hoge Veluwe section that follows are but a stone's throw away and can easily be visited from your base in Apeldoorn, the best access being from the Keizerskroon hotel situated so close to the palace that you can almost feel the blue blood pulse.

Begun in 1685 on the site of a 14th- and 15th-century castle and hunting lodge in the midst of the Royal Forest (nearly 25,000 acres), and serving as a country residence for Dutch William III and his wife Mary Stuart (daughter of James II of England), famously known as "William and Mary," **Paleis Het Loo** (Het Loo Palace, i.e., The Woods Palace) expanded into a full-blown royal palace when the couple became king and queen of England. As was the case in many royal (and many not-so-royal) households, Mary's quarters were in the east wing and William's in the west; some say they had the best of both worlds. Constructed of brick and outfitted with what are said to be the world's first sash windows, the spectacularly beautiful palace—one of the most glorious examples of Dutch Neoclassicism—and its Dutch Baroque gardens exemplify symmetry, order, and unity.

A vaulted avenue of tall beeches leads to the central courtyard, where you enter through a grilled, blue-and-gold gate. Special exhibits fill some of the rooms, and there is a video that documents the building's history and restoration prior to its opening to the public in 1984. Many rooms are furnished as they were for William and Mary, but are also maintained in the manner in which they were used by later Dutch monarchs, including Queen Wilhelmina, grandmother of the current Queen Beatrix. Wilhelmina became queen at the age of 10 and was the last regent to make this her summer home, residing in The Hague and Amsterdam throughout much of the year. She died here in 1962. A peek at her playroom may make you envious, but consider that, besides her English nanny, her tutors were all elderly men and that she had no brothers or sisters with whom to play, only a donkey, a pony, and the doll collection on display. Indeed, her office used in later life has a decidedly manly feel, and she was known to be a very intense, serious woman of large stature.

Certain rooms deserve particular attention, such as Queen Mary's petite and homey kitchen where she made jam; the shell grotto next to it, an exotic retreat once filled with birds; her bedroom with its lavish canopied four-poster bed brought from Kensington Palace in London where she formerly lived, as well as her lovely red-and-green antechamber with its English lacquer cabinet (1690) and Delft and Chinese porcelain; Queen Sophia's closet room, garishly decorated in Moorish style; the hunting trophy room of Prince Henry, husband of Queen Wilhelmina; and the Chancellory of Orders of Knighthood, where you can see one of the world's most important collections of orders and decorations. Chandeliers cleverly hung with ribbons and an abundance of fresh flowers so characteristic of The Netherlands, the world's biggest bloomer, complete the regal but inviting scene.

Four gardens, meticulously planted in the same fashion as they were in the 17th century after being designed by Daniel Marot, an ancestor of the late actress Audrey Hepburn, are decorated with statues and fountains fed by the waters of the Rhine, including two in the form of globes. The terrestrial one shows the world as it was perceived in the 17th century, and the celestial one corresponds to the sky above the palace at the time of Princess Mary Stuart's birth. Rivaling Versailles, the king's fountain was meant to shoot water higher than that of Louis XIV's. Separate king's and queen's gardens provide respective views from their individual domains; the king's is dominated by plantings in blue and orange, the colors of the Dutch royal family, and the queen's by pastel flowers and fruit trees.

If you are here around Christmastime, the entire palace is decorated in a festive manner and the tables set as if to say, Come join us. If you have other plans, you can always feast at one of the two palace restaurants offering short-order fare: the self-service **Theehuis** (Teahouse) near the exit and part of the old stables, a favorite of many with its wicker chairs and an outdoor café complete with strutting, well-bred peacocks, or the **Balzaal** (Ballroom) in the West Wing with the same simple fare in a more lavish setting. You could also grab a snack, albeit minimal, at the snack bar by the back garden terrace and overlook (which you should be sure to ascend for a picture-perfect view of the palace and gardens). Catering to every whim (that *is,* after all, what palace life is all about), there is also an ice-cream stand as you exit. Guided tours in English are available by appointment, and concerts are held the last Friday of every month at 8:15 PM (contact the palace or VVV for tickets). A map of walking routes in the palace park is available at the entrance. If you don't have a car, take Bus No. 102 or 104 from the bus/train station to get to Het Loo. ⊠ *Koninklijk Park, 7315 JA* ☎ *055/577–2448* ⊕ *www.hetloo.nl* ⊠ *€9, parking €3* ☉ *Tues.–Sun. 10–5.*

What kid hasn't wondered what it's like to be a policeman or policewoman and wear a bulletproof vest? Now's their chance to do just that at **Het Nederlands Politie Museum,** where they can also be fingerprinted, climb into police cars and helicopters, and get a close-up look at 200 years of Dutch uniforms, weapons, and equipment. May the force be with you. ⊠ *Arnhemseweg 346* ☎ *055/543–0691* ⊕ *www.politiemuseum.nl* ⊠ *€3* ☉ *Tues.–Fri. 10–5, weekends 1–5.*

Mingle with your primate relatives at the **Apenheul** park, the only such zoo in the world where more than 350 monkeys, apes, chimpanzees, and gorillas wander freely in the woods and, some of them, all over you. Among bright flocks of tropical birds, your evolutionary cousins will saunter right up to you—in fact, they'll even get in your bags, highly adept pickpockets that the squirrel monkeys can be (bags can and should be checked to avoid problems). Situated in **Park Berg & Bos,** a beautiful nature park with walking routes and a large lake, it's the perfect spot for a family outing and picnic—that is, if your hairy friends don't eat it first. On summer nights, a romantic light-and-sound show, **Lumido,** takes place in the park. An awesome playground features a child-friendly wooden observation tower without a single nail in it, perfect for the little monkeys in *your* family. ⊠ *JC Wilslaan 21, 7313 HK* ☎ *055/357–5757* ⊕ *www.apenheul.nl* ⊠ *€13, parking €4* ☉ *Apr.–June, Sept.–Nov. 1, daily 9:30–5; July and Aug., daily 9:30–6.*

Located only five minutes by car from the Apenheul monkey park is the **Koningin Juliana Toren** (Queen Juliana's Tower) amusement park geared to kids up to about 12 years old. One admission charge gets them reeling on trains, motorboats, a bat flight, a water coaster, and a literal "roller" coaster with seats that resemble Rollerblades—indeed, every imaginable moving mechanism made. ⊠ *Amersfoortseweg 35, 7313 AC* ☎ *055/355–2015* ⊕ *www.julianatoren.nl* ⊠ *€13.50* ☉ *Apr.–Oct., daily 10–5.*

off the beaten path

STEAM TRAIN TO DIEREN – At various times of the year you can ride a nostalgic steam train (☎ 055/506–1989 ⊕ www.stoomtrein.org ⊠ €9.50 round-trip, €6.50 one-way) from Apeldoorn to the town of Dieren. Reservations are not necessary, and the train leaves from the central station. Food and drinks are available on board, and bikes are allowed.

Where to Eat & Stay

$$$–$$$$ ✕ **Echoput.** Not far from Het Loo Palace and the royal hunting grounds, Echoput is a much-honored and gracious country restaurant offering fine game dishes nearly year-round, often sublimely accented with fresh mushrooms and berries from surrounding woods. The large fireplace in the lounge is welcoming in winter, as is the terrace in summer. ⊠ *Amersfoortseweg 86, Hoog Soeren* ☎ *055/519–1248* ⊕ *www.echoput.nl* ⚑ *Reservations essential* ⊟ *AE, DC, MC, V* ⊗ *Closed Mon.*

★ **$–$$$** ✕ **Spicebrush.** If you've been traveling too long and your shoes are beginning to feel wooden, Spicebrush will sweep you off your feet and transport you back to the good ol' USA, complete with not one but two copies of the Statue of Liberty, Chicago Bulls horns, a neon Bud Beer sign, and good vibrations on tap. Specializing in steaks, barbecue ribs, seafood, and a bold Tex-Mex menu, Spicebrush's only failing is that it's not open for lunch. The Mexican fajitas were *numero uno* in our book, their quality equaled by the fresh green salad, great garlic bread, and Dutch coffee-flavor chocolates called *koffieboontjes* (coffee beans) served with java. ⊠ *Marktplein 9* ☎ *055/522–5064* ⊕ *www.spicebrush.nl* ⊟ *AE, MC, V.*

¢–$$ ✕ **Grand Café de Notaris.** A cozy place to sit in the old town center and watch the world go by, this outdoor café specializes in *saté*, pork on a skewer with a peanut sauce worth writing home about. ⊠ *Raadhuisplein 1* ☎ *055/578–5887* ⊟ *AE, DC, MC, V.*

★ **$$$** ☷ **De Keizerskroon Bilderberg.** Royal service . . . what else would you expect from a savvy hotel within walking distance of Het Loo Palace? It's so close, in fact, that you can almost hear the walls speak of its privileged past. A grand country inn once patronized by Czar Peter the Great, the Keizerskroon was a haunt of visiting royalty and those living vicariously. Princely attention to detail is their forte (wonder if the czar ever had heated towels . . .), with every manner of organized adventure, from bicycle tours and horseback riding through the adjacent forests, to sightseeing flights over castles (or your own flying lessons at a nearby airfield), and game tracking through the Royal Forest. Rooms are everything one would expect, and more. There is a bus stop close to the hotel, for a 10-minute trip to the center. ⊠ *Koningstraat 7, 7315 HR* ☎ *055/521–7744, 800/024–5245 from U.S.* ⊜ *055/521–4737* ⊕ *www.bilderberg.nl* ⧉ *89 rooms, 5 suites* ⚑ *Restaurant, minibars, cable TV, indoor pool, gym, sauna, Turkish bath, bicycles, bar, some pets allowed; no a/c in some rooms* ⊟ *AE, DC, MC, V* ◎ *EP.*

$ ☷ **Astra.** On a quiet residential side street within walking distance of the center, Astra is a bed-and-breakfast furnished in the manner of a comfortable Dutch home. Rooms are large for this type of accommodation, and there is a pleasant garden terrace behind the house. ⊠ *Bas Backerlaan 12–14, 7316 DZ* ☎ *055/522–3022* ⊜ *055/522–3021* ⊕ *www.hotelastra.nl* ⧉ *28 rooms* ⚑ *Cable TV; no a/c* ⊟ *AE, DC, MC, V* ◎ *BP.*

Nightlife & the Arts

Incomparable for atmosphere are the concerts on the last Friday of every month at the beautiful **Paleis Het Loo** (⊠ Koninklijk Park 1 ☎ 055/521–2244). Although there are no discos in town at this time, the main hive of nightlife buzzes around **Caterplein** square.

The Outdoors

Apeldoorn has several stunning parks—Oranjepark, Prinsenpark, Emmapark, and Wilhelminapark—and is known for its much-loved cycle paths along the Apeldoorn Canal and through the surrounding forest.

Shopping

Market days in Apeldoorn are Monday and Wednesday mornings and all day Saturday at Marktplein in the city center. An attractive mall, **De Oranjerie** (⊠ Oranjerie 265), with underground parking, is in the center. Late shopping night is Thursday.

en route

If you have a car, head out to the village of Hoog Soeren from Apeldoorn, a must-drive through a real enchanted forest. Only a higher power and the Dutch could have such manicured, pristine forests. The dappled light in early spring and summer, starkly contrasted with the Hoge Veluwe turf that you enter just beyond the forest, is like a slice of heaven on earth.

Otterlo/De Hoge Veluwe

▶ ⑲ *78 km (49 mi) southeast of Amsterdam, 20 km (13 mi) south of Apeldoorn, 35 km (22 mi) southeast of Amersfoort.*

When German heiress Hélène Müller married Dutch industrialist Anton Kröller at the turn of the 20th century, their combined wealth and complementary tastes were destined to give pleasure to generations to come. She loved art and could afford to collect it; he bought up land in Gelderland and eventually created a foundation to maintain it as a national park, building a museum to house the fruits of their expensive and discriminating taste. Today you can wander through the vast forests, heath, dunes, and moors of the Hoge Veluwe National Park, Kröller's land, and see the descendants of the wild boar and deer with which he stocked the estate. Or you can visit the world-famous museum in the middle of the park, established by Hélène and containing one of the best collections of Van Goghs in the world, as well as an excellent selection of late-19th-century and modern art. Additionally, you can visit the philanthropists' own house and hunting lodge. Children can caper about the largest sculpture garden in Europe, and the whole family can pick up one of the free bikes that are available in the park and trundle off down wooded lanes. (Note that Otterlo is only one entrance of several to the Hoge Veluwe, but it is widely considered the main gateway to the park.)

FodorśChoice ★ **De Hoge Veluwe,** once the private property of the Kröller-Müller family, is the largest national park in Holland, covering 13,300 acres of forest and rolling grassland, moors, and sand dunes, where it is possible to stroll without limit, apart from a few areas reserved for wildlife. The traditional hunting grounds of the Dutch royal family, it is populated with red deer, boar, roes, mouflons, and many birds; it is also filled with towering pines and hardwood trees (oak, beech, and birch), dotted with small villages (**Hoge Soeren,** near Apeldoorn, is particularly charming), and laced with paths for cars, bicycles, and walkers, more than 42 km (27 mi) of which are specifically designated for bicycling. Indeed, there are more than 1,000 white bicycles at your disposal here, free to use with the price of entrance (available at the entrances to the park, at the visitor center, De Koperen Kop restaurant, and at the Kröller-Müller museum; return them to any bike rack when you are finished).

There is a landlocked, always shifting sand dune to marvel at; the world's first museum of all things that live (or have lived) underground; plus an old hunting lodge beside a pond that provides a nice stopping place. At the heart of the park is the visitor center (**Bezoekers Centrum**), which contains exhibits on the park and an observation point for game-watching. **Jachthuis Sint Hubertus** (St. Hubert Hunting Lodge) was the private home and hunting lodge of the Kröller-Müllers, a monumental house planned in the shape of antlers, built between 1914 and 1920 by Dutch architect H. P. Berlage around the legend of St. Hubert, the patron saint of hunters. Rooms with art deco furniture follow in sequence from dark to light, representing Hubert's spiritual development and path of enlightenment from agnostic to saint. Free guided tours of the lodge, which is still used as a residence for visiting dignitaries, may be arranged at the park entrance only.

Museonder is the first underground museum in the world, offering visitors a fascinating look at life below the surface, including a simulated earthquake. A campsite at the Hoenderloo entrance is open from April to the end of October (☎ 055/378–2232), and there are four restaurants in the park: the stylish Rijzenburg, at the Schaarsbergen entrance (☎ 026/443–6733; closed Monday and February); and De Koperen Kop, a self-service restaurant in the center of the park opposite the visitor center (☎ 031/859–1289), another self-service one at the Kröller-Müller Museum, and a kiosk near the Jachthuis (open only in summer). The best opportunity for game-watching is at the end of the afternoon and toward evening, and park officials advise that you stay in your car when you spot any wildlife. Special observation sites are signified by antlers on the maps that are provided at the entrances. To enter the park from the A1, A50, or A12 motorways, follow the signs to "Park Hoge Veluwe." ⊠ *Entrances at Hoenderloo, Otterlo, and Schaarsbergen* ☎ *0318/591627, 0900/464–3835 at €.45 per min* ⊕ *www.hogeveluwe. nl* ⊠ *€5, cars €5; half-price entrance after 5 PM, May–Sept.; weekly tickets available* ☉ *Nov.–Mar., daily 9–5:30; Apr., daily 8–8; May, daily 8–9; June and July, daily 8–10; Aug., daily 8–9; Sept., daily 9–8; Oct., daily 9–7.*

Fodor'sChoice
★ The **Kröller-Müller Museum** ranks as the third-most important museum of art in The Netherlands, after the Rijksmuseum and the Vincent van Gogh Museum in Amsterdam. Opened in 1938, it is the repository of a remarkable private collection of late-19th-century and early-20th-century paintings, the nucleus of which are 285 works by Van Gogh (about 50 of which rotate on display at any given time) that, when combined with the collection in the Amsterdam museum, constitutes nearly four-fifths of his entire oeuvre. Hélène Kröller, née Müller, had a remarkable eye as well as a sixth sense about which painters created art for the ages. Her first purchase was most likely Van Gogh's *Faded Sunflowers.* Among his other well-known paintings in her collection are the *Potato Eaters, Bridge at Arles,* and *L'Arlesienne,* copied from a drawing by Gauguin.

But Hélène Kröller-Müller was not myopic in her appreciation and perception. She augmented her collection of Van Goghs with works by Georges Seurat, Pable Picasso, Odile Redon, Georges Braque, and Piet Mondriaan. The museum also contains 16th- and 17th-century Dutch paintings, ceramics, Chinese and Japanese porcelains, and contemporary sculpture. The building itself, designed by Henry van de Velde, artfully brings nature into the galleries through its broad windows, glass walkways, and patios. The gardens and woods around the museum form a stunning open-air gallery, the largest in Europe with a collection of 20th-century sculptures by Auguste Rodin to Richard Serra; works by Barbara Hepworth and Alberto Giacometti are in a special pavilion added in 1953. There is a gift shop and self-service restaurant on-site. For more information on the Kröller-Müllers, *see* the Close-Up box, "Passion and Paint: Hélène Kröller-Müller and Van Gogh." ⊠ *Houtkampweg 6, in National Park De Hoge Veluwe, 6730 AA Otterlo* ☎ *0318/591241*

CloseUp

PASSION & PAINT: HÉLÈNE KRÖLLER-MÜLLER & VAN GOGH

DESCRIBING HIM AS "ONE OF the great souls of our modern art, on whom the spirit of the times had no grasp . . .," heiress Hélène Kröller-Müller fed on Dutch artist Vincent van Gogh's (1853–90) elusive disparity. As such, he occupied a special place in her thinking and, hence, in her visionary art collection. While her industrialist husband was busy buying up wasteland as his own visionary enterprise (later to become the Hoge Veluwe National Park), Hélène, inspired by art appreciation classes, was fervently buying art, some of it with the brushstrokes still damp.

In 1912 alone, she added 35 Van Gogh paintings to her collection, the first of which was most likely his Faded Sunflowers (1887), the nucleus of a burgeoning collection that now includes 92 paintings, 183 drawings, one etching, and two lithographs by a misunderstood genius.

Reputed to have sold only a single painting in his lifetime, Van Gogh committed suicide at the age of 37, penniless and plagued by deep depression. An individualist, the servant of no school but the unwitting master of many a painter, Van Gogh left Holland to bring his private revolution in art to Paris and southern France.

Because, as it turns out, many of those lovely southern vistas have been completely changed, you have to go to Amsterdam, to Moscow, or to the museum here to view Van Gogh's great canvases. People continue to make the trek to Arles in southern France, forgetting that it was a completely inhospitable place to the artist—the town folk, in fact, formed a petition to ban him from their town, setting into motion his retreat into a mental institution and final despair and death.

His posthumous fame, of course, accelerated to such proportions that in 1990, his portrait of Dr. Gachet, his personal medical and psychological guru of sorts, sold at Christie's auction house in New York for the most money ever paid for one painting—a staggering $82 million. Not bad for a basically untrained artist and former lay preacher—a man who desperately longed to be loved yet repeatedly met with in-your-face rejection and unrequited love.

His greatest lost love was a mousy, plain, Dutch woman named Margot Begemann, next-door neighbor to his parents in Nuenen, where he returned for a brief stint in Holland. Despite their mutual affection and deep love, however, she was, at the "tender" age of 40-something (10 years older than Vincent), forced by her own parents to deny his existence, so unpromising (oh, ship of fools) they felt poor Vincent was. She attempted suicide; Vincent saved her, but after helping her back to her parents' doorstep, they were forever banned from mutual sight.

Little wonder, then, that Vincent, succumbing to madness, cut off a piece of his ear in a self-deprecating argument with fellow-artist and friend Paul Gauguin. (Incidentally, such an "homage" mirrored those given in the bullrings in southern France, when a matador would cut off a vanquished bull's ear and then offer it to his amorata sitting in the stands.) Ultimately, he shot himself in a cornfield outside of Paris, dragging his defeated body back to his one-room apartment where a viewless skylight served as his final window on life, a seemingly dire fate for someone whose eyes were the root of his soul.

For Vincent, fame came too late. The Kröller-Müllers, on the other hand, were perceptive enough to recognize his poignant talent, and accumulated the vast holding of his work that makes up the foundation of their now-public collection, the Kröller-Müller Museum at the core of Hoge Veluwe National Park.

⊕ *www.kmm.nl* ✆ *Park and museum €10* ⊗ *Park and museum Tues.–Sun. 10–5; sculpture garden closes at 4:30.*

See and buy is the game plan at the **Nederlands Tegelmuseum** (Netherlands Tile Museum), where all manner of Dutch tiles, from as far back as the 13th century, including those old Dutch standbys, Makkum and Delft, are displayed in a former summerhouse in the village of Otterlo, not far from the Hoge Veluwe. For those with a decorative eye, the tiles for purchase in the gift shop will be irresistible. ⊠ *Eikenzoom 12, 6731 BH Otterlo* ☎ *0318/591519* ✆ *€2.75* ⊗ *Tues.–Fri. 10–5, weekends 1–5.*

Where to Eat & Stay

$$–$$$ ✗ **Restaurant Rijzenburg.** In an old farmhouse dating from 1860 and brimming with antiques, this popular restaurant is known far and wide for its fine Dutch/French cuisine, and is conveniently located at the most southerly entrance to the Hoge Veluwe National Park. ⊠ *Koningsweg 17, Arnhem, at Rijzenburg entrance to Hoge Veluwe near Schaarsbergen* ☎ *026/443–6733* ⊕ *www.rijzenburg.nl* ☰ *AE, DC, MC, V* ⊗ *Closed Mon.*

¢ ✗ **'t Pannekoekhuis Schaarsbergen.** The Schaarsbergen Pancake House, housed in a Brabant-province-style Dutch farmhouse from the 1800s, is a sweet and savory answer to the "Let's eat something different today" dilemma. Offering up 100 different varieties of pancakes (yes, it is possible), there's something to suit every fancy—except that you can't eat them in The Netherlands at breakfast time. Remember, when in Rome . . . ⊠ *Kemperbergweg 673, Arnhem* ☎ *026/443–1434* ⊕ *www.pannenkoek.net* ☰ *MC, V* ⊗ *Closed Mon.*

¢–$ ✗▦ **Engelanderhof.** Known just as much for its restaurant (closed end of October to April) as for the quality of its accommodations, the Engelanderhof is only a few minutes' drive from the Hoge Veluwe National Park, and you can relax around the cozy fire in winter before dining on fresh fish or wild game in season. ⊠ *Arnhemseweg 484, 7361 CM* ☎ *055/506–3318* 🖷 *055/506–3220* ⊕ *www.engelanderhof.nl* ☞ *28 rooms* ♿ *Cable TV; no a/c* ☰ *AE, DC, MC, V* ⦿ *BP.*

$ ▦ **Hotel Oranjeoord.** In a small woodland village right out of Grimm's fairy tales 5 km (3 mi) west of Apeldoorn, the Oranjeoord is a relaxed, simple country hotel offering garden rooms, terraces, and a sunny dining room at reasonable prices, although the quality of the rooms tends to vary. Owned at one time by the Dutch royal family, it was used to accommodate guests for hunting parties. The surrounding forest and gateway to the Hoge Veluwe make for a truly spectacular drive or bicycle outing. A public golf course is in the vicinity. Consider booking for the high tea here—it's quite a Sunday occasion. ⊠ *Hoog Soeren 134–138, 7346 AH Hoog Soeren* ☎ *055/519–1227* 🖷 *055/519–1451* ⊕ *www.oranjeoord.nl* ☞ *35 rooms, 1 apartment* ♿ *2 restaurants, bicycles, some pets allowed; no a/c* ☰ *AE, MC, V* ⦿ *EP.*

¢ ▦ **De Wittehoeve.** Cozy on up to this bed-and-breakfast in a 100-year-old farmhouse where guests are invited to "bring your own horse." If you'd rather just saddle in for the night than arrive on horseback, just come as you are. This hotel is only a 10-minute walk from the Hoge Veluwe National Park. ⊠ *Brouwersweg 30, 7351 BS Hoenderloo* ☎ *055/378–2012* 🖷 *055/378–2015* ⊕ *www.hoenderloo.nl/wittehoeve* ☞ *8 rooms* ♿ *Restaurant, cable TV in some rooms, bicycles, some pets allowed; no a/c, no room phones* ☰ *No credit cards* ⦿ *BP.*

The Outdoors

CAMPING One of the best recommended campsites in the Hoge Veluwe park area is **De Pampel** (⊠ Woeste Hoefweg 35 ☎ 055/378–1760), a large, five-star campsite at €16.50–€22.50, near the Hoenderloo entrance to the

park. A popular camping option in the Hoge Veluwe is **Veluws Hof**
(✉ Krimweg 154 ☎ 055/378–1777), a moderate-size campsite at €22.24
per night per site, also near the Hoenderloo entrance to the park.

Zutphen

⓴ *17 km (11 mi) southeast of Apeldoorn, 64 km (40 mi) east of Amersfoort, 107 km (67 mi) east of Amsterdam.*

Don't be put off when you spot the hideous green, yellow, and orange
bridge as you're coming into town over the IJssel River, or by the matching green Town Hall evident when you arrive, for Zutphen defies any
attempt to modernize its very obvious medieval core. Enveloping the visitor with its Middle Age cloak, this "Tower City," known for its many
spires, is justifiably prized for its ancient library, the only medieval one
in continental western Europe, and where numerous specialty shops on
its three central market squares evoke images from its former Hanseatic
culture. Like an illuminated manuscript balanced on a lectern between
the Hoge Veluwe to the west and the Achterhoek and Germany to the
east, Zutphen was one of the region's wealthiest towns during the 14th
and 15th centuries. Today the once-walled town is a patchwork quilt
made up of prized medieval houses and courtyards, churches and towers, and remnants of old city gates. Guided walking tours, including a
special Hanseatic package with reduced-price museum tickets, are conducted by the local VVV office from April to September, and there are
boat tours along the canals.

★ A feast for the eyes both inside and out, **Sint Walburgiskerk** (St. Walburga's
Church), begun in the 12th century in Romanesque style and enlarged
in the 16th century in Gothic style, is ornamented with 14th- to16th-century frescoes on the walls and vaulted ceiling, a 17th-century pulpit
with an intricately carved lectern, a stunning Bader organ from 1643,
a brass baptismal font cast in Belgium in 1527, and a magnificent
Gothic, tiara-shape wrought-iron chandelier depicting the names of the
Apostles around its base. The **Librije** (Library), originally constructed
for that purpose in a chapel-like room connected to the church, is where
you'll find the true treasures of Zutphen (library must be toured with
a guide and times can be somewhat irregular). Dating from 1561, this
medieval library, built by a church warden to enable regular citizens,
tempted by reform, to read about Catholicism under its starch-white,
vaulted ceiling, still houses some 750 rare and beautiful early works (including 85 incunabula, or books printed before 1501), more than 300
of which are chained to the original rows of carved-wood reading stands
with adjoining monastic benches.

Highlights of the collection include 20 editions by Erasmus, including
a small schoolbook he wrote, works of all the western church fathers
(St. Augustine, St. Jerome, St. George, and St. Ambrose), a first edition
of the work of Copernicus, one edition of Martin Luther's complete works
(1564–70), as well as the oldest book in the library, a 1469 commentary by Thomas Aquinas. It took almost a full year to complete a book
in those days, making them prohibitively expensive and therefore available only to the sinfully rich. Also, *very* few people were able to read,
particularly in Latin, so the books were a privilege merely to behold for
those educated few, as it is our privilege today to see them in this setting. ✉ *Kerkhof 3, 7201 DM* ☎ *0575/514178* ⊕ *www.walburgiskerk.
nl* 🎫 *€1.20, combined with library €3* ☉ *Mid-May–June, Aug.–mid-Sept., Mon.–Sat., call for opening times; July and Aug., Mon. 1:30–4:30,
Tues.–Sat. 10:30–4:30.*

Shelved behind the Sint Walburgiskerk is the **Grafisch Museum** (Graphics Museum), a two-level, shoplike exhibit of printing presses, typesetting, and bookbinding implements, including one man's amazing collection of some 1,600 seals used to emboss the leather tomes. ⊠ *Kerkhof 16, 7201DM* ☏ *0575/542329* ⌦ *€2.50* ⊙ *Wed.–Fri. 1–4:30, Sat. 11–3.*

The small **Henriette Polak Museum** offers changing exhibitions from its substantial collection of 20th-century Dutch figurative art and paintings, most notably *Landschap* (Landscape) by Wim Oepts. Climb the stairs to the attic to see the tiny room used in the 17th century as a *schuilkerk,* a secret Roman Catholic church. ⊠ *Zaadmarkt 88, 7200 VB* ☏ *0575/516878* ⌦ *€2.27, includes admission to Stedelijk Museum Zutphen* ⊙ *Tues.–Fri. 11–5, weekends 1:30–5.*

The **Stedelijk Museum Zutphen** houses an eclectic collection of historical art, archaeology of the region, modern house interiors, and vintage toys. ⊠ *Rozengracht 3, 7201 JL* ☏ *0575/516878* ⌦ *€2.27, includes admission to Henriette Polak Museum* ⊙ *Tues.–Fri. 11–5, weekends 1:30–5.*

Where to Eat & Stay

$$–$$$ ✕ **'t Spyshuys Apotheek/Restaurant 't Schulten Hues.** A tough choice of two entirely different restaurants, the brother establishments are run on the same premises. The ground floor 't Spyshuys is a brasserie in the refurbished premises of a former pharmacy, and downstairs in a 14th-century vaulted cellar the fare is French with Dutch influence. (Credit cards are taken only at 't Schulten Hues.) ⊠ *Houtmarkt 79* ☏ *0575/510005* ⊟ *AE, DC, MC, V* ⊙ *Closed Mon. Lunch by reservation only at 't Schulten Hues.*

★ **$$** ✕☎ **Best Western Zutphen Museumhotel.** Facing the Sint Walburgiskerk and medieval library in a 17th-century building on the oldest square in Zutphen, this high-standard hotel has completely modernized rooms in the main wing and carriage house. For drinks on the front terrace, just ring up the waiter (the buzzer is on the pillar). Their **De Gravin** restaurant (closed Sunday) features Dutch/French cuisine with a Hanseatic flair. ⊠ *'s Gravenhof 6, 7201DN* ☏ *0575/546111* 🖷 *0575/545999* ⊕ *www. zupthen-museumhotel.nl* ⇱ *74 rooms* ⚹ *Minibars, cable TV, bar, dry cleaning, some pets allowed; no a/c* ⊟ *AE, DC, MC, V* ¶⊙ *BP.*

¢–$ ✕☎ **Berkhotel.** Old-world English charm is at the core of this country-style inn with a town heart. A grand restaurant, **De Kloostertuin,** with chandeliers, palms, and candlelight features an eclectic mix of French, Thai, Indian, Moroccan, Russian, and vegetarian cuisine. ⊠ *Marspoortstraat 19, 7201 JA* ☏ *0575/511135* 🖷 *0575/541950* ⇱ *19 rooms, 10 with bath; 1 suite* ⚹ *Restaurant, cable TV, bar, lounge, some pets allowed; no a/c* ⊟ *AE, MC, V* ¶⊙ *BP.*

Nightlife

Café 't Winkeltje (⊠ Groenmarkt 34 ☏ 0575/511804) is a welcoming "brown café" where the walls are desirably (to the Dutch, anyhow) left stained with years' worth of tobacco smoke, home, in this instance, to a mixed crowd, rock and golden oldies over the sound system, and a good assortment of specialty beers.

Bronkhorst

㉑ *9 km (5 mi) south of Zutphen.*

Fodor'sChoice
★ It's as though Dickens's Tiny Tim has left his thumbprint on Bronkhorst, the tiniest official town in The Netherlands, with a population of just 160. The entire hamlet, established in 1344, has been declared a National Monument, and it's easy to see why as you wander along its cob-

blestone streets paved with nostalgia and punctuated with a dickens of a lot of curiosity shops where local craftsmen ply their traditional trades. Pick up an English copy of "A Town Walk—Bronkhorst" (€1.79, available at local restaurants or the Zutphen VVV). The most curious spot *is*, in fact, the **Charles Dickens Museum**, the passion-turned-museum-shop of Sjef de Jong, a lifelong Dickens fan and devotee, and Scrooge imitator, where, among a good collection of memorabilia, you can see Dickens's walking stick and a ticket used by the British royal family for his last performance. Literary fans will swoon over the museum's antiquarian bookshop, The Old Curiosity Shop, where copies of Dickens's works are available for purchase. About a week before Christmas, Mr. de Jong, with the help of the locals, turns Bronkhorst into an animated *Christmas Carol* tableau with street and church performances in a completely illuminated village. (The shop does not take credit cards.) ☒ *Onderstraat 2, 7226LD* ☎ *0575/451623* ⊕ *www. dickensmuseum.nl* ☒ *Free* ☉ *Easter–late Oct., daily 10–5; late Oct.–Easter, weekends 11–5.*

Where to Stay & Eat

★ **$$–$$$** ✕⌂ **Herberg de Gouden Leeuw.** Experience the best that Dutch hospitality and ambience have to offer in this stunning 16th- and 17th-century farmhouse inn combining country-style Dutch with English decor. In a village so cute and quaint it almost squeaks, this luxurious farmhouse is the next best thing to hearth and home, perhaps even better. Set just across from the town's Dickens Museum and a 14th-century chapel, this romantic inn complete with 17th-century tile tableaux is worth fighting for a reservation, even if it's only for dinner at their excellent restaurant, 't Pietshuus (closed Monday and Tuesday), which serves local game, asparagus, and lobster in season. Bicycle and walking paths abound along the nearby IJssel River, providing tranquility and repose. For a luxurious but oh-so-homey experience, head here. ☒ *Bovenstraat 2, 7226 LM* ☎ *0575/451231* 🖨 *0575/450123* ⊕ *www. herbergdegoudenleeuw.com* ⇆ *8 rooms* ㊅ *Restaurant, bar* ▤ *AE, MC, V* ⊌ *BP.*

Shopping

Local artisans can be found at **Lötters Edelstenen** (☒ Bovenstraat 1 ☎ 0575/452657), a gem and mineral shop. **Kaasboerderij Hoga Huys** (☒ Bovenstraat 12a ☎ 0575/452598) is a cheese farm and adjacent art gallery. **Heren van Bronkhorst** (☒ Onderstraat 1 ☎ 0575/452535) is a well-known antiques shop.

Arnhem

❷❷
Fodor'sChoice
★

99 km (62 mi) southeast of Amsterdam, 50 km (31 mi) southeast of Amersfoort, 25 km (16 mi) southwest of Bronkhorst.

In war log and movie terms, Arnhem may be known as the basis for *A Bridge Too Far,* but this historic city is certainly not out of reach for military buffs who like to combine their field research with great shopping, parks, and castles in the sky, all in close proximity to the great Hoge Veluwe National Park. Central to what was the largest airborne operation of World War II, Arnhem's famous bridge over the Rhine, the Rynbrug, now called **John Frostbrug,** became the rope of the four-day tug-of-war between the Allies and the German forces intent on trying to further penetrate the area. Left with the short end of the rope, 1,748 Allied troops lost their lives in the fight for the bridge.

Today, trolley buses unique to Arnhem weave their environmentally friendly way around this largely pedestrianized town, the fifth-largest shopping area in The Netherlands. Although much of Arnhem was destroyed during World War II, there are a few bastions that survived the bombing, namely the **Korenmarkt** square of old warehouses, which now throbs nightly with a mix of pubs, cafés, restaurants, and dance clubs. A weekly market is held in the shadows of Arnhem's **Grote Kerk** (Great Church) or **Eusebiuskerk** as it is properly called, a three-aisle cross-basilica that dates back to the 15th century. Accessible by a glass-enclosed elevator that passes one of the largest carillons in Europe, the reconstructed tower offers a panoramic view of the town and its famous bridge. ⊠ *Kerkplein* ☎ *026/443–5068* ▱ *€2.50* ◷ *Apr.–Oct., Tues.–Sat. 10–5, Sun. noon–5; Nov.–Mar., Tues.–Sat. 11–4, Sun. noon–4.*

Lurking around one side of the Grote Kerk is the 16th-century Stadhuis or **Duivelshuis** (Devil's House) at Koningstraat 38, which, strangely enough, suffered no damage whatsoever during World War II. The demonic sculptures on the building's facade were carved by order of General Maarten van Rossum, allegedly as payback for the city fathers' refusal to allow him to pave the front steps of his town hall with gold. (Dutch hellfire-and-brimstone painter Hieronymus Bosch could have had a field day with this one, particularly in light of the fact that it was the city church tower that fell.)

Oosterbeek, now a very posh town just west of Arnhem, where 10,000 of the First British Airborne Division parachuted down on September 17, 1944, is today the setting for the **Airborne Museum Hartenstein**, where all manner of military memorabilia, weapons, and equipment depict the crucial battle that took place. An English-language audiovisual presentation brings it to life. Ask at the desk for a map of other nearby war-related sites or a guided tour. ⊠ *Utrechtseweg 232, Oosterbeek* ☎ *026/ 333-7710* ⊕ *www.airbornemuseum.org* ▱ *€4.50* ◷ *Apr.–Oct., Mon.–Sat. 10–5; Nov.–Mar., Mon.–Sat. 11–5, Sun. noon–5.*

Just to the north of Oosterbeek lies the **Arnhem/Oosterbeek War Cemetery,** also known as the Airborne Cemetery, resting place of those Allies who fell during the Battle of Arnhem.

For a small-dose culture break, the **Historisch Museum Arnhem** (Historic Museum), just on the rim of Arnhem's main shopping area, offers a gratifying range of art, furniture, silver, ceramics, and town history served up in a delightful 18th-century mansion, a former soap factory, and orphanage. Highlights include an 1800 dollhouse in a china cabinet, a wax portrait of a 12-year-old girl (who drowned along with her mother and brother when their ship sank on the Rhine River while en route to a friend's estate in Arnhem), paintings of the town by Bartholomeus Springer and others on the top floor, and old photos taken before and after the World War II siege. ⊠ *Bovenbeekstraat 21, 6811 CV* ☎ *026/ 442-6900* ⊕ *www.hmarnhem.nl* ▱ *€3.50* ◷ *Tues.–Fri. 10–5, weekends 11–5.*

For a look at daily civilian life in wartime Arnhem, go to the **Arnhem Oorlogsmuseum '40–'45.** ⊠ *Kemperbergweg 780, 6816 RX* ☎ *026/ 442-0958* ▱ *€3* ◷ *Tues.–Sun. 10–5.*

Captured in Arnhem's **Museum voor Moderne Kunst** (Museum for Modern Art) is the magic realism and contemporary art of modern Dutch masters Charlie Toorop, Dick Ket, and Carel Willink, plus a sculpture garden overlooking the Rhine River. If you dare, take a gander at the statue of a man in the phone booth–like structure outside (warning: he's rated X). ⊠ *Utrechtseweg 87, 6812AA* ☎ *026/351-2431* ⊕ *www. mmkarnhem.nl* ▱ *€6* ◷ *Tues.–Fri. 10–5, weekends 11–5.*

<table>
<tr><td>

**need a
break?**

</td><td>

Withdraw to **Coffee Grounds** (✉ Korenstraat 6–8 ☎ 026/370–5110) for an American blast of bagels, brownies, doughnuts, muffins, cheesecake, and perhaps the only take-out coffee on Dutch soil (excepting McDonald's). If you haven't tried raw herring yet, head for **Gamba's** (✉ Jansstraat 12 ☎ 026/351–2224), where the freshest seafood delicacies are served. (Go on, smother it in onions and pickles like the Dutch do. You'll be donning wooden shoes before you know it.)

</td></tr>
</table>

★ ☯ If time doesn't allow you to make it to every province of The Netherlands, why not "cheat" a little by visiting the **Nederlands Openlucht Museum** (Open Air Museum), a 109-acre park that re-creates Dutch country life through a colorful cross section of historic buildings and dwellings transported from all over the country, complete with windmills, fully furnished thatched-roof farmhouses, craft shops, and the "klomp" of wooden shoes. Children can participate in farm life, ride old-fashioned toys, play in a 1930s playground, and when they tire, take a tram to the next stop. For those who still don't get the picture, a *HollandRama* mobile time capsule provides a glimpse of life in Holland. (The museum is on the northern outskirts of town.) ✉ *Schelmseweg 89, 6818 SJ* ☎ *026/357–6111* ⊕ *www.openluchtmuseum.nl* ☞ *€11.20* ☉ *Apr.–Oct., daily 10–5; Nov.–Mar., Tues.–Sun. 10–4:30.*

Not far from Arnhem's train station lies the verdant, 185-acre **Sonsbeek Park** with its striking 15th-century white mill house, the **Witte Molen,** and a visitor center, **Bezoekerscentrum,** where you can get information about the park, see the inner workings of an old water mill, and buy some homemade "windmill bread," *Molenbrood,* or the flour to mill your own. Take time to wander through the woodlands past lakes and streams, peer out over Arnhem from the **Belvedere** lookout point, and ogle the stately **Huis (House) Sonsbeek,** the massive white villa on the hill, now an art gallery. ✉ *Zijpendaalseweg 24a* ☎ *026/445–0660* ⊕ *www.dewatermolen.nl* ☞ *Free* ☉ *Visitor center Tues.–Fri. 10–5, weekends 11–5; water mill Tues.–Thurs. 10–4:30.*

Up the hill from the water mill in **Sonsbeek Park** rises one of four beckoning castles in the Arnhem area, the 1762 **Kasteel (Castle) Zijpendaal** where you can catch a glimpse into another realm. ✉ *Zijpendaalseweg 44, 6814 CL* ☎ *026/355–2555* ⊕ *www.hgl-vhk.nl* ☞ *€2.50* ☉ *Guided tours mid-Apr.–Oct., Tues.–Fri. and Sun. at 1, 2, 3, and 4.*

<table>
<tr><td>

**off the
beaten
path**

</td><td>

THE CASTLES OF ARNHEM – A castle tour in surrounding Arnhem should first take you to medieval **Kasteel Doorwerth** (✉ Fonteinallee 2, Doorwerth ☎ 026/333–2532). Authentically furnished and magnificently decorated, **Kasteel Middachten** (✉ Landgoed Middachten 3, De Steeg ☎ 026/495–4998) is a fun outing, but mind the trick floor. **Kasteel Rozendaal** (✉ Rozendaal 1, Rozendaal ☎ 026/364–4645) crowns a town that is on a par with Wassenaar (near The Hague) as the wealthiest in The Netherlands. Contact the local VVV information office for details.

</td></tr>
</table>

Where to Eat & Stay

★ $$–$$$ ✗ **Kasteel Doorwerth.** If 200 candles lit in the chandeliers of a moated castle overlooking the Rhine don't "get you in the mood," then your significant other had better drop you off and drive on. The ultimate romantic dinner is what we're after here, only 8 km (5 mi) from Arnhem, and featuring a timbered dining room, once the castle's coach house, furnished with antiques, not that you'll notice. In the unlikely event that food is your priority, the cuisine is classic French with a twist of local

Dutch ingredients. Upon advance request, large groups can be entertained in medieval style (who needs them?) and the main house can be toured for €4.50. Surrounding woods keep the world at bay. ⊠ *Fonteinallee 4, Doorwerth* ☎ *026/333–3420* ⊕ *www.bilderberg.nl* 🚗 *Reservations essential* ▤ *AE, DC, MC, V* ☻ *Closed Mon. and Tues. No lunch.*

★ $$ ✕ **Bistro in den Vollen Pot.** One of the original places in Arnhem (more are planned) where you can eat underground in a 15th-century cave/cellar, this bistro features a varied menu, the highlight of which is their *Stoofpannetje* (Little Oven Pan), a fish casserole in lobster sauce, served with a clay pot of spinach, fried potatoes, and carrot knobs. ⊠ *Varkensstraat 48a* ☎ *026/351–0106* ▤ *AE, DC, MC, V* ☻ *Closed Mon. No lunch.*

$$ ✕ **Zilli & Zilli.** Casual or dressy, Zilli's is the place to don your favorite duds and Italian taste buds for a choice of informal or formal dining in the casual *trattoria* or full-scale *ristorante.* ⊠ *Marienburgstraat 1* ☎ *026/442–0288* ▤ *MC, V* ☻ *Closed Mon. No lunch Sun.*

$$ ▦ **Best Western Hotel Haarhuis.** By American standards, this hotel offers all the comforts of home in the center of town, directly across from the train station. ⊠ *Stationsplein 1, 6800 AG* ☎ *026/442–7441* 🖨 *026/442–7449* ⊕ *www.hotelhaarhuis.nl* ⟿ *84 rooms* 🚗 *Restaurant, cable TV, gym, hair salon, sauna, bar, some pets allowed; no a/c* ▤ *AE, DC, MC, V* ❏ *BP.*

$–$$ ▦ **NH Rijnhotel.** If you want to be in the middle of the action and still have a view of the Rhine—since that seems to be the thing to do when you come here—it's only a 10–15 minute walk to the center of town from this serene hotel where all the rooms and the terrace offer magnificent river views. If you'd rather bike than walk or cruise, two-wheelers can be reserved in advance in summer. It's only a short pedal to the nearby Openlucht Museum. ⊠ *Onderlangs 10, 6812 CG* ☎ *026/443–4642* 🖨 *026/445–4847* ⊕ *www.nhhotels.com* ⟿ *68 rooms, 5 suites* 🚗 *Restaurant, minibars, cable TV, some pets allowed; no a/c* ▤ *AE, DC, MC, V* ❏ *EP.*

$ ▦ **Hotel Blanc.** This small hotel, directly across from the railway station in central Arnhem, is situated in a turn-of-the-20th-century town house and offers bright, comfortable rooms and a friendly café. ⊠ *Coehoornstraat 4, 6811 LA* ☎ *026/442–8072* 🖨 *026/443–4749* ⊕ *www. hotel-blanc.nl* ⟿ *22 rooms* 🚗 *Restaurant, cable TV, bar, lounge, parking, some pets allowed; no a/c* ▤ *AE, DC, MC, V* ❏ *BP.*

★ $ ▦ **Molendal.** By far our favorite choice for Arnhem, this Jugendstil-style city mansion, on a Boston-row-house-look-alike street close to the town center and station (and bordering the magnificent Sonsbeek Park), is a joy to behold with its imposing staircases, light-filled, spacious rooms, and modern bathrooms. Enjoy your buffet breakfast in the cozy sunroom while Fleur, the resident pooch, makes you feel at home. ⊠ *Cronjestraat 15, 6814 AG* ☎ *026/442–4858* 🖨 *026/443–6614* ⊕ *www. hotel-molendal.nl* ⟿ *17 rooms* 🚗 *Minibars, cable TV, bar, lounge, some pets allowed; no a/c* ▤ *AE, DC, MC, V* ❏ *BP.*

Shopping

You may want to increase your credit-card limit before you travel to Arnhem, because the shops are a booby trap waiting to blast you into debt. Market days are Friday morning and Saturday at Kerkplein, and late shopping is on Thursday until 9. A few of the best picks, in addition to the pocket of antiques shops on Bakkerstraat, are the following: **De Bijenkorf** (⊠ Ketelstraat 45 ☎ 026/371–5700) is the Dutch version of Bloomingdale's, with a superb cafeteria upstairs. **Wim Pollmann** (⊠ Vijzelstraat 18 ☎ 026/442–4103), a tableware emporium extraordinaire, has a bargain basement at medieval prices and shipping to the United

States. **Hendriksen** (✉ Vijzelstraat 11–12 ☎ 026/443–7454) is a men's and women's European fashion house with only good taste for sale. **Alexander van den Hoven** (✉ Bentinckstraat 4 ☎ 026/443–4086), a designer jewelry shop, has pearls to make your pupils dilate. **Brassa** (✉ Bakkerstraat 11a ☎ 026/442–7589) is the place for clocks, kitchenware, fun postcards, and funky gifts such as the stuffed-animal heads for that incessantly needy child back home. **Black Point** (✉ Nieuwstad 2 ☎ 026/443–0073) is a gasping breath of fresh-air fashion for women who think that black and white are the only respectable colors. **Noack** (✉ Vijzelstraat 23 ☎ 026/442–4861), an old-world delicatessen and Dutch souvenir/specialty shop, is perfect for Aunt Mary's last-minute gift.

Nijmegen

㉓ *18 km (11 mi) south of Arnhem, 71 km (44 mi) southeast of Amersfoort, 122 km (76 mi) east of Amsterdam.*

If every pocket has a silver lining, then Nijmegen is no exception. Ravaged by World War II—being so close to the border with Germany, the town was inadvertently bombed by the Allies—it wears a split personality of modernity strutting in a straitjacket of Roman heritage. Pocketed with the scattered remains of ancient settlement, *Noviomagum,* or "New Market," as the Romans called it, is a city that can be enjoyed for its diversity but pitied for its legacy. Devastatingly bombed and worse for the wear, it has very little character remaining. Even its motto, "Up to date for 2,000 years" bemoans its identity crisis. Seeming to bear witness to that, the town's casino sits on the remains of a Roman underfloor heating system. Claiming to be the oldest town in The Netherlands (roundly disputed by Maastricht) with a debut in AD 104, Nijmegen starts out appearing a bit stiff, but then grows on you like a pair of well-fitted jeans.

Built on seven hills, like Rome, which makes it clearly unique in an otherwise linear topography, Nijmegen has an upper and a lower town skirting the River Waal near the strategic junction of the Maas/Waalkanal, an understructure of medieval passageways and cellars, and the highest concentration of outdoor cafés, so they say, in The Netherlands. The resident Catholic University Nijmegen gives the town a young, hip style at designer discount prices, making your stay here almost as good a value as it was in its days as a medieval trading center, which can still be explored vicariously in the area of the Begijnenstraat. Splendid river views are afforded from **Valkhof,** the hilltop site of a revolt against Rome in AD 69–70, and **Belvedere Park,** where there's a fine restaurant in a tower. Nearby is the **Waalkade riverfront esplanade,** lined with restaurants, shops, and a casino, in back of which is an embarkation point for riverboat trips in July and August.

Forgiven, barely, for its aqua-hue, boxlike exterior "design"—at which Emperor Charlemagne, whose castle remains border the premises, would have decidedly turned up his nose—the **Valkhof Museum** is, nevertheless, a very important archaeological and modern art museum rolled into one. The bright, pleasant space on the inside (despite the questionable accordion-like stairway) features a truly fine exhibit of prehistoric, Roman, and medieval artifacts found (and still being found) in the very backyards of local residents. A veritable department store of antiquity balanced by a fast-forward selection of pop art and expressionism designed to tease those reluctant to test both waters, the museum's showpieces include the oldest wine in all of Europe (in a glass bottle some 2,000 years old; no sampling, please); a hoot of a drinking vessel in the shape of an owl-like creature with a coconut-shell body and silver trim (belief was that if given poison, one could see it in the coconut); and the showstopper, an iron mask with silver and bronze, dating from AD 100 and found nearby in the river. ⊠ *Kelfkensbos 59, 6501BL* ☏ *024/360–8805* ⊕ *www.museumhetvalkhof.nl* ☒ *€4.50* ☼ *Tues.–Fri. 10–5, weekends noon–5.*

The ubiquitous bicycle is given its due at the **Nationaal Fietsmuseum Velorama** (Velorama National Bicycle Museum), where more than 250 historic spokesters are on view. ⊠ *Waalkade 107, 6511 XR* ☏ *024/322–5851* ⊕ *www.velorama.nl* ☒ *€4.60* ☼ *Mon.–Sat. 10–5, Sun. 11–5.*

In an area once besieged by war and since face-lifted from the fallout, it's appropriate that the **Nationaal Bevrijdingsmuseum 1944–1945** (National Liberation Museum), some 10 km (6 mi) southeast of Nijmegen, occupies beautiful surroundings between hills and woods. Experience here the ebb and flow of man's conflicts: the occupation, the liberation, and the rebuilding of a war-torn Europe, through interactive displays, dioramas, models, and films in a positive tribute to freedom, democracy, and international cooperation. Take the No. 5 bus to Groesbeek and get off at De Oude Molen. ⊠ *Wylerbaan 4, 6560 AC Groesbeek* ☏ *024/397–4404* ⊕ *www.bevrijdingsmuseum.nl* ☒ *€5.50* ☼ *Mon.–Sat. 10–5, Sun. noon–5.*

If you'd like to say that you've gone underground, visit the subterranean **Museum De Stratemakerstoren** (The Road Workers' Tower Museum), where a series of cannons is still positioned under a fortress tower built between the 14th and 16th centuries and used to repel invaders, with audiovisuals depicting what it was like to approach the medieval city gates at night. ⊠ *Waalkade 83–84, 6511 XR* ☏ *024/323–8690* ⊕ *www.stratemakerstoren.nl* ☒ *€3.20* ☼ *Tues.–Fri. 10–5, weekends 1–5.*

off the beaten path

Several offbeat but very impressive museums are located just outside of Nijmegen. **Afrika Museum** (⊠ Postweg 6, 6571 CS Berg en Dal ☏ 024/684–1211) is an outdoor oasis replicating the living and working conditions in various parts of Africa, including a Ghanaian living compound, an authentic reconstruction of a village in Mali, houses on stilts from Benin, and a life-size reproduction of a Pygmy settlement, with dance and cooking workshops in summer. The **Bijbels Openluchtmuseum** (⊠ Profetenlaan 2, 6564 BL Heilig Landstichting ☏ 024/382–3110), the Open Air Bible Museum, literally transports you into major scenes from the Bible. At the Dutch-German border, northeast of Nijmegen, 3,705 acres of riparian habitat, known as **De Gelderse Poort**, are being returned to their original wildness along the Waal River. Trek by bike or foot from Kekerdom along the extensive network of trails, or forge your own way through this unrestrictive natural domain of flora and fauna. Ask the VVV Nijmegen for information.

Where to Eat & Stay

$$$ ✗ **Belvedere.** Housed in a 16th-century watchtower high on a hill in the middle of Belvedere Park, overlooking a wide bend in the River Waal, this restaurant, with only a handful of tables, has possibly the best river view in The Netherlands. The menu features contemporary French cooking, including choices such as lobster and sweetbreads in a lobster sauce. ⊠ *Kelfkensbos 60* ☏ *024/322–6861* ⊕ *www.restaurant-belvedere.nl* ⌕ *Reservations essential* ▤ *AE, DC, MC, V* ☼ *Closed Sun. No lunch Sat.*

★ **¢–$$** ✗ **Pasta e Fagioli.** Anna Maria and Nino Casella, he the chef from the Naples area in Italy, she the Dutch half, together make a delectable feast in this pretty yellow restaurant where everything is prepared to perfection. Down to the last mussel, the fish soup is worth an oversize postcard in itself, but who has time to write when the broccoli pasta has just arrived and there are more than 65 kinds of grappa to choose from. (Reserve the lovely back conservatory for a romantic or family affair.) ⊠ *Van Welderenstraat 105* ☎ *024/323–4283* ⊟ *AE, DC, MC, V* ☉ *Closed Mon.*

$ ✕ **De Waagh.** Dishing up an international array of food in the most Gothic monument in town, with an atmosphere to match, the Weigh House was a former marketplace with still-visible weights, pulleys, and scales suspended from the vaulted ceiling. Nijmegen's main-square showpiece, it has comfortable cushioned benches inside and a bustling outdoor café. The Thai fish soup or cold cucumber soup might just whet your appetite. ⊠ *Grote Markt 26, 6511 KB* ☎ *024/323–0757* ⊕ *www.de-waagh.nl* ⊟ *No credit cards.*

★ $$$ ⌘ **Scandic Hotel Sanadome.** In need of a total body tonic? You've come to the right place, because Sanadome offers a mega-cure for what ails you, head to toe. A totally pampering, ultramodern spa in a four-star luxury hotel, this spot allows you to immerse yourself in everything from body wraps, facials, manicures, pedicures, and massages, to yoga; work out in the fitness center or aqua-gym; tan in the solarium; sweat in the sauna; flip around the pool, then luxuriate in a saltwater bath or one of several whirlpools, including one with lavender; have your hair coiffed in the beauty salon and your makeup applied by specialists—all before going out on the town or retiring to your luxurious room. Or just use the spa, from €16 to €22, depending on time and day, without staying over. Body farmers, unite. This is what hotels were meant to be. ⊠ *Weg Door Jonkerbos 90, 6503 CC* ☎ *024/359–7200* 🖷 *024/ 359–7294* ⊕ *www.sanadome.nl* ⇄ *85 rooms* ⌂ *2 restaurants, some in-room data ports, minibars, cable TV, pool, health club, bar; no a/c in some rooms* ⊟ *AE, DC, MC, V* ⎚ *BP.*

$–$$ ⌘ **Hotel Belvoir.** Thanks to the Dutch (the tallest people in the world), there are extra-long beds at this high-standard hotel, plus a pool for Junior and a modern bathroom for Mom, all in a quiet residential area within walking distance of the center of Nijmegen and the casino. ⊠ *Graadt van Roggenstraat 101, 6522 AX* ☎ *024/323–2344* 🖷 *024/ 323–9960* ⊕ *www.belvoir.nl* ⇄ *60 rooms, 14 suites* ⌂ *Minibars, indoor pool, gym, some pets allowed; no a/c* ⊟ *AE, DC, MC, V* ⎚ *EP.*

Nightlife & the Arts

Given the number of university students in Nijmegen and their incumbent academic pressures, there is an overabundance of nightlife here. Number one on many tourists' lists is the **Holland Casino** (⊠ Waalkade 68 ☎ 024/381–6381). A popular option for dancing couples is the **Tangoschool El Corte** (⊠ Graafseweg 108b ☎ 024/323–3063) for which Nijmegen is particularly renowned. The nightclub **De Drie Gezusters** (⊠ Molenstraat 79–81 ☎ 024/322–6674) even has a revolving bar. **Grote Griet** (⊠ Molenstraat 83 ☎ 024/322–6674) is a pub replete with its own library room.

Major concerts take place at the **Concerthall De Vereeniging** (⊠ Keizer Karelplein 2d). Contact the VVV office for listings and ticket information.

Shopping

Reputedly the oldest Roman city in The Netherlands, Nijmegen boasts the oldest shopping street, the **Lange Hezelstraat,** an ancient Roman road still vaguely recognizable today as a medieval thoroughfare, lined with more than 100 shops, which leads toward the **Grote Markt.** **Vestiti** (⊠ Lange Hezelstraat 81 ☎ 024/322–2554) is a top place for Dutch,

Italian, and English country wear, including blouses and tees with a subtle "Dutch" insignia from the line by that name, great for gifts or memories of your trip, and handmade silk tweed jackets from Ireland. **De Engelbewaarder** (✉ The Guardian Angel, Lange Hezelstraat 40 ☎ 024/360–8004), a well-known shop for children's wooden furnishings and toys, has a stock that includes unique music boxes. **Curly Corner** (✉ Sint Stevenskerkhof 44 ☎ 024/322–5028) is a hip gift shop in one of the oldest and prettiest medieval corners of town, tucked behind St. Stevens' Church. **'t Winkeltje** (✉ The Little Shop, Sint Stevenskerkhof 45 ☎ 024/323–0829), a cozy antiques shop, is set in a 14th-century priest's house. **Het Begin** (✉ The Beginning, Lange Hezelstraat 104 ☎ 024/322–7605) is a fine spot for frivolous children's decorations made by local artists, including handmade photo albums, music boxes, and crazy mirrors. Molenstraat and Broerstraat also offer good shopping, as does the Marikenstraat, the newest shopping area akin to an open-air mall where **David Mulder** (✉ Marikenstraat 75 ☎ 024/322–4764) will fill your china cabinet with fine European tableware. Late-night shopping takes place on Thursday night until 9.

THE GREEN HEART A TO Z

To research prices, get advice from other travelers, and book travel arrangements, visit www.fodors.com.

BICYCLE TRAVEL
Free bicycles are provided for visitors in the De Hoge Veluwe National Park. You can also rent bicycles at most railway stations.
🚲 Bike Rentals **Blakborn** ✉ Soerenseweg 3, Apeldoorn ☎ 055/521–5679. **Hotel Restaurant De Harmonie** ✉ Beulakerweg 55, Giethoorn ☎ 0521/361372. **Prinsen** ✉ Beulakerweg 137, Giethoorn ☎ 0521/361261. **Scholten** ✉ Luttekestraat 7, Zwolle ☎ 038/421–7378.

BUS TRAVEL
A comprehensive network of local and regional bus services in the Green Heart provides a useful supplement to the train service.
🚲 Bus Information **Public transportation** ☎ 0900/9292.

CAR RENTAL
🚲 Major Agencies **Alamo** ☎ 023/556–3666 in Holland. **Avis** ☎ 0800/235–2847 in Holland. **Budget** ☎ 023/568–8888 in Holland. **Europecar** ☎ 070/381–1812 in Holland. **Hertz** ☎ 0900/235–4378 in Holland.

CAR TRAVEL
From Amsterdam, take A1 to Amersfoort, Apeldoorn, and Deventer or Zutphen; A2 and A12 to Arnhem; or A1 and A28 to Zwolle, continuing on, if you like, to Staphorst. Likewise, Giethoorn is in the same neighborhood via the N331 and N334 from Zwolle. Kampen is another good detour en route to Zwolle, with a deviation via the N50. Nijmegen is easily reached from Arnhem by A325. Bronkhorst is accessible either from Arnhem on the A348, or from Zutphen via the N345 or N314.

CURRENCY EXCHANGE
The best place to get cash is at an ATM (*geld automat*). Thanks to the euro, much of Europe is on the same system in case you decide to do some country hopping.

EMERGENCIES
🚲 Emergency Services **National Emergency Alarm Number** for police, fire, and ambulance ☎ 112.

TAXIS
Taxis wait at city railway stations; additional stands may be available in central shopping and hotel districts.

TOURS
The tourist offices in most cities in the region organize walking tours in summer months. Inquire for times, minimum group size, and whether or not English translation is offered or can be arranged.

In summer (late June–late August) the VVV Apeldoorn offers a variety of tours through the surrounding nature parks.

🚩 Fees & Schedules **VVV Apeldoorn** ☎ 0900/1681636 or 055/578-8884.

TRAIN TRAVEL
Frequent express Intercity trains link Amsterdam with Amersfoort, Apeldoorn, Deventer, Zwolle, Arnhem, and Nijmegen. To reach Zutphen by train, change in either Arnhem or Zwolle.

🚩 Train/Public Transportation Information ☎ 0900/9292 ⊕ www.ns.nl.

VISITOR INFORMATION
🚩 Tourist Information **VVV Amersfoort** ⊠ Stationsplein 9–11, 3818 LE ☎ 033/463-2804, 0900/112-2364 in Holland ⊕www.vvvamersfoort.nl. **VVV Apeldoorn** ⊠Stationstraat 72, 7311 MH ☎ 055/578-8884, 0900/168-1636 in Holland [€.45 per min] 🖳 055/521-1290 ⊕ www.vvvapeldoorn.nl. **VVV Arnhem Region** ⊠ Willemsplein 8, 6811 KB ☎ 026/442-6767, 0900/2024075 in Holland 🖳 026/442-2644 ⊕ www.vvvarnhem.nl. **VVV Deventer** ⊠ Keizerstraat 22, 7411 HH ☎ 0570/691410, 0900/353-5355 in Holland 🖳 0570/643338 ⊕ www.vvvdeventer.nl. **VVV Giethoorn** ⊠ Beulakerweg 114a, 8355 AL ☎ 0900/567-4637 **VVV Kampen** ⊠ Oudestraat 151, 8261 CL ☎ 038/331-3500 🖳 038/332-8900 ⊕ www.vvvkampen.nl. **VVV Nijmegen** ⊠ Keizer Karelplein 2, 6511 NC ☎ 024/329-7878, 0900/112-2344 in Holland ⊕ www.vvvnijmegen.nl. **VVV Zutphen** ⊠ Stationsplein 39, 7200 BC ☎ 0575/519-355 or 0900/269-2888 🖳 0575/517928 ⊕ www.vvvzutphen.nl. **VVV Zwolle** ⊠ Grote-Kerkplein 14, 8011 PK ☎ 038/421-6798 🖳 038/422-2679 ⊕ www. vvvzwolle.nl. There is no VVV in Bronkhorst (contact Zutphen VVV) or Staphorst (contact Zwolle VVV).

THE NORTH & THE WADDEN SEA ISLANDS

6

FODOR'S CHOICE

Eise Eisinga Planetarium, *Franeker's 17th-century wonder*

Groningen, *the Amsterdam of the North*

Harlingen, *a gem of a harbor town*

Hindeloopen, *"the painted lady" of Friesland*

Leeuwarden, *origin of the Elfstedentocht race*

Menkemaborg, *a manor house oozing with Vermeerian charm*

The Princess's Palace, *Leeuwarden's decorative arts delight*

Royal Tichelaar Museum, *Makkum's legendary ceramics trove*

Sloten, *a village pretty as a postcard*

Texel, *an island getaway beloved by Amsterdammers*

HIGHLY RECOMMENDED

RESTAURANTS　De Passage, *Assen*

Muller, *Groningen*

HOTELS　Het Rentmeesterhuis, *Fraeylemaborg*

Hotel de Ville, *Groningen*

Hotel-Restaurant Van der Werff, *Schiermonnikoog*

Logement t'Olde Hof, *Assen*

Schimmelpenninck Huys, *Groningen*

Vuurtoren van Harlingen, *Harlingen*

Many other great sights, restaurants, and hotels enliven this region. For other favorites, look for the black stars as you read this chapter.

By Shirley J. S.
Agudo

Updated by
Shirley J. S.
Agudo and
Carol Conover

IF THE DUTCH COUNTRYSIDE IS ONE OF THE BEST-KEPT TRAVEL SECRETS, then Holland's North and its islands are its softest whisper. A fairy-tale land, these northern reaches conjure up images of Hans Christian Andersen, Hans Brinker, and Don Quixote rolled into one—the wooden shoes (*klompen*) worn mostly by the farmers in the province of Drenthe to guard their feet against the dampness of the fields; the ice skates of Friesland's tour de force, the Elfstedentocht 11-city skating tour; and the windmills, those lyrical symbols of mind over matter. As Danish writer Andersen, himself the son of a shoemaker, wrote in 1847, "The housemaids here wear wooden shoes which look like Chinese shoes seen through a magnifying glass." Such is still the case in the North, although it is now the farmer and his wife, rather than the housemaid, who wear them. Fabled images perhaps, but here in never-never land, the dream comes true.

Home to Holland's earliest settlers, the Stone Age inhabitants who left mysterious, megalithic boulder configurations here as proof of their presence, the northern provinces of Friesland, Groningen, and Drenthe—which include four of the five islands canopied across their Wadden Sea coast and linked to the North Sea—retain much of the past, flavoring today's quintessentially Dutch villages with a spicy blend of prehistoric and medieval tartness unique to this area. Formerly cut off from the rest of the country before the Afsluitdijk—the 32-km-long (21-mi-long) dike spanning the sea from the province of North Holland to Friesland—was opened in 1932, the northern provinces are now easily accessible from the main hubs of Amsterdam and The Hague.

Friesland, the rebel of the pack, with its own language and customs, is mostly a waterway linked by patches of land, offering every conceivable water sport known to mankind, as well as some known only to the Frisians. Famous for its sailing regattas and the rare and timeless 11-city tour on ice (which takes place only once in a cold blue moon), Friesland is an outdoor temple of sport. Terps, those earthen-mound precursors to dikes, lie like goose bumps on an otherwise pancake-flat terrain, mere humps in the perennial war against the inroads of water at a below-sea-level existence.

Groningen, bordering Germany on the east, is the hopping hub of the North, an unlikely linkage of manorial splendor with university panache. Surrounded by *borgen,* those manor houses of the once-rich-and-famous, the port city of Groningen, which is also capital of the province, pulses with the academic vibrancy of its ancient seat of learning and the inherent nightlife. Despite its extra buzz of brain cells, however, this province to the east of Friesland still favors old-fashioned local traditions, such as using richly tapestried rugs as tablecloths.

Drenthe, "*mooi* (beautiful) Drenthe," as the Dutch automatically respond when you mention this province, which lies southeast of Groningen, is the noble matriarch of the Dutch family and consequently rich in history, her bodice a vestment of idyllic beauty . . . corseted by meandering Drentse Aa streams and an endless procession of poplar-lined country roads interlaced by some 300 km (187 mi) of bicycle paths winding through green fields and moors. Van Gogh himself wanted to live here forever, so intense was the painterly effect the region had on him. A worse fate could have befallen him (and did, unfortunately), and he not only cut off his ear to spite his face but also shot himself in a cornfield in France. If only he had stayed in Drenthe . . .

Clinging to the North Sea, the four Wadden Sea islands of Vlieland, Terschelling, Ameland, and Schiermonnikoog, belonging to the province of Friesland, are havens of nature for beach, bird, and bike lovers alike,

6

Coming into view as the mist rises, like a curtain being raised on a play, are these iconic images of Holland's north. First, the water-locked, seemingly unassuming land. Then the farmers, their clog-shod feet still as entrenched in the fields as Van Gogh's potato eaters. Enter the tranquil cows favored in old-master paintings and, finally, ice-skaters right out of a 17th-century Avercamp painting. In the North, the sky takes center stage, its vastness interrupted only by the sails of windmills and the spires of church towers, standing sentrylike over this land of low horizons. Here, you'll find the provinces of Friesland, Groningen, and Drenthe—three Vermeer-stock lasses adorned with pearl earrings and a strand of island beads—bowing to the audience, clear pigments of your imagination.

In addition to the local **VVV** tourist information offices in almost every town in the North and on every island, the **Noord Nederland Board of Tourism** (☎ 0900/9222, 011/31/5125/85000 from the U.S.)—whose jurisdiction covers the three provinces of Friesland, Groningen, and Drenthe—can be contacted for more information.

Numbers in the text correspond to numbers in the margin and on the North/ Islands and the Groningen maps.

If you have **4 days** With only four days, you could fly from Amsterdam into the Eelde airport near Groningen, and rent a car or take the train from there, or you could drive across the Afsluitdijk, the dike running from North Holland province to Friesland. With Eelde as your starting point—incidentally, this town has a fine Museum Voor Figuratieve Kunst De Buitenplaats (De Buitenplaats Country Estate Museum for Figurative Art), which concentrates on figurative art in The Netherlands after 1945, and merits equal attention for its organic architecture and landscape design—make for ⌘ **Groningen** ❾–⓰ ☞ for an injection of nightlife, taking in the Groninger Museum and perhaps a canal boat ride around the city before heading for the Grote Markt area and preparing for an all-nighter. Next day, a quiet tour of the Groningen countryside could be in order, either to the **Menkemaborg** ⓱ or ⌘ **Fraeylemaborg** ⓲ manor house; to the mustard-vinegar-candle-making complex in Eenrum and the seal sanctuary in nearby Pieterburen if you have children; or to the megalithic *hunebedden* tomb and information center in **Borger** ⓳, in Drenthe, and perhaps the WWII transition camp, Kamp Westerbork, near Assen if you're a history or military buff. While you're in the neighborhood, stop at the Royal Goudewaagen Delft factory in Nieuwe Buinen and ship home some hand-painted pottery. Your third day could be spent in Friesland, west of Groningen, in one of the 11 medieval towns on the famous Elfstedentocht ice-skating tour or, if it's summer, on one of the Wadden Sea islands easily accessible by ferry, and then backtrack to Amsterdam if that is your base. Leading sights in Friesland include the museums in ⌘ **Leeuwarden** ❶, that gem of a harbor town, ⌘ **Harlingen** ❸, and **Hindeloopen** ❼, famous for its elaborately painted interiors and furniture. If you decide to drive across the dike, you could do this tour in reverse, as you will be crossing into Friesland first.

If you have
9 **days**

Nine days allows you to explore both Leeuwarden and Groningen, the major cities of Friesland and Groningen provinces. Take advantage of your extra time to do some shopping in both towns. While in ⊡ **Groningen ❾**–**⓰**, rent a canoe or water bike for an afternoon, and allow some time for outdoor café sitting on the Grote Markt. Expand your repertoire in Drenthe to include an afternoon or a full day of bicycling through Van Gogh's favorite countryside, and if you have munchkins along, take them to the Verkeerspark in ⊡ **Assen ⓴** for a half day in this driving-course park for youngsters where they learn and practice the rules of the road in kid-friendly vehicles. As you traverse through Friesland, be sure to catch Mata Hari at the Fries Museum in ⊡ **Leeuwarden ❶**; visit the one-of-a-kind planetarium in **Franeker ❷**; buy some world-famous ceramics at the Royal Tichelaar factory in **Makkum ❺** and some ornately painted wooden pieces in **Hindeloopen ❼** (where you can see rooms full of the local art at the Hidde Nijland Stichting Museum, and ice skates galore chronicling the Elfstedentocht tour at Het Eerste Friese Schaatsmuseum). From there, you could spy on Jopie Huisman's unique junk collection, which he turned into art at his one-man museum in **Workum ❻**; have a Kodak moment in postcard-perfect **Sloten ❽**; and do the daylong Aldfaers Erf Route of traditional homes and shops, beginning in ⊡ **Bolsward ❹** (by car or bike). Be sure to allow time, weather permitting, to visit one or more of the Wadden Sea islands, such as **Texel ㉑**–**㉓**, **Terschelling ㉔**, or ⊡ **Schiermonnikoog ㉕**, to comb them with a leisurely bike outing. If you're really lucky and it's hot, beach it.

---

and for the city-weary. Although similar in many respects, each island has its own character and appeal, the closest being only a 20-minute ferry ride from the coast and the farthest just two hours away. Of Caribbean clime they are not, but they do enjoy about twice as much sunshine as the mainland, albeit more breeze. Two of the islands are off-limits to visitors' cars, making them particularly captivating refuges of peace and quiet, and the tidal mudflats of the Wadden Sea make for a uniquely curious approach.

Late spring, summer, and early fall are, of course, the best times to tour the North and the islands, especially if you like water sports, camping, biking, and hiking. For ice-skating fans, a good Dutch winter replete with frozen canals and the chance-in-a-lifetime Elfstedentocht is a chilling enticement.

Exploring the North & the Islands

You can get a good taste of the area by beginning in Leeuwarden, capital of Friesland, then looping through the Frisian countryside and heading either westward to the Elfstedentocht towns and on to one or more of the islands, or eastward to the thriving city of Groningen and the idyllic Drenthe countryside. If you are driving, there is no problem in getting around these relatively off-the-beaten-track provinces. If not, your best bet maybe to take the train from Amsterdam to Enkhuizen, from which you can catch the ferry that crosses the IJsselmeer to Stavoren in Friesland, where another train continues to Leeuwarden via Hindeloopen, Workum, and Sneek. From Leeuwarden there are trains and buses that thread out through the northern sector.

About the Restaurants & Hotels

Although Vincent van Gogh's brooding painting of "The Potato Eaters" was based on the province of Noord Brabant, it could just as easily depict this area. When the lakes and canals begin to freeze over and the promise of another 11-city ice tour, the Elfstedentocht, approaches, northerners rely on their most satiating staples to get them by, one of which is the potato. Dishes such as *stamppot,* a wedding of cabbage and the spud, often laced with a vegetable or two, have wedged their way into the comfort zone and stomachs of the North where fields are starched with potato crop. Other marriages of hearty ingredients such as brown beans and bacon *bruine bonen met spek,* and lamb (*lamsvlees*) with mustard and honey sauce, all local products, are abundant here. One of the most hearty of Dutch foods, the thick, sausage-studded pea soup known as *erwtensoep,* which typically kicks in as the leaves begin to fall, is a national—and Fodor's—favorite that also seems to line the extensive waterways of this region. Spicy mustard soup, with its kick-in-the-pants flavor, is equally popular and a must-try on your culinary byways. Rounding out the menu are cranberries, homegrown on the island of Terschelling, shrimp and mussels crawling in from the North Sea, and *suikerbrood,* literally sugar bread, a Frisian quick energy fix from the northwestern province of Friesland that's punctuated and coated with enough locally processed sugar to set you reeling on your route. Not surprisingly, with all that heavy food and a tad more oppressive climate, life tends to move a bit slower in the North. The 6 PM dinner hour is still sacred, as in the rest of the country, and often arrives even a bit earlier given the preponderance of early-rising farmers in the area. Doors also seem to shut a bit earlier in all but perhaps the livelier city of Groningen and a few other outposts. Cafés are your best bet for standard Dutch fare, while other ethnic restaurants are abundant and recommended.

Manor house or lighthouse tonight? The North and the islands have a particularly varied range of places to prop your pillow, from the decked-out luxury of the romantic lighthouse, the Vuurtoren, in Harlingen, to the oh-so-idyllic but classy bed-and-breakfast lodgings such as Logement 't Olde Hof in Westervelde near Assen, to the gracious old country houses, such as De Klinze in Oudkerk, or Landgoed Lauswolt in Beetsterzwaag. The Erfgoed Logies group (☎ 050/535–0202 for color brochure ⊟ 050/535–0203 ⊕ www.erfgoedlogies.nl) of historic B&B properties offers a very high standard of accommodation in a wide variety of characteristically Dutch farmhouses and estates. In July and August rates are higher and rooms are at a premium, so be sure to make reservations in advance. Many hotels are closed from November to March, particularly on the islands. Do not assume that all rooms have air-conditioning, but you can normally count on room TV and telephones.

WHAT IT COSTS In euros*					
	$$$$	$$$	$$	$	¢
RESTAURANTS	over €30	€22–€30	€15–€22	€10–€15	under €10
HOTELS	over €230	€165–€230	€120–€165	€75–€120	under €75

*Restaurant prices are per person for a main course only, excluding tax (6% for food and 19% for alcoholic beverages) and service; note that if a restaurant offers only prix-fixe (set-price) meals, it has been given the price category that reflects the full prix-fixe price. Hotel prices are for a standard double room in high season, including the 6% VAT (value-added tax); higher prices (inquire when booking) prevail for any meal plans.

Timing

Though the fields and pastures of Friesland stay green practically all year around, the drizzles and showers of late fall and early spring have much to do with it. Your best chances of good weather, then, are the traditional months, May through September. Since Gelderland and Limburg are more popular vacation destinations for Hollanders, the peak holiday months of July and August are not as packed here and there is a better chance of landing a hotel room without advance reservations. When it comes to Drenthe and Groningen, however, their popularity with the vacationing Dutch means you need to be sure you have reservations.

FRIESLAND

Throughout eternity, the Dutch have had to keep their heads above water, living as they do on land reclaimed from the sea and surrounded by dikes—the saucer effect. But the Frisian people of the province of Friesland seem to delight in keeping their heads at water's edge in a land stenciled over a fluid background of seemingly endless waterways. Floating, as it were, this outdoor sports haven is second to none, home to every imaginable water sport, including the popular sailing regatta that ignites the Frisian town of Sneek near Bolsward the first Friday in August, and the infamously grueling Elfstedentocht 11-city ice-skating race and tour, which takes place only when this piece of heaven totally freezes over. At last count there were 14,184 acres of water, including 13 large lakes and 17 smaller ones, not to mention the network of canals and streams. Clean air, a profusion of nature reserves, lush pastureland, 22,487 acres of forest, with scenery dotted by Frisian cows and horses and steeply sloping farmhouse roofs, all primly and properly reflected in the underpinning maze of waterways, make this northwestern province very seductive.

Fiercely independent, the feisty Frisians boast their own language (Frisian), an ancient tongue that has Germanic roots with traces of Dutch, English, and German still apparent; their own flag, bearing the leaves of the water lily—their "national" plant—appearing like red hearts on a white and blue ground; their own "national" anthem; their own "national" animal, the swan, whose image adorns the peaks of many rooftops; and, indeed, their own outlook on life. Generally regarded as hospitable, reliable, and straightforward, Frisians are also known to be fiercely stubborn in their individuality. Leeuwarden, capital of the province, is the largest Frisian town, with bustling markets, shopping, and a decent nightlife, and Sloten, a mere dot of a village, is so picturesque that it challenges art itself.

Leeuwarden

1 *132 km (83 mi) north of Amsterdam.*

Fodor'sChoice
★

Eclectic and electric Leeuwarden, capital of the province of Friesland, was the official residence of the first king of The Netherlands, William I, and was also the birthplace of two artists specializing in deception: Escher, master of geometric distortions and tricks of perspective, and Mata Hari, the dancer-turned-spy who flaunted her notorious brand of deceit. Also born here was Saskia, wife of the great Dutch master of art, Rembrandt, whose portrait of her is in Leeuwarden's Fries Museum. When the ice thickens, which happens quite infrequently, Leeuwarden is also the starting and finishing point for a uniquely Dutch ice-skating race, the Elfstedentocht, that traverses 11 medieval cities across Friesland (see the Close Up box, "Poetry In Motion–The Elfstedentocht"). During the thaw of the year, it's the cows who get all the attention here in one of the largest cattle markets in Europe, a weekly event proving Leeuwarden's position as the focal point of the Dutch dairy industry. Just ask "Us Mem," the cow that stands over the town (at the plaza off Harlingersingel) as a proud symbol of Frisian prosperity. Leeuwarden has a strong U.S. connection as well, for it was here in 1782 that the

Dining: Eet Smakelijk! Cordon Bleu it's not, but Dutch cuisine *is* making a bit of headway over what it used to be, and the North offers its share of star chefs, although the emphasis is still on simple, hearty food—much akin to the Dutch character itself. Savory winter stews, such as *hutspot*, and soups such as *erwtensoep* (thick pea soup with bacon or sausage) and *mosterdsoep* (mustard soup) are comfort foods that slide down really well when the ice takes over outside. Top it off with a Hooghoudt *jenever* (gin) from Groningen, or a Beerenburg liqueur from Bolsward, touted as Friesland's national drink, traditionally sipped from *fûgeltsjes*, special stemless glasses, and you'll be ready for the Elfstedentocht. Fill up those extra corners with a slice of *karnemelkbrood* (buttermilk bread) and wash it down with *anijsmelk* (warm milk flavored with aniseed), or a mug of Frisian tea served extra sweet. *Lekker!* (Delicious!) The Frisians also have their own *Frysk Menu*, a three-course menu, which often includes the local delicacy known as *Flielânske fiskskûtel*, a fish stew with potatoes and onions that originally hails from the island of Vlieland. Throughout the North, there are always the advertised *Dagschotels*, the daily special menus or "tourist menus," which are a good three-course value. Eet Smakelijk! ("Enjoy!" Indeed).

The Great Outdoors If it's sleep you're after, don't come here; if it's rest and repose with some physical activity and fresh air mixed in, then turn down the corners on that Amsterdam chapter and go north, young man or lady. Don your wellies (that's waterproof boots to a Brit) and your woolies, depending on the season you arrive in the North or the Wadden Islands, because this is action country, despite its reputation as a sleepy, somewhat backward region (what isn't, in all fairness, compared to Amsterdam?). If you can't find a sport or outdoor activity in the North, you haven't yet crossed the threshold into Friesland, Groningen, and Drenthe. The entire area, comprising some of the most splendid scenery found in Europe, is nearly overrun with miles and miles of cycling and rambling paths and is home to annual biking races and walking tours. And if you want to kick up a bit more dust, try horseback riding, all manner of water sports (particularly in Friesland), and, in winter, ice-skating on the innumerable canals and lakes gracing the lowlands. Those with a penchant for the obscure will certainly want to try a local version of pole vaulting called *fierljeppen,* which takes place across canals and ditches, and "horizontal mountain climbing" called *Wadlopen* (mudflat walking)—wading thigh-deep across the mudflats to the Wadden Sea island of Schiermonnikoog. If luck is with you, you'll hit an Elfstedentocht winter and can watch or participate in the 11-city ice-skating race and tour through Friesland's most picturesque medieval towns. Throughout the year, you can also imitate the famous tour by bike, canoe, horseback, boat, motorbike, car, or even foot. Route information and imitation stamp cards to support your claim that you've traversed each town in the legendary manner are available at local VVV information offices.

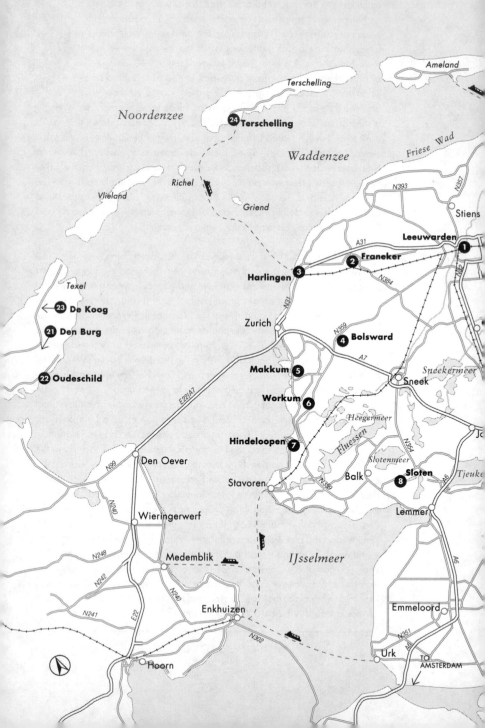

The North & the Islands

Ameland

Terschelling

Noordenzee

24 Terschelling

Waddenzee

Friese Wad

N393

N357

Richel

Griend

Stiens

Vlieland

N392

A31

1

Leeuwarden

2 Franeker

N384

3 Harlingen

Texel

De Koog **23**

Zurich

N359

4 Bolsward

A7

Sneekermeer

21 Den Burg

N31

5 Makkum

Sneek

22 Oudeschild

6 Workum

Heegermeer

N354

E22/A7

Fluessen

Jo

7 Hindeloopen

Slotenmeer

8 Sloten

Tjeuke

N99

Den Oever

N240

Stavoren

Balk

N359

Lemmer

A6

Wieringerwerf

IJsselmeer

N248

Medemblik

Emmeloord

N242

N240

E22

Enkhuizen

N351

N241

N302

Urk

TO AMSTERDAM

Hoorn

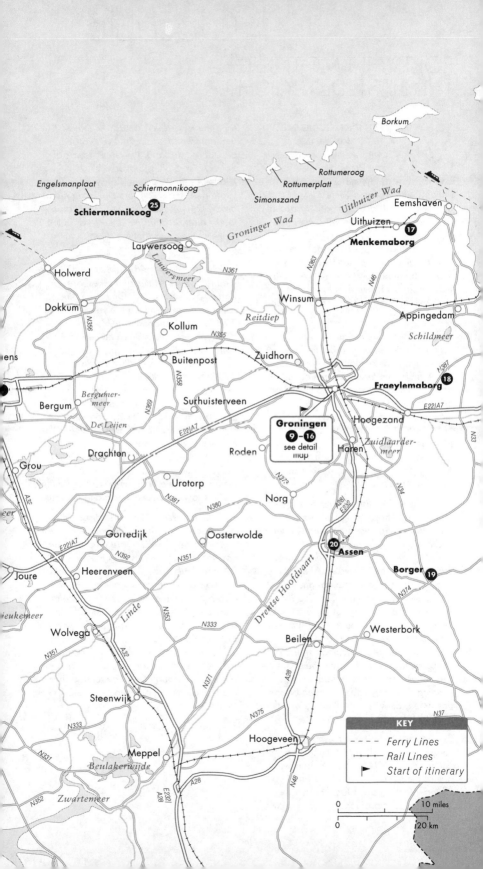

CloseUp

POETRY IN MOTION: THE ELFSTEDENTOCHT

WHEN IT'S FREEZING IN FRIESLAND, the most northwestern province, the Dutch become frantic . . . with joy, that is. No other nation waits for frigid winters like Holland does—and with good reason. It's one of the few times during the year when the otherwise anti-nationalistic Dutch rally in anticipation of the Elfstedentocht, the one-day, magical mystery ice-skating marathon that methodically and lyrically winds its way through 11 medieval towns over 200 km (130 mi) of solidly frozen canals and waterways.

Today, it's become the most cherished sporting event embraced by the Dutch and draws hundreds of thousands of spectators to the Frisian waterways when conditions are ripe. Most of the other 15-million-plus inhabitants adhere like veritable icicles to their television sets, with press coverage beginning at 5 AM for the 5:30 AM start (there is no particular day or month to start, only when the ice is ripe; usually in January or February and, of course, many years not at all).

To be anywhere along the route is to be part of a real happening with wooden-shoe-clad oom-pah-pah musicians, banners and Frisian flags flying, policemen parading on skates, and hundreds of foodies lining the in-town stretches where hearty pea soup (erwtensoep) and hot chocolate are served up. Capping it off is Beerenburg juniper liqueur to help insulate the spectators under their sea of symbolic orange attire, reveling in Royal Dutch House of Orange pandemonium. In the background, windmills wave their sails as the "schuss" of skaters can be heard, winding their way under wooden bridges, possessed, as was Hans Brinker, with the poetry of motion.

For the race to be run it must be, of course, bitter cold; in fact, it must be below -15°C (5°F) for more than a week before the Ice Master declares an Elfstedentocht year. In fact, there have only been 15 marathons run since 1909

(and the record is 6 hours, 47 minutes). Beginning and ending in Leeuwarden, capital of Friesland, the circuit towns of Sneek, IJlst, Sloten, Stavoren, Hindeloopen, Workum, Bolsward, Harlingen, Franeker, and Dokkum (in that order) light up like neon indicators on a tourist map, bristling with ice fever in the wake of the news that the race is on.

It's a grueling competition, but one to which the long-legged, hardy Dutch, weaned on ice skates and bikes, are particularly well suited. Of the 15 official races to date, spanning the years from 1909 to the last one in 1997, only the doggedly tenacious Dutch have ever triumphed, although foreigners do dare to compete against the stalwart natives. In 1933, an American diplomat, L. Süssdorf, was the first foreigner to finish the official tour, although he did not come in first. Of the more than 16,000 who normally participate, only about 300 qualify for the actual competitive part of the race, whereby they are given a number (and a prayer) along with an official card that they must get stamped as they whiz by the various towns' checkpoints along the route.

The official racers, limited to those who glaze across the finish line within the winning-time-plus-20%, are awarded the coveted Eleven Cities Cross medal, the Elfstedenkruis. "Tour riders," as the rest of the 16,000 contingency are called, will also receive the cross if they finish before the ice curtain falls at midnight. Official winners (distinguished from the large pack of "tour riders") receive no prize money, just a crack at eternal fame, in addition to the cross, a medallion, and their name on a perpetual trophy that they relinquish to the skating museum in Hindeloopen.

first official recognition of the new American nation was declared, prompting a much-needed loan from the Dutch government. Local ties go back even further than that, however, because Peter Stuyvesant, an early governor of New York, then called Nieuw Amsterdam, hailed from this area. All in all, it's a charming town where the carillon bells peal out over tiled roofs and canals.

Fodor'sChoice Home to one of the world's finest collections of ceramics, the **Neder-**
★ **lands Keramiekmuseum Het Princessehof** (The Netherlands Ceramics Museum—The Princess's Palace) takes pride of place in Leeuwarden's old part of town near the Oldehove tower. The birthplace of artist M. C. Escher in 1898 and the former residence of Marie Louise of Hessen-Kassell, widow of the first prince of Orange, Johan William Friso (whose 1740 dining room has been preserved) is a grand Baroque monument. A treasure trove of international ceramics, both ancient and modern, the museum documents the history of Asian and European pottery, featuring a remarkable collection of Chinese stoneware and porcelain dating from the 3rd millennium BC through the 20th century. By pattern and subject matter, it displays one of the largest tile collections in the world and is especially famous for its Spanish, Portuguese, Italian, and Dutch tiles, the Spanish ones displayed in a vaulted room reminiscent of Spain's Alhambra palace. There is a fine café and also affordable ceramic giftware in the museum shop. ⊠ *Grote Kerkstraat 11, 8911 DZ, from railway station, follow wide street across Nieuwestad canal, then left to next bridge and continue along Kleine Kerkstraat* ☎ *058/294–8958* ⬚ *€5, free on Wed., combination ticket to the Fries Museum €7.50* ⊙ *May–Aug., daily 11–5; Sept.–Apr., Tues.–Sun. 11–5.*

Tinker, tailor, soldier, spy . . . they're all here at the **Fries Museum en Verzetsmuseum** (Frisian Museum and Museum of the Resistance), where 19th-century Frisian shops and period rooms, costumes, a war resistance exhibit, and Mata Hari are all featured in this ornate Renaissance-era building, the **Kanselarij**, or the Chancellery (linked on two sides of the street by an underground tunnel), where George of Saxony lived when he governed the region in the 16th century. An unlikely place, then, for Rembrandt's treasured portrait of his wife to end up? Not at all, for she was born in this town as the daughter of a former mayor of Leeuwarden and married in 1634 in the nearby village of Sint Annaparochie.

Mata Hari, the other renowned local daughter, has been accorded an entire room crammed with memorabilia, including her original scrapbook, her perfume bottle, and a monogrammed linen napkin. There's also a multimedia display about her mysterious life. Born Margaretha Zelle (Leeuwarden 1876–Paris 1917), Mata Hari—a Malaysian nickname literally translated as "eye of the day," which she certainly became—found herself divorced and poor and set her sights on Paris, where she sensationalized the world as one of the highest-paid exotic dancers in Europe. During World War I, she found herself once again in an even more precarious position: suspected double agent for both the Germans (code name "H-21") and the French, a role for which she proved naively unsuitable. In 1917, she was arrested in Paris as a pro-German spy and was ultimately sentenced to death. Twelve French rifle shots put an end to her femme fatale life, but her enigmatic story lives on here. The Fries Museum also houses a world-famous collection of silver, highlighted by the Beerenburg Cup, a 16th-century test of "spirit" whereby the procurer spun the windmill on it while trying to down the liquor inside before the *molen* (windmill) stopped turning; failing, he became responsible for a round of drinks. Look for the silver *Rinkelbels,* akin to present-day rattles, given to celebrate the birth of a child. Dutch ones had whistles on them, and sometimes a stone or animal tooth to ward off evil spirits. ☒ *Turfmarkt 11, 8911 KS* ☎*058/255–5500* ⊕*www.friesmuseum. nl* ☒ *€5, free on Wed., combination ticket for the Nederlands Ceramics Museum €7.50* ⊘ *May–Aug., daily 11–5; Sept.–Apr., Tues.–Sun. 11–5.*

Standing in a blissfully peaceful square in the old part of town and close to the Ceramics Museum, the 13th-century **Grotekerk** (Great Church), a Jacobin church, was reconstructed and restored over a span of centuries. It is the traditional burial place of the Nassau line, ancestors of the royal family, and is well known for its large Müller organ, frescoes, and stained-glass windows. ☒ *Jacobinerkerkhof* ☎ *058/212–8313* ☒ *Free* ⊘ *June–Aug., Tues.–Sat. 2–4.*

need a break?

In an old wooden sailing boat, you can enjoy no fewer than 90 kinds of traditional Dutch pancakes, both sweet and savory. The **Pannekoekschip** (Pancake Ship; ☒ Willemskade 69 ☎ 058/212–0903) is moored midway between the railway station and the center of town and is open Tuesday 5–9 and Wednesday–Sunday noon–9 (note that pancakes are not breakfast fare for the Dutch).

Mata Hari lived in Leeuwarden from 1883 to 1890, and her house is now the **Frysk Letterkundich Museum en Dokumintaasjesintrum** (Frisian Literary Museum and Document Center), which promotes the use of the Frisian language through exhibitions on Frisian literature. (A rather small statue of the famed dancer-spy can be seen at the Korfmakerspijp bridge near her birthplace, now a hair salon, at No. 33 De Kelders.) For a special peek at some interesting house gables, one of Leeuwarden's secret treasures, take a stroll along Wijde Gasthuissteeg, accessible from the Grote Kerkstraat, and look at the back sides of the houses. ☒ *Grote Kerkstraat 212, 8911 EG* ☎ *058/212–0834* ⊕ *www.flmd.nl* ☒ *€.50* ⊘ *Tues.–Fri. 9–12:30 and 1–5, Mon. 1–5.*

Facing each other across the leafy **Hofplein** are Leeuwarden's **Stadhuis** (Town Hall) and **Hof,** which was the former residence of the Frisian *stadhouders* (governors). In the center of the square is a statue of William Louis, the first stadhouder, locally known as *Us Heit* ("Our Father").

No, you're definitely not in Pisa, but the **Oldehove** tower also leans. Although when building began in 1529 it was designed to be the tallest tower in The Netherlands, the foundation along with its future started to sink, and it was left at a height of merely 130 feet. Fine views are yours if you climb the tower. ☒ *Oldehoosterkerkhof, 8911 DH* ☒ *€1.15* ⊘ *May–Sept., Tues.–Sat. 2–5.*

Where to Eat & Stay

$–$$ ✕ **De Grote Wielen.** After a day on your feet, treat yourself to dinner lakeside where the ripple of the water, reeds swaying in the breeze, serenading waterfowl, and the soft light of evening will surely put you at ease. Saucy choices include eel with rémoulade sauce, salmon with white wine sauce, a vegetarian combo, rabbit stroganoff, pork with creamed mushroom sauce, or veal with calvados sauce. ☒ *Butlan 1* ☎ *0511/431777* ▤ *MC, V* ⊘ *Closed Mon.*

$–$$ ✕ **Eetcafé Het Leven.** After 10 years waitressing, Manon Planting up and bought this intimate but lively eatery and has made it into a huge success with a good-value menu full of ethnic surprises and vegetarian dishes. *Gado Gado met Kip* is an exotic mix of rice, chicken, stir-fried vegetables, and peanuts in a peanut sauce worth writing home about (a veggie version is also available). There is a small salad bar (ask to partake from it first, if you like, because Dutch custom is to eat it *with* your meal). "Swingnight," with funk, soul, mellow, R&B, and disco, is Saturday night 10–2 or 3 AM, free admission, in their Café Alfred Silbermann next door. *Kwark,* a yogurt tart with fruit, is the dessert specialty. ⊠ *Druifstreek 57 (down the street from the Fries Museum)* ☎ *058/212–1233* ⊟ *AE, V.*

¢–$$ ✕ **Spinoza.** Three rooms, a 1600s cellar bar, and the shady garden courtyard of an 18th-century city mansion make up this popular, cozy restaurant. It is one of those cavernous spaces that, through the patina of age and subtle lighting, manages also to be intimate. Specialties include a Frisian stew with Beerenburg liqueur, a beef and chicken dish in a spicy tomato sauce, and spareribs. Their special menu features ethnic foods and changes every three months. There is also a grill room, a theater-restaurant for live performances, and regular medieval dinners where food served on wooden plates is meant to be eaten with the hands (call for times and reservations). Another section, Jefferson's Wine & Dine Room, caters to students and is less expensive. Friday night, a DJ finds himself in the cellar, and Spinoza really becomes a fun place. ⊠ *Eewal 50–52* ☎ *058/212–9393* ⊟ *AE, DC, MC, V.*

★ $–$$$$ ▦ **Hotel-Paleis Het Stadhouderlijk Hof.** History precedes you at this former royal palace, where the standard rates aren't princely but the room styles and quality of accommodations are fit for any king and his queen. Built in 1550, the palace was originally inhabited by William I, Prince of Orange, Duke of Nassau 1580–84. At one time or another, the current Queen Beatrix's ancestors have reportedly all stayed here, the house having been in their possession until 1971. The red carpet now awaits you. Ideally located in the old part of town, just opposite the Town Hall, it's the only place in The Netherlands where you can sleep in a royal palace. For true luxe, the William Ludovicus Suite has a cast-iron, four-poster bed and an enormous bathroom with a Roman tub under a lighted star ceiling supporting three showerheads. So-called "business rooms" are a high-tech indulgence featuring CD players, leather lounge chairs, and showers with six sense-surround heads. Depending on the season, breakfast, featuring scrumptious homemade bread, may be served in the garden. For dinners with a royal touch, head to the hotel's Restaurant Bellfleur, replete with haute cuisine, garden views, and grand bouquets. The oldest room of the palace, a 15th-century vaulted cellar called the *hofkelder* is reserved for special parties. Adding to the allure here, room rates range from the luxe to the very affordable. ⊠ *Hofplein 29, 8911 HJ* ☎ *058/216–2180* 🖷 *058/216–3890* ⊕ *www. stadhouderlijkhof.nl* ➳ *28 rooms* ♨ *Restaurant, café, cable TV, some pets allowed; no a/c* ⊟ *AE, DC, MC, V* ⎟◎⎟ *BP.*

$$$ ▦ **Bilderberg Oranjehotel.** Right in the city center directly across from the train station in this royal capital of Friesland, this hotel offers a very high standard with a king's ransom of amenities to choose from, depending on the level of room, and is part of the Bilderberg group of highly individualized hotels found throughout Holland. Pip's Pub is a popular, English-style meeting place, and the restaurants serve both Frisian (hearty cooking with meat, potatoes, and pea soup) and international cuisine. Bike and boating excursions, typically offered by this chain of hotels, introduce you to the wealth of sites and waterways for which Friesland is famous. A champagne breakfast will set you back €13.50. ⊠ *Stationsweg 4, 8911 AG* ☎ *058/212–6241* 🖷 *058/212–1441* ⊕ *www. bilderberg.nl* ➳ *78 rooms* ♨ *2 restaurants, in-room data ports, minibars, cable TV, tennis court, pool, gym, hair salon, sauna, some pets allowed* ⊟ *AE, DC, MC, V* ⎟◎⎟ *BP.*

$$–$$$ ▦ **Landgoed De Klinze.** In a wooded town not far from Leeuwarden, De Klinze is a semi-resort created from a 17th-century country estate. The roomy suites in the manor house are furnished with vintage furniture and antiques; the bright and spacious guest rooms are in a separate, mod-

ern wing that also houses a spa. Frisian horses and carriage rides complete the fantasy. Dinner is in the former parlors, with views of the woods, and the cuisine is Mediterranean. Bicycles are available for jaunts through the countryside. ⊠ *Van Sminiaweg 32–36, 9064 KC Oudkerk, (10 km [6 mi] northeast of Leeuwarden)* ☎ *058/256–1050* 🖷 *058/256–1060* ⊕ *www.klinze.nl* ⇝ *22 rooms, 5 suites* ♿ *Restaurant, cable TV, indoor pool, hair salon, spa, bicycles, meeting rooms; no a/c in rooms* ▭ *AE, DC, MC, V* ℱ⊙ℱ *EP.*

¢ 🖫 **Bed & Brochje A. de Haas.** If you don't mind sharing a place with another family (complete with three children and two cats) in a nonsmoking environment, including a shared bathroom, and you're looking for a friendly and inexpensive option, then this one's for you. This spot is 10 minutes from the station by bus (Line 1) and is open only in July and August. ⊠ *Jelle Brouwerwei 18, 8915 KA* ☎ *058/216–0456* ◿ *a. dehaas@zwo.nhl.nl* ⇝ *2 rooms* ♿ *Cable TV, some pets allowed; no a/c, no room phones* ▭ *No credit cards* ℱ⊙ℱ *BP.*

Nightlife

Café Mukkes (⊠ Grote Hoogstraat 26 ☎ 058/215–9800) brings a rousing selection of local bands to a crowd of enthusiastic young fans. The only Guinness to be found for miles around is served at the **Irish Pub** (⊠ Gouverneursplein 37 ☎ 058/213–7740) along with lilting Irish music (and even an Irish breakfast). **Toog** (⊠ Ruiterskwartier 91 ☎ 058/212–9360) is a popular option. **Vat 69** (⊠ Nieuwestad 63–65 ☎ 058/213–4792) plays a variety of music.

Sports & the Outdoors

Leeuwarden is a great base from which to set out to enjoy the area's many water sports and quirky indigenous activities or the islands covered in this chapter. It is from here that the celebrated **Elfstedentocht** 11-city ice-skating tour begins and ends; for more information on this famous event, *see* the Close Up box in this chapter.

CANOEING Friesland offers a wealth of canoeing opportunities along quiet countryside waterways and the connecting canals that course through attractive towns. Printed canoeing routes and special maps are available; check with the respective tourist offices. Five of the largest canoe-renting facilities in Friesland are **Watersportbedrijf De Drijfveer** (⊠ U. Twijnstrawei 31, 8491 CJ Akkrum ☎ 0566/652789); **Konoverhuur Hollema** (⊠ Tsjerkepaed 5, 9264 TG Earnewald ☎ 0511/539213); **De Kievit** (⊠ Jousterweg 82, 8465 PL Oudehaske ☎ 0513/677658); **De Ulepanne/Balk** (⊠ Tsjamkedijkje 1, 8561 HA Balk ☎ 0514/602982); and **Makkumerstrand** (⊠ Suderseewei 19, 5784 GK Makkum ☎ 0515/232285).

FIERLJEPPEN A uniquely Frisian sport is *fierljeppen*, called *polsstokverspringen* in Dutch, which involves pole vaulting over canals (and sometimes in them). It originates, so they say, from farmers having to negotiate the drainage ditches between their fields. For a taste of canal hopping, don't miss the main competition held in Winsum in August—truly for the odd-event seeker. Further information is available from the VVV.

SAILING & Friesland is bordered by the large and windswept IJsselmeer (Lake IJssel) and cut through with a swath of lakes, canals, and small rivers that offer myriad sailing and boating opportunities. Throughout summer you will find weekend racing on the Frisian lakes, including the main event, a two-week series of **Skûtjesilen Races** (late July) using the uniquely Dutch vessels, *skûtjes*, wide-bottom sailing barges built to navigate shallow waters. More than 150 companies throughout Friesland rent boats and sailboats, including **De Blieken** (⊠ Garde Jagersweg 4–5, 9001 ZB Grou ☎ 0566/621335); **Top En Twel Zeilcentrum** (⊠ It Ges 6, 8606

JK Sneek ☎ 0515/419192); and **Watersportcamping Heeg** (✉ De Burd 25a, 8621 JX Heeg ☎ 0515/442328).

Shopping
The biggest market in Friesland takes place in Leeuwarden every Friday 8–4 at Wilhelminaplein/Zaailand. Late shopping (until 9 PM) is on Thursday; and the old-time shops on Nieuwesteeg, including the **Museumwinkel** (Museum Shop; ☎ 058/215–3427) at No. 5–7, are nostalgically rewarding.

Franeker

❷ *17 km (11 mi) west of Leeuwarden, 20 km (13 mi) north of Makkum, 120 km (78 mi) north of Amsterdam.*

In the Middle Ages, Franeker was a leading academic town. Although there is no university here today, there are Renaissance gables aplenty, pretty canals, and a highly unusual museum.

Fodor'sChoice
★
A late 17th-century, still fully functioning planetarium built, by candlelight, into his living room ceiling by a self-educated, amateur astronomer using 10,000 handmade nails: that's the marvel of the **Eise Eisinga Planetarium,** the creation of math prodigy and wool comber Eise Eisinga, hand-fashioned between 1774 and 1781. His motive? To allay the fears of the local townspeople who were panicked by a local clergyman's prediction that May 8, 1774, would mark the end of the world, when a constellation of the planets Mercury, Venus, Mars, and Jupiter was set to collide with the moon. Eisinga, who had written a brilliant mathematics text at the age of 17 (on display here), set about to prove him wrong with an elaborate reconstruction of the planetary system, including multiple moving moon and sun dials, so ingeniously calibrated that it still precisely indicates the current day, date, and times of sunrise and sunset, not to mention every solar and lunar eclipse. Amazingly, no essential part has ever had to be replaced. Eise's motto? Before you enter the gabled house, look to the right of the main door above a little gate. In Frisian it says: "Voersint eer Ghy begint." (Look before you leap.) ✉ *Eise Eisingastraat 3, 8801 KE* ☎ *0517/393070* ⊕ *www.planetariumfriesland.nl* 🎫 *€3* ⊙ *Apr.–Oct., Tues.–Sat. 10–5, Sun. and Mon. 1–5; Nov.–Mar., Tues.–Sat. 10–5, Sun. 1–5.*

> **need a break?**
> Travel back in time (but right next door) from the Eise Eisinga Planetarium to the cozy Jugendstil/art nouveau tea and coffee shop **De Tuinkamer** (✉ Eise Eisingastraat 2 ☎ 0517/397474 ⊙ Tues.–Sun. 9:30–6). It has, arguably, the best Dutch *appelgebak* (apple pie) in The Netherlands. Afternoon or evening high tea with scones is also available, as are soups, sandwiches, and pancakes. A summer-garden room is in back.

Harlingen

❸ *30 km (20 mi) west of Leeuwarden.*

Fodor'sChoice
★
A pin drop of a seaport, fitted out with gabled merchant houses that wouldn't be out of place in Amsterdam, Harlingen is a place where you may want to linger instead of using it merely as a departure point for the Wadden Sea islands of Terschelling or Vlieland. It's a gem of a harbor town, with none of the seediness of some ports. One of the best reasons to come here, however, is its famous lighthouse hotel, the Vuurtoren. From the main Noorderhaven canal, go one street over to Voorstraat for some of the best local shops. At night, walk along Zoutsloot street

to see how the locals live in their prim little lace-curtained houses fronted by gas lanterns. **Gemeentemuseum Het Hannemahuis** (Hannemahuis Municipal Museum), in a lovely old merchant's house, features local Harlingen history, shipping, and tile production. ⊠ *Voorstraat 56, 8861 BM* ☎ *0517/413658* ⊿ *€1.55* ⊘ *Mid-Mar.–late June, Tues.–Sat. 1:30–5; late June–late Sept., Tues.–Sat. 10–5, Sun. 1:30–5; late Sept.–late Nov., Tues.–Sat. 1:30–5.*

At Voorstraat 84 in Harlingen, just down the street from the Hannemahuis museum, you can visit the workshop and purchase ceramics at the **Harlinger Aardewerk en Tegelfabriek** (Pottery and Tile Factory), but we recommend saving your money for the considerably more beautiful ceramics only 16 km (10 mi) south in Makkum at Koninklijke Tichelaar Makkum.

Where to Eat & Stay

¢–$$ ✕ **Restaurant de Gastronoom.** A *très chic* French overture begins with lobster soup, an aperitif glass of potato cocktail with a smidgen of seafood and succulent brown rolls, then open ravioli with spinach and mussels in a crab sauce . . . and that's just for starters. Dine by candlelight to the sound of the nearby carillon while you contemplate saving enough money for the surrounding shops. Friendly owners Marco and Inez keep it oh so classy. (There is a special arrangement with the Vuurtoren lighthouse hotel for a six-course dinner with a different wine for each course at €55 per person.) ⊠ *Voorstraat 38* ☎ *0517/412172* ⊕ *www.degastronoom.nl* ⋒ *Reservations essential* ▭ *AE, DC, V.*

★ $$$$ ▥ **Vuurtoren (Lighthouse) van Harlingen.** Romance is the real reason to come to Harlingen. For once in a lifetime, experience the unparalleled rush that comes from sleeping at the top of a luxurious lighthouse—two people only, please. The romantic dream of Gosse Beerda, a visionary and former journalist in his mid-thirties, was to do just that, so he bought a lighthouse whose lights had been extinguished and renovated it to the hilt. The ultimate getaway, the Vuurtoren features a deluxe circular shower with heated-tile surround and piped-in music, a glamorous, contemporary lounge-bedroom with a kidney-shape bed (with built-in CD player) that doubles as a sofa, and an enclosed hull with dishes and silverware, all encircled by a 360-degree view of the harbor and Harlingen. Take your coffee or tea, champagne or wine, from the minibar—or even the breakfast feast left discreetly inside the door by lighthouse keeper Hilda—up to the top observation deck, from where, on a clear day, you can see the Wadden Sea islands and their respective lighthouses. A VHF radio lets you eavesdrop on the dialogue between sailing vessels and the harbormaster, and there's a wind-force direction meter for those with nothing better to do. Beerda now also offers, canal-side in Harlingen, a two-person luxury lifeboat fitted out with a red-cedar bath. Reserve far in advance for either. ⊠ *Lighthouse, Havenweg 1 (information office, Voorstraat 34), 8861 BL* ☎ *0515/540550* ▤ *0515/543605* ⊕ *www.vuurtoren-harlingen.nl* ⇨ *1 room* ⚘ *Minibars, cable TV; no a/c, no room phones* ▭ *No credit cards* ⦿❘ *BP.*

$ ▥ **Het Heerenlogement.** Once the home of a wealthy family, this imposing, all-white 16th-century building has been converted to a prim and proper hotel and overlooks one of the many rippling harbor canals snaking through Harlingen. Beerenburg, a special Frisian borrel or drink made with a secret recipe of spices and herbs, is a specialty served in the hotel pub, and the restaurant food is Dutch with a French accent. Access to the harbor, if you're setting off to one of the islands, is only a 10-minute walk or a cab ride away. ⊠ *Franekereind 23, 8861 AA* ☎ *0517/415846* ▤ *0517/412762* ⊕ *www.heerenlogement.nl* ⇨ *25 rooms* ⚘ *Restaurant, cable TV, some pets allowed; no a/c* ▭ *AE, V* ⦿❘ *BP.*

Bolsward

④ *20 km (13 mi) southeast of Harlingen, 108 km (70 mi) northeast of Amsterdam.*

A neatly wrapped bundle of Frisian charm, Bolsward was settled by AD 715. One of the 11 cities on the Elfstedentocht ice-race tour, it sparkles at night with its illuminated canals with *posten* (wooden footbridges) and Hanseatic monuments. Built on two terps, or mounds, as protection against flooding before the Zuider Zee was closed off by the dike, it's a good overnight bump if you fancy a bit of fun and culture in a single swoop. Two imposing lions greet you at the exuberantly decorated, red-shuttered **Stadhuis** (Town Hall) dating from 1614–17, one of the finest Renaissance buildings in Friesland and considered one of the most beautiful in all of Holland. An external Rococo flight of stairs dating from 1768 takes you up to a magnificently carved door (1614), and inside to the monumental council hall and *burgemeester* (mayoral) rooms. Housed inside are a local archaeological museum (with a magnificent silver collection) and a lyrical carillon. ⊠ *Jongemastraat 2* ☎ *0515/578735* 🖾 *€4* ☉ *Museum Apr.–Nov. 1, daily 9–noon and 2–4.*

For a real kick, check out the whimsical wooden fisherman and his child at the bridge on Kerkstraat behind the Bolsward Town Hall, heading toward the Martinikerk. In summer, you can watch the wood-carver himself, Mr. Bosma, at work behind his house there.

One of the largest churches in Friesland, the **Martinikerk** (Martini Church), built 1446–66 on a mound, has extraordinary choir stalls and a magnificent Hinsz organ (1775–81). Since the church is famed for its acoustics, try to catch a concert here—organ recitals are every Tuesday evening at 8, late June–late September. ⊠ *Broereplein 1* ☎ *0515/573977* ☉ *May–late Sept., Mon.–Sat. 10–noon and 1:30–4; Oct.–Apr. 1:30–4.*

Watch them make the famous dark-brown Frisian, 17-herb, juniper-flavored Beerenburg liqueur at the **Distilleerderij F. J. Sonnema** (Sonnema Distillery) and don't forget to sample the wares. Tours include coffee and tea, cookies, and sample sips. ⊠ *Stoombootkade 12* ☎ *0515/572949* 🖾 *€1* ☉ *Guided tours June–Aug., Tues.–Thurs. at 1:30 and 3.*

Visit the smallest brewery in Holland, the **Us Heit Bierbrouwerij**, where no fewer than eight types of beer are brewed. ⊠ *Snekerstraat 43* ☎ *0515/577449* 🖾 *€3.50, including drink* ☉ *Mon., Tues., Thurs., Fri. 3–6, Sat. 10–6 (guided tour every hr).*

Where to Stay

$ 🏨 **Hid Hero Hiem Hotel.** This spartan hotel is ideally situated in a serene courtyard just off the very center of Bolsward in what, for 400 years, served as an orphanage (founded in 1553). All rooms have kitchenettes and pristine bathrooms. There are some facilities and apartments for guests with disabilities. Private terraces on the ground floor lead out to large, grassy play areas. ⊠ *Kerkstraat 51, 8700 AC* ☎ *0515/575299* 🖨 *0515/573052* 🛏 *14 rooms* ♨ *Cable TV, some pets allowed; no a/c* ⊟ *V* ⊙| *BP.*

off the beaten path

ALDFAERS ERF ROUTE – In a triangle framed by Bolsward, Makkum, and Workum, Aldfaers Erf Route, or Our Forefathers' Heritage Route, is a 25-km (16-mi) signposted living-museum trail through idyllic countryside where you can stop in four villages (Allingawier, Exmorra, Piaam, and Ferwoude) at different historical buildings dating from the 18th and 19th centuries. Visit a grocer's shop, bakery, smithy, carpenter's shop, farmhouse, school, church, and typical Frisian cargo vessel, all set up as if still occupied. Cycling the route is even more fun. The historic buildings in Allingawier are open from April to the end of October, daily 1–5; other villages from May to the end of October. Admission, for Allingawier only, is €3.90; for all four villages €7.50. Tickets may be purchased in each participating village at host buildings flying the Dutch flag. ⊠ *Stichting Aldfaers Erf [or local VVV office]* ☎ *0515/231631* ⊕ *www.aldfaerserf.nl.*

Makkum

⑤ *20 km (13 mi) south of Franeker, 37 km (23 mi) southwest of Leeuwarden.*

A shard of a town on the IJsselmeer lake harbor where world-sought-after ceramics are commissioned by the likes of Yoko Ono and the Dutch royal family, Makkum is a real Frisian find. This delightful fishing village can easily be your first stop after crossing the Afsluitdijk (Enclosing Dike) from North Holland province and turning south.

Fodor'sChoice Treasures have been created out of local clay by the same family for more than 400 years, making **Koninklijke (Royal) Tichelaar Makkum** ceramics
★ factory the oldest business in The Netherlands (about 60 years older than the more well-known Delft factory). Metamorphosed into 900 different pieces of hand-painted tiles and decorative earthenware in the popular blue and white, as well as a range of colors in motifs ranging from floral, aviary, country, and humanistic to sleek contemporary lines, the products are of an unsurpassed quality and beauty. After visiting the extensive collection in the factory museum, you'll want to pay a call on the shop. Beware: a visit here may well prove a real lesson in moderation. ⊠ *Turfmarkt 65* ☎ *0515/231341* ⊕ *www.tichelaar.nl* ☒ *€3.50* ☉ *Guided factory tours Mon.–Thurs. at 11, 1:30, and 3; Fri. at 11 and 1:30. Ongoing video presentation Sat. in lieu of tours. Shop, weekdays 9–5:30, Sat. 10–5.*

Where to Eat & Stay

¢ ✕🏨 **Hotel-Restaurant de Waag.** If you'd rather spend your extra cash on the pottery for which Makkum is famous than on a 5-star hotel, this small but tastefully decorated family hotel, situated in an old weigh house in the center of historic Makkum, just may suit the bill. Located near the IJsselmeerstrand, ideal for swimming or walking along the beach, it provides an entrée to a great area for walking or biking. A cozy restaurant with beamed ceilings prides itself on a chef who creates an imaginative Dutch-French style of cooking—but then it *does* take a fair amount of creativity to combine those cuisines. Why not take them up on the challenge? ⊠ *Markt 13, 8754 CM* ☎ *0515/231447* 🖷 *0515/ 232737* ⊕ *www.makkum.nl* ⌧ *14 rooms* ⌖ *Restaurant, cable TV, some pets allowed; no a/c* ☰ *AE, DC, MC, V* ⊠⦿ *BP.*

Workum

⑥ *10 km (6 mi) south of Makkum, 38 km (24 mi) southwest of Leeuwarden.*

Work your way into Workum, one of the oldest towns in Friesland. Albeit a pinch of salt, this seaside town harks back to its former trading days as an eel exporter, as witnessed by its elegant 16th- and 17th-century architecture; note the fine gable of Sleeswijckhuys at Noard 5, dating back to 1663. Workum's claim to fame, however, rests with a junk collector–turned–famous artist, a role model for clutter-prone children and adults alike. "One man's junk is another man's treasure." Workum-born Jopie Huisman (1922–2000) could have coined that phrase, but he was more interested in painting it. A junk collector without rival, he saw beauty in banality and transferred it to canvas. Uneducated and uninterested in accumulating wealth, he passionately painted found objects as well as portraits of his cronies. The one-man show at the **Jopie Huisman Museum** features a very clever room where a large portion of his spider-web-laden props, such as rags, worn shoes, and discarded dolls, are displayed. Hauntingly reminiscent of Van Gogh's work in many ways, not many of Huisman's paintings were made available while he lived; indeed, after three of his paintings were stolen from an exhibition, he refused to sell anything again, instead handing it all over to a museum foundation. Today, his work commands five figures. Not bad for a junkyard man. ⊠ *Noard 6* ☎ *0515/543131* ⊕ *www.jopiehuismanmuseum.nl* 🖂 *€3* ☉ *Mar. and Nov., daily 1–5; Apr.–Oct., Mon.–Sat. 10–5, Sun. 1–5.*

Where to Eat

$$ ✕ **Ne Nynke Pleats.** Follow the dike and the signs from Workum to Piaam for lunch or dinner at a typical 18th-century Dutch farmhouse restaurant, run by two young sisters in an achingly bucolic village; find it just past the church and worth the diversion. There's a free mini–wooden shoe (while supplies last) with cheese appetizer on the Menu of the Day (*Fries Menu*), and outdoor tables overlook a lovely patch of countryside. ⊠ *Buren 25* ☎ *0515/231707* 🖃 *No credit cards.*

Hindeloopen

❼ *6 km (4 mi) south of Workum, 44 km (28 mi) southwest of Leeuwarden.*

Fodor'sChoice
★
Considered the painted lady of Friesland, Hindeloopen is known for its ornately hand-painted furniture and interiors. In the 18th and 19th centuries, virtually every interior surface was sprayed with elaborate floral, religious, and Renaissance motifs influenced by rich, local sea captains who sailed to Scandinavian and Russian ports. When the town was cut off from the open sea in 1932 with the construction of the Afsluitdijk (Enclosing Dike), its prosperity disappeared along with the fishermen—indeed, there's only one fisherman left here today, still clinging like the village's patchwork canals and cross-stitched wooden bridges to a seafaring past. Today Hindeloopen attracts as many yachters and other water-sports enthusiasts as it does sentimental dreamers. If the ice cooperates in winter, it turns into a Siberian wonderland scene of figure skaters in colorful, traditional costumes, speed skaters (it's one of the towns on the 11-city Elfstedentocht ice-race tour), and horse-drawn-sleigh races. The only word for all of this: enchanting.

★ Wedged under the dike in a building that served as the Town Hall from 1683 to 1919 is the **Museum Hidde Nijland Stichting** (Hidde Nijland Foundation Museum), a vibrant snapshot of 18th- and 19th-century Hindeloopen. Stunning period rooms feature the richly hand-painted, mostly floral-motif furniture and decor for which the village is famous, plus Chinese porcelain and wonderful examples of Dutch *bedsteden,* cupboard beds where families slept sitting up to ward off coughs or the devil and potential death (so they believed). Walls are covered in 18th-century Frisian tiles, and there's a good display of costumes, including traditional red-and-white Hindeloopen bridal dresses whose telltale colors were referred to as "milk and blood." Married women wore a stiff, tall hat and a scarf across the heart to indicate they were "taken." (Wear yours on the right if you're still looking.) ⊠ *Dijkweg 1–3, 8713 KD* ☎ *0514/521420* 🖂 *€2.75* ☉ *Mar.–Nov. 1, Mon.–Sat. 10–5, Sun. 1:30–5.*

The largest collection of skates in the world is to be found at **Het Eerste Friese Schaatsmuseum** (First Frisian Skate Museum), where all manner of memorabilia from the fast and famous Dutch Elfstedentocht ice race is displayed, including a once-frozen toe donated by a die-hard skater who pushed his limits. The wooden-shoe skates conjure up images of Hans Brinker, and the bones carved in the form of skates, dug up by archaeologists, reveal the sport's long history. There is also a restaurant and a shop that sells decorative arts. ⊠ *Kleine Weide 1–3, 8713 KZ* ☎ *0514/521683* ⊕ *www.schaatsmuseum.nl* 🖾 *€1.50* ⊙ *Mon.–Sat. 10–6, Sun. 1–5.*

Shopping

For authentic Hindeloopen art, furniture, and decorative pieces, the Nieuwestad and Nieuwe Weide streets house a number of shops. The style can best be described as folk art, using bright colors—mostly reds and greens—with motifs of flowers, biblical themes, and sea imagery all painted on wood. **Hindelooper Kunst W. H. Glashouwer** (⊠ Nieuwestad 25 ☎ 0514/521480 ⊕ www.hindeloopen.com) showcases the work of the Glashouwer family, whose stylistic origins date dates from the 17th century and whose techniques were passed from father to son. Family Zweed's 18th-century classical style painting decorates the chairs, cabinets, tables, and seemingly every other object within their reach, a veritable feast for the eyes on view at **Hindelooper Kunst Meine Visser** (⊠ Buren 26 ☎ 0514/521253).

Sloten

❽
Fodor'sChoice
★

120 km (78 mi) from Amsterdam, 25 km (16 mi) southeast of Hindeloopen.

Discerning travelers opt to bypass the nearby town of Balk and head instead to Sloten. As the elf of the 11-city Elfstedentocht ice-race towns, Sloten seems to have been frozen in time. Once a fortress at the southwestern gate to Friesland and settled around 1063, it can probably all be seen in about three hours, including museum time and maybe lunch, but there's not a drop in its bucket to be missed. It's one of those park-just-outside-the-village-and-walk-toward-the-church-tower places (only residents' cars allowed within) where time seems to wake up only when the Elfstedentocht connects its fourth dot here. The epitome of charming towns, Sloten has a sleepiness that is to be savored. About as big as a single, priceless postcard image, this walled village comprises in one panoramic view a moat, old sluice gates, a high-water warning cannon, cobbled roads flanked by 17th- and 18th-century gabled facades, and a 1755 windmill for grinding corn. Be sure to see the guillotine in front of the footbridge over the water gate where, according to local legend, a Spanish captain whose crew hid themselves in beer barrels for surprise attacks on Sloten lost his head in 1586, cerebrally "hung up to dry" for two weeks as a warning to others. Still shaking in their boots, the current population numbers only 700. Neck- and step-gabled houses, along with lime trees, are reflected in the Diep canal. In summer, yachts skirt the village, a very popular destination for water-sports lovers.

Next to the centrally located Dutch Reformed Church (1647) with its Renaissance, double-stepped gable, the **Stedhus Sleat Museum** is in the old Town Hall (1757). Collections deftly showcase Sloten's history through artifacts, fans, clothes, costumes, jewelry, clocks, and antique cameras. ⊠ *Heerenwal 48, 8556 XW* ☎ *0514/531541* 🖾 *€3* ⊙ *Tues.–Fri. 11–5, weekends 1–5.*

Where to Eat

$ ✕ **Taveerne 't Bolwerk.** In the old center of Sloten you can enjoy canal-side dining in a 17th-century former mayor's house complete with original beams, high ceilings, and tile roof, all of which have been preserved. Every day, from the classic Dutch menu, a surprise concoction from the chef is offered, a welcome overture in an otherwise sleepy, but dreamy, village. ⊠ *Voorstreek 116, 8556 XV* ☎ *0514/531405* 🖃 *AE, DC, MC, V.*

GRONINGEN: PULSE OF THE NORTH

Fodor'sChoice Groningen rocks. As the largest city in the province of the same name, ★ with 178,000 people, half of whom are under 35 years old, it is the throbbing pulse of the North. Historically mentioned by name in 1040 but believed to have been inhabited as early as the 1st century, it was a walled city and member of the Hanseatic League in medieval times that enjoyed six centuries of prosperity as a grain market. Today the city—62 km (39 mi) east of Leeuwarden and 181 km (113 mi) northeast of Amsterdam—is a hotbed of 36,000 university students from two schools and a major commercial center of the northern provinces. In addition to being the sugar capital of Western Europe, it is also a primary shipbuilding hub and an area rich in natural gas. The nightlife scene, in particular, is one of the liveliest in Holland. Culture, punctuated by the daring Groninger Museum, and spectacular countryside drives past manor houses of former silver-spoon merchants round out its rip-roaring repertoire.

Exploring Groningen

Because Groningen has been dubbed the "the world's best cycling city" by American magazine *Bicycle*, it goes without saying that the best way to get around in this town of less than a square mile is on two wheels, or by foot (if you don't get run over by the bicyclists first, that is). Bikes have the run of the road here, as they do in all of The Netherlands—if you hit a bicyclist with your car, it may be deemed your fault regardless of the circumstances. More than half of the city's residents go to work or school by pedaling. Get in the act by renting bikes at the train station (note its art nouveau architecture) or in the center at Oude Boteringestraat 14. There's even a bike taxi and tour service, **TrapTaxi** (☎ 050/577–0782; Apr.–Sept., daily 11–8), which hauls passengers around the center via wagon-type carts hitched behind bikes (pick-up point is at the ABN-Amro bank across from the VVV).

If you come by car, there are several parking garages around town, marked by blue-and-white "P" signs, or you can leave your car just outside the center at either Sontweg on the southeast side or Zaanstraat behind the train station and take the **P & R City Bus** into the center (a bargain at €1.80 per car). Much of the center is closed off to cars, but be extra cautious around the bike paths when walking. For a relaxing way to see the city, take the hour-long canal boat cruise **Rondvaartbedrijf Kool Groningen** (⊠ Stationsweg 1012 ☎ 050/312–8379), which docks just in front of the Groninger Museum across from the train station and departs year-round at various times throughout the day. Candlelight cruises run from mid-November to the end of December, and there are charters to several local villages from April to September.

a good walk Groningen is a classic walking city. Full of countless cafés and carefully preserved historic buildings and monuments, it also has museums as well as some avant-garde, contemporary structures, the most striking of which are the highly touted Groninger Museum and the so-called "organic" Gasunie, a gas company headquarters whose pastel pink, fluid structure seems to sprout organically from Concourslaan 17, the street where it is located. The following route, which will take you approximately two hours to dust the perimeter, begins at the VVV information office at Grote Markt 25, where a friendly staff will help you assemble a package of materials detailing the city highlights you choose to explore in further depth. Be sure to ask for a city map, as well as the walking tour booklet and complete guide to Groningen in English.

For a caffeine boost from a great cappuccino or a rich hot chocolate with whipped cream before you set off, the **De Kosterij** (Martinikerkhof 2), directly across from the VVV, is a perfect spot. Weather permitting, you can sit outside and contemplate your day, or perhaps life's big questions . . . like how you're going to finagle moving to Europe. Whether you're sitting at the café or heading out the door from the VVV, you're facing the **Grote Markt,** the main square in Groningen where it all happens, from one of the biggest daily markets—selling everything from vegetables to vintage clothing (except for Monday and Sunday, unless it happens to be *Koopzondag,* or Shopping Sunday)—to the throbbing hub of nightlife that it is, particularly with the large population of university students in the vicinity. The columned Town Hall, built in Neoclassical style and dating from 1810, is also situated on this central square.

If the caffeine hasn't kicked in yet and you haven't noticed the Gothic tower above your head, it's time to look up at the **Martinikerk and Martinitoren** ❾ ► (St. Martin's Church and Tower). Go right, down St. Jansstraat, to the **Provinciehuis** (Provincial Government Building). Although the front facade dates from 1916, the left facade is quite a bit older, going back to 1599. Head up the narrow street to the left of the building, the Kleine Snor, which means "little mustache"; it's the smallest street in Groningen. You'll come directly to the **Prinsenhof** (Princes' Court), originally a cloister-cum-friary, governor's palace, military hospital, and boarding school, but now the Radio/TV Noord studio. Just around the corner on Turfsingel is the entrance to an ancient rose-and-herb garden, an oasis in the middle of a bustling city, the **Prinsenhoftuin** ❿ (Princes' Court Gardens), which has been there since 1625. A canopy of beech hedge creates a covered walkway, and there's a dreamlike alfresco garden "tearoom."

From the garden, you have a choice. Either take a side detour down W. A. Scholtensstraat to the **Anatomisch (Anatomy) Museum** ⓫ at Oostersingel 69, or make your way down Hofstraat and cross over the Noorderhaven canal to the **Spilsluizen North Side,** an area of landing wharves in earlier days. Proceed down Spilsluizen to the **Ossenmarkt,** in use as a cattle market until 1892, with a square surrounded by houses with striking facades, past the **Gerechtsgebouw** (Court of Justice) and back across the canal to the **Corps de Garde,** a former watch post dating from 1634. Continue down Oude Boteringestraat, where there's a large number of monumental buildings, including No. 44, the former residence of the Queen's Commissioner to Groningen (now a university building) and No. 24, the **Calmerhuis,** one of the oldest stone houses in the city of Groningen. Turn right on Broerstraat to Academieplein and the **Academiegebouw** (University Seat), the main building of the **Rijksuniversiteit Groningen (RUG)** ⓬, the University of Groningen, a fine example of the Neo-Renaissance style.

Continue on to the Oude Kijk in 't Jatstraat and turn left; go all the way until you hit another square called the **Vismarkt** (Fish Market). To the right side of the plaza is the **Korenbeurs** (Corn Exchange), where grains used to be traded; today it is a warren of ever-changing shops and restaurants. Proceed down the A-Kerkhof NZ to the right of the Ko-

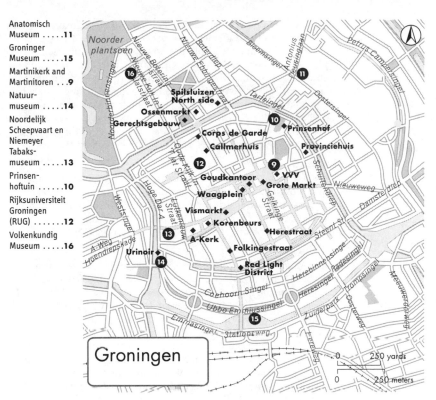

renbeurs, past the A-Kerk (A-Church), a Romanesque structure dating from the 15th century, with origins from 1247, and on to the **Noordelijk Scheepvaart en Niemeyer Tabaksmuseum** ⑬ (Northern Shipping and Niemeyer Tobacco Museum), in two stone houses considered to be among the oldest in the city. If you have the urge, take a quick detour down Brugstraat, left at Kleine Der A before the bridge, and over to one of the strangest sites in the city—the Urinoir. Is it art or is it . . . well, you guessed it, a public toilet? Actually, it's both, the creation of superstar Dutch designer Rem Koolhaas with opaque glass and decorated with human figures by Erwin Olaf.

Whiz along now down Reitemakersryge and turn right on Museumstraat to the **Natuurmuseum** ⑭ (Museum of Natural History) for a glimpse of regional flora, fauna, and geology. Resist the temptation (or not) to shop along Folkingestraat, an eclectic concentration of ethnic shops in the former Jewish Quarter, which just so happens to cut through the Red Light District on Nieuwestad where scantily clad ladies of the night legally display themselves in picture windows and doorways; then continue down Ubbo Emmiusstraat. Just before you reach the canal is a very special shop worth a 10-minute investment: the Minimuseum Shop, at No. 34A, has the largest selection of art postcards anywhere. Inspired by the collection, forge on over across the grassy Ubbo Emmiussingel to the unmissable, floating modern structure begging for attention, the much-talked-about **Groninger Museum** ⑮. This houses a permanent collection of art and objects from the province, Chinese porcelain, and both old and modern works of art, in addition to an ever-changing array of exhibits. If you're hankering by this time to take in some shopping, backtrack to the main thoroughfare of town, the Gedempte Zuiderdiep, and go right until you hit Herestraat to the left, the main shopping, pedestrians-only street. Halfway up the street on the left is a great place for another cappuccino and a sandwich made to order, the Croissanterie Paris at No. 41. If you proceed up this street, you'll end up back at the **Waagplein,** the square modernized by Italian architect Natalini, and to the **Goudkantoor** (Gold Office), perhaps the most beautiful building in Groningen, a 17th-century gabled and red-shuttered former office for weighing gold and silver that is now a restaurant. Facing the front of the Goudkantoor is the Grote Markt, where you began your walk. As a postscript, you can trek out to the northern reaches of the city to explore the town ethnographic collection, the **Volkenkundig Museum** ⑯.

Sights to See

⑪ **Anatomisch Museum** (Museum for Anatomy). Located in the Groningen Academic Hospital, this very specific museum is, as you might imagine, only for those with ironclad stomachs. Exploring medical history from 1760 to the present, this exhibition has been compiled by various local professors. ⊠ *Oostersingel 69* ☎ *050/363–2455* 💰 *€1* ⊗ *Wed. and Sun. noon–4.*

★ ⑮ **Groninger Museum.** "The most startling museum in The Netherlands," as it has been often called, rises majestically like a ship from the canal directly opposite the train station. A zany architectonic work of art, the Groninger comprises a splash of four brightly colored pavilions connected by below-water walkways. This flashily mosaicized, trapezoidal structure was conceived by Italian designer and architect Alessandro Mendini and made even more capricious by additions from several guest architects. Once across the museum drawbridge, which, when raised to let sailing vessels pass through, reveals a tongue-in-cheek Delft tile motif worth viewing, you'll find exhibits on Groningen history, arts and crafts, and visual art from the 16th century to the present, in addition to some always exciting temporary exhibits. Pride of place is given over to the fabulous Geldermalsen Porcelain treasure, salvaged only in 1985 from a sunken Dutch trading vessel in the South China Sea—lovers of Asian porcelain will be in heaven. Opened in 1994, the museum is full of surprises, such as the Coop Himmelblau Pavilion, an example of Deconstructivism, a new stream of architecture incorporating fallout from fields of tension, the latest movement rejecting tradition and embracing emotion. "Unity in diversity" was Mendini's intent. Seeing is believing. The museum has an audio guide and offers guided English-language tours by reservation for groups of 10 or more. A museum shop and popular Italian café round out the many attractions here. ⊠ *Museumeiland 1* ☎ *050/366–6555* ⊕ *www.groninger-museum.nl* 💰 *€6* ⊗ *Tues.–Sun. 10–5; also Mon. 1–5 in July and Aug.*

➤ ⑨ **Martinikerk and Martinitoren** (St. Martin's Church and Tower). Dominating the central Grote Markt square, this church dates from 1230 and was begun as a Romanesque-Gothic cruciform basilica. Finished in the 15th century, it has a Baroque organ, first installed in 1470, as well as splendid murals, the oldest fresco dating from the 13th century; the stained-glass windows date from the late 18th century. The 315-foot-high tower dubbed *d'Olle Grieze* (The Old Gray) by locals is only a little less tall than the mighty Dom Tower of Utrecht, the highest in the country. Groningen's five-storied spire has been struck and felled by lightning no fewer than four times since original construction began in 1215; it caught fire in the 1500s from a bonfire set on top to commemorate the retreat of Spanish and Walloon troops; later, it was damaged by grenade fire during the fight for liberation in 1945. Concerts are given with the 52-bell carillon made by the Hemony brothers every Tuesday noon to 1, Saturday 11 to noon, and in summer also on Thursday evening 7:30 to 8:30.

(Find a seat at an outdoor café in the square and enjoy.) The foundation of the tower, replaced during World War II with concrete, used to consist entirely of cowhides, perhaps not so strange considering the industry of the region. You can climb the tower up to the third level (323 steps) for a magnificent view of Groningen. St. Martin *is* the patron saint of tourists, but check first to be sure a storm is not impending. ⊠ *Martinikerkhof 3* ☎ *050/311–1277* 🎟 *Church €1, tower €2.50* ⊙ *Church, June–Aug., Tues.–Fri. noon–5; tower, daily 11–5.*

⑭ **Natuurmuseum.** Woolly mammoths, creepy-crawlies, the Ice Age, geology, wildlife, and land reclamation all feature in this kid-friendly natural history museum. ⊠ *Praediniussingel 59* ☎ *050/367–6170* ⊕ *www.natuurmuseum.org* 🎟 *€2.80* ⊙ *Tues.–Fri. 10–5, weekends 1–5.*

> **need a break?**
>
> Groningen has a lot of great places for a break, such as the Italian deli **Basarz** (⊠ Vismarkt 34 ☎ 050/318–5319), where you can get fresh bread, a wide assortment of olives, cheeses, salads, sandwiches, and wines, and, voilà, it's a picnic. At **Croissanterie Paris** (⊠ Herestraat 41 ☎ 050/314–8143) you can design your own sandwich (the grilled *provencette* and the *Italianse Bol,* or "Italian Roll," are particularly good, as are the huge cappuccinos). For a quick fish pick-me-up *à la Dutch,* head to the Vismarkt on market days where **Bert Zwier Zeevishandel** sets up his temporary stand selling herring, fish sandwiches, fish-and-chips, and, a great favorite, *kibbeling* (fried cod) pieces with a tartar-type sauce.

⑬ **Noordelijk Scheepvaart en Niemeyer Tabaksmuseum** (Northern Shipping and Niemeyer Tobacco Museum). This combination museum is housed in the oldest building in Groningen, which dates from the 13th and 14th centuries. Today still immersed in the shipbuilding and shipping industry, Groningen has amassed a large collection of memorabilia from a diverse range of merchants, from the Hanseatic days to the peat-barge skippers of Granny's days. The maritime section of the museum weaves the story of the ships, the crews, and the voyages they made, right down to the typical skipper's home and the contents of his sea chest. The famous tobacco collection of Royal Theodorus Niemeyer B. V. traces the history of the weed from thousands of years of Native American culture, including objects and folklore touting the healing properties of tobacco, to present-day usage and antismoking campaigns. ⊠ *Brugstraat 24–26* ☎ *050/312–2202* 🎟 *€2.75* ⊙ *Tues.–Sat. 10–5, Sun. 1–5.*

★ ⑩ **Prinsenhoftuin** (Prinsenhof Garden). Fancy a cup of tea in a priceless 17th-century rose and herb garden? A haven of peace and quiet in a bustling city, and the result of more than 250 years of topiary cultivation and hedge growing, the Prinsenhoftuin is one of the purest examples of Renaissance garden style in The Netherlands, and the best part is that you can feast on dainties in its glorious outdoor "tearoom." A wonderful sundial above the entrance gate welcomes you with a Latin saying: "The past is nothing, the future uncertain, the present unstable; ensure that you do not lose this time, which is yours alone." Noted for its promenade walk with hedges cut in the shapes of the letters *A* and *W* (after the first names of former governors of Friesland and Groningen provinces), the garden is neatly tucked away behind the Martinikerk. ⊠ *Turfsingel* 🎟 *Free* ⊙ *Apr.–mid-Oct., daily 10–sunset; tearoom during good weather only.*

⑫ **Rijksuniversiteit Groningen (RUG)** (University of Groningen). Founded in 1614, this celebrated university was chosen by Descartes in 1645 to arbitrate his conflicts with Dutch theologians. It is the second oldest, and today one of the largest, in The Netherlands. The main university building, the **Academiegebouw** (University Seat) was built in 1909 in florid Neo-Renaissance style; allegorical figures of Science, History, Prudence, and Mathematics adorn its gable. Some students still don the signature caps of the university: pink for chemistry, blue for theology, red for medicine, white for law, and yellow for math. In the surrounding streets are a number of fashionable houses built by prominent 18th-century citizens. ⊠ *Oude Boteringestraat.*

⑯ **Volkenkundig Museum** (Ethnographic Museum). This adventure into the history and development of various cultures is devoted to the study of the creative capabilities of humankind and their cultural interaction. The fascinating collection includes a mummy and other archaeological artifacts from ancient Egypt. ⊠ *Nieuwe Kijk in 't Jatstraat 104* ☎ *050/363–5791* ⊕ *www.netsign.nl/volkenkundig.museum* 🖾 *Free* ☉ *Tues.–Fri. 10–4, weekends 1–5.*

Where to Eat & Stay

As a university town and commercial hub of the North, Groningen has something for everyone, from the cheapest to the chicest eateries and lodgings. There are some great ethnic restaurants catering to a more diverse palate, but the penchant for Dutch standbys is still evident, from the raw herring stands at the markets to the hearty winter menus of thick stews and soups. There are also overnight accommodations to suit everyone, from the understated classiness of the Hotel de Ville and Schimmelpenninck Huys to the **Erfgoed Logies group** (☎ 050/535–0202 🖶 050/535–0203 for color brochure ⊕ www.erfgoedlogies.nl) of historic manor- and farmhouses catering to those wanting a unique experience away from the hubbub of the city. In fact, be mindful of double-pane windows and courtyard versus street-side rooms; in case you've forgotten, university students are known to be nocturnal, especially in a town where there are no closing hours imposed on bars and clubs, and in a country where the legal drinking age is 16 for beer and wine and 18 for hard liquor.

★ **$$$** ✕ **Muller.** A great place for a romantic rendezvous if one of you has the euro wherewithal, this classic restaurant has a softly lighted and sumptuous interior with cozy, cushy corners. The six-course menu is a culinary delight, especially the imaginative vegetarian option. The wine list and service are excellent. ⊠ *Grote Kromme Elleboog 13* ☎ *050/318–3208* ⚷ *Reservations essential* 🖃 *AE, DC, MC, V* ☉ *Closed Sun. and Mon.*

$$ ✕ **De Pauw.** This chic, highly styled restaurant, done in cream and soft yellows, has a sophisticated and imaginative menu influenced by the cuisines of Provence, Italy, Asia, and the rest of Europe. Dishes include delicate white asparagus shoots (in season), lobster with pesto, and a royal selection of desserts from the trolley. ⊠ *Gelkingestraat 52* ☎ *050/318–1332* ⊕ *www.depauw.nl* ⚷ *Reservations essential* 🖃 *AE, DC, MC, V* ☉ *No lunch.*

★ **$$** ✕ **Goudkantoor Café Restaurant.** Situated in the most striking building in Groningen—a 17th-century red-shuttered and gabled former tax office–cum–gold and silver exchange (19th century), this is a particularly atmospheric place to have a typical but slightly more inventive Dutch lunch or dinner, complete with spicy *mosterdsoep* (mustard soup). ⊠ *Waagplein 1* ☎ *050/589–1888* ⊕ *www.goudkantoor.nl* 🖃 *AE, DC, MC, V* ☉ *Closed Sun. and Mon.*

$–$$ ✕ **'t feith huis.** A hip place for lunch or dinner close to the Martini Church (of which it used to be part in the 16th century), this spot has a trendy reading room–café just off the entrance along with two levels for dining. Specialties include mustard soup and warm breads topped with mozzarella, tomato, and pesto, as well as salads and pastas. Try the champagne brunch (€21) every Sunday 11–4:30 (with reservations), or the English-style afternoon tea served daily replete with scones. ⊠ *Martinikerkhof 10* ☎ *050/313–5335* ⊕ *www.feithhuis.nl* ⊟ *V.*

★ ¢–$$ ✕ **Four Roses.** Olé to owner Ton Alferin: this place has the best Mexican-American food this side of Texas, with huge portions, small but mighty margaritas, great guacamole dip, and to-die-for burritos with chicken or beef, black beans, and rice (they'll leave out the black beans if you ask, but why would you?). A rare find (for Holland) is the special room allotted to nonsmokers. Go before 7 PM on weekends if you don't want a long wait; reservations are taken only for parties of eight or more. ⊠ *Oosterstraat 71* ☎ *050/314–3887* ⊟ *V.*

¢–$ ✕ **Da Carlo.** This Italian trattoria on the main street offers 87 different kinds of pizza and almost as many pastas and meat dishes. If you can't decide, order the *Sorpresa della Casa*, the "surprise of the house" with three different pastas. The owner promises "you'll fall in love directly." It's a good late-night stop after a movie (the Pathé cinema is just down the street). ⊠ *Gedempte Zuiderdiep 36* ☎ *050/313–5796* ⊟ *AE, DC, MC, V.*

★ ¢–$ ✕ **'t Pannekoekschip.** Kids adore the more than 100 kinds of pancakes at this popular pancake ship—yes, it's literally a ship—just down the street from the casino. Adults, of course, will love these sizzling delights, too (but be aware that pancakes are not breakfast fare in Holland). ⊠ *Schuitendiep* ☎ *050/312–0045* ⊟ *No credit cards.*

¢ ✕ **Vroom & Dreesman (La Place Café).** Located in a well-regarded department-store chain Vroom & Dreesman (fourth floor, counting ground as "0"), this is a great spot for a quick, delicious, low-cost cafeteria-style lunch, where you can see what you're getting without any command of Dutch. Everything is consistently good and fresh, from the sandwiches and soups to the best—and maybe the only—real salad bar on Dutch soil, hot meals, great desserts, and one of the most generous cappuccinos anywhere. There's also an outside sandwich bar in front of the shop. ⊠ *Grote Markt 21* ☎ *050/308–0680* ⊟ *AE, MC, V.*

★ $$$–$$$$ ✕🔲 **Landgoed Lauswolt.** Get out the camera and your wallet, Scarlet, and be gone with the wind at this classic and historic country estate-cum-spa resort with a sprawling manor house behind a sweeping lawn, all in a quiet wooded village about 30 minutes from Groningen. Splendor and spoils are the keys to indulgence here, with large rooms and suites with separate living rooms, and a setting to die for. Restaurant de Heeren van Harinxma prides itself on its mix of ingenuity, purity, and contrast in the French-country style and is a member of the Alliance Gourmandise Néerlandaise. Special golf, spa, and gastronomic packages are available. From Groningen, head toward Heerenveen-Drachten via A7, exit Beetsterzwaag, and go through the village; the estate is on the right. ⊠ *Van Harinxmaweg 10, 9244 CJ Beetsterzwaag, 40 km (25 mi) southwest of Groningen* ☎ *0512/381245* 🖷 *0512/381496* ⊕ *www.bilderberg.nl* ↪ *55 rooms, 10 suites* ⟁ *Restaurant, minibars, cable TV, tennis court, 2 pools (1 indoor), hair salon, sauna, some pets allowed; no a/c* ⊟ *AE, DC, MC, V* ⟊ *EP.*

★ $–$$$ ✕🔲 **Hotel de Ville.** This central, classy hotel with contemporary accents occupies a group of gracious houses once used by the university. Soft lighting, chandeliers, bold antique mirrors, and the warmth of a fire lure you to an inner sanctum of tranquillity. Favored by the likes of Bono of U2, it's the *in* place to stay. Rave reviews are accorded to its Bistro 't Gerecht restaurant. Breakfast is served in the conservatory or on the garden terrace. A thoughtful welcome list of local "musts," in English, adds a ribbon to the package. ⊠ *Oude Boteringestraat 43, 9712 GD* ☎ *050/318–1222* 🖶 *050/318–1777* ⊕ *www.deville.nl* ⇆ *43 rooms, 3 suites ⸂ Restaurant, room service, in-room safes, minibars, bar, lobby lounge, free parking, some pets allowed, no-smoking floor; no a/c* ▭ *AE, DC, MC, V* ⦿I *EP.*

$–$$ ▦ **City.** If you're casino-bound, this trendy, central Best Western hotel is the place to consider, as it is directly across from the gambling mecca and offers special entrance and dinner arrangements. Amenities include a sleek breakfast room and bar adjoining the free 24-hour Internet corner, a coffee- and tea-making cubby on every floor, and a free "relaxation room" with sauna and Turkish steam bath. Rooms with water beds and Jacuzzis are available. (Ask for a room with an unobstructed view, as the architect has annoyingly blocked out the windows with a "creative" design in some rooms.) ⊠ *Gedempte Kattendiep 25, 9711 PM* ☎ *050/588–6565* 🖶 *050/311–5100* ⊕ *www.edenhotelgroup.com* ⇆ *93 rooms ⸂ Cable TV, massage, sauna, bar, parking (fee); no a/c* ▭ *AE, DC, MC, V* ⦿I *EP.*

★ $–$$$ ✕▦ **Schimmelpenninck Huys.** Reeking with history all the way back to the 11th century, this grand old patrician mansion with a Dutch *klok* (bell) gable from the 1600s, once a warren of streets and courtyards, has been cleverly melded into 50 pristine, modern boudoirs and apartments. The scene of revolutionary plotting in the 18th century, it was requisitioned as an officers' barracks during the Eighty Years' War. In 1988 the building was rescued from occupation by squatters and lovingly restored. Reflecting its checkered history, there's a vaulted 14th-century wine cellar–bar set against the foundation walls of the old city, Baroque- and Empire-style dining rooms, and a Jugendstil Grand Café, the last very popular with the locals for fine French cuisine. Sweetly enough, they even have their own chocolate shop, La Bonbonnière, a Greek restaurant, and the Parelvissen, where fish is the chef's specialty. Be sure to ask for a room either in the newer wing or facing the courtyard, as street-side rooms can be incredibly noisy from university fallout. ⊠ *Oosterstraat 53, 9711 NR* ☎ *050/318–9502* 🖶 *050/318–3164* ⊕ *www.schimmelpenninckhuys.nl* ⇆ *50 rooms, 6 suites ⸂ 2 restaurants, minibars, cable TV, bar, some pets allowed; no a/c* ▭ *AE, DC, MC, V* ⦿I *EP.*

$ ▦ **Auberge Corps de Garde.** Near the ancient fortification wall and facing the city center's encircling canal, this small family-owned hotel is in a gracious 17th-century barracks-house where the elite sector of the Dutch military was once housed. Partially furnished with antiques, it is a congenial place with spacious, modernized rooms. ⊠ *Oude Boteringestraat 74, 9712 GN* ☎ *050/314–5437* 🖶 *050/313–6320* ⊕ *www.corpsdegarde. nl* ⇆ *24 rooms ⸂ Cable TV, some pets allowed; no a/c* ▭ *AE, DC, MC, V* ⦿I *EP.*

Nightlife

Groningen will knock your socks off with its party-all-night panache. With a prescription to howl, university students turn academia into urban mania in a town with no imposed closing hours on bars, clubs, or discos (such as exist even in Amsterdam) and virtually no cover charges. The hostess-with-the-mostest, Groningen has the most pubs per square mile, after its sister rivals Amsterdam and Maastricht. To top it off, catering to a student population keeps prices low, so you can have a good time for less money here. Curiosity seekers may want to check out the so-called "coffee shops" (as opposed to "koffie shops" or "cafés")— these are places where soft drugs, not legal but tolerated, grace the menu, or the Red Light District on Nieuwestad, a now-legal haven of prostitution where ladies display themselves all day and night in picture windows and doorsteps illuminated by red lights. A former corner café called **Eureka** on the corner seems to say it all. On the other side of the spectrum, classic opera, theater, and cabaret are featured at the **Stadsschouwburg** (✉ Turfsingel 86). Pop music, as well as cabaret and classical music, are on tap at the **Oosterpoort** (✉ Trompsingel 27). Ask the VVV office for performance schedules.

Bars & Pubs

The high concentration of university students here is proportionate to the high density and variety of bars and pubs found in Groningen. Perhaps the largest of them, **De Drie Gezusters** (The Three Sisters; ✉ Grote Markt 39 ☏ 050/313–4101) is an absolute warren of 19 intimate and innovative bars, 4 of them rotating, 3 of which feature an elevator-like shaft where the DJ shifts from one level to another. Among the theme rooms are a sports bar, a library room with a fireplace, and a ski hut with a chalet motif. There is even a hotel (De Doelen) and café-restaurant spread throughout the bar rooms. Needless to say, this is an experience in itself. Of the 19 bars, the Scottish Lady is a student favorite.

Particularly popular, **O'Ceallaigh's Irish Pub** (✉ Gedempte Kattendiep 13 ☏ 050/314–7694 ⊕ www.oceallaighs.nl) is a low-profile home-away-from-home offering traditional Irish music. **Sally O' Brien's Irish Pub** (✉ Oosterstraat 33 ☏ 050/311–8039) has beef, booze, Irish breakfasts, and a big-screen TV. For an archetypal Dutch, time-stained "brown café," try **De Pintelier** (✉ Kleine Kromme Elleboog 9 ☏ 050/318–5100). **Mulder** (✉ Grote Kromme Elleboog 22 ☏ 050/314–1469) is a happening place for jazz. **Wolthoorn & Co.** (✉ Turftorenstraat 6 ☏ 050/312–0282) draws in jazz and soft-rock aficionados.

Casino

The Las Vegas-y **Holland Casino** (✉ Gedempte Kattendiep 150, 9711 PV ☏ 050/317–2317 ⊕ www.hollandcasino.nl), the only casino in the northern half of The Netherlands, is open daily from 1:30 PM. You must be 18 years of age with a valid ID to be admitted.

Dancing & Live Music

The most vibrant discos and music venues in Groningen are peppered on or around **Peperstraat**, near the Grote Markt. Up-to-the-minute DJs and a long happy hour attract hordes of students and other young Groningers to **De Blauwe Engel** (✉ Grote Markt 39 ☏ 050/313–7679). **Jazz Café De Spieghel** (✉ Peperstraat 11 ☏ 050/312–6300) swings nightly to mainstream jazz, with live bands over the weekends. If your taste is for salsa and other Latin rhythms, head for the lively **Troubadour** (✉ Peperstraat 19 ☏ 050/313–2690). Best known for being an all-nighter that doesn't get started until midnight is **Benzine Bar** (Gasoline Bar; ✉ Hoekstraat 44 ☏ 050/312–8390), where the music pumps until 10 or 11 in the morning. For alternative rock, try **De Kar** (✉ Peperstraat 15 ☏ 050/312–6215). R&B nights are a big feature at **Index** (✉ Poelestraat 53–55 ☏ 050/313–6466). The posher, tamer crowd heads to the **News Café** (✉ Waagplein 5 ☏ 050/311–1844).

Gay Bars

A complete listing of gay bars and clubs is available on the **Web** (⊕ www.homogroningen.nl). Groningen's largest and most popular gay disco, **De Golden Arm** (✉ Hardewickerstraat 7 ☏ 050/313–1676), has two dance floors and three bars and is popular with students during the week. With a terrace on a busy shopping street, **El Rubio** (✉ Zwanestraat 26 ☏ 050/314–0039) is a camp way to start an evening among a mixed crowd of gay men and lesbians. **Bite Me** (✉ A-Kerkstraat 20 ☏ 050/312–2213) is a gay dinner café–bar that speaks for itself.

The Outdoors

Canoeing through the waterways of the province of Groningen can be great fun. Maps with special canoeing routes are available from the VVVs. To rent canoes, contact **Kano 't Peddeltje Groningen** (⊠ Herebrug ☎ 050/318–0330), at the bridge to the right of the Groninger Museum and across from the train station. **Hinrichs Watersport** (⊠ Damsterweg 32, Schildmeer ☎ 0596/629137), 30 km (19 mi) from Groningen, is a popular starting point for boat rentals.

Shopping

With a large pedestrian-only area and university students to cater to, Groningen is a great place to shop. Markets are held on the Grote Markt, Tuesday–Saturday. Late-shopping night is Thursday until 9. There's an eclectic range of international shops on **Folkingestraat,** just off the Vismarkt. Best general shopping, including many well-known fashion houses, can be found on Herestraat, Zwanestraat, and Waagstraat. Antiques lovers will find a web of shops on **Gedempte Zuiderdiep.** Antique-book dealers are especially thick in this university city. **Isis Antiquarian Bookshop** (⊠ Folkingestraat 20 ☎ 050/318–4233) specializes in philosophy and history, as well as translated and Dutch literature. For imported table and giftware, **Tafelgoud** (⊠ Oude Boteringestraat 7 ☎ 050/311–2707) has a stunning selection, tops being the hand-painted German glass plates. Shipping to the United States is available, and you can pay by credit card. For the largest selection of art postcards and prints anywhere, visit the **Minimuseum** (⊠ Ubbo Emmiusstraat 34A ☎ 050/314–6365), where you can also visit Mr. Oegemas's private museum of World War II mementos and photos, particularly pertaining to the Jewish community.

SIDE TRIPS FROM GRONINGEN

Although there's much to do in the bustling city of Groningen, a day trip through its provincial countryside may be in order. Replete with 16 manor houses, or *borgen* (⊕ www.borgen.nl) that are open to the public (ask the VVV for the brochure), you're sure to encounter a fantasy en route. To jolt you back to reality before returning to Groningen, sample some of Abraham's spicy mustard at his factory-museum-café in Eenrum, where you can also see or stay at the smallest hotel in the world and visit the nearby seal sanctuary. The more intrepid traveler may want to walk the Pieterpad, a 488 km (305 mi) walking trail beginning in Pieterburen and ending in Maastricht.

Menkemaborg

⑰ *25 km (16 mi) north of Groningen.*

Fodor's Choice
★

To the manor born . . . is how you'll wish you'd been when you visit Menkemaborg, a glorious, double-moated, fortified manor house, or *borg,* considered to be one of the finest in the province of Groningen and oozing with exquisite Vermeerian settings down to the finest detail. The furniture, including a showpiece 1777 pipe organ disguised as a phantom secretary, represents the 17th and 18th centuries, all housed in a 14th-century structure. King William III of The Netherlands rested his weary head in the huge 18th-century four-poster bed. Manorial magic pervades the house as a medley of clocks banter at the same time.

As if the master and his lady's digs were not enough to behold, saunter on down to the basement servants' quarters, a remnant of the original house destroyed in 1400, and you'll find the most *gezellig*, or cozy, kitchen and bedroom, complete with Dutch *bedsteden*, cupboard beds where the servants slept sitting up with mouths closed to prevent devils or the smoke from open hearths from entering their bodies (as they believed in those days). Hygiene consisted of hand washing at the fountain in the main upper corridor, which was fed by a reservoir, and although they look like sentry boxes at the outside entrance, the two little "houses" are really the former privies. The table is always set in the dining room, and the rooms have been furnished as though the manor is still occupied. (If only you didn't have to go home . . .) Reconstructed according to an 18th-century plan found at the house, the garden comes complete with a teahouse and a maze, both fancies of the last inhabitant, the nobleman Gerhard Alberda van Menkema en Dijksterhuis, a bachelor who died in 1902 amidst this Dutch splendor. Red-check tablecloths bring you back down to earth at the 1686 carriage house–turned–café adjacent to the manor house. Elevate your deflated status with a typical English high tea featuring scones and sweet delights, or remain a commoner with Dutch *pannekoeken* (pancakes). Go quickly, fair maidens. You can at least *pretend* that Gerhard has never left. ⊠ *Menkemaweg 2, Uithuizen* ☎ *0595/431970* ⊕ *www.menkemaborg.nl* ⊠ *House and garden € 4, garden only €3* ⊘ *Mar.–late Apr., Tues.–Sun. 10–noon and 1–4; late Apr.–late Sept. 10–5.*

Museum 1939–1945, across the street from Menkemaborg manor house, depicts World War II with everything from a parabike to a fully restored Sherman tank, plus all the paraphernalia that went with the cause. Nearby you can explore a 30 km (19 mi) Atlantic Wall bunker route with the help of an explanatory booklet. ⊠ *Dingeweg 1, Uithuizen* ☎ *0595/434100* ⊕ *www.museum1939-1945.nl* ⊠ *€5* ⊘ *Apr.–Oct., daily 9–6.*

Fraeylemaborg

★ ⑱ *20 km (13 mi) east of Groningen.*

A well-preserved, 17th-century moated manor house with 16th-century wings, Fraeylemaborg boasts many portraits and mementos of the Dutch royal family and an equally manorial dollhouse with pink brocade walls and matching carpet. Both Johan de Witt and William III graced Fraeylemaborg's premises at one time—and so can you, if you opt to book a room in the old steward's house, now a classy B&B. Other enticements at the manor include a restaurant, an art gallery, a park, and a February antiques fair. ⊠ *Hoofdweg 30, Slochteren,* ☎ *0598/421568* ⊕ *www.borgen.nl/fraeylemaborg* ⊠ *€4.50* ⊘ *Mar.–Dec., Tues.–Fri. 10–5, weekends 1–5.*

A perfect day out for kids only 20 km (12 mi) from Groningen can be had in the village of Eenrum at **Abraham's Mosterdmakerij,** a factory museum–restaurant where the congenial manager invites you into the mustard factory to see how mustard (a local specialty) and vinegar are made, and then welcomes you to his charming café serving, what else, mustard soup and other luncheon fare. It's right next to the village windmill, which you can go inside on Saturday 10–5 from May to September. Then head on over to the resident candle maker where children (yes, you too) can make their own candles in about 20 minutes. As an added attraction, "the smallest hotel in the world," **De Kromme Raake** is also on-site. From Groningen, head north taking the N361 past Winsum and go right on the N984 to Eenrum. ⊠ *Molenstraat 5, Eenrum, 20 km (12 mi) north of Groningen* ☎ *0595/491600* ⊠ *€1.50* ⊘ *June–Sept., Tues.–Sun. 11–8; Oct.–Apr., Wed.–Sun. 11–6.*

An amazing research facility and rehabilitation sanctuary for ill or injured seals rescued in or near the Wadden Sea, the **Zeehondencrèche** (Seal Creche) is a marvelous place to take children. Since the start of the center in 1971, more than 1,000 seals have been rehabilitated and released back into their natural habitat. ✉ *Hoofdstraat 94a, Pieterburen, Groningen ring road, exit Winsum, toward Baflo to Pieterburen* 🕾 *0595/526526* ⊕ *www.zeehondencreche.nl* ⌨ *€1* ⊙ *Daily 9–6.*

The longest walking route in The Netherlands, the **Pieterpad** (⊕ www. wandelnet.nl) passes through towns, fields, marshes, woods, and areas rich in nature. It begins in Pieterburen—28 km (18 mi) northwest of Groningen (take the N361 north through Winsum, direction Baflo to Pieterburen)—and ends 488 km (305 mi) later in Sint-Pietersberg near Maastricht (hence the name Pieterpad). It can be walked in small segments, and a handbook with routes, cafés, and accommodations is available at VVVs or bookstores.

Where to Stay

★ $$$ 🏨 **Grand Hotel "De Kromme Raake."** Listed in the *Guinness Book of Records* as the Smallest Hotel in the World (and part of Abraham's Mosterdmakerij, the mustard museum), this 1920s-style villa-cottage sports one bed, albeit double the size of a normal Dutch bedstede, or old-fashioned cupboard bed, contained in a wall, complete with a time-warp radio and TV. The "Winding Stream" comes complete with full-scale check-in concierge area and is backdropped by a massive windmill. The flashy black-and-white-tile bath features a luxury tub-shower, with a hidden entrance to the cupboard bed behind a mirror. Breakfast arrives surreptitiously at your door in the morning. Just in case you were interested: yes, the hotel sleeps only two (€175 with champagne; €275 with afternoon coffee and dessert, four-course dinner with wine and coffee, and champagne breakfast). ✉ *Molenstraat 5, 9967 SL Eenrum, 23 km (14 mi) northwest of Groningen* 🕾🕾*0595/491600* 🕾*0595/491400* ⊕*www. eenrum.com* ↩ *1 room* ⌂ *No a/c* ▭ *AE, MC, V* ⏀ *BP.*

★ $ 🏨 **Het Rentmeesterhuis.** For a perfect night away from lively Groningen (a 15–20 minute drive), this posh bed-and-breakfast is in a beautifully renovated house dating from 1720, which served as the steward's residence for the noted Fraeylemaborg manor-house museum. Charming owner Susan Engelbertink's discriminating taste is evident in each of the guest rooms. Ask for the Romantic Suite, whether your romancer is along or not, and soak in the hot tub by candlelight in a bathroom cum laude. Then see if you can awaken at all for the magnum of all breakfasts, served in the antiques-filled country kitchen, or out in the garden. From Groningen, take A7 east to Hoogezand intersection, then north toward Slochteren (about 15 km [10 mi] total). ✉ *Hoofdweg 15, 9621 AC Slochteren* 🕾🕾 *0598/423006* ⊕ *www.rentmeesterhuis.nl* ↩ *2 rooms* ⌂ *Minibars, cable TV; no a/c, no room phones* ▭ *No credit cards* ⏀ *BP.*

DRENTHE: A STORYBOOK LAND

The oldest, and considered by many to be the most traditional and most beautiful, province of The Netherlands, Drenthe is a storybook land of farmers in wooden shoes (*klompen*), meandering streams called the Drentse Aa, vast heather fields, fens and forests fairy-dusted with lakes, steeply sloping thatched-roof farmhouses, 500 km (325 mi) of cycling paths, and more horses, cows, and sheep, it seems, than people—all accentuated with quixotic windmills on a seemingly endless horizon. Life *is* but a dream here.

Van Gogh himself was captivated by Drenthe, the quintessential Dutch landscape, so much so that, while painting its alluring scenes, he wrote to his brother Theo, ". . . Drenthe is fantastic. It would give me great peace of mind if I could come and live here forever . . . It is so entirely everything that I think is beautiful here. I mean, it is peaceful here." Historically, Drenthe is home to the country's oldest prehistoric monuments, the oldest canoe in the world, peat settlements, and, a bit more recent in history, a World War II transit camp where Anne Frank and her family spent a month after their arrest by the Nazis in Amsterdam. Today, it's also where a world-famous motorcycle race takes place every summer, a four-day bike tour takes place every July (contact Assen VVV), and one of the best zoos in the world is located.

Borger

⑲ *40 km (26 mi) south of Groningen, 200 km (130 mi) east of Amsterdam.*

Eat your heart out, Fred Flintstone. Those Stone Age boulder formations, of which 54 still exist throughout the Hondsrug ridge running between Groningen and Emmen, are the real thing, and Borger is home to the largest one, an 82-foot-long, 44-stone dolmen, or *hunebed* as the Dutch call them, adjacent to what is now the **Nationaal Hunebedden Informatiecentrum** (National Dolmen Information Center). Its largest capstone weighs an incredible 20 tons. Almost 4,000 years older than Stonehenge, these most ancient of all monuments in The Netherlands are believed to be the megalithic skeletons of burial tombs used by the first farmers in this area, although local legend purports them to have been built by giants referred to as *huynen,* thus the name *hunebed.* Previously covered with a mound of earth, these partially excavated funerary sites have revealed some of the finest known prehistoric implements and pottery, characteristically in the form of funnel-shape beakers, hence the name "Beaker Culture." Strangely, almost all hunebedden (plural for hunebed) lie in a southwest direction, with the entrance to the south. They are believed to have been initially transported from Scandinavia by glacier movement during the Ice Age more than 100,000 years ago, a theory explored in a well presented exhibition at the museum. You, too, can traverse the Flintenroute, as they call it ("flint" means "hard stone"), a 42-km (27 mi) biking, walking, or driving route past the area's dolmens. Children visiting the Hunebedden Information Center are invited to dress up as Stone Age characters, build their own mini-hunebed, and crawl inside a scaled-down thatched-roof house thought to be typical of that era. (The Drents Museum in Assen further explores the archaeology of this area.) ✉ *Bronnegerstraat 12* ☎ *0599/ 236374* 🖼 *€2.80* ⊙ *Weekdays 10–5, weekends 11–5.*

A stone's throw away from Borger in Nieuwe Buinen is a blue-and-white fancier's paradise at **Royal Goudewaagen,** a ceramics factory with a museum as well as one of the best places in The Netherlands to overdose on Delftware shopping. Rock-bottom prices can be had in the seconds shop, where errors, barely detectable, mean bliss—less than half the cost of items in the adjacent first-quality room. It is a little-known fact that Royal Goudewaagen produces pottery for Colonial Williamsburg in Virginia. ✉ *Glaslaan 29a, Nieuwe Buinen* ☎ *0599/616090* ⊙ *Weekdays 10–4* ⊙ *Closed last 2 wks of Dec., May vacation.*

Assen

⑳ *27 km (17 mi) south of Groningen.*

The provincial capital of Drenthe, Assen used to be a center of contemplation for Cistercian nuns beginning in the 13th century; the convent and former abbey church now house the local museum, which is worth a visit, especially to see its display of bog bodies (preserved in wet, spongy ground composed of decomposing vegetation).

By contrast, Assen is most famous today for its annual Grand Prix qualifying motorcycle races, the **Rizla & Dutch TT** (Tourist Trophy; ☎ 0900/388–2488 ⊕ www.tt-assen.com), which take place in June. True introspection on a more serious note, however, takes place at the WWII transit camp just outside town. And where else can you visit a street-organ museum and hear street organs in concert? For children, the attractions are Europe's largest traffic park (where they can "drive" long before they're 16) and one of the best zoos, bar none, in nearby Emmen.

A large part of the center has been pedestrianized for shopping, but keep an eye out for those two-wheelers who do own the bike paths. Wednesday and Saturday are market days, and late-night shopping is on Friday until 9.

If you're traveling by train or bus, it's an easy five-minute walk from the Assen station to the **Drents Museum**, where you will find the Pesse Canoe (from the village of Pesse south of Assen), the oldest water vessel ever found, dating from about 6800 BC, as well as the extremely well-preserved body of a 16-year-old girl, dubbed "Yde" for the nearby village in which she was found in a peat bog by two Drenthe farmers in 1897 (peat was used as fuel to heat homes). Remains of other bodies, clothing, and artifacts at the museum are those of the prehistoric, megalithic tomb builders (such as those found at Borger). Authentic period rooms of the Drenthe area are also worth seeing, as well as a collection of Dutch art from around 1900 (including Van Gogh's *De Turfboot* (The Turfboat), a fine decorative arts and costume collection, and a jewelry collection from AD 400 excavated from the neighboring area of Beilen. For children, there's a Geo Explorer room where they can experience the thrill of the birth of Mother Earth. There is also a 1900s-era café. ⊠ Brink 1 ☎ 0592/377773 ⊕ *www.drentsmuseum.nl* ▨ €5 ⊙ *Tues.–Sun. 11–5.*

Nine kilometers (5 mi) south of Assen in **Hooghalen** is the World War II transit camp **Herinneringscentrum Kamp Westerbork,** where heroine Anne Frank and her family were brought upon their arrest in Amsterdam after having hidden from the Nazis for two years in her now-famous house in Amsterdam. Although all the camp buildings, except for the commander's house and watchtower, have been destroyed, you can walk through the area where the sites of the buildings are marked off and see a remaining section of the train track on which more than 105,000 Jews and Gypsies were transported, most to their deaths, to concentration camps throughout Europe. (The Frank family was on the very last train out of Camp Westerbork; destination: Auschwitz, Poland. Anne was later transferred to the Bergen-Belsen camp in Germany, where she died of typhus.) An excellent museum depicts life in the camp, with actual memorabilia, photos, videos, and even a makeshift barracks room. On-site is a bookshop and café; a bus takes visitors from the museum to the camp site, a healthful 3-km (2-mi) walk or bike ride for those so inclined, through beautiful woods. English tours are available on request. Adjacent to the camp is the largest radio telescope in western Europe. ⊠ Oosthalen 8, Hooghalen ☎ 0593/592600 ⊕ *www.kampwesterbork. nl* ▨ €3.85 ⊙ *Feb.–Dec., weekdays 10–5, weekends 1–5 (July and Aug., weekends 11–5).*

For a unique experience, visit the **Draaiorgelmuseum** (Street Organ Museum) in Assen, where you can hear concerts on a fine collection of barrel street organs on the second and fourth Sunday of each month 1–5:30 (in December, the second and third Sunday). ✉ *Rode Heklaan 3* ☎ *0592/356718* ⌧ *€3* ⊙ *Tours only, weekdays; open on selected Sun. for concerts.*

ⓒ At the **Verkeerspark Assen** (Traffic Park Assen), a unique park for fledgling pedal-pushers ages 4–12, the kids will drive you crazy when let loose on a driving circuit with all manner of minicars. For teenagers 13 and older, there is a motorized jeep circuit. The mobile motive here is to learn and observe the traffic signs and rules while having fun in the process. ✉ *De Haar 1/1a* ☎ *0592/355700* ⊕ *www.verkeersparkassen. nl* ⌧ *€8.25* ⊙ *Apr.–Aug., daily 9:30–5, but call ahead for variations* ⊙ *Closed on TT races day (1 wk before Easter).*

ⓒ Head east to Emmen, where the **Noorder Dierenpark** (North Animal Park) does a smashing job of presenting all manner of beasts in their natural habitats with no cages, bars, or fencing whatsoever. Famous for its African savanna and tropical butterfly garden, the zoo also has a 264,172-gallon shark tank featuring seven lemon sharks, the largest such display in Europe. Three restaurants are on-site. Less than an hour from Assen, the zoo can be reached by taking A28 to Beilen, then follow the signs to Emmen on N381 (50 km [32 mi] total); by train, it's a 10-minute walk from the station. ✉ *Hoofdstraat 18, Emmen* ☎ *0591/ 850850* ⊕ *www.zoo-emmen.nl* ⌧ *€16* ⊙ *Daily 10–3:30 (July and Aug. 10–6).*

Where to Eat & Stay

★ **$$–$$$** ✕ **Ribhouse Texas.** You'll think you're on American soil when you arrive at this steak house, although it's in beautiful Drenthe countryside only 11 km (7 mi) from Assen. Dutch owner Jim Hogevorst and his pardner, Monica, love the States and have transformed their restaurant into a hoot'n'holler of a place complete with servers in chaps, line dancing, and peanut shells on the floor. Steaks are as good as the place is fun, with the Fred Flintstone rib eye weighing in at 26.5 ounces and a smaller, very tender Lady's Steak, plus ribs and a mixed grill, and good ol' corn on the cob. ✉ *Hoofdweg 42, Zeegse* ☎ *0592/541360* ▭ *MC, V* ⊙ *Closed Mon. and Tues.*

★ **$–$$** ✕ **De Passage.** For the best in local Dutch fare in the center of Assen, try Alyce Dijkstra's home cooking. Particularly good are *Oma's mosterdsoep* (Grandma's mustard soup) and, in winter, the heartiest pea soup (*erwtensoep*) this side of the Atlantic. All entrées come with generous portions of refillable vegetable and potato side dishes. Children up to 12 years eat for half price. ✉ *Gedempte Singel 1* ☎ *0592/300020* ▭ *MC* ⊙ *Closed Sun.*

★ **$–$$** ▣ **Logement 't Olde Hof.** Pure, unadulterated heaven may be experienced here in your own luxury cottage at a very reasonable price. Dirkje Heida has turned her Drenthe-style 1860 farmhouse into a classy, completely restored B&B with several unique options for spending the night (or a lifetime). Our favorite is Het Achterhuis ("the house behind"), a haven that sleeps six but is a dream escape for two. Every whim is catered to, from candles to coffee in your own kitchen and Andrea Bocelli on CD. But the tour de force is your own private sauna entered through a very modern bathroom. Luxurious thick bathrobes await. Walk out onto private tennis courts and a pool, or linger on your own garden patio. Other options include three equally decked-out rooms in the main house, or the ultimate honeymoon cottage—a thatched, one-room delight featuring a hot tub in the adjacent woods, all overlooking the water of a beautiful fen. The gazebo runs €250 for three nights—but any room here is bliss. ✉ *Olde Hofweg 5–7, 9337 TD Westervelde (10 km [6 mi]* *northwest of Assen)* ☎ *0592/612733* 🖶 *0592/612016* ⌨ *3 guest houses* ♨ *Minibars, cable TV, some pets allowed; no a/c, no room phones* 🗏 *No credit cards* 🍽 *BP.*

THE WADDEN SEA ISLANDS

Faced with the choice of visiting one or more of the five islands sandwiched between the North Sea and the Wadden Sea along the northern coastline, you should be aware of the subtle differences that characterize each bead of sand and surf, all rich in shifting dunes, marvelous stretches of beach, particularly varied flora and fauna, and quiet, open spaces stenciled with miles of intricate cycle paths and a proportionate number of bike rental shops. Strung together by island-hopping ferries in summer, the archipelago is also, curiously, accessible by foot. If you're a real stick-in-the-mud for taking life one step at a time, you may enjoy wallowing in knee-to-neck-deep water and mud to get there by *Wadlopen,* literally "mudflat walking," whereby you traipse, trample, and trudge alongside an experienced guide (many bravado types have drowned attempting this alone) from various departure points on the coast across the shallow Wadden Sea, at low tide, of course, to Schiermonnikoog, and return by boat. Wadlopen takes place between mid-March and early October and can be arranged in Groningen (☎ 0595/528300) or in Friesland (☎ 0519/561656); you can also opt for a private guide, Mr. Lammert (☎ 0594/622029), or just go through the auspices of a local VVV information office. Enjoying more sunshine than the Dutch mainland, the islands just may turn out to be the pearled oyster in your movable feast. For a superb review of all the islands, in English, including hotel information and precise ferry schedules, ask for the "Wadden Travel Guide," available at the VVV office or at the Web site (🌐 www.vvv-wadden.nl).

Texel

85 km (53 mi) north of Amsterdam.

Fodor'sChoice ★ Texel (pronounced "Tessel") is the most westerly of the Dutch islands and has long been considered a key getaway for Amsterdam's citizenry—masses travel north from Amsterdam to the port of Den Helder, which is the mainland jumping-off port for Texel. By ferry, it's a 20-minute ride to the island. Uniquely belonging to the province of North Holland, Texel is the largest, and some think most touristy, of the Wadden island group. Nicknamed "Holland in miniature" because of its highly varied landscape featuring woodlands, open meadows, saltwater marshes, dunes, and broad beaches, it lends itself to the widest variety of sporting and cultural activities and is, therefore, a firecracker of activity in July and August—not a good time to visit if you dislike crowds. Sheep, which outnumber the people, a large variety of birds, 30 km (19 mi) of wide, sandy beaches, and 135 km (88 mi) of cycle paths are characteristic of Texel, as are activities for the more adventuresome, such as surf-kayaking, catamaran sailing, island flights, and parachute jumping. A famous 100-km (60-mi) catamaran race, the Ronde om Texel, takes place around the island in mid-June and is preceded by a week of other maritime events. Of the seven villages, Den Burg is the main one with the most shops, not surprisingly heavy on fleece products; De Waal and Oosterend are the more silent partners, and Oudeschild is a fishing haven. De Koog is the night owl in a neon frock. For the ultimate back-to-nature experience, there are nudist beaches at Den Hoorn and south of De Cocksdorp. The **Telekom Taxi** (☎ 322211 locally) takes you from the ferry terminal to your lodgings on the island and picks you up for the return journey if you call an hour ahead. Buy your ferry tickets at the terminal in Den Helder.

One of Texel's remarkable natural features is **De Hoge Berg** (the High Mountain), the 50-foot-high (okay, so it's a mountain to the Dutch) pinnacle of a ridge formed by glacier movement during the last Ice Age and declared a natural monument in 1968. Climbing its grass-covered pathways is hardly a problem, and it offers a stunning overview of the whole island. Throughout the island you can spot the unusual *schapeboet,* sheep shelters that look like truncated barns, some thatched with local reed, with their sloping rumps turned to the westerly winds.

㉑ **Den Burg,** in the island's center, offers the best choice of places to eat and shop. The step gabled house occupied by the **Oudheidskamer** (Museum of Antiquities) dates from 1599 and gives a sense of local life in times gone by, with exquisitely tiled fireplaces and antique furniture in a homey setting, in addition to a display of local costumes and the smallest herb garden in the country. ✉ *Kogerstraat 1* ☎ *0222/313135* 🖻 *€1.60* ⏱ *Apr.–Oct., weekdays 11–5.*

㉒ **Oudeschild,** the island's historic harbor town, is still used as a port by Texel's modern fishing fleet. During the 17th century, VOC (Dutch East India Company) ships would anchor here, awaiting favorable winds to take them off on their adventurous journeys, and smaller boats would bring them provisions. Sportfishing trips and shrimping fleets now set out from here. The **Maritiem en Jutters Museum** (Maritime and Beachcomber's Museum) contains a bemusing collection of beachcombers' finds and is just next door to the landmark **Traanroier Molen** (Tear Rower Windmill), which was used for hulling grain. This harbor museum also has exhibitions about the local fishing industry, lifeboats, furnished fishermen's cottages, and marine archaeology, including the finds from a VOC ship that sank in the Wadden Sea in 1640. ✉ *Barentszstraat 21, Oudeschild* ☎ *0222/314956* ⊕ *www.texelsmaritiem.nl* 🖻 *€4.10* ⏱ *Tues.–Sat. 10–5; July and Aug., Mon.–Sat. 10–5.*

㉓ **De Koog,** a modern seaside town, is a practical base for exploring the North Sea coastline and its nature reserves. In high season it is subject to hordes of sun-seeking tourists. Much of northwestern Texel is new, the result of dikes built early in the 17th century. Sand was deposited on the seaward side of these dikes, forming a second row of dunes that protected the land behind. However, if the sea breaks through the dunes or man-made dikes during a storm, the valleys behind them can become tidal salt marshes. This is how the **De Slufter** and **De Muy** nature reserves were formed, ideal feeding and breeding grounds for birds such as the spoonbill, sandpipers, and even the rare avocet.

☾ Plenty of live animals are on tap at the **Ecomare** nature center for the Wadden Sea and the North Sea, a good starting point for discovering the natural wonders of these abundant habitats. There is a seal rehabilitation center, a bird sanctuary, a dogfish shark breeding tank (replete with some mean-machine babies), a natural history museum, and a visitor information center about the Wadden tidal flats, the North Sea, and the island's nature areas. Interactive games for children are available in English, and you can book excursions through the nature areas. ✉ *Ruyslaan 92, De Koog* ☎ *0222/317741* ⊕ *www.ecomare.nl* 🖻 *€7* ⏱ *Daily 9–5.*

Where to Eat & Stay

While you're out counting Texel's sheep, count on the culinary delights that go hand and hoof with them. These include sheep's-milk cheese and succulent *pré-salé* lamb (with a natural saltiness acquired from grazing in meadows sprayed by the salt-laden sea winds). Organic dairy products and vegetables are also prevalent on the island, the salt marshes making it possible to farm unusual vegetables such as sea aster, a leaf that makes a tasty addition to salads. Holiday accommodations are abundant on Texel, from campsites in the dunes to private villas hidden in woodlands. Contact the VVV for further information, including a variety of packages that can reduce your hotel costs considerably.

$$$ ✕ **Het Vierspan.** This intimate but sophisticated restaurant serves carefully prepared Continental cuisine emphasizing local products, such as a starter of carpaccio of duck's breast followed by saddle of Texel lamb, or the freshest catch of the day. Popular with the locals—always a good sign—Vierspan is perhaps the finest restaurant on Texel. ⊠ *Gravenstraat 3, Den Burg* ☎ *0222/313176* ⊟ *AE, MC, V* ⊙ *Closed Mon. and Tues.*

$ ▦ **Hotel and Villa Opduin.** Get your dune buggy out . . . this establishment, which aims to uphold the values of the family hotel from which it has developed, is in the middle of the island dunes. Though the building is architecturally nothing short of a modern, blocklike monstrosity, the rooms are spacious and filled with light. For a panoramic sea view, opt for one of the luxury top-floor suites; the hotel's original section, Villa Opduin, has simple, cheaper rooms with shared bathrooms. ⊠ *Ruyslaan 22, 1796 AD De Koog* ☎ *0222/317445* 🖷 *0222/317777* ⊕ *www.opduin.nl* 🛏 *59 rooms, 42 suites, 6 apartments* ⚹ *Restaurant, in-room safes, minibars, tennis court, indoor pool, sauna, bicycles, bar, lobby lounge, children's programs, convention center, meeting rooms, some pets allowed; no a/c* ⊟ *AE, DC, MC, V* ❭◯❬ *BP.*

¢–$ ▦ **Hotel De Lindeboom.** This 105-year-old gentleman's house offers spacious, light rooms with modern furnishings. Above a popular café-restaurant with a sunny terrace, it overlooks an open square in the peaceful center of town. ⊠ *Groeneplaats 14, 1791 CC Den Burg* ☎ *0222/ 312041* 🖷 *0222/310517* ⊕ *www.lindeboomtexel.nl* 🛏 *22 rooms* ⚹ *Cable TV, some pets allowed; no a/c in some rooms* ⊟ *MC, V* ❭◯❬ *BP.*

¢ ▦ **Hotel-Restaurant De Zeven Provinciën.** This old-fashioned tavern, paradoxically with no bar, has simple rooms and nestles safely behind the sea dike on the eastern side of the island. The restaurant, which indeed serves traditional Dutch food, is open throughout the day. ⊠ *De Ruyterstraat 60, 1792 AK Oudeschild* ☎ *0222/312652* 🖷 *0222/313149* 🛏 *14 rooms* ⚹ *Cable TV, some pets allowed; no a/c, no room phones* ⊟ *MC, V* ⊙ *Closed Oct.–Easter* ❭◯❬ *BP.*

Sports & the Outdoors

Bicycling: Bicycles can be rented from the ferry terminal and all over the island. **Catamaran Sailing:** Training courses and rentals are available at **Zeilschool De Nieuwe Eilander** (⊠ Paal 33, De Cocksdorp ☎ 0222/ 316699). **Westerslag** (⊠ Paal 15, Den Burg ☎ 0222/314847 or 0222/ 312013) offers courses in catamaran sailing. **Kayaking:** Sea and surf excursions as well as courses are offered by **Zeekanocentrum Texel** (⊠ Schumakerweg 3, De Koog ☎ 0222/316699). **SeaMount Tracks** (⊠ Rommelpot 19, Den Hoorn ☎ 0222/319393) offers weeklong certificate courses. **Parachuting: Paracentrum Texel** (⊠ Vliegveld Texel ☎ 0222/311464) offers training and supervised jumps.

Terschelling

㉔ *35 km (18 mi) northwest of Texel, 28 km (17 mi) west of Leeuwarden, 115 km (71 mi) north of Amsterdam.*

East of Vlieland we find Terschelling, the largest of the Frisian pearls (second only to North Holland's Texel), with just over 5,000 permanent residents. This 27,180-acre member of the Wadden Island chain experiences a population explosion during high season, as it is a favorite Dutch vacation spot with 30 km (19 mi) of beautiful dunes and endless beaches and 70 km (44 mi) of bike trails, about two hours by passenger and car ferry from Harlingen. The island was settled around AD 900, its main industries originally fishing and whaling. Today, 80% of the island is nature reserve. The **Oerol Festival** (for information, contact the VVV) was started in 1986 as the brainchild of a local landlord. Held during the second and third weeks of June using the whole island as the set for theatrical productions, it appropriately ends on Midsummer Night and has grown into an international event attracting thousands of visitors. June is also the time when fields of orchids are in bloom, and in August and September the heather and sea lavender burst open. Cranberries grown on the island are used for local jams, liqueurs, and wine.

West-Terschelling is the island's main port, surrounding the only natural coastal bay in the whole of Holland. De Brandaris lighthouse has kept sailors safe for the last 400 years and towers 150 feet high. The island retains its natural beauty and interest partly because most of the eastern end is a world-class nature reserve, the **Boschplaat Vogelreservaat** (Boschplaat Bird Sanctuary)—off-limits to wingless visitors from mid-March to mid-August. **Museum 't Behouden Huys** (Keeper's House Museum) explains the cultural-historical background of the island and its people. It occupies the former homes of two naval captains dating from 1668; the rooms are richly decorated with tiles and ornate wooden furniture. Also on display are local traditional costumes and tools. ⊠ *Commandeurstraat 30–32, West Terschelling* ☎ *0562/442389* ⊕ *www.behouden-huys.nl* ⛃ *€3* ☉ *Weekdays 10–5, Sat. 1–5, Sun. (July and Aug. only) 1–5.*

♻ The **Centrum voor Natuur en Landschap** (Center for Nature and Countryside) incorporates an enormous aquarium for marine life from the North Sea and Wadden Sea. During off-season, it opens for the Christmas holiday and one week at the end of February. ⊠ *Burgemeester Reedekkerstraat 11, West Terschelling* ☎ *0562/442390* ⛃ *€4* ☉ *Apr.–Oct., weekdays 9–5, weekends 2–5.*

Where to Eat & Stay

★ **$$–$$$** ✕ **De Grië.** Situated in a typical Terschelling farmhouse, this top-flight restaurant has a reputation as being the best on all of the islands. Specialties include mouthwatering local lamb and duck in season and pastries with locally grown cranberries. Call, as the opening hrs and days vary considerably. ⊠ *Oosterend 43, Oosterend* ☎ *0562/448499* ⊕ *www.terschelling.net* ⚲ *Reservations essential* ▤ *MC, V.*

$$–$$$ ▥ **Golden Tulip Hotel Schylge.** This modern hotel overlooking the harbor has all the conveniences you might ever need if the weather turns inclement. The rooms are standard but practical for a beach vacation. Ask about weekend and midweek rates. ☒ *Burg. Van Heusdenweg 37, 8881 ED West Terschelling* ☎ *0562/442111* 🖷 *0562/442800* ⊕ *www. terschelling.net* ⇱ *98 rooms* ♿ *2 restaurants, minibars, cable TV, indoor pool, hair salon, spa, bowling, 2 bars, meeting rooms; no a/c* ☰ *AE, DC, MC, V* ⦿⦿ *BP.*

$ 🖭 **Hotel Oepkes.** This family hotel on the quiet outskirts of town is only two minutes from the ferry terminal. The rooms are simple and clean. ☒ *De Ruyterstraat 3, 8881 AM West Terschelling* ☎ *0562/442005* 🖷 *0562/443345* ⊕ *www.oepkes.nl* ⇱ *20 rooms* ♿ *Cable TV, bicycles, some pets allowed; no a/c, no room phones* ☰ *AE, DC, MC, V* ⦿⦿ *BP.*

Schiermonnikoog

❷⑤   *42 km (26 mi) northeast of Leeuwarden, 42 km (26 mi) northwest of Groningen, 181 km (112 mi) northeast of Amsterdam.*

Farthest east on the strand lies impossible-to-pronounce (unless you're Dutch) **Schiermonnikoog,** a vast national park known for its 4-km-wide (2½-mi-wide) beach and its role as a migration stop-off for birds heading south in autumn. A total of 30 km (19 mi) of bike trails wend their way around the island. The second smallest on the chain, this car-free Wadden island, just 16 km (10 mi) long, has only 1,000 permanent residents and only one village, of the same name. Named after Cistercian monks—the first-known inhabitants who had a monastery here until it was dissolved and appropriated during the Reformation—for their gray *schier* (habits), plus *monnik* for monk, and *oog* for island, it was at successive times privately owned by a Dutch nobleman and a German count, then confiscated by The Netherlands after World War II. It takes about 45 minutes by passenger ferry to reach it from the mainland port of Lauwersoog—set 188 km (118 mi) north of Amsterdam—where you can safely leave your car. Section 7 of the beach has a lifeguard patrol, making it ideal for families with young children.

The village, the only residential center, was started circa 1720 and is landmark protected. Here you can savor the relaxing pace of life on broad, peaceful terraces. Many of the older private houses are also protected. **Bezoekerscentrum Schiermonnikoog** (Schiermonnikoog Visitor Center) has information about the island's wildlife and guided tours. ☒ *Torenstreek 20* 🖷 *0519/531641* ⊕ *www.waterland.net/npschierm* ⊙ *Mar.–Oct., Mon.–Sat. 10–noon and 1:30–5:30; Nov.–Feb., Sat. 1:30–5:30.*

Where to Eat & Stay

$–$$ ✕ **Steakhouse Brakzand.** As an alternative to the rather pricey food at the hotel restaurants, daily specials at this dormered house in the middle of the village include specialty T-bones, plus an extensive selection of fresh local fish, all at reasonable prices. ☒ *Langestreek 66* ☎ *0519/ 531382* ☰ *MC* ⊙ *Closed Dec.–Feb.*

★ $ ✕🖭 **Hotel-Restaurant Van der Werff.** Renowned as the preferred residence of the Dutch royal family when they visit, and a hotel since 1726, the Van der Werff has a characterful but fusty atmosphere. The grandly spacious restaurant also serves as the breakfast room, and the lounge is maturely comfortable. Full pension is available. From the ferry you can take the complimentary bus, which must be a good 30 years old. ☒ *Reeweg 2, 9166 PX* ☎ *0519/531203* 🖷 *0519/531748* ⇱ *49 rooms* ♿ *Restaurant, cable TV, tennis court, some pets allowed; no a/c* ☰ *DC, MC, V* ⦿⦿ *BP.*

THE NORTH & THE ISLANDS A TO Z

To research prices, get advice from other travelers, and book travel arrangements, visit www.fodors.com.

AIR TRAVEL

The quickest way to reach the northern provinces from Amsterdam is to fly from Schiphol airport to the Eelde airport near Groningen. There are five flights per day, and the flight takes only 30 minutes.

BOAT & FERRY TRAVEL

Ferries transport people and bicycles across the IJsselmeer between Enkhuizen and Urk and Enkhuizen and Stavoren May–September. To reach Texel, take the ferry from Den Helder. A return trip costs about €4 and takes 20 minutes each way. The ferry to Terschelling departs from Harlingen and costs €23 and takes 2 hours. For more information about getting to Schiermonnikoog, see (⊕ www.wpd.nl). The ferry from Lauwersoog takes you to Schiermonnikoog in 45 minutes and costs €13.

🛂 Boat & Ferry Information Contact the VVV Enkhuizen ☎ 022/831–3164 for the ferry schedule to and from Urk and Stavoren. For information on the ferry schedules to the Wadden islands, log onto the Den Helder ferry web site ⊕ www.teso.nl. and contact the VVV offices in Den Helder ☎ 022/362–5544, Leeuwarden ☎ 0900/202406, or Groningen ☎ 0900/202–3050 or ⊕ www.vvv-wadden.nl. For information on Schiermonnikoog, call ☎ 0900/455–4455 and press 3 for English.

BUS TRAVEL

A comprehensive network of local and regional bus services provides a useful supplement to the train service.

🛂 Bus Information Public transportation ☎ 0900/9292.

CAR RENTAL

🛂 Major Agencies Alamo ☎ 023/556–3666 in Holland. Avis ☎ 0800/235–2847 in Holland. Budget ☎ 023/568–8888 in Holland. Europcar ☎ 070/381–1812 in Holland. Hertz ☎ 0900/235–4378 in Holland.

CAR TRAVEL

In less than two hours, you can drive to the north via E22 through Noord Holland province, crossing the 32-km (21-mi) Afsluitdijk (Enclosing Dike) that divides the IJsselmeer from the North Sea; from the end of the Enclosing Dike, continue on E22 to Groningen or take A31 to Leeuwarden. You can also take A31 if you are heading to the Wadden Islands, but stop at Harlingen, where there are ferries to Terschelling. The ferry for Schiermonnikoog leaves from Lauwersoog: take N361 from Groningen or N355, then N361 from Leeuwarden. Alternatively, if you are heading straight for Groningen or Leeuwarden, you can follow A6 across the province of Flevoland to Joure and then take the E22 for Groningen or turn north on A32 for Leeuwarden. A third option is to drive to Enkhuizen and take the car ferry to Urk. From Urk, take N351 to A6 and continue as above.

To reach the island of Texel, travel north from Amsterdam on N203, N8, A9, N9, and N250 to the port of Den Helder.

EMERGENCIES **Wegenwacht** (☎ 0800–0888) is a national breakdown and towing service.

RULES OF THE ROAD In Friesland signs are in two languages, with the town names shown in Frisian as well as in Dutch. As in the rest of the country, you must know which main city or town you are traveling toward, as there are no directional signs of east, west, etc., in The Netherlands. Good planning is key.

EMERGENCIES

⌘ Emergency Services National Emergency Alarm Number for police, fire, and ambulance ☎ 112.

MONEY MATTERS

CURRENCY EXCHANGE ATM machines (*geld automat*) are the most convenient source of local currency. Many train stations also have GWK offices for currency exchange.

TAXIS

Taxis wait at most railway stations in The Netherlands.

TOURS

BOAT TOURS Canal cruise trips are available in summer; in Leeuwarden, contact Party Cruise Prinsenhof; in Groningen, Kool Groningen.

⌘ Fees & Schedules Party Cruise Prinsenhof ⊠ P. Midamaweg 19 ☎ 0511/539334. Kool Groningen ⊠ Stationsweg 1012 ☎ 050/312-8379.

WALKING TOURS *Wadlopen* (mudflat walking) excursions are permissible *only* with a guide who knows well the timing of the tidal waters on the Wadden Sea (between mid-March and early October). The VVV tourist offices can give you information and recommend qualified guides, or you can contact **De Stichting Wadloopcentrum Pieterburen** (⊠ Postbus 1, Pieterburen ☎ 0595/528300 ⌨ 0595/528318 ⊕ www.wadlopen. com). Mr. Lammert is a popular private Wadlopen guide from Friesland (☎ 0594/622029). Wadlopen guides from Groningen can be hired (☎ 0595/528300).

TRAIN TRAVEL

Intercity express trains operate once an hour direct from Amsterdam to both Leeuwarden and Groningen. Be sure you are in the right car; trains often split en route, so there are separate cars for each destination in both classes of service. In addition to the national rail lines connecting Leeuwarden and Groningen with the south, local trains link up Leeuwarden with the Enkhuizen–Stavoren ferry service; another line connects Leeuwarden with Harlingen (departure point for ferry and hydrofoil services to the Wadden Islands) every half hour; and another links Leeuwarden with Groningen and continues to the German border. A small local train in Groningen province connects Groningen with Winsum (a canoeing center), Uithuizen (departure for guided walks to the Wadden Islands at low tide), and the port of Eemshaven. Connections to Assen run regularly every hour as well.

For Texel, Intercity trains run direct to Den Helder every hour, with connecting trains to the ferry terminal. The Waddenbiljet all-inclusive return ticket, the easiest and most economical method for getting to Texel, includes bus service on the island itself. Take the train to Harlingen for the ferry to Terschelling. Take the train to Groningen and then a bus to Lauwersoog to get to the ferry terminal for Schiermonnikoog. Since the best way to get around The Netherlands is by train, you can search ⊕ www.ns.nl for all train schedules and the amenities provided at each station. An English version is also provided.

CUTTING COSTS If you intend to tour the region by train and you will be including a visit to one of the Wadden Islands, it is worth considering a *Waddenbiljet,* an all-inclusive return ticket including all connecting services and ferries. Ask for this arrangement at the train station.

⌘ Train Information Train/public transportation ☎ 0900/9292 ⊕ www.ns.nl.

VISITOR INFORMATION

7 Tourist Information **VVV Assen-Drenthe** ☒ Marktstraat 8-10, 9401 JH ☎ 0592/314324 ᗡ 0592/317306. **VVV Bolsward** ☒ Marktplein 1, 8701 KG ☎ 0900/123-4888. **VVV Den Helder** ☒ Bernhardplein 18, 1781 HH ☎ 022/362-5544 ᗡ 022/361-4888 **VVV Groningen** ☒ Grote Markt 25, 9712 HS ☎ 0900/202-3050 in Holland, 0503/139741 ᗡ 050/311-0258 ⊕ www.vvvgroningen.nl. **VVV Leeuwarden** ☒ Achmeatoren-Sophialaan ⊕ www.vvvleeuwarden.nl. **VVV Schiermonnikoog** ☒ Reeweg 5, 9166 PW ☎ 0519/531233 ᗡ 0529/531325. **VVV Terschelling** ☒ Willem Barentszkade 19a, 8881 BC ☎ 0562/443000 ᗡ 0562/442875. **VVV Texel** ☒ Emmalaan 66, 1791 AV ☎ 0222/314741 ᗡ 0222/314129. **VVV Wadden Islands** ⊕ www.vvv-wadden.nl.

WHERE TO STAY

HOTELS Hotels, bed-and-breakfasts, vacation homes, apartments, and bungalows abound on all the islands. Special arrangements including the ferry, transportation to your hotel, lodging, bikes, museums, and information packets can save money and time. Ask the appropriate VVV office for choices and offers.

CAMPING With more than 100 campgrounds in the province of Friesland alone, the North offers plenty of opportunity for camping. Unfortunately, there is no national or central reservation service for campsites, so you have to contact sites individually. For camping in Leeuwarden, De Kleine Wielen, open April–October, has sites for 350 tents and RVs, as well as places for hikers. In Groningen, Camping Stadspark, open March–October, has 200 sites; it also has accommodation for hikers. In the Assen (Drenthe) area, try Witerzomer in Witten (5 km [3 mi] from Assen), which is open all year. The ANWB office (akin to AAA in the United States) has a wide range of information on campsites throughout Holland.

7 **ANWB** ☒ Kloekhorstraat 12, 9401 BD Assen ☎ 0592/314100. **Camping Stadspark** ☒ Campinglaan 6, 9727 KH ☎ 050/525-1624. **De Kleine Wielen** ☒ De Groene Ster 14, 8926 XE ☎ 0511/431660. **Witerzomer** ☎ 0592/393535.

UNDERSTANDING
HOLLAND

GOING DUTCH

I F YOU COME TO HOLLAND EXPECTING to find all its residents shod in wooden shoes, you're years too late; if you're looking for windmills at every turn, you're looking in the wrong place. Although the wings of windmills do still turn on government subsidy and the wooden shoe recently has been recognized by the European Union (EU) as acceptable safety footwear, the bucolic images that brought tourism here in the decades after World War II have little to do with The Netherlands of the 21st century. *Ja*, this may be a country where you can find the old world in spades, but this is very, very far from a senile land. Walk through the Red Light District of Amsterdam—gorgeously adorned with some of the most historic structures in town—and be startled by scarlet women sitting immobile behind scarlet-neon framed windows, their pose suggesting that of Whistler's Mother (the resemblance ends there, however). Or marvel at today's Vermeers and Mondriaans now globally championed as being on the very cutting edge of both Web design and urban planning. Holland is bustling, busy, and clangorous, filled with noise and hullabaloo, festivals and floodlights.

But for visitors, it is also a land where you can happily and effortlessly trade in sophisticated modernity for medieval mellowness or the featherbed finesse of the 17th-century Golden Age. A walk down a time-stained alley in Amsterdam or a horseback ride up a dune path along the North Sea often lets you lose five or six centuries in six or seven minutes. And rest assured: there also remains a wealth of villages that have changed little since the time of Hobbema, interiors seemingly plucked from the paintings of Terborch and Rembrandt, and landscapes that suggest the work of Van Ruysdael and—on particularly windy days—even Van Gogh. Holland, in fact, is one big throbbing canvas.

The Netherlands has always had great press agents in its Golden Age painters, who portrayed a shimmering and geometric landscape of fields and orchards sporadically dotted with stretches of color-coded tulips, windmills keeping the sea at bay, cozy villages burnished with age and history, and bustling cities bursting with culture and merchant spirit—all forming a grand tapestry by the lacework of canals. The local saying "God made the world but the Dutch made The Netherlands" would sound cocky if it were not true. But one can certainly call the Dutch stubborn: half of this New Jersey–size democratic monarchy's 15,450 square miles has been reclaimed from the sea, and to this day, it remains a full-time job of many to stop this land from slipping back whence it came. As the primary element, water does much to define this country's landscape, history, people, and politics, and the predominance of water and the relative lack of terra firma have also helped create the image of the Dutch for visitors of days long past. To wit, Sir F. B. Head called the Hollanders a "heavy, barge built, web-footed race," and that 18th-century English snob William Beckford said, "A certain oysterishness of eye, and flabbiness of complexion, are almost proofs sufficient of their aquatic descent." Although these observers were obviously victims of propagandists of the various Dutch-Anglo Wars, it cannot be denied that the nation's long-ingrained respect for how water derives its power through its flexibility accounts for the Dutch being more renowned for their pragmatism than their stubbornness. And perhaps it was as compensation that the Dutch developed a humor best described as "earthy."

But a certain visionary pragmatism has seen Holland evolve beyond the bucolic images with which it's long been associated to embrace the future and its accompanying flurry of—mostly happy—contradictions. Certainly its greatest enigma is the fact that although it is one of Europe's smallest countries, the modern and sophisticated Netherlands has an economic strength and cultural wealth that far surpass its size and population. It may be small enough to drive through in a few hours, but with more art treasures per square mile than any other country on Earth and with an international clout that has led it to become one of the largest investors in the U.S. economy, you will need more than a few weeks to unlock all its secrets.

Besides striving to make things as *gezel-lig*—an endemic word that describes a feeling of comfort and coziness in a social situation—as possible, you should also come equipped with the maximum respect for the concept of the *individual*. After all, it was the painters of the Low Countries who realized that the 17th-century variations of our present-day Mr. Smiths, Mr. Browns, and Mr. Johnsons were just as worthy subjects for the artist's brush as were the St. Marks, St. Matthews, St. Jeromes, St. Sebastians, and the rest. It was these painters who dared to paint simple subjects for the little, though usually extremely well-off, patrons. It was the painters of the Dutch School who first came to the conclusion that the minimum acceptable size for a picture was not 30 by 25 feet. Frescoes and paintings executed to the order of the church and intended to be displayed in cathedrals must be large; but it took the Dutch masters to realize that the private dwellings of the well-to-do bourgeoisie were also suitable places for their works.

And it was the Dutch who first thought of building houses—that is to say, dwellings where these pictures might suitably be hung. Until then, "architecture" meant the building of churches, cathedrals, royal and ducal palaces, or huge municipal buildings. It was the Dutch who were not ashamed to start building pretty, charming, and often beautiful houses—just for ordinary people to live in. That a private house might be or should be tasteful and lovely was practically a revolutionary idea in the 17th century, and it is the upper-middle-class burghers and merchants of Holland to whom we owe so much of our present-day delight in our domestic surroundings. The Dutch were the first people to enshrine the concepts of coziness, intimacy, and privacy in everyday life.

Their pride in home and hearth is one reason why nearly every square inch of the country looks as though it were scrubbed with Dutch cleanser. If the state of a Dutch cottage or apartment is today best explained as a coping mechanism of living in a densely populated land that now numbers more than 16 million souls, that is because, in spite of constant elbow-rubbing in this crowded country, Hollanders retain a strong sense of personal privacy. They also respect your privacy—on first meeting, the Amsterdammer can occasionally be reserved to the point of seeming brusque, but this is not because he is cold or hostile; rather, he regards over-friendliness as an imposition on you. Still, in Holland folks are comfortable with living without curtains and having their lives and possessions open to viewing by passersby. When summer comes, many pack their curtainless trailers and head south, only to cluster together again in crowded trailer parks. Although these actions may help you understand why The Netherlands was the birthplace of TV's *Big Brother* concept—a show that bloomed with the turn-of-the-21st-century's infatuation with "reality TV"—do not conclude that the Dutch are an exhibitionist people. They are merely the "live and let live" philosophy personified.

Centuries of international trade and the welcoming of endless streams of immigrants have also played their role in creating a form of conflict resolution that requires long meetings that strive to make everyone happy; the Dutch have long loved to organize themselves and form societies (as witnessed by the famous group portraits of the 17th century, such as Rembrandt's *Syndics of the Cloth Guild*) for every conceivable purpose. On the opposite side of the coin, the country's brand of liberalism ironically runs on encyclopedias filled with laws, both strict and elastic but always based on libraries full of reports and studies, that seek to give the greatest possible freedoms to the individual. It is, therefore, understandable why The Netherlands is a tangle of inner conflicts—Catholic versus Protestant (it leans 60–40 toward the latter, that 60% still functioning as one of Europe's Reformation strongholds); puritanical versus prurient (you can't buy liquor on Sunday in some areas, and in others prostitutes sit, whalebone-stayed, in display windows).

It is, in fact, a luxury that The Netherlands can afford to take the time and effort to experiment with alternative—and, dare one say, more pragmatic—ways of dealing with the realities of sex and drugs. Its economic power, rooted in the 17th century when it was *the* great colonial power, also accounts for its cultural wealth. In days of seafaring yore, money raised through its colonial outposts overseas was used to buy or commission portraits and paintings by young artists such as Rembrandt, Hals, Vermeer, and Van Ruysdael. But it was not only the arts that were encouraged: The Netherlands was home to the philosophers Descartes, Spinoza, and Comenius; the jurist Grotius; the naturalist Van Leeuwenhoek, inventor of the microscope; and other prominent people of science and letters, who flourished in the country's enlightened tolerance. This tradition continues today with The Netherlands still subsidizing its artists and performers and supporting an educational system in which creativity in every field is respected, revered, and given room to express itself.

Contemporary Dutch design and architecture, in particular, are enjoying a new golden age of sorts. In a tiny land where space has always been maximized and where much is essentially artificial, these arts have long been dealing with issues that the rest of the rapidly shrinking world is only now beginning to recognize. The influence of such homegrown luminaries as Rem Koolhaas, whose architecture springs from a reaction to realities instead of historical legacies, and Viktor & Rolf, whose fashions showcase the country's more flamboyant side, have filtered across the globe. So please enjoy Amsterdam's historical legacy but also keep yourself open to the new. You will then have a well-rounded trip indeed. Now if only the Dutch could do something about their impeccable English—you are abroad, after all . . .

—Steve Korver

FURTHER READING

For a magical peek into Golden Age Holland, read the best-selling novel by Tracy Chevalier, *Girl with a Pearl Earring,* which evocatively paints a picture of the Delft household and its emotional undoing of the great 17th-century painter Johannes Vermeer. The film version, directed by Peter Webber and starring Colin Firth as Vermeer and Scarlett Johansson as the maid Griet, who became the subject (so Chevalier feels) of one of the greatest portraits every painted, premiered in late 2003. Numerous art-history books are devoted to Vermeer, and you'll find many of them discussed in Anthony Bailey's enjoyable biography, *Vermeer: A View of Delft.* For a view into Golden Age Amsterdam, check out David Liss's novel, *The Coffee Trader,* which is set in the city's Jewish community of the 17th century and deals with the attempts of its merchants to market the then-new coffee bean in Europe.

Colin White's *The Undutchables* is more than an observation of The Netherlands, its culture, and its inhabitants—it is everything you ever wanted to learn about the Dutch and that they'd rather you never found out. Jacob Vossestein takes you under the surface in getting to grips with Netherlanders in his *Dealing with the Dutch. The Low Skies* offers good background reading from Han van der Horst. From beloved U.S. author John Irving, *The Widow for One Year* is set partly in Amsterdam's Red Light District. Booker Prize winner Ian McEwan's *Amsterdam,* a craftily engineered thriller, is also set in the first city to decriminalize euthanasia (a very salient point). To get an idea of the current literary scene, *The Dedalus Book of Dutch Fantasy* is an anthology of short stories from modern Dutch writers. Cees Nooteboom has written several books worth looking out for, *Rituals* and *In the Dutch Mountains* especially, but his *The Following Story* is a provocative exploration of the differences between platonic and physical love. Renowned Dutch journalist Renate Rubinstein's moving diary *Take It or Leave It* deals with her fight against multiple sclerosis.

Another diary, this one set in war-ravaged Amsterdam, is Anne Frank's famous *Diary,* which has been translated into 55 languages; read it in conjunction with *Anne Frank Remembered,* a collection of essays retelling the story of the woman who helped the Frank family during the war. In *Bitter Herbs,* Marga Minco traces the tragedy of the breakup of a Jewish family during and after World War II. To put a historical spin on your visit, try Multatuli's classic, *Max Havelaar (or the Coffee Auctions of the Dutch Trading Company),* which relates the story of a colonial officer and his clash with a corrupt government; this novel did much to uncover the evils of Dutch colonialism. The celebrated Scot Irvine Welsh set one of his short stories in Amsterdam's dodgy narcotics underworld in *The Acid House.* Tim Krabbé's *The Vanishing,* relating one man's search for his vanished lover, was made into a nightmarish, unforgettable feature film.

Super-Dutch is the unforgettable name for a new tome devoted to that hotter-than-hot subject, contemporary architecture in The Netherlands. Published by the Princeton Architectural Press—and as graphically striking as the subject it covers—the incisive text by Bart Lootsma and dazzling photographs make this the perfect introduction and survey of the subject.

Ideal for taking a highly personalized and lovingly picturesque stroll around the capital, Derek Blyth's *Amsterdam Explored* describes nine walks around the city. A magisterial overview of the city's history is found in Geert Mak's *Amsterdam.* Mike Dash's *Tulipomania* is an unbelievably fascinating account of the great tulip craze of the 17th century. And hand in hand with that volume, take a long and lingering look at Barbara Abbs's *The Garden Lover's Guide to The Netherlands and Belgium.* If you're looking to find the most gorgeous and magisterial gardens, estates, and manors in Holland, this text, fitted out with lovely photos, is certainly a must-read. The philosopher Witold Rybczynski devotes a chapter to the history of Dutch domesticity in his thought-provoking *Home: A History of an Idea.*

If you want to get into the legendary art tradition of Holland, the first place to start is Simon Schama's award-winning *The Embarrassment of Riches,* a lively social and cultural history of The Netherlands) that deals with the country's infatuation with the visual arts during the 17th century. A dazzling perspective on the Golden Age, it provides the context and the "why" behind such great artists as Rembrandt, Vermeer, and Hals. Schama's biography of sorts, *Rembrandt's Eyes,* is also definitely worth a read, as is Anthony Bailey's fascinating tome, *Rembrandt's House.* For a comprehensive guide to Dutch painting, see Rudolf H. Fuchs's guide on that very subject, *Dutch Painting.* Another comprehensive guide is Seymour Slive's volume on *Dutch Painting, 1600–1800,* for the Pelican History of Art Series, published by Yale University Press. Any general survey, of which there are many published, will yield unbelievably rich bibliographies, detailing hundred of volumes devoted to Dutch art and artists. Finally, Paul Overy's *De Stijl* unravels the greatest 20th-century Dutch art movement.

DUTCH VOCABULARY

	English	Dutch	Pronunciation
Basics			
	Yes/no	Ja, nee	yah, nay
	Please	Alstublieft	**ahls**-too-bleeft
	Thank you	Dank u	**dahnk** oo
	You're welcome	Niets te danken	neets teh **dahn**-ken
	Excuse me, sorry	Pardon	pahr-**don**
	Good morning	Goede morgen	**hoh**-deh **mor**-ghen
	Good evening	Goede avond	**hoh**-deh **ahv**-unt
	Goodbye	Dag!	dah
Numbers			
	one	een	ehn
	two	twee	tveh
	three	drie	dree
	four	vier	veer
	five	vijf	vehf
	six	zes	zehss
	seven	zeven	**zeh**-vehn
	eight	acht	ahkht
	nine	negen	**neh**-ghen
	ten	tien	teen
Days of the Week			
	Sunday	zondag	**zohn**-dagh
	Monday	maandag	**mahn**-dagh
	Tuesday	dinsdag	**dinns**-dagh
	Wednesday	woensdag	**voons**-dagh
	Thursday	donderdag	**don**-der-dagh
	Friday	vrijdag	**vreh**-dagh
	Saturday	zaterdag	**zah**-ter-dagh
Useful Phrases			
	Do you speak English?	Spreekt U Engels?	sprehkt oo **ehn**-gls
	I don't speak Dutch	Ik spreek geen Nederlands	ihk sprehk **ghen** **Ned**-er-lahnds
	I don't understand	Ik begrijp het niet	ihk be-**ghrehp** het neet
	I don't know	Ik weet niet	ihk **veht** ut neet
	I'm American/English	Ik ben Amerikaans/Engels	ihk ben Am-er-ee-**kahns**/Ehn-gls

Where is . . .	Waar is . . .	vahr iss
the train station?	het station?	heht stah-**syohn**
the post office?	het postkantoor?	het **pohst**-kahn-tohr
the hospital?	het ziekenhuis?	het **zeek**-uhn-haus
Where are the restrooms?	waar is de WC?	**vahr** iss de **veh**-seh
Left/right	links/rechts	leenks/rehts
How much is this?	Hoeveel kost dit?	hoo-**vehl** kohst deet
It's expensive/ cheap	Het is te duur/ goedkoop	het ees teh **dour**/ **hood**-kohp
I am ill/sick	Ik ben ziek	ihk behn zeek
I want to call a doctor	Ik wil een docter bellen	ihk veel ehn **dohk**-ter **behl**-len
Help!	Help!	help
Stop!	Stoppen!	**stop**-pen

Dining Out

Bill/check	de rekening	de **rehk**-en-eeng
Bread	brood	brohd
Butter	boter	**boh**-ter
Fork	vork	fork
I'd like to order	Ik wil graag bestellen	Ihk veel khrah behs-**tell**-en
Knife	een mes	ehn mehs
Menu	menu/kaart	men-**oo**/kahrt
Napkin	en servet	ehn ser-**veht**
Pepper	peper	**peh**-per
Please give me . . .	mag ik [een] . . .	mahkh ihk [ehn] . . .
Salt	zout	zoot
Spoon	een lepel	ehn **leh**-pehl
Sugar	suiker	**sigh**-kur

INDEX